A Progressive History of American Democracy Since 1945

A Progressive History of American Democracy Since 1945: American Dreams, Hard Realities offers a social, political, and cultural history of the United States since World War II.

Unpacking a period of profound transformation unprecedented in the national experience, this book takes a synthetic approach to the history of the 1940s to the present day. It examines how Americans descended from a mid-century apogee of boundless expectations to the unsettling premise that our contemporary historical moment is fraught with a sense of crisis and national failure. The book's narrative explores the question of decline and more importantly, how the history of this transformation can point the way toward a recovery of shared national values. Chris J. Magoc also gives extensive treatments to the following:

- Grassroots movements that have expanded the meaning of American democracy, from the 1950s human rights struggle in the South to contemporary movements to confront systemic racism and the existential crisis of climate change.
- The resilience of American democracy in the face of antidemocratic forces.
- The impacts of a decades-long economic transformation.
- The consequences of America's expanding global military footprint and national security state.
- Fracturing of a nation once held together by a post-war liberal consensus and broadly shared societal goals to an America facing an attack from within on empirical truth and democracy itself.

This book will be of interest to students of modern U.S. history, social history, and American Studies, and general readers interested in recent U.S. history.

Chris J. Magoc is Professor of History at Mercyhurst University in Erie, Pennsylvania, U.S.A.

A Progressive History of American Democracy Since 1945

American Dreams, Hard Realities

Chris J. Magoc

Routledge
Taylor & Francis Group

NEW YORK AND LONDON

First published 2022
by Routledge
605 Third Avenue, New York, NY 10158

and by Routledge
2 Park Square, Milton Park, Abingdon, Oxon, OX14 4RN

Routledge is an imprint of the Taylor & Francis Group, an informa business

Library of Congress Cataloging-in-Publication Data
Names: Magoc, Chris J., 1960- author.
Title: A progressive history of American democracy since 1945 : American
dreams, hard realities / Chris J. Magoc.
Description: New York, NY : Routledge, 2022. | Includes bibliographical
references and index. |
Identifiers: LCCN 2021032756 (print) | LCCN 2021032757 (ebook) | ISBN
9780367749774 (hardback) | ISBN 9780367749767 (paperback) | ISBN
9781003160595 (ebook)
Subjects: LCSH: Social change--United States--History. | Democracy--United
States--History. | United States--Politics and government--1945-1989. |
United States--Politics and government--1989- | United
States--History--1945- | United States--Social conditions--1945-
Classification: LCC E743 .G27 2022 (print) | LCC E743 (ebook) | DDC
320.973--dc23
LC record available at https://lccn.loc.gov/2021032756
LC ebook record available at https://lccn.loc.gov/2021032757

ISBN: 978-0-367-74977-4 (hbk)
ISBN: 978-0-367-74976-7 (pbk)
ISBN: 978-1-003-16059-5 (ebk)

DOI: 10.4324/9781003160595

Typeset in Bembo
by SPi Technologies India Pvt Ltd (Straive)

For America

Contents

Preface viii

1 A "People's War" and the Dawn an "American Century" 1

2 Containing Communism, Advancing "the American System" 25

3 Affluence and Angst: The Politics and Culture of Cold War America 49

4 Through the Looking Glass: Discontent and Rebellion in the Fifties 74

5 Let Us Begin: The Promise of the Early 1960s 98

6 Mississippi to Saigon: The Tragedy of Lyndon Johnson and the Turning of the Sixties 126

7 "People of This Generation:" The New Left and the Counter-culture 150

8 1968: The Rupture 173

9 Richard Nixon and the Resilience of American Democracy 197

10 Confronting Limits, Turning Right 226

11 The Reagan Revolution 251

12 The End of Nothing: History Lurches On 279

13 America Under Attack 302

Index 339

Preface

Although a work of history and not a memoir, this has been an inescapably personal book to write. Beyond a kind of summing up of thirty years of teaching courses in modern American history and American Studies, my own life as a former organizer and still actively engaged citizen informs the progressive interpretation of post-1945 U.S. history found in these pages. More recently, any pretense of objectivity I once held for this book evaporated in the attack on our democracy that intensifies as I write this. Writing in an historical moment fraught with great division, a seemingly intractable, ceaseless series of crises, and most frighteningly, an embrace of antidemocratic illiberalism unprecedented in our national experience, I have found it impossible to produce a clinically "objective" chronicle of events.

Our divided hour demands works of history that critically examine how Americans landed here, descending from a 1945 apogee of boundless expectations, shared values, and generally unified confidence. While this is an unabashedly progressive history, it is my hope that the book will shed just a little light on questions now haunting Americans across the political divide, beginning with *what happened to that country?* There are no definitive answers here. But in the spirit of Herbert Hoover's wisdom that "the supreme purpose of history is a better world," my lofty aspiration is that in honoring a nation bound together not so long ago by a broadly shared commitment to democracy, the book might in its best moments help to inform conversations about the health and future of our republic.

I am indebted to Mercyhurst University for granting me a sabbatical in 2018, to my students, and to my colleagues in the history department whose support allowed me to complete this project over the past several years. My deepest appreciation extends also to the good people at Routledge in particular Kimberley Smith and Emily Irvine, for recognizing the potential value of this project and for their patient support over the past year, and the careful editorial efforts of Hamish Ironside and Jenny Guildford. Errors of any sort that remain in the following pages belong solely to the author.

An autobiographically informed history owes its greatest debts to the people who have mattered most to the writer, beginning with my parents Stephen and Frances Magoc, who instilled in my brothers Dan, Jim, Gerard, Ron, and me a deep and unshakeable fidelity to this country's highest ideals. It is an abiding patriotism that my wife and soul mate Mary Ellen, with whom I have traveled and loved America for nearly four decades, have tried to pass on to our beloved children, Ethan and Caroline. I am profoundly grateful for all that my Scout has contributed and surrendered to this project's completion. As with so much else of my life, this book would not have happened without her.

Erie, Pennsylvania, June 2021

1 A "People's War" and the Dawn an "American Century"

[The] fundamental trouble with America has been … [that Americans] have failed to play their part as a world power—a failure which has had disastrous consequences for themselves and for all mankind. And the cure is this: to accept wholeheartedly our duty and our opportunity … to exert upon the world the full impact of our influence, for such purposes as we see fit and by such means as we see fit.
—Henry Luce, "The American Century," *Life*, February 17, 1941[1]

Some have spoken of the "American Century." I say that the century on which we are entering—the century which will come into being after this war—can be and must be the century of the common man … No nation will have the God-given right to exploit other nations. Older nations will have the privilege to help younger nations … There can be no privileged peoples. We ourselves in the United States are no more a master race than the Nazis.
—Henry Wallace, "The Price of Free World Victory,"
New York City, May 8, 1942[2]

The clash of these two Henrys, both towering American figures early in World War II, was no minor skirmish. Luce's dominion of Time–Life–Fortune publishing made him, by one account, "the most influential private citizen" in the country and a force in the Republican Party.[3] Wallace had long been among the most ardent of President Franklin Roosevelt's New Dealers, and after being elevated from agriculture secretary to vice president in 1940, was FDR's heir apparent. Although ideological opposites, Luce and Wallace each believed that the United States was destined to play a more central role in global affairs, proponents of what would soon be termed "American exceptionalism." There, the common ground ended. Framed by sharply divergent philosophies, the outcome of the contesting Luce-Wallace global visions would also shape the direction of American politics and society in the postwar era.

In February 1941, with continental Europe having fallen to the Nazis and London absorbing nightly bombing, Henry Luce's argument for U.S. intervention in World War II, housed inside a grand vision of postwar internationalism, was bound to land with force. Directed in part at confronting the considerable influence of the isolationist America First Committee, the editorial appeared in Life, a lavishly pictorial magazine read by nearly 13 million Americans that

DOI: 10.4324/9781003160595-1

helped shape the national mood.[4] Beyond summoning Americans to abandon their lingering reservations about the need to confront the Axis powers, Luce implored readers to reconcile themselves to America's rightful position of global leadership. Once the United States accepted its responsibility and fortified its position through the experience of war, Luce argued, the nation would emerge with an unprecedented opportunity to lead a new world order of peace and prosperity. With unflinching audacity, Luce proclaimed the United States the "intellectual, scientific and artistic capital of the world," prestige that should now be leveraged toward the next logical stage of global hegemony.

More than a foreign policy treatise, Luce's appeal laid bare his disdain for the "socialist doctrines and collectivist trends" emanating from Washington, claiming that many isolationist Americans opposed engagement because they believed Franklin Roosevelt would exploit the war to bring about "the end of our constitutional democracy."[5] Luce and many of the bankers and businessmen of his class had fought virtually all of Roosevelt's New Deal. More than a few were proto-fascists. Fellow publisher William Randolph Hearst expressed admiration for Benito Mussolini and Adolf Hitler and ran columns celebrating the fascistic miracles of the Italian and German economies.[6] Others, including Irénée du Pont and Alfred B. Sloan, were implicated in the 1933 Wall Street Putsch, a plot to oust FDR and replace him with an authoritarian, business-friendly regime.[7] No far-right coup conspirator, Luce acknowledged the necessity of some Roosevelt's reforms, and later insisted "The American Century" had not called for a postwar American empire.[8] Intended or not, the essay stood as a conceptual blueprint for multinational corporate globalization, backed by immense U.S. military power. Luce earned endorsements from unabashed champions of American hegemony like columnist Dorothy Thompson who echoed, "To Americanize enough of the *world* so that we shall have a climate favorable to our growth is indeed a call to destiny [emphasis original]."[9]

Five months after Pearl Harbor came the address from Vice President Henry Wallace. That the speech served in part as a rebuke to Luce could have been lost in the shared messianic language Wallace used to characterize the stakes of a war in which Americans were now fully engaged. The vice president framed the conflict against the Axis powers as the latest chapter in the long democratizing "march of freedom for the common man," grounded in "the Bible, with its extraordinary emphasis on the dignity of the individual" and "social justice." What began with America's founding, said Wallace, had continued in 150 years of "the long-drawn-out people's revolution" around the world. And now, the Roosevelt administration's domestic program epitomized the ongoing struggle for a more democratic world, one envisioned in FDR's Four Freedoms. Articulated by Roosevelt in his January 1941 State of the Union address, they would be immortalized in a series of paintings by *Saturday Evening Post* illustrator Norman Rockwell, and embedded in the charter of the United Nations: freedom of worship and speech, and freedom *from* fear and want. A primary U.S. obligation in the postwar era, declared Wallace, was to foster a more egalitarian world where "common" men and women would be educated and enjoy economic security. This, he pledged further, would guard against the rise of despotic demagogues, "the curse of the modern world." The anti-imperialist vision of American moral leadership was met with thunderous applause in the ballroom.

"Century of the Common Man" carried far greater impact than "The American Century" in these dark early moments of the war. The speech was nearly universally praised, even by Wallace critics like Walter Lippman, who advised Wallace to "have no qualms about letting it be circulated not only all over the country but all over the world." Indeed it was. The address was widely reprinted in newspapers, reproduced in pamphlet form, and translated into 20 languages for distribution by American soldiers all over the globe. Musically enhanced recordings were sold as LPs. Paramount and the Office of War Information collaborated to produce *The Price of Victory*, a short film featuring Wallace reading excerpts of the speech. Screened nationwide, the film earned an Academy Award nomination.[10] More enduring was *Fanfare for the Common Man*, Aaron Copland's brilliant musical composition inspired by the address, his response to a request from the conductor of the Cincinnati Symphony Orchestra to 18 American composers to create original fanfares that could "make stirring and significant contributions to the war effort."[11] Premiering at income tax time in 1943, "Fanfare for the Common Man" was an instant triumph. Like *The Spirit of '43*, a Walt Disney cartoon in which Donald Duck delivers the patriotic message of paying one's "taxes to defeat the Axis," Copland's soaring composition amplified the sense of a unified citizenry engaged in an epic battle for freedom.

The phenomenal resonance of "Century for the Common Man" reflected the heightened profile of its orator. Preceded in the vice presidency by conservative John Nance Garner—best remembered for dismissing the office as "not worth a bucket of warm piss"—Henry Wallace was assigned an expanded portfolio.[12] Reflecting the confidence he had in his new number two man, Roosevelt placed Wallace in charge of two critically important agencies, one overseeing the delivery of war materiel to the allies, the other the Board of Economic Welfare (BEW). That post placed him in charge of all matters concerned with U.S. economic relations abroad, including contracts with corporations in allied countries, where he would insist on minimum standards of wages and conditions. The *Des Moines Register* summarized Wallace as "the American minister of economic defense, and the chief planner of the new world order when the war is over."[13] He had become the most powerful vice president in U.S. history.

Wallace spent much of 1943–1944 barnstorming for popular causes he believed part of the fight against fascism. He campaigned alongside African Americans fighting racial hatred, with women fighting for the Equal Rights Amendment, Jewish Americans protesting an ugly wave of anti-Semitism, and on behalf of returning service members concerned about their postwar readjustment.[14] While standing with these core elements of a more democratic postwar future, Wallace railed *against* the forces aligned with American fascism (Figure 1.1). Beyond the most visible—the German American Bund, the Silver Legion, the Fascist League of North America—there were more insidious currents,

Figure 1.1 German American Bund Parade, East 86th Avenue, New York City, October 1939.

Courtesy of the Library of Congress (LC-USZ62-117148).

including corporate dominance of American life and racism. In Detroit on July 24, 1943 Wallace linked the recent deadly riots there against African Americans to Nazi ideology. He left no doubt as to the battle lines on the home front:

> Our choice is not between a Hitler-slave world and an out-of-date holiday of "normalcy." The defeatists who talk about going back to the good old days of Americanism mean the time when there was plenty for the few and scarcity for the many, when Washington was a way-station in the suburbs of Wall Street ... nor is our choice between an Americanized fascism and the restoration of prewar scarcity and unemployment ... Our choice is between democracy for everybody or for the few—between the spreading of social safeguards and economic opportunity to all the people—or the concentration of our abundant resources in the hands of selfishness and greed.[15]

Newspapers nationwide gave the speech glowing reviews, many reprinting the entire speech.

Wallace was hardly alone. The fight against domestic fascism remains one of the most important, largely untold stories of the World War II era. Historian Stephen Ross has recounted the extraordinary story of Los Angeles attorney and World War I veteran Leon Lewis who, beginning in 1933, organized and directed a band of citizen spies to disrupt the Nazi threat in LA. For 12 years, Lewis and his espionage recruits thwarted a wide-ranging campaign of planned terror by American fascists and their Third Reich masters. They foiled Nazi plots to blow up key defense factories and military bases, machine gun Jewish Americans in Boyle Heights, fumigate the homes of Jewish residents with cyanide, publicly hang twenty of Hollywood's most prominent actors and filmmakers, and assassinate American leaders.[16] No corner of America was safe from homegrown fascism. Father Charles Coughlin, the popular Detroit Catholic "radio priest" began spewing vile anti-Semitic poison as the rise of fascism took hold in Europe. By the eve of the war, Coughlin was arguing outright for American fascism and helped inspire the Christian Front, an armed political organization pledging to defend America from alleged Jewish-communist conquest. Fascist Americans packed Madison Square Garden in 1939, hailing George Washington as "America's First Fascist." Franklin Roosevelt's opponents often took to defaming him as "Rosenfeld," the New Deal as the "Jew Deal." From Long Island to LA, expressions of an American far-right underscored the very real possibility that Wallace and others like Sinclair Lewis had been warning about for the previous decade: It *could happen here.*[17] Yet as Stephen Ross has recounted, those working under Leon Lewis's espionage wing—only one of whom was Jewish—demonstrated that a more righteous current was also flowing in American life:

> They knew that the Nazis and the fascists hated Jewish-Americans, they hated Catholic-Americans, they hated black Americans. They never saw their ... undercover operation, as working for the Jews; they saw it as an American campaign. And what they argued is ... what we all have in common is the noun, American. And they saw this as an American crusade, 'cause they said, if you attack one—if you allow an outside group and their American allies to attack one group of Americans, you attack all Americans.[18]

Civil rights leaders drew the same connections between the fight against fascism in Europe and the struggle for human rights in America. In Nazism, many African Americans saw a more extreme version of a racist ideology they recognized at home. As Baltimore Urban League leader Alexander J. Allen recalled, "Fascism was ... something that we saw every day on the streets of Baltimore and in other places," he said. "It made a mockery of wartime goals to fight overseas against fascism only to come back to the same kind of discrimination and racism in this country.[19] The War Department recognized it as well. In their short 1943 film *Don't Be a Sucker*, a crowd listens with rapt attention to a bigot warning of "negroes holding jobs that belong to me and you," wondering, "what's going to happen to us real Americans?" An immigrant in the crowd[20] walks away distraught, saying, "I have heard this kind of talk before," in Nazi-occupied Hungary. "I was a fool then. I thought Nazis were crazy people, stupid fanatics ... They knew they were not strong enough to conquer a unified country, so they ... used prejudice as a practical weapon to cripple the nation."[21]

Henry Wallace's outspoken views and close relationship with First Lady Eleanor Roosevelt and other notable figures of the American left gave him a growing national profile, but also made him vulnerable to attack. With the 1944 campaign looming, those seeking to oust Wallace as vice president began their offensive. He may have had the support of most voters and the president to be re-nominated, but the forces arrayed against him were formidable: southern congressmen outraged at Wallace's opposition to segregation, businessmen chafing at Wallace's anti-imperialism and plans to expand the New Deal after the war, and national security officials wary of Wallace's purported appeasement of the Russians. British Prime Minister Winston Churchill voiced his indignation privately to Roosevelt over Wallace's repeated calls for an end to colonial empires, including that of Great Britain.[22] Henry Wallace was supplanted at the Democratic National Convention by Missouri Senator Harry S. Truman. Followed months later by the death of FDR, it proved a turning point within the larger watershed of World War II. For beyond the progressive direction the Democratic Party would almost certainly have pursued at home with a President Wallace, his ouster signaled the triumph of a U.S. foreign policy that more closely mirrored the outlook of Henry Luce. The war, meanwhile, rendered the pathogens of American-style fascism dormant but not defeated.

The People's War

> This is not only a war of soldiers in uniform; it is a war of the people, of all the people. And it must be fought not only on the battlefield, but in the cities, and in the villages, in the factories and in the farms, in the home and in the hearts of every man, woman and child who loves freedom! … This is the people's war! It is our war! We are the fighters. Fight it then! Fight it with all that is in us. And may God defend the right.
>
> —*Mrs. Miniver* (1942)[23]

In June 1942, Americans flocked to see *Mrs. Miniver*, William Wyler's Oscar-winning film that concludes with these moving words. The homily by the vicar of a war-ravaged church begins as an elegy to residents of a village outside London killed in a German bombing raid. The original ending called for him to read the 91st Psalm as the camera panned through his bombed-out church roof to the heavens, but on the night before shooting, Henry Wilcoxon, the actor playing the vicar, and director William Wyler rewrote the scene. Wilcoxon had just joined the British Navy, and Wyler had Jewish family members living under German occupation. The film began shooting weeks before the Japanese attack on Pearl Harbor, but by the time *Mrs. Miniver* hit theatres, Americans had been at war for six months. The film's affectionate depiction of the courage and grit of a British family and their fellow villagers hit home in a country now united in an all-consuming "people's war" that spared no one. Just months earlier in August 1941, Franklin Roosevelt and Winston Churchill had put forward the democratic rhetorical framework of the Allied Powers in the Atlantic Charter, the Anglo-American declaration of "common principles" and "hopes for a better future for the world" for which the war would be fought.[24] FDR saw immediately the resounding power of the vicar's homily, ordering it broadcast over the Voice of America in Europe and reprinted as a leaflet to be dropped throughout the Nazi-occupied continent.[25]

The scope of American engagement on a mobilized home front was without limit, beginning with the staggering volume of munitions produced by American workers: 300,000 aircraft, 3,600,000 trucks, 87,620 warships, 5,600 merchant vessels, 44 billion rounds of ammunition, 6,000,000 tons of bombs. At Henry Ford's Willow Run plant, workers produced one B-24 Liberator Bomber every 63 minutes. Pennsylvanians produced more steel than the Axis powers combined. Production of what Roosevelt had called the "arsenal of democracy" brought immediate economic prosperity, as Americans enjoyed near-full employment. Most industrial workers enjoyed the benefits of belonging to a union, courtesy of the decades-long struggle of the labor movement to win the right to organize without fear of reprisal. That historic victory had come in 1935 with the National Labor Relations Act, establishing collective bargaining rights for American workers, and now the defense boom sent membership soaring. By 1945, unions represented more than 35 percent of the non-agricultural work force, a strength triggering a counterattack from business and their allies in congress. On the whole, World War II represents the pinnacle of union power, a time when most Americans appreciated the vital connection between democracy on the shop floor and its defense on the battlefield.[26]

The strength of labor unions, combined with high tax rates on the wealthy and corporations, significant overtime hours and other federal policy, brought the most progressive, short-term redistribution of wealth in American history. During World War II, the richest one-fifth of Americans enjoyed an annual growth in after-tax income of roughly four percent, while the poorest one-fifth saw their real incomes soar by more than 13 percent every year. The share of the nation's disposable income controlled by the top 5 percent fell from 23 to 17 percent, as the middle-class doubled in size. The rich and corporations did well enough, with after-tax corporate profits also doubling.[27] Without question, however, the egalitarian nature of American prosperity was without precedent and raised expectations for the postwar era.

The extraordinary mobilization of American society depended on close cooperation between business leaders and the federal government—a sharp departure from the antagonism of the Depression years when FDR had "[welcomed the] hatred" of the "economic royalists" of Wall Street and the business world.[28] With "cost-plus" profits guaranteed, corporate leaders famously took "dollar-a-year" positions to help coordinate planning of a wartime economy. Conversion of civilian to military production required new plant construction and massive federal investment, much of it headed South or West. Nearly half of all ships and airplanes produced during World War II came from the west coast. Charleston shipbuilding, Birmingham steel, petroleum refining along the Gulf Coast seeded the growth of an emerging new southern economy. The War

Production Board (WPB) coordinated allocation of critically needed strategic materials, and also instituted nationwide rationing of such favored consumer goods as gasoline, cigarettes, chocolate and beef. Ration books delivered strict instructions on the use of ration stamps. From rural fields to city rooftops, Americans planted 18 million Victory Gardens, allowing large-scale agriculture to be directed toward the war effort. In 1943, the Office of War Mobilization (OWM), coordinated production among the armed services and between military and civilian goods.[29]

Staffed by scientists from universities and industry, the Office of Scientific Research and Development (OSRD) led a wave of developments in electronics, radar and communications technologies, medicines, and chemicals, many of which would have postwar civilian uses. Massive, vacuum tube-based electronic computers used in code breaking and ballistics accelerated the application of computers after the war. New plastics that proved essential in aircraft production would find limitless applications in a booming consumer society.[30] Japan having cut off the supply of natural rubber, nationwide gas rationing was instituted to reduce civilian tire usage, along with a national 35 mph speed limit, an intensive scrap rubber drive, and rapid development of a synthetic rubber industry. Collaborating with companies like Union Carbide, the federal government invested $700 million in building 51 new plants, making the U.S. the world's greatest exporter of synthetic rubber.[31]

As mobilization moved into high gear, large cities and small towns with defense plants and military and naval bases were flooded with new arrivals. By 1945 fifteen million Americans were living somewhere other than where they resided in 1939. The wartime adage to "make do or do without" was tested in the housing crunch, as resourceful Americans slept wherever and however they could: in crowded boarding houses, "hot bunk" rotating shifts, or makeshift Quonset huts. The National Defense Housing Act brought construction of more than 600,000 individual housing units in nearly every state, invariably built on time and under budget. In New Kensington, Pennsylvania, Marcel Breuer and Walter Gropius, two architects of the famous Bauhaus school and refugees of Nazi Germany, designed Aluminum City Terrace to accommodate workers at the nearby Aluminum Company of America (Figure 1.2). The complex was designed by the modernist architects in a frenetic 36 hours in August 1941 and then erected in two months.[32] More famously, builder William Levitt built 2,350 war worker homes in Norfolk, Virginia, mass-producing the complex in a process resembling Henry Ford's assembly line, establishing a model he would replicate after the war.[33]

Raising the $341 billion[34] cost of the war came primarily through the imposition of taxes and War Bonds. The most progressive tax rates in American history propelled the wartime redistribution of wealth downward and underscored a sense of shared sacrifice. By 1945, incomes above $200,000 were taxed at 94 percent, excess corporate profits at 90 percent.[35] Alongside the patriotic message on taxes were ubiquitous appeals to purchase War Bonds. Redeemed at 2.9 percent after 10 years, War Bonds were hardly a shrewd financial investment.

Figure 1.2 Lower Terrace Building 29b (Units 245–250), Facing West. Aluminum City Terrace, New Kensington, Westmoreland County, PA.

Courtesy of the Library of Congress.

Effectively serving as a citizen loan to the government, they deepened the stake of ordinary Americans in the cause of victory.

When the war began, some of FDR's advisors recommended a regimented system in which Americans would be assigned to work in a defense plant designated by the federal government—a scheme he resisted, knowing it would have borne a distressing resemblance to those of the Soviet Union and the German Third Reich. Instead, Roosevelt established the War Manpower Commission, which balanced the demands of the home front with the armed services. Although the agency worked to deploy specialized workers where their skills were needed, the agency generally reflected FDR's confidence in the practical instincts of Americans. If their government told them where need and opportunity were great, they would pack up and go. In one of his legendary fireside chats, Roosevelt urged listeners to procure maps to assist them in finding their destination of employment; the Hammond company in New York soon sold out their entire stock.[36] Since the onset of the New Deal, FDR's regular radio addresses had forged an abiding, unprecedented level of trust between the president and the American people, in the process lifting the veil on the workings of "your government" to millions of listeners.[37] On October 12, 1942, he reiterated Americans' unified purpose:

> This whole nation of one hundred and thirty million free men, women and children is becoming one great fighting force. Some of us are soldiers

or sailors, some of us are civilians. Some of us are fighting the war in airplanes ... and some of us are fighting it in mines deep down in the earth of Pennsylvania or Montana ... [but] each of us playing an honorable part in the great struggle to save our democratic civilization ...

And ... a word of praise and thanks to the more than 10,000,000 people ... who have volunteered for the work of civilian defense ... [who] are helping to fortify our national unity and our real understanding of the fact that we are all involved in this war.[38]

One final, generally unsung story in America's mobilization underscores the spirit of the people's war. In 1933, public book burnings unfolded across Nazi Germany, one hundred million volumes eventually going up in flames. Luce's *Time* damned it a "bibliocaust."[39] Americans poured into the streets in massive public protests. When the nation went off to war against that despotism, librarians urged Americans to send books to soldiers and sailors in the armed forces. Some 20 million hardcover books were donated, filling makeshift libraries set up in military camps around the world. In 1943, the U.S. War Department collaborated with the publishing industry to orchestrate the Victory Book Campaign, producing 120 million small, paperback books of every subject and genre. "Armed Service Editions" were the lifeblood of countless American soldiers. Carried by men into battle, the books filled many idle hours, and served as touchstones of home and the democratic future for which they were fighting.[40]

During World War II, more than 1,100 young women flew military aircraft as Women Airforce Service Pilots (WASP), enduring rigorous military training commensurate with men who flew combat operations. WASP flew 60 million miles, testing new aircraft, ferrying military planes from factories to military installations and other points of overseas departure across the country, and transporting live ammunition for air and ground gunner training exercises. Thirty-eight of the women perished, among them Mabel Rawlinson of Kalamazoo, Michigan, who on August 23, 1943 was returning from night training exercise when her plane went down. "We ran out onto the field," remembered Marion Hanrahan. "We saw the front of her plane engulfed in fire, and we could hear Mabel screaming. It was a nightmare."[41] Classified as civil servants, WASP were entitled to no military recognition, no honors, or benefits. Families absorbed the cost of transporting and burying loved ones in a non-military funeral with no flag-draped coffin, nor a gold star service flag in the window. In Rawlinson's case, her WASP comrades pitched in to help get her casket home, two of them escorting her. It took the women's movement of the 1960s and the introduction of women pilots for the WASP to receive recognition as honored patriots.

In the spring of 1944, WASP Teresa James took flight in *Ten Grand*, the ten-thousandth P-47 Thunderbolt fighter plane produced at Republic Aviation in Farmingdale, New York. The workers there called themselves "Racers," for the speed at which they turned out P-47s, the heaviest and most devastating single-engine fighter plane in the Allied bombing campaign over occupied Europe. James delivered the plane to the Newark (NJ) Army Base, from whence it joined the fleet of P-47s based in England.[42] Fully one-half the Racer workforce in Farmingdale were women. It is no exaggeration to say—as Joseph Stalin said of American production overall—that without the female Racers and the efforts of all American women on the home front, the war could not have been won.[43] From 1941 to 1945, six million women joined the 13 million already in the workforce. They served as riveters, welders, locomotive engineers, boilermakers, and mechanics. Women ran farms, roped cattle, ran streetcars, and drove buses. Many more assumed clerical jobs and positions in radio, health care, and finance. Betty Friedan, author of *The Feminine Mystique* that helped ignite the women's movement in 1963, began her career as a wartime journalist. More than 300,000 joined one of the women's units of the armed services. The sexism and gender discrimination women endured on the job often fueled their determination to succeed. Frankie Cooper moved from Kentucky to East St. Louis when the war began and took a job operating a fifty-ton crane in a steel mill. "Almost scared to death," Cooper later recalled how she overcame her trepidation:

> Pouring steel was the hardest job in the mill, and the men said, "It's too big a responsibility for a woman. She'll never last." But I did. The hardest part for me was sanding the rails ... They're way up in the air over the concrete floor, and they have to be sanded every eight-hour shift ... I thought, I can't do that. I can't look down at that concrete and maneuver this little bucket of sand ... And one of the men said, "Well, that'll get her. She'll never sand them tracks." That's what made me sand them. After that, I had to ... show them I could do it.[44]

Women endured not only widespread sexual harassment, but also discrimination in job type and pay. Despite the National War Labor Board's call for "equal pay for equal work," and support from most unions, women in manufacturing made 65 cents for every dollar a man made for equal work.[45] Still, most made more money than they ever had in their lives. "The money was in defense," said Margarita Salazar, who left her beauty shop to help fabricate aircraft. "The more hours you made, the more money you made. And it was exciting ... You figured you were doing something for your country—and at the same time making money." Hundreds of laundries and restaurants closed because they lost their workforce.[46] Starting from a lower socioeconomic position, the impact for African American women was even more dramatic. More than 400,000 left their jobs as domestic maids or servants for jobs in the defense industry.[47] Although subjected to the added insult of pervasive racism, most black women enjoyed more respect in their workplace than they had ever received from their white employers. "Hitler," Fanny Christina Hill recalled, "was the one that got us out of the white folks' kitchen."[48]

Newspapers and magazines featured scandalous reports of working women abandoning their children at home, leaving them in their car with sandwiches, or with strangers—all contradicting the War Manpower Commission's admonition that mothers not abandon their "first responsibility."[49] The WMC encouraged women to find work in their own communities where friends and grandparents might care for children, advice that fell far short of addressing the need. The 1940 Lanham Act authorizing war-related grants to local communities facilitated the establishment of more than 3,000 "Lanham Nursery Schools," "daycare" centers. Although they only cared for 600,000 children for the duration of the war—10 percent of what was needed—Lanham daycare established what advocates hoped would be an important precedent for further federal investment in affordable childcare for working mothers. Alas, despite studies conducted later documenting the life-changing impact of Lanham daycare on the children, it was not to be.[50]

Whether they served in the military or on the home front, women's lives were transformed. Adele Erenberg, who went from the cosmetics counter in a local LA drugstore to working in the Boeing machine shop, put it this way:

> For me defense work was the beginning of my emancipation as a woman … I had the consciousness-raising experience of being the only woman in this machine shop and having the mantle of challenge laid down by the men, which stimulated my competitiveness and forced me to prove myself.[51]

Notwithstanding a 1944 study indicating that 80 percent of women wanted to retain their jobs, most were "furloughed," replaced by returning GIs. Yet their experience had planted an important seed of women's liberation.

The Struggle for Democracy at Home

Against the background of the global fight to save democracy was a struggle over its very meaning at home, beginning with one of the most shameful episodes in American history. In February 1942, President Roosevelt signed Executive Order 9066, authorizing the forced internment of nearly 120,000 Japanese Americans—nearly two-thirds of whom were *Nisei*, naturalized citizens. Tens of thousands were forced to abandon their homes, sell their farms and possessions at rock-bottom prices, and move to desolate internment camps for the duration of the war. From 1942 to 1945, 33,000 *Nisei* volunteered for service in the military, roughly 14,000 of whom served in the legendary 442nd Regimental Combat Team, which became the most decorated unit of its size in the history of the U.S. military. The men of the 522nd Field Artillery, a special unit of the 442nd, were among those who liberated the Dachau death camp in April 1945. By the time Americans made their approach to the ghastly scene of dead bodies and emaciated survivors, many blindfolded about to be shot, the German guards had fled. Survivor Janina Cywinska described what happened next:

> I was standing with a blindfold waiting to be shot, but the shot didn't come. So I asked the woman next to me, "Do you think they're trying to make us crazy, so we'll run and they won't have to feel guilty about shooting us?" She said, "Well, we're not going to run. We'll just stand here." So we stood

and stood and suddenly someone was tugging at my blindfold. He tugged this way and that way, and then he jumped up because he was short and he pulled it off. I saw him and I thought, Oh now the *Japanese* are going to kill us. And I didn't care anymore. I said, "just kill us, get it over with." He tried to convince me that he was an American and wouldn't kill me. I said, "Oh no, you're a Japanese and you're going to kill us." We went back and forth, and finally he landed on his knees, crying, with his hands over his face, and he said, "You are free now. We are *American* Japanese. You are free."[52]

American Japanese they were, and the fact that two-thirds of those who served did so from the U.S. territory of Hawaii points to one of the underlying reasons for the internment policy. Japanese Americans in Hawaii were not subjected to internment and dispossession of their land and homes, largely because the influential Hawaiian business community was heavily dependent on their labor. By contrast, powerful white agricultural interests of California had been agitating for years against Japanese vegetable growers. As support for interring all Japanese hit fever pitch after Pearl Harbor, Austin Anson, managing secretary for the Grower-Shipper Vegetable Association, offered this candid admission:

> We're charged with wanting to get rid of the Japs for selfish reasons ... We do. It's a question of whether the White man lives on the Pacific Coast or the brown men. They came to this valley to work, and they stayed to take over ... If all the Japs were removed tomorrow, we'd never miss them ... and we don't want them back when the war ends.[53]

Another Association official wrote that "the Japanese cannot be assimilated as the white race [and] we must do everything we can to stop them now as we have a golden opportunity now and may never have it again." White growers seized the opportunity, commandeering for pennies on the dollar $72 million of valuable Japanese American agricultural land and property.[54] State Department official Eugene V. Rostow pointed out the glaring hypocrisy of American policy:

> We believe that the German people bear a common political responsibility for outrages secretly committed by the Gestapo and the SS. What are we to think of our own part in a program which violates every democratic social value, yet has been approved by the Congress, the President and the Supreme Court?[55]

Other episodes of discrimination tainted West Coast war mobilization. By 1945 California was home to 100,000 migrant laborers who came from Mexico through the *bracero* program, aimed at meeting a farm labor shortage. *Braceros* were ostensibly guaranteed decent living and working conditions, a minimum wage, and protections from discrimination, yet contractual violations and racist treatment were routine.[56] Mexican Americans had long endured pervasive discrimination in employment, housing, the justice system, and voting rights. In the Depression-era "Repatriation" program, nearly one million had been forcibly deported to Mexico—60 percent of them, U.S. citizens. In June 1943, thousands of white sailors and servicemen engaged in several days and nights of assaults against Mexican, Filipino, and African Americans in the infamous "Zoot Suit Riots." The attacks, aided by civilians and abetted occasionally by the police, occurred on the streets, in bars, restaurants, and theaters.[57]

Alongside xenophobic repression stood inspiring moments of struggle, including that in Dayton, Washington in July 1943. There, *braceros* labored beside some of the 10,000 Japanese Americans released from internment to ease the farm labor shortage in the Pacific Northwest. On July 20, a white female worker accused a man "looking Mexican" of assaulting her. Lacking a suspect, local authorities immediately imposed restrictions on the movement of all workers. In a remarkable demonstration of solidarity, more than 400 Mexican and Japanese American farm workers immediately struck the cannery. With pea-picking and canning season at its peak, the restrictive order was lifted within 48 hours.[58]

No home front struggle had more far-reaching impact than that of African Americans, the overwhelming majority of whom responded to the war with a profoundly felt, but complicated, patriotism. Jim Crow and Klan terror still ruled the South. Across the country, blacks experienced discrimination in employment and housing, police brutality, and pervasive racism. The U.S. war against the Nazi ideology of white Aryan supremacy laid bare more starkly than ever what Swedish Nobel laureate Gunnar Myrdal in 1944 called *The American Dilemma*. Myrdal's thickly documented study revealed the contradictions of American ideals versus the realities of life for black Americans. Myrdal's evidence provoked sobering debate among officials in Washington about America's image around the world. Black patriots did not need to read the book. German prisoners being held in Salina, Kansas could dine in restaurants that black soldiers dare not enter.[59] African Americans watching Frank Capra's documentary *Why We Fight*, in segregated theatres everywhere, learned that Americans "hate war … but—let our freedoms be endangered and we'll pay and suffer to the last man."[60] Black freedom had been endangered for more than three centuries.

The war galvanized African Americans. Civil rights leaders, led by A. Philip Randolph, head of the Brotherhood of Sleeping Car Porters, launched the March on Washington Movement (MOWM). Founded primarily to protest segregation in the armed forces, the MOWM took up the issue of discrimination against African Americans in the defense industry. In January 1941, Randolph proposed the idea of a march on Washington of tens of thousands under the banner: "WE LOYAL NEGRO AMERICAN CITIZENS DEMAND THE RIGHT TO WORK AND FIGHT FOR OUR COUNTRY." The event would culminate with a rally at the Lincoln Memorial, capped by an address, Randolph proffered, from "the greatest living champion of the cause of liberty and democracy," President Roosevelt.[61] Demonstrations on the capitol were an uncommon sight in 1941, a gathering of 25,000 Klan members in 1925 having been the largest. Not only was FDR averse to speaking, he had his War

Department reject the integration request and tried to dissuade Randolph from the march. Randolph resisted FDR's entreaties, for, "we feel as you have wisely said: 'No people will lose their freedom fighting for it.'" In the end, the president signed Executive Order 8802, prohibiting discrimination in the defense industry—at least on paper.[62] A Fair Employment Practices Committee (FEPC) was established to enforce the measure.

Randolph suspended the march, but the MOWM persisted, staging marches around the nation calling for desegregation of the military and to hold the FEPC accountable. Just one third of the 8,000 charges of discrimination received by the FEPC were resolved favorably. Still, there was progress. By war's end, African Americans accounted for eight percent of defense-related jobs—up from three in 1941. The number of blacks employed by the federal government tripled. The most dramatic episode of the FEPC's effectiveness unfolded in 1944 in Philadelphia. When the local transit company responded to agency pressure by hiring eight black trolley drivers, white drivers reacted with a wildcat strike, shutting down the city's transit system. The president deployed 8,000 soldiers to the city to break the strike, restore order, and ensure protection of the eight drivers.[63] However imperfect, the FEPC set an important precedent of federal action against discrimination in the private sector.

Expanded opportunity for African Americans triggered episodes of violent resistance, none worse than Detroit in June 1943. A center of war production, Detroit saw tens of thousands of blacks arrive from the South. The majority huddled in dreadful conditions in a segregated area unironically called "Paradise Valley." White Detroiters fought any hint of black integration of their neighborhoods. In 1942, when African Americans tried to move into the Sojourner Truth Homes—designated for black residents but adjacent to a white neighborhood—a white mob assaulted them and set a large cross afire. Police brutality in the city was egregious, as was FEPC resistance; when three black workers were promoted at Packard, 3,000 whites struck the plant.[64] Racial street brawls became a common sight. In August 1942, *Life* declared ominously, "Detroit can either blow up Hitler or it can blow up the U.S."[65] In June 1943 tensions boiled over on Belle Isle, the city's recreation jewel. Fueled by rumors of murder and rape, 24 hours of riotous attacks resulted in the deaths of nine whites and 25 blacks and 600 injured. President Roosevelt sent 6,000 soldiers backed by tanks to end the violence.[66]

With the war winding down, African American leaders urged that the FEPC be extended and other measures taken to ensure the protection of what the *Pittsburgh Courier* called the "Double V"—Victory over America's enemies and discrimination at home. Although the shifting political climate of 1945 made an extension of the FEPC impossible, the modern civil rights struggle had been joined.

Recovering from the flu in early January 1944, President Roosevelt decided to return to the longstanding practice of American presidents submitting the State of the Union message to congress in written form. The American people, however, would hear it as a fireside chat. The speech was no rhetorical masterpiece, one historian calling much of it a disparate "pastiche" of observations and assessments of the war's progress.[67] After summarizing results of his recent discussions with Allied leaders, the president applauded "the overwhelming majority" of Americans who had risen to their nation's hour of need, suffering tremendous "inconveniences … hardships … [and] tragic sacrifices." He then contrasted the cooperative spirit of most Americans with the deplorable "selfish agitation" of a "noisy minority" of "pests" who "swarm through the lobbies of the Congress and the cocktail bars of Washington" seeking to profit from the war. The return to the populist language of the Depression era set up the memorable portion of the speech: his proposal for a "Second Bill of Rights." As had been his wont, FDR selected portions of the address to be filmed as newsreels to be shown in theaters—this, at a time when more than two-thirds of Americans went to the movies at least once a week. The selection of the economic bill of rights for filming underscored its importance for Roosevelt. Delivered months before the Democratic Party jettisoned Henry Wallace from the 1944 ticket, FDR's second bill of rights reminds us just how closely aligned the two men were. Echoing his vice president, Roosevelt declared that a just and permanent peace required "a decent standard of living for all individual men and women and children in all nations." In the end, "freedom from fear is eternally linked with freedom from want." [68]

The address envisioned an expansive postwar program guaranteeing broad security for Americans, including rights

> to a useful and remunerative job … to earn enough to provide adequate food and clothing and recreation … to adequate medical care … to adequate protection from the economic fears of old age, sickness, accident, and unemployment; … and a good education.

Further, President Roosevelt reiterated the need for a strong social democracy as a bulwark against illiberal authoritarianism: "We have come to a clear realization of the fact that true individual freedom cannot exist without economic security and independence … People who are hungry and out of a job are the stuff of which dictatorships are made."

The vision was well received internationally. The Universal Declaration of Human Rights, inspired by the second bill of rights and adopted by the United Nations in 1948, includes basic guarantees for social and economic security as one important means to ensuring global peace. Nations around the world incorporated similar provisions into their constitutions.[69] There was broad support at home, as well. Labor, civil rights and religious leaders rallied behind the second bill of rights, as did nearly three quarters of Americans.[70] Yet the consolidation of a conservative coalition of Republicans and Democrats, coupled with the rising climate of anti-communism immediately after the war that made anything smacking of enlarged government sound like Soviet communism, doomed the package. Roosevelt's death in April 1945 and the ascension of Harry Truman to the presidency marked the onset of more a decade and a half of stasis for social reform, unions and liberals doing well simply to defend the gains of the New Deal era. Washington's power would grow, but almost exclusively with respect to the size and authority wielded by the military and the national security establishment.

"We Are All Jews Here"

The righteous peace for which Franklin Roosevelt declared soldiers were fighting was grounded in what the ancient Greeks called *agape*. The highest form of human love, *agape* is fueled by the capacity for empathy. Essential to an effective modern democracy that tries to care for all of its citizens, *agape* speaks to the essence of military service. Among the countless acts of heroism committed by Americans during the war, few distill with greater moral clarity the universal value of selfless duty than that of Master Sergeant Roddie Edmonds of the 442nd Infantry Regiment of the 106th Infantry Division of the U.S. Army. On December 19, 1944, Edmonds and his men were captured during the Battle of the Bulge, the final German offensive of the war. Within weeks, Edmonds and over 1,200 other Americans found themselves imprisoned at Stalag IX-A, a POW camp near Ziegenhain, Germany. With defeat approaching, the Nazis' extermination of Jewish POWs accelerated that winter. On January 27, 1945, Edmonds, a stoic, respected leader of his men and the highest non-commissioned officer among the Americans at the camp, received an order from the commandant, Major Siegmann: "Tomorrow morning at roll call all Jewish Americans must assemble at the Appelplatz [the site of roll call]—only the Jews—no one else. All who disobey this order will be shot."[71]

"We're not doing that," Edmonds told his men. The word went down the line from barracks to barracks to fall out at the Appelplatz, including those barely able to stand by this point from malnourishment—Americans with names like "McCoy and Walker, Smith and Nicholson, Miller and Bruno," right alongside Lester Tannenbaum, Paul Stern, and 200 other Jewish American soldiers. *"Raus! Raus!"* came the order at 0600. With all 1,292 men standing in formation, Major Siegmann approached Edmonds. "Were my orders not clear, Sergeant? Only the Jews were to fall out." Edmonds replied that under the rules of the Geneva Convention, his men would provide "name, rank, and serial number," nothing more. "Only the Jews!" the major yelled. "They cannot all be Jews." Edmonds responded, "We are all Jews here." Siegmann then pointed his Luger between the eyes of the young Tennessean, "Sergeant, one last chance." "Major," Edmonds coolly replied, "you can shoot me, but you'll have to kill *all* of us—because we know who you are—and you *will* be tried for war crimes when we win this war. And you will pay."[72] Following the war, Edmonds said nothing to anyone about the episode. It was left to his son decades later to dig out the story, mainly by speaking with survivors, many of whose lives had been saved and changed forever. As Paul Stern put it, "Sergeant Edmonds's shining example is something for all of us to remember, and try to emulate in our own lives."[73] On February 10, 2015, Israel's Yad Vashem recognized Master Sergeant Roddie Edmonds as

"Righteous Among the Nations," awarded to non-Jews who risked their lives to save the lives of Jews during the Holocaust.

"A God-Sanctioned Invincible Holy Power"

> When the war was over we felt really good about ourselves. We had something no other nation had. We had saved the world from an unspeakable evil. We were a God-sanctioned invincible holy power and it was our duty to show that our way was the right way for the world. I think all of us felt that way. We were so innocent and naïve … Life was going to be glorious from now on, because we deserved it.
>
> —Idahoan Laura Briggs[74]

Sixteen million Americans served in the armed forces, and although the number of casualties paled in comparison to the more than 25 million dead in the Soviet Union and the 65 million suffered worldwide, more than 400,000 paid the ultimate price to preserve their nation and the values of a democratic free world. Americans at home had rationed, sacrificed, and worked around the clock in the greatest war in history. The exuberant patriotism and nationalistic confidence of Americans recalled by Laura Briggs echoed the hubris of Henry Luce and was indeed widely felt. In contrast to the Soviet Union and much of Europe, the United States had not been ravaged by the war and in 1945 enjoyed unparalleled economic strength. Policy makers in Washington anticipated the grand opportunity to, as Luce envisioned, "exert upon the world the full impact of [American] influence."

The way the war ended punctuated dramatically America's "invincible holy power." The "Manhattan Project," the $2 billion effort to build the world's first atom bomb, proved a success with the "Trinity" test in New Mexico on July 16, 1945. Three weeks later, the United States dropped atomic bombs on the Japanese cities of Hiroshima and Nagasaki, killing nearly 250,000 instantly and forcing the capitulation of the Japanese Empire. In announcing the news, President Harry Truman captured that spirit of a victorious nation acting in accord with its divine mission:

> Having *found* the atomic bomb we have used it … in order to shorten the agony of war, in order to save the lives of thousands and thousands of young Americans … It is an awful responsibility which has *come to us*. We thank God that it has *come to us*, instead of to our enemies; and we pray that He may guide us to use it in His ways and for His purposes (emphasis added).[75]

Even in the calculated decision to produce and use the world's first atomic bombs, Truman asserted the nation's righteous innocence, in the process declaring that it had been a military necessity to drop the bomb to force a Japanese surrender. Nearly all high-ranking military officials at the time disputed the president's assertion, which nonetheless became firmly implanted in America's popular memory of the war.[76] Admirals William Leahy and Chester Nimitz were among the many officials who argued that the Japanese would have surrendered by November 1945 without the need for a U.S.-led invasion. The decision that launched the world into the nuclear age was at a minimum driven by additional factors, including its demonstration of American power in the looming postwar struggle against the Soviet Union.

There were other, less dramatic indicators of the coming U.S. hegemony. A full fourth Roosevelt term or a Henry Wallace administration would almost certainly have meant a different kind of global American footprint from the one emerging by 1945. Throughout World War II, a growing number of State Department officials and business elites anticipated a postwar world in which the United States would emerge from the war an economic juggernaut with the capacity to reshape the global business environment. In July 1944, representatives of 44 Allied nations met at Bretton Woods, New Hampshire, for the United Nations Monetary and Financial Aid Conference to chart the postwar economic order. The Bretton Woods Conference established the pillars for an American- and Anglo-European–directed global financial system. Leaders conceived the foundations of the International Monetary Fund, the World Bank, and the General Agreement on Tariffs and Trade. Haunted by the memory of 1920s economic nationalism and the Great Depression, and with a nervous eye on the international appeal of communism, the goals of western officials were to promote free-market economic growth and political stability. A fixed rate of currency exchange pegged to a gold-backed U.S. dollar solidified America's position as an economic hegemon. The ability to heavily capitalize reconstruction efforts in postwar Europe gave the United States dominant influence at the World Bank and IMF, steering reconstruction, development, and monetary policies in its favor for the next quarter century. In addition, Secretary of State Cordell Hull was instrumental in forging creation of the United Nations. While democratic principles like the right of nations to self-rule, human rights, and a prohibition against preemptive war were embedded in the UN Charter, it was clear from the outset that U.S. officials viewed the body as another instrument through which to advance both American values and U.S. interests.

Another sign came with the February 1945 meeting between the ailing Franklin Roosevelt, en route home from his final wartime conference in Yalta, and Abdul Aziz, the founder of the Saudi Arabian kingdom. Taking place aboard the U.S. cruiser *Quincy*, the discussions marked a symbolic beginning to a valuable, albeit exceedingly fraught, strategic relationship for the United States. During the war the U.S. sent millions to the kingdom, facilitating Saudi assistance in ferrying Allied troops and munitions. Now with the war underscoring the paramount importance of petroleum to an ascendant global power, and the sun setting on British influence, key figures in the Roosevelt administration made filling an emerging power vacuum in the Middle East a strategic priority. A U.S.–Saudi alliance would provide not only a crucial fortification against Soviet influence, but also a cornerstone for America's own aspirations. Tension emerged when the president reiterated U.S. support for a Jewish state in Palestine—a position Aziz rejected as a betrayal of Arab sovereignty. Roosevelt pledged further aid and reassured Abdul Aziz that he "would make no move hostile to the Arab people."[77] How the American president would have reconciled that promise with the strategic advantage and moral urgency of supporting a Jewish state in a post-Holocaust world is unknown. In 1948, after much debate inside the Truman administration, the U.S. formally recognized Israel, complicating but by no means rupturing the Saudi partnership.

Winston Churchill regretted the decline of the British Empire, but he consoled himself with the arrival of the American colossus. Churchill and FDR had forged an Anglo-American alliance that the much-admired British statesman trusted would protect western values and the imperial interests for which he believed the war had been fought. On August 16, 1945, one day after the announcement of the Japanese surrender, Churchill put the newfound position of American leadership in these grandiloquent terms:

> The United States stand [sic] at this moment at the summit of the world. I rejoice that this should be so. Let them act up to the level of their power and their responsibility, not for themselves but for others, for all men in all lands, and then a brighter day may dawn upon human history.[78]

How the United States exercised this extravagant vision—and what that portended for peoples around the world with visions of freedom of their own, no less what it meant for Americans at home—proved far more complex than Churchill could have imagined.

Notes

1 Henry Luce, "The American Century," *Life*, February 17, 1941, 63.
2 Henry Wallace, "The Price of Free World Victory," remembered as "The Century of the Common Man," Grand Ballroom, Commodore Hotel, New York City, May 8, 1942.
3 Robert Edward Herzstein, *Henry R. Luce, Time, and the American Crusade in Asia* (New York: Cambridge University Press, 2005), 1.
4 David Plotz, "The Greatest Magazine Ever Published," *Slate*, December 27, 2013, https://slate.com/human-interest/2013/12/life-magazine-1945-why-it-was-the-greatest-magazine-ever-published.html, retrieved December 16, 2020.
5 Luce, 62.
6 Dana Frank, "The Devil and Mrs. Hearst," *The Nation*, June 22, 2000, review of David Nasaw's *The Chief* (Boston, MA: Mariner Books, 2001), www.thenation.com/article/archive/devil-and-mr-hearst, retrieved December 16, 2020.
7 See Sally Denton, *The Plots Against the President: FDR, A Nation in Crisis, and the Rise of the American Right* (London: Bloomsbury, 2012).
8 Luce, 64; and Alan Brinkley, *The Publisher: Henry Luce and His American Century* (New York: Alfred A. Knopf, 2010), 271.
9 Thompson, quoted in Brinkley, 270.
10 John Nichols, *The Fight for the Soul of the Democratic Party: The Enduring legacy of Henry Wallace's Anti-Fascist, Anti-Racist Politics* (New York: Verso, 2020), Kindle edition, 41.

11 "Aaron Copland and Fanfare for the Common Man," Kennedy Center, n.d., www.kennedy-center.org/education/resources-for-educators/classroom-resources/media-and-interactives/media/music/aaron-copland--fanfare-for-the-common-man, retrieved December 19, 2020.

12 J. Michael Martinez, *Congressional Giants: Influential Leaders of Congress and How They Shaped American History* (Lanham, MD: Rowman & Littlefield, 2020), 171.

13 Quoted in Nichols, 47–8.

14 Nichols, 73.

15 Wallace, in Nichols, 55.

16 Steven J. Ross, *Hitler in Los Angeles: How Jews Foiled Nazi Plots Against Hollywood and America* (New York: Bloomsbury, 2017).

17 The reference is to Sinclair Lewis's 1935 dystopian political novel warning of American fascism.

18 "Fighting Nazis in the U.S., Then and Now," Robert Scheer, interview with Steven J. Ross, December 22, 2017, www.truthdig.com/articles/fighting-nazis-america-now-audio, retrieved December 22, 2020.

19 Alexander Allen, quoted in Mark Jonathan Harris et al., *The Home Front: America During World War II* (New York: Putnam, 1984), 96.

20 Portrayed by Hungarian American actor Paul Lukas, who won an Oscar for his performance in the 1941 anti-Nazi film *Watch on the Rhine*.

21 U.S. Department of War, *Don't Be a Sucker* (Washington, DC, 1943, shorter version 1947), www.youtube.com/watch?v=sAu41SpYtl4, retrieved December 18, 2020.

22 Nichols, ch. 4.

23 *Mrs. Miniver*, directed by William Wyler (Hollywood, CA: Metro-Goldwyn-Mayer, 1942).

24 The Atlantic Charter, August 14, 1941, https://avalon.law.yale.edu/wwii/atlantic.asp, retrieved December 19, 2020.

25 Mark Harris, *Five Came Back: A Story of Hollywood and the Second World War* (New York: Penguin, 2014), 138; and n.a., "The Wilcoxon Speech," Reel Classics, www.reelclassics.com/Movies/Miniver/miniver-dialog3.htm, retrieved December 20, 2020.

26 Harvard Sitkoff, "The American Home Front," in Barbara McLean Ward, ed., *Produce & Conserve, Share & Play Square* (Portsmouth, NH: Strawbery Banke Museum, 1994), 37–39.

27 Sitkoff, 45; and Doris Goodwin, "The Way We Won: America's Economic Breakthrough During World War II," *The American Prospect*, December 19, 2001, https://prospect.org/health/way-won-america-s-economic-breakthrough-world-war-ii, retrieved December 19, 2020.

28 Roosevelt's Announcement of the Second New Deal, October 31, 1936, http://docs.fdrlibrary.marist.edu/od2ndst.html; and Speech before the Democratic National Convention, June 27, 1936, www.austincc.edu/lpatrick/his2341/fdr36acceptancespeech.htm, retrieved December 20, 2020.

29 Herman Miles Somers, *Presidential Agency: OWMR, The Office of War Mobilization and Reconversion* (Cambridge: Harvard University Press, 1950).

30 Carroll W. Pursell, "Science Agencies in World War II: The OSRD and Its Challengers," in Nathan Reingold, ed., *The Sciences in the American Context: New Perspectives* (Washington, DC: Smithsonian Institution Press, 1979).

31 Marilyn M. Harper et al., *World War II and the American Home Front: A National Historic Landmarks Theme Study* (Washington, DC: Department of Interior, National Parks Service, 2007), 17, citing Allan M. Winkler, *Home Front U.S.A.: America during World War II*, 2nd ed. (Wheeling, IL: Harlan Davidson, 2000), 11–12; William M. Tuttle, Jr., "The Birth of an Industry: The Synthetic Rubber 'Mess' in World War II," *Technology and Culture* 22 (1981): Vatter, U.S. Economy, 28–29.

32   Chris J. Magoc, "The Aluminum City: Prepared as part of the Feasibility Study on the Development of Aluminum Heritage in New Kensington, Pennsylvania" (Johnstown, PA: Westsylvania Heritage Corp, 2003), 16–17.

33   Harper et al., 43.

34   More than $4 trillion in 2021.

35   Sitkoff, 45.

36   Goodwin.

37   Jonathan Alter, *The Defining Moment: FDR's Hundred Days and the Triumph of Hope* (New York: Simon and Schuster, 2007), 263–271.

38   Franklin D. Roosevelt, "Fireside Chat 23, October 12, 1942: On the Home Front," https://millercenter.org/the-presidency/presidential-speeches/october-12-1942-fireside-chat-23-home-front, retrieved December 21, 2020.

39   "Bibliocaust," *Time*, May 22, 1933, quoted in Molly Guptill Manning, *When Books Went to War: The Stories That Helped Us Win World War II* (New York: Houghton Mifflin, 2014), 6.

40   Manning's book richly covers this generally unheralded story.

41   Susan Stamberg, "Female WW II Pilots: The Original Flygirls," National Public Radio: *Morning Edition*, March 9, 2010, www.npr.org/2010/03/09/123773525/female-wwii-pilots-the-original-fly-girls, retrieved December 19, 2020.

42   Penny Colman, *Rosie the Riveter: Women Working on the Home Front in World War II* (New York: Crown Publishers, 1995), 19.

43   Quoted in "One War Won," *Time*, December 13, 1943.

44   Colman, 93.

45   William Chafe, *The Paradox of Change: American Women in the 20th Century* (New York: Oxford University Press, 1991), 154–158.

46   Colman, 42–43.

47   Karen Tucker Anderson, "Last Hired, First Fired: Black Women Workers during World War II," *Journal of American History* 69 (June 1982): 82–97.

48   Colman, 31.

49   Agnes Meyer, "War Orphans, U.S.A.," *Reader's Digest* 43 (August 1943): 98–102.

50   Rhaina Cohen, "Who Took Care of Rosie the Riveter's Kids?" *The Atlantic*, November 18, 2015, www.theatlantic.com/business/archive/2015/11/daycare-world-war-rosie-riveter/415650, retrieved December 22, 2020.

51   Erenberg, quoted in Harris et al., 128–129.

52   Judy Y. Kawamoto, *Forced Out: A Nikkei Women's Search for a Home in America* (Boulder, CO: University Press of Colorado, 2020), 18; and Martin W. Sandler, *Imprisoned: The Betrayal of Japanese Americans During World War II* (New York: Bloomsbury, 2013), 107–109.

53   *Korematsu v. United States*, 323 U.S. 214, Dissenting opinion by Justice Frank Murphy, footnote 12 (Supreme Court of the United States, 1944).

54   Stephen B. Caudill, "Special Interests and the Internment of Japanese-Americans During World War II," Foundation for Economic Education, July 1, 1995, https://fee.org/articles/special-interests-and-the-internment-of-japanese-americans-during-world-war-ii, retrieved December 22, 2020.

55   John Morton Blum, *V Was for Victory: Politics and American Culture During World War II* (New York: Harcourt Brace, 1976), 166, quoting Eugene V. Rostow, "The Japanese American Cases—A Disaster," *Yale Law Journal*, June 1945.

56   Martin Camps, ed., *Dialogues on the Delta: Approaches to the City of Stockton. (Newcastle, UK: Cambridge Scholars Publishing, 2018), 143.*

57   Blum, 205–206.

58   Robert Longley, "The Bracero Program: When the U.S. Looked to Mexico for Labor," ThoughtCo., December 3, 2020, www.thoughtco.com/the-bracero-program-4175798, retrieved December 22, 2020.

59 Clayborne Carson, "African Americans at War," in I. C. B. Dear, ed., *The Oxford Companion to the Second World War* (New York: Oxford University Press, 1993), https://web.stanford.edu/~ccarson/articles/oxford_companion.htm, retrieved December 22, 2020.

60 Frank Capra and Anatole Litvak, *Why We Fight*, part seven, "War Comes to America" (Washington, DC: U.S. Office of War Information, 1945).

61 Blum, 186.

62 Ibid., 187.

63 Lingeman, 163–164.

64 Ibid., 323; Vivian M. Baulch and Patricia Zacharias, "The 1943 Detroit Race Riots," www.mtholyoke.edu/courses/rschwart/clio/detroit_riot/DetroitNewsRiots1943. htm, retrieved December 22, 2020.

65 Quoted in "A Race Riot There Will Be," n.a., n.d., www.detroits-great-rebellion. com/Detroit---1943.html, retrieved December 22, 2020.

66 Lingeman, 326–329.

67 Cass R. Sunstein, *The Second Bill of Rights: FDR's Unfinished Revolution and Why We Need It More than Ever* (New York: Basic Books, 2004), 10.

68 Franklin D. Roosevelt, "State of the Union Message to Congress," January 11, 1944, www.fdrlibrary.marist.edu/archives/address_text.html, retrieved December 23, 2020.

69 Sunstein, 2–3.

70 Harvey J. Kaye, "Remembering Franklin Delano Roosevelt and the Second Bill of Rights," *Bill Moyers on Democracy*, March 7, 2014, https://billmoyers.com/2014/03/07/ remembering-franklin-delano-roosevelt-and-the-second-bill-of-rights, retrieved December 23, 2020.

71 Chris Edmonds and Douglas Century, *No Surrender: A Father, A Son, and An Extraordinary Act of Heroism That Continues to Live on Today* (New York: Harper One, 2019), 225.

72 Ibid., 226–230.

73 "Roddie Edmonds," Yad Vashem, World Holocaust Remembrance Center, www.yad-vashem.org/righteous/stories/edmonds.html, retrieved December 23, 2020.

74 Laura Briggs, quoted in Harris et al., 245.

75 President Harry S. Truman, "Radio Address to the American People Announcing the Dropping of the Atomic Bomb," August 9, 1945, www.pbs.org/perilousfight/psy-chology/the_atomic_option/letters, retrieved December 23, 2020.

76 Admiral William Leahy, Truman's Chief of Staff, as well as top Army Air Force General Henry "Hap" Arnold, Admiral William "Bull" Halsey, Admiral Chester Nimitz, and General Dwight D. Eisenhower were among those who argued the bomb was unnec-essary to force Japanese surrender. See Gar Alperovitz, "The War Was Won Before Hiroshima—and the Generals Who Dropped the Bomb Knew It," *The Nation*, August 6, 2015, www.thenation.com/article/world/why-the-us-really-bombed-hiroshima, retrieved December 24, 2020.

77 Memorandum of Conversation Between the King of Saudi Arabia and President Roosevelt, February 14, 1945, Aboard the U.S.S. *Quincy* (Washington, DC: U.S. Department of State), https://history.state.gov/historicaldocuments/frus1945v08/ d2, retrieved June 1, 2021.

78 Quoted by "David M. Kennedy on World War II," Humanities Texas, July/August 2011, www.humanitiestexas.org/news/articles/david-m-kennedy-world-war-ii, retrieved December 26, 2020.

Further Reading

Alter, Jonathan. *The Defining Moment: FDR's Hundred Days and the Triumph of Hope*. New York: Simon and Schuster, 2007.

Barber, William J. *Designs within Disorder: Franklin D. Roosevelt, the Economists, and the Shaping of American Economic Policy, 1933–1945*. Cambridge, MA: Cambridge University Press, 2006.

Black, Edwin. *Nazi Nexus: America's Corporate Connections to Hitler's Holocaust*. Westport, CT: Dialog Press, 2009.

Blum, John Morton. *V Was for Victory: Politics and American Culture During World War II*. New York: Harcourt Brace, 1976.

Brown, Daniel James. *Facing the Mountain: A True Story of Japanese-American Heroes in World War II*. New York: Viking Press, 2021.

Doherty, Thomas P. *Projections of War: Hollywood, American Culture, and World War II*. New York: Columbia University Press, 1999.

Harris, Mark. *Five Came Back: A Story of Hollywood and the Second World War*. New York: Penguin, 2014.

Harris, Mark Jonathan et al. *The Home Front: America During World War II*. New York: Putnam, 1984.

Herzstein, Robert Edward. *Henry R. Luce, Time, and the American Crusade in Asia*. New York: Cambridge University Press, 2005.

Higham, Charles. *Trading with the Enemy: The Nazi-American Money Plot, 1933–1949*. New York: Lowenstein Associates, 1983.

Kryder, Daniel. *Divided Arsenal: Race and the American State During World War II*. Cambridge, UK: Cambridge University Press, 2001.

Lingeman, Richard. *Don't You Know There's a War On? The American Home Front, 1941–1945*. New York: Thunder's Mouth Press, Nation Books, 1970, 2003.

Lipset, Seymour Martin. *American Exceptionalism: A Double-Edged Sword*. New York: W. W. Norton & Company, 1997.

Malloy, Sean Langdon. *Atomic Tragedy: Henry L. Stimson and the Decision to use the Bomb Against Japan*. Ithaca, NY: Cornell University Press, 2008.

Manning, Molly Guptill. *When Books Went to War: The Stories That Helped Us Win World War II*. New York: Houghton Mifflin, 2014.

Miscamble, Wilson D. *From Roosevelt to Truman: Potsdam, Hiroshima, and the Cold War*. New York: Cambridge University Press, 2007.

Nichols, John. *The Fight for the Soul of the Democratic Party: The Enduring Legacy of Henry Wallace's Anti-Fascist, Anti-Racist Politics*. New York: Verso, 2020.

O'Sullivan, Christopher. *FDR and the End of Empire: The Origins of American Power in the Middle East*. New York: Palgrave Macmillan, 2012.

Ross, Steven J. *Hitler in Los Angeles: How Jews Foiled Nazi Plots Against Hollywood and America*. New York: Bloomsbury, 2017.

Sandler, Martin W. *Imprisoned: The Betrayal of Japanese Americans During World War II*. New York: Bloomsbury, 2013.

Sunstein, Cass R. *The Second Bill of Rights: FDR's Unfinished Revolution and Why We Need It More than Ever*. New York: Basic Books, 2004.

Winkler, Allan M. *Home Front U.S.A.: America During World War II*, 2nd ed. Wheeling, IL: Harlan Davidson, 2000.

2 Containing Communism, Advancing "the American System"

At the present moment in world history nearly every nation must choose between alternative ways of life … One … is based upon the will of the majority, and is distinguished by free institutions, representative government, free elections, guarantees of individual liberty, freedom of speech and religion, and freedom from political oppression.

The second way of life is based upon the will of a minority forcibly imposed upon the majority. It relies upon terror and oppression, a controlled press and radio; fixed elections, and the suppression of personal freedoms. I believe that it must be the policy of the United States to support free peoples who are resisting attempted subjugation …

—President Harry S. Truman, March 12, 1947[1]

The joint session of Congress that was the president's audience for this historic address responded at first not with thunderous approval as we might imagine, but apprehensive silence. The applause that came minutes later as the president exited had, as one observer described, "a bewildered quality about it."[2] President Truman's immediate purpose was to persuade legislators to deliver a $400 million aid package to defend a besieged British-backed government in Greece, then engaged in a civil war against a communist-led army of partisans. British leaders had recently informed the U.S. State Department that given the United Kingdom's own postwar challenges, Britain could no longer prop up the regime. A smaller portion of the assistance would go to Turkey, whose efforts to defend its "national integrity," said Truman, demanded aid only America could provide. "Preservation of order in the Middle East" depended on it. Should congress reject the appeal, the president warned, "unspeakable tragedy" would befall both nations—and worse, "disastrous" consequences "for the world" if America stood by and permitted the "collapse of free institutions and loss of independence" in Greece and Turkey.[3]

In one slight-of-hand stroke of magniloquence, President Truman asked congress not only to defend Greece and Turkey, but to commit to a grand global struggle. Members of congress and much of the country sensed that what the president was seeking represented a watershed in America's relationship with the world. In the days that followed, newspaper editorials captured the historic

DOI: 10.4324/9781003160595-2

weight of what became known as the Truman Doctrine, noting its clear departure from the hemisphere-bound Monroe Doctrine that had for over a century largely framed, rhetorically if not always in action, U.S. foreign policy. Just two years removed from a terrible war, Americans received the speech with some ambivalence: even as two-thirds believed the U.S. should "take a strong stand in European affairs," and Truman's favorability shot up 15 points to 63 percent support, a majority thought aid to Greece and Turkey was a United Nations responsibility.[4] Senator Claude Pepper worried that such a unilateralist approach to world affairs would "sabotage" the UN. Even pillars of the national security establishment were alarmed by the president's tone. Concerned about the Soviet reaction, Secretary of State George Marshall said the president had "overstated the case a bit." Senior statesman Bernard Baruch called the speech "tantamount to a declaration of … an ideological or religious war."[5] America's European allies, who sat on the war's front lines, offered a generally cool response—stemming from not having been consulted on a speech that represented the first major rupture in Soviet relations with the West, as well as the fact that Communist parties were fully integrated into the democracies of France and Italy.[6] The most prescient critique may have come from Republican Congressman George Bender of Ohio:

> Let there be no mistake about the far-reaching implications of this plan. Once we have taken the historic step of sending financial aid, military experts and loans to Greece and Turkey, we shall be irrevocably committed to a course of action from which it will be impossible to withdraw. More and larger demands will follow. Greater needs will arise throughout the many areas of friction in the world.[7]

Joining Bender was Henry Wallace, who derided the Truman Doctrine for "betraying the great tradition of America," predicting it would send the United States into endless "reckless adventure" overseas.[8] When Wallace took his show on the road to Europe, members of congress called for revoking his passport; George Bender was nearly alone in defending the right of a former government official to speak out.[9]

Seen from the age of a costly American empire when millions in military aid are spent daily all around the world, the Truman request seems reasonable. But in 1947, Truman's call for direct intervention in the affairs of nations six thousand miles away represented a break from pre-World War II isolationism, and from longstanding American tradition. Moreover, the fusion of a crisis in the eastern Mediterranean into a summons to take up the role of what would later be characterized euphemistically as "global policeman" sounded as portentous to most Americans as it proved to be. The president's decision to frame the appeal in epic terms came after State Department drafts of the speech focused too much on the material conditions of Greece and the economic stakes of what could be lost to the U.S. in the Middle East if a communist-led government were to assume power in Athens—sounding too much to the president's ears "like an investment prospectus."[10] Undersecretary of State Dean Acheson, who led the process that produced the speech the president ultimately delivered, understood what was at stake: British "abdication of the Middle East" and the "obvious implications" for their successors."[11] The struggle in Greece would be made epic. As Acheson later wrote, "like apples in a barrel infected by one rotten one, the corruption of Greece would infect Iran and all to the east … to Africa through Asia Minor and Egypt, and to Europe through Italy and France …"[12]

Taken together, the complex of forces—the precipitating events and impact of Truman's speech, the subsequent U.S. role in the Greek Civil War, and equally fateful actions in Italy, Berlin and most bloodily, Korea—checked the communist advance. They further established the stable, liberal postwar international order, conditions for expanding what the National Security Council in 1950 would call "the American system." The full implications were impossible to predict then, but the Greek Civil War that triggered the Truman Doctrine and a worldwide crusade to contain communism signaled a new paradigm in human affairs that would be backed by a muscular projection of U.S. military power.

"Free Peoples" and an "Iron Curtain"

Not once in Truman's 2,204-word address did he mention the Soviet Union, or "Soviet communism." He did not need to. Combined with a deep-seated antipathy toward communism in America, events elsewhere—particularly the recent denial by Soviet leader Joseph Stalin of free elections in Poland, had freshly stoked anti-communist fervor. In March 1946, revered American ally Winston Churchill declared that an "Iron Curtain" of communism was falling over Eastern Europe. Thus, as Republican Senator Arthur Vandenberg urged him, Truman needed to paint only in broad strokes in order to "scare the hell out of the American people."[13] In the shadow of World War II, the costs of a return to isolationism would need to be made starkly clear to breach the resistance of anti-interventionists led by Ohio Republican Senator Robert A. Taft.

With sweeping declarations of freedom and democracy, Truman shrouded the recent history of Greece as a client state of the British, one whose freedom from Nazi occupation could not have been won without the blood of anti-fascist Greek communists. The president said nothing about the secret "Percentages Agreement" of October 1944 between wartime allies Churchill and Stalin that traded away the sovereignty of Greece. In what Churchill later called a "naughty document," the Percentages Agreement divided the postwar spoils of much of southeast Europe, pledging to Britain a free hand in reestablishing a far-right government in Greece. In exchange, the Soviets received varying percentages of control of the governments of Romania, Bulgaria, Hungary, and Yugoslavia.[14] Missing also was mention of the bloody crackdown against Greece's free press, labor unions, and political dissidents that followed the return of British rule that fall.[15] In the culminating event December 12, 1944, British-backed government soldiers gunned down 28 peaceful protesters in Athens' Constitution Square.

The violence prompted Churchill to visit the capital city, where he urged the government to "hold and dominate Athens … with bloodshed if necessary."[16]

Most importantly, Americans did not hear of the Soviets *not* intervening in Greece; indeed, Stalin had chastised Josip Broz Tito, the maverick communist leader of Yugoslavia, over Tito's efforts to supply arms to the Greek insurgents. Stalin's respect for Greek sovereignty underscores the fact that while the Soviet dictator had presided over the deaths of up to 20 million of his own people in punitive famines and murderous purges, in the immediate postwar era he had neither the capacity for, nor intentions of, worldwide communist revolution. The Soviet decision to withdraw from Iran in 1946 with little more than a promise of future oil concessions, as well as the steady demobilization of the Red Army in the late 1940s were indicative of the larger reality that the great Russian project after the war was rebuilding their shattered country, not expansion. Depictions of Stalin by American politicians and in the press as another Hitler bent on global conquest infuriated the Soviet despot.[17]

Meanwhile, the actions of Americans drove Soviet behavior further in the very direction U.S. leaders claimed was already reality. The secrecy and detonation of the atomic bomb at Hiroshima had reignited and heightened Stalin's insecurities. "A single demand of you, comrades," Stalin decreed to his top scientists in August 1945. "Provide us with atomic weapons in the shortest possible time. You know that Hiroshima has shaken the whole world. The equilibrium has been destroyed. Provide the bomb—it will remove a great danger from us."[18] Now it was Truman's reaction that proved decisive. He leaned heavily on the arguments of Russian expert George Kennan. From his post at the U.S. embassy in Moscow, in February 1946 Kennan authored a 5,500-word cable to the State Department that provided the policy underpinnings of the Truman Doctrine. The diplomat's influential "Long Telegram" and subsequent article in *Foreign Affairs* written under the pseudonym "X" argued that Russians held a "neurotic view of world affairs" stemming from a deep history of insecurity. Informed by centuries of fending off repeated invasion—Germany most recently, at catastrophic cost—the Soviet Union responded only to the "logic of force," Kennan argued. U.S. policy should work to "increase enormously the strains under which Soviet policy must operate" in the world.[19] Soon Kennan would regret that his arguments would be misappropriated in service to a policy of imperial adventures having little or nothing to do with Soviet ambitions.

A case can be made that the generally obscured U.S. intervention in Greece in the late 1940s is the most important episode of the entire Cold War. After Congress approved the Truman request—in the end, decisively—more than $300 million of American aid flowed into the American Mission to Aid Greece (AMAG) in Athens. It arrived mostly in the form of bombs, small arms, and incendiary napalm. As armed struggle waged by the Greek People's Liberation Army (ELAS) of the communist-led Greek National Liberation Front (EAM) continued in 1947, Greek authorities imposed a crackdown on those who criticized the government. In a campaign of state terror, a regime saturated with former Nazi collaborators declared martial law and arrested thousands, sending many to prisons or "reeducation camps" where many were tortured. Three-quarters of Greek citizens were investigated for "subversive activities."[20] Journalists were targeted for persecution. CBS correspondent George Polk was especially vocal in condemning the government and the AMAG. On May 16, 1948, Polk's body was found in Salonika Bay, a victim of assassination. In an investigation of his murder headed by William Donovan, former head of the U.S. Office of Strategic Services, the lead investigator found evidence pointing not to the communist who had been found guilty in a show trial, but to the U.S.-backed rightist government. The investigator was soon recalled to Washington. Journalist I. F. Stone called Polk "the first casualty of the Cold War."[21]

The Greek justice system was its own kingdom of atrocity. While the arrest and prosecution of Greek collaborators of the fascist wartime occupation essentially ended in 1945, prosecutors went after leftists with a vengeance. In the late 1940s, the number of leftist leaders put to death by Greek authorities and their British and American sponsors outnumbered executed fascist collaborators more than 100 to one, the number in prison seven to one. More than 20,000 leftwing political prisoners still languished in Greek prisons in 1950. Hundreds were still rotting there in the 1960s, their only crime having fought against the fascists.[22] The backing of the anti-human rights, Nazi-friendly regime in Athens by the United States is all the more appalling when seen against the background of the Nuremberg War Crimes Trials (1945–1946) then unfolding. In his opening statement to the International Military Tribunal, Chief of Counsel for the United States and U.S. Supreme Court Justice Robert H. Jackson, warned: "Civilization can afford no compromise with the social forces which would gain renewed strength if we deal ambiguously or indecisively with the men in whom those forces now precariously survive."[23] Tragically, that was precisely what happened in Greece.

After nearly three years of fighting and pressure from Stalin for a ceasefire, in the fall of 1949 the communists surrendered. Americans had gotten little of the truth of what had transpired in their defense of "free people." More than 100,000 people were killed, more than three-quarters of a million left homeless, and 30,000 children were now refugees. In the corridors of power, U.S. military planners and policymakers saw in the successful pacification of the Greek insurgency a model to be replicated elsewhere in the Cold War. The ink had barely dried on the Truman Doctrine when Dean Acheson formed an Ad Hoc Committee to study the globe for "situations elsewhere [that] ... may require analogous financial, technical, and military aid on our part."[24]

The Truman Doctrine was followed that September by the National Security Act, carrying the greatest restructuring and peacetime enlargement ever of the U.S. military. The law brought the armed services under the unified command structure of the Joint Chiefs of Staff and established the National Security Council to advise the president. The colossal new Pentagon housed the Defense Department, signifying the enlarged importance of a permanent military establishment. So, too, did the creation of the Central Intelligence Agency, the first peacetime agency empowered to gather intelligence on America's enemies. Less than a year later, Truman signed National Security Council Directive 10/2, unleashing the CIA with authority to conduct the widest possible range of covert operations against America's enemies and in support of states or groups friendly to U.S. interests.[25]

Just in time, for across the Mediterranean the United States launched an extraordinarily elaborate campaign to manipulate the outcome of Italy's 1948 general election in which the Italian Communist Party and the Socialists united as the Popular Democrat Front (PDF). Their showing in local elections early that year suggested that national victory against the ruling conservative Christian Democrats was within reach. Although the Christian Democrats were riddled with hard-right authoritarians, a number of them fascists, the Central Intelligence Agency's massive propaganda effort in Italy and at home depicted the party as an instrument of "freedom-loving" people everywhere and the PDF as liberty-crushing communists whose victory would align Italy with the Soviets. Millions of letters and postcards were mailed by Italian Americans, newspapers, the Catholic church, American Legion and other organizations to Italian citizens warning of a U.S. aid cut-off, and that "a world war will come" if the PDF won. Radio broadcasts declared the election a "choice between democracy and communism, God and godlessness, order and chaos." Truman's Justice Department threatened PDF supporters with ineligibility to emigrate. Italian American musicians toured the country in support of a Christian Democrat victory. As the election approached, Italian premier Alcide De Gasperi ousted socialists and communists from his cabinet. Generous food and reconstruction aid suddenly arrived, accompanied by reminders that it could all end with a PDF victory.[26]

As newsman Howard K. Smith reported, "there was no resisting what amounted to a tidal wave" of coercive brainwashing. Italians handed Christian Democrats a decisive victory, the election scored as one of the most blatant campaigns of foreign meddling in an election in Cold War history. The interference continued, as the CIA funneled millions annually into Italy to fortify the Christian Democrats' hold on power. Reverberations of the election were felt in France, where the government moved to oust Communists and Socialists. These events further solidified the liberal-capitalist breakwater of Western Europe, despite the stubbornly persistent popularity of Communist and socialist parties throughout the continent.[27] All promoted policies calling for the nationalization of various sectors of the economy. The victory of the Christian Democrats sent clear signals to European governments that continued cooperation with leftwing political parties would not be welcome in Washington.

Meanwhile, in February 1948 the Kremlin-backed communists in Czechoslovakia handed the United States all the justification it could have needed for its anti-democratic activities when it seized power in a *coup d'état*, overthrowing what had been a broadly representative governing coalition. The alleged "suicide" of the last remaining Eastern European anti-communist government minister Jan Masryk, son of the beloved founder of the Czechoslovakian republic, triggered suspicion that communist henchmen had orchestrated Masryk's murder. Following the Czech coup, Secretary of Commerce Averell Harriman declared Stalin a "greater menace than Hitler." [28] Military officials prepared possible atomic strikes. Secretary of Defense James Forrestal believed war with the Soviets imminent, while President Truman called for the return of military conscription and declared that "moral, god-fearing peoples" would act to "save the world from Atheism and totalitarianism."[29]

Simultaneous with the anti-communist crusade abroad was the launch of a corollary program at home. On March 21, 1947, nine days after the containment speech, the president issued Executive Order 9835 establishing a Loyalty Review program for federal employees. Truman acted in part to shield himself and the Democrats from an endless barrage of accusations from rightwing congressmen that the federal government harbored communists.[30] On its face, there was truth in the allegation. Left-wingers, from moderate liberals to socialists to members of the American Communist Party, had joined the federal government in droves in the heady days of the New Deal. Many had long drawn the attention of J. Edgar Hoover's FBI, the Justice Department, and the House Un-American Activities Committee (HUAC). Investigations turned up a raft of far-left radical idealists, but scarce evidence of the kind of genuine security risk posed by fascists and Nazis during the war—which both Hoover and HUAC had mostly ignored.[31]

What the president called a cynical distraction of Republicans was unfolding publicly in a domestic political climate sharply different from the 1930s, a fearful atmosphere intensified by the president's own foreign policy. Following the Republicans' victory in the 1946 elections, Speaker of the House Joseph Martin declared there was "no room in the government of the United States" for those "who do not believe in the way of life which has made this the greatest country of all time."[32] Truman authorized Attorney General Tom Clark to draw up a list of "totalitarian, fascist, communist, or subversive organizations" whose activities were deemed a threat to the government. Clark's successor J. Howard McGrath asserted that "communists [were] everywhere—factories, offices, classrooms, butcher stores, street corners, in the movies. And each," he warned, "carries the death of our society." The Justice Department built a thick catalog of organizations, many of them alleged "communist front" groups. Past "sympathetic association" with such organizations, ranging from the National Lawyers Guild and Unitarian Service Committee to the Nature Friends of America, brought one under the scope of Loyalty Review.[33] For the next nine years, more than five million federal employees were investigated for alleged disloyalty, often without due process. The probes resulted in more than 2,700 terminations and 12,000 more resignations. States, school districts, the Catholic Church, and private businesses followed with their own versions. From factory workers to university professors and Catholic nuns, more than 13.5 million Americans were subjected to a loyalty oath in some form.[34] Long before Loyalty Review ended over a decade later, it had paved the road for ever more draconian attacks on American constitutional liberties.

"Dollar Imperialism": The Marshall Plan and the Berlin Crisis

The appeal of socialism and communism across Europe was fueled in part by the grim postwar conditions of the continent. Hundreds of cities had been partially or wholly destroyed. Bewildered orphaned children and refugees wandered through the rubble of bombed out buildings. In Germany and Ukraine alone, thirty million were homeless. Survivors and occupying soldiers described the scenes as "hideous," "devastated beyond all comprehension," like "the face of the moon."[35] In the unscarred United States, U.S. Secretary of State George Marshall issued the first public call for a comprehensive European reconstruction program in June 1947. Inspiration for the scheme stemmed from not only altruism, but important sectors of the American business community. "Let us admit right off," said William Clayton, Undersecretary of State for Economic Affairs, "that our objective [in reconstruction aid] has as its background the needs and interests of the people of the United States. We need markets—big markets—in which to buy and sell," he said. As a partner in Anderson, Clayton & Company, the largest cotton-trading business in the world, Clayton was in a good position to know.[36]

The European Recovery Program (ERP), better known as "the Marshall Plan," was, said its namesake, "not directed against any country or doctrine but against hunger, poverty, desperation and chaos."[37] Despite the high-minded rhetoric and ostensibly open invitation to Eastern European states and the Soviet Union to participate, Marshall directed the plan be developed "in such a way that eastern European countries would either exclude themselves by unwilling-ness to accept proposed conditions" on such matters as currency, trade and investment policies, or more unlikely, succumb to the strict requirements.[38] President Truman understood immediately the economic framework as neatly complementing the military muscle of containment. As he put it in characteris-tically blunt terms, the Marshall Plan and Truman Doctrine were "two halves of the same walnut."[39] Although congress's immediate response to the proposal was cool, events abroad, particularly the Czechoslovakian coup, ratcheted up an atmosphere of approaching war and turned the corner toward passage. The plan's multiple objectives—staving off depression at home, expressing America's noble humanitarianism, exercising influence over the future of Europe, Germany in particular, and fighting communism abroad (which came with a fanciful promise of reduced military spending)—offered an irresistibly compelling ratio-nale.[40] There was something for everyone in the package.

At the initial ERP planning conference that June, American insistence that Germany be included in the plan was met with resistance from virtually every European nation. No representative complained more loudly about Germany's inclusion, as well as the imposition of U.S. strings on the aid, than Soviet Foreign Minister V. M. Molotov. The Russians saw the Marshall Plan for what Truman himself had acknowledged: an instrument of U.S. hegemony. Soviet anger had been brewing for three years—first over a U.S. refusal to respond to a final request for wartime Lend-Lease Aid as the conflict was winding down, then to even consider what Stalin considered a promise by FDR at Yalta for some degree of reparations from Germany, given the enormously disproportionate cost borne by the Soviet Union in the Allied victory. Thus a Marshall Plan-driven reconstruction of all of Europe appeared to Russia as an American takeover. The Soviets left the conference enraged and determined to prevent its satellite nations from participating. Further, both "halves of the walnut" provoked the Russians to intensify their consolidation of economic and political control over Eastern Europe, Stalin's position becoming all the more strident in the face of what Soviet officials labeled America's "dollar imperialism." Stalin purged non-communist political dissidents, ended the quasi-independence of Bulgaria and Hungary, imposed exploitive trade agreements, declared united communist opposition to western capitalist imperialism, and generally secured a firm grip on governments and economies from Poland to Romania.[41]

The Russians were not alone in grieving the imposition of what even conservative voices in London labeled "shameful," and "humiliating" violations of British sovereignty by their new American overlords. Notwithstanding the enormous psychological lift given to shattered peoples by Marshall Plan aid and the genuine economic stimulus it provided to recovery, the conditions and assorted other mechanisms of ERP funding cultivated economies whose chief benefits by the 1950s increasingly tilted toward Europe's upper classes and American interests. Left-wing politicians decried the "Yankee businessmen's invasion of Europe" that saw U.S. business investment in Britain and across western Europe soaring. By the early 1960s, majority control of whole sectors of European economies lay in the hands of American corporations. According to one member of the British Parliament, ERP programs "filled our shops with luxuries and our streets with unemployed." American journalist Theodore White observed that the Marshall Plan

> had yielded no love for America and little diminution of communist loyalty … The rich and well-to-do rolled about once more in automobiles … but the workers had barely held their own; they lived in stinking, festering slums, dressed in shabby second-hand clothes.[42]

Throughout this critical period, U.S. policymakers read every destabilizing event in Europe, Asia and elsewhere as emanating from the Kremlin. Soviet capabilities and territorial ambitions were constantly overstated and U.S. defenses consistently misrepresented as weaker and more vulnerable than they were. Anti-Soviet hardliners led by Forrestal protégé Paul Nitze assumed key posts in the national security establishment. Most held the conviction that the Russians were bent on launching an imminent war. Reflecting back on this period, George Kennan later lamented:

> The image of a Stalinist Russia, poised and yearning to attack the West, and deterred only by our possession of atomic weapons, was largely a fiction of the western imagination, against which some of us who were familiar with Russian matters tried in vain … to make our voices heard.[43]

To Kennan's chagrin, the die had been cast.

The next flashpoint, Berlin, was presented as a simple case of overbearing Soviet aggression, when in fact it resulted from a combination of U.S. ambition, western strength, and Russian weakness and desperation. At the Potsdam Conference in July 1945, the Allies determined that Germany would be temporarily divided into four occupation zones: the eastern half by the Soviet Union, and the west apportioned to the United States, Great Britain, and France. The capital city of Berlin, located 100 miles inside the Soviet zone, was similarly divided into four zones, although Stalin continued to insist that it be governed solely by the Soviets. Having paid by far the greatest price of Hitler's aggression, the Soviets (like the French in this regard) demanded that Germany remain a weakened postwar power. Yet as aid began pouring into western Germany, Britain, the U.S., and France combined their three zones into one "Tri-Zone," paving the way for the creation of the Federal Republic of (West) Germany in May 1949. The three powers then introduced the Deutsche Mark, a common unified currency for western Germany. Stalin immediately saw its implications: it would not only fortify the anti-communist alliance, but also hasten the recovery of western Germany and accelerate migration from the east. Indeed, the Deutsche Mark advanced the remarkable industrial revitalization of western Germany, while putting inflationary pressure on Stalin's woeful economic system in the east, isolating it from the rest of Europe. Meanwhile, in what appeared a desperate act of larceny to stave off the economic juggernaut emerging in the west, the Russian dictator commandeered massive quantities of industrial capacity in the Soviet zone, relocating it eastward.

The more dramatic move came June 27, 1948, when Stalin blocked all water, rail and road access from the Tri-zone into Berlin. Electricity from the east was cut, and the Soviets declared they would prevent any more supplies from reaching West Berlin, which had food and fuel for only a few weeks. Aiming for control of the entire city, what Stalin got instead was a further hardening of the Truman administration's position. The blockade served as undeniable proof of the rapacious ambitions of the Russians. General Lucius Clay, senior U.S. military official in Berlin, who just weeks earlier had voiced optimism about the prospects of rapprochement with the Soviet Union, now asked the president for authority to shoot his way through the blockade. Resistant to military action, Truman instead authorized the Berlin Airlift, an extraordinary effort by American and British pilots to deliver thousands of tons of coal, food, and other supplies around-the-clock from bases in Britain and West Germany into West Berlin's Tempelhof airport. More than 250,000 individual sorties would be flown before the airlift ended more than a year later. Major General Curtis LeMay, chief Air Force officer in Europe who had helped orchestrate the savage bombing of Hamburg and Dresden, now presided over the "LeMay Coal and Feed Company." While LeMay took pride in his bombardiers sustaining the people of West Berlin, he geared up for a possible atomic attack on the Soviets should they dare shoot down any of his planes, a position that was earning White House support. Twenty-eight of LeMay's B-29s were transported to bases in Germany and then to a safe remove in Britain. Although the planes were not yet configured for atomic bombs, the Soviets were unaware of that fact.[44]

The Berlin crisis magnified the larger confrontation. In April 1949, U.S. officials led Canadian and western European allies in establishing the North Atlantic Treaty Organization (NATO), obligating all member states in a pact of mutual defense; an attack on one was an attack on all. Although Stalin soon relented and access eased, the use of American air power to defend what it now viewed as vital strategic interests had been established. Backed by the Kremlin, the regime in East Berlin soon established the Federal Republic of (East) Germany, and the Soviets in 1955 would meet NATO with the Warsaw Pact of communist satellite states. Further, the principle of "extended deterrence" emerged from the crisis, signaling the onset of a nuclear-armed Europe. Kennan privately complained to Dean Acheson that NATO created a "defense against an attack no one is planning," bemoaning the fact that it "virtually forced [European] nations to choose up sides."[45] It ignored, too, the independence of Josip Tito's communist Yugoslavia, which might have opened the door toward peaceful accommodation with other communist states. Instead, NATO pronounced a bipolar Europe that was absolute.

Two Minutes to Midnight

By the time of the Berlin crisis, the Truman administration had little interest in the sort of nuanced understanding of Russian actions or historical insecurities that George Kennan was urging. A bipartisan consensus was now fixed on stemming a "Red tide" now sweeping Asia. The dramatic news from China in October 1949 that Chiang Kai-shek's militarily superior nationalist government— recipient of $3 billion in U.S. aid since the end of the war—had fallen to Mao Zedong's communists shook Washington. Coming as it did just weeks after the shocking announcement of the Soviet's first atomic bomb test, the "loss of China" brought a wave of charges that Truman's State Department and the whole of the Democratic Party was, as Senator Joseph McCarthy would soon put it, "thoroughly infested with communists."[46] Refusing to recognize the new government in Beijing, the Truman administration granted formal diplomatic relations only to Chiang's "China," whose regime decamped to Formosa (Taiwan).

The mood in Washington grew dark. Vitriol was directed at the Truman administration for alleged weakness and ineptitude. Sounding the alarm about the defense of Formosa, Congressman Richard Nixon warned ominously that if Chiang's fortress were not successfully defended, "the next frontier" of communist expansion would be "the coast of California."[47] The State Department tried to argue that there was nothing the United States could have done to prevent Mao's forces from claiming victory, given the failures of Chiang's government. Foreign service officers did little to tamp down the China hysteria, nor offer an accurate picture of why Chiang's regime had collapsed. Dean Rusk, Assistant Secretary of State for Far Eastern Affairs, claimed the People's Republic of China a Soviet satellite—a "colonial Russian government ... It is not even Chinese."[48]

After China, the Soviet bomb, and rumors of a Sino-Soviet Non-Aggression Pact, it was hardly a surprise when President Truman gave the green light to develop the hydrogen bomb, or "Super," a weapon up to 1,000 times the destructive energy of the atom bomb. Given the climate, it may seem that it was a *fait accompli*, and yet the Super would not have happened if America's leading nuclear physicists had had their way. Among veterans of the Manhattan Project, Hungarian-American physicist Edward Teller, was in the minority arguing for its development. In the fall of 1949, the eight-member General Advisory Committee of the Atomic Energy Commission (AEC) recommended unanimously against pursuing the H-bomb. The full AEC voted 3–2 against its development. Unsatisfied, Truman formed a special three-person committee that gave him the vote (2–1) he was seeking. "General annihilation beckons,"[49] Albert Einstein declared. In 1952 the United States exploded its first hydrogen bomb, followed soon by the Soviets. In that moment, the "Doomsday Clock" of the Bulletin of Atomic Scientists, created by veterans of the Manhattan Project to monitor the degree of danger facing humanity in the nuclear age, moved the clock "two minutes to midnight."[50]

The cascading events drove officials in the State Department and National Security Council to formulate a tougher policy toward communist expansion. What became known as NSC-68 appeared on President Truman's desk the morning of April 7, 1950. Chiefly authored by Paul Nitze, who tellingly held the position at State formerly held by George Kennan, the 66-page document implied that containment was an inadequate response to what it declared was now an aggressive, existential threat to the very existence of America and its interests around the world. NSC-68 asserted the Soviet Union was "animated by a new fanatic faith, antithetical to our own," which sought "to impose its absolute authority over the rest of the world ..." It followed that U.S. policy could not possibly remain one entirely of "defense":

> Our overall policy at the present time may be described as one designed to foster a world environment in which the American system can survive and flourish ... This broad intention embraces two subsidiary policies. One is a policy which we would probably pursue *even if there were no Soviet threat*. It is a policy of attempting to develop a healthy international community ...
> [emphasis added][51]

The document noted that the UN, the Marshall Plan, and "most of our international economic activities" fall under advancing the "American system." Obliquely subsumed were the increasing volumes of military and economic aid to nations in the "free world" whose people were anything but free. Beyond Greece, the United States supported authoritarian regimes from fascist Spain to Cuba and throughout the Middle East and Latin America. The newly established racist apartheid regime of South Africa, where American and European investments in gold and plutonium reserves proved lucrative and strategically valuable, enjoyed growing U.S. economic and military assistance.

These contradictions were of little consequence in the petrified atmosphere of 1950. NSC-68 called for the United States to go on the offense. Wherever "free institutions" were threatened by "communism," American personnel and weaponry would now defend those interests from a global network of military bases from Asia to the Antarctic. Local, anti-colonial insurgencies in the heart of Africa were seemingly as great a menace as armed soldiers in East Berlin. Along with a more aggressive use of the Central Intelligence Agency, a massive military buildup was essential "to check and to roll back the Kremlin drive for world domination." Even at the expense of domestic priorities, any and all means— "overt or covert, violent or non-violent, which serve the purposes of frustrating the Kremlin design"—would be deployed. NSC-68 opened the door to a world of morally vacuous decision making where virtually any action abroad could be justified. Although the document aligned with much of his own doctrinal thinking, Truman—nervous about the Soviet response and fearing its release would short-circuit his domestic policy agenda—had all copies of NSC-68 brought to him and locked in his safe.[52]

Korea: "An Entirely New War"

The president soon faced even greater pressure to take the fight to the communists. On June 25, 1950 the North Korean government of Kim Il-sung launched an invasion of South Korea. "Korea saved us," said Dean Acheson, reflecting the sentiments of a national security establishment determined to act on the "roll-back" mandate of NSC-68.[53] As David Halberstam has written, Korea "was, if not a godsend, then something perilously close, because they [the national security establishment] wanted a massive increase in the military budget."[54] They surely got it, from $13.5 billion in 1950 to nearly four times that by 1953—more than 60 percent of the entire federal budget.[55] The invasion of Korea triggered U.S. involvement in a three-year conflict that took the lives of nearly 40,000 Americans and almost five million Koreans and Chinese. It also brought the full-scale militarization of American society, and set the stage for an even more brutal Asian land war to follow in Vietnam.

In the summer of 1950, few Americans understood they were entering a dangerous conflict of complex origins. The end of the Second World War brought an end to the decades-long brutal occupation of Korea by the Japanese Empire. On September 6, 1945, a nationwide left-dominated alliance of resistance organizations calling itself the Korean People's Republic met in Seoul to determine the future of the country. "People's Committees" called for a series of wide-ranging measures, beginning with land reform. The Soviet Union and the United States, however, began acting independently of the Koreans. In part fearing a Japanese–American alliance in the Far East, the Russians aimed minimally at influence—ideally, control—in northern Korea through the nation's Communist Party to gain a security buffer to the east. The United States proposed the division of Korea at the 38th parallel and the two great powers settled on a five-year joint trusteeship of the country. After being anointed Communist

Premier in the north, Kim Il-sung coercively integrated the Peoples Committees into his governing structure. By 1949 Stalin had allowed a regime to emerge that began to resemble in its independence Yugoslavia. Kim welcomed Stalin's support, mimicked his tyrannical rule, but resisted outright Soviet control.[56]

To the south, the American Military Government (AMG) quickly abolished the People's Committees and aligned itself with the most reactionary elements of the military and larger society, including those most closely associated with the hated Japanese. In 1946, the AMG tapped 71-year-old Syngman Rhee, a nationalist who had lived most of his life in the United States, to head a "Representative Democratic Council." The body began confiscating lands from peasants that had been liberated from the Japanese, and introduced a free market economy that produced inflation and shrinking incomes for workers. When a general strike was called in February 1948, it was met with assault by the Korean National Police, a brutally despotic remnant of the Japanese, that left dozens dead. Sporadic declarations of martial law followed. Thousands were tortured or killed by soldiers, the police, or paramilitary terror groups. Conditions deteriorated so badly that an AMG poll indicated that 49 percent of respondents would have preferred the return of the hated Japanese.[57] American authorities often deflected criticism and responsibility for the repressive autocracy they were birthing by resorting to anti-oriental prejudice, alleging that "simon-pure democracy" was beyond reach of Asian peoples.[58] As one scholar has written, "the theory of native despotism not only made the violence seem inevitable, but also helped to deflect attention from American support of the brutal suppression."[59]

In the meantime, the United States engineered a process through the United Nations that led to elections in what was soon the Republic of Korea (ROK). Scheduled for May 1948, the elections prompted mass demonstrations against the idea of dividing Korea, which in turn were met with a bloody crackdown. Rightwing youth organizations, aided by the police and sanctioned by U.S. military authorities, arrested thousands and killed hundreds more in the weeks leading up to the vote. Nowhere was the violence more horrific than the island of Jeju, 50 miles southwest of the Korean peninsula, where opposition to the elections and Rhee's government was especially strong. U.S. officials orchestrated the arrest of 2,500 left-leaning political dissidents as "terrorists." The South Korea Labor Party attacked polling places, triggering a merciless response from the U.S.-backed government. Over the next year, more than 30,000 residents of Jeju were slaughtered in a state-sanctioned wave of terror.[60] With leftwing groups either banned or boycotting the election, Rhee swept into the presidency. His election was certified at the UN amid criticism from the Soviet Union and its allies in the north, which soon thereafter established the (communist) Democratic Republic of Korea. Even as U.S. military personnel withdrew in 1949, the cycle of opposition to Rhee and resulting state repression continued. He closed down newspapers, jailed their editors, and launched government surveillance of prominent critics. Nevertheless, a deluded Rhee continued to entertain fantasies of "liberating" the north through force.[61]

Clear-eyed observers could see that it was South Korea that was vulnerable to invasion and unification by the north. Joseph Stalin initially rebuffed Kim Il-sung's request to support an invasion, but he and China's Mao Zedong ultimately gave the green light—though both feared the U.S. response.[62] On June 25, well-equipped North Korean forces stormed across the 38th parallel. Rhee's army melted. State Department officials rushed a pre-worded resolution to the UN calling on it to "furnish such assistance to the ROK as may be necessary to repel the armed attack and to restore international peace and security." The Security Council approved it overwhelmingly. The Soviets, boycotting the body because of its refusal to recognize the People's Republic of China, issued their futile condemnation from afar. As ever, events in Korea were perceived in sweeping, apocalyptic terms that bore little relationship to geopolitical realities. Some advisors thought the action in Korea a diversion for a full-scale assault on Berlin or all western Europe. In an Oval Office meeting with advisors that week, the president spun the globe and pointed to Iran:

> Here is where they will start trouble ... Korea is the Greece of the Far East. If we are tough enough now, if we stand up to them like we did in Greece three years ago, they won't take any next steps. But if we just stand by, they'll move into Iran and they'll take over the whole Middle East.

"By God, I'm going to let them have it!" the president exclaimed.[63]

Shortly after noon on June 27, Truman announced that he had ordered air and naval support to the South Korean military. Ten days later, a UN resolution set in motion full-scale military operations to roll back the invasion. Simultaneously, the president stepped up support for the French in Indochina, and also ordered the Seventh Fleet into the Taiwan Straits to protect Chiang's regime, in the process attempting to quiet the China critics. Eight of ten Americans supported the president's response. With communists taking Seoul and memories of the Munich appeasement of Hitler in the air, when Robert Taft declared from the Senate floor, "there is no legal authority for what he has done," few stood with him.[64] Bravely sounding the founders' fears of investing war-making authority in one man, Taft was a rare voice as colleagues of both parties in both chambers overwhelmingly abdicated their constitutional responsibility. Even at a White House meeting with congressional leaders, most endorsed the president's actions and did not urge him to seek a declaration of war.[65] Authorizing the war through the United Nations in fact won the hearts of many liberals, assuaging concerns about American unilateralism. "For the first time in history," Truman declared later, "the nations who want peace have taken up arms under the banner of an international organization to put down aggression ... a tremendous step forward in the age-old struggle to establish the rule of law in the world."[66] Truman might have added that for the first time a president had committed the nation to a major military conflict without seeking a constitutionally required declaration of war. Succeeding presidents would be pleased to follow the precedent.

Leading the U.S. military effort was 70-year-old General Douglas MacArthur, the decorated, vainglorious leader of American forces in the South Pacific during World War II. Since 1945, MacArthur had served as Supreme Commander of occupied Japan. From there he managed an operation in Korea he saw as indisputably American, later boasting that he had no contact with anyone at the UN. What direction he received from the U.S. Joint Chiefs of Staff he was happy to ignore.[67] The combination of a megalomaniacal general who took his own counsel and the aggressive posture from Washington portended doom. By mid-September, North Korean forces had penetrated deep into South Korea, pinning UN forces inside a shrinking perimeter around the southwestern port of Pusan. MacArthur devised an audacious strategy to land 80,000 marines deep inside enemy lines at Inchon. Coupled with a redoubled force at Pusan, the counterassault took the North Koreans by surprise. Within weeks, UN forces had retaken Seoul and pushed the fight north of the 38th parallel.

Although UN authorization mandated only the restoration of conditions to the pre-invasion dividing line, North Korean forces were now on the run, and the temptation to "liberate" and unite the entire Korean peninsula under anti-communist leadership proved irresistible. In late September, with remarkable temerity the U.S. Ambassador to the UN declared that, "the artificial barrier which has divided North and South Korea has no basis in law or reason."[68] One week later, the General Assembly approved the revised American goal of Korean unification. The "rollback" objective demanded by NSC-68 and a subsequent directive that fall had now been imposed on and sanctioned by the UN, a few nations feebly abstaining.

Truman dismissed as "Communist propaganda" Mao's anger over the move to defend Taiwan, as well as an explicit warning of Chinese intervention transmitted via the Indian ambassador. From his post in Tokyo where he managed operations—never spending a single night in Korea—MacArthur remained supremely confident.[69] On October 15, he met with President Truman at Wake Island and assured him that there were no Chinese in Korea and that even if they were to enter the war, his forces would annihilate them. Receiving independent reports from the field, the Joint Chiefs were far less certain, yet gave MacArthur qualified authority to press his momentum toward the Chinese border.[70] Reports of a clash on October 25 between Chinese "volunteers" and UN forces near Unsan heightened Washington's anxiety. With remarkable hubris, MacArthur simply refused to believe that what he had termed "grossly overrated" Chinese communists could have been so wily as to move such vast numbers of men without detection.[71] It turned out they had been doing so since late summer, mostly at night, right under his Tokyo nose.

When in 1949 Mao Zedong was briefed on MacArthur's vanity-saturated biography, he replied, "Fine! Fine! The more arrogant and stubborn he is the better. An arrogant enemy is easier to defeat."[72] Exacerbating the danger was the fact that the narcissistic MacArthur, ensconced in his palatial court in Tokyo, was surrounded exclusively with what Joseph Alsop described as "almost wholly simpering and reverential" sycophants who dared not deliver a discouraging word to the general for fear of derailing their careers. MacArthur's chief of staff, Major General Charles Willoughby, was the worst of the lot. A far-right anti-Semitic racist of fascist sympathies, Willoughby was rightly regarded by senior officers as an ideologue who fed his boss's worst instincts. Willoughby routinely disregarded or distorted beyond recognition intelligence reports that did not comport with his own extreme views, or with his and the general's warped perception of events on the ground.[73]

With 300,000 Chinese troops amassed near the border and U.S. allies counseling a diplomatic solution for fear of a wider war, a Chinese representative flew to New York November 24 to address an anxious UN General Assembly. With the U.S. Eighth Army now facing heavy assault from the Chinese, MacArthur ordered 100,000 men toward the Yalu, triggering a major counter assault. Trapped in dangerous terrain and increasingly brutal winter conditions, poorly supplied American and ROK forces were suddenly overrun by seemingly endless Chinese artillery units and ground forces. The fighting that ensued over the next three months produced some of the worst casualty rates in U.S. military history. At what went down in the annals of the U.S. Marines as the "Frozen Chosin" Reservoir, 120,000 Chinese assaulted an American force of 30,000. As temperatures plunged to 35 below zero, guns refused to fire. Many suffered frostbite, unprepared and ill-supplied in remote mountainous country.[74] The rout in North Korea that winter of 1950–1951 was the worst defeat of an American military force since the First Battle of Bull Run in the Civil War.

MacArthur was right about one thing: it was, he declared, "an entirely new war."[75] By January, the communists had retaken Seoul and once more moved the fighting south of the 38th parallel. By March, UN forces managed to halt the communist counteroffensive. The war now entered its final protracted phase—a slow, bloody grind back and forth across the 38th parallel that would continue for more than two years. On December 29, the president notified MacArthur that he had given up the possibility of Korean unification. Sobered by the realities of "the new kind of war," and facing sinking poll numbers, Truman began moving toward a negotiated ceasefire near the 38th parallel. Ever defiant, MacArthur criticized "the politicians in Washington" and called for a major "expansion of our military operations into [China's] coastal areas and interior bases," including the deployment of Chinese Nationalist forces from Formosa. The final straw came April 5, when MacArthur ally and House Minority Leader Joseph Martin read aloud the general's letter criticizing the president's strategy in Korea, specifically suggesting that "the forces of Generalissimo Chiang Kai-shek on Formosa … be employed in the opening of a second Asiatic front to relieve the pressure on our forces in Korea." "Rank insubordination," an angry Truman wrote in his diary.[76] He relieved MacArthur of command, an action that had been recommended by senior military officials for months.

Returning home to a demigod's welcome, MacArthur delivered a memorable, thoroughly embroidered address to a joint session of Congress. "There is no substitute for victory," he declared. Laden with maudlin self-aggrandizement— "old soldiers never die, they just fade away"— the address further immortalized him. One Congressman swore he had seen "God in the flesh, the voice of God." A ticker tape parade in New York City was punctuated by shouts of, "Hang that bastard Harry Truman!"[77] Among the unimpressed minority, the president grumbled privately the speech was "nothing but a bunch of damn bullshit." He later wrote that he fired MacArthur "because he wouldn't respect the authority of the President ... I didn't fire him because he was a dumb son of a bitch, although he was."[78]

Implicit in MacArthur's call for total victory was the very real possibility of using atomic weapons. Since July, the Joint Chiefs had been planning to deliver to MacArthur up to 20 "tactical" atomic bombs to support combat operations. MacArthur anxiously awaited them to "sweeten up [his] B-29 force." In later interviews, the general asserted that he "would have dropped 30 or so atomic bombs ... strung across the neck of Manchuria." "My plan was a cinch," he declared. MacArthur was hardly alone. U.S. Air Force supporters on the National Security Council argued for an atomic assault on China from General Curtis LeMay's Strategic Air Command (SAC), and a secondary plan to hit the Soviet Union, confident in the U.S. superiority of nearly 500 atomic bombs to the Soviets' 25.[79] At a news conference on November 30, 1950, five days into the Chinese assault, Truman himself declared that there had "always been active consideration of [the atomic bomb's] use" in Korea, and further, that "the military commander in the field will have charge of the use of the weapons, as he always has." Within hours, his press secretary made clear that America's atomic arsenal remained under the president's sole authority. Truman's fear of what a desperate MacArthur might do almost certainly figured into his firing.[80]

Unwilling to launch a wider, apocalyptic conflict, what Truman did preside over was massive bombing of North Korea through conventional and incendiary firepower. Beginning in September 1950, Americans unleashed a hellacious napalm assault—more than 800 tons *every day* unloaded on the north that fall—further intensified after the Chinese stormed over the border. Macarthur's orders to deploy incendiary weapons on every "installation, factory, city, and village," rendering thousands of square miles of North Korea an inferno, belied American press reports of "precision bombing." What MacArthur's forces left behind as they were routed south that winter was a "wilderness of scorched earth."[81]

When retired General Dwight D. Eisenhower ran for president in 1952, he pledged to "go to Korea" should he win the White House to bring an end to the war. Following his victory, he made good on the promise. By the following July, a combination of events—most notably, Stalin's death and resultant pressure from new Soviet leader Nikita Khrushchev on Kim Il-sung's regime, as well as Eisenhower squeezing a recalcitrant Syngman Rhee—a ceasefire on July 26, 1953 brought an end to combat operations at roughly the diving line of 1948. Just five months in, Eisenhower presided over the last death of an American service member of his presidency—a feat that no president for the next 70 years would be able to claim.[82]

By the time the Korean War ended, Americans had endured 36,914 combat deaths and more than 100,000 wounded—80 percent of the casualties occurring *after* the provocative triggering of Chinese intervention (Figure 2.1). The suffering of the Korean population is nearly beyond comprehension. More than twelve percent of North Korea's population was lost. Dramatically shifting front lines of the war often left civilians even more vulnerable to bombing and ground operations. Horrific atrocities were still being unearthed decades later.[83] For generations of survivors in the north, it remained the "Victorious Fatherland Liberation War." It is perhaps not surprising that the dynastic and brutally authoritarian Kim regime sought to defend itself with nuclear weapons.

For Americans, Korea may be less "the forgotten war," a term often used to characterize it, than a conflict they have never known. Easily suppressed from memory are the complex nature of the war's origins, the moral contortions of defending a South Korean government that would not move toward genuine democracy until the 1970s, the unpopular defrocking of a dangerously egoistic general, and in the end a less than satisfying feeling about a less than total, very costly victory. Moreover, the war illustrates the disquieting truth that America's ability to shape world events in a nuclear-armed Cold War would have limits.

More unsettling were the deeper implications of Korea, which crowned this formative period of the U.S. global project. Neither America's imperial aspirations, nor the nation's capacity to delude itself about its rhetorically stated aims,

Figure 2.1 Two U.S. Marines visit the grave of a Korean Marine buddy to pay their respects.

Bettman/Getty, www.gettyimages.co.uk/detail/news-photo/two-u-s-marines-visit-the-grave-of-a-korean-marine-buddy-to-news-photo/514675150

began with the Truman Doctrine. Yet African slavery, the decimation of Native America, a war of conquest against Mexico, even the Spanish–American War were continental, hemispheric transgressions. The first years of the American Century had brought a profound change, relinquishing the founders' revulsion of the United States as an imperial power. As John Quincy Adams declared on Independence Day 1821, America went "not abroad, in search of monsters to destroy." For by doing so, said Adams, "she would involve herself beyond the power of extrication, in all the wars of interest and intrigue, of individual avarice, envy, and ambition, which assume the colors and usurp the standard of freedom."[84] Cloaking that transformation in the strategic objectives and rhetoric of the Cold War would not shield the nation forever from its ramifications.

Notes

1   President Harry S. Truman, "Address Before a Joint Session of Congress," March 12, 1947, https://avalon.law.yale.edu/20th_century/trudoc.asp, retrieved December 28, 2020.
2   Quoted in Charles L. Mee, Jr., *The Marshall Plan: The Launching of the Pax Americana* (New York: Simon and Schuster, 1984), 50–51.
3   Truman, "Address Before a Joint Session."
4   Lydia Saad, "Gallup Vault: Truman's Doctrine Earned Him Public Kudos," March 9, 2017, https://news.gallup.com/vault/205742/gallup-vault-truman-doctrine-earned-public-kudos.aspx, retrieved December 28, 2020.
5   Quoted in Lawrence S. Wittner, *Cold War America: From Hiroshima to Watergate* (New York: Praeger, 1974), 33–34.
6   Mee, 74–75.
7   Quoted in Justin Raimondo, *Reclaiming the American Right: The Lost Legacy of the Conservative Movement* (Wilmington, DE: Intercollegiate Studies, 2008), 174–176.
8   Quoted in Mee, 66; and Raimondo, 175.
9   Henry Wallace served briefly as Truman's Commerce Secretary—until they parted ways over the Truman Doctrine.
10 Quoted in Mee, 47.
11 Quoted in Mee, 36.
12 Dean Acheson, *Present at the Creation: My Years in the State Department* (New York: W.W. Norton, 1970), 219.
13 Quote attribution in Robert L. Ivie, "Fire, Flood, and Red Fever: Motivating Metaphors of Global Emergency in the Truman Doctrine Speech," *Presidential Studies Quarterly* 29, no. 3 (September 1999): 570.
14 Albert Resis, "The Churchill–Stalin Secret "percentages" Agreement on the Balkans, Moscow, October 1944," *American Historical Review* 83, no. 2 (April 1978): 368–387.
15 Mee, 16.
16 Joëlle Fontaine, "How Churchill Broke the Greek Resistance," *Le Monde diplomatique*, July 2012, https://mondediplo.com/2012/07/Churchill-Greece, retrieved December 28, 2020.
17 Ralph B. Levering, *The Cold War: A Post-Cold War History* 3rd ed. (Malden, MA: Wiley Blackwell, 2016), 29; and Mee, 17.
18 Quoted in Levering, 26.
19 George Kennan, The Charge in the Soviet Union to the Secretary of State, Telegram, February 22, 1946, https://nsarchive2.gwu.edu//coldwar/documents/episode-1/kennan.htm, retrieved December 28, 2020.

20 Wittner, 34–36; and William Blum, *Killing Hope: U.S. Military and C.I.A. Interventions Since World War II* (Monroe, ME: Common Courage Press, 2004), 34–38.

21 Sandra L. Ellis, "Polk, George, 1913–1948," http://cw.routledge.com/ref/radio/polk. pdf, retrieved December 28, 2020.

22 Keith Lowe, *Savage Continent: Europe in the Aftermath of World War II* (New York: St. Martin's Press, 2012), 313.

23 Chief of Counsel Robert H. Jackson, "Opening Statement Before the International Military Tribunal," November 21, 1945, Robert H. Jackson Center, www.roberth-jackson.org/speech-and-writing/opening-statement-before-the-international-military-tribunal, retrieved December 29, 2020.

24 Quoted in Mee, 75.

25 "Note on U.S. Covert Action Programs," National Security Archive, George Washington University, n.d., https://nsarchive2.gwu.edu/NSAEBB/NSAEBB52/docXXXIII.pdf, retrieved December 29, 2020.

26 Blum, 27–34.

27 Ibid., 33; and Mee, 230–234.

28 Quoted in Wittner, 52.

29 Quoted in Walter L. Hixson, *George Kennan: Cold War Iconoclast* (New York: Columbia University Press, 1991), 75.

30 Quoted in David McCullough, *Truman* (New York: Simon and Schuster, 1992), 652.

31 Richard M. Freeland, *The Truman Doctrine and the Origins of McCarthyism: Foreign Policy, Domestic Politics, and Internal Security, 1946–1948* (New York: Alfred A. Knopf, 1972), 117–120; and Steven J. Ross, *Hitler in Los Angeles: How Jews Foiled Nazi Plots Against Hollywood and America* (New York: Bloomsbury, 2017), Chapter 1.

32 Rep. Joseph Martin, reported by the *New York* Times, January 4, 1947, p. 2; quoted by Freeland, 131.

33 Wittner, 37, 86–89.

34 Ellen Schrecker, *Many Are the Crimes: McCarthyism in America* (New York: Little Brown, 1998), pp. 209–211, 266–269, 288–291; and Wittner, 38.

35 Lowe, *Savage Continent*, 5–8.

36 Quoted by Mee, 78–79.

37 Secretary of State George Marshall, June 5, 1947, www.archives.gov/exhibits/trea-sures_of_congress/text/page22_text.html, retrieved December 30, 2020.

38 Quoted in Sam O'Brien, "Questioning the Marshall Plan in the Buildup to the Cold War," University of New Hampshire *Inquiry Journal*, www.unh.edu/inquiryjournal/spring-2014/questioning-marshall-plan-buildup-cold-war, retrieved December 30, 2020.

39 Quoted in Joseph M. Jones, *The Fifteen Weeks: An Inside Account of the Genesis of the Marshall Plan* (New York: Viking, 1955), 233.

40 Mee, 239.

41 Wittner, 43–46.

42 Quoted in Mee, 258–259.

43 Quoted in Wittner, 52.

44 James Carroll, *House of War: The Pentagon and the Disastrous Rise of American Power* (New York: Mariner, 2007), 147.

45 Quoted in Wittner, 67.

46 Senator Joseph McCarthy, "Lincoln Day Speech Delivered to the Republican Women's Club of Wheeling, West Virginia," February 9, 1950, at https://liberalarts. utexas.edu/coretexts/_files/resources/texts/1950%20McCarthy%20Enemies.pdf, retrieved December 30, 2020.

47 Richard Nixon, Speech During the California Senate Campaign, September 18, 1950, in *China and U.S. Foreign Policy* (Washington, DC: Congressional Quarterly, 1971), 19.

48 Dean Rusk, U.S. State Department *Bulletin* xxiv: 621 (May 28, 1951), 843 ff, in Keith S. Peterson, "Non Recognition of Red China: Reasons and Realizations," *Journal of the Arkansas Academy of Sciences* 7, article 21 (1955), 77, at https://scholarworks.uark.edu/cgi/viewcontent.cgi?article=1206&context=jaas, retrieved December 30, 2020.

49 Carroll, 180; and "Einstein Sees 'Annihilation' in Hydrogen Bomb," *New York Times*, February 13, 1950, https://timesmachine.nytimes.com/timesmachine/1950/02/13/84813039.html?pageNumber=1, retrieved December 30, 2020.

50 This had been the closest the clock ever got to midnight until 2018, by which time the scientists had begun to consider the added danger of climate change.

51 National Security Council, "NSC 68: United States Objectives and Programs for National Security," April 14, 1950, https://fas.org/irp/offdocs/nsc-hst/nsc-68.htm, retrieved December 30, 2020.

52 Carroll, 186.

53 Quoted in Lloyd C. Gardner, "Korean Borderlands: Imaginary Frontiers of the Cold War," in William Stueck, ed., *The Korean War in World History* (Lexington, KY: University Press of Kentucky, 2004), 142.

54 David Halberstam, *The Coldest Winter: America and the Korean war* (New York: Hyperion, 2007), 93.

55 Carroll, 186.

56 Joel R. Campbell, "The Wrong War: The Soviets and the Korean War, 1945–1953," *International Social Science Review* 88, no. 3 (2014): 3–7, https://digitalcommons.northgeorgia.edu/cgi/viewcontent.cgi?article=1017&context=issr, retrieved December 31, 2020.

57 Su-kyoung Hwang, "South Korea, the United States, and Emergency Powers During the Korean Conflict," *Asia Pacific Journal* 12, issue 5, no. 1 (January 30, 2014), https://apjjf.org/2014/12/5/Su-kyoung-Hwang/4069/article.html, retrieved December 31, 2020.

58 Gregory Henderson, "A Memorandum Concerning United States' Political Objectives in Korea," November 30, 1950, Box 1, RG 84, NACP, MD, quoted by Hwang.

59 Hwang.

60 Ibid.; Bruce Cumings, "Epilogue to (De)memorializing the Korean War: A Critical Intervention, *Cross-Currents—East Asian History and Culture Review*, n.d., https://crosscurrents.berkeley.edu/sites/default/files/e-journal/articles/cumings.pdf, retrieved December 31, 2020; and Elizabeth Shim, "South Korea Jeju Massacre Haunts the Memories of the Survivors," UPI, June 20, 2019, www.upi.com/Top_News/World-News/2019/06/20/South-Korea-Jeju-Massacre-haunts-the-memories-of-survivors/1491561083862, retrieved December 31, 2020.

61 Blum, 47, quoting the *New York Times*, June 26, 1950.

62 "Causes, Course and Conclusion of the Conflict," Association for Asian Studies, n.d., www.asianstudies.org/publications/eaa/archives/the-korean-war-101-causes-course-and-conclusion-of-the-conflict, retrieved December 31, 2020.

63 Halberstam, 92–93.

64 Quoted in Clarence E. Wunderlin, Jr., *The Papers of Robert A. Taft*, vol. 4, 1949–1953 (Kent, OH: Kent State University Press, 2006), 169.

65 James M. Lindsay, "The Water's Edge Remembers: Truman's Decision to Intervene in Korea," Council on Foreign Relations, June 27, 2020, www.cfr.org/blog/twe-remembers-trumans-decision-intervene-korea, retrieved December 31, 2020.

66 President Harry S. Truman, "Address in San Francisco, October 17, 1950," Department of State *Bulletin* 23, no. 521 (October 30, 1950), 683.

67 James F. Schnabel and Robert J. Watson, *History of the Joint Chiefs of Staff: The Joint Chiefs of Staff and National Policy* vol. III, 1950–1951 (Washington, DC: Office of the Chairman of the Joint Chiefs of Staff, 1998), 117–118; and Wittner, 76.

68 Quoted in Wittner, 76.
69 David Halberstam, "MacArthur's Grand Delusion," *Vanity Fair*, September 24, 2007, www.vanityfair.com/news/2007/10/halberstam200710, retrieved December 31, 2020.
70 Schnabel and Watson, 118.
71 Halberstam, *Coldest Winter*, 370.
72 Halberstam, "Grand Delusion."
73 Ibid.
74 Halberstam, *Coldest Winter*, 427–448.
75 The Commander in Chief, Far East (MacArthur) to the Joint Chiefs of Staff, November 28, 1950, https://history.state.gov/historicaldocuments/frus1950v07/d888, retrieved December 31, 2020.
76 Halberstam, *Coldest Winter*, 602–604.
77 Excerpt from Stanley Weintraub, *MacArthur's War: Korea and the Undoing of an American Hero*, http://catdir.loc.gov/catdir/samples/simon031/99035870.html, retrieved December 31, 2020.
78 Quoted in Robert Dallek, *Harry S. Truman* (New York: Henry Holt, 2008), 119.
79 Carroll, 189–191; and Bruce Cumings, "Why Did Truman Really Fire MacArthur?" *History News Network*, January 10, 2005, https://historynewsnetwork.org/article/9245, retrieved January 1, 2021.
80 Cumings, "Why Did Truman Really Fire MacArthur."
81 CumingsIbid., quoting MacArthur Archives, RG6, box 1, Stratemeyer to MacArthur, 8 November 1950;, Public Record Office, FO 317, piece no.° 84072, Bouchier to Chiefs of Staff, 6 November 1950;, piece no.° 84073, 25 November 25, 1959, sitrep.
82 Jean Edward Smith, "How to End a War, Eisenhower's Way," *History News Network*, April 11, 2009, https://historynewsnetwork.org/article/76191, retrieved January 1, 2021.
83 For a powerful corrective history, see Bruce Cumings, *The Korean War: A History* (New York: Modern Library, 2011).
84 John Quincy Adams, "Speech to the U.S. House of Representatives on Foreign Policy," July 4, 1821, https://millercenter.org/the-presidency/presidential-speeches/july-4-1821-speech-us-house-representatives-foreign-policy, retrieved January 1, 2021.

Further Reading

Appy, Christian G., ed. *Cold War Constructions: The Political Culture of United States Imperialism, 1945–1966.* Amherst, MA: University of Massachusetts Press, 2000.

Beisner, Robert L. *Dean Acheson: A Life in the Cold War.* New York: Oxford University Press, 2006.

Blum, William Blum. *Killing Hope: U.S. Military and C.I.A. Interventions Since World War II.* Monroe, ME: Common Courage Press, 2004.

Borstelmann, Thomas. *The Cold War and the Color Line: American Race Relations in the Cold War Arena.* Cambridge, MA: Harvard University Press, 2003.

Bostdorff, Denise M. *Proclaiming the Truman Doctrine: The Cold War Call to Arms.* College Station, TX: Texas A & M University Press, 2008.

Cullather, Nick. *Secret History: The CIA's Classified Account of Its Operations in Guatemala, 1952–1954.* Redwood City, CA: Stanford University Press, 2006.

Cumings, Bruce. *The Korean War: A History.* New York: Modern Library, 2011.

Doherty, Thomas Patrick. *Cold War, Cool Medium: Television, McCarthyism, and American Culture.* New York: Columbia University Press, 2003.

Dudziak, Mary L. *Cold War Civil Rights: Race and the Image of American Democracy.* Princeton, NJ: Princeton University Press, 2011.

Eisenberg, Carolyn Woods. *Drawing the Line: The American Decision to Divide Germany, 1944–1949.* New York: Cambridge University Press, 1998.

Gaddis, John Lewis. *George F. Kennan: An American Life.* New York: Penguin, 2012.

Gerolymatos, Andre. *Red Acropolis, Black Terror: The Greek Civil War and the Origins of the Soviet-American Rivalry, 1943–1949.* New York: Basic Books, 2004.

Halberstam, David. *The Coldest Winter: America and the Korean War.* New York: Hyperion, 2007.

Harper, John Lamberton. *America and the Reconstruction of Italy, 1945–1948.* Cambridge, UK: Cambridge University Press, 2002.

Harrington, Daniel F. *Berlin on the Brink: The Blockade, The Airlift and the Early Cold War.* Lexington, KY: University Press of Kentucky, 2012.

Heiss, Mary Ann. *Empire and Nationhood: The United States, Great Britain, and Iranian Oil, 1950–1954.* New York: Columbia University Press, 1997.

Hixson, Walter L. *Parting the Curtain: Propaganda, Culture, and the Cold War, 1945–1961.* New York: Palgrave Macmillan, 1997.

Johnson, Chalmers. *Blowback: The Costs and Consequences of American Empire.* New York: Holt, 2004.

Levering, Ralph B. *The Cold War: A Post-Cold War History*, 3rd ed. Malden, MA: Wiley Blackwell, 2016.

Lowe, Keith. *Savage Continent: Europe in the Aftermath of World War II.* New York: St. Martin's Press, 2012.

Manchester, William. *American Caesar: Douglas MacArthur 1880–1964.* New York: Hachette Book Group, 2008.

McCullough, David. *Truman.* New York: Simon and Schuster, 1992.

Mee, Jr. Charles L. *The Marshall Plan: The Launching of the Pax Americana.* New York: Simon and Schuster, 1984.

Stueck, William, ed. *The Korean War in World History.* Lexington, KY: University Press of Kentucky, 2004.

Weiner, Tim. *Legacy of Ashes: The History of the CIA.* New York: Anchor, 2008.

Wittner, Lawrence S. *Cold War America: From Hiroshima to Watergate.* New York: Praeger, 1974.

Woodhouse, C. M. *The Struggle for Greece, 1941–1949.* New York: Ivan R. Dee, 2002.

3 Affluence and Angst

The Politics and Culture of Cold War America

On September 16, 1947, Philadelphians began streaming into the Freedom Train, a railway museum of 133 documents and objects spanning the history of the republic and beyond, from the Magna Carta to George Washington's copy of the U.S. Constitution to the Truman Doctrine. The Freedom Train exhibition soon embarked on a tour of more than 300 cities, where it was viewed by three and a half million Americans.[1] Organized under the banner of the American Heritage Foundation whose board was dominated by bankers and businessmen, the Freedom Train's clear purpose was anticommunist civic education based on a conflict-free view of history that reinforced American ideals and the principles of liberal capitalism.

Freedom Train champion and Attorney General Tom Clark called it "an American program which seeks to re-establish the common ground of *all* Americans"—a purpose seemingly made more urgent by the greatest wave of labor unrest in American history in 1945–1946.[2] It was telling that the National Archives professionals who curated the Freedom Train selected the Wagner Act that legalized collective bargaining rights for American workers, only to have it rejected by the Foundation. In the same vein, Confederate General Robert E. Lee's acceptance of a university presidency made the cut of the Freedom Train exhibit, but not the Nineteenth Amendment granting women's suffrage, nor FDR's "Four Freedoms." These documents would have celebrated a group-oriented social democracy on the move, an honoring of American dissidence that was unwelcome among the principals of American Heritage. *Freedom*, in fact, had been chosen over the unruly-sounding "Democracy Train."[3]

Other tensions soon emerged, most pointedly surrounding the issue of race. African Americans greeted news of the Freedom Train with a hopeful skepticism, especially given what appeared to be contradictory messages. On the one hand, the American Heritage Foundation rejected for inclusion in the exhibit documents overly suggestive of the black freedom struggle: the Reconstruction-era Fourteenth and Fifteenth Amendments granting citizenship and voting rights, as well as FDR's executive order establishing the Fair Employment Practices Committee. At the same time, the Foundation insisted on an integrated Freedom Train; host communities were required to not separate visitors by race. Forty-seven thoroughly segregated cities complied. When authorities in

DOI: 10.4324/9781003160595-3

Memphis and Birmingham announced their defiance, the Foundation cancelled the stops. Disappointed Memphis citizens boarded buses for Nashville, where black and white together awaited their turn without incident.[4] Upon learning of the decision, NAACP executive secretary Walter White declared, "for one of the very first times in history, the rest of the country had called the bluff of the reactionary South." Foundation vice president Louis Novins thought the Memphis cancellation "had a better education impact than the appearance of the train itself."[5] Moreover, accounts of trouble-free stops throughout the South seemed, if only symbolically, to point toward the possibility of racial progress in postwar America.

No matter one's background or politics going in, citizens were to exit the Freedom Train wholly American, a patriotic refurbishing capped by visitors signing the Freedom Scroll and taking a Freedom Pledge.[6] For critics on the left, the coercive patriotism of the Freedom Train, combined with its carefully delineated exhibition, appeared to undercut the meaning of American democratic freedom. All criticism was carefully monitored by FBI Director J. Edgar Hoover and his agents. In just the first few months, Hoover sent nine field reports on Freedom Train dissidents to Tom Clark—the same attorney general who, as the Freedom Train rolled across America that winter, declared, "those who do not believe in the ideology of the United States shall not be allowed to stay in the United States."[7]

The conflicted story of the Freedom Train offers a window onto much of what would unfold in America over the coming decade. For even as millions of white middle-class citizens enjoyed an expanding, unprecedented economic prosperity, the apparent triumph of American consumer capitalism contained its own complicating blemishes. Moreover, the early Cold War era produced policy outcomes at home and abroad that often subverted the very democratic ideals the Freedom Train was ostensibly celebrating.

"Have You No Sense of Decency?"—America's Second Red Scare

Better known as the era of "McCarthyism," the Second Red Scare was not the first time Americans suppressed constitutional liberties in a fear-driven crusade to stamp out communism. In the "Red Scare" following World War I, reactionary opposition to an insurgent labor movement stoked fears of American-style Bolshevism, triggering the arrest of several thousand radicals and mass deportations. Leading the Justice Department's efforts then was J. Edgar Hoover, who in 1924 became head of the new Bureau of Investigation (FBI), a post he would hold for 48 years, eventually amassing more power than most presidents. The efforts of his "G-men" in taking down gangsters elevated Hoover a national hero, fortifying his ability to assemble a Red-hunting surveillance network that included the Chamber of Commerce, the American Legion, and a dubious cast of paid informants across the country. Among them were dozens of former Nazis and Third Reich collaborators like Laszlo Agh. A war criminal and unrepentant fascist, in the 1950s Agh was leading a far-right, anti-Soviet Hungarian American organization in New Jersey. When immigration officials moved to deport him, Hoover intervened. He and his agents also protected Belorussian John Avdzej, who had presided over the execution of thousands of Jews.[8]

Among the many lists compiled by Hoover's G-men were Hollywood films, actors, screenwriters, and directors deemed communist. Long before the House Un-American Activities Committee (HUAC) came to town, the FBI had been tracking Hollywood leftists. With roots in the Depression-era "Popular Front," an amalgam of communists, socialists, and liberal Democrats, the leftward strain of 1930s filmmaking was characterized by New Deal-style populism, some of it explicitly anti-fascist. During the war, such movies drew large audiences, but also the attention of FBI agents concerned about their use as communist propaganda. In the late 1940s their efforts zeroed in on films like *Crossfire*, a brilliant noir production that confronted postwar anti-Semitism. The film's director, Edward Dmytryk, received not only an Oscar nomination, but also FBI scrutiny.

Also earning surveillance was Oscar-winning director Frank Capra, whose 1941, quintessentially American *Mr. Smith Goes to Washington* had been judged "decidedly socialist in nature." Capra's Christmas classic, *It's a Wonderful Life*, released in 1946 while a free wind still blew in Hollywood, was found by the FBI to be a work of communist indoctrination. The picture's pitting of the small-town virtues of everyman George Bailey against mercenary banker Henry Potter "deliberately maligned the upper class." Worse, in Jimmy Stewart's inimitably sympathetic Bailey, viewers received "a subtle attempt ... to magnify the problems of the so-called 'common man' in society."[9] Also likely produced just in time was William Wyler's *The Best Years of Our Lives*. One of the great films of the century, its central theme was the sobering readjustment of returning servicemen to postwar America. Ayn Rand denounced it as communist propaganda partly for its less-than-flattering treatment of bankers, as well as a scene in which the film's central heroic figure, veteran Harold Russell who had lost both hands during the war, confronts a fascist bigot.[10]

In 1947 HUAC assumed command of the inquest. Public hearings summoned dozens of actors, screenwriters, directors, and film executives before the committee for endless interrogations of their political beliefs and alleged Communist Party associations. "Friendly witnesses," led by Gary Cooper, Walt Disney, and Screen Actors Guild President Ronald Reagan, said enough to confirm committee fears of a shadowy communist conspiracy in the film industry. Less friendly were the Hollywood Ten, mostly screenwriters, who defiantly refused to cooperate. When a group of Hollywood luminaries that included Humphrey Bogart, Lauren Bacall, and Judy Garland formed the Committee for the First Amendment and flew to Washington to testify against the inquisition, most Americans supported their efforts. But the press soon turned on them as Hollywood elites, naïve to the fact that the Hollywood Ten included Stalin apologists. The Hollywood Ten were cited for contempt and given short sentences. By the early 1950s, hundreds of individuals in Hollywood were either blacklisted or, because of their reputed associations, simply stopped receiving offers of work.[11]

The cleansing of Hollywood's left spared few. Charlie Chaplin—long in Hoover's sights despite never joining the Communist Party—was unwilling to disassociate himself from long-time friends in the industry who were, nor stop making the kind of films of thoughtful social content that made him a Hollywood icon. Chaplin fled to Europe. "These days," he said, "if you step off the curb with your left foot, they accuse you of being a communist."[12] Actor John Garfield was targeted for working in films like *Body and Soul*, which dramatized capitalism's capacity to consume a good man—here, a working-class boxer trying to make it big. Garfield's performance earned an Oscar nomination. A patriot who labored tirelessly for the war effort, Garfield was enough of an outspoken liberal to merit a HUAC subpoena. Refusing to name names he did not have, Garfield's testimony left committee members unsatisfied:

> I have nothing to be ashamed of and nothing to hide. My life is an open book. I was glad to appear before you and talk with you. I am no Red. I am no "pink." I am no fellow traveler. I am a Democrat by politics, a liberal by inclination, a loyal citizen of this country by every act of my life.[13]

The persecution continued, impacting Garfield's career and health. He died of a heart attack at age 39, by most accounts prematurely.[14]

One of the Hollywood Ten, Herbert Biberman, led other blacklisted refugees to New Mexico to make *Salt of the Earth*, a film based on a recent zinc mine strike. Shooting in semi-documentary, neorealist style, Biberman and producer Paul Jarrico employed mainly miners and families as actors. That the film was produced at all is something of a miracle, as actors had to contend with FBI surveillance and threats of violence from local vigilante patriots. In Washington, Congressman Donald L. Jackson of California condemned the film "as a new weapon for Russia ... deliberately designed to inflame racial hatreds and to depict the United States as the enemy of all colored peoples."[15] After its premiere in New York City, *Salt of the Earth* was banned. When it emerged in the 1960s, the film earned appreciation for its depiction of democratic unionism and sympathetic portrayal of the Mexican American community—particularly the women, whose courage and dignity in fighting for justice anchors the film. Biberman was proud of having "created eight thousand feet of freedom in America."[16]

The fear began to lift in 1960 when legendary actor and producer Kirk Douglas determined to give Hollywood Ten screenwriter Dalton Trumbo on-screen credit for his film, *Spartacus*. Trumbo had survived the fifties writing screenplays, including two Oscar winners, under pseudonyms. Despite being told that engaging Trumbo would end his career, Douglas had seen too many "friends who went into exile when no one would hire them; actors who committed suicide in despair." Besides, he said later, "there are times when one has to stand up for principle."[17] His courage freed Trumbo from the shadows and helped end the darkest chapter in Hollywood's history.

The labor movement suffered its own share of casualties. Workers felt the winds shifting against them in a series of measures taken by President Truman during the postwar labor turmoil. When oil industry employees struck in October 1945, Truman ordered them back to work. He did the same with John L. Lewis's United Mine Workers when they shut down bituminous coal mines. The president generally championed worker interests, but standing up to what the press now pejoratively termed "Big Labor" suited the temperament of a "buck stops here," no-nonsense president, and played well with conservative southern Democrats. Planted firmly at mid-field, the president could also swing at opponents to his right, as he did in vetoing the 1947 Taft–Hartley Act, which allowed states to declare themselves union-free by claiming the "right to work." Granting employers greater latitude to subvert organizing, the law arrested union growth in the South and West. The greatest damage came from a provision that compelled unions to ban communists in order to retain protections of the National Labor Relations Board (NLRB). After a conservative congress passed Taft–Hartley by a wide margin, unions in the Congress of Industrial Organizations (CIO) deluged Truman with the largest volume of mail ever received by the White House.[18] The president vetoed the law but was overridden.

Taft-Hartley brought internecine warfare within the CIO. Unions purged themselves of communists in an effort to survive. One revealing episode unfolded at the General Electric plant in Erie, Pennsylvania, where 10,000 workers were represented by Local 506 of the United Electrical, Radio and Machine Workers Union (UE)—one of the most democratic, progressive unions in the country. UE found itself battling the entwined forces of anticommunism and GE, then headed by Charles E. Wilson, who in 1946 declared "the problems of America … summed up in two words: Russia abroad, Labor at home."[19] Two years later, the CIO-created International Union of Electrical Workers (IUE) denounced the UE as communist and began raiding their locals.[20] Local 506 was led by the charismatic John Nelson, who after serving his country in Germany, led members in the successful 1946 strike. For over a decade, a legion of federal investigators, together with the predatory rival union, and abetted by the local press that condemned the "communist-saturated" UE 506 for its "big-government" advocacy, aimed their fire at Nelson, a member of the Communist Party. Notwithstanding John Nelson's demonstrated patriotism and multiple signed loyalty affidavits, GE fired him. Also terminated was Nelson's mentor, Jim Kennedy, who at one point responded to the withering attack on 506 with a full-page ad titled "Who Is Loyal?" that reminded readers of GE's collaboration with I. G. Farben, producer of Zyklon-B used in the Holocaust and an indispensable power in the rise of the Nazis. For Johnny Nelson, a decade of public scourging took a toll. He died in 1959 at the age of 42.[21]

The CIO's capitulation to anti-communist hysteria foreshadowed the cozy business relationship the reunited AFL-CIO would seek with corporate America. Perceived later as halcyon years of peak membership, strong contracts, and political influence, the postwar era in fact marked the beginning of labor's decades-long decline. Another harbinger was the ill-fated "Operation Dixie," a multi-racial campaign to organize the South in 1946–1948. As the CIO flooded southern textile and lumber mill towns with organizers, and black veterans marched to courthouses demanding the right to vote, southern businessmen retaliated with fear mongering of communists and "race-mixing," and with violence. The assassination in Charleston of white progressive organizer, Bob New—a "Communist and a nigger-lover" to his assassin—provided a cruel reminder of the barriers to organizing a multi-racial alliance of workers in the South.[22]

Senator Joseph McCarthy's ignominious turn on the stage was made possible by all that preceded him. Wisconsin's junior senator had been watching HUAC member Richard Nixon's star rising for four years. The California congressman had a nose for Red-baiting opportunism, and by 1950 was mounting a run for the U.S. Senate, slandering Democratic opponent Helen Gahagan Douglas as "pink right down to her underwear."[23] Two years earlier, Nixon smelled blood when repentant former communists Elizabeth Bentley and Whitaker Chambers testified to HUAC that they had managed a Washington spy network dating to the 1930s. Chambers zeroed in on former State Department aide Alger Hiss, then head of the Carnegie Endowment for International Peace. Nixon attacked Hiss for complicity in a vast web of Soviet-American espionage, a charge that rocked Washington. Having served as one of the erudite intellects of the New Deal only made Hiss more vulnerable amid a spasm of American anti-intellectualism. Purporting to have the inside scoop on the capital's communist cabal, the *Washington Confidential* declared, "where you find an intellectual, you will probably find a Red."[24]

Hiss's sympathetic view of the Russians during World War II had indeed inspired him, and hundreds more government employees, to transmit information. Whether he was guilty of espionage was a very different question. The debate resurfaced in the 1990s following the declassification of cables from the Venona Project, a nearly 40-year counterintelligence effort of the National Security Agency to decipher more than 3,000 messages between U.S. government employees and Soviet agents. Among the mountain of communications were a small number from those sympathetic to Soviet interests conveying information threatening to U.S. security, including Julius and Ethel Rosenberg, charged and later executed for passing atomic secrets to the Soviets. Most of the communications tracked by Venona were innocuous, concerned with domestic politics and echoing the hopes of internationalists like Alger Hiss for postwar U.S.-Soviet cooperation. As historian Ellen Schrecker has argued, Venona underscored the obligation to examine not only the threat posed by communists, but also the motivations of anticommunist warriors.[25]

Indeed, the Hiss affair went to the heart of the larger rightwing project to destroy "New Dealism," an effort embodied in HUAC's fascistic bent. Nixon's lead Hiss investigator, Robert Stripling, was a former publicist for the German American BUND who used his perch at HUAC to prevent the deportation of two Nazis. HUAC member John Rankin of Mississippi was an unabashed white supremacist and anti-Semite—"the No. 1 bigot, hatemonger, and fascist in America," by one account.[26] Rankin did not think much of prosecuting the

Nazis after the war, because, he said, the Germans had been persecuted by "a racial minority" [Jews]. Nor was he a fan of the wartime decision of the Red Cross to integrate human blood, which Rankin damned as "one of the most vicious movements that has yet to be instituted by the crackpots, the communists, and the parlor pinks of this country."[27]

This was the fevered atmosphere that launched McCarthy, who in his February 9, 1950 speech in Wheeling, West Virginia claimed to "have here in my hand a list of 205" Communists working in the State Department.[28] By the next day in Salt Lake City, the figure had shrunk to 57. The number was as slippery as "Tail-Gunner-Joe"—a self-inflating nickname derived from a faked service record.[29] Within days, the Tydings Committee, already investigating loyalty in the State Department, demanded that McCarthy produce evidence. He had none.[30] That did not stop him from naming names—the loftier the better—the shock value of each allegation calibrated for bigger headlines, often singling out "cosmopolitan" intellectuals. A favorite target was Owen Lattimore, an Asian scholar whose views had helped shape China policy. "I am willing to stand or fall on this one," McCarthy said.[31] He fell. Lattimore had the temerity to argue for a nuanced understanding of the complex forces that brought the rise of communist China. For McCarthy, he became the man who "lost China," Hiss's "boss in the espionage ring." As McCarthy candidly admitted to a group of journalists, he was working from "a pailful of shit and [was] going to use it where it [did] him the most good."[32] The feces kept flying, even after the Tydings Committee reported McCarthy's charges constituted a "fraud and a hoax ... on the American people."[33]

Five years after Truman's loyalty program had helped to loose the madness, the president framed McCarthyism as a master of the Nazi demagogic tactic of the "Big Lie":

> The technique of the "big lie" consists of two things. It consists first of making a charge ... [so] frightening and horrible and so extreme that nobody could believe that a decent person would make it if it were not true ... The second part of the "big lie" technique is to keep repeating the lie over and over again, ignoring all proof to the contrary ...
>
> Unfortunately, there is a tendency in this country today to resort to the use of the "big lie" in order to reap personal and partisan advantage. It is a "big lie," for example, to say that we tolerate Communists and other disloyal persons in our Government. It is a "big lie" to attack one of the greatest generals and patriots whom this country ever had and call him a traitor.[34]

The patriot general was former Secretary of Defense and State George C. Marshall. McCarthy declared him tied to a "conspiracy ... so black that, when it is finally exposed, its principals shall be forever deserving of the maledictions of all honest men." Presidential candidate Dwight Eisenhower, to whom Marshall, as FDR's Chief of Staff, had given command of American forces in Europe, and with whom he shared a mutual respect, said ... nothing. On October 3, 1952,

Ike was set to publicly rebuke McCarthy and defend Marshall's "singular selfless-ness and profoundest patriotism." But advisors feared the consequences of taking on McCarthy just weeks before the election, and Eisenhower excised the pas-sage.[35] Most Republicans cravenly kept their concerns to a whisper. One notable exception was Maine Senator Margaret Chase Smith, who took to the Senate floor June 1, 1950 and delivered a "Declaration of Conscience" that read in part:

> I think that it is high time that we remembered that we have sworn to uphold and defend the Constitution … Those of us who shout the loudest about Americanism in making character assassinations are all too fre-quently those who, by our own words and acts, ignore some of the basic principles of Americanism: … As an American, I want to see our nation recapture the strength and unity it once had when we fought the enemy instead of ourselves.[36]

For nearly four years, Smith stood virtually alone in her party as a profile in courage.

Ultimately breaking the fever were two of the most powerful moments in the history of television. On March 9, 1954, revered broadcast journalist Edward R. Murrow devoted his entire *See It Now* program to exposing McCarthy. Murrow brilliantly intercut McCarthy's slander and hypocrisy with truth-telling: an allega-tion that the A.C.L.U. had been listed as a communist front organization—no, said the venerable newsman, neither the Justice Department nor the FBI had deemed it so; McCarthy's purported evidence that was "never supposed to see the light of day," Murrow revealed "anyone can buy for two dollars"; he laid bare the absurdity of McCarthy's charge of "treason" by the Democratic Party and an "extreme lef-twing" press that had at last begun to expose him as a reckless demagogue. Even the arch-conservative *Chicago Tribune* that had waged war against the New Deal and championed McCarthy was now outraged by his assault on the fealty of U.S. Army officials. Nearly an hour of this culminated with Murrow looking straight into the camera, his steely voice announcing the curtain beginning to fall:

> We will not walk in fear, one of another. We will not be driven by fear into an age of unreason if we dig deep in our history and our doctrine and remember that we are not descended from fearful men …
>
> This is no time for men who oppose Senator McCarthy's methods to keep silent … We can deny our heritage and our history, but we cannot escape responsibility for the result.[37]

It was not McCarthy's fault, concluded Murrow, that the anti-communist cru-sade he led was now undermining American democracy from within and alarm-ing U.S. allies. "He didn't create this situation of fear, he merely exploited it," said Murrow. "Cassius was right. 'The fault, dear Brutus, is not in our stars, but in ourselves.'" [38] By 1:30 a.m., CBS was flooded with telegrams, their switchboard overloaded with phone calls, nearly all supportive. Murrow was hailed at home and in Europe. In confronting Americans' complicity, the New York *Herald Tribune's* John Crosby keenly observed, Murrow had "put his finger squarely on the root of the true evil of McCarthyism, which [was] its corrosive effect on the souls of hitherto honest men."[39]

Three months later came the dramatic denouement of the "Army-McCarthy" hearings. It began with charges from the Army that McCarthy's truculent, take-no-prisoners attorney Roy Cohn had used his position to pressure officials to gain special treatment for his associate and close companion David Schine. Although not acknowledged publicly, Schine, wealthy heir to a hotel fortune, was rumored to be Cohn's lover since their much-publicized junket in 1953 across Europe scrutinizing the libraries of the United States Information Agency for alleged communist writings. Fiercely loyal to Cohn, McCarthy alleged the attack was motivated by his red-hunting investigation of the Army. The longer the hearings went on, the more American viewers turned away in disgust from McCarthy's surly badgering, ultimately culminating in an immortal rebuke from the army's lead defense attorney, Joseph N. Welch, who drilled in on the well-documented timeline of Cohn's work on Schine's behalf. With the cameras rolling, McCarthy then went after Fred Fisher, one of Welch's young attorneys, for his association many years earlier with the allegedly communist National Lawyers Guild. "Until this moment, Senator, I think I never really gauged your cruelty or your recklessness," Welch responded with plaintive indignation. "Let us not assassinate this lad further, senator. Have you no sense of decency, sir, at long last? Have you left no sense of decency?"[40] More Americans than not knew the answer. By year's end, the Senate had formally censured him, and over the next three years, he drank himself to death.

As recent scholars have noted, an undercurrent of homophobia added greater potency to the question of McCarthy's "decency." Beyond the Cohn–Schine relationship, there was the widely publicized photograph of Cohn whispering into McCarthy's ear during the hearing that seemed to feminize him and undercut the uber-masculine line of attack that had been central to the bipartisan anticommunist crusade. Homosexuals, the "lavender lads," had by this point largely been hounded out of the federal government by an Eisenhower executive order and a broadly shared antipathy toward queerness in America. In that context, the fact that there was something vaguely "off" about the Cohn–Schine–McCarthy triad further ensured McCarthy's finish.[41]

Neither homophobia nor the exploitation of communist fear to slander civil rights activism, nor even *McCarthyism*, ended with the senator's demise. Hate mail besieged senators who had voted to censure him:

> Red Skunk. You are not fit to clean Senator McCarthy's shoes. Hope you are struck by God … I am an ex-marine who fought in the South Pacific, to open the gates of this Nation for the commie Jews that Hitler did not kill?[42]

In flinging stones at Washington giants like George Marshall, McCarthy anticipated the madness of the far-right John Birch Society, which fermented throughout the fifties in the mind of a candy manufacturer named Robert Welch. Birchers would declare that Joe McCarthy had been murdered, that Franklin Roosevelt had led an international cabal of "Illuminati" masterminds of the Great Depression, that fluoridation of public drinking water was a communist plot, the UN was waging "war on Christmas," and that presidents Truman and Eisenhower, and Secretary of State John Foster Dulles were "communist agents." Fueled by conspiracy theories and saturated with Nazi sympathizers and racists, the Birch Society provided good material for standup comics, a generally marginalized force in American life. It was also a breeding ground for extremist bacterium that would eventually creep into the public square.[43]

The "End of Ideology"

In Washington, it was an era of political equilibrium. Sociologist Daniel Bell famously proclaimed in 1960 *The End of Ideology*, arguing that expanding prosperity had ushered in a new age of political stability and the demise of radical ideologies. Capitalism's worst abuses had been cured by the New Deal, cornerstone elements of which—Wall Street regulation, Social Security, agricultural supports—were accepted as permanent by most Republicans. A widening middle class had eliminated the need for further domestic spending and reduced the appeal of radical thinking that challenged the postwar world order. One could see it in the once-progressive CIO eating its own and the elevation of union leaders who did not contest the globalization of American business nor exorbitant levels of defense spending. It was evident in Harry Truman's pitching right and then leftward, an oscillation more temperamental and calibrated for survival than ideological. Hostility toward "Big Labor," coupled with Henry Wallace's Progressive Party candidacy, threatened Truman's reelection in 1948, but the president's veto of Taft–Hartley led most unions to close ranks, ensuring his stunning comeback.

An era celebrating American exceptionalism presided over by a president seeking the center did not welcome a debate over structural racism. But as we have seen, the war made the issue impossible for Roosevelt to ignore, a reality that only intensified with the Cold War and America's global leadership role. Harry Truman, genuinely outraged by reports of violent repression suffered by returning black veterans across the South, and recognizing that America's moral failure on race was a propaganda weapon for the Soviets, in 1947 established a commission to study the issue and present him with recommendations. Its landmark report, *To Secure These Rights*, constituted the first formal acknowledgment by the federal government of racism as a fact of American life. Among its recommendations were the establishment of a permanent Fair Employment Practices Committee and bold action on lynching, voting rights, and segregation. In February 1948, Truman sent congress a civil rights message that included elements of the report. Met mostly with indifference and hostility, he began buckling as the Democrats convened that summer in Philadelphia. He issued executive orders desegregating the military and the federal workforce, but did not propose civil rights legislation and encouraged a watered-down plank in the party platform.[44]

Led by the young mayor of Minneapolis, Hubert Humphrey, northern liberals remained resolute even as southern opposition brewed on the convention floor. Humphrey took the stage and delivered a speech for the ages, challenging Democrats to renounce southern claims of states' rights. "There are those who say to you—we are rushing this issue of civil rights. I say we are a hundred and seventy-two years too late," his voice rising. "The time has come for the Democratic Party to get out of the shadow of states' rights and walk forthrightly into the bright sunshine of human rights!" Truman fumed—calling Humphrey and the liberals "crackpots"—but thunderous approval from delegates carried a strong civil rights position into the platform. [45] It came with a price: thirty southerners bolted the convention, forming the States' Rights Democratic Party with South Carolina Governor Strom Thurmond as their presidential candidate. The "Dixiecrats" carried just four states, but initiated a decades-long exodus of southern Democrats into the Republican Party.

There would be little progress on civil rights, nor on what Truman called a "Fair Deal" for Americans that featured national health insurance and the repeal of Taft-Hartley. A bipartisan block of conservatives thwarted nearly all of it, casting "New Dealism" throughout the era in varying shades of red.[46] It would be much the same under Eisenhower, who generally proposed only modest initiatives that had broad bipartisan support like Social Security and minimum wage increases, funds to disseminate the polio Salk vaccine, and a new Department of Health, Education and Welfare. It was through HEW that Eisenhower proposed a health "reinsurance" plan to support private insurance companies who offered expanded coverage. Like Truman's plan, it was condemned by the AMA as "socialized medicine" and went nowhere.[47]

"People of Plenty": Rising Affluence and Its Consequences

In the September 1954 issue of *Reader's Digest*, Henry Wallace regaled readers with the wonders of the new science of "hybridizing" farm animals. Joining one genus of species to another had gone from the laboratory to quite literally reshaping American pastoralism. The former Agriculture Secretary was bullish, describing hybridization as "the joy of working with nature to create something new, something better [so that] farm animals and vegetables … would be of higher quality and far more productive." Americans could anticipate heftier beef cattle, and the "Super-Chicken-1954 model," "meatier, juicier, more tender and pleasing to the eye"—and available year-around![48] Industrial agriculture's leap forward coincided with the publication of *People of Plenty*, historian David Potter's celebratory study placing American abundance at the center of national identity. Potter argued that the uniquely American capacity to produce a veritable avalanche of affordable goods and services for greater numbers of citizens than ever before gave the nation its exceptional place in history.[49] Technological and scientific innovation, a sturdy work ethic, and a political system that encouraged entrepreneurial risk-taking had produced, "per capita, more auto-mobiles, more telephones, more radios, more vacuum cleaners, more electric lights, more bathtubs, more supermarkets and movie palaces and hospitals than any other nation."[50]

Seemingly frivolous expressions of the American dream packed a punch in the early Cold War. Pitching for two California shopping centers, newsman George Putnam glowed that "the eighty stores and glittering assortment of goods that one would find there [were] concrete expressions of the practical idealism that built America." And, he reminded, there was "plenty of free parking for all those cars we Americans seem to drive. Who can help but con-trast all of this to what you'd find living under Soviet communism?"[51] Although there were glaring racial and regional breaches in American afflu-ence, rising white middle-class prosperity was indeed something to behold. In the decade and a half after the war, Americans moved into the middle class in record numbers. By 1960, three out of four households owned an automobile, six in ten their own home, and almost 90 percent had at least one television. The longer the boom continued, the more it became an article of faith that 76 million Baby Boom children would be more economically secure than their parents. Although often forgotten, much of the prosperity was powered by government policy, including progressive taxation that funded critical pub-lic investments. The generous educational benefits of the GI Bill of Rights made possible many of the nation's greatest postwar achievements, including the genesis of the computer age, the space program, and life-saving advances in medical care.[52]

Patriotism had a way of obscuring the darker consequences of American affluence. Mountains of new forms of garbage—paper plates, frozen TV dinner trays, Styrofoam cups, plastic packaging, spent toys, diapers and more—poured into landfills. In the Cold War, this was not mere rubbish. The *freedom* to discard was another marker of American plenty, a liberating sign of unprecedented abundance, material evidence of national superiority. In 1959 *Look* magazine glowed about the "kitchen freedom" facilitated by a "revolution in food packag-ing and processing."[53] The "convenience, cleanliness, and labor savings" embod-ied in disposable packaging, as one historian has written, signified "the freedom of modernity," and the difference "between the freedom of capitalism and the bondage of communism."[54]

By contrast, the "waste" of free-flowing rivers was to be arrested. Through an eruption of dozens of dams and other water projects, the Bureau of Reclamation and Army Corps of Engineers—bolstered by a phalanx of western politicians, business interests, and ranchers—worked to bring water and hydroelectric power to every corner of the arid west. Presiding over much of the dam-building jug-gernaut was the Bureau's indomitable Floyd Dominy. In pressing for major development of the Colorado River, Dominy announced he had "seen all the wild rivers [he] ever [wanted] to see," which were "useless to anyone."[55] Not to be outdone, the rival Corps of Engineers promised, "TOTAL USE FOR GREATER WEALTH." Reclamation's momentous significance in the early

Cold War was made clear by oil tycoon and former Oklahoma governor Robert Kerr in congressional testimony:

> Can a pagan Communist nation, by enslaving and regimenting its people, make more efficient use of soil and water resources than the most advanced and enlightened nation in the world? Can ruthless atheists mobilize and harness their treasures of God-given wealth to defeat and stifle freedom-loving peoples everywhere?[56]

The rivers may have been God-given, but damming them required federal largesse: the annual cost of western water development soared from $33 million in 1939 to outlays of nearly $250 million. Beyond powering the region's growth, the reengineered West left a very mixed legacy, exacerbating the concentration of wealth and power throughout the region and leaving behind a radically transformed environment.[57] Within decades, the long-term sustainability of American civilization in the arid West would be in doubt. Dominy could make water run uphill, but by the 1960s the Colorado River failed to reach the sea.[58]

The era's more celebrated public investment was the 1956 Federal-Aid Highway Act. More than 41,000 miles of limited access highways linked the nation coast to coast and wrapped cities with beltways, hastening suburban development. Inspired in part by the illusory belief of civil defense planners that multi-lane highways would allow millions to evacuate cities in the event of a Soviet nuclear strike, interstates were resoundingly popular with travelers, truckers and aspiring entrepreneurs like Ray Kroc, whose ingenious transformation of a San Bernardino, California hamburger stand called McDonald's pioneered a wave of nationally franchised retail operations that soon grew like mushrooms in the Interstate-suburban ecosystem.

For all the economic activity it spawned, the postwar project to construct an auto-centric culture left a trail of collateral destruction. Interstates bypassed small towns and independently owned businesses, increasingly abandoned as beguiling relics of an older America. They gutted historic urban neighborhoods and vintage structures in the rural countryside, displaced residents and preservationists standing defenseless against the blitz. Simultaneously, even as automobiles remained out of reach for many city residents, their growing dominance turned the final screws on what were once impressive urban trolley systems. Neither trolleys nor passenger rail could compete with taxpayer-subsidized highway and airline travel. And there were other costs: in an age of rising incomes, many Americans failed to notice that by 1960 they were spending 15 percent of their income on transportation—more than double a generation before.[59] The length of car loans was extended, if only to match the widening spread of new models styled with fins and dripping in heavy chrome gorp. Despite poor fuel efficiency of the American automobile fleet, ads from the American Petroleum Institute promoted consumption of oil and gasoline as testament to the new equation that consumerism was Americanism.[60]

Intensified resource development was the subject of a 1952 presidential commission. Its report, *Resources for Freedom*, did not mince words, declaring that the defeat of communism demanded "maximum production of natural resources to be found at home and in every corner of the globe." In that spirit, the U.S. Forest Service called for increases in the "allowable cut" of lumber production—over and above what decades of the agency's own scientific studies specified. Swept aside were conclusions about rates of forest regeneration, the areas suitable for timbering, the amount of wood fiber extractable from a given forest. The sky was now the limit as forest managers complied with demands from Washington for more timber. To deny requests for additional board feet meant saying no to budget increases and to America's can-do spirit. It meant saying no to *Peter Pine*, star of a timber industry radio program who lived a lonely life in the forest until a kind forester discovered and marked him. Soon a logger arrived to "free" Peter from the forest. The ecological consequences of such thinking became clear soon enough in degraded watersheds throughout the Rocky Mountain West.[61]

Pressure for the accelerated cut derived in part from a home building industry furiously responding to the postwar housing shortage. With the onset of the baby boom and GI bill-backed low-interest mortgages, young families fled cramped cities for new housing developments in the suburbs. The archetype, Levittown, New York, was a marvel of the age—a former 4,000-acre potato farm magically converted into a community of 17,000 homes for 80,000 residents (Figure 3.1). Not one was black. Builder William Levitt coolly remarked that "we can solve a housing problem, or we can try to solve a racial problem. But we cannot combine the two."[62] He was hardly the first to espouse such a view. On the specious assumption that integration would degrade property values, since the 1930s appraisers and surveyors of the federal Home Ownership Loan Corporation had been creating maps for private lenders that indicated on a graded color-coded scale, "high and low risk areas" of urban areas. Mixed race neighborhoods and those dominated by minorities were colored red and variously labeled, "racial hazards."[63] The Federal Housing Administration perpetuated the practice, consistently denying loans to prospective minority buyers. Developers and banks followed suit, racially restrictive "covenants" serving to exclude minorities.

Other insidious costs accompanied suburbanization. New homes often came fully equipped with modern appliances and were heated and cooled with cheap, coal-fired electricity—polluting, but sent from a distant remove. Developers gorged on wetlands, woodlands, farms, and meadows—drained, cut, and paved over at a rate of more than 2,000 square acres a day, compounding the unseen problem of non-point source water pollution.[64] There was also the visible contamination: many suburbanites had foamy "septic cocktails" flowing from their faucets, the result of thousands of backyard septic tanks being crammed into a few square miles of development. Finally, the new obsession with the lawn sent Americans warring against crabgrass and an assortment of pests, applying fertilizers and an avalanche of insecticides and pesticides, most notably DDT. Hailed as the "atomic bomb of the insect world," DDT was sprayed to kill mosquitoes, to combat polio before the Salk vaccine, embedded in wallpaper to ward off

Figure 3.1 Aerial view of Levittown, New York.
Bettman/Getty, www.gettyimages.co.uk/detail/news-photo/aerial-view-of-levittown-li-news-photo/514677930?adppopup=true

bedbugs, and laid on "almost anything that flew, crawled, or walked."[65] In the years ahead, suburban Americans concerned with these issues quietly became a force in the environmental movement.[66]

A Culture of Conformity

While most residents found a welcoming sense of community in the suburbs, for critics outside it seemed an oppressive landscape that reinforced a culture of white-bread homogeneity. As Lewis Mumford acidly observed, the suburbs delivered

> a multitude of uniform, unidentifiable houses, lined up inflexibly, at uniform distances on uniform roads, in a treeless command waste, inhabited by people of the same class, … witnessing the same television performances, eating the same tasteless prefabricated foods, from the same freezers, conforming in every outward and inward respect to a common mold.[67]

Residents may have come from ethnically heterogeneous urban neighborhoods, but once arrived they melted in as *Americans*. And they worshipped.

Fears of nuclear war, anti-communism, social pressure, and a desire for community drove religious affiliation to an all-time high of more than 60 percent. Radio and TV preachers seamlessly fused Christian piety and eternal salvation with messianic anticommunism and the material rewards of virtuous living in a free enterprise system.

Young suburban mothers took their cues about a colicky infant not from their mother next door as they once might have, but from Dr. Benjamin Spock's *Common Sense Book of Baby and Child Care*. Women were returning to work, but in a narrow range of positions where they endured multiple forms of discrimination, while many African American women were driven from wartime assembly lines back to mostly menial positions. The message echoed throughout the culture: women's primary responsibilities concerned the home and children, and "liberating" their husbands to succeed at work. When accompanying husbands to social events, women were to mute themselves on political affairs. If a woman wanted something more in life than home and family, she suffered some sort of mental affliction or sexual disorder. One ad from the Brand Names Corporation called it "an inferiority complex." The cure? Shopping! Women "should feel mighty important," because "only in the USA are there so many brands of so many good things—all dependent upon just one person—*You!*"[68] Out of sight were darker realities like domestic violence, the most salient reflection of which may have come in the popular TV sitcom, *The Honeymooners*. The show featured a frequent gag in which Ralph Kramden, lovable, bus-driving blowhard "master" of the house, would threaten Alice his wife, with "Pow! To the moon!" Ralph invariably ended up the fool, but the mocking caricature of wife beating was more revealing than many viewers would have admitted.[69]

Americans took up new hobbies to fill expanded leisure time. One of the era's great commercial success stories, paint-by-number kits epitomized a democratic people of plenty, where a Nebraska 12-year-old's "da Vinci Last Supper" mirrored that of the American president. An endless variety of inexpensive paint-by-number pictures were turned out by millions of "filler-inners," including Eisenhower and fittingly enough, J. Edgar Hoover—it was, after all, a popular art that demanded compliance. Though mocked by art critics as "regimented" art "for self-indulgent philistines," painting-by-number brought artistic verisimilitude within reach of the masses.[70] As with the era's jigsaw puzzle craze, much of the subject matter reinforced nostalgic affection for an idealized American past. In the same spirit, the popularity of Lionel Trains and miniature villages romanticized the disappearing world of small towns and passenger rail. These and other pursuits offered enjoyment, as well as a small measure of control in an anxious age characterized by increasing complexity and a loss of individual agency.

The "New Look"

Dwight Eisenhower's election brought the most revered military figure to the White House since Ulysses S. Grant. Promising to end the fighting in Korea, the retired general pledged a policy calibrated to avoid similarly protracted military confrontations. Emphasizing deterrence centered on the threat of "massive retaliation," Eisenhower and Secretary of State John Foster Dulles deployed a strategy of nuclear "brinksmanship," threatening North Korea, and then China—twice, over the Taiwan Straits.[71] Eisenhower presided over modest reductions in conventional forces, but expanded the hydrogen bomb arsenal from 1,000 warheads to 18,000, augmented with increases in the bomber fleet. The "New Look" policy aimed to give Americans "better bang for the buck" in arresting the communist threat, deterring aggression through "a capacity to retaliate instantly," as Dulles declared.[72]

The New Look did not imply the absence of an offensive strategy. His national security team, led by the Secretary of State and his brother, CIA Director Allen Dulles, deployed covert operations to advance both U.S. security interests and the overseas investments of multinational corporations. For John Foster Dulles, a corporate attorney whose specialization was international finance, these were "interrelated and mutually reinforcing."[73] The Dulles brothers presided over an epoch of increasingly aggressive actions abroad that protected American interests, even as they damaged the image of the United States in areas of the globe being swept up in a rising tide of nationalism. It began in Iran, where the British held a lucrative grip on the nation's oil supply through its Anglo-Iranian Oil Company, paying a paltry 16 percent royalty to the government for extracting the country's oil.[74] In 1951, Prime Minister Dr. Mohammad Mossadegh and the Iranian Parliament moved to nationalize the oil industry. Mossadegh offered compensation, but the British reacted in fury, threatening military action. While Iran's government stood firm, the Truman administration cautioned Prime Minister Clement Atlee against using force. Atlee was replaced by the ardent defender of Britain's shrinking empire, Winston Churchill, whose government settled on a covert coup orchestrated by British intelligence and the American CIA. Truman resisted authorizing the CIA to engage in covert operations—especially against Mossadegh, a democratic leader who reviled communism.[75]

Months later, however, Eisenhower was in the White House and the Dulles brothers made the case for Mossadegh's overthrow. In March 1953—just as the president lamented privately that America "seemed unable to get some of the people in these downtrodden countries to like us instead of hating us"—Allen Dulles wired $1 million to CIA officers in Tehran with instructions to carry out the coup.[76] Led by Kermit Roosevelt, Jr., grandson of Theodore Roosevelt, the CIA "[bribed] journalists, editors, Islamic preachers, and other opinion leaders" to whip up a storm of disinformation about Mossadegh, fomenting hostility toward his government. Two more bags of cash went to parliament and members of the military. On August 19, Mossadegh was deposed. Left in charge of the country was reliable U.S. ally, Shah Reza Pahlavi. Backed by U.S. weapons and a CIA-trained secret police, the SAVAK, the Shah's despotic rule lasted for a quarter-century. Iran become a strategically important outpost of operations for the growing U.S. military footprint in the Middle East. By 1960, a consortium of U.S. oil companies had firm command of Iran's oil industry.[77]

One year later it was Guatemala, where the CIA aimed at the democratic government of Juan Jacobo Árbenz Guzmán. Elected president in 1951, Árbenz followed Juan José Arévalo, who since 1944 led a season of remarkable reform in a country that had lived in tyranny, where three American companies controlled most of the economic life. Arévalo brought social security, a fixed work week, and collective bargaining rights, a legacy Árbenz hoped to build on by forging an independent, progressive "modern capitalist state."[78] The centerpiece of his program was the Agrarian Reform Law, authorizing the government to commandeer and redistribute vast acreages of uncultivated land. Much of it was owned by the United Fruit Company (UFC), known throughout Latin America as *el pulpo* ("the octopus"). The government seized 234,000 acres, less than half the company's holdings, and offered $1.185 million as compensation. United Fruit rejected it, demanded $19 million, and looked to its friends in Washington for salvation.[79]

It had many. John Foster and Allen Dulles had performed UFC legal work, Allen owned substantial stock, other top State Department officials were shareholders, as were various congressmen and the UN Ambassador. The chief of the Madison Avenue PR firm representing United Fruit was married to Eisenhower's personal secretary. Soon after the dust had settled in Iran, the CIA launched an operation headquartered out of Opa Locka, Florida to overthrow Árbenz. Coordinating with U.S.-backed dictators in the region, the campaign funneled cash to student groups, labor unions, and the Catholic Church to saturate Guatemala with anti-Arbenz propaganda, depicting him as a tool of international communism. From the *New York Times* to the *Reader's Digest*, a parallel campaign unfolded in the United States. The Secretary of State claimed Guatemalans were living under a "Communist type of terrorism." U.S. Ambassador to Guatemala John Peurifoy declared that a "Soviet republic" could not be permitted to stand "between Texas and the Panama Canal."[80]

Árbenz was dumbfounded by the slander. His Foreign Minister Guillermo Toriello wondered how the United States could condemn "as 'communism' every manifestation of nationalism or economic independence, any desire for social progress, any intellectual curiosity, and any interest in progressive liberal reforms."[81] After his only meeting with Arbenz in December 1953, Peurifoy nearly admitted the truth to Dulles: "If he is not a communist, he will certainly do until one comes along."[82] The inevitable coup came in June 1954. Árbenz's replacement, Colonel Carlos Castillo Armas, terminated all reform and inaugurated decades of rule by military junta and a savage civil war that took the lives of nearly 200,000 Guatemalans.

That summer, Dulles rued the "unfortunate fact [that] … most of the countries of the world do not share our view that communist control of any government anywhere is in itself a danger and a threat."[83] The secretary was referring specifically to the Geneva Conference, called to determine the future of Vietnam following an eight-year conflict between the communist-led Viet Minh and colonial French forces. The Geneva Agreement's most important provision called for the temporary division of Vietnam near the 17th parallel, and for internationally supervised elections to unify the country under one government. American officials refused to sign the accords, claiming elections could not be held with a communist government in the north allegedly menacing the country. In truth, the CIA knew the communist leader, Ho Chi Minh, would have won the election decisively. Eisenhower later admitted that Ho could have won as much as 80 percent of the vote.[84]

Geneva was the latest in a series of decisive turning points toward deepening American involvement in Vietnam. Near the end of World War II, American diplomats in Saigon had advocated to Washington that then-U.S. ally Ho Chi Minh was an independent communist leader with whom the United States could accommodate itself, as it seemed prepared to do with Yugoslavia's Tito. Although schooled in Marxist thought and a determined nationalist committed to a radical restructuring of Vietnam, Ho Chi Minh admired much about both America and the French. Having led the Viet Minh to victory against the Japanese, in September 1945 Ho Chi Minh proclaimed his nation's independence, famously quoting the "undeniable truths" of Thomas Jefferson's seminal document and the French Revolution. Offering a litany of 80 years of abuses heaped upon the Vietnamese by their French overlords, he finished by asserting the Vietnamese were prepared to sacrifice everything "in order to safeguard their independence and liberty."[85] As the French reoccupied the south, Ho warned that they "could kill ten of our men" for every Frenchman his forces killed, "and in the end it will be you who will tire of it"—pointed advice that would be ignored.[86] He directed eight letters to Harry Truman seeking recognition of Vietnamese sovereignty. Not one received an answer. Seeking to bolster the anti-Soviet bulwark in Europe, the United States threw its support behind the doomed French war against the Viet Minh. Three years in, the "fall of China" further raised the stakes, and soon the United States was bearing 80 percent of the cost of the French war.[87]

Just weeks before the culminating siege at Dien Bien Phu in the spring of 1954, Eisenhower offered this tragically prescient response to questions of growing U.S. involvement: "I cannot conceive of a greater tragedy for America than to get heavily involved now in an all-out war" in Vietnam.[88] By April, however, with French troops surrounded and the White House considering both conventional and nuclear strikes, the president spoke of "what you would call the 'falling domino' principle. You have a row of dominoes set up, you knock over the first one," and before you knew it, Vietnam's fall would mark the "beginning of a disintegration that would have the most profound influences."[89] In 1954, the image of communist dominoes falling from Saigon to San Diego was not the paranoid phantasm it became. After Geneva, the United States moved to establish the Republic of Vietnam in the south. Its head was Ngô Đình Diệm, a Vietnamese nationalist and devout Catholic monk, soon hailed by prominent Americans as the savior of democracy in Asia. Having rejected unifying elections, in 1955 U.S. officials had Diệm stage a referendum to give him a fig leaf of legitimacy. In an absurd parody of a free election, he earned 98.2 percent of the vote and proclaimed himself president. More than 600,000 votes were cast for him in the Saigon capital, 150,000 more than the electorate.[90]

This was the opening act of one of the most thoroughly corrupt, nepotistic, authoritarian regimes to ever receive American support. Edward Lansdale, who headed the CIA's clandestine operations in the country, called Diem's regime "fascistic"—an apt descriptor for many reasons, not least among them his brother Ngô Đình Nhu, an admirer of Adolph Hitler who ran the government's Gestapo-like secret police.[91] For the next eight years, boatloads of U.S. military aid floated to Saigon. It was not enough, nor could it ever have been. The deeper the U.S. investment, the more repressive the regime seemed to become. Through a savage internal security program, Nhu's forces rounded up suspected opponents of the government, the majority not communist but demanding a democratic end to the repression, which increasingly fell on Buddhist spiritual leaders. Tens of thousands of South Vietnamese were herded into "reeducation centers," many mercilessly tortured and killed.[92] Urgings by the U.S. Ambassador in Saigon to condition the continued flow of U.S. aid on Diệm moderating his policies and implementing land and other political reforms were rejected.[93] By 1960, anti-Diem opposition crystallized into the National Liberation Front that would soon be fighting American GIs.

By the late 1950s, the New Look appeared to have run its course, as national security officials increasingly argued for a more "flexible response" to the communist threat. Its limits were most tragically realized with the anticommunist 1956 democratic uprising in Hungary. A genuinely democratic, non-CIA-sponsored revolt inspired partly by liberalizing policies of new Soviet leader Nikita Khrushchev, and further encouraged by U.S. radio propaganda, the Hungarian Uprising was left to stand alone without U.S. assistance when the inevitable crackdown arrived. Looking down the barrel of a wider war with a nuclear-armed Soviet Union, the threat of a massive U.S. strike proved useless, the promise of American democracy vacuous.[94] That the American Freedom Train did not run through Budapest seemed a crowning finale to an era when U.S. policy often fell short of its ideals at home and abroad.

Notes

1 Eric Foner, "The Idea of Freedom in American History," n.d., http://www2.law. columbia.edu/law_culture/Faclunch_sp04/Foner_Feb26.pdf, retrieved January 7, 2021.

2 Clark, Department of Justice Press Release, December 11, 1946, quoted by Stuart J. Little, "The Freedom Train: Political Citizenship and Postwar Political Culture, 1946–1949," *American Studies* 34, no. 1 (Spring 1993): 36.

3 Ted Widmer, "Remembering the Freedom Train," *The New Yorker*, November 26, 2017, www.newyorker.com/culture/culture-desk/remembering-the-freedom-train, retrieved January 7, 2021.

4 Widmer.

5 Greg Bradsher, "The Freedom Train, 1947–1949" (National Archives, *The Text Message*, April 7, 2020), https://text-message.blogs.archives.gov/2020/04/07/the-freedom-train-1947–1949, retrieved January 7, 2021.

6 Little, 51–52.

7 Ibid., 54; Bradsher; Clark quoted in Stephen J. Whitfield, *The Culture of the Cold War*, 2nd. ed. (Baltimore, MD: Johns Hopkins University Press, 1996), 53.

8 Eric Lichtblau, *The Nazis Next Door: How America became a Safe Haven for Hitler's Men* (New York: Mariner, 2014), 37–40; and Richard Rashke, "The FBI's Shameful Recruitment of Nazi war Criminals," Reuters, March 6, 2013, http://blogs.reuters.com/great-debate/2013/03/06/the-fbis-shameful-recruitment-of-nazi-war-criminals, retrieved January 8, 2021. The bootlegging of Third Reich refugees into the United States extended to the CIA. As Eric Lichtblau has recounted, the agency smuggled and shielded as many as ten thousand former SS men, Gestapo agents, and Nazi officers who melted into American society, becoming used car salesmen, mechanics, and suburban anticommunist patriots.

9 John Sbardellati, *J. Edgar Hoover Goes to the Movies: The FBI and the Origins of Hollywood's Cold War* (Ithaca, NY: Cornell University Press, 2012), 2.

10 Ibid., 100–101.

11 "Bogie and the Blacklist," *Slate*, March 4, 2016, https://slate.com/culture/2016/03/you-must-remember-this-on-the-blacklist-humphrey-bogart-and-the-african-queen.html; and Ellen Schrecker, "Blacklists and Other Economic Sanctions," in *The Age of McCarthyism: A Brief History with Documents* (New York: St. Martin's Press, 1994), www.writing.upenn.edu/~afilreis/50s/schrecker-blacklist.html, retrieved January 8, 2021.

12 Quoted by John Sbardellati and Tony Shaw, "Booting a Tramp: Charlie Chaplin, the FBI, and the Construction of the Subversive Image in Red Scare America," *The Pacific Historical Review* 72, no. 4 (November 2003): 495–530.

13 Carl Steward, "John Garfield: Real-Life Noir Hero," Film Noir Foundation (Summer 2012): 44, http://filmnoirfoundation.org/noircitymag/John-Garfield.pdf, retrieved January 8, 2021.

14 Ibid.; and Robert David Jaffee, "Witness to a Persecution: In Search of Blacklistee John Garfield," *HuffPost*, December 6, 2017, www.huffpost.com/entry/witness-to-a-persecution-_b_2735083, retrieved January 8, 2021.

15 Quoted in Herbert Biberman, *Salt of the Earth: The Story of a Film* (New York: Sag Harbor, 2003), 86.

16 Ibid., 162.

17 Pete Hammond, "Kirk Douglas on 'Trumbo': 'I Was Threatened That Using a Blacklisted Writer Would End My Career,'" *Deadline*, November 19, 2015, https://deadline.com/2015/11/kirk-douglas-speaks-out-trumbo-career-threatened-blacklist-1201629542, retrieved January 9, 2021.

18 Lawrence S. Wittner, *Cold War America: From Hiroshima to Watergate* (New York: Praeger, 1974), 48.

19 Quoted in James Young, *Union Power: The United Electrical Workers in Erie, Pennsylvania* (New York: Monthly Review Press, 2017), 73.

20 "John Nelson, 1917–1959 Historical Marker" (Pennsylvania Historical and Museum Commission, dedicated September 18, 2004, https://explorepahistory.com/hmarker.php?markerId=1-A-BF, retrieved January 10, 2021.

21 Young, 146–167, 178; at the 2004 dedication of a state historical marker for Johnny Nelson, his sons wept as they recalled the pain their family endured.

22 James Patterson, *Grand Expectations: The United States 1945–1974* (New York: Oxford University Press, 1996), 53; and J. H. O'Dell, "Operation Dixie: Notes on a Promise Abandoned," *Labor Notes*, April 1, 2005, https://labornotes.org/2005/04/operation-dixie-notes-promise-abandoned, retrieved January 10, 2021.

23 Quoted in David McCullough, *Truman* (New York: Simon and Schuster, 1992), 814.

24 Quoted in Wittner, 100.

25 Ellen W. Schrecker, Comments on John Earl Haynes's, "The Cold War Debate Continues: A Traditionalist View of Historical Writing on Domestic Communism and Anti-Communism, *Journal of Cold War Studies* 2, no. 1 (Winter 2000), https://sites.fas.harvard.edu/~hpcws/comment15.htm; and Victor Navasky, "Cold War Ghosts," *The Nation*, June 28, 2001, www.thenation.com/article/archive/

cold-war-ghosts, retrieved January 12, 2021; Schrecker and Navasky were responding to John Earl Haynes and Harvey Klehr, *Venona: Decoding Soviet Espionage in America (New Haven, CT: Yale University Press, 2000)*.

26 Reynold Humphries, *Hollywood's Blacklists: A Political and Cultural History* (Edinburgh University Press, 2008), 57–59, 111; and Stanley Frank, "The Rancorous Mr. Rankin," *Liberty: The Magazine of a Free People*, October 6, 1945, 19, quoted in "John Rankin," *Densho Encyclopedia*, https://encyclopedia.densho.org/John_Rankin, retrieved January 11, 2021.

27 Quoted in Michael S. Sherry, *In the Shadow of War: The United States Since the 1930s* (Yale University Press, 1995), 175.

28 In Senator Joseph McCarthy, "Communists in Government Service," February 9, 1950, www.senate.gov/about/powers-procedures/investigations/mccarthy-hearings/communists-in-government-service.htm, retrieved January 12, 2021.

29 Richard H. Rovere, *Senator Joe McCarthy* (New York: Harper Row, 1959), 95.

30 Ibid., 148–150.

31 Quoted in ibid., 151.

32 Geoffrey Wheatcroft, "Hell, There Ain't No List: Will Trumpism Be Remembered as McCarthyism Is?," Review of Larry Tye's *The Life and Long Shadow of Senator Joe McCarthyism* (New York: Houghton Mifflin, 2020), December 11, 2020, www.the-tls.co.uk/articles/demagogue-larry-tye-book-review-joseph-mccarthy, retrieved January 12, 2021.

33 Quoted in Wittner, 95.

34 Quoted by William D. Zeranski, "The 'Big Lie' Explained By a Good Man," American Thinker, February 19, 2010, www.americanthinker.com/blog/2010/02/the_big_lie_explained_by_a_goo.html, retrieved January 12, 2021.

35 Jon Meacham, *The Soul of America: The Battle for Our Better Angels* (New York: Random House, 2018), 197.

36 Excerpted from Margaret Chase Smith, *Declaration of Conscience* (Garden City, NY: Doubleday, 1972), 13–14.

37 Edward R. Murrow, *See It Now*, March 9, 1954, www.youtube.com/watch?v=OtCGlqA2rrk, retrieved January 12, 2021.

38 Ibid.

39 A. M. Sperber, *Murrow: His Life and Times* (New York: Freundlich Books, 1986), 436–440.

40 Army-McCarthy Hearings, McCarthy-Welch Exchange, June 9, 1954, www.youtube.com/watch?v=8llS0ZkLVGA, retrieved January 12, 2021.

41 Rebecca Onion, "We're Never Going to Get Our 'Have You No Sense of Decency Sir?' Moment," *Slate*, July 26, 2018, https://slate.com/news-and-politics/2018/07/that-have-you-no-sense-of-decency-sir-moment-from-the-1954-army-mccarthy-hearings-isnt-quite-what-we-remember.html, retrieved June 3, 2021.

42 Ibid.

43 Claire Conner, *Wrapped in the Flag: A Personal History of America's Radical Right* (Boston, MA: Beacon Press, 2013), xi, 10, 27–28, 34–35, 40.

44 McCullough, 587–588.

45 Quoted in McCullough, 639–640.

46 Howard Markel, "Give 'Em Health, Harry," *Millbank Quarterly* 93, no. 1 (March 2015), www.ncbi.nlm.nih.gov/pmc/articles/PMC4364422, retrieved January 12, 2021.

47 Jean Edward Smith, *Eisenhower in War and Peace* (New York: Random House, 2012), 560, 654.

48 In David Peterson Del Mar, "'Our Animal Friends': Depictions of Animals in *Reader's Digest* During the 1950s," *Environmental History* 3, no. 1 (January 1998), 34.

49 David Potter, *People of Plenty* (1954), 137.

50 Ibid., 84.

51 In The Archives Project, *The Atomic Café* (Thorn Emi Video, 1982).

52 Milton Greenberg, *The GI Bill: The Law That Changed America* (New York: Lickle Publishing, 1997), 36–37, 47.

53 Quoted in Susan Strasser, *Waste and Want: A Social History of Trash* (New York: Holt, 1999), 268.

54 Strasser, 268–269.

55 Quoted in Marc Reisner, *Cadillac Desert: The American West and Its Disappearing Water* (New York: Penguin Books, 1986), 242.

56 Quoted in Donald Worster, *Rivers of Empire: Water, Aridity, and the Growth of the American West* (New York: Pantheon Books, 1985), 264.

57 Ibid., 265–275.

58 Reisner, Chapter 7–8.

59 "100 Years of U.S. Consumer Spending" (Washington, DC: U.S. Department of Labor, Bureau of Labor Statistics, 2006), www.bls.gov/opub/100-years-of-u-s-consumer-spending.pdf, retrieved January 14, 2021.

60 American Petroleum Institute ad, ca. 1955, author's collection.

61 Paul W. Hirt, *A Conspiracy of Optimism: Management of the National Forests Since World War II* (Lincoln, NE: University of Nebraska Press, 1994), xxi–xxii, Jack Shepherd, *The Forest Killers: The Destruction of the American Wilderness* (New York: Weybright and Talley, 1975), 49; and Harold K. Steen, *The U.S. Forest Service: A History* (Seattle, WA: University of Washington Press, 1980), 281.

62 Quoted by David Halberstam, *The Fifties* (New York: Random House, 1993), 141.

63 Becky M. Nicolaides, *My Blue Heaven: Life and Politics in the Working-Class Suburbs of Los Angeles, 1920–1965* (Chicago, IL: University of Chicago Press, 2002), 193.

64 Adam Rome, *Bulldozer in the Countryside: Suburban Sprawl and the Rise of American Environmentalism* (New York: Cambridge University Press, 2001), 8.

65 Thomas R. Dunlap, *DDT: Scientists, Citizens, and Public Policy* (Princeton, NJ: Princeton University Press, 1981), 65.

66 See Rome, Chapter 2–5.

67 Lewis Mumford, *The City in History: Its Origins, Its Transformation, and Its Prospects* (Orlando, FL: Harcourt, 1961, 1989), 486.

68 Brand Names Corporation ad, n.d., author's collection.

69 Virginia Lee Cronin, "Silence is Golden: Older Women's Voices and the Analysis of Meaning Among Survivors of Domestic Violence" (Syracuse University, 2013), https://surface.syr.edu/cgi/viewcontent.cgi?article=1029&context=etd, retrieved January 14, 2021.

70 Karal Ann Marling, *As Seen on TV: The Visual Culture of Everyday Life in the 1950s* (Cambridge, MA: Harvard University Press, 1994), 50–84.

71 Smith, *Eisenhower in War and Peace*, 641.

72 Quotes from Diggins, *The Proud Decades*, 140; John Lewis Gaddis, *John Foster Dulles and the Diplomacy of the Cold War* (Princeton, NJ: Princeton University Press, 1992), 50; Smith, *Eisenhower in War and Peace*, 643.

73 James A. Bill, quoted in Stephen Kinzer, *Overthrow: America's Century of Regime Change from Hawaii to Iraq* (New York: Holt, 2006), 122.

74 Less than one-third the 50–50 split the United States negotiated with the Saudis.

75 Kinzer, 118–121.

76 NSC Meeting, March 4, 1953, quoted in P.G. Boyle, *Eisenhower* (New York: Routledge, 2014), 54.

77 Kinzer, 123.

78 Quoted in Kinzer, 132.

79 Richard H. Immerman, *The CIA In Guatemala: The Foreign Policy of Intervention* (Austin, TX: University of Texas Press, 1982), Chapter 6 and 7; and Kinzer, 133.

80 *New York Times*, June 16, 1954 and *Time*, January 11, 1954, quoted in William Blum, *Killing Hope: U.S. Military and CIA Interventions Since World War II* (Monroe, ME: Common Courage Press, 2004), 73.

81 In Stephen Schlesinger and Stephen Kinzer, *Bitter Fruit: The Untold Story of the American Coup In Guatemala* (New York: Doubleday, 1982), 143–144.

82 Quoted in Kinzer, 137.

83 Quoted in Jerry Carrier, *Hard Right Turn: The History and the Assassination of the American Left* (New York: Algora Publishing, 2015), 50.

84 Dwight Eisenhower *The White House Years: Mandate for Change, 1953–1956* (New York: Doubleday, 1963), 372.

85 Ho Chi Minh, *Selected Works*, vol. 3 (Hanoi: Foreign Languages Publishing House, 1960–1962), 17–21.

86 Quoted in Robert Shaplen, "Ho Chi Minh: The Untried Gamble," in Andrew J. Rotter, ed., *Light at the End of the Tunnel*, revised ed. (Wilmington, DE: Scholarly Resources, 1999,), 14.

87 George C. Herring, *America's Longest War: The United States and Vietnam, 1950–1975*, 2nd ed. (New York: Knopf, 1986), 25–29.

88 President Eisenhower's News Conference, February 10, 1954, *Public Papers of the Presidents, 1954*, p. 253.

89 President Eisenhower's News Conference, April 7, 1954, in *The Pentagon Papers*, Gravel Edition, vol. 1 (Boston, MA: Beacon Press, 1971), 597–598.

90 James H. Wilbanks, *Vietnam War: A Topical Exploration and Primary Source Collection* (Santa Barbara, CA: ABC-CLIO Press, 2017), 96.

91 U.S. Department of Defense, *United States – Vietnam Relations, 1945–1967* (U.S. Government edition, Pentagon Papers), book 2, IV, A.5, tab 4, 66.

92 *The Pentagon Papers*, Gravel Edition, vol. 1, Chapter 5, "Origins of the Insurgency in South Vietnam, 1954–1960" (Boston, MA: Beacon Press, 1971), section I, 242–269.

93 David L. Anderson, "Dwight D. Eisenhower and Wholehearted Support of Ngo Dinh Diem," in Rotter, 41.

94 Dave Davies, "'The Quiet Americans' Examines Tragic Miscalculations in the CIA's Formative Years," National Public Radio: Fresh Air, September 1, 2020, www.npr. org/2020/09/01/908267554/the-quiet-americans-examines-tragic-miscalcula-tions-in-the-cia-s-formative-years, retrieved December 4, 2020; Davies was interviewing Scott Anderson, author of *The Quiet Americans: Four CIA Spies at the Dawn of the Cold War—A Tragedy in Three Acts* (New York: Doubleday, 2020).

Further Reading

Biberman, Herbert. *Salt of the Earth: The Story of a Film*. New York: Sag Harbor, 2003.

Carrier, Jerry. *Hard Right Turn: The History and the Assassination of the American Left*. New York: Algora Publishing, 2015.

Conner, Claire. *Wrapped In the Flag: A Personal History of America's Radical Right*. Boston, MA: Beacon Press, 2013.

Fried, Richard M. *Nightmare in Red: The McCarthy Era in Perspective*. New York: Oxford University Press, 1990.

Gasiorowski, Mark J. and Malcom Byrne, eds. *Mohammad Mosaddeq and the 1953 Coup in Iran*. Syracuse, NY: Syracuse University Press, 2004.

Gleijeses, Piero. *Shattered Hope: The Guatemalan Revolution and the United States, 1944–1954*. Princeton, NJ: Princeton University Press, 1992.

Halberstam, David. *The Fifties*. New York: Random House, 1993.

Haynes, John Earl and Harvey Klehr. *Venona: Decoding Soviet Espionage in America*. New Haven, CT: Yale University Press, 2000.

Herring, George C. *America's Longest War: The United States and Vietnam, 1950–1975*, 2nd ed. New York: Knopf, 1986.

Hirt, Paul W. *A Conspiracy of Optimism: Management of the National Forests Since World War II*. Lincoln, NE: University of Nebraska Press, 1994.

Humphries, Reynold. *Hollywood's Blacklists: A Political and Cultural History*. Edinburgh: Edinburgh University Press, 2008.

Kinzer, Stephen. *The Brothers: John Foster Dulles, Allan Dulles, and Their Secret World War*. New York: Times Books, 2013.

Kinzer, Stephen. *Overthrow: America's Century of Regime Change from Hawaii to Iraq*. New York: Times Books, 2007.

Lichtblau, Eric. *The Nazis Next Door: How America became a Safe Haven for Hitler's Men*. New York: Mariner, 2014.

Marling, Karal Ann. *As Seen on TV: The Visual Culture of Everyday Life in the 1950s*. Cambridge, MA: Harvard University Press, 1994.

Meacham, Jon. *The Soul of America: The Battle for Our Better Angels*. New York: Random House, 2018.

Oshinsky, David M. *A Conspiracy So Immense: The World of Joe McCarthy*. New York: Free Press, 1983.

Patterson, James. *Grand Expectations: The United States 1945–1974*. New York: Oxford University Press, 1996.

Potter, David M. *People of Plenty: Economic Abundance and the American Character*. Chicago, IL: University of Chicago Press, 1958.

Reisner, Marc. *Cadillac Desert: The American West and Its Disappearing Water*. New York: Penguin Books, 1986.

Rome, Adam. *Bulldozer in the Countryside: Suburban Sprawl and the Rise of American Environmentalism*. New York: Cambridge University Press, 2001.

Rovere, Richard H. *Senator Joe McCarthy*. New York: Harper Row, 1959.

Sbardellati, John. *J. Edgar Hoover Goes to the Movies: The FBI and the Origins of Hollywood's Cold War*. Ithaca, NY: Cornell University Press, 2012.

Schrecker, Ellen. *Many Are the Crimes: McCarthyism in America*. New York: Little Brown, 1998.

Schrecker, Ellen. *The Age of McCarthyism: A Brief History with Documents*. New York: St. Martin's Press, 1994.

Smith, Jean Edward. *Eisenhower in War and Peace*. New York: Random House, 2012.

Sperber, A.M. *Murrow: His Life and Times*. New York: Freundlich Books, 1986.

Strasser, Susan. *Waste and Want: A Social History of Trash*. New York: Holt, 1999.

Tye, Larry. *The Life and Long Shadow of Senator Joe McCarthyism*. New York: Houghton Mifflin, 2020.

Whitfield, Stephen J. *The Culture of the Cold War*, 2nd ed. Baltimore, MD: Johns Hopkins University Press, 1996.

Young, James. *Union Power: The United Electrical Workers in Erie, Pennsylvania*. New York: Monthly Review Press, 2017.

4 Through the Looking Glass

Discontent and Rebellion in the Fifties

Just before dawn on January 27, 1951, "Test Able," the first detonation of a nuclear weapon at the Nevada Proving Grounds, ignited a flash so bright it was seen from San Francisco. "Able" bore the same moniker as a July 1946 atomic test at Bikini Atoll in the South Pacific, the first of 23 conducted there over 12 years, most of them hydrogen weapons exponentially more destructive than the bombs dropped at Hiroshima and Nagasaki. U.S. officials had evacuated Bikini natives to nearby Kili island after their King Juda convinced them the test was "in God's hands-," as a Navy commander promised, "for the good of mankind."[1] Generations of displaced Bikinians would look back on those assurances with bitter regret after radioactivity rendered their paradisiacal home uninhabitable. To author E. B. White's eyes, Bikini, in the days preceding the blast, "[seemed] unspeakably precious, like a lovely child stricken with a fatal disease."[2] The deadly exposure of Marshall Islanders (then under U.S. trusteeship) inaugurated one of the darkest chapters in the history of the American government's treatment of its own people.

The decision to develop the H-bomb, coupled with the outbreak of the Korean War and the Soviet Union's successful atomic bomb test, made the need for a remote testing location on the mainland more urgent. Frenchman Flat, a remote dry lake bed 65 miles northwest of Las Vegas, fit the bill. As at Bikini, the exposure of Americans living downwind was a marginal concern of military planners. One Atomic Energy Commission (AEC) memo described the region's Mormon and Native American communities as a "low-use segment of the population." Presented with the prospect of endangering American citizens, President Eisenhower reportedly said, "we can afford to sacrifice a few thousand people out there in the interest of national security."[3] Sacrifice they did. Many of the 126 nuclear bombs detonated over the Nevada desert plastered downwind communities like St. George, Utah with radioactive fallout. Residents received AEC booklets reading, "We can expect many reports that 'Geiger Counters were going crazy here today.' Reports like this may worry people unnecessarily. Don't let them bother you." St. George physicians who had never seen a child afflicted with leukemia were suddenly overcome with cases, along with various adult cancers.[4] From Oak Ridge, Tennessee to Hanford, Washington, workers engaged in nuclear weapons production experienced rising cancer rates

DOI: 10.4324/9781003160595-4

in the decades ahead. "Atomic soldiers" suffered a variety of malignancies, sterility, and infertility, some enduring the agony of seeing their children born with mutations and hideous defects. One test site commander prepared his men for nuclear maneuvers with this chilling advice:

> The radiation level may be high, but if you follow orders you'll be moved out in time to avoid sickness. Finally, if you receive enough gamma radiation to cause sterility or severe sickness, you'll be killed by blast, flying debris, or heat anyway. Well, that's the story. Don't worry about yourselves. As far as the test is concerned, you'll be fine.[5]

Far beyond the Southwest, continental weather patterns produced radioactive "hot spots," rendering residents from Kansas to New York unwitting "downwinders"—a predictable meteorological outcome that began coming into view following the March 1, 1954 Castle Bravo test at Bikini.[6] The largest ever U.S. nuclear test, Bravo produced a 15-megaton explosion—three times what was expected. It contaminated a 7,000 square-mile area of the Pacific. Fallout was detected in Europe. Military personnel arrived to inspect the damage and issued no warnings to the Marshall Islanders whose children played in the radioactive "snow." An AEC report declared one island population to have suffered "no ill effects." In 1957, the Marshallese were returned to islands still contaminated, studied in the years ahead for the ongoing effects of radioactivity.[7] Castle Bravo might have remained just an exceptional blast had it not been for the *Fukuryū Maru* (*Lucky Dragon*), a Japanese tuna fishing vessel caught inside the fallout zone. Its crew suffered acute radiation poisoning; one did not survive. What Japan's press corps called "the second atomic bombing of mankind" panicked the country's tuna market and poisoned U.S.-Japanese relations. A compensatory settlement of fifteen million dollars to the government did not quell the outrage of a people made nuclear victims twice in a decade.[8] Americans, too, grew alarmed at reports of strontium-90 in the bones of their children. Delivering the message that no place on Earth was safe, Bravo fueled the first truly global protest movement. Scientists around the world endorsed a call for a moratorium on atmospheric testing. From London, the Campaign for Nuclear Disarmament (CND) mounted an international effort to "Ban the Bomb," while in the U.S., the Committee for a SANE Nuclear Policy published full-page advertisements featuring America's foremost pediatrician, Dr. Benjamin Spock.

The movement to end nuclear testing may appear startling given the popular memory of the fifties as a golden age of civic faith. Indeed, in 1958 73 percent of citizens trusted the federal government to act in their best interest "all or most of the time."[9] That figure reflects an era of rising expectations about Washington's central, positive role in American life, buttressed by a broadly shared understanding of values. Public skepticism of nuclear testing brought some of the first postwar tremors in civic confidence, as scientists and activists scrutinized a terrifying fact of life in the Cold War, a project carried out by American citizens' own government with often-sinister operational secrecy. The anti-nuclear movement implied other questions. For beyond the quiescent world of suburbia, fallout and the omnipresent threat of nuclear war shared much with Jim Crow racism and other insidious forces menacing Americans. As the test site commander said to his men before sending them on their atomic maneuvers, "you can't see radiation, feel it, smell it, or taste it."[10] One could, however, fight against its release into the atmosphere. In the late 1950s, the incipient anti-nuclear movement went forward alongside other currents of angst, discontent, and outright resistance that were churning throughout American society.

Rumblings of Anxiety and Dissent

Pervasive Cold War anxieties found multiple forms of cultural expression. As psychiatrist Robert Lifton later documented, children performing "Duck and Cover" drills and wearing military-style dog tags so they could be identified in the rubble of the apocalypse found their dreams haunted by nuclear nightmares.[11] In 1954, many of them went to Saturday matinees of the Japanese-produced *Gojira (Godzilla)*, a film inspired by Bravo. Ishirō Honda's film opens with a fishing crew enjoying a moment of respite aboard their vessel when a white flash on the horizon is followed by a concussion and the boat's sinking. Awakened by an atomic blast, Godzilla wreaks destruction upon Tokyo. Like *The Beast From 20,000 Fathoms*, a 1953 American release, *Godzilla* enjoyed enormous box office success and led to a wave of atomic monster-themed films. *Them!* featured a colony of monstrous ants irradiated by the 1945 Trinity test in New Mexico, rampaging through the desert Southwest until they are finally destroyed.

The best films provided thoughtful critiques of nuclear technology and left viewers more apprehensive than reassured about the future. As one scientist intoned at the end of *Them!*, "When Man entered the Atomic Age, he opened the door to a new world. What we may eventually find in that new world, nobody can predict." *The Day the Earth Stood Still* (1951) radically challenged the Cold War mindset. An alien spaceship arrives in Washington, provoking hysteria and a militarized reaction from civil authorities. Humanoid alien Klaatu determines to meet with *all* world leaders to convey his ultimatum to abandon the current course toward nuclear war. Granting no deference to the United States, he dismisses the "petty squabbles" of the two great powers. Questioning scientists are depicted favorably at a time when many had turned against the H-bomb and were falling from public favor. Professor Barnhardt, portrayed by Sam Jaffe, bears a resemblance to Albert Einstein, already marked by congressman John Rankin as a "foreign-born agitator."[12] The casting was notable: Jaffe had been publicly identified as a subversive, and soon found himself on the receiving end of a HUAC subpoena.[13]

Television, envisioned in its infancy as an instrument for broad social enlightenment and human uplift, fell a bit short of those utopian visions. Early TV did produce some extraordinary moments, among them *See It Now*. In addition to confronting Joe McCarthy, Edward R. Murrow and producer Fred Friendly took on other controversial subjects such as the link between cigarettes and lung cancer. A number of reports brought, as one Murrow biographer has summarized, "the concerns of black Americans into the all-white world of prime-time TV: an all-night vigil with a family sending a child off on a school bus amid threats of violence" following court-ordered integration.[14] Despite numerous awards, *See It Now* repelled major corporate sponsors like Alcoa and General Motors.[15] After being shuffled around CBS's schedule, the final program aired in July 1958. Three months later, Murrow delivered a trenchant speech to the Radio and Television News Directors Association in which he excoriated the pressures of corporate sponsorship and "timidity" of network executives that left television largely devoid of meaningful programming—"in the main [insulating] us from the realities of the world in which we live."[16]

Murrow's fall coincided with the rise of the TV game show, by 1956 the most profitable genre of network programming. Featuring contestants competing for various prizes, the game show with its commercial breaks was a consumer feast. *Queen for a Day* may have topped them all for its vintage fifties amalgam of shallow materialism and condescending sexism—the latter performed by the show's oily host, Jack Bailey. Contestants shared with Bailey the reason they should be crowned "Queen for a Day": a husband's lost job, a husband away in the service, an ailment afflicting her child—anything but a woman's own unfulfilled aspirations. Many aspirants broke down, with the gallant Bailey dabbing their tears with his handkerchief. A live audience registered their sympathies by applause meter, the most dire victim crowned the winner. Out came the velvet-trimmed queen's robe, the poor sovereign often finding herself overcome.[17] A number of the most popular game shows were soon revealed to be rigging outcomes in order to drive up ratings, a scandal that seemed just desserts for a genre that had done much to diminish TV's early promise.

The sitcoms were mostly schlock, but there were exceptions. Most notable was *I Love Lucy*. The show became a cultural landmark for many reasons, beginning with the comedic brilliance of Lucille Ball and the pioneering television techniques of her husband, Cuban American actor and bandleader, Desi Arnaz. Among Arnaz's innovations was the introduction of three-camera production in front of a live audience which brought life to what had been stilted TV production. The on-screen "mixed" marriage of Lucy and Ricky Ricardo broke ground, made possible only when Ball demanded it from CBS. While Arnaz often played for comic effect the stereotyped features of a hot-tempered Latin, they insisted contractually that only Lucy could make fun of Ricky's accent, a distressing reminder of the real-world prejudice Arnaz faced in Hollywood. In addition, a frequent plot line featured Lucy scheming to break into show business against Ricky's wishes. Although those efforts inevitably ended in farcical failure, Lucy's desires for a meaningful life outside her domestic sphere reflected the aspirations of millions of women. Moreover, Ball and Arnaz's production company, Desilu, became hers alone upon the couple's divorce, a rarity in Hollywood—or anywhere in America for that matter.[18]

Desilu brought many classic shows to TV, none of more potent social content than *The Twilight Zone*, the ingenious creation of Rod Serling. Seeking to make sense of his harrowing military service in the Philippines, after the war Serling poured himself into script writing. He began in radio, but found the medium stifling and moved into television. Focusing on serious subjects like bigotry, war, and the ethics of the corporate world, by 1957 Serling's work for live television theatre was drawing critical and popular acclaim. *Patterns*, a complex, fascinating teleplay that shined a light on corporate culture and earned him an Emmy award. As was true for Murrow, such accolades did not insulate Serling from corporate sponsors wanting to censor his work. Determined to have greater control, in 1958 Serling wrote a script intended as the pilot for a science fiction anthology program that would allow him greater artistic freedom. Centered on a psychiatric patient who time travels back to Pearl Harbor before it is bombed, the pilot for what became *The Twilight Zone* was picked up by Desilu.[19] For five seasons, the show's stable of brilliant writers took on salient issues addressed nowhere else, including the struggle for dignity among society's marginalized, the loss of individualism, and the dark absurdity of nuclear fallout shelters. Death figured prominently—as did racism, reflecting Serling's conviction "that the singular evil of our time is prejudice. It is from this evil that all other evils grow and multiply."[20] One of the most imaginative programs in television history, *The Twilight Zone*'s cultural impact was immense, stirring the imagination and the questioning impulse of young viewers.

For socially informed comedy one looked to the stage. Trailblazer of a new generation of comics, Mort Sahl moved to San Francisco in the mid-1950s, where he landed an audition at "the hungry i" (for intellectual), a North Beach nightclub that stood at the center of the emerging Beat literary movement. Sahl pioneered much that would become standard among comics in the years ahead: exuberant, rapid-fire delivery, political satire that was both interrogatory and rooted in traditional American idealism, spontaneous riffs on current events—seemingly informed by the folded newspaper under his arm. Until Sahl, no comedian had recorded a live album, none whose jokes carried a higher social purpose. And like so much else that shook the culture in the 1950s, he seemed to come out of nowhere. As historian Gerald Nachman has written, "Nobody saw Mort Sahl coming. When he arrived, the revolution had not yet begun. Sahl was the revolution."[21] Sahl helped another young comedian get a chance at the hungry i: Lenny Bruce, whose improvised comic rants on notorious subject matter like drugs, Jewish identity, and abortion earned him multiple arrests for obscenity.

The fast-talking, risk-taking comedy of Sahl and Bruce recalls the importance of the era's bebop jazz that helped inspire them. Originating in the 1940s with the complex, improvisational playing of saxophonist Charlie Parker and trumpet virtuoso Dizzy Gillespie, bebop emerged partly as a reaction to the increasingly conventional forms that jazz had assumed in the big band era. By the early fifties, Gillespie, Parker and Miles Davis had opened new frontiers of musical experimentation that featured breakneck pacing, daring solo riffs, and changeable chord and harmonic structures. Neither radio-friendly nor danceable, bebop was adventurous, intellectual jazz, challenging the listener to find their way into the music.

Beyond their influence on Sahl and Bruce, bebop musicians also fired the Beat literary movement. Two neighborhoods west of the hungry i stood the Six Gallery, a former auto repair shop converted to a literary art space. Here, on October 7, 1955 Kenneth Rexroth, a leader of San Francisco's postwar literary renaissance, introduced six young poets who read from their latest works. A groundbreaking event for the Beats, the "Gallery Six Reading" is best remembered for Allen Ginsberg's inaugural recitation of "Howl," a monumental semi-autobiographical work that instantly earned a hallowed place in American poetry. In its first major section, "Howl" vocalizes Ginsberg's journey from a sexually and psychologically tormented market research analyst to a carnally liberated, psychedelic-drug-inspired visionary surveying the personal pain, social repression and wreckage of the McCarthy era. In part two, Ginsberg, aided by a peyote-induced vision, deployed Moloch—the ancient false idol of the Canaanites and the hellish industrial beast of Fritz Lang's brilliant classic film, *Metropolis*—as a metaphor for the monstrous forces afflicting America. Howl's indictment of a materialistic, conformist, fear-driven culture resonated well beyond the walls of Gallery Six. Standing in the rear that night was Lawrence Ferlinghetti, owner of City Lights Bookstore, who invited Ginsberg to publish "Howl," a decision that landed them in court on obscenity charges. In a landmark First Amendment decision, Ginsberg and Ferlinghetti emerged victorious, Judge Clayton Horn—a Sunday School-teaching conservative Republican—determined the obscenity charge irrelevant to a work of "redeeming social significance."[22]

A number of images pouring out of "Howl" suggested the allure of African American culture for leading Beat writers. Much of Jack Kerouac's *On the Road* (1957), a novel based on Kerouac's adventures across America and into Mexico with a colorful cast of fellow searchers, including Ginsberg, William S. Burroughs, and the legendary Neal Cassady, was written in stream-of-consciousness style that mimicked bebop. Write, Kerouac urged, "as jazz musicians drawing breath between outblown phrases … free association of mind into limitless blow-on-subject seas of thought, swimming in a sea of English."[23] Not the first nor the last white American artist to appropriate African American culture without being *of* it, Kerouac was enamored of minority communities who were *beat* down, but still managed to produce art of greater vitality and authentic power than anything else in America. Kerouac's descriptions of Mexico, though penned by a privileged white American traveler, offered an affectionate glimpse of the Mexican *other* that was exceptional in 1957 America. Ignore the stereotypes of the Mexican "sleeping gringo" and "greasers," Kerouac urged. The "people here are straight and kind," he wrote, "and don't put down any bull."[24]

Kerouac found the Beat spirit in Neal Cassady, "Dean Moriarty" in the novel. A hypermanic genius from another dimension, Cassady was a "great artist whose art form was his life," Grateful Dead bassist Phil Lesh recalled. Among his mystical attributes, according to Lesh bandmate Bob Weir, Cassady could carry on a half dozen conversations simultaneously while driving 55 miles per hour in downtown rush-hour San Francisco without incident.[25] Like a meteoric visitor,

Cassady's star burned just long enough to leave an indelible impact on Beat consciousness and what became the counterculture. He died in 1968 in Mexico, just short of his forty-second birthday.

For all the invective directed at them as communist-inspired Bohemian delinquents, the Beats channeled some of America's highest literary traditions, including the defiance of literary constraint, the urge for sexual liberation, and a re-sanctification of nature. Their best work suggested that a meaningful life and a more humane social consciousness were to be found in ecstatic engagement with the world. As Ginsberg declared, "The only thing that can save the world is the reclaiming of the awareness of the world. That's what poetry does."[26] Poetry, and psychoactive drugs. Mood-altering enhancements figured prominently for the Beats, marijuana naturally migrating from bebop. Benzedrine famously propelled Kerouac to write *On the Road* in three weeks' time on an endless ribbon of paper taped end to end. William S. Burroughs fell into a heroin addiction and found his first success with the semiautobiographical novel, *Junkie*. However, it was only the journey into hallucinogenic drugs that stirred mystical visions. On one of several expeditions to South America, in 1953 Burroughs had a serendipitous encounter with Harvard ethnobotanist Richard Evans Schultes, the leading expert on psychoactive botanicals, including *ayahuasca*, an ancient entheogenic brew used by Amazon peoples for over a thousand years to produce transcendent visions of the sacred. *The Naked Lunch* author's first *ayahuasca* journey was a bit bumpy, but subsequent attempts paralleled Ginsberg's own psychedelic report of having fused with "the Great Being."[27]

They were not alone. None other than Henry Luce announced in 1964 that he had been taking LSD "under doctor's supervision" for years. His wife, Clare Boothe Luce, reported seeing the world "through the eyes of a happy and gifted child." *Life* featured regular "travel accounts" from psychedelic pilgrims on the wondrous and clinically psychotherapeutic attributes of hallucinogenic drugs. By the late 1950s, extensive clinical studies at prestigious institutions including Harvard were under way on the transformative, healing potential of psychotherapeutic drugs, including LSD. Bill "W" Wilson, founder of Alcoholics Anonymous, took an early trip and found it immensely helpful in revealing the divine power that helped liberate him from alcohol. After more than 60 sessions, Hollywood actor Cary Grant reported in 1959 that he had been "born again," his "ego stripped away." The consciousness-raising current that came to define much of the sixties' counterculture may have begun in that moment.[28]

Music as a Force for Change

Music journalist Greil Marcus recalled the arrival of rock and roll was

> like something that came from another planet … And what was so strange was that so many people responded to someone very weird like Little Richard—instantly, with no sense of questioning—just 'of course, I've been waiting all my life for this and I never knew it.'[29]

Until that moment, Baby Boomers had been listening to their parents' music: Big Band, swing, jazzy standards, banal covers of country and western music. Erupting across that tranquil soundscape was "Rocket 88," a song memorably put on vinyl by the legendary Memphis record producer, Sam Phillips. A spirited rhythm and blues number inspired by a flashy new Oldsmobile, "Rocket 88" was penned by Jackie Brenston and backed by Ike Turner and his "Kings of Rhythm." The group's journey from Mississippi to Phillips's studio in Memphis on the fabled "Blues Highway" 61 was not uneventful: a stop by state troopers—"too many little niggers in the car," they ruefully joked later—and then the overstuffed car suffered a flat. A hurried tire change damaged a speaker cone in Turner's amplifier, which Phillips tried to remedy by stuffing a wad of paper inside. The quick fix produced a buzzing distortion that left the group dejected. Phillips, however, loved it. Laid underneath the horns and piano, the fuzz-tone amplified the song's raw energy, a "sound you had not heard before," Phillips recalled.[30] The rough edges made "Rocket 88" a hit, establishing the improvisational spirit and electrifying sound of both Sun Records and rock and roll.

Rock's arrival served as more than just racially integrated background music for the civil rights movement. Beyond disturbing the decade's placid façade, its interracial nature revealed the rich vitality of African American culture, as well as the absurdity of American apartheid. Rolling like the Mississippi into the heart of America, the river of rock and roll was fed by gospel, spirituals, Texas "boogie-woogie," "jump blues," and rhythm and blues—R&B—known in the late 1940s as "race music." Music from predominantly white America poured in: Western swing, the honky-tonk sound of Hank Williams, folk and bluegrass from the mountains and hollows of Appalachia. Other cosmically timed forces contributed to rock's dynamic growth, including the proliferation of jukeboxes and locally controlled radio stations, the arrival of 45-rpm vinyl singles, the hand-held AM transistor radio, and pioneering innovations by Les Paul and Leo Fender of rock's signature instrument, the electric guitar.

With a sign in the window reading, "We record anything, anywhere, anytime," Phillips's Sun Records epitomized rock's democratic vitality. Growing up poor in rural Alabama, he had picked cotton alongside African Americans, infusing a genuine respect for black folk and deep admiration for their music. By the late 1940s Phillips had become a radio disc jockey featuring an "open format" of racially integrated music. He brought that spirit to Sun, where he recorded R&B singers, bluesmen like B. B. King, and a rockabilly–country–gospel musician named Johnny Cash. Word of the "Sun Sound" got around. On the evening of July 5, 1954 Phillips recorded a 19-year-old truck driver from Mississippi who, so goes the story, wanted to make a birthday record for his mother. Taking a break in a session dominated by ballads, Elvis Presley spontaneously broke into an unvarnished, electrifying version of Mississippi Delta blues musician Arthur "Big Boy" Crudup's "It's All Right." Another serendipitous moment—"raw and ragged," guitarist Scotty Moore called it—the song sent Elvis on his way.[31]

From the start, Elvis Presley both appropriated and honored the black music of his youth. He had learned "It's All Right" from Crudup. "If I ever got to the place where I could feel all old Arthur felt," Presley mused, "I'd be a music man like nobody ever saw." In press interviews, he invariably deferred to "the colored folks [who have] been singing it and playing it for more years than I know ... let's face it, nobody can sing that kind of music like colored people. I can't sing it like Fats Domino can. I know that."[32] Presley's mimicking of a black aesthetic exposed him to the racist attack aimed at all of rock and roll; his movements on stage, said one critic, were akin to "an aborigine's mating dance."[33] Elvis's enormous popularity helped kick the door open for artists of similar frenetic energy like Little Richard, while further stoking the ongoing interrogation of race in America.

Early in the decade, nearly half the buyers of "race music" were white. Its crossover appeal was evident when Alan "Moondog" Freed, a Cleveland disc jockey, persuaded his manager to give him a show. Among the hits Freed played was "Sixty-Minute Man" by the Dominoes. An R&B hit containing sexually charged lyrics ("rock 'em and roll 'em") "Sixty-Minute Man" scored success on the white-dominated Billboard pop chart, inspiring Freed to begin calling the music "rock 'n' roll." Along with legions of white artists soon covering songs of African Americans (many not compensated), the new label might have deflected the music's black roots, but it could not hide them.[34] For segregationists, rock and roll implied a communist plot to destroy America from within. "We're setting up a twenty-man committee to do away with this vulgar animalistic nigger rock and roll bop," declared the Chairman of the North Alabama White Citizens Council.[35] Freed's "rock 'n' roll revues" in urban arenas often featured acts that were entirely African American and audiences predominantly white. Replicated in many cities, the events became the largest, most consistently integrated social setting in America, though not without resistance. One night in Atlanta, the Platters marveled at their name on the marquee of the theatre where they were to perform, only to be forbidden from entering the front doors. Local officials often draped a rope between the races, or restricted blacks or whites to the balcony—a line that proved dissoluble by the emotional force of the music. "A lot of places had the line when we first walked in, and after we started playing, they let them cross the line," the Coasters' Leon Hughes remembered. "It was beautiful."[36]

It was a very different scene at the American Legion Auditorium in Roanoke, Virginia May 4, 1956, where Fats Domino was performing. With 2,000 whites jammed into the balcony, some escaped the crush by fleeing to the blacks-only main floor, where much to the horror of the local press, they "actually danced" with black attendees. This triggered the rage of some whites, who hurled bottles and other objects down on the integrated scene below. The fracas spilled into the street, teens bloodied by fists and flying glass. At other Domino performances that year, the big man had to take cover under his piano (Figure 4.1).[37] Despite such eruptions of racist fury, rock and roll's inherent capacity to transcend color heralded the arrival of a more liberated culture.

With a history reaching back to pre-colonial America, folk music was a communal experience—an inherently subversive quality in the 1950s. Having receded from popular view during the war, folk music was enjoying a revival, in part because of the migration of rural Americans to the city. Its rebirth also owed

Figure 4.1 Fats Domino.

Michael Ochs Archives/Getty, www.gettyimages.co.uk/detail/news-photo/american-pianist-fats-domino-on-stage-at-the-apollo-theater-news-photo/1061706514

much to Woody Guthrie, whose songs during the Great Depression inspired both fortitude and social protest. Entwined with the history of social movements, folk music drew from the lived experience of working people and a rich musical palette, from Appalachian bluegrass to the Caribbean sounds of Harry Belafonte and Maya Angelou. It could be heard at clubs from San Francisco to New York City's Greenwich Village, where in 1948 the Weavers, a profoundly influential folk group, formed. Taking their name from a play about an uprising of Selesian weavers, the group included Ronnie Gilbert, Lee Hays, Fred Hellerman, and Pete Seeger.[38] A string of commercial hits for the Weavers coincided with the worst years of McCarthyism. Hays and Seeger ran afoul of HUAC, and the group was dropped by their record company and largely disappeared from view. By the late fifties the folk music left on the airwaves was politically vacuous. A few years later, *Hootenanny*, a folk-centered TV show, refused to allow Seeger to appear unless he signed a loyalty oath at the insistence of sponsor Proctor and Gamble—prompting Bob Dylan, Joan Baez, and others to boycott the program. "We have all this richness and variety in our country, but a bunch of schmoes, out to sell soap, keep the whole country seeing the same dreary things night after night," Seeger lamented.[39]

Seeger persevered on the road, touring campuses, coffeehouses, and folk festivals. In 1959, he found himself at a weekend meeting of civil rights activists at the Highlander Folk School in Monteagle, Tennessee, a long-time activist training center. It was there that Seeger and fellow folk musician Guy Carawan would help make the song "We Shall Overcome" the anthem of the southern human rights struggle. The song was a classic folk amalgam of wide-ranging influences. In 1901, Philadelphia minister Rev. Charles Tindley published "I'll Overcome Someday," a song that borrowed from an eighteenth-century European hymn called "Oh, Sanctissima," but lyrically evoking the plantation spiritual, "I'll Be All Right Someday." Tindley's composition was about personal, eternal salvation—very different from the song's first activist iteration in 1908, "I Will Overcome," which was inspired by an interracial miners' strike in Birmingham, Alabama. In 1946, after striking South Carolina tobacco workers grafted new verses on to the song, two of them traveled to Highlander and taught it to music director Zilphia Horton. On a visit to New York City, she taught it to Seeger, who upped the tempo and changed it to "*Shall* Overcome"— because "it opens the mouth wider." Over time, the collective "We" firmly supplanted "I."[40] A simple but resoundingly determined vow of social change, "We Shall Overcome" was easily learned, eventually becoming a global anthem that has been sung from Northern Ireland to North Korea. That storied tradition began with Seeger and Carawan at the Highlander gathering, where according to Seeger, "We Shall Overcome" was the "hit song." Soon it would be carried aloft by the courage of young people joining a movement then nearly a decade under way.[41]

"If We Are Wrong, God Almighty Is Wrong"

The struggle to end Jim Crow and expand the meaning of American freedom stands as the most consequential force of social change in the twentieth century. Its modern roots lay in the Niagara Movement, which in 1909 birthed the National Association for the Advancement of Colored People (NAACP). Along with the efforts of individuals like activist historian W. E. B. Dubois and educator and journalist Ida B. Wells, who relentlessly forced the issue of lynching into public view, the NAACP carried the civil rights movement to mid-century. Other events insistently drove the issue of race onto the nation's agenda, including the Cold War that loomed over everything. For civil rights proponents, until the nation took concrete steps to confront statutory, deep-seated racism, America's rhetorical promise of democracy in the face of Soviet totalitarianism rang hollow.

As historian Danielle McGuire has shown, another long-hidden but powerful current of activism propelled the civil rights movement forward early in the postwar era. On September 3, 1944, 24-year-old Recy Taylor was walking home from church in Abbeville, Alabama when a car loaded with six men stopped and ordered her into the vehicle at gunpoint. Driven to a patch of woods, Taylor was told "to get them rags off" and "act just like you do with your husband or I'll cut your damn throat."[42] Gang-raped, Recy Taylor managed to get home where she reported the crime to her husband. Soon the Taylors were on the phone to E. D. Nixon, president of the NAACP in Montgomery, who sent his best investigator, Rosa Parks, to Abbeville to launch an inquiry.[43] By spring 1945, the "Committee for Equal Justice for Mrs. Recy Taylor" was establishing Taylor advocacy groups across the country and bringing her story to national attention. The *Chicago*

Defender called it the "strongest campaign for equal justice to be seen in a decade."[44] Despite a firebombing of the Taylor home, and Parks earning a menacing threat from the sheriff, Recy Taylor determined to exercise the agency long denied to black women. But there would be no justice. Two all-white male grand juries refused to indict the men. One admitted to the events, but slandered Taylor as a prostitute, insisting they had paid for the sex.[45]

The rape of Recy Taylor reflected the pervasive abuse of black women that was rooted in slavery and remained deeply ingrained in the South. From rape to daily humiliation at the hands of white employers and harassment in the streets, the assault on black women reinforced white rule. Black women who dared report their rape were invariably dismissed as promiscuous "jezebels," or met with the perverse defense that black women were "unrapable"—a lie rendered about women of color across centuries.[46] In the years after World War II, scores of first-hand accounts of violated women languished in file drawers of inaction of the Alabama Attorney General's office. Many, however, were published in the black press through the determined efforts of E. D. Nixon and Rosa Parks. Throughout the postwar era, campaigns to reclaim the dignity of black women and expose the brutal assault on their bodies became inseparable from the larger human rights struggle. Courageously finding their voice, women tested organizing strategies and established community networks that were deployed in Montgomery and throughout the south.

The sexual terror of black women transpired with ironic brutality alongside the lynching of more than 4,000 black men since the Civil War—most often for bogus charges of violating white women. Rumors of rape incited some of the worst mob violence against black communities since the Civil War. The gruesome photographs of Emmett Till, whose body was found at the bottom of Mississippi's Tallahatchie River in August 1955 with a cotton gin wired around his neck, lynched for the unforgivable alleged[47] transgression of an unsolicited advance toward a white woman, helped galvanize the civil rights movement. Published only in the black press, the images of a 14-year-old boy in an open casket who had been shot, beaten to a pulp with his eye gouged out, came to black America only because Mamie Till-Mobley, his mother, determined to "let the people see what they did to my boy."[48]

Three months later came the Montgomery bus boycott, an event linked to both Till and the story of sexual terror. Here in the capital of Alabama, bus drivers routinely leveled racist slurs and sexual insults, and carried blackjacks to enforce racial order on a ridership that was 70 percent black, the majority women. Soon after Jo Ann Robinson arrived as a newly hired English teacher at Alabama State College, she sat down in the front section of a city bus, inattentive to the color line. The verbal abuse Robinson endured from the driver brought her to tears and moved her to deeper involvement with the Women's Political Council (WPC), urging the group to prioritize the issues suffered by black women in city transportation.[49] The WPC began meeting with the mayor, proposing modest changes to the bus system. When those demands were ignored, preparations began for a citywide boycott, a strategy attempted by activists in other cities without success.

On March 2, 1955, it appeared the time had come. That afternoon, Claudette Colvin, a 15-year-old member of the NAACP Youth Council was in a black history class studying nineteenth-century freedom fighters Harriet Tubman and Sojourner Truth. Students turned the discussion toward the present painful realities of Jim Crow, including the shameful ritual African Americans endured when simply buying a pair of shoes. Because they could not use the store's fitting room or try shoes on, Colvin later recalled, "you had to take a brown paper bag and draw a diagram of your foot ... and take it to the store." Her outrage awakened, Colvin boarded the bus for the ride home, taking her seat in the front row of the colored section. The enforced custom required that when the white section filled and a white person boarded, the entire front row of the black portion had to vacate. When a white woman entered, three blacks in Colvin's row removed themselves, but she, her "head just too full of black history," would not. The police arrested her, the driver sneering that he had "had trouble with that *thing* before."[50] But Colvin would not take center stage in the story. E. D. Nixon determined that Claudette's pregnancy—she "done took a tumble," her mother lamented—combined with the Colvins' residing in a part of Montgomery with "a bad reputation," made her a less than ideal public figure.[51]

By contrast, Rosa Parks was a respected 42-year-old seamstress (Figure 4.2). When Parks boarded the bus on Thursday evening, December 1, the black history on her mind was the body of Emmett Till. Four nights earlier, she attended a talk at Dexter Avenue Baptist Church by Dr. T.R.M. Howard, who was leading the investigation into Till's lynching. The driver demanded she surrender her seat, but Parks "thought about him and just couldn't go back."[52] E. D. Nixon and Jo Ann Robinson moved into action. Working through the night, Robinson mimeographed and organized the distribution of more than 35,000 leaflets reading in part:

> Another Negro woman has been arrested and thrown into jail because she refused to get up out of her seat on the bus for a white person to sit down ... This has to be stopped ... If you do not do something to stop those arrests, they will continue. The next time it may be you, or your daughter or your mother. ... We are, therefore, asking every Negro to stay off the buses Monday in protest of the arrest and trial ... If you work, take a cab or walk. But please, children and grownups, don't ride the bus at all on Monday.[53]

They did not. In the streets of Montgomery, women and children walked, black cabbies offered ten-cent rides (bus fare), men and women rode horse-drawn buggies or mules. That evening, more than 5,000 Montgomery black citizens gathered to hear Dr. Martin Luther King, Jr., the newly arrived minister of Dexter Avenue Baptist Church, speak of "the great glory of American democracy" and the right of peaceful protest. "And we," he reminded them, "are not wrong in what we are doing."

Figure 4.2 A booking photo of American civil rights activist, Rosa Parks, following her February 1956 arrest during the Montgomery bus boycott.

Universal History Archive/Getty Images, www.gettyimages.co.uk/detail/news-photo/booking-photo-of-american-civil-rights-activist-rosa-parks-news-photo/113491410?adppopup=true

If we are wrong, the Supreme Court of this nation is wrong. If we are wrong, the Constitution of the United States is wrong. If we are wrong, God Almighty is wrong ... If we are wrong, justice is a lie. Love has no meaning. And we are determined here in Montgomery to work and fight until justice runs down like water, and righteousness like a mighty stream.[54]

Dr. King was elected to head the Montgomery Improvement Association, a new organization formed in part to circumvent the state of Alabama having outlawed the NAACP. As the months passed, with each pair of shoes they exhausted, with every fine they were leveled for violating a nineteenth-century law against boycotts, Montgomery's black citizens grew more determined. Nothing deterred, not telephone threats to black women, nor acts of violence, including the bombing of King's home. Their resolute spirit was immortalized by Mother Pollard, a Dexter Avenue Church elder, who despite her age, insisted on walking. King later recalled that when Pollard was asked months into the boycott if she wasn't tired. "My feets is tired, but my soul is rested," she said.[55]

In the meantime, Claudette Colvin and three other women filed a NAACP federal lawsuit challenging the unconstitutionality of Montgomery's segregated bus system. The case sought more than the original boycott demands, which had been limited to courteous treatment by bus drivers, opportunity for blacks to apply for positions, and the establishment of first-come, first-served seating. On June 5, 1956, a federal district court ruled that segregated seating in Montgomery was unconstitutional, a decision upheld by the U.S. Supreme Court. Led by the organizing of Jo Ann Robinson and the WPC, the eloquent vision of Dr. King, African American citizens earned more than they set out to achieve. When blacks boarded the buses December 20, 1956, it symbolized not an end but a beginning. As civil rights leader Eldridge Cleaver later put it, as Rosa Parks looked out the window of a seat of her choosing that morning, "somewhere in the universe a gear in the machinery had shifted."[56]

In the empowering wake of the Montgomery victory, black ministers and other leaders formed the Southern Christian Leadership Conference (SCLC), headed by King. Inspired by the moral vision of Henry David Thoreau's "Essay on Civil Disobedience" and more recently, Mohandas Gandhi, leader of the resistance movement that ended British rule in India, the SCLC determined to win the righteous high ground against white supremacy by applying the principles and tactics of nonviolent direct action elsewhere. They would become, as Vincent Harding later described King, "[disturbers] of all unjust peace."[57] Through acts of nonviolent resistance, they would reveal the chasm between American ideals and the unconstitutional realities of racism. With assistance from the national press—since Till increasingly covering the civil rights story—activists would pierce the conscience of the nation.

The busing decision ratified the victory won in the streets of Montgomery and further signaled the U.S. Supreme Court as an ally. When the court agreed to hear the cluster of school desegregation cases that fell under *Brown vs. the Board of Education*, the Chief Justice was Fred Vinson, who like some of his colleagues, appeared averse toward overturning the doctrine of "separate but equal" facilities in public education. Fate intervened when Vinson died suddenly of a heart attack in September 1953, leaving President Eisenhower with an immediate vacancy. He looked to California governor Earl Warren, who he believed shared his own centrist political views. Warren proved a more complex figure than the president assumed, decidedly more liberal on questions of civil rights. Although he never expressed it publicly, Warren regretted his role as state attorney general in the internment of Japanese Americans.[58] As governor, he signed legislation ending the segregation of Mexican American in California public schools. There was, too, the influence of Louisiana native Edgar Patterson, Governor Warren's African American driver, whose daily chauffeuring, along with long drives in the Sierra Nevada foothills, proved instrumental in the education of the future chief justice. Among other aspects of being black in America, Patterson "told him about black people who had college degrees and who could not get a decent job, who had to work as Pullman porters and garbage collectors," about restrictive covenants that prevented African Americans from home ownership.[59]

With this heightened understanding, Warren led the Supreme Court in thoroughly reviewing the voluminous social science evidence of discrimination in public education presented by NAACP lead attorney, Thurgood Marshall. State funding disproportionately favored white schools over black, leaving teachers poorly paid compared to their white counterparts, black children with school books too tattered and outdated for white kids, and wide disparities in transportation and the condition of schools. In the namesake case emerging from Topeka, Kansas, Oliver Brown alleged denial of equal treatment as his daughter Linda, forced to walk six blocks to take a bus to her school, could have gone to a neighborhood white school. In a unanimous decision authored and read by Chief Justice Warren Monday, May 17, 1954, the Supreme Court declared the "separate but equal" doctrine, infamously sanctioned by the court in 1896 in *Plessy v. Ferguson*, was inherently unconstitutional, a violation of the Fourteenth Amendment's equal protection clause.

Hoping to speak to Americans' sense of fairness and decency, Warren's language was clear, direct, and morally authoritative. There was little hope of persuading the man who had appointed him. Although Eisenhower had helped advance integration of the armed forces, he did not support court-ordered integration, a view reflecting much of the nation. Knowing the court had to speak definitively on an issue sure to provoke fierce resistance, Warren worked to address the divisions on the court and reach unanimous accord. The specter of Soviet communism loomed, several justices noting during their deliberations the injustices endured by minorities at home undermined the U.S. effort to advance democracy across the globe.[60] The implications of *Brown* were large indeed. Earl Warren's progressive reading of the U.S. Constitution as it applied to school desegregation, combined with the rigorous review of the real-world impacts of Jim Crow, foretold the liberal direction he would lead the Supreme Court for the next 15 years on a host of issues.

The decision met angry opposition throughout the south. Virginia's "Massive Resistance" campaign called for abandoning public schools to "Negroes," and furtively steering funding to segregated private schools. Mississippi Circuit Judge Tom P. Brady published a widely disseminated address entitled "Black Monday" (the date of the *Brown* decision) that called for abolition of public schools, outlawing the NAACP, and establishing a forty-ninth state for Negroes.[61] In March 1956, the "Southern Manifesto," calling for "all lawful means" of resistance to *Brown*, was endorsed by dozens of newspapers and 101 congressmen.[62] Suddenly ubiquitous were Confederate battle flags, complemented by a fresh wave of statues honoring soldiers of the Lost Cause. White Citizens Council membership soared, as did Klan activity.

Some school districts integrated without incident, while others made a mockery of the decision. Two incidents from Tennessee are revealing of the nation's[63] conflicted response. On the first day of school in 1955, Mary Brent, principal of what had been the all-white Glenn Elementary School in Nashville, warmly welcomed black and white students.[64] It was a different story at Clinton High School in Anderson County. Poised in the fall of 1956 to become the first southern high school to integrate, Clinton was rocked by a wave of violence incited by White Citizens Council leaders, including bombings, sniper fire, cross burnings, and the severe beating of a white minister who had helped escort the "Clinton 12" students to school. The students persevered. On May 17, 1957 Bobby Cain became the first black student in the south to graduate from a court-ordered integrated high school. The racial terror continued, as did the good will of those in the white community who saw a different future: after a bomb destroyed Clinton High on October 5, 1958, Reverend Billy Graham led a fundraising effort to rebuild.[65]

The most dramatic test came in Little Rock, Arkansas, where NAACP president Daisy Bates urged local officials to move forward with school desegregation. Another black woman whose activism had been spurred by sexual violence—her mother having been raped and murdered by three white men—Bates and her husband published the *Arkansas State Press*, which pressed for civil rights and justice for black women victimized by assault.[66] As parents of the "Little Rock Nine" prepared to register their children at Central High School, it was apparent they would be met with organized resistance. Governor Orval Faubus used the pretext of local opposition to call out the Arkansas National Guard, effectively positioning them on the side of a growing white mob. Bates and local ministers arranged to have the students escorted in a group on the first day, but one of the nine, Elizabeth Eckford, did not have a telephone and did not receive the message. Arriving alone that morning, Eckford was steered frighteningly as she recalled, "*into the crowd*" by National Guardsmen.[67] As one reporter described the scene, "Elizabeth Eckford had walked into the wolf's lair, and now that they felt she was fair game, the drooling wolves took off after their prey. The hate mongers, who look exactly like other, normal white men and women, took off down the street after the girl."[68]

With the confrontation intensifying, on September 14 President Eisenhower summoned Faubus to a meeting at his Newport, Rhode Island retreat. Although sympathetic to Faubus's position, Eisenhower insisted he comply with federal law and place his guardsmen on the side of the students. It did not bode well that after the meeting Faubus claimed a desire "to harmonize [his] actions under the Constitution of Arkansas" with the U.S. Constitution.[69] He returned to Arkansas but soon departed the state, leaving behind the threat of mob violence. On September 20, a federal judge ordered Faubus to remove his soldiers and allow local police to escort the students. Three days later, African American reporters tried shielding the students as they made their way into the building, but were viciously attacked. The president issued a cease-and-desist order that evening, yet the chaos continued. Facing the greatest constitutional crisis since the Civil War, the president seized control of the National Guard and deployed 1,200 members of the 101st Airborne Division of the U.S. Army to restore order, announcing to the nation that night that "mob rule cannot be allowed to override the decisions of our courts."[70]

While federal officials moved haltingly toward protecting the lives and liberties of American citizens, the SCLC was building a network of affiliated churches and community organizations across the South. Most SCLC affiliates were led by Christian ministers and modeled on the Montgomery Improvement Association and similar groups elsewhere. Nearly the entire SCLC leadership was male and came from the upper echelon of the urban black middle-class. The organization was autocratic, much of its energy fixed on building a public image of Dr. King as *the* leader, not only of SCLC, but the larger movement.[71] Although inevitable tensions between the SCLC and the venerable NAACP persisted throughout the civil rights era, in the late 1950s the two organizations shared a goal of passing civil rights legislation.

By 1960, the limitations of that approach were apparent. In 1957, Eisenhower's attorney general sent a civil rights bill to Congress. As congressional hearings and debate ensued, the president remained mute. Most definitely not silent was South Carolina's Strom Thurmond, the former Dixiecrat standard bearer, who had once said this: "There's not enough troops in the army to force the Southern people to break down segregation and admit the nigger race into our theaters, into our swimming pools, into our homes, and into our churches."[72] On the evening of August 28, 1957 Thurmond delivered the longest filibuster in U.S. Senate history, inveighing against the bill's alleged evils. Thurmond held the floor for 24 hours and 18 minutes, reading everything from the Declaration of Independence to his grandma's biscuit recipe. Segregationists succeeded in stripping the bill of its more important provisions. Ethel L. Payne, "the First Lady of the Black press" in those years, called the legislation "almost unrecognizable ... after all the teeth had been pulled." When both NAACP president Roy Wilkins and Martin Luther King opted to support the law, they were met with scorn by the black press. "How silly can you get?" asked the *Chicago Defender* of King.[73] Advocates tried again in 1960, but the outcome was little better, lacking meaningful enforcement mechanisms to prosecute civil and voting rights violations.

Although Wilkins remained hopeful of further progress in Washington and through the courts, the disappointments bolstered King's conviction that SCLC resources were best invested at the grassroots level. It was a direction that did not come naturally, given SCLC's makeup and aversion to working directly with rural impoverished sharecroppers. In 1958, an ambitious voter registration plan, the "Crusade for Citizenship," was led by Ella Baker, SCLC's first director, whom King agreed to hire on an interim basis.[74] An experienced organizer, Baker chafed at King's high-handed style and the supercilious culture of SCLC leadership. Lacking organizational infrastructure and facing pressure for quick results, the Citizenship Crusade fizzled before it really began. Meanwhile, Septima Clarke, a long-time educator from South Carolina who had been fired when she refused to renounce her NAACP membership, became the lead workshop facilitator at Highlander. There, she launched a "citizenship school" aiming to transform illiterate sharecroppers into educated citizens and organizers. Recognizing the potential of Clark's work for expanding the SCLC mission and its reach into the rural South, Baker adopted the concept as SCLC's Citizenship Education Program (CEP), headed by Clark. Carried out by thousands of teachers, primarily women, the CEP became a tool of educational empowerment of far-reaching impact. Along the way, Clark, Baker, and their mostly female colleagues struggled with the ingrained sexism of SCLC's male leadership. As Baker said, "I wasn't one to say yes, just because [an idea] came from Dr. Martin Luther King, Jr … It's a strange thing about men … if they haven't ever had a woman say no to them, they don't know what to do sometimes."[75]

Parallel to this civic literacy work was the nonviolence training carried out by James Lawson under SCLC auspices. A deeply committed pacifist, in the early 1950s Lawson journeyed to India to study *satyagraha*, Gandhi's method of nonviolent resistance. He returned in 1955, enrolling in theology at Oberlin College in Ohio, where he met and struck an immediate affinity with King, who appealed to him to go South. "We don't have any Negro leadership in the South that understands nonviolence."[76] Soon the Gandhian disciple was in Nashville where as a divinity student at Vanderbilt University he began leading SCLC workshops on nonviolent direct action from a church basement. Lawson introduced the philosophy and strategy of nonviolent direct action to young students enrolled at area black colleges, efforts that resulted in his expulsion. He pressed on with greater fire, impatient with the NAACP's court-obsessed strategy, "Uncle-Tom Negroes," the "futile middle-class technique of sending letters to the centers of power," and other "half-way efforts to deal with radical social evil."[77]

Very much of the same mind, James Lawson's disciples were about to be swept away by what one of them, John Lewis, called "the Spirit of History" that would define the early 1960s.[78] The preceding decade had sown the seeds of social, cultural, and political change that were now beginning to bloom.

Notes

1 Quoted in Jack Niedenthal, "A Short History of the People of Bikini Atoll," http://marshall.csu.edu.au/Marshalls/html/History_Varia/Bikini_History/Bikini_History.html, retrieved January 31, 2021.

2 E. B. White, "Bikini," *New Yorker*, March 9, 1946, in his *The Wild Flag: Editorials from the* New Yorker *on Federal World Government and Other Matters* (New York: Houghton Mifflin, 1946), 33.

3 Quoted in Carole Gallagher, *American Ground Zero: The Secret Nuclear War* (Cambridge, MA: MIT Press, 1993), xxiii–xxiv, xxviii.

4 Gallagher, 145–147, 149–151.

5 Army training film, in Kevin Rafferty, Jayne Loader, and Pierce Rafferty, *The Atomic Café* (documentary film, 88 minutes, distributed by Ben Barenholtz, 1982).

6 "6 July 1962, Shot Sedan—Massive Crater, Massive Contamination," Comprehensive Nuclear-Test-Ban Treaty Organization, www.ctbto.org/specials/testing-times/6-july-1962-sedan-massive-crater-massive-contamination, retrieved January 31, 2021; and Matthew L. Wald, "Radiation from 1953 Nuclear Test Fell on Albany," *New York Times*, May 2, 1982, sec. 1, 48.

7 April L. Brown, "No Promised Land: The Shared Legacy of the Castle-Bravo Nuclear Test," Arms Control Association, n.d., www.armscontrol.org/act/2013_03/No-Promised-Land-The-Shared-Legacy-of-the-Castle-Bravo-Nuclear-Test%20, retrieved January 31, 2021.

8 "60th Anniversary of Castle-Bravo Nuclear Test," February 28, 2014 (George Washington University: National Security Archive), https://nsarchive2.gwu.edu/nukevault/ebb459; and David Ropeik, "Godzilla and the Birth of Modern Environmentalism," *Psychology Today*, June 10, 2014, retrieved January 31, 2021.

9 Pew Research Center for the People and the Press, "The People and Their Government: Distrust, Discontent, Anger, and Partisan Rancor" (Washington, DC, April 18, 2010), 13, www.pewresearch.org/wp-content/uploads/sites/4/legacy-pdf/606.pdf, retrieved January 31, 2021.

10 Rafferty et al.

11 Robert Jay Lifton, "Beyond Nuclear Numbing," *Educational Perspectives* (1982): 15–16, https://scholarspace.manoa.hawaii.edu/bitstream/10125/47208/EDPVol21%233_10-18.pdf, retrieved February 20, 2021.

12 David E. Rowe and Robert Schulmann, "What Were Einstein's Politics," *History News Network*, n.d., https://historynewsnetwork.org/article/39445, retrieved February 21, 2021.

13 "Hope for America: Performers, Politics, and Pop Culture," Library of Congress, n.d., www.loc.gov/exhibits/hope-for-america/a-climate-of-fear.html, retrieved February 21, 2021.

14 A. M. Sperber, *Murrow: His Life and Times* (New York: Freundlich, 1986), 485.

15 Ibid., 482–483, 492.

16 Edward R. Murrow, "Wires and Lights," October 15, 1958, www.rtdna.org/content/edward_r_murrow_s_1958_wires_lights_in_a_box_speech, retrieved February 21, 2021.

17 This discussion leans on the analysis of Susan Douglas, *Where the Girls Are: Growing Up Female with the Mass Media* (New York: Three Rivers Press, 1995), 32–33.

18 Sonari Glinton et al., "How Desi Invented Television," January 22, 2021 (NPR, Planet Money), www.npr.org/transcripts/959609533, retrieved March 5, 2021.

19 Ann Serling, "Birth of *The Twilight Zone*," Rod Serling Books, December 31, 2014, www.rodserlingbooks.com/thoughts/2014/12/31/birth-of-the-twilight-zone, retrieved March 5, 2021.

20 Rod Serling, *Los Angeles Times*, undated 1967 interview, in Lisa Lopez Levers, *Trauma Counseling: Theories and Interventions* (New York: Springer Publishing, 2012), 264.

21 Gerald Nachman, *Seriously Funny: The Rebel Comedians of the 1950s and 1960s* (New York: Pantheon, 2009), from Chapter 1: http://catdir.loc.gov/catdir/samples/random044/2002030713.html, retrieved February 1, 2021.

22 Quoted in Bill Morgan and Nancy J. Peters, eds., *Howl on Trial: The Battle for Free Expression* (San Francisco, CA: City Lights Books, 2006), 199.

23 Jack Kerouac, "Essentials of Spontaneous Prose," n.d., http://ivanbrave.com/wp-content/uploads/2015/08/Kerouac_SPONTANEOUS_PROSE.pdf, retrieved February 4, 2021.

24 Jack Kerouac, *On the Road* (New York: Penguin Books, 1991, edited and with an introduction by Ann Charters), 278.

25 Lesh quoted in David Gans, *Playing in the Band: An Oral and Visual Portrait of the Grtateful Dead* (New York: St. Martin's Press, 1996), 43; Weir, in Mike Fleiss, dir., *The Other One: The Long Strange Trip of Bob Weir* (Netflix documentary, Next Entertainment, 83 minutes, 2014).

26 Although the origins of this widely reproduced Ginsberg quote were difficult to trace, it is found here: https://kentuckypress.wordpress.com/2019/04/02/national-poetry-month, retrieved February 4, 2021.

27 Roger Keen, "The Beat Writers and the Psychedelic Movement," *Oak Tree Review*, March 3, 2017, www.oaktreereview.com/the-beat-writers-and-the-psychedelic-movement, retrieved February 25, 2021; William S. Burroughs and Allen Ginsberg, *The Yage Letters* (San Francisco, CA: City Lights Bookstore, 1963), 57.

28 Richard Gehman, "Ageless Cary Grant," *Good Housekeeping*, September 1960, 64; and Sarah Rense, "Cary Grant Was Once One of LSD's Biggest Fans," *Esquire*, June 13, 2017, www.esquire.com/lifestyle/health/a55611/cary-grant-took-acid, retrieved April 6, 2021; and Michael Pollan, *How to Change Your Mind: What the New Science of Psychedelics Teaches Us About Consciousness, Dying, Addiction, Depression, and Transcendence* (New York: Penguin Press, 2018), 104–105, 113, 152–153, 156–157.

29 David Hoffman and Carol Rissman, *Making Sense of the Sixties* (Alexandria, VA: PBS Video, six-part documentary series, 1990), from part one.

30 Peter Guralnick, *Sam Phillips: The Man Who Invented Rock and Roll* (New York: Little Brown, 2015), 103–106.

31 Quoted in ibid., 213.

32 Peter Guralnick, "How Did Elvis Get Turned into a Racist?" *New York Times*, August 11, 2007, www.nytimes.com/2007/08/11/opinion/11guralnick.html, retrieved February 8, 2021.

33 Noah Berlatsky, "Getting Elvis's Legacy Right," *The Atlantic*, July 8, 2014, www.the-atlantic.com/entertainment/archive/2014/07/whats-so-great-about-elvis-he-didnt-invent-or-steal-anything/374081, retrieved February 8, 2021.

34 Quoted in R. Serge Denisoff and William D. Romanowski, *Risky Business: Rock in Film* (Piscataway, NJ: Transaction Publishers, 1991), 37.

35 Michael T. Bertrand, *Race, Rock, and Elvis* (Urbana, IL: University of Illinois Press, 2004), 161.

36 Steve Knopper, "The Rope: The Forgotten History of Segregated Rock and Roll Concerts," *Rolling Stone*, November 16, 2017, www.rollingstone.com/music/music-features/the-rope-the-forgotten-history-of-segregated-rock-roll-concerts-126235; and Steve Thornton, "Rock and Roll vs. Racism," (Connecticut Humanities Council, March 19, 2020), https://connecticuthistory.org/rock-and-roll-vs-racism, retrieved February 8, 2021.

37 Tad Dickens, "Fats Domino's Career Included 'Racial Disturbance' in 1956," *Seattle Times*, October 29, 2017, www.seattletimes.com/nation-world/fats-dominos-career-included-racial-disturbance-in-1956, retrieved February 8, 2021.

38 Allan M. Winkler, *"To Everything There Is a Season": Pete Seeger and the Power of Song* (New York: Oxford University Press, 2011), 56.

39 Winkler, 89–90; and Jon Pareles, "Pete Seeger, Champion of Folk Music and Social Change, Dies at 94," *New York Times*, January 28, 2014, www.nytimes.com/2014/01/29/arts/music/pete-seeger-songwriter-and-champion-of-folk-music-dies-at-94.html, retrieved February 9, 2021.

40 Winkler, 98; Allan M. Winkler, "We Shall Overcome," *American Heritage* 62, no. 5 (Fall 2017), www.americanheritage.com/we-shall-overcome, retrieved February 10, 2021.

41 Winkler, 99.

42 Danielle McGuire, *At the Dark End of the Street: A New History of the Civil Rights Movement from Rosa Parks to the Rise of Black Power* (New York: Vintage, 2010), xv–xvi.

43 Ibid., xvi–xvii.

44 Fred Atwater, "$600 to Rape Wife?" Alabama Whites Make Offer to Recy Taylor Mate!," *Chicago Defender*, January 27, 1945, 1, in McGuire, 15.

45 McGuire, 6.

46 See Leigh Gaskin, "Rape Culture: Power, Profit, Punishment" (Washington State University: Doctoral Dissertation, May 2019), 38, citing such scholars as Dorothy Roberts, *Killing the Black Body: Race, Reproduction, and the Meaning of Liberty* (New York: Vintage, 1998), and Andrea Smith, *Conquest: Sexual Violence and American Indian Genocide.* (Durham, NC: Duke University Press, 2005).

47 In 2017, Carolyn Bryant, the woman who reported varying accounts of Till's alleged menacing behavior, confessed to historian Timothy B. Tyson that the allegation was fabricated.

48 Maureen Corrigan, "'Let the People See': It Took Courage to Keep Emmett Till's Memory Alive," (National Public Radio: Fresh Air), October 30, 2018, www.npr. org/2018/10/30/660980178/-let-the-people-see-shows-how-emmett-till-s-murder-was-nearly-forgotten, retrieved. Corrigan reviews Elliott J. Gorn, *Let the People See* (New York: Oxford University Press, 2020, illustrated edition).

49 McGuire, 78–79.

50 Margot Adler, "Before Rosa Parks, There was Claudette Colvin," National Public Radio, Weekend Edition, March 15, 2009, www.npr.org/2009/03/15/101719889/ before-rosa-parks-there-was-claudette-colvin, retrieved February 14, 2021.

51 McGuire, 90–91.

52 "Jesse Jackson Recalls Bus Boycott," National Public Radio, December 5, 2005, www.npr.org/templates/story/story.php?storyId=5039020, retrieved February 14, 2021.

53 Quoted in Fred D. Gray, *Bus Ride to Justice: The Life and Works of Fred Gray* (Montgomery, AL: NewSouth Publishing, 2002), 54.

54 Dr. Martin Luther King, Jr., "MIA Mass Meeting, Holt Street Baptist Church," December 5, 1955, https://kinginstitute.stanford.edu/king-papers/documents/mia-mass-meeting-holt-street-baptist-church, retrieved February 16, 2021.

55 Dr. Martin Luther King, Jr., "Letter from Birmingham Jail," April 16, 1963, www. africa.upenn.edu/Articles_Gen/Letter_Birmingham.html, retrieved February 16, 2021.

56 Quoted in Harvard Sitkoff, *The Struggle for Black Equality* (New York: Hill and Wang, 1981), 42.

57 Vincent Gordon Harding, "Beyond Amnesia: Martin Luther King, Jr. and the Future of America," *Journal of American History* 74, no. 2 (September 1987): 468.

58 Earl Warren, *The Memoirs of Earl Warren* (New York: Doubleday, 1977), 149.

59 Michael R. Belknap, *The Supreme Court Under Earl Warren, 1953–1969* (Columbia, SC: University of South Carolina Press, 2005), 30; and Carol Nolte, "Edgar Patterson, Jurist's 'Teacher,'" *SFGate*, February 28, 2001, www.sfgate.com/news/article/Edgar-Patterson-Jurist-s-Teacher-2947439.php, retrieved February 17, 2021.

60 See Mary L. Dudziak, "Brown as a Cold War Case," *Journal of American History* 91, no. 1 (June 2004), 32–42.

61 Thomas P. Brady, "A Review of Black Monday," October 28, 1954 (University of Mississippi Citizens Councils Collection), https://egrove.olemiss.edu/cgi/viewcontent.cgi?article=1027&context=citizens_news, retrieved February 17, 2021.

62 *Southern Manifesto* on Integration, March 12, 1956. From Congressional Record, 84th Congress Second Session, vol. 102, part 4 (Washington, DC: Governmental Printing Office, 1956).

63 "The nation" includes the north, where de facto segregation was often the norm.

64 Digital photograph (Washington, DC: Library of Congress, 1957), www.loc.gov/ item/00651013, retrieved February 17, 2021.

65 Heather Flood, "Chaos in Clinton" (East Tennessee State University, Master's Thesis, December 2007), https://dc.etsu.edu/cgi/viewcontent. cgi?article=3509&context=etd, retrieved February 17, 2021.

66 McGuire, *At the Dark End of the Street*, 138–139.

67 "In Her Own Words: Elizabeth Eckford," n.d., www.facinghistory.org/resource-library/her-own-words-elizabeth-eckford, retrieved February 17, 2021.

68 Buddy Lonesome, *St. Louis Argus*, quoted in "Crisis Timeline," n.d. (National Park Service), www.nps.gov/chsc/learn/historyculture/timeline.htm, retrieved February 17, 2021.

69 Statement by the Governor of Arkansas," September 14, 1957, www.umass.edu/legal/Hilbink/lpsc/LittleRockDocs.pdf, retrieved February 17, 2021.
70 Dwight Eisenhower, September 24, 1957, at www.nps.gov/chsc/learn/historyculture/timeline.htm, retrieved February 17, 2021.
71 Adam Fairclough, "The Preachers and the People: The Origins and Early Years of the Southern Christian Leadership Conference, 1955–1959," *Journal of Southern History* 52, no. 3 (August 1986): 424–426, 430.
72 Quoted by Barbara Spindel, "Strom Thurmond's America," *Christian Science Monitor*, September 7, 2012, www.csmonitor.com/Books/Book-Reviews/2012/0907/Strom-Thurmond-s-America, retrieved February 17, 2021.
73 Payne quoted in William Sturkey, "The Hidden History of the Civil Rights Act of 1960," *Black Perspectives*, February 8, 2018, www.aaihs.org/the-hidden-history-of-the-civil-rights-act-of-1960, retrieved March 3, 2021; and *Defender* quoted in Taylor Branch, *Parting the Waters: America in the King Years, 1954–1963* (New York: Touchstone, 1988), 221–222.
74 Branch, 232.
75 *Fundi: The Story of Ella Baker* (Icarus Films, 1981); and "Male SCLC leaders tend to ignore the contributions of women leaders," in Oral History Interview with Septima Poinsette Clark, July 25, 1976 (Chapel Hill, NC: University of North Carolina Wilson Library, Southern Oral History Program Collection), #4007, Interview G-0016.
76 Branch, 205.
77 Adam Fairclough, *To Redeem the Soul of America: The Southern Christian Leadership Conference and Martin Luther King Jr.* (Athens, GA: University of Georgia Press, 1987, 2001), 63.
78 John Lewis with Michael D'Orso, *Walking with the Wind: A Memoir of the Movement* (New York: Simon and Schuster, 1998), 3.

Further Reading

Belknap, Michael R. *The Supreme Court Under Earl Warren, 1953–1969.* Columbia, SC: University of South Carolina Press, 2005.

Bertrand, Michael T. *Race, Rock, and Elvis.* Urbana, IL: University of Illinois Press, 2004.

Branch, Taylor. *Parting the Waters: America in the King Years, 1954–1963.* New York: Touchstone, 1988.

Charters, Ann, ed. *The Portable Beat Reader.* New York: Penguin, 1992.

Douglas, Susan. *Where the Girls Are: Growing Up Female with the Mass Media.* New York: Three Rivers Press, 1995.

Engel, Joel. *Last Stop, The Twilight Zone: The Biography of Rod Serling.* Brooklyn, NY: Antenna Books, 1989, 2014.

Fairclough, Adam. *To Redeem the Soul of America: The Southern Christian Leadership Conference and Martin Luther King Jr.* Athens, GA: University of Georgia Press, 1987, 2001.

Fuller, John G. *The Day We Bombed Utah.* New York: New American Library Press, 1984.

Gallagher, Carole. *American Ground Zero: The Secret Nuclear War.* New York: Random House, 1994.

Ginsberg, Allan. *Collected Poems, 1947–1980.* New York: HarperCollins, 1984.

Gorn, Elliott J. *Let the People See.* New York: Oxford University Press, 2020.

Guralnick, Peter. *Sam Phillips: The Man Who Invented Rock and Roll.* New York: Little Brown, 2015.

Kerouac, Jack, with an Introduction by Ann Charters. *One the Road.* New York: Penguin Classics, 1991.

McGuire, Danielle. *At the Dark End of the Street: A New History of the Civil Rights Movement from Rosa Parks to the Rise of Black Power*. New York: Vintage, 2010.

Miller, Richard L. *Under the Cloud: The Decades of Nuclear Testing*. The Woodlands, TX: Two Sixty Press, 1999.

Morgan, Bill, and Nancy J. Peters, eds. *Howl on Trial: The Battle for Free Expression*. San Francisco: City Lights Books, 2006.

Murnaghan, Sheila, and Ralph M. Rosen, eds. *Hip Sublime: Beat Writers and the Classical Tradition*. Columbus, OH: Ohio State University Press, 2018.

Nachman, Gerald. *Seriously Funny: The Rebel Comedians of the 1950s and 1960s*. New York: Pantheon, 2009.

Roberts, Dorothy. *Killing the Black Body: Race, Reproduction, and the Meaning of Liberty*. New York: Vintage, 1998.

Sitkoff, Harvard. *The Struggle for Black Equality*. New York: Hill and Wang, 1981.

Winkler, Allan M. *Life Under a Cloud: American Anxiety About the Atom*. Chicago, IL: University of Chicago Press, 1993.

Winkler, Allan M. *"To Everything There Is a Season": Pete Seeger and the Power of Song*. New York: Oxford University Press, 2011.

5 Let Us Begin

The Promise of the Early 1960s

For I can assure you that we love our country, not for what it was, though it has always been great—not for what it is, though of this we are deeply proud—but for what it someday can, and, through the efforts of us all, someday will be.
—John F. Kennedy, February 13, 1961[1]

Science fiction writer Arthur C. Clarke called Sputnik 1, the world's first unmanned satellite launched by the Soviet Union October 4, 1957, "one of the greatest scientific advances in world history."[2] Better reflecting a national mood of alarm greeting the Soviet achievement, physicist Edward Teller declared it a "greater and more important defeat than Pearl Harbor."[3] With the presumption quickly taking hold that the Russians would use the same technology to launch intercontinental ballistic missiles at the United States, Americans soon viewed Sputnik as a dual crisis of national confidence and security.[4] Assertions from some corners that the Russians must have stolen the technology were cold comfort. Worse still, the attempted U.S. liftoff in December of a satellite to be carried by the Vanguard rocket collapsed four feet into the air, a humiliating spectacle that reporters branded "kaputnik." Defense Secretary Charles Wilson chastised the press and asserted Sputnik was little more than a "neat scientific trick."[5]

Wilson's claim might have carried greater weight if not for the conspicuously timed leak of a top-secret report on America's defenses two weeks after the Vanguard disaster. *Deterrence and Survival in the Nuclear Age*, known as the "Gaither Report,"[6] had been authorized by Eisenhower, mainly to examine the viability of a nationwide fallout shelter program to protect the country from nuclear attack. The military establishment had criticized the president for allegedly penny-pinching defense budgets which it argued left America vulnerable. Especially strident were Air Force claims that Eisenhower's trimming of their requests had led to a "bomber gap" between the Strategic Air Command (SAC) and a supposedly superior Soviet fleet.[7] Eisenhower dismissed the criticism, assured by highly classified U-2 spy plane surveillance that since 1956 revealed the relative weakness of Soviet forces. The president anticipated that Gaither would confirm overall U.S. strategic superiority, diminishing the need for a massively expensive shelter program. He was therefore stunned when the

DOI: 10.4324/9781003160595-5

committee went beyond its mandate, and warned of Soviet military supremacy. The *Washington Post* did nothing to reassure:

> The still-top secret Gaither Report portrays a United States in the gravest danger in its history … It shows an America exposed to an almost immediate threat from the missile-bristling Soviet Union. It finds America's long-term prospect one of cataclysmic peril in the face of rocketing Soviet military might …

"Only through an all-out effort," the Post concluded, could the United States stave off destruction. Encompassing shelters, increases in ballistic missile technology, strategic offensive capabilities and conventional armed forces, Gaither's price tag was a whopping $44 billion.[8]

Eisenhower was not buying. Trying to exceed the Soviets weapon-for-weapon, missile-for-missile, was more of what he had dismissed as "the numbers racket." Just as he came to see "the bomber gap" as a self-interested ploy by SAC and the aerospace industry, the president dismissed most of the recommendations as gratuitous excess. "There comes a time," said Eisenhower, "when the destructiveness of weapons is so great as to be beyond imagination … and you do no good, as I see it, by increasing these numbers."[9] Even as he presided over an enormous expansion of the U.S. nuclear arsenal, Eisenhower had grown frustrated by his inability to control spending on weapons he believed unnecessary. He feared the nation was becoming a "garrison state," led there by a complex of forces: generals, admirals, profit-driven defense corporations, congressmen whose reelection was tied to weapons contracts, university-based scientists developing new weapons systems, and a citizenry vulnerable to fear-mongering. Eisenhower famously articulated his apprehension in his January 1961 farewell address. "In the councils of government," he advised, "we must guard against the acquisition of unwarranted influence, whether sought or unsought, by the military industrial complex. The potential for the disastrous rise of misplaced power exists and will persist."[10]

But the *Sputnik* panic of October 1957 was no time for such sobering counsel. Eisenhower advanced a series of typically measured actions, first pressing the Army and Navy to get their satellite projects on track for a successful launch in January 1958. He then signed the National Aeronautics and Space Act establishing NASA, and the National Defense Education Act, which appropriated $800 million to strengthen the teaching of mathematics, science, and foreign languages—the largest direct federal investment in education to date. The measure galvanized liberal proponents of aid to education, muting the charge from some Republicans that such spending was tantamount to socialism. Indeed, the political reverberations of the hyperventilated *Sputnik* crisis signaled the end of one era and the genesis of the next. As the 1960 campaign dawned, Democratic presidential hopefuls Stuart Symington and John F. Kennedy seized on Gaither's charge that the Soviets had gained the edge in the development of intercontinental ballistic missiles. Symington warned of an imminent Soviet arsenal of 3,000 ICBMs; in 1958 they had four.

Not to be outdone, Kennedy alleged a "missile gap" now endangered American security. JFK soon learned the gap ran the other way: it was the U.S. that held the overwhelming advantage in land and sea-based missile systems.[11]

Kennedy's charge presaged a broader frontal attack in the 1960 campaign against Vice President Richard Nixon in which he argued that pressing national issues had been ignored by a moribund Republican administration. It was a critique that reinforced a general awakening in the late fifties to what historian and Kennedy advisor Arthur Schlesinger, Jr. called Americans' immersion in "self-indulgent values." The obsession with climbing the ladder and acquiring material comforts had led to anomic social isolation, he argued, a withering of common purpose and commitment to a greater good that characterized the New Deal–World War II era.[12] Liberals like Schlesinger contended that a self-interested culture focused on the private acquisition of goods produced a government of stagnation that inevitably led to *Sputnik*, as well as a lengthening agenda of domestic policy concerns. In *The Affluent Society* (1958), economist John Kenneth Galbraith summoned the nation to apply its enormous wealth to solving problems like education and urban degradation. A revealing moment came during the July 1959 "Kitchen Debate" between Nixon and Khrushchev at the American National Exhibition in Moscow. As the vice president boasted of the glorious features of the modern American kitchen on display, he and Khrushchev moved into a broader colloquy about the relative merits of the two societies. At one point, Nixon acknowledged that, "there are some instances where you may be ahead of us—for example, in the development of the thrust of your rockets for the investigation of outer space. There may be some instances, for example, color television, where we're ahead of you."[13] And there it was: an inadvertent acknowledgement of what liberal critics believed were the misplaced priorities of Eisenhower's America.

A New Frontier

Tapping into a broadly felt desire to, as he put it, "get America moving again," Kennedy promised a "New Frontier" of renewed energy.[14] Declaring the 1960 election a choice "between the public interest and private comfort—between national greatness and national decline … between determined dedication and creeping mediocrity," he draped around Nixon the disquieting sense of lost national purpose, and animated his campaign with a revival of FDR-style liberalism.[15] Kennedy' pilgrimage that summer to Roosevelt's beloved Hyde Park to celebrate with Eleanor the twenty-fifth anniversary of Social Security was symbolic of a larger effort to galvanize the Roosevelt coalition. Besides courting favor with a Democratic Party luminary, he used the occasion to promote a piece of unfinished New Deal business, health insurance for the elderly.[16]

At the center of Kennedy's call for a New Frontier were young people, whose nascent desire to move beyond the fifties' success ethos was reflected in a late-night campaign stop at the University of Michigan. Arriving well after midnight, Kennedy's staff looked to find a bed. But when the candidate saw several hundred students waiting at the university union, he delivered an impromptu address, floating an idea that had been germinating in Democratic circles: to challenge college students to serve America abroad, working in their chosen field to assist peoples of underdeveloped nations. On "your willingness to contribute part of your life to this country," said Kennedy, could rest the fate of the nation. The state of Michigan, he continued, was not funding the university "merely to help its graduates have an economic advantage in the life struggle. There is certainly a greater purpose, and I'm sure you recognize it." Students erupted in applause. Days before the election, Kennedy proposed a "peace corps of talented young men and women, willing and able to serve their country." Nixon denounced the proposal as a "cult of escapism" and "a haven for draft dodgers," an attack that appeared small and out of touch with the budding idealism of the moment.[17]

The 1960s, said Kennedy, would be a "contest between the comfortable and the concerned," a tension revealed in another episode that fall.[18] In late October, Dr. Martin Luther King, Jr. was arrested at an Atlanta sit-in and transferred to a Georgia maximum-security prison. Fearing for her husband's life, Coretta Scott King reached out to both campaigns. Nixon, pressed by Jackie Robinson to express concern for the civil rights leader, said nothing. By contrast, Kennedy appealed to Governor Ernest Vandiver to help secure King's release, and against the objections of aides called Coretta King, which he knew would become public.[19] When King was freed days later, leading black newspapers and church leaders, led by Reverend "Daddy" King, pronounced Kennedy the more promising civil rights leader. Strong black turnout on November 8 made a difference in key northern states that went to Kennedy by slim margins.

It was bitter cold in Washington that Friday, January 20, 1961 as John F. Kennedy stood at the east portico of the Capitol. His inaugural address, best remembered for its *Ask not ...* crescendo that tapped the teeming well of sixties idealism, took its place in the pantheon of great inaugurals, alongside Lincoln's "malice toward none" at the end of the Civil War, and FDR's "fear itself" in the worst hour of the Great Depression. Although the speech is often recalled as a forceful reiteration of U.S. Cold War policy—Americans, he pledged, would "pay any price, bear any burden ... oppose any foe" in the cause of liberty—the greater part of it aspired to break free of the calcified thinking that had produced diplomatic stalemate in the Cold War. After acknowledging the "balance of terror that stays the hand of mankind's final war," Kennedy offered a litany of proposals pointing toward a new epoch in world history:

> Let both sides explore what problems unite us instead of belaboring those problems which divide us. Let both sides, for the first time, formulate serious and precise proposals for the inspection and control of arms—and bring the absolute power to destroy other nations under the absolute control of all nations. Let both sides seek to invoke the wonders of science instead of its terrors. Together let us explore the stars, conquer the deserts, eradicate disease, tap the ocean depths and encourage the arts and

commerce … All this will not be finished in the first one hundred days. Nor will it be finished in the first one thousand days, nor in the life of this Administration, nor even perhaps in our lifetime on this planet. But let us begin.

The words echoed far beyond the national mall. "Let the word go forth from this time and place, to friend and foe alike, that the torch has been passed to a new generation of Americans."[20] Braided with elegant phrasing, the address summoned America's highest ideals of duty and sacrifice in a great national cause, reawakening them for an age bursting with promise.

The president's first executive order that afternoon increased the surplus food allotment to four million needy Americans, prelude to a broader effort aimed at addressing poverty in America.[21] Many Americans first confronted the issue in March 1962 when Michael Harrington published *The Other America*, a shocking portrait of a world beyond suburbia. Harrington offered a compelling look at the millions of Americans living in poverty. Across rural Appalachia, in urban communities, on Indian reservations, more than one out of five were poor in the richest nation on earth. Kennedy's own awakening began during his 1960 primary campaign in West Virginia, where he turned a yawning deficit against Hubert Humphrey into a stunning 20-point victory, overcoming deep anti-Catholic prejudice in the overwhelmingly Protestant state —in no small part by simply listening to West Virginians. Coal miner John Mendez remembered how Kennedy sat on rail cars and often "broke away from the security, and … just [mingled] with the people just like he was one of us." He ventured into mountain hollows, where the sight of malnourished children living without electricity and indoor plumbing left him shaken.[22] It was not happenstance that the first federal food authorization that inauguration day went to Alderson Muncy, an unemployed West Virginia miner he had met with 13 children to feed. The spring of 1961 saw passage of key economic development measures and authorization of one billion dollars in public works for Appalachia.[23]

The Other America was one of a number of pivotal books in this period that focused national attention on critical issues. None had greater impact than Rachel Carson's *Silent Spring*. A biologist who spent her early career with the U.S. Fish and Wildlife Service, Carson was by 1962 an acclaimed author of bestselling books on the world's oceans. In *Silent Spring*, she assailed the indiscriminate use of pesticides and insecticides and their resulting impacts on the environment. With exacting detail and eloquent prose Carson explained the threats posed to bird life, and ultimately to humans, by the bioaccumulation of DDT and other chemicals. The bald eagle was among the North American birds that had been brought to the edge of extinction.[24] Noting "the 500 new chemicals to which the bodies of men and animals are required somehow to adapt each year," Carson warned of the damage to all life from the "violent crossfire" of a "chemical war." She linked the chemical menace to the threat of nuclear war, twin pillars of the "central problem of our age … the contamination of man's total environment."[25] The ramifications of *Silent Spring* went well beyond pesticides, to the inescapable truth that the fate of humanity was inextricably bound to that of the natural world. Further, Carson shattered the postwar illusion that experts in corporations and the government could always be trusted. Not surprisingly, the book ignited a firestorm. Rachel Carson faced a withering assault from industry officials like American Cyanamid chemist Robert White-Stevens, who labeled her "a fanatic defender of the cult of the balance of nature." [26]

The sea-loving Kennedy had read Carson's ocean books. The two found common cause in her warning of the perils of the U.S. military's ocean dumping of radioactive waste, and of atmospheric nuclear testing. Carson volunteered for the Kennedy campaign, and along with Supreme Court Justice and conservationist William Douglas, advised him on environmental issues. By the time of *Silent Spring*, the administration had embarked on a vigorous conservation agenda headed by Secretary of Interior Stewart Udall. Shortly after excerpts were published in *The New Yorker*, anticipating industry's attack, the Kennedy conservation team—Udall, Douglas, and the president's brother, Attorney General and Douglas hiking partner Robert F. Kennedy—quietly built a bulwark of public support for the book. At a news conference, the president announced that "Miss Carson's book" had triggered an investigation into the health impacts of pesticides and insecticides (Figure 5.1).[27] Issued in May 1963, the report called for decreased use and the eventual phase-out of DDT.

If *Silent Spring* struck like lightning across the summer sky, *The Feminine Mystique* arrived in February 1963 as if women had been waiting for it. Since the end of the war, white middle-class women had been consumed with childrearing and housekeeping, even as more of them returned to work outside the home. Millions of women tried to numb the pain of their repressed aspirations with martinis and anti-anxiety drugs like Miltown.[28] A journalist who had directly experienced discrimination in the workplace, Betty Friedan seemed perhaps destined to write a book affirming a woman's inner truth that she was not mad for wanting something more from life. Conversations with dispirited former classmates at a Smith College reunion provided final inspiration. "We can no longer ignore that voice," Friedan wrote, "that says: 'I want something more than my husband and my children and my home.'"[29] Friedan shattered the idea, "the feminine mystique," that every woman could find total fulfillment waxing her kitchen floor and catering to everyone's needs but her own. "The problem," she said,

> lay buried, unspoken, for many years. … As she made the beds, shopped for groceries, matched slipcover material, ate peanut butter sandwiches with her children, chauffeured Cub Scouts and Brownies, lay beside her husband at night—she was afraid to ask even of herself the silent question— "Is this all?"[30]

Suddenly the author of one of the most important books of the century, Friedan was deluged with letters from women variously thanking her for affirming they were not mad, or unreasonable for wanting to return to school. Others sought

Figure 5.1 Scientist and author Rachel Carson.

Bettman/Getty, www.gettyimages.co.uk/detail/news-photo/washington-d-c-rachel-carson-stirred-up-a-roaring-national-news-photo/517350968?adppopup=true

counsel on how to escape domestic entrapment.[31] Friedan's psycho-cultural study of the limitations imposed on affluent white women excluded many of the issues that would soon be encompassed by the women's liberation movement. Even with its limited sphere, Friedan "was cursed, pitied, told to get psychiatric help, to go jump in the lake and accused of 'being more of a threat to the United States than the Russians.'"[32]

The Feminine Mystique reflected a broader set of tensions regarding the changing role of women. Thirty percent of married women worked outside the home, though the door to many professional careers remained shut. Although white women were paid less than 60 cents for every dollar a man earned doing the same work, and black women just 45 cents, to complain about pay inequity or sexual harassment risked termination. Women labor leaders debated whether it was time to abandon gender-specific protective legislation for women in the workplace—often used by employers to discriminate—and instead to advocate for equality across-the-board: the long-delayed Equal Rights Amendment (ERA) to the Constitution.[33]

With that debate simmering, and convinced that a presidential-level examination of the issues would produce mostly good news and prove less divisive than Truman's effort on race, John Kennedy authorized the President's Commission on the Status of Women to study a broad range of policy matters. Although embedded in Cold War ideology, the commission's report ("American Women") nonetheless reflected women's shifting realities and higher aspirations. While celebrating the traditional position of American women vis-à-vis their Russian counterparts, "American Women" documented systematic gender discrimination and called for sweeping change: affordable childcare, equal opportunity in the professions, paid maternity leave, legal reforms, women in public office. It offered the most progressive vision of women's lives ever produced by the federal government.[34] Together with *The Feminine Mystique*, the commission helped pave the way for Kennedy's executive order halting gender discrimination in federal hiring, the Pay Equity Act of 1963, and Title VII of the 1964 Civil Rights Act prohibiting gender discrimination. Further, the federal effort spawned dozens of state- and university-level commissions aimed at gender discrimination, in the process establishing a network of activists who in 1966 formed the nucleus of the National Organization for Women.[35]

Making America What It Must Become

> [If] the word "integration" means anything, this is what it means, that we with love shall force our brothers to see themselves as they are, to cease fleeing from reality and begin to change it, for this is your home, my friend. Do not be driven from it. Great men have done great things here and will again and we can make America what America must become.
>
> —James Baldwin, "My Dungeon Shook," 1963[36]

Author James Baldwin did more in this essay than capture the hopeful zeitgeist of the early sixties. Ostensibly a letter to his nephew marking the centennial of black emancipation, "My Dungeon Shook" delivered a cutting indictment of America's willful ignorance of its racist past, the mythology of white supremacy, and the grim conditions facing young black men. White Americans were "trapped in a history which they do not understand," a version of the past that told them "black men are inferior to white men." Overcoming that historical illiteracy demanded courage, an understanding of black Americans' place in the nation's history, and the audacious conviction that change was possible. In 1963, the letter served as a preamble for Baldwin's *The Fire Next Time*, a searing dissection of American racism centered on institutions from Christianity to the police—his instinctual suspicion of men in blue drawn from both history and years of personal harassment. "The brutality with which Negroes are treated in this country simply cannot be overstated," declared Baldwin,

> however unwilling white men may be to hear it. In the beginning—and neither can this be overstated—a Negro just cannot *believe* that white

people are treating him as they do; he does not know what he has done to merit it.[37]

Making America what it must become was the mission of a civil rights movement whose pace had been quickening since Monday, February 1, 1960. That afternoon, four black university students strode to the Woolworth's lunch counter in Greensboro, North Carolina and were denied service. The next day, their numbers grew to 25, confronted by whites yelling racist epithets. By Thursday, 300 students took shifts and extended their sit-in to nearby Kress's, both stores opting to close lunch counters rather than integrate. The students kept coming, to more establishments, their growing ranks hauled off to jail. Within weeks, 90 percent of the area's black students were sitting in, picketing, or boycotting segregated businesses.[38] Victory came in July as storeowners surrendered to integration.

Independently, in Nashville, Tennessee, James Lawson's pupils had also moved into action. Diane Nash and John Lewis led the Nashville Campaign to desegregate lunch counters, theatres, and other facilities, achieving victory in May. Young *Tennessean* reporter David Halberstam later recounted the trepidation of Chicagoan Diane Nash, who on the eve of the sit-ins acknowledged the immensity of their challenge. "We're children, bright and idealistic, but we are children and we are weak. We have no police force, no judges, no cops, no money." Rev. Lawson, wrote Halberstam, "is a fine man and a good leader, she thought, but this is nothing but a dream."[39] Although Halberstam may have overstated Nash's pessimism for dramatic effect, it was also true that the 21-year-old could not have imagined the power of civil disobedience. Shocked by Jim Crow segregation when she first arrived in Nashville, Nash recalled with delight the reaction of whites on day one:

> Waitresses dropped things. Store managers and personnel perspired. Several cashiers were led off in tears … Two Negro students, who had sat in at the lunch counter, went into [a department store] ladies restroom … marked "white" and were there as a heavy-set, older white lady, who might have been seeking refuge from the scene … Upon opening the door and finding the two Negro girls inside, the women threw up her hands and, nearly in tears, exclaimed, "Oh, Nigras everywhere!"[40]

Sit-ins spread to more than 100 cities and towns across the South. Students sat-in at lunch counters and theatres, staged library read-ins, and swam-in at public beaches and pools. By June, 70,000 students had participated, with 1,500 arrested. One facility at a time, the sit-ins battered Jim Crow in a dramatic demonstration of the moral authority and power of nonviolent civil disobedience. Even if they disagreed with the tactic, when the majority of Americans looked at their televisions and saw white mobs pouring hot coffee and pressing lighted cigarette butts into the backs of peaceful Americans asking for a hamburger, it was not difficult to choose sides. As their movement gained momentum, the SCLC's Ella Baker organized a conference in Raleigh, North Carolina, unifying the students under the Student Non-Violent Coordinating Committee (SNCC, "Snick").[41]

SNCC's dedication to nonviolence was tested the following spring in the Freedom Rides. In December 1960, the U.S. Supreme Court struck down segregation in interstate travel, but months later "Colored" and "Whites Only" still hung in bus and train stations throughout the South. The Congress of Racial Equality decided to revive the idea of an integrated bus ride, a tactic attempted without success in 1947. In a more hopeful political environment that spring of 1961, thirteen black and white Freedom Riders prepared for a journey from Washington DC to New Orleans, a dangerous test of the federal government's willingness to enforce the law. With no illusions about what lay ahead, the activists prepared wills. The response from civil rights leadership was decidedly mixed. Thurgood Marshall decried the action as "suicide," certain it would provoke violence and a backlash against goals better pursued in the courts. Dr. King offered support but not his participation. Preparing for his first summit with Soviet Premier Nikita Khrushchev, John Kennedy feared racial violence would hand Moscow a propaganda coup and tried unsuccessfully to dissuade CORE leadership from going forward.[42]

On May 4 the Freedom Riders boarded two buses. Traveling unmolested through the upper South, the first assault came in Rock Hill, South Carolina—for a "shoe-in" at a shoeshine stand. It proved a mild overture to what transpired May 14, Mother's Day. As the buses pulled into the station in Anniston, Alabama, the Greyhound driver yelled to a waiting mob, "Well, boys, here they are. I brought you some niggers and nigger-lovers."[43] Wielding baseball bats and iron bars, the crowd besieged the bus, breaking windows and slashing tires. Police arrived but made no arrests. The bus escaped with a police escort and the mob in pursuit, but five miles outside Anniston could go no further. As the police drove off, the defenders of white Alabama resumed their assault—at one point barring the exit door as the bus was firebombed. Screams and shouts of "burn the niggers alive!" filled the air before riders forced open the door of a bus engulfed in flames. Photographs taken by photographer Joseph Postiglione flashed around the globe. Eclipsed by the horror was one moment of grace: Janie Miller, a 12-year-old white girl, defied the Klansmen and waded into the chaos. "I picked me out one person," she said. "I washed her face. I held her, I gave her water to drink, and soon as I thought she was gonna be okay, I got up and picked out somebody else."[44]

Meanwhile, the Trailways bus arrived in Birmingham where a crowd of 200 wielding bricks, bats, and lead pipes lay waiting. Birmingham Police waited fifteen minutes before intervening, allowing the mob time to deliver a ferocious assault. Jim Peck needed 53 stitches to close a head wound. Police Chief Eugene "Bull" Connor blamed the late arrival on Mother's Day, while FBI director J. Edgar Hoover, whose agents busied themselves conducting surveillance on movement leaders, offered no excuse to Robert Kennedy. Hoover's Klan informant alerted him to the attack and still he did nothing.[45]

If not for Diane Nash, the story could have ended very differently. The assault in Anniston led CORE director James Farmer to call for an end to the rides. Learning of the decision in Nashville, Nash resisted, arguing that surrender could prove fatal to the Freedom Rides, and to nonviolence as a strategy. Ten Nashville SNCC students headed for Birmingham determined to continue, only to be arrested by Bull Connor and driven back to the Tennessee state line. The ten found their way to Nashville, where Nash organized their return to Birmingham.[46] Meanwhile, Robert Kennedy pressured Greyhound to find another driver and dispatched aide John Siegenthaler south to attempt mediation. Siegenthaler persuaded Alabama Governor John Patterson to pledge state police protection for the Freedom Riders from Birmingham to Montgomery. An early Kennedy supporter, Patterson now turned on the White House, refusing at one point to accept a phone call from the president. Alabama troopers escorted the bus to Montgomery city limits and disappeared. When the bus pulled into the station, the activists encountered eerie silence until suddenly a mob swarmed, wielding every weapon imaginable. First off the bus and meeting the full force of the violence were "Nigger lover" Jim Zwerg and John Lewis. Attempting to intervene, Siegenthaler was clobbered with a lead pipe. From his hospital bed, Zwerg later told a reporter, "We're going to keep coming until we can ride from anywhere in the South ... as American citizens."[47]

The violence brought extensive national television coverage, inspiring more activists to organize more Freedom Rides. "It was like a wave or a wind, and you didn't know where it was coming from but you knew you were supposed to be there," one student recalled. "Nobody asked me, nobody told me."[48] Mississippi officials made a last desperate effort to stem the tide, arresting hundreds of Freedom Riders and sending them to the notorious Parchman State Penitentiary. By November, nearly 500 Americans had participated in more than 60 Freedom Rides.[49] Given their impact, it mattered little that few reached New Orleans. The Kennedy administration, although it had intervened reluctantly, began enforcing desegregation of interstate travel and had by year's end grown more committed to civil rights.

In 1961, James Meredith applied for admission to the University of Mississippi in Oxford—"Ole Miss" to white Mississippians. The Air Force veteran's decision to crash this great southern bastion of whiteness was partly inspired by the JFK summons to *do something for your country*.[50] When Meredith's application was rejected, the NAACP filed suit. After the Supreme Court ordered his admission, Governor Ross Barnett defied the ruling. On September 13, 1962, he took to the airwaves: "There is no case in history where the Caucasian race has survived racial integration. We will not drink from the cup of Genocide."[51] The White House found itself on familiar fractious ground, confronting another obstinate southern Democratic governor. Self-deputized as university registrar, Barnett personally blocked Meredith's admission. A federal court found him in contempt and ordered Meredith admitted. Barnett responded with an incendiary half-time appearance at an Ole Miss football game on September 29. "I love

Mississippi, I love her people!" the governor bayed, prompting the frenzied throng to break into the words of a new Ole Miss fight song:

Never, no-o-o never, never, never …
Ross's standin' like Gibraltar
He shall never falter
Ask us what we say, it's to hell with Bobby K
Never shall our emblem go from Colonel Reb to Old Black Jo.[52]

Led by Reb Barnett, this citadel of the Lost Cause prepared for the Battle of Oxford the following night.

The front in this deadly engagement was the elegant Lyceum, a neoclassical structure that had served as a makeshift Confederate hospital during the Civil War. Now the administration building where Meredith was to enroll, the Lyceum was surrounded that Sunday evening by a self-appointed militia of 2,500. As Meredith lay coolly on a dorm cot in another building, shouts of "lynch the nigger" and Confederate rebel yells filled the night air. Inside the Lyceum, several hundred besieged federal marshals and various other deputized officials held their ground with tear gas, under orders from the White House not to draw weapons unless the mob attempted a lynching. The long night saw everything *but* that. Blasts of sniper gunfire, gasoline-filled Coke bottles, pipes, and other makeshift weapons assaulted the defenders. Dozens were injured, blood spattering the walls as medical supplies grew short. To Mississippians it felt like 1863. For Deputy Attorney General Nicholas Katzenbach and Ed Guthman, who spent much of the night calling Robert Kennedy from a Lyceum pay phone, the experience evoked memories of World War II combat.[53]

Through the long night of terror, President Kennedy paced the floor of the Cabinet Room, confounded by the slow response of the Army's riot control team. As the violence spun out of control, officials could not explain to the commander-in-chief why the Memphis-based 503rd Military Police Battalion had not yet arrived. Incompetence bordered on the preposterous, as wayward soldiers stopped at service stations seeking road maps to find their way to Oxford. An exasperated president was told that the United States Army had no place to land its helicopters. Increasingly it looked like insubordination, a perception heightened by the arrival of rightwing demagogue Edwin Walker. A decorated major-general, Walker was forced into retirement in 1961 for promoting to men under his command the crackpot conspiracies of the John Birch Society. Rallying the mob, Walker mounted a Confederate statue, hollering: "Go get 'em, boys!"[54] By the time 30,000 troops began arriving at dawn to end the siege, more than 200 had been injured and two persons killed. As James Meredith headed to class the next day, he saw a campus strewn with tear gas canisters and other debris of a war zone. More than 300 were arrested, including Walker who was charged with fomenting insurrection.[55]

Ole Miss proved a turning point, less for the movement than the Kennedys' relationship with the white South. For JFK, the confrontation ended the illusion that there could be any accommodation with southern Democrats. Even if governors and congressmen were privately willing to bend slowly toward ending segregation, the most extreme elements of their states were now more defiant, not less. Leaflets littering the Ole Miss campus and disseminated to soldiers on the streets of Oxford read, "KENNEDY is out to destroy AMERICA because he is a sick, sick COMMUNIST. ... [Join] with your fellow Americans ... [and] we will remove RED JACK KENNEDY." The antipathy was not confined to Oxford. That summer a movie marquee in a small Georgia town for *PT-109*, a film dramatizing the president's World War II naval heroism, read: "See the Japs Almost Get Kennedy."[56] The picture of 30,000 soldiers in an American city handed Republicans an opportunity many were willing to exploit. Arizona Senator Barry Goldwater, preparing a 1964 presidential run, compared the president to Adolf Hitler.[57]

"If you come to Birmingham, you will not only gain prestige, but really shake the country. If you win in Birmingham, as Birmingham goes, so goes the nation."[58] The appeal from Reverend Fred Shuttlesworth to Martin Luther King early in 1963 came at precisely the right moment. The SCLC had spent much of the previous year attempting without success to desegregate Albany, Georgia. The city made promises to King that went unmet, law enforcement exercised restraint, and activists ultimately grew demoralized. Birmingham, larger and bitterly segregationist, promised to be different if only because of Bull Connor. His assault on the Freedom Riders epitomized years of repression. Connor shamelessly blamed African Americans for more than 50 unsolved bombings of black churches, homes and businesses that had given the city the moniker, "Bombingham." Shuttlesworth believed King's stature and SCLC resources could crack Birmingham open, producing a victory that could force the president to introduce civil rights legislation. Notwithstanding promises of moderation from an incoming new city government, Shuttlesworth aimed to carry out a broad campaign focused on desegregation and an end to discriminatory hiring by the city.

The campaign launched April 3 with a business boycott, marches to city hall, mass meetings, sit-ins, church kneel-ins, and library read-ins. Black citizens filled the jails. Seeking to dramatize the campaign, on April 12, Good Friday, King and Rev. Ralph Abernathy subjected themselves to arrest. Placed in solitary, King read in the *Birmingham News* a letter from fellow clergymen condemning the protests and his arrival in the city. Stung by the public censure, King asked the guards for composition paper. He proceeded to write "Letter from Birmingham Jail," a powerful treatise on the strategy and moral authority of nonviolence. After shredding the preachers' patronizing arguments on the timing of the protests, King schooled the ministers on the distinctions between just and unjust laws, drawing disturbing parallels between the immorality of American apartheid and the horrors of ignoble legal systems with which readers were familiar: "We should never forget that everything Adolf Hitler did in Germany was 'legal,'" King admonished, "and everything the Hungarian freedom fighters did ... [in the 1956 uprising] was 'illegal.'" Alarmed at the growing appeal of black nationalism and the violence beginning to break out around the country, he delivered this warning:

> Oppressed people cannot remain oppressed forever. The yearning for freedom eventually manifests itself, and that is what has happened to the American Negro ... [He] has been caught up by the Zeitgeist, and with his black brothers of Africa and his brown and yellow brothers of Asia, South America and the Caribbean, the United States Negro is moving with a sense of great urgency toward the promised land of racial justice ... So let him march ... If his repressed emotions are not released in nonviolent ways, they will seek expression through violence; this is not a threat but a fact of history.[59]

Victory in Birmingham would come not on paper but in early May as young protesters filled the streets and parks and the city unleashed the full force of segregationist race hatred. It came in the form of Bull Connor's white tanks roaming the streets. It came most viciously from attack dogs sicced on peaceful demonstrators, from fire hoses pummeling black children in the streets. The brutality shocked the conscience of Americans and many around the globe, offering the Soviets a propaganda coup. White Alabamans were indifferent. That fact was reaffirmed days later when Governor George Wallace, defying a court order, blocked the University of Alabama "schoolhouse door" with Robert Kennedy's deputy looking on. Wallace stepped aside once he'd had his moment for the cameras, settling for a futile condemnation of the history now rolling over him.[60]

It is worth noting briefly the extraordinary power and contradictory nature of those TV cameras in the early sixties. Network coverage of Birmingham held an irresistible, loathsome mirror up to the nation that was propelling history forward. At the same time, viewers gripped by televised coverage of Birmingham experienced a confounding dissonance as they tuned from CBS news anchor Walter Cronkite to their evening programming. The televised portrait of southern white law enforcement in Birmingham contrasted starkly with that of one of the era's top-rated TV programs, *The Andy Griffith Show*. In Mayberry, benevolent sheriff Andy Taylor carried no gun, deployed no dogs or hoses, and did not collaborate with the Klan. Nor did Andy or deputy Barney Fife ever encounter a single black citizen. The westerns dominating television programming featured sheriffs violently but honorably enforcing law and order, further enshrining the mythology of righteous white lawmen and rendering the actions of Bull Connor all the more jarring. It was James Baldwin inside out: most white viewers just "[could] not *believe* that white people" in uniform could wield state power so savagely.

John Kennedy *could* believe it, and had seen enough. On the afternoon of June 11, the president arranged for airtime and had speechwriter Ted Sorensen draft an address on civil rights, remarks the president edited right up to airtime. Channeling King, Kennedy made clear that troubled race relations was not a southern problem. "Every American, regardless of where he lives," the president urged, should "stop and examine his conscience." Indirectly chastising his own administration, he ticked off some of the prevailing gross injustices of racial discrimination, asking, "Who among us would then be content with the counsels of patience and delay?" Referencing both the Cold War and Nazism, he confronted the hypocrisy of a nation that:

> [preaches] freedom around the world, and we mean it, and we cherish our freedom here at home, but are we to say to the world, and much more importantly, to each other that this is the land of the free except for the Negroes; that we have no second-class citizens except Negroes; that we have no class or caste system, no ghettoes, no master race except with respect to Negroes? … We face, therefore, a moral crisis as a country and as a people …[61]

As he closed, the president announced the introduction of the long-promised civil rights bill.

Progress that summer of 1963 did not come without retribution. The night of Kennedy's speech, in Jackson, Mississippi, revered civil rights leader Medgar Evers, a veteran who fought on the beaches of Normandy, was shot dead by a Klansman in his driveway. And then on a quiet mid-September morning, just weeks after King delivered his historic "I Have a Dream Speech" at the Lincoln Memorial, a horrific explosion rocked the 16th Street Baptist Church in Birmingham, killing four young girls and wounding dozens more.

"Not a Pax Americana"

On July 2, 1957, John F. Kennedy took to the Senate floor to condemn U.S. support for the French colonial war in Algeria. "The single most important test of American foreign policy today," the Massachusetts senator declared, "is how we meet the challenge of imperialism, what we do to further man's desire to be free." U.S. backing of the doomed French effort, Kennedy argued, was only delaying the inevitable and inciting anti-Americanism on the African continent. The speech was denounced by French officials and many of his fellow Democrats. Former presidential candidate Adlai Stevenson damned Kennedy's "self-righteous preaching." No one should have been surprised. During the siege of the French at Dien Bien Phu three years earlier, Kennedy argued against U.S. intervention in Vietnam, declaring that "no amount of American military assistance in Indochina can conquer an enemy which … has the sympathy and covert support of the people."[62] Speaking on behalf of Stevenson's 1956 campaign, Kennedy denounced the Truman and Eisenhower administrations for failing to see the complexity of rising nationalism in Asia and Africa and reducing U.S. policy to crude, counterproductive anti-communism. Stevenson quietly asked the senator to restrict his speeches to domestic policy.[63]

John F. Kennedy's anti-imperialist thinking seems discordant with the popular mythology of an iron-willed president committed to victory at any cost in the

Cold War. Mounting scholarship over decades has challenged that narrative with the record of a president determined to avoid armed confrontation with the communists, who challenged fundamental assumptions about both the Cold War and the U.S. relationship with the developing world. To be sure, Kennedy believed America had a preeminent role to play in shaping global events, but it needed to do so by repositioning itself amid the forces sweeping Africa, Asia, and Latin America. Among the first statesmen of his generation to recognize that the age of imperialism was dying, Kennedy asserted that the sooner the United States placed itself on the side of nationalist struggles around the world, the greater the odds of influencing those forces. He voiced support for leaders of emerging "non-aligned" nations like Sukarno of Indonesia determined to avoid being swept into either Cold War camp. Leaders like Patrice Lumumba of the Congo,[64] whose anti-imperialist rhetoric marked him as anti-American at the CIA, earned Kennedy's support. His anti-colonialism and courting of African leaders made Kennedy a celebrity figure in remote corners of the continent, where portraits of the slain president would hang years afterward.[65]

In Latin America, Kennedy pinned his hopes on an ambitious development initiative called the "Alliance for Progress" (AFP). After decades of U.S. imperialism followed by a period of postwar indifference, the AFP was to be a Marshall Plan for the Western hemisphere, a non-militarized anti-communist counterweight to the influence of Fidel Castro. The grand hopes proved grandiose. Governments remained resistant to democratization, especially when it came to land reform. AFP funding remained stingy, given the tremendous need. Moreover, this was not like rebuilding Europe, but ground-up development for a region that had been colonized and still lived partly under military dictatorship. Despite some successes, the AFP would be regarded by the end of the 1960s as a disappointment.[66]

The Bay of Pigs invasion is much better remembered, albeit through the distorting prism of Kennedy the cold warrior. Long obscured is the essential fact that the episode became the crucible for a foreign policy antithetical to Cold War orthodoxy. In 2005, the CIA declassified its history of the operation, confirming what some scholars and White House insiders had long argued. The evidence makes clear that from December 1960 through the launch of the operation April 17, 1961, CIA Director Allen Dulles and Director of Special Plans Richard Bissell lied repeatedly to John Kennedy about the operation's prospects for successfully overthrowing the government of Fidel Castro. The plan counted on an uprising of Cubans to support the landing by 1,500 CIA-trained exiles of the corrupt, ousted regime of Fulgencio Batista. The spy chiefs knew well that was not going to happen; support for Castro was, if anything increasing. Yet in mid-March 1961 Dulles and Bissell told the president that Castro had the support of barely one-quarter of the Cuban people, and that once the exiles landed, most of Castro's forces would join the invaders.[67] America's top spies understood the operation was doomed, that it would not reprise Bissell's overthrow of Árbenz in Guatemala, that it could only succeed with direct involvement from the U.S. military.

They knew also that John Kennedy had insisted he wanted no part of an operation requiring U.S. combat forces. The president made clear that while he supported *Cuban* resistance against Castro, an American coup would undermine the Alliance for Progress before it even began, and undercut any leverage he had with Khrushchev over Berlin. It was, moreover, antithetical to his larger anti-imperialist policy goals. Yet having had free reign to launch one operation after another under Eisenhower, Dulles and Bissell, along with Navy Chief Admiral Arleigh Burke, simply could not believe that "the president would let [the invasion] openly fail when he had all this American power" at his disposal, advisor Walt Rostow recalled.[68] During a midnight meeting on the eve of the invasion, Kennedy and the three men went at it over the scale of U.S. involvement, including the number of aircraft, the president cutting their request in half. Admiral Burke called for use of a destroyer to "knock the hell out of Castro's tanks." The president asked what would happen if the destroyer were hit. "Then we'll knock the hell out of them!" Burke howled. "Burke, I don't want the United States involved in this." "Hell, Mr. President," the admiral shouted, "we *are* involved!"[69] The meeting ended at 3 am, Kennedy reluctantly green-lighting a scaled-down operation.

Within hours, more than 1,200 exiles had been taken captive and 118 killed. The United States faced widespread condemnation for an attempted overthrow of a sovereign government. Kennedy appalled the spy chiefs and military brass by refusing to rescue the operation with airstrikes, preferring to accept the consequences of the disaster. He knew he had been set up by the CIA, that the arrogant agency heads were convinced Kennedy would accede to their emergency request for intervention in order to avoid personal humiliation. "They couldn't believe that a new president like me wouldn't panic and try to save his own face. Well, they had me figured all wrong."[70] JFK exercised his fury by firing Dulles, Bissell and Deputy Director, Charles Cabbell, and signing a series of National Security Action Memoranda that aimed to assert presidential control over covert operations.[71] After the Bay of Pigs, the president declared privately he would "shatter the CIA into a thousand pieces and scatter it to the winds." As for the Joint Chiefs, he would "never trust the generals again."[72]

Part two of the Cuba saga, the October 1962 Missile Crisis, began with the discovery via U-2 surveillance aircraft of dozens of medium and intermediate range missiles capable of launching nuclear weapons at the United States. Castro sought the weapons as a means of defense against ongoing CIA efforts to topple his government; Khrushchev obliged partly to gain strategic leverage on Berlin. The Missile Crisis is another familiar story often half told—beginning with the Kennedy-Khrushchev relationship that proved crucial to its resolution. Relations between the two men unfolded through not only contentious public pronouncements, but also secret correspondence that began after their first summit in Vienna in June 1961, a tense affair marked by bellicose rhetoric over the fate of Berlin. That fall, Khrushchev penned a 26-page epistle from the shore of his Black Sea retreat. After suggesting that Kennedy would appreciate the site's beauty, Khrushchev confronted the awful responsibility that had befallen them, leading their nations under the threatening shadow of nuclear destruction. Invoking a biblical metaphor, the Soviet leader proposed a relationship in which they would steer the global ark of "the clean and unclean" to a safe and secure future. Receiving the newspaper-wrapped dispatch from press secretary Pierre Salinger, Kennedy responded immediately from his oceanside haven in Hyannis Port.[73]

It went on from there. By November 1963, they had exchanged 21 letters, a consistent theme of which were the hardline forces each man faced to escalate the Cold War. Throughout the terrifying 13 days of the Cuban Missile Crisis, Khrushchev faced pressure from generals in the Kremlin to strike the United States. Simultaneously, despite casualties potentially counted in millions, Kennedy endured relentless arguments for military action from the Joint Chiefs who dominated the National Security Council's ExCom. The loudest voice in the room, Air Force Chief General Curtis LeMay, argued for bombing the missile sites. Late in the crisis, a Soviet surface-to-air missile shot down a U-2 plane, killing the pilot and ratcheting up the pressure for reprisal. "There was the feeling," Robert Kennedy later recalled, "that the noose was tightening on all of us, on Americans, on mankind, and that the bridges to escape were crumbling."[74] Without presidential authorization, LeMay ordered his bombers beyond their turn-around points over the Arctic and toward Soviet airspace, and test-fired an unarmed missile. Khrushchev's men saw these moves as provocation and pressured him to respond. At the White House, General LeMay argued that the president's "quarantine," a naval blockade of Cuba coupled with an ultimatum to remove the missile sites, signaled American weakness—"almost as bad as appeasement at Munich"—a cutting reference for Kennedy, whose father had been complicit in that seminal moment of Hitler appeasement in 1938. "Can you imagine LeMay saying a thing like that?" he said to advisor Kenny O'Donnell. "Those brass hats have one great advantage in their favor," Kennedy brooded. "If we listen to them and do what they want us to do, none of us will be alive later to tell them they were wrong." As James Douglass has argued, the two leaders' back-channel appreciation of the pressures each was under provides an essential window into understanding their exercise of mutual restraint in resolving the crisis.[75]

It is striking that months earlier, Kennedy had invited a very different set of voices to the White House to discuss the subject of nuclear arms. On May 1, 1962 the president listened as a delegation of the Society of Friends pressed him on his stated commitment to "general and complete nuclear disarmament." The Quakers pointed out the contradiction between his aspirations for a "peace race" and the recent resumption of nuclear testing. On this, Kennedy did not disagree. He then raised the recent Navy recommendation that a new Polaris submarine be named the "William Penn," recognizing the awful contradiction in naming a weapon capable of killing millions for a Christian pacifist. "I can assure you that this will not be done." The conversation covered a range of matters, attendees recalling the president did far more listening than talking. When Kenny O'Donnell interrupted to announce his next appointment, Kennedy said, "Let them wait. I'm learning things from these Quakers." When the president did speak, he repeatedly referenced the pressures he faced from the

Pentagon, one attendee characterizing Kennedy as feeling "frustrated and trapped" by the war hawks.[76]

In the harrowing hours of October 1962, he was surrounded not by Quakers but militarists. As America's children ducked-and-covered, with the activation of plans to keep the federal government running after the apocalypse at the Greenbrier Nuclear Bunker in West Virginia, Robert Kennedy conveyed to Soviet Ambassador Anatoly Dobrynin that the president believed the situation was spinning out of his control. As Khrushchev later wrote, Dobrynin informed him that Kennedy even feared that if he did not use military force, the generals might seize power. It was in this dire moment that Dobrynin was authorized to accept a deal that surely would look lopsided to Soviet generals and Castro: removal of the Cuban sites in exchange for a public pledge to not invade and the promise to withdraw U.S. missiles from Turkey—kept secret so as to ensure that Kennedy could appear the victor. Hopeful of working with the president for another six years to improve the U.S.–Soviet relationship, sensitive to the reelection pressures Kennedy faced, Khrushchev accepted a deal that proved critical to his own fall from power less than a year after JFK's assassination.[77]

Hiding in plain sight has been clear evidence of a sustained pattern of Kennedy the peacemaker. Rarely mentioned in public remembrances of Kennedy and Cuba is the secret back-channel communication with Castro after the missile crisis that aimed at a more constructive relationship following his reelection.[78] Similarly, Kennedy's *ich bin ein Berliner* declaration that all peoples stood with free West Berlin is enshrined in the iconography of the Cold War, alongside his fearful July 1961 warning of the increasing possibility of nuclear war over the defense of the city. Eclipsed is the president who refused the generals' recommended military response to the building of the Berlin Wall.[79] JFK's break with Cold War orthodoxy continued in Southeast Asia. In Laos, the CIA had been supporting military strongman Phoumi Nosavan who could, so they believed, fend off a growing communist insurgency. Publicly, Kennedy spoke of holding the line in Laos and stationed troops in the region as a show of resolve—even as he resisted Pentagon calls for combat forces, ended support for Nosavan, and badgered the State Department to negotiate a fragile coalition government that represented all factions, including the communist Pathet Lao.[80]

In Vietnam, the consensus has long held that Kennedy laid the groundwork for a disastrous war by sending an additional 15,000 American soldiers to South Vietnam, publicly supporting the corrupt Ngo Dinh Diem, and then most fatally, authorizing Diem's overthrow in the fall of 1963 that firmly bound U.S. policy to the Saigon government and the defense of South Vietnam. Other scholars have argued convincingly that Kennedy's independent foreign policy was also underway in Vietnam—indeed, was long in the making. His 1951 visit to the country and discussions with diplomat Edmund Gullion informed Kennedy's longstanding opposition to western intervention.[81] Even as he sent additional forces to Vietnam, in the spring of 1962 the president demanded a withdrawal plan from the Joint Chiefs. By the time the withdrawal plan— National Security Action Memorandum 263—was approved on October 11,

1963, the president had to write much of it himself, continually rejecting the generals' longer timetable and accompanying military escalation. Conversations with advisors, Washington figures like Representative Tip O'Neil, Senator Mike Mansfield, and journalist Charles Bartlett, as well as Pentagon documents all point in the same direction: American troops would be gone from Vietnam by the end of 1965.[82] General Maxwell Taylor remembered the singular voice opposing escalation in 1963: "I don't recall anyone who was strongly against [sending ground troops], except one man and that was the President. The President just didn't want to be convinced that this was the right thing to do."[83] On November 26, 1963, President Lyndon Johnson signed National Security Action Memorandum 273. Although it indicated "continuity" with the previous policy, in fact Kennedy had rejected a document that called for intensified military activity in Vietnam.[84]

We Are All Mortal

> JFK. JFK the murder and the aftermath
> Everything that was before was not after that.
>
> —Paul Kantner[85]

After the standoff in Cuba, Kennedy and Khrushchev wrestled with how they might transform the urgency summoned by the crisis into a diplomatic breakthrough. Norman Cousins, editor of the *Saturday Review* and president of the Committee for a SANE Nuclear Policy, served as Kennedy's emissary to Khrushchev and the Vatican, where Pope John XXIII lent encouraging support. After Cousins reported Khrushchev's willingness to negotiate on issues of nuclear disarmament, JFK offered this blunt observation:

> One of the ironic things about this entire situation is that Mr. Khrushchev and I occupy approximately the same political positions inside our governments. He would like to prevent a nuclear war but is under severe pressure from his hard-line crowd, which interprets every move in that direction as appeasement. I've got similar problems.[86]

Kennedy therefore had no illusions when he arrived at American University June 10, 1963 to deliver the commencement address billed as "a Strategy of Peace," the contents of which were known only to close advisors. An aspirational vision of a more secure world, the address began with a paradigm-challenging redefinition:

> What kind of peace do I mean? What kind of peace do we seek? Not a Pax Americana enforced on the world by American weapons of war … the kind of peace that makes life on earth worth living, the kind that enables men and nations to grow and to hope and to build a better life for their children …

Humanizing America's enemy, the president praised Russian achievements and declared their abhorrence of war borne of the staggering price paid in World

War II—and then challenged Americans to "reexamine our own attitude" toward the Cold War. Acknowledging the repugnance of communism, the president rejected the calcified logic of the arms race and the inevitability of armed conflict with the Soviet Union that could likely, even *logically* climax in nuclear war. Fatalist assumptions had become matters of faith for national security hardliners.[87] Referencing the "total war" nearly triggered by Cuba, Kennedy laid bare the stakes: "All we have built, all we have worked for, would be destroyed in the first 24 hours." Americans should reject the deadly nuclear embrace, "for, in the final analysis, our most basic common link is that we all inhabit this small planet. We all breathe the same air. We all cherish our children's future. And we are all mortal."[88]

"One of the great documents of the twentieth century," Robert McNamara called it,[89] the speech received a lukewarm reception at home, while Khrushchev ordered an unprecedented nationwide broadcast. The address served as Kennedy's most explicit call for an end to Cold War thinking and a redirection of the resources toward more positive ends. In that spirit, the president proposed in September a joint U.S.-Soviet manned mission to the moon.[90] More immediately, the speech launched an effort to win Senate ratification of the Partial Test Ban Treaty (PTBT). Signed July 25, 1963, the agreement banned the testing of nuclear weapons in the atmosphere, underwater, and outer space. The first breakthrough in the nearly two-decade arms race, the treaty met strong criticism from Edward Teller, the press, retired generals, and the Joint Chiefs. Constituent mail to senators voting on ratification ran 15–1 in opposition.[91] Undeterred, the president mounted a vigorous campaign, supported by the anti-nuclear movement, to turn popular sentiment around. In a televised address, he declared, "Yesterday a shaft of light cut into the darkness" of the nuclear threat. While acknowledging the treaty's limitations, the president hailed it as a step in reviving the long-abandoned goal of international control of nuclear weapons—and more immediately, confronting "the fears and dangers of radioactive fallout." The treaty, he said, was for the "children and grandchildren with cancer in their bones, with leukemia in their blood, or with poison in their lungs" resulting from nuclear testing. The Senate ratified the treaty 80–19, capping one of the most remarkable legislative feats ever earned by a president, and as Kennedy told aides, the proudest achievement of his public life.[92]

At 12:21 p.m. Central Standard Time on Friday, November 22, 1963, shots rang out in Dealey Plaza in the heart of Dallas, Texas—a city seething with far-right extremist hatred, much of it aimed at the President of the United States.[93] Nearly an hour later, CBS anchor Walter Cronkite labored to deliver the news: *From Dallas, Texas, the flash apparently official: President Kennedy died at 1 p.m. Central Standard Time.* In September 1964, the official report of the Warren Commission investigating the assassination concluded that Lee Harvey Oswald acted alone, firing from a "sniper's nest" on the sixth floor of the Texas School Book Depository Building. Almost immediately, independent investigators, forensics experts, and other scholars launched a methodical dismemberment of the Warren Report. In 1978, a congressional inquiry echoed much of their work, concluding that the president had been murdered by a conspiracy likely involving the Mafia. More than a half-century later, aided by countless books and films (some better than others to be sure), the event had seeped so deeply into the national consciousness that elements of a plot to murder John F. Kennedy still ring familiar: shots from the Grassy Knoll; forensic shredding of the "magic bullet theory"—linchpin of Oswald as the lone gunman; the FBI's deliberate investigatory malfeasance; Jack Ruby shooting on live television the accused killer of the president.

Americans who were alive on 11/22/63 remained haunted by the JFK assassination even decades later. As the sixties transpired and the nation sank deeper into the tragedy of Vietnam, many became most interested in the *why*—the Cold War context of powerful forces arrayed against Kennedy that provided the most likely motive for his murder. As James Douglass has argued, the details of how the president was murdered and by whom, while fascinating, obscure the central questions of *Why He Died and Why It Matters*. That they remain officially unanswered leaves them suspended in what he calls an *unspeakable*, enduring void of national complicity.[94] From that abyss, for decades on November 22, historians, pundits masquerading as historians, and journalists from FOX to MSNBC dutifully dismissed "the conspiracy kooks and nuts"[95]—that is, learned experts who had been dissecting the assassination for years. It served as an annual reminder of the deeply inscribed denial that frames one of the most important events of modern American history.

This discussion merely sketches the outlines of the consensus of serious assassination scholars, that a tight circle of men associated with the CIA, the Mob, and a nexus of military officials and figures on the far-right established the circumstances and means for Kennedy's elimination. The president's turn away from war in Cuba and Southeast Asia, coupled with his aspiration to end the Cold War, threatened the interests of the military industrial complex, and as Kennedy himself worried, marked him for death. The president's grim fixation on his mortality was driven by more than the severe health issues that long afflicted him.[96] Intersecting with an intuitive sense of his demise were equally strong fears of an overthrow of U.S. civilian government by the military. It was why he encouraged Hollywood director John Frankenheimer to make *Seven Days in May*, a film dramatizing a rightwing general resembling a composite of Curtis LeMay and Edwin Walker leading a military plot to topple a peace-making president. Determined to see the book made into a film, Kennedy took his family to Hyannis Port on a weekend in July 1963, making the White House available for filming. As press secretary Pierre Salinger later recalled to David Talbot, "Kennedy wanted *Seven Days in May* to be made as a warning to the generals. The President said, 'The first thing I'm going to tell my successor is, "Don't trust the military men—even on military matters."'"[97]

As 1960s rock musician Paul Kantner put it, the Kennedy assassination "shut the door"—on an era of endless possibility, on the hopeful expectations and innocence that defined America in those years, on what the sixties might have been. Secretary of Defense Robert McNamara, who would preside over the escalation of the war in Vietnam that JFK tried to stop, put it this way: "If he had lived, the world would have been different … [It] would have been a less dangerous world, I'm certain of that."[98]

Notes

1 John F. Kennedy, "Address at a Luncheon Meeting of the National Industrial Conference Board (33)," February 13, 1961, Public Papers of the Presidents: John F. Kennedy, www.jfklibrary.org/learn/about-jfk/life-of-john-f-kennedy/john-f-kennedy-quotations, retrieved September 4, 2018.

2 Arthur C. Clarke, quoted in Gerard Degroot, *Dark Side of the Moon: The Magnificent Madness of the American Lunar Quest* (New York: New York University Press, 2006), 63.

3 Fred Kaplan, *Wizards of Armageddon* (Stanford, CA: Stanford University Press), 135.

4 International Affairs Seminars of Washington, "American Reactions to Crisis: Examples of Pre-Sputnik and Post-Sputnik Attitudes and of the Reaction to other Events Perceived as Threats," October 15–16, 1958, U.S. President's Committee on Information Activities Abroad (Sprague Committee) Records, 1959–1961, Box 5, A83-10, Dwight D. Eisenhower Library, Abilene, Kansas; and Martin Walker, *The Cold War: A History* (New York: Holt, 1993), 114.

5 Charles Wilson, quoted in Gerard Degroot, *Dark Side of the Moon: The Magnificent Madness of America's Lunar Quest* (New York: New York University Press, 2006), 63.

6 Named for its chairman, H. Rowan Gaither, former president of the Ford Foundation.

7 James Carroll, *House of War: The Pentagon and the Disastrous Rise of American Power* (New York: Houghton Mifflin, 2006), 220–225.

8 Chalmers Roberts, "Enormous Arms Outlay is Hekd Vital to Survival," *Washington Post*, December 20, 1957, Sec. A, 1, 19.

9 Gerard H. Clarfield and William M. Wiecek, *Nuclear America: Military and Civilian Nuclear Power in the United States, 1940–1960* (New York: Harper and Row, 1984), 159.

10 John Newhouse, *War and Peace in the Nuclear Age* (New York: Vintage, 1990), 146; and Dwight D. Eisenhower, January 17, 1961, www.eisenhower.archives.gov/research/online_documents/farewell_address/Reading_Copy.pdf, retrieved September 4, 2018.

11 Carroll, 225–226; and Greg Thielman, "The Missile Gap Myth and Its Progeny," Arms Control Association, May 3, 2011, www.armscontrol.org/act/2011_05/Thielmann, retrieved September 4, 2018.

12 Arthur M. Schlesinger, Jr., *The Politics of Hope and The Better Heritage: American Liberalism in the 1960s* (Princeton, NJ: Princeton University Press, 1963), 106–108.

13 "The Kitchen Debate—Transcript," July 24, 1959, www.cia.gov/library/reading-room/docs/1959-07-24.pdf, retrieved September 4, 2018.

14 "Remarks of Senator John F. Kennedy at Allentown, Pennsylvania, October 28, 1960, www.jfklibrary.org/archives/other-resources/john-f-kennedy-speeches/allentown-pa-19601028, retrieved June 5, 2021.

15 "John F. Kennedy accepting the Liberal Party Nomination," New York City, New York, September 14, 1960, www.jfklibrary.org/Research/Research-Aids/JFK-Speeches/Liberal-Party-Nomination-NYC_19600914.aspx, retrieved September 5, 2018.

16 Theodore C. Sorensen, *Kennedy* (New York: Harper Row, 1965), 342–324.

17 James Tobin, "JFK at the Union: The Unknown Story of the Peace Corps Speech," University of Michigan, http://peacecorps.umich.edu/Tobin.html, retrieved September 5, 2018.

18 Thurston Clarke, *Ask Not: The Inauguration of John F. Kennedy and the Speech that Changed America* (New York: Henry Holt, 2004), 173.

19 Sorensen, 215–216.

20 John F. Kennedy Inaugural Address, January 20, 1961, www.jfklibrary.org/Research/ Research-Aids/Ready-Reference/JFK-Quotations/Inaugural-Address.aspx, retrieved September 12, 2018.

21 Arthur Schlesinger, Jr., *A Thousand Days: John F. Kennedy in the White House* (New York: Houghton Mifflin, 1965), 166.

22 John Mendez, quoted in Anthony W. Ponton, "John F. Kennedy and West Virginia, 1960–1963," (Marshall Digital Scholar, Theses, Dissertations and Capstones, Marshall University, 2004), 45; Ken Hechler, *West Virginia Memories of President Kennedy*, private printing, 27, in Ponton, 60.

23 Ponton, Chapter 3 and 4.

24 Rachel Carson, *Silent Spring* (New York: Houghton Mifflin, 1962).

25 Ibid., 8.

26 Quoted in Chris J. Magoc, *Chronology of Americans and the Environment* (Santa Barbara, CA: ABC-CLIO Press, 2011), 106.

27 Douglas Brinkley, "Rachel Carson and JFK, An Environmental Tag Team," *Audubon Magazine*, May–June 2012, www.audubon.org/magazine/may-june-2012/rachel-carson-and-jfk-environmental-tag-team, retrieved September 13, 2018.

28 Alan V. Howitz, "How an Age of Anxiety Became an Age of Depression," *The Milbank Quarterly* 88, no. 1 (March 2010), 112–138.

29 Betty Friedan, *The Feminine Mystique* (New York: W.W. Norton, 1963), Chapter 1.

30 Ibid.

31 Ruth Rosen, *The World Split Open: How the Modern Women's Movement Changed America* (New York: Penguin, 2000), 5–7.

32 Rosen, 6–7 (Friedan quote, 7).

33 Elizabeth Singer More, "Report of the President's Commission on the Status of Women: Background, Content, Significance," www.radcliffe.harvard.edu/sites/ default/files/documents/report_of_the_presidents_commission_on_the_status_of_ women_background_content_significance.pdf. retrieved September 14, 2018.

34 Rosen, 64–68.

35 Singer More, "Report of the President's Commission on the Status of Women.

36 James Baldwin, "My Dungeon Shook," in *The Fire Next Time* (New York: The Dial Press, 1963), 23–24.

37 Ibid., 22, 82–83.

38 Stewart Burns, *Social Movements of the 1960s: Searching for Democracy* (New York: Twayne, Simon and Schuster Macmillan, 1990), 11.

39 David Halberstam, *The Children* (New York: Random House, 1998), prologue, 3–4.

40 Diane Nash, "Interview," in *The New Negro*, ed. Matthew Ahman (Notre Dame: Fides, 1961), quoted in Peter B. Levy, *Let Freedom Ring: A Documentary History of the Civil Rights Movement* (Westport, CT: Praeger, 1992), 69.

41 SNCC, "Statement of Purpose," April 1960, in Levy, 74.

42 John Lewis, with Michael D'Orso, *Walking With the Wind: A Memoir of the Movement* (New York: Simon and Schuster, 1998), 134–135, 144–145.

43 Raymond Arsenault, *Freedom Riders: 1961 and the Struggle for Racial Justice* (New York: Oxford University Press, 2006), 143.

44 Stanley Nelson, *Freedom Riders*. American Experience, PBS documentary, 2011.

45 Lewis, *Walking with the Wind*, 134.

46 Ibid., 150–151.

47 Tony Gonzalez, "Accidental Advocate Risked Life to Fight Segregation." *USA Today*, May 26, 2013, www.usatoday.com/story/news/nation/2013/05/26/accidental-advocate-fought-segregation/2362391, retrieved September 16, 2018.

48 "Meet the Players: Freedom Riders," PBS: American Experience, n.d., www.pbs.org/ wgbh/americanexperience/features/meet-players-freedom-riders, retrieved March 21, 2021.

49 See Arsenault's definitive account of the Freedom Rides.

50 David Talbot, *Brothers: The Hidden History of the Kennedy Years* (New York: Free Press, 2007), 152.

51 Barnett, JFK Library and Museum, http://microsites.jfklibrary.org/olemiss/chronology; and Detroit's Great Rebellion, www.detroits-great-rebellion.com/James-Meredith.html, accessed September 16, 2018.

52 James W. Silver, *Mississippi: The Closed Society* (Jackson, MI: University Press of Mississippi, 1966), 119–120.

53 Talbot, 152–159.

54 John Neff et al, "A Brief Historical Contextualization of the Confederate Monument at the University of Mississippi," University of Mississippi, May 2016, p. 5, https://history.olemiss.edu/wp-content/uploads/sites/6/2017/08/A-Brief-Historical-Contextualization-of-the-Confederate-Monument-at-the-University-of-Mississippi.pdf, retrieved September 16, 2018; and Talbot, 154–155.

55 Al Kuettner, "Ole Miss enrolls Meredith after riots kill 2," UPI, October 1, 1962, retrieved September 16, 2018 at www.upi.com/blog/2012/09/20/On-this-day-in-history-James-Meredith-barred-from-Ole-Miss/3931348149557;   and   Talbot, 155–162.

56 Jeremy D. Mayer, "LBJ Fights the White Backlash," *Prologue: Quarterly of the National Archives and Records Administration* 33, no. 1 (Spring 2001), 8, quoting Peter O'Donnell, Jr., "Progress Report #2," Letter to Goldwater state chairmen, September 23, 1963, box 8, W Series, GP.

57 Talbot, 160–162.

58 Henry Hampton and Steve Fayer, *Voices of Freedom: An Oral History of the Civil Rights Movement from the 1950s through the 1980s* (New York: Bantam, 1991, reissue), 125.

59 Martin Luther King, Jr., "Letter from Birmingham Jail," in the *New Leader*, June 24, 1963, 3–11, quoted in Levy, 110–114.

60 Henry Hampton, producer. *Eyes on the Prize: No Easy Walk, 1961–1963* (Washington, DC: Public Broadcasting Service, documentary, 60 minutes, 1987).

61 John F. Kennedy, "Address to the Nation on Civil Rights," June 11, 1963, retrieved September   16,   2018,   www.jfklibrary.org/learn/about-jfk/historic-speeches/televised-address-to-the-nation-on-civil-rights.

62 John F. Kennedy, United States Senate, Washington, DC, July 2, 1957, JFK Presidential Library   and   Museum,   at   www.jfklibrary.org/Research/Research-Aids/JFK-Speeches/United-States-Senate-Imperialism_19570702.aspx, retrieved September 16, 2018; and Kennedy, U.S. Senate speech, April 6, 1954, quoted by Michael O'Brien, *John F. Kennedy: A Biography* (New York: Thomas Dunne Books, 2005), 353.

63 Philip E. Muehlenbeck, *Betting on the Africans: John F. Kennedy's Courting of African Nationalist Leaders* (New York: Oxford University Press, 2012), 34–36, citing Kennedy, "The Proper Role of Foreign Policy in the 1956 Campaign," remarks to the World Affairs Council, Los Angeles, September 21, 1956.

64 Lumumba was assassinated in December 1960 with CIA complicity.

65 Muehlenbeck's *Betting on the Africans* offers a comprehensive look at JFK's commitment to forming alliances with African nationalist leaders. Among the best works reexamining Kennedy's foreign policy more broadly are David Talbot's *Brothers*, James W. Douglass, *JFK and the Unspeakable: Why He Died and Why It Matters* (New York: Orbis, 2008); Jeffrey D. Sachs, *To Move the World: JFK's Quest for Peace* (New York: Random House, 2013); John M. Newman, *JFK and Vietnam: Deception, Intrigue, and the Struggle for Power* (New York: Grand Central Pub, 1992); David Kaiser, *American Tragedy: Kennedy, Johnson, and the Origins of the Vietnam War* (New York: Belknap Press, 2000); see also the work of Peter Dale Scott and former CIA official Fletcher Prouty.

66 Christopher Hickham, "The Kennedy Administration's Alliance for Progress and the Burdens of the Marshall Plan," *Federal History* 5 (2013), 75–98.

67 James DiEugenio, *Destiny Betrayed: JFK, Cuba, and the Garrison Case* (New York: Skyhorse, 1992, 2nd ed. 2012), 33–37.

68 Rostow, quoted in Bradley Podliska, *Acting Alone: A Scientific Study of American Hegemony and Unilateral Use-of-Force Decision-Making* (Lanham, MD: Rowman & Littlefield, 2010), 166.

69 Talbot, 46–47.

70 Kenneth O'Donnell and David F. Powers, *Johnny, We Hardly Knew Ye* (New York: Little Brown, 1972), 274.

71 National Security Action Memoranda 55, 56, 57, signed by the president June 28, 1961, www.jfklibrary.org/archives/other-resources/national-security-action-memoranda-nsams, retrieved June 17, 2020; and Peter Kornbluh, ed., *Bay of Pigs Declassified* (New York: New Press, 1998), 269–275, 293–305, 319–322.

72 Tom Wicker, John W. Finney, Max Frankel, E. W. Kenworthy, "C.I.A." Maker of Policy, or Tool?" *New York Times*, April 25, 1966, 20, quoted in Douglass, 15.

73 Douglass, 20–31, 59–60.

74 Robert Kennedy, *Thirteen Days* (New York, Signet, 1969), 98.

75 O'Donnell and Powers, *Johnny, We Hardly Knew Ye*, 318, quoted in Douglass, 29.

76 Douglass, 322–326.

77 Nikita Khrushchev, *Khrushchev Remembers* (New York: Little Brown, 1970), 497–498, quoted in Douglass, 27.

78 "Kennedy Sought Dialogue With Cuba," National Security Archive, November 24, 2003, https://nsarchive2.gwu.edu/NSAEBB/NSAEBB103/index.htm, retrieved March 23, 2021.

79 Talbot, 69–70; and Douglass, 109–113.

80 Douglass, 101.

81 Daniel Ellsberg, *Secrets: A Memoir of Vietnam and the Pentagon Papers* (New York: Viking, 2002), 196.

82 Douglas, 181; and National Security Action Memorandum No. 263, October 11, 1963, *Foreign Relations of the United States, 1961–1963, Volume IV: Vietnam: August–December 1963* (Washington, DC: Government Printing Office, 1991), 396; Pentagon documents calling for withdrawal are referenced by Arthur Schlesinger, Jr., *Robert Kennedy and His Times* (New York: Ballentine, 1978), 82.

83 Maxwell Taylor, recorded interview by L. J. Hackman, November 13, 1969, 47, cited by Schlesinger, *Robert Kennedy*, 761.

84 James K. Galbraith, "Exit Strategy: In 1963, JFK Ordered a Complete Withdrawal from Vietnam," *Boston Review*, September 1, 2003, http://bostonreview.net/us/galbraith-exit-strategy-vietnam, retrieved June 12, 2020.

85 Paul Kantner, "Introduction," in Jeff Tamarkin, *Got a Revolution: The Turbulent Flight of Jefferson Airplane* (New York: Atria Books, 2005), viii, 19.

86 Quoted in Talbot, 208–209.

87 To cite two examples: Leading strategist Herman Kahn spoke in *Life* of "acceptable losses" of up to 50 million in a nuclear "exchange." At a Washington dinner party in July 1961, General LeMay told a senator's wife that nuclear war was inevitable by year's end, recommending the desert southwest as the safest refuge.

88 John F. Kennedy, "Commencement Address at American University," June 10, 1963, www.jfklibrary.org/Asset-Viewer/BWC7I4C9QUmLG9J6I8oy8w.aspx, retrieved September 19, 2018.

89 McNamara quoted by Talbot, 206.

90 W. D. Kay, "John F. Kennedy and the Two Faces of the U.S. Space Program, 1961–1963," *Presidential Studies Quarterly* 28, no. 3 (Summer 1998), 573–586; and John M. Logsdon, "John F. Kennedy and NASA," National Aeronautics and Space Administration, May 22, 2015, www.nasa.gov/feature/john-f-kennedy-and-nasa, retrieved January 3, 2020.

91 Douglass, 52.
92 President John F. Kennedy, Radio and Television Address to the American People on the Nuclear Test Ban Treaty, July 26, 1963, www.jfklibrary.org/Research/Research-Aids/JFK-Speeches/Nuclear-Test-Ban-Treaty_19630726.aspx, retrieved September 19, 2018.
93 Bill Minutaglio and Steven L. Davis, *Dallas 1963* (New York: Twelve Books, 2014).
94 Douglass, Introduction.
95 The quote belongs to Chris Matthews MSNBC, ca. 2010.
96 Ralph G. Martin, *A Hero for Our Times: An Intimate Story of the Kennedy Years* (New York: Ballantine, 1983), 503.
97 Quoted by Patrick Kiger, "The Movie that JFK Wanted Made, But Didn't Live to See," May 13, 2014, https://blogs.weta.org/boundarystones/2014/05/13/movie-jfk-wanted-made-didnt-live-see, retrieved September 20, 2018.
98 Kantner, quoted in Tamarkin, xix; McNamara, quoted in Talbot, 206.

Further Reading

Arsenault, Raymond. *Freedom Riders: 1961 and the Struggle for Racial Justice*. New York: Oxford University Press, 2006.

Baldwin, James. *The Fire Next Time*. New York: The Dial Press, 1963.

Burns, Stewart. *Social Movements of the 1960s: Searching for Democracy*. New York: Twayne, Simon and Schuster, 1990.

Carroll, James. *House of War: The Pentagon and the Disastrous Rise of American Power*. New York: Houghton Mifflin, 2006.

Carson, Rachel. *Silent Spring*. New York: Houghton Mifflin, 1962.

Clarfield, Gerard H., and William M. Wiecek. *Nuclear America: Military and Civilian Nuclear Power in the United States, 1940–1960*. New York: Harper and Row, 1984.

Clarke, Thurston. *Ask Not: The Inauguration of John F. Kennedy and the Speech that Changed America*. New York: Henry Holt, 2004.

Degroot, Gerard. *Dark Side of the Moon: The Magnificent Madness of America's Lunar Quest*. New York: New York University Press, 2006.

DiEugenio, James. *Destiny Betrayed: JFK, Cuba, and the Garrison Case*. New York: Skyhorse, 1992, 2nd ed. 2012.

Douglass, James W. *JFK and the Unspeakable: Why He Died and Why It Matters*. New York: Orbis, 2008.

Friedan, Betty. *The Feminine Mystique*. New York: W.W. Norton, 1963.

Halberstam, David. *The Children*. New York: Random House, 1998.

Hampton, Henry, and Steve Fayer. *Voices of Freedom: An Oral History of the Civil Rights Movement from the 1950s through the 1980s*. New York: Bantam, 1991.

Kaiser, David. *American Tragedy: Kennedy, Johnson, and the Origins of the Vietnam War*. New York: Belknap Press, 2000.

Kennedy, Robert. *Thirteen Days*. New York, Signet, 1969.

Levy, Peter B. *Let Freedom Ring: A Documentary History of the Civil Rights Movement*. Westport, CT: Praeger, 1992.

Lewis, John, with Michael D'Orso. *Walking With the Wind: A Memoir of the Movement*. New York: Simon and Schuster, 1998.

Martin, Ralph G. *A Hero for Our Times: An Intimate Story of the Kennedy Years*. New York: Ballantine, 1983.

Minutaglio, Bill, and Steven L. Davis. *Dallas 1963*. New York: Twelve Books, 2014.

Muehlenbeck, Philip E. *Betting on the Africans: John F. Kennedy's Courting of African Nationalist Leaders*. New York: Oxford University Press, 2012.

Newhouse, John. *War and Peace in the Nuclear Age*. New York: Vintage, 1990.

Newman, John M. *JFK and Vietnam: Deception, Intrigue, and the Struggle for Power*. New York: Grand Central Publishing, 1992.

Rosen, Ruth. *The World Split Open: How the Modern Women's Movement Changed America*. New York: Penguin, 2000.

Sachs, Jeffrey D. *To Move the World: JFK's Quest for Peace*. New York: Random House, 2013.

Schlesinger, Jr. Arthur J. *The Politics of Hope and The Better Heritage: American Liberalism in the 1960s*. Princeton, NJ: Princeton University Press, 1963.

Schlesinger, Jr. Arthur J. *A Thousand Days: John F. Kennedy in the White House*. New York: Houghton Mifflin, 1965.

Scott, Peter Dale. *Deep Politics and the Death of JFK*. Berkeley, CA: University of California Press, 1993.

Sorensen, Theodore C. *Kennedy*. New York: Harper Row, 1965.

Talbot, David. *Brothers: The Hidden History of the Kennedy Years*. New York: Free Press, 2007.

6   Mississippi to Saigon

The Tragedy of Lyndon Johnson and the Turning of the Sixties

With two key decisions within 48 hours of the Kennedy funeral, Lyndon Baines Johnson established the essential framework of his domestic and foreign policy, actions that profoundly influenced the course of the 1960s. In a moving address to Congress on November 27, 1963, the president gave voice to the nation's grief by vowing to pursue the unfinished domestic agenda of the slain Kennedy. As the resolute Texan put it, "*let us continya*," first by advancing passage of the civil rights bill then stalled in Congress. In an extended debate with advisors the night before, he was warned not to expend his considerable political capital— LBJ enjoyed 75 percent approval following the assassination—on the divisive issue of civil rights.[1] Other priorities would suffer from the enmity sure to be aroused among his fellow southerners. "Well," asked Johnson, "what the hell's the presidency for?"[2] Johnson's evolution on race had begun decades earlier with a teaching stint at a "Mexican School" in Cotulla, Texas, and then as state director of FDR's National Youth Administration. As a congressman in 1949, he arranged for the re-interment at Arlington National Cemetery of Felix Longoria, a World War II soldier of Mexican American descent whose family had been denied a burial request by a local funeral home "because the whites wouldn't like it."[3] Introducing himself now to Americans as their president in a moment of deep division over race, he appealed for "tolerance" and "mutual understanding," and called for passage of Kennedy's bill.[4] It was just the beginning. Building on JFK's legacy, Johnson would propel himself toward a resounding reelection around a visionary domestic agenda he called the Great Society.

The second action, mentioned only briefly that evening, promised an uninterrupted transition from Kennedy's foreign policy. "This nation," he declared, "will keep its commitments from South Vietnam to West Berlin."[5] Hidden inside the reassuring rhetoric of continuity was an abrupt policy shift. The nature of the U.S. commitment had changed significantly the day before when Johnson huddled with his national security team and quietly signed National Security Memorandum 273, which rescinded the Kennedy withdrawal plan signed weeks earlier, and authorized aggressive U.S. air and naval attacks against communist North Vietnam. Further, the goal was now an American victory, not merely supporting the Saigon government. Johnson told aide Bill Moyers the U.S. needed to "stand by our word. I want 'em to get off their butts and get out there in those

DOI: 10.4324/9781003160595-6

jungles and whip hell out of some Communists," declaring he would not be blamed for "losing" Vietnam as Truman had on China.[6] As Secretary of Defense Robert McNamara observed, LBJ was far more deferential to the generals and embraced the view that Vietnam was essential in the global struggle to contain Russia and China.[7]

Lyndon Johnson's signature that November morning proved portentous in launching what six years later he damned as that "bitch of a war."[8] The operations authorized by NSAM 273 led, purposefully, to the fateful incidents in the Gulf of Tonkin nine months later. In the spring of 1964, Pentagon officials devised a series of covert operations in North Vietnam, including attacks by South Vietnamese patrol boats against North Vietnamese coastal installations. To support these actions, the U.S. naval destroyer Maddox was deployed to the Gulf of Tonkin. On July 30–31, South Vietnamese and U.S. forces directed raids on two islands in the gulf. Two days later, after months of increasingly aggressive U.S.–South Vietnamese provocations, three North Vietnamese patrol boats began close observation of the Maddox, which attacked, prompting return torpedo fire. The next night, Johnson directed the USS *Turner Joy* to join the Maddox. Late on August 4, an unclear radar blip on the *Turner Joy* and pings bouncing from the *Maddox*'s rudder induced confusion aboard both vessels and a barrage of fire on a phantom enemy. The *Turner Joy* commander concluded that enemy contact was "very doubtful" and a "complete evaluation [should be made] before further action."[9]

The advice was ignored. Shortly before midnight, Johnson appeared on television to announce that American ships "on routine patrol" in "international waters" had been attacked by North Vietnamese forces. Following an address to Congress, the Gulf of Tonkin Resolution passed with just two dissenting votes. The measure had been drafted several months earlier, LBJ having ordered Bill Bundy, Assistant Secretary of State for the Far East, to draft "a war resolution to be sent to Congress when the moment was ripe."[10] The barely debated resolution gave the president full authority to launch a military escalation against communist forces that included ground troops, massive bombing, and much more. It was, he joked, "like Grandma's nightshirt—it covers everything."[11]

Although the Tonkin Gulf episode would bring utter devastation to Southeast Asia and tragedy for both Johnson and his country, in the short run it was shrewd political opportunism. It insulated the president from attacks by his Republican opponent, Arizona Senator Barry Goldwater, that he was ignoring the threat in Vietnam. Johnson could assert that he was confronting the communists even as he reassured Americans that he was not Goldwater, who offered the imprudent assertion that he would allow military commanders to use nuclear weapons. That message was driven home in a campaign ad in which a young girl stands in a field picking petals from a daisy as a voice intones, "TEN—NINE— EIGHT ..." culminating with a mushroom cloud. Out of the nuclear abyss came LBJ's voice imploring viewers "to make a world in which all of God's children can live ... We must either love each other. Or we must die." Over the black screen a voice warns ominously to vote for Johnson, or else.

With the launch of both the Great Society and the war in Southeast Asia, Lyndon Johnson reaffirmed the fatally antithetical pillars of Cold War liberalism: a vigorous federal government working to expand social and economic progress at home, coupled with the use of America's vast military power to suppress communism abroad. It was the foundation for a tragic presidency that would shape the larger trauma of the nation. A president who could reassure a grief-stricken nation and rekindle the soaring expectations of limitless progress at home, also proved capable of waging a senseless, savage war that would drive him from the White House and tear the nation apart.

"A Change Is Gonna Come"

The fulcrum of social and political change on which the sixties was about to turn was heard in pop music. In August 1963, producer Phil Spector and the Ronettes released "Be My Baby," one of the most influential songs in the history of rock and roll. In addition to its signature, much-imitated opening drum beat, the song featured richly layered vocals and an echoing, fully immersive instrumentation that shattered the limits of what seemed possible in a recording studio. The same month, Bob Dylan's "Blowin' in the Wind," with its urgent questioning around matters of war and human freedom, further stirred the currents of social change in the air. In February 1964, the Beatles landed in New York City for their first U.S. tour, lifting the mood of a grieving nation and changing American music forever. One month later, soul music legend Sam Cooke included a song on his new album that was inspired by both Dylan's classic, and a painful experience a few months earlier. Having made a phone reservation at a Shreveport, Louisiana Holiday Inn, Cooke and his band were turned away upon arriving at the whites-only motel and later arrested for disturbing the peace. The musical result was "A Change is Gonna Come," composed instantly, as if it had been waiting for Cooke to receive it from the muse.[12] Unlike any of his Top 40 hits, "A Change is Gonna Come" featured elaborate strings, horns, timpani, and complex orchestration. The song's determined refrain gave it an anthemic, timeless quality, even as it spoke to the tidal force of history on the move in 1964.

A different tune was playing in the United States Senate that spring. In late March, southern senators launched a filibuster of the civil rights bill that had passed the House of Representatives. With Democrats divided, Johnson knew the measure needed Republican support. He charged the man soon to be his vice president, Minnesota Senator and civil rights champion Hubert Humphrey, with reeling in Republican Minority Leader, Everett Dirksen. "You make up your mind now," he commanded, "that you've got to spend time with Ev Dirksen. You've got to let him have a piece of the action." If necessary, Humphrey was to "kiss Dirksen's ass on the capitol steps."[13] It was a brilliant LBJ masterstroke: to have the leader of the party of Lincoln, a senator from Lincoln's own state of Illinois, stake a shared moral claim to the bill that would in effect complete the martyred president's work.

There was no courting a bloc of southern Democrats who stood in rock solid opposition. West Virginia's Robert Byrd, the pride of South Carolina, Strom Thurmond, and Georgia's Richard Russell led segregationists in a 60-day filibuster aimed at killing the bill. An expert filibusterer of federal lynching laws, Russell promised Georgia voters he would, "go as far and make as great a sacrifice [as necessary] to preserve and insure white supremacy" in his state.[14] But as Dirksen declared in the spring of 1964, "stronger than all the armies is an idea whose time has come." Speaking for a filibuster-ending cloture vote, Dirksen compared the civil rights bill to woman's suffrage, child labor and other historic measures that initially faced great opposition. "The time has come," said Dirksen, "for equality of opportunity in sharing in government, in education, and in employment. It will not be stayed or denied. It is here!" The measure's most poignant moment arrived when the roll call vote to end the filibuster came to California Senator Clair Engle. Suffering terminal brain cancer and unable to speak, Engle slowly raised his arm and pointed to his right eye.[15] The final vote on the legislation ten days later was anti-climactic, and overwhelming: two-thirds of Democrats, and even higher numbers of Republicans voted to end discrimination on the basis of race and gender in the United States.

Alongside the legislative drama on Capitol Hill were life-and-death events unfolding in St. Augustine, Florida. One of America's premier tourist destinations, St. Augustine seemed an unlikely site of civil rights confrontation. Yet almost ten years after *Brown*, even minimal school integration here met violent Klan resistance. In 1963 the city's segregated quadricentennial celebration was marked by NAACP protests. Its Youth Council began staging sit-ins, one ending with four activists sentenced to "reform" school. Release of the "St. Augustine Four" came only after appeals from figures like Jackie Robinson. As the Klan continued to provoke violent confrontations, local leader Dr. Robert Hayling issued an appeal to college students to descend on St. Augustine for a series of nonviolent protests. Joining the students were several well-heeled Boston women, including Mary Parkman Peabody, the mother of Massachusetts Governor Endicott Peabody, whose arrest at a sit-in brought St. Augustine more unwanted attention.[16]

Deploying resources to the city, the Southern Christian Leadership Conference organized nightly demonstrations that triggered more Klan assaults, one nearly killing Andrew Young. Swim-ins on segregated white beaches incited further violence. On June 11, Dr. King took part in one of a growing number of demonstrations at the segregated Monson Motor Lodge, prompting his arrest. King then appealed to his long-time compatriot Rabbi Israel Dresner, urging him to "send as many rabbis as you can" to St. Augustine. A week later, Dresner led 15 other Jewish clerics in a motel "pray-in," resulting in the largest mass arrest of rabbis in American history. In a public letter explaining their actions, the rabbis wrote, "We came as Jews who remember the millions of faceless people who stood quietly, watching the smoke rise from Hitler's crematoria."[17] That same day, activists staged a swim-in at the Monson swimming pool, precipitating one of the era's dramatic moments: desperate to end the action at his motel, owner James Brock poured muriatic acid into a pool of protesters. The Senate voted for the Civil Rights Act that afternoon.

"The Decisive Battleground": Mississippi, Selma, and the Struggle for Voting Rights

In November 1963, Paul Johnson snarled his way to the Mississippi governor's mansion declaring the NAACP stood for, "Niggers, Apes, Alligators, Coons and Possums." "The only real and truly white state left in this nation is ours," he declared.[18] He was correct in one sense: 42 percent of Mississippians were African American, but less than seven percent were registered to vote.[19] As we have seen, a special kind of race hatred prevailed in the dark heart of the old Confederacy. In May 1955, minister George Lee had his face blown off for daring to encourage black voter registration. The local press called Lee's murder "an odd accident." On August 13 that same summer, two weeks before Emmett Till's body was dragged from the Tallahatchie River, voting rights activist Lamar Smith was murdered on the steps of a county courthouse. Over the next six years, dozens more black bodies floated down rivers or surfaced in Mississippi swamps; "common as a snake," observed a local.[20]

Change in Mississippi seemed as distant as the flat horizon until SNCC activist Bob Moses, a math teacher from the Bronx, arrived in Amite County in the summer of 1961 and met a successful farmer named Herbert Lee. One of few blacks in the county to own a car, Lee introduced Moses to black farmers with whom he discussed voter registration. On September 25, E. H. Hurst, a state legislator who had known Lee, shot him in cold blood in front of twelve witnesses. Claiming Lee had come at him with a tire iron, Hurst was never charged. One witness, black businessman Louis Allen, returned home one day to find three white men in his living room brandishing shotguns and threatening to kill him if he testified against Hurst. After initially backing Hurst in his lie, Allen confided the truth to Bob Moses and then the FBI, rendering himself a marked man. On January 31, 1964, one day before he planned to depart for Milwaukee, Louis Allen was assassinated.[21]

Devastated by the murders of Lee and Allen, Bob Moses led endless SNCC deliberations that winter toward the decision to proceed with the Mississippi Freedom Summer Project. One of the most courageous and visionary campaigns of the civil rights era, Freedom Summer was committed to three goals: register 200,000 new voters, conduct "Freedom Schools" to empower black Mississippians, and establish an interracial Mississippi Freedom Democratic Party (MFDP) that could challenge the all-white Democratic Party power structure. The Mississippi Democrats' delegation to the national party convention in Atlantic City that year had no plans to endorse Lyndon Johnson for reelection because of the president's support for civil rights. The interracial MFDP aimed to appeal to the Democratic National Committee and unseat the segregationists as the true Democrats from the Magnolia State.

That spring, more than 1,000 Freedom Summer volunteers from around the nation—ninety percent white—determined to spend the summer risking their lives in Mississippi. In mid-June, they descended on a small women's college in Ohio for intensive preparation. Within days of arriving, the volunteers learned that three of their peers had disappeared while investigating the burning of a church in Neshoba County. Former Freedom Rider James Chaney, social worker Andrew Goodman, and Michael Schwerner, who with his wife Rita, ran the CORE office in Meridian, had been arrested by Deputy Sheriff Cecil Price on an alleged traffic violation and released. While returning to Meridian, they were intercepted by Klansmen and murdered, their bodies dumped at the bottom of an earthen dam. For 44 days, the FBI-led search for their bodies made Freedom Summer a national story. It did not take a cynic to believe the FBI presence and national coverage were due to the white skin of Goodman and Schwerner. Deploying hundreds of America's white middle-class idealists to this perilous ground had in fact been a leading consideration in the decision to launch the project. They all knew the danger. As Mickey Schwerner told a friend early that summer:

> I belong right here in Mississippi. Nothing threatens peace among men like the idea of white supremacy … So this is the decisive battleground for America, and every young American who wants to have a part in the decision should be here.[22]

Battleground it was. More than 60 bombings or burnings of black churches, homes and business, 75 beatings, and three additional murders of black Mississippians marred Freedom Summer.

Through a hot and sultry Mississippi summer, through violent repression, despite surveillance and harassment by state authorities and FBI officials, the best of America went about the work of redeeming the nation. "Shack by shack," as Bruce Watson has recounted, "canvassers dragged the bottom of Mississippi and came up with just enough hope to keep them going." From throughout the nation came voluminous supplies, teams of medical clinicians, monetary support, and celebrities like folk singer Phil Ochs, basketball star Bill Russell, and actors Shirley MacLaine, Sidney Poitier, and Harry Belafonte. Welcomed into the homes of black sharecroppers, volunteers slept on wooden floors, ate southern food, and soaked in the Delta blues. They registered only 17,000 Mississippians, far short of project goals. Yet the seeds planted that summer bore 300,000 voters by 1975, by which time more black Mississippians had been elected to public office than any state in the nation.[23] Beyond those achievements were the profound impacts of Freedom Schools that unfolded in churches, on porches, and under the shade of magnolia trees. Young and old engaged in a curriculum that taught literacy and math skills, and was grounded in American history and civic education. One poignant incident recounted by Watson illustrates their transformative power. Volunteer Fran O'Brien turned her students one day to the founding of America:

Opening the 1930 text, she read, "The history of America really begins in England." "Now," she said, "what might be wrong with that sentence?" A hand went up.

"Well, lots of people came here who weren't from England."

Fran smiled. And what other countries might Americans have come from? Her students began touring the globe.

"France?"

"Yes."

"Italy?"

"Certainly."

"Germany?"

They moved on to Mexico and South America. Fran was impressed with their geography, but couldn't help wonder. After they tried China and India, Fran asked, "Well, what about Africa?" The classroom fell silent. Finally, a little girl raised her hand. "Does that count?" Fran began to blink back tears. "Yes," she said softly. "Yes, that counts."[24]

The dramatic climax to Freedom Summer came more than a thousand miles away in late August in Atlantic City, where 68 MFDP delegates looked to win the support of the convention's credentials committee and be seated on the floor. They brought dramatic evidence documenting the violent repression they had endured. On the boardwalk outside the convention hall, black and white activists maintained solemn demonstrations in support of the MFDP.[25] In the White House, Lyndon Johnson grew indignant. The MFDP's arrival threatened to upstage his celebratory re-nomination. Worse, in LBJ's estimation, the delegation's insistent demands portended further alienation of not just southern Democrats, but northern white voters already growing alarmed that summer after a major uprising in Harlem. The first of a five-year wave of urban rebellions across the nation, Harlem signaled the coming "white backlash" of resistance to any further legislative efforts to address racial injustice. Johnson feared too much attention on race could sabotage his campaign, as he complained to labor leader Walter Reuther: "Hell, the Northerners are more upset [than southern segregationists]." "They wire me to tell me the Negroes are taking over the country, they're running the White House, they're running the Democratic Party ... it's not [only] Mississippi and Alabama anymore."[26] One month earlier, the night after the senate passed the Civil Rights Act, Bill Moyers found him despondent in his bedroom. When Moyers asked why, Johnson said, "I think we've just delivered the South to the Republican Party for the rest of my life, and yours."[27]

Determined to repel the appearance of a takeover of his party by upstart negroes, Johnson fumed as he watched the networks' coverage of impassioned MFDP activists appealing to the credentials committee. Much anticipated was the testimony of Fannie Lou Hamer. After attending her first SNCC meeting in 1962, the 46-year-old sharecropper began registering others to vote, resulting in eviction from the plantation she had worked for 18 years. Hired as a SNCC organizer, Hamer's inspirational singing of black spirituals to nourish activists' spirits soon became legendary. When her turn came to testify, Hamer recounted the merciless beating she and colleagues had endured a year earlier (Figure 6.1). Returning from a voter registration workshop, they were hauled from their bus and into a jail in Winona, Mississippi.

> [It] wasn't too long before three white men came to my cell … And [one of them] said, "We are going to make you wish you was dead." I was carried out of that cell into another cell where they had two Negro prisoners. The

Figure 6.1 Fannie Lou Hamer, Mississippi Freedom Democratic Party delegate.

State Highway Patrolmen ordered the first Negro to take the blackjack ... I laid on my face and the first Negro began to beat ... After the first Negro had beat until he was exhausted, the State Highway Patrolman ordered the second Negro to take the blackjack ... [who] began to beat ...

All of this is on account of we want to register, to become first-class citizens. And if the Freedom Democratic Party is not seated now, I question America. Is this America, the land of the free and the home of the brave, where we have to sleep with our telephones off the hooks because our lives be threatened daily, because we want to live as decent human beings, in America?[28]

Midway through Hamer's riveting testimony, the networks cut to the White House for a hastily staged, phony news conference in which Lyndon Johnson announced the ... nine-month anniversary of the Kennedy assassination. The ham-fisted attempt to get Hamer removed from Americans'TV screens misfired, as that evening's newscast featured replays of her remarks. Support for the seating of the MFDP poured in from around the country, but Johnson was not having it. He charged his anointed vice-presidential candidate Hubert Humphrey to orchestrate a "compromise" solution that the civil rights champion would impose on Martin Luther King to take to the MFDP. They could take or leave it: two "at-large" seats and a pledge of no more segregated delegations at future conventions. King resisted, but was threatened with the loss of SCLC United Auto Workers funding. Humphrey warned Democratic state officials that promised federal appointments would likely be pulled should they not back the offer. When Humphrey appealed to Hamer, she told him with tears in her eyes (and some said his), "Mr. Humphrey, I've been praying about you and you're a good man, and you know what's right ... But Mr. Humphrey, if you take this job, you won't be worth anything."[29]

The MFDP voted down the compromise unanimously and went home empty-handed, bitter, and profoundly disillusioned. Atlantic City proved a watershed in the sixties, an alienating turning point away from the belief that the Democratic Party—viewed increasingly by human rights and antiwar activists as an irredeemable instrument of "the system"—could be counted on to advance positive change. Atlantic City became a kind of metonym for liberalism's failures, amplifying more militant voices in the movement. As SNCC leader Cleveland Sellers recalled, "never again were we lulled into believing that our task was exposing injustices so that the 'good' people of America could eliminate them ... After Atlantic City, our struggle was not for civil rights, but for liberation."[30] Lyndon Johnson's short-term fears were not groundless. Yet his coercive bullying in Atlantic City proved an undeniably tragic moment in the larger heartbreak of his presidency. No matter what LBJ did from this point, Democrats had already lost the South; Goldwater carried his home state of Arizona and five others—all in the Deep South. LBJ was reelected by one of the biggest landslides in American history. White backlash came on not because of the president's ambitious program of opportunity for all, but because racial insecurity and white supremacy claimed as much ground in the nation's soul as its higher aspirations. Atlantic City is all the more lamentable in light of Johnson's continued vocal support for civil rights that fall. Ignoring aides' advice to avoid the subject, aware of how poor southern whites had long been exploited by the region's elites—Dylan called them "Only a Pawn in Their Game"—LBJ confronted the cynical politics of racial resentment and beckoned southerners to support his program of interracial social uplift. Speaking in New Orleans in October, he denounced "the people that would use us and … all these years … have kept their foot on our necks by appealing to our animosities and dividing us."[31]

Although it left many activists embittered, the struggle in Mississippi thrust voting rights onto the nation's agenda as the movement turned its focus toward Alabama. The SCLC's "Project for an Alabama Political Freedom Movement" aimed to work with a cadre of voting rights activists in Selma, at work for nearly a decade under the banner of the Dallas County Voters League (DCVL). In Selma, less than one percent of eligible African Americans were registered, a reality enforced by Sheriff Jim Clark and his "posse" of deputies. The "NEVER!" button on Clark's uniform spoke volumes.[32] Confronting this repression, on Friday, January 22, 1965, 110 black schoolteachers began marching from Clark Elementary School, located across from a black housing project, toward the courthouse determined to register. Many held toothbrushes, signaling their expectations of arrest. DCVL president Reverend Frederick Reese recalled the scene:

> The faces of men and women who had, due to their will power and faith, survived under one of the most oppressive and discriminatory systems in a Southern town met our eyes. It is difficult to say to whom this march meant the most, the teachers or the observers … Many Black bystanders in the projects were weeping and sobbing openly as we passed by their homes.[33]

The teachers bravely marched not toward the customary back door but up the front steps of the courthouse where they were met by a wall of Clark's deputies bearing cattle prods and Billy clubs. Informed the registrar was closed, the teachers refused to leave. Suddenly the officers began pushing them down the steps like dominoes. The group persisted twice more, officers deploying greater force each time. They had not been arrested, nor breeched the courthouse. Their courage had been enough. Reese led the teachers toward Brown Chapel where students and parents received them as heroes.[34]

An atmosphere increasingly fraught with danger saw Martin Luther King physically assaulted by a leader of the American Nazi Party (ANP), prompting black nationalist leader and King critic, Malcolm X, to telegram ANP head George Lincoln Rockwell:

> [I]f your present racist agitation against our people there in Alabama causes physical harm to Reverend King or any other black Americans … you and your Ku Klux Klan friends will be met with maximum physical retaliation

from those of us who ... believe in asserting our right of self-defense—by any means necessary.[35]

By February 1965 Malcolm X had renounced the Nation of Islam, even as he remained a Muslim committed to black self-determination, self-defense, and an awakening of pan-African identity and unity. Malcolm's 1964 pilgrimage to Africa broadened his view of the struggle, including the need for interracial alliances. He came to Selma in early February for what became one of his last appearances, his assassination coming just weeks later. Speaking in Brown Chapel, Malcolm X declared "100 percent" support for the effort in Selma, avoiding the sort of criticism of King and nonviolence for which he was known, yet reaffirming black America's right of self-defense.[36] "I didn't come to Selma to make his job more difficult," Coretta Scott King later recalled Malcolm telling her, "but I thought that if the white people understood what the alternative was that they would be more inclined to listen to your husband."[37]

The growing appeal of Malcolm X was in large measure a response to the conditions of urban black America that were also drawing King's attention by 1965: high rates of poverty and unemployment that stood in glaring contrast to affluent whites, disproportionately high rents for substandard housing and "redlined" barriers to better neighborhoods, limited access to health care and other services, and largely white police forces who often treated the black residents of neighborhoods they patrolled like colonial subjects. The Selma encounter, combined with the hopes for an interracial struggle for economic justice that became King's focus after 1965, is a reminder of one of the great tragedies of the sixties: with the intellectual distance between King's radical imagination and the global, fundamentally humanist vision of Malcolm X closing at mid-decade, the assassins' bullets that violently ended their lives also snuffed out the possibility of a formidable alliance between the two men.

By mid-February, more than 3,500 residents of Selma had been jailed. Clark's posse had forced 160 teenagers out of Selma on a run for their lives. Then on the night of February 18, nearly 500 residents of nearby Marion began marching from the Zion Methodist Church to the city jail where an SCLC staffer was being held, intending to sing freedom songs outside his cell. Suddenly the streetlights went dark. Violent pandemonium ensued, Alabama state troopers pummeling marchers and reporters. Paint was sprayed on photographers' lenses. Jimmie Lee Jackson, a 26-year-old veteran and church deacon, ran with his mother and grandfather into a nearby café, seeking refuge. As he tried to shield them from the troopers' assault, Jackson was shot by a state trooper at close range. Governor Wallace denounced the events as the work of "professional agitators with pro-communist affiliations." When Jimmie Lee Jackson died eight days later, James Bevel proposed marching his coffin 54 miles to the steps of the capitol in Montgomery—an action sure to increase pressure on the White House to act on promised voting rights legislation. A March 5 meeting between the president and King was not encouraging, Johnson offering no firm commitment and chastising the civil rights leader to exercise caution. Jackson was buried in

Marion, but the idea of the march took hold. When SCLC announced its plans for Sunday, March 7, Governor Wallace denounced it as a threat to public safety. King returned to Atlanta, partly at the urging of aides who learned of a serious threat to his life. Promising to return, he urged marchers to wait.[38]

There was no waiting. Burning to carry the memory of Jimmie Lee Jackson to Montgomery, 600 activists lined up two abreast in downtown Selma. In front were SCLC's Hosea Williams and SNCC chairman John Lewis. As the marchers—"somber and subdued … just the sound of scuffling feet," as John Lewis remembered—reached the end of the Edmund Pettus Bridge on the edge of town, they confronted several hundred state troopers and Clark's posse, many on horseback. Troopers brandished tear gas and billy clubs, while many of Clark's men held bullwhips or rubber hoses pierced with barbed wire. "This is an unlawful assembly," came the warning. "You have two minutes to turn around and go back to your church." One minute later, Lewis heard "the clunk of the troopers' heavy boots, the whoops of rebel yells … the voice of a woman shouting, 'Get 'em! Get the niggers!'" Tear gas filled the air, clubs flew at heads like sickles in a wheat field, horses landed atop fallen bodies. The assault lasted 20 minutes. More than 90 were injured, including John Lewis who suffered a fractured skull, and Amelia Boynton, a 53-year-old organizer who suffered throat burns from the tear gas and was beaten unconscious.[39] That night, with 48 million Americans tuned into ABC's television premier of the film *Judgment at Nuremberg*, the network broke in with footage from Selma. Viewers could hear the voice of Jim Clark, "*Get those goddamned niggers …*" The juxtaposition of a film dramatizing Nazi crimes with what appeared to be American stormtroopers in Selma was jarring, heightening Americans' palpable shock and outrage.[40]

The nationwide response to the brutality was unprecedented. Sympathy marches in nearly 80 cities, a flood of telegrams to Lyndon Johnson, and numerous congressional speeches all urged passage of a voting rights bill. As activists from across the nation mapped out the road to Selma, King and Andrew Young resolved to lead a second march. On Monday morning, they filed a request for a federal injunction against the state of Alabama on First Amendment grounds. It landed in the courtroom of Frank M. Johnson, who had cast the decisive vote on the unconstitutionality of segregated busing in Montgomery, the first of several pro-civil rights decisions. Johnson had endured death threats, a cross burning on his lawn, and the dynamiting of his mother's home. Although the SCLC was confident of a favorable ruling, the hearing's postponement until Thursday forced a dilemma. Debate ensued among King and his advisors as they weighed the risks of waiting or acceding to local demands for a second march and potentially undermining support with Judge Johnson—and the Johnson in the White House.[41]

Having decided to respect the restraining order, King arrived Monday night at Brown Chapel to convey the news—only to be overwhelmed by the fervor in the room and reverse himself. Determined to avoid bloodshed, the president dispatched former Florida governor LeRoy Collins to Selma to implore King to halt the march. On Tuesday morning, as 2,000 marchers strode across the

Edmund Pettus Bridge they sang with a mix of trepidation and confidence the old Negro spiritual, "Ain't Gonna Let Nobody Turn Me Around." Upon reaching the site of the violence two days before, the marchers faced a sea of blue. King asked marchers to kneel for a prayer, and then to turn around and proceed back into Selma. Collins had prevailed on King to not provoke the inevitable reprise of violence and live to march another day. Only the top SCLC echelon knew of what appeared to some as an underhanded move to appease the same president who betrayed the MFDP. "Turnaround Tuesday" deepened the chasm between King—the skillful tactician determined to hold White House support—and far less patient activists who had seen too much bloodshed. Confrontations between SNCC firebrands and mounted policemen in Montgomery that week portended the direction of the movement.[42] Meanwhile, James Reeb, a white Unitarian minister who came to Selma after Bloody Sunday, was savagely beaten in downtown Selma and died two days later.

During Thursday's hearing, Judge Johnson became "visibly disgusted" at the Bloody Sunday footage.[43] George Wallace, meanwhile, traveled to Washington in a desperate, delusional effort to persuade Lyndon Johnson of his position. The president delivered a vintage iteration of the "Johnson Treatment," his legendary capacity for merciless, physically intimidating cajolery. He had Wallace seated low on a soft-cushioned couch, barely off the floor, while Johnson perched himself high in a rocking chair. "Don't you shit me, George," LBJ spat back at Wallace's assertions that he had no control over local officials. Johnson bore in, nose-to-nose, drubbing him into the couch. Then he tried an appeal to Wallace's better instincts. "Don't you think about 1968. Think about 1988," Johnson admonished. "You and me, we'll be dead and gone then, George ... What do you want left after you when you die? Do you want a great, big, marble monument that reads, 'George Wallace – He Built,' or do you want a little piece of pine board lying across that harsh caliche soil that reads, 'George Wallace – He Hated'"? After three hours of this, the governor had about sunk into the Oval Office floorboards. Johnson emerged to announce he was sending his voting rights bill to Congress the following week.[44] Judge Johnson lifted the restraining order, and activists began planning a four-day march from Selma to Montgomery on Sunday, March 21. Wallace continued to disgorge aggrieved states' rights rhetoric, but appealed for federal troops to protect the marchers.

On Tuesday night, March 15, the president spoke to a nationally televised joint session of congress seeking support for voting rights legislation. In the noblest moment of his presidency and one of the most eloquent presidential orations ever delivered, Johnson elevated the cause of voting rights to hallowed ground:

> I speak tonight for the dignity of man and the destiny of democracy.
>
> I urge every member of both parties, Americans of all religions and of all colors, from every section of this country, to join me in that cause.
>
> At times history and fate meet at a single time in a single place to shape a turning point in man's unending search for freedom. So it was at Lexington

and Concord. So it was a century ago at Appomattox. So it was last week in Selma, Alabama.[45]

He ended with an emphatic, "And we *shall* overcome," bringing a tear to King's eye as he watched the speech on television. Six days later 8,000 marchers crossed the Edmund Pettus Bridge headed toward Montgomery. Twenty-five thousand strong by the time they reached the capital, the throng encamped at City of St. Jude, a Catholic social services complex, where they were entertained by Hollywood luminaries and musicians including Leonard Bernstein, Mahalia Jackson, and Tony Bennett.[46] The next day's address from King on the steps of the Montgomery Capitol, blocks from where the boycott had commenced a decade earlier, ended with a soulful crescendo of hope:

> How long? Not long, because the arc of the moral universe is long, but it bends toward justice.
> How long? Not long, because:

> *Mine eyes have seen the glory of the coming of the Lord;*
> *He is trampling out the vintage where the grapes of wrath are stored;*
> *He has loosed the fateful lightning of, his terrible swift sword;*
> *His truth is marching on.*[47]

That night, Viola Liuzzo, a Detroit mother of five, was assassinated as she transported marchers back to Selma. The violent defiance would not stop the bipartisan passage of the landmark Voting Rights Act. Signed by President Johnson August 6, the law subjected states with a history of voting suppression to rigorous oversight from the Justice Department. Its impact was immediate and so profound that reactionary politicians immediately commenced decades of scheming to subvert it.

Other events that summer of 1965 signaled both a quickening pace of change and a more restless, agitated atmosphere taking hold in the country. There were musical milestones: in July, Bob Dylan "went electric" at the Newport Folk Festival and the Rolling Stones had their first number one hit, "Satisfaction." More ominously, five days after the Voting Rights Act became law, a commonplace incident of police brutality triggered an uprising in the Watts section of Los Angeles, resulting in 34 deaths and 3,000 arrests. The smoke was still rising from Watts when Jonathan Daniels, a white Episcopalian seminarian and activist, was murdered in Lowndes County, Alabama, a place 80 percent black with not one registered voter. Eighty-six white families owned 90 percent of the land. In this forbidding environment, SNCC's Stokely Carmichael and local activists organized an independent grassroots political party, the Lowndes County Freedom Organization (LCFO), whose black farmer membership asserted a willingness to use their shotguns to enforce the Voting Rights Act in the face of continued racist violence. Although short-lived, the organization's black panther logo and Carmichael's slogan, "Black Power!" was soon borrowed by two organizers from Oakland, California—Bobby Seale and Huey Newton—who in 1966 formed the Black Panther Party for Self-Defense.[48]

The "Quality of their Goals": The Great Society

Almost immediately shrouded by the trauma of Vietnam, Lyndon Johnson's presidency never recovered in Americans' collective memory. Because of the carnage wrought by the death of Cold War liberalism and the generally gloomy narrative of the sixties that quickly took hold in the country, Democratic politicians for decades consistently avoided association with the legacy of LBJ. Americans in the twenty-first century could be forgiven, then, for not knowing they live in a nation transformed by Lyndon Johnson and a congress dominated by liberal Democrats from 1964–1966. In that very short window Lyndon Johnson sent to Capitol Hill nearly 200 legislative proposals, 95 percent of which passed in some form. Beyond the goal of a society that "rests on abundance and liberty for all," and "an end to poverty and racial injustice," LBJ's grand vision of a Great Society reached higher, to "a place where the city of man serves not only … the demands of commerce but the desire for beauty and the hunger for community. It is a place where man can renew contact with nature." In a Great Society, citizens would be "more concerned with the quality of their goals … [than the] quantity of their goods."[49] High-flown as the west Texas sky, it was rhetoric that reflected the spirit of the emerging counterculture.

Yet Johnson's program was grounded in a pragmatic vision of improving the lives of not just the poor, but all Americans. The consummate politician, LBJ knew time was not on his side; he needed to move quickly before the deep well of support in the country he enjoyed evaporated. Fecund economic conditions made the mid-1960s the absolute optimum time of the twentieth century to launch an ambitious program of expanded government action. Even after passage of a long-debated tax cut, government revenues continued to expand, owing partly to a growing workforce. Average mean family income grew across all income groups by more than three percent throughout the decade.[50] Twenty years into a mostly uninterrupted postwar boom, white middle-class Americans possessed an unprecedented degree of economic confidence. Equally important, the Depression-World War II generation and their JFK-weaned children very much believed in the capacities of the federal government, a buoyant conviction made evident in the language of the Economic Opportunity Act that launched the War on Poverty: "The United States is the first major nation in history which can look forward to a victory over poverty."[51]

The Office of Economic Opportunity (OEO) suffered many failures born of inherent flaws, not least an inability to confront an often-impenetrable local white power structure that blocked access to decision making in communities of greatest need. A number of OEO programs were ill conceived, while others were not given adequate resources or time to adapt before they were attacked and defunded. Nevertheless, extensive empirical evidence demonstrates that programs such as Head Start, Job Corps and Job Training, the Elementary and

Secondary Education Act, VISTA (Volunteers in Service to America), Legal Aid for the Poor, and the Community Action Program transformed lives and helped build the capacities of community-based organizations across the nation. Medicaid, Medicare and Community Health Centers *saved* countless lives. Native American communities witnessed declines in infant mortality and expanded economic opportunity. The cynical fallacy perpetrated by critics that the War on Poverty was a failure is belied by the data: the percentage of Americans living in poverty fell dramatically, from just over 22 percent in 1964 to less than 12 in 1973.[52]

Continuing the Kennedy reliance on policy experts drawn from both academe and long-time government service, President Johnson charged fourteen task forces with devising proposals on everything from cultural enrichment and higher education to environmental protection and urban transportation policy. Again, much was imperfect. The Clean Air and Water Quality Acts contained weak standards and few dollars to help restore polluted air and waterways; stronger measures would be needed. Urban housing and transportation initiatives brought a mixed legacy: "slums"—many of them still-vital, historic neighborhoods—were cleared to make way for poorly conceived public housing projects; on the other hand, the Urban Mass Transportation Act funneled the largest federal investment ever into energy efficient, vitally needed mass transit projects that served as catalysts for revitalizing urban corridors and reducing the loss of green space for further highway development.[53] The National Historic Preservation Act established a process for slowing down the wrecking ball that had since the war resulted in the loss of thousands of historic sites and structures. National Endowments for the Arts and Humanities, and the Corporation for Public Broadcasting have immeasurably enriched the nation's cultural life.

The list goes on. Generations of college students on Pell Grants or government-financed low-interest loans; preservation of millions of acres of unspoiled wild places and waterways through the Wilderness and Wild and Scenic Rivers Acts; consumer protection laws providing Americans with greater levels of confidence in the safety of everything from automobiles to children's toys—thanks in part to the investigative and advocacy work of Ralph Nader. The 1965 Immigration and Nationality Act (INA) ended the racist quota system of the 1920s that dictated immigration on the basis of race and country of national origin, rendering the "nation of immigrants" less exclusively white and European in origin.[54]

Vietnam: "The Guys on the White Horses"

> We must weaken the enemy by drawing him into long protracted campaigns … When the enemy is away from home for a long time and produces no victories and families learn of their dead, then the enemy population at home becomes dissatisfied and considers it a Mandate from Heaven that their armies be recalled. Time is always in our favor.
>
> —Trần Hưng Đạo[55]

If only the Americans had read Trần Hưng Đạo. The legendary Vietnamese statesman warrior spoke these words in 1284 as he led what some historians call the world's first guerilla army to the second of three stunning defeats of Mongol warrior Kublai Kahn's invading army. They could have been spoken 650 years later when Ho Chi Minh began organizing his forces to drive the French out of Vietnam, or during World War II when the invader was Imperial Japan. By the time of Dien Bien Phu in 1954, the French were demanding "their armies be recalled." Indeed, Trần Hưng Đạo's political and tactical brilliance were subjects of fascination for Võ Nguyên Giáp, Ho's chief military strategist for the Vietnam People's Army that defeated the Japanese, French—and the Americans. Vietnamese history was a matter of great interest for Bernard Fall, the leading analyst at the time of America's growing involvement. For more than a decade until he was killed by a landmine in 1967, Fall warned of arrogant U.S. indifference to the French experience and strategic wrongheadedness. As ever, policymakers saw little outside the myopic containment tunnel. Beating off repeated foreign occupation for a millennium deeply influenced Vietnamese identity, but as far as Washington was concerned, the history of the country began with the arrival of Americans.[56]

In 1965, relatively few Americans questioned the nation's intentions in Vietnam. Embedded deep in frontier mythology and given renewed strength out of the Second World War, the idea of America's exceptional divine mission in the world never held greater potency than in the critical early years of its commitment to South Vietnam. Racially charged ideas of a superior western nation arriving in the Asia-Pacific region to lift up a wayward repressed people were Americanized in the Philippine–American War era, and endlessly reinforced in 1950s popular culture. *Deliver Us From Evil*, a best-selling book by American physician Tom Dooley about his humanitarian (and secretly CIA-funded) efforts in Vietnam, promulgated the fiction that America's growing presence there was a benevolent extension of its providential destiny to bring racial tolerance, humanitarian aid, and democracy to communist-threatened nations.[57] Hollywood westerns and World War II movies amplified images of virtuous—and invariably victorious—heroic white men fighting "savage" Indians and Japanese. The memoirs of Vietnam veterans are replete with boyhood recollections of the power such films held, particularly in the context of JFK's call to service.[58]

It was not long after an American soldier landed in Vietnam that he comprehended the brutal realities of a conflict that looked nothing like his father's war. Secretary of Defense Robert McNamara and U.S. commander, General William Westmoreland, believed they could win a war of attrition against the combined enemy forces of the North Vietnamese Army (NVA) and the guerilla soldiers of the South Vietnamese National Liberation Front (NLF—the Viet Cong, "VC" to Americans). The first major battle of the war seemed to confirm U.S. thinking. In November 1965, 1,000 American soldiers engaged 2,500 NVA in the Ia Drang Valley in the first major battle of the war. Although nearly 500 Americans were killed, wounded, or went missing, U.S. officials put the number of enemy casualties at nearly 1,200 and proclaimed victory. The fight bolstered a confidence bordering on hubris. Surely there was no way the communists could sustain losses of the magnitude they endured at Ia Drang, and for much of the first year of the war, for very long.[59] Americans did not anticipate Giap changing strategy after Ia Drang, away from conventional battles in relatively open terrain in which the U.S. could bring to bear significant advantages of firepower from the skies. Communist forces would "cling to the belt," forcing Americans to come after them in the mountains and rice paddies, while guerilas could melt in among the people from which they had come. Under cover of a mountainous, thick rainforest they knew well and could nimbly navigate, the enemy could ambush Americans in nighttime fire fights, set landmines and booby traps, and take cover in a vast network of underground tunnels. It would be *they* who would win a war of attrition, outlasting the Americans. Echoing Trần Hưng Đạo, Giap surmised early on that as "the number of dead American boys" begins to climb, "their mothers will want to know why. The war will not long survive their questions."[60]

Ever confident, Westmoreland pushed on in 1966–1967 with a strategy first attempted in Korea, where success had been measured in KIAs—"killed in action." As data poured in from the field and was sent on to be ciphered in shiny new IBM computers at the Pentagon, American commanders continued an elusive search for what Westmoreland termed the "crossover point"—the instant when U.S. capacity to level unforgiving destruction upon the enemy would outstrip Ho Chi Minh's ability to replenish his losses. *Everything* was calculated and reported as an indicator of "progress": number of sorties flown (from 3,000 monthly to 8,000 by 1967); bomb tonnage dropped (8 million by war's end, nearly three times that of the entire Second World War); gallons of Agent Orange dropped (20 million, defoliating one-quarter of Vietnam by 1973); number of "strategic hamlets" of relocated, supposedly "pacified" villagers taken from their ancestral homelands that were then destroyed because they were harboring VC, and the resulting square kilometers of South Vietnam under "control" of the Saigon government.

Above all else stood the body count. American soldiers in every sector received relentless pressure from lieutenants and sergeants, who heard it from colonels and majors, who received it from generals in Saigon and Washington. "It seemed that securing or pacifying an area was secondary to 'getting some kills,'" recalled one officer. "Stack 'em like cordwood," Phil Caputo remembered the orders to kill VC—or *suspected* VC. "Victory was a high body-count, defeat a low kill-ratio, war a matter of arithmetic," he said. At one point in his tour, Caputo was assigned as keeper of a commander's "scoreboard" tabulating body counts and displaying dead bodies to visiting officers like trophies. The rewards for high body count were both frivolous and consequential: R&R in Hong Kong, cold beer, an assignment in Saigon or stateside for officers. "Your success," said one captain, "was measured by your body count. It came down through channels." Inflated, falsified reporting was routine. Water buffalo were counted. A guerilla blown to pieces counted as two. It mattered little if a South Vietnamese casualty thought to be VC turned out to be a villager farming his rice crop. As Caputo recalled, "If it's dead and Vietnamese, it's VC"—or as some soldiers called it, the "MGR," the "Mere Gook Rule."[61]

Americans would win the arithmetical war, by a long shot. Far from insignificant, the 58,200 dead Americans still paled to the more than 1.1 million VC and NVA killed over the course of the war, along with more than two million civilian casualties. It was a war not of numbers, but for "the hearts and minds" of the South Vietnamese people, as Americans termed it—a battle Americans lost the minute they chose to support the colonial enterprise of the French, and put further out of reach with every B-52 sortie, every village hut "Zippoed." "They killed a lot of Communists," said journalist Michael Herr, "but that was all they did, because the number of Communist dead meant nothing, changed nothing."[62]

"Grunt" infantrymen were forced on operations into remote mountainous villages in a desperate attempt to "search and destroy" NLF guerillas and their places of refuge. As American soldiers took on casualties in their units, with pressure to drive up body counts, and having been trained to effectively ignore the rules of engagement respecting civilian life, "over a relatively short period of time, you begin to treat all of the Vietnamese as though they are the enemy," as marine sergeant W.D. Ehrhart recalled. "If you can't tell, you shoot first and ask questions later." Ehrhart would be haunted by the memory of shooting an unarmed old woman, "who I shot in the rice field one day, just because she was running away from the Americans who were going to kill her."[63] With every innocent peasant killed—whether for body count, the justified fear of a scared 18 year-old, the acts of special "Vengeance patrols," or a unit like Tiger Force that killed hundreds of innocent villagers in the Central Highlands in 1967—the necessary goal of winning South Vietnamese hearts and minds receded further into the distance.[64] In April 1967, Marine Ed Austin wrote home to his parents:

> I'm not surprised that there are more VC. We make more VC than we kill by the way these people are treated. I won't go into detail but some of the things that take place would make you ashamed of good old America.[65]

The war was built on a bedrock of American exceptionalism that proved difficult to crack—even after the revelation of what happened in the village of My Lai on March 16, 1968. Lieutenant William Calley, commander of a unit that had taken heavy casualties, led his men in the slaughter of 450 unarmed women, children, and old men. Journalist Seymour Hersh's story one year later, followed by a 1971 court martial finding him guilty of premeditated murder, triggered a wave of "Calley Rallies" and "Free Calley" bumper stickers. Some Americans reasoned that "gooks" got what was coming to them. My Lai quickly sank into a dark cavity of the American soul, alongside events like the 1868 Sand Creek Massacre and the Tulsa Race Massacre of 1921—racially fueled horrors suppressed from memory, or otherwise explained away as aberrant episodes of immoral psychopaths.

At the Pentagon, however, My Lai triggered the Vietnam War Crimes Working Group (VWCWG), a task force charged with investigating the extent, and credibility of a growing wave of alleged atrocities being reported through various forums since the start of the war. As journalist Nick Turse made clear decades later when the VWCWG records were briefly declassified, My Lai was no aberration. His book, *Kill Anything That Moves*—Calley's order to his men upon entering the village—documents the grim fact that war crimes took place throughout Vietnam. Senior officers not only were often aware of the incidents, they sometimes gave cover to soldiers accused, and punished those who tried to report them. An especially contemptible episode concerned Lieutenant Colonel Anthony Herbert. Highly decorated in Korea and wounded fourteen times in Vietnam, Herbert had his distinguished career derailed when he witnessed American officers torturing and executing South Vietnamese civilians in Phu Mhy province in South Vietnam in 1969, and then had the courage to report the incidents to a general. Herbert was relieved of command, and suddenly this star-spangled soldier of honor faced abrupt career termination and character assassination. As was true with the quashing of many post-My Lai inquiries, the attack on Herbert and discrediting of his allegations was orchestrated from on high—in his case, directly involving General Westmoreland. When Major Carl Hensley was assigned to investigate Herbert's charges, he not only found them truthful, but discovered how widespread they were. Subsequently prevented by superiors from pursuing justice, Hensley became deeply despondent and took his own life.[66]

That Americans could not win over the people of South Vietnam is not difficult to understand. More confounding is that policymakers could not bring themselves to see that, as Ehrhart put it, "what was happening here was nuts ... America might not be the guys on the white horses."[67] It was clear to GIs on the ground that the U.S.-sponsored government, which had grown more stable after the revolving door of generals that followed Diem, was no more supported by its people. The government proved incapable of ridding itself of the repression and corruption that had marked it from the beginning. Why the world's beacon of democracy was employing atrocious means to defend an authoritarian regime in Vietnam remained an incomprehensible riddle to most South Vietnamese. Meanwhile, no matter the military pounding they absorbed, NVA units continued to reconstitute themselves, month after grueling month—"like a sledgehammer on a floating cork" as one officer observed,[68] keenly aware that the ancient cause of national liberation—and time—were on their side.

Notes

1 David Coleman, "LBJ's Presidential Approval Ratings," compiled from Gallup, https://historyinpieces.com/research/lbj-presidential-approval-ratings, retrieved April 1, 2021.

2 Robert A. Caro, *The Years of Lyndon Johnson: The Passage of Power* (New York: Alfred A. Knopf, 2012), 428.

3 John J. Valadez, *The Longoria Affair* (PBS Independent Lens, Documentary, 60 minutes, 2010).

4 Lyndon B. Johnson, "Let Us Continue," address before a Joint Session of Congress, November 27, 1963, www.americanrhetoric.com/speeches/lbjletuscontinue.html, retrieved September 22, 2018.

5 Ibid.

6 Caro, 402; and John M. Newman, *JFK and Vietnam: Deception, Intrigue and the Struggle for Power* (Grand Central, 1992), 420–445.

7 Robert S. McNamara, *In Retrospect: The Tragedy and Lessons of Vietnam* (New York: Vintage Books, 1996), 102.

8 Doris Kearns Goodwin, *Lyndon Johnson and the American Dream* (New York: Harper and Row, 1976), 251.

9 Marilyn Young, *The Vietnam Wars: 1945–1990* (New York: Harper Perennial, 1991), 117; and "The Gulf of Tonkin Resolution" in Marvin E. Gettleman, Jane Franklin, Marilyn B. Young, and Howard Bruce Franklin, eds., *Vietnam and America: The Most Comprehensive Documented History of the Vietnam War* (New York: Grove Press, 2005), 248–273.

10 Tim Weiner, *Legacy of Ashes: The History of the CIA* (New York: Anchor Books, 2008), 280

11 Julian Zelizer, "A War's Legacy," *Princeton Alumni Weekly*, April 1, 2015, https://paw.princeton.edu/article/war%E2%80%99s-legacy, retrieved September 24, 2018.

12 Quoted in NPR Staff, "Sam Cooke and the Song that Almost Scared Him," All Things Considered, February 1, 2014, www.npr.org/2014/02/01/268995033/sam-cooke-and-the-song-that-almost-scared-him, retrieved September 25, 2018.

13 Robert Dallek, *Lyndon B. Johnson: Portrait of a President* (New York: Oxford University Press, 2004),168.

14 Ian Millhiser, "Senate Office is Named for a Virulent Racist," Think Progress, August 27, 2018, https://thinkprogress.org/a-third-of-the-senate-works-in-a-building-named-for-a-virulent-racist-schumer-plans-to-fix-that-5c7fd8e392d2/, retrieved September 25, 2018.

15 "Civil Rights Filibuster Ended," United States Senate, June 10, 1964, www.senate.gov/artandhistory/history/minute/Civil_Rights_Filibuster_Ended.htm, retrieved September 25, 2018.

16 Karen Grigsby Bates, "Why a Proper Lady Found Herself Behind Bars" (NPR: All Things Considered, Code Switch, March 28, 2014), www.npr.org/sections/codeswitch/2014/03/28/294816965/why-a-proper-lady-found-herself-behind-bars, retrieved April 4, 2021.

17 Rachael McNeal, "What St. Augustine Can Teach Us About the Importance of Interfaith Literacy," *Huffington Post*, April 6, 2017, www.huffingtonpost.com/rachael-mcneal/what-st-augustine-fl-can-teach-us_b_9611508.html, retrieved September 29, 2018.

18 Jerry Demuth, "A Guide to Mississippi," Spring 1964, in Michael Edmonds, ed., *Risking Everything: A Freedom Summer Reader* (Madison: Wisconsin Historical Society Press, 2014), 2.

19 "'Niggers, Apes, Alligators, Coons, and Possums,': Mississippi: Battle of the Kennedys," *Newsweek*, August 19, 1963, 24, quoted in Bruce Watson, *Freedom Summer: The Savage Season of 1964 That Made Mississippi Burn and Made America a Democracy* (New York: Penguin, 2010), 6–7.

20 Watson, 48, 10.

21 Ibid., 64–65.

22 William Bradford Huie, *Three Lives for Mississippi* (Jackson, MI: University Press of Mississippi, 2000), 117.

23 Watson, 19, 60, 115–119, 171–174; and John Lewis with Michael D'Orso, *Walking With the Wind: A Memoir of the Movement* (New York: Harcourt, 1998), 282.

24 Watson, 187.

25 Lewis with D'Orso, 286–287.

26 Recording of Telephone Conversation between LBJ and Walter Reuther, Aug. 24, 1964, 8:25 p.m., Citation #5165, Recordings of Telephone Conversations— White House Series, LBJ Library; quoted by Jeremy D. Mayer, "LBJ Fights the White Backlash," *Prologue* 33, no. 1 (Spring 2001), www.archives.gov/publications/prologue/2001/spring/lbj-and-white-backlash-2.html#nt70, retrieved September 29, 2018.

27 Bill Moyers, Symposium, "LBJ: The Difference He Made." Johnson Presidential Library, Austin, Texas, May 4, 1990, www.lbjlibrary.org/page/library-museum/memorable-moments-at-the-lbj-library, retrieved September 29, 2018.

28 Hamer, "Testimony Before the Credentials Committee."

29 Watson, 253.

30 Joshua Zeitz, "Democratic Debacle," *American Heritage*, June/July 2004 (vol. 55, n. 3), www.americanheritage.com/content/democratic-debacle, retrieved September 29, 2018.

31 "Remarks of the President at a Dinner in the Grand Ballroom of the Jung Hotel," New Orleans, Oct. 9, 1964, box 125, Confidential Files, LBJ Library, quoted by Mayer.

32 Dallek, 202.

33 Quoted in Wally G. Vaughn and Mattie Campbell Davis, eds., *The Selma Campaign, 1963–1965: The Decisive Battle of the Civil Rights Movement* (Dover, MA: The Majority Press, 2006), 46.

34 Ibid, 49.

35 Malcolm X to George Lincoln Rockwell, www.malcolm-x.org/docs/tel_rock.htm, retrieved October 1, 2018.

36 Quoted by Jack Barnes, "A Malcolm-Martin Convergence?" *The Militant* 79, no. 6 (February 23, 2015), www.themilitant.com/2015/7906/790650.html, retrieved March 30, 2021.

37 Coretta Scott King, Interview with Jackie Shearer, November 21, 1988 (Washington University), http://digital.wustl.edu/e/eii/eiiweb/kin5427.0224.089corettascottking.html, retrieved March 30, 2021.

38 Lewis with D'Orso, 326–328.

39 Ibid, 340–345.

40 "#Selma 50: What the Media and Hollywood Got Wrong About 'Bloody Sunday,'" NBC News, August 8, 2017, www.nbcnews.com/news/nbcblk/media-studies-selma-n319436, retrieved April 2, 2021.

41 Jack Bass, "Judge Johnson Played Key Role in Historic March," *Montgomery Advertiser*, March 20, 2015, www.montgomeryadvertiser.com/story/opinion/contributors/2015/03/20/judge-johnson-played-key-role-historic-march/25082443/, retrieved March 30, 2021.

42 Craig Brandhorst, "Turnaround for Justice," University of South Carolina, March 6, 2015, https://sc.edu/uofsc/posts/2015/03_carl_evans_selma_montgomery_march.php#.W7N4SFJRe9Y, retrieved October 2, 2018; and Lewis with D'Orso, 346–349.

43 Lewis with D'Orso, 351.

44 Nick Kotz, *Judgment Days: Lyndon Baines Johnson, Martin Luther King, Jr., and the Laws that Changed America* (New York: Houghton Mifflin, 2005), 305–306.

45 President Lyndon John, "Special Message to the Congress: The American Promise," March 15, 1965, www.lbjlibrary.org/lyndon-baines-johnson/speeches-films/president-johnsons-special-message-to-the-congress-the-american-promise, retrieved October 2, 2018.

46 "Stars for Freedom Rally," March 24, 1965; Selma-to-Montgomery Trail, National Park Service, U.S. Department of the Interior, http://npshistory.com/brochures/semo/stars-for-freedom-rally.pdf, retrieved October 2, 2018.

47 Martin Luther King, Jr., "Our God is Marching On!" March 25, 1965; at https://kinginstitute.stanford.edu/our-god-marching, retrieved October 2, 2018.

48 Hasan K. Jeffries, *Bloody Lowndes: Civil Rights and Black Power in Alabama's Black Belt* (New York: NYU Press, 2009), 2–17.

49 Lyndon B. Johnson, "Remarks, University of Michigan," May 22, 1964; LBJ Presidential Library, www.lbjlibrary.org/exhibits/social-justice-gallery, retrieved October 3, 2018.

50 "The 'Lost Decade' of the American Middle Class," Economic Opportunity Institute, August 31, 2012, citing U.S. Census Bureau, Historical Income Tables, www.opportunityinstitute.org/blog/post/the-lost-decade-of-the-american-middle-class, retrieved March 30, 2021.

51 Public Law 88-452, August 20, 1964, Economic Opportunity Act of 1964.

52 Official poverty data from http://americanradioworks.publicradio.org/features/poverty/whospoor.html; on the success (and failures) of the War on Poverty, see, among other works, Annelise Orleck and Lisa Hazirjian, eds., *The War on Poverty: A New Grassroots History, 1964–1980* (Athens, GA: University of Georgia Press, 2011); and Martha J. Bailey and Sheldon Danziger, eds., *Legacies of the War on Poverty*, National Poverty Center Series on Poverty and Public Policy (New York: Russell Sage Foundation, 2013).

53 Richard F. Weingroff, "A Great Day in America: USDOT's 50th Anniversary," *Public Roads* 80, no. 2 (Washington, DC: U.S. Department of Transportation, Sept/Oct 2016), www.fhwa.dot.gov/publications/publicroads/16sepoct/04.cfm, retrieved March 31, 2021.

54 Tom Gjelten, "In 1965, a Conservative Tried to Keep America White. His Plan Backfired." (National Public Radio, Weekend Edition Saturday, October 3, 2015), www.npr.org/2015/10/03/445339838/the-unintended-consequences-of-the-1965-immigration-act, retrieved October 3, 2018.

55 Quoted in Patrick Hearden, *The Tragedy of Vietnam* (New York: Pearson, 2012), 3.

56 On Bernard Fall, see Dorothy Fall, ed., *Last Reflections on a War* (New York: Doubleday, 1967); Bernard Fall, *Viet-Nam Witness* (New York: Praeger, 1966); Gary Hess and John McNay, "'The Expert': Bernard Fall and His Critique of America's Involvement in Vietnam," in David L. Anderson, ed., *The Human Tradition in the Vietnam Era* (Wilmington, DE: Scholarly Resources, 2000), 63–80; and Michael Herr, *Dispatches* (New York: Random House Vintage International, 1991; first published 1977), 49.

57 Christian G. Appy, *American Reckoning: The Vietnam War and Our National Identity* (New York: Penguin Books, 2015), 16–20.

58 See, for example, Phil Caputo, *A Rumor of War* (New York: Henry Holt, 1977); Ron Kovic, *Born on the Fourth of July* (New York: Pocket, 1990, 1976); and W. D. Ehrhart, *Vietnam-Perkasie* (Amherst, MA: University of Massachusetts Press, 1995).

59 Guenter Lewy, *America in Vietnam* (New York: Oxford University Press, 1978), 51–52.

60 Gerard J. DeGroot, *A Noble Cause? America and the Vietnam War* (London: Longman, Pearson, 2000), 148; Giap quoted in James S. Olson and Randy Roberts, *Where the Domino Fell: America and Vietnam, 1945–1995* (New York: St. Martin's Press, 1996), 145.

61 Caputo, xix–xx, 74, 168–169; and Nick Turse, *Kill Anything That Moves: The Real American War in Vietnam* (New York: Henry Holt, 2013), 42–51.

62 Herr, 96.

63 Andrew Pearson, Director, "America Takes Charge," Episode 5, *Vietnam: A Television History* (PBS, 13-part Documentary Series, 1987).

64 Michael Sallah and Mitch Weiss, *Tiger Force: A True Story of Men and War* (New York: Little Brown, Back Bay Books, 2007).

65 Quoted in Turse, 120, from James R. Evert, *A Life in A Year* (New York: Presidio, 1993), 392.

66 Ronald Kaiser, *Herbert's War* (Tarentum, PA: Word Association Publishers, 2019).

67 Pearson, "America Takes Charge."

68 Journalist Malcolm Browne, quoted in Robert K. Brigham, *Iraq, Vietnam, and the Limits of American Power* (New York: Public Affairs, 2006, 2008), 44–45.

Further Reading

Anderson, David L., ed. *The Human Tradition in the Vietnam Era*. Wilmington, DE: Scholarly Resources, 2000.

Appy, Christian G. *American Reckoning: The Vietnam War and Our National Identity*. New York: Penguin Books, 2015.

Bailey, Martha J., and Sheldon Danziger, eds. *Legacies of the War on Poverty*. New York: Russell Sage Foundation, 2013.

Bradford, Huie William. *Three Lives*. Jackson, MI: University Press of Mississippi, 2000, 1965.

Brigham, Robert K. *Iraq, Vietnam, and the Limits of American Power*. New York: Public Affairs, 2006.

Caputo, Phil. *A Rumor of War*. New York: Henry Holt, 1977.

Caro, Robert A. *The Years of Lyndon Johnson: The Passage of Power*. New York: Alfred A. Knopf, 2012.

Dallek, Robert. *Lyndon B. Johnson: Portrait of a President*. New York: Oxford University Press, 2004.

DeGroot, Gerard J. *A Noble Cause? America and the Vietnam War*. London: Longman, Pearson, 2000.

Edmonds, Michael, ed. *Risking Everything: A Freedom Summer Reader*. Madison, WI: Wisconsin Historical Society Press, 2014.

Ehrhart, W.D. *Vietnam-Perkasie*. Amherst, MA: University of Massachusetts Press, 1995.

Fall, Bernard. *Viet-Nam Witness*. New York: Praeger, 1966.

Goodwin, Doris Kearns. *Lyndon Johnson and the American Dream*. New York: Harper and Row, 1976.

Hearden, Patrick. *The Tragedy of Vietnam*. New York: Pearson, 2012.

Herr, Michael. *Dispatches*. New York: Random House Vintage International, 1991.

Huie, William Bradford. *Three Lives for Mississippi*. Jackson, MI: University Press of Mississippi, 2000.

Jeffries, Hasan K. *Bloody Lowndes: Civil Rights and Black Power in Alabama's Black Belt*. New York: NYU Press, 2009.

Kotz, Nick. *Judgment Days: Lyndon Baines Johnson, Martin Luther King, Jr., and the Laws that Changed America*. New York: Houghton Mifflin, 2005.

Lewy, Guenter. *America in Vietnam*. New York: Oxford University Press, 1978.

McNamara, Robert S. *In Retrospect: The Tragedy and Lessons of Vietnam*. New York: Vintage Books, 1996.

Olson, James S., and Randy Roberts. *Where the Domino Fell: America and Vietnam, 1945–1995*. New York: St. Martin's Press, 1996.

Orleck, Annelise, and Lisa Hazirjian, eds. *The War on Poverty: A New Grassroots History, 1964–1980*. Athens, GA: University of Georgia Press, 2011.

Sallah, Michael, and Mitch Weiss. *Tiger Force: A True Story of Men and War*. New York: Little Brown, Back Bay Books, 2007.

Turse, Nick. *Kill Anything That Moves: The Real American War in Vietnam*. New York: Henry Holt, 2013.

Vaughn, Wally G., and Mattie, Campbell Davis, eds. *The Selma Campaign, 1963–1965: The Decisive Battle of the Civil Rights Movement*. Dover, MA: The Majority Press, 2006.

Watson, Bruce. *Freedom Summer: The Savage Season of 1964 That Made Mississippi Burn and Made America a Democracy*. New York: Penguin, 2010.

7 "People of This Generation"

The New Left and the Counter-culture

> We are people of this generation, bred in at least modest comfort, housed now in universities, looking uncomfortably to the world we inherit.
> —The Port Huron Statement 1962[1]

This was the weighty, fraught opening of the Port Huron Statement, founding manifesto of the Students for a Democratic Society (SDS). The quintessential expression of early sixties idealism, the Port Huron Statement also served as intellectual bedrock for what sociologist C. Wright Mills termed the New Left. Unlike the Depression-era left of communists and labor leaders whose chief concern was working class struggle, New Left activists sought nothing less than to challenge the fundamental underpinnings of American society. Drafted by University of Michigan student Tom Hayden, the Port Huron Statement had been thoroughly debated for four days and nights in mid-June 1962 by SDS leaders from around the nation at the "FDR Four Freedoms Camp,"[2] a rustic CIO retreat near Detroit. Having endorsed the manuscript, the students who remained on the final night walked to the shore of Lake Huron to revel in their achievement. "We were sure we had done something visionary," recalled Sharon Jeffrey. Suddenly an aurora borealis appeared over the lake. "It was euphoric, deeply profound," said Jeffrey. "Some of the kids went swimming and we watched the end of the night and the coming of dawn. We were elated." "It was," Hayden mused, "like God was sending us a message."[3] SDS leaders could not know what lay ahead, but their exalted recollections were not entirely overblown.

The Port Huron Statement is a remarkable document for many reasons, not least for its introspective discussion of "Values." Rejecting what they saw as the amoral and anomic tenets of postwar American life, the authors declared an aspirational search for a more "authentic" self that would be guided by "uniqueness rooted in love, reflectiveness, reason, and creativity." Faced with looming nuclear annihilation and the dark realities of segregation—"events too troubling to dismiss"—the students announced a conviction in America's unfulfilled promise that was at once hopelessly idealistic and determinedly pragmatic. Port Huron's potency derived from the moral force and tactical verve of the civil rights movement that "compelled most of us from silence to activism." Hayden and fellow SDSer Al Haber had already suffered the physical blows of

DOI: 10.4324/9781003160595-7

segregationists in McComb, Mississippi. The human rights struggle in the south made real the exuberant possibilities of what the statement famously called "participatory democracy." Opposite a postwar politics rendered alien to most Americans, the students posited an understanding of democratic civic engagement that could "[bring] people out of isolation and into community."[4] "Participatory democracy" was vulnerable to charges from liberals that it was impossibly naïve, nebulous, and arrogantly dismissive of a strong representative government that was delivering real progress for Americans. Yet in that rarefied era of doing something for one's country, the challenging promise contained in the phrase was enthralling.

In 1962, the American university sat at the dawn of an explosion in size, economic and societal influence that would last nearly two decades. It was a highly bureaucratic institution where students were governed by a legal doctrine known as *in loco parentis* ("in place of parents"), empowering universities to direct every aspect of students' lives, including what could be printed in the college newspaper, classroom dress, and "parietal rules" severely restricting student opportunities for social interaction. Behavioral guidance could reach levels of the absurd—for example, requiring couples to keep three feet on the floor at all times while visiting in dormitories. At the University of Chicago, women whose dates returned them to their dorms repeatedly a few minutes after curfew could be "campused"—effectively grounded—and her parents notified. Young women, generally assumed to be in college in order to find a husband, often found a climate indifferent to their own educational aspirations and frequently hostile to their personal safety. When Judith Karpova reported her rape to local police, they immediately informed university administrators and expelled her—a double victimization then common in higher education.[5]

Students overall found lifeless curricula focused on training the future managers of American society, not educating them to think critically about the nature of that world. Large universities, increasingly dependent on research contracts from the Defense Department and partnerships with multinational corporations, were inherently averse to cultivating critically thinking citizens. Nowhere was this truer than at the University of California at Berkeley, the center of the state's university system. Berkeley's president was Clark Kerr, a preeminent figure in American higher education who had positioned himself as a voice of reason in the McCarthy era—refusing, for example, to fire professors who would not sign a loyalty affidavit. In those same years, he led Berkeley's research laboratories to their central role in the nation's nuclear weapons complex. In an influential 1963 address at Harvard University, Kerr famously celebrated "the growth of the knowledge industry" that had already "[permeated] government and business." American higher education, he declared, was now responsible for nearly one-third of the nation's gross national product. Like the railroad and the automobile of previous epochs of America's economic ascendancy, "the knowledge industry" would now "serve as the focal point for national growth."[6] In the early 1960s, Berkeley, a "crown jewel" of America's "knowledge factory,"[7] was about to be overwhelmed by the rising tide of participatory democracy—which, together with the counterculture taking root across the bay in San Francisco, would define the forces of transformational change in the 1960s.

"The Operation of the Machine"

It began innocently enough, with sporadic protests against U.S. support for South African apartheid and nuclear testing. And then in 1960 the House Un-American Activities Committee (HUAC), by this point a relic of McCarthyism, came to San Francisco for hearings into alleged subversive activities of leftwing intellectuals. HUAC's inquisition was met with protest from UC Berkeley students who at one point rose to sing "The Star-Spangled Banner" in defense of the First Amendment. The students were then forcibly removed from the buildings, police pummeling them down the steps of city hall with fire hoses. That scene, predating Bull Connor's hoses by three years, was featured in *Operation Abolition*, a HUAC propaganda film. Screened on campuses around the country with the intent to smear the protesters as communist dupes, *Operation Abolition* backfired, inciting solidarity with Berkeley and further awakening student activism.[8]

In the 1963–1964 school year, students launched a campaign targeting the discriminatory hiring practices of San Francisco hotels, auto dealerships, and retail stores. Dozens of nonviolent actions followed, many targeting William F. Knowland, owner and editor-in-chief of the Oakland *Tribune*, and a vehement critic of the civil rights movement. The campaign culminated in a peaceful occupation of the Sheraton Palace Ballroom involving more than 2,000 Berkeley students. Hundreds were arrested. With the national spotlight turned on it, the city's hotel industry surrendered to an historic agreement committing to specific measures to end racial discrimination. Reaction to the students' victory was swift. Knowland led the university's board of regents in ordering a ban on the dissemination of literature on "the Bancroft Strip," an area just outside the Berkeley gates that served as a "lifeline" for groups across the political spectrum.[9]

Because the crackdown on free speech applied to all organizations, student outrage was universal. Following the arrest and suspension of eight student leaders for defying the ban, on October 1, 500 students marched toward Sproul Hall, the administration building, for a peaceful sit-in. The police arrested Jack Weinberg, and placed him in a police car that was immediately surrounded by hundreds of student protesters singing, "We Shall Overcome," preventing the vehicle from moving. A microphone was arranged and placed on the roof of the car. Students from a crowd now several thousand strong began removing their shoes and climbing atop the car to speak. For 32 hours, Weinberg sat in the back of the police car while students orated above him, passionately invoking ideas of human rights and constitutional liberties from the likes of Aristotle, Jefferson, and Thoreau.[10] The Free Speech Movement (FSM) had begun.

FSM student leaders deliberated throughout the fall, determined to hold together a broad coalition extending from Goldwater activists on the right to the Young Socialist Alliance of the far left. The regents attempted a divide and conquer strategy that Kerr tried to sell as liberal—allowing the use of the Bancroft Strip for all but organizations advocating civil disobedience. They rescinded the punishment of six of the original students, yet two activists associated with civil rights—Art Goldberg and Mario Savio—remained suspended. Instead of ending the whole affair, the crackdown on the campus left led to one of the luminous moments of the sixties. In a demonstration on Sproul Plaza on Wednesday, December 2, Mario Savio, son of a proud union machinist and just weeks removed from running a Freedom School and facing down the Klan in McComb, Mississippi, addressed a crowd of several thousand:

> We were told the following: If President Kerr actually tried to get something more liberal out of the Regents in his telephone conversation, why didn't he make some public statement to that effect? And the answer we received—from a well-meaning liberal—was the following: He said, "Would you ever imagine the manager of a firm making a statement publicly in opposition to his Board of Directors?" ...
>
> Well I ask you to consider—if this is a firm, and if the Board of Regents are the Board of Directors, and if President Kerr in fact is the manager, then I tell you something—the faculty are a bunch of employees and we're the raw material! But we're a bunch of raw materials that don't mean ... to end up being bought by some clients of the University, be they the government, be they industry, be they organized labor, be they anyone! We're human beings!
>
> There's a time when the operation of the machine becomes so odious, makes you so sick at heart, that you can't take part; you can't even passively take part. And you've got to put your bodies upon the gears and upon the wheels, upon the levers, upon all the apparatus, and you've got to indicate to the people who own it that unless you're free, the machines will be prevented from working at all![11]

Equal parts Tom Paine, Henry David Thoreau, and Charlie Chaplin, the impassioned oration moved 1,200 students to march into Sproul Hall for what became a festive occupation. Late that night Chancellor Edward Strong announced that the "assemblage had developed to such a point that the purpose and work of the university has been impaired," a declaration met with exuberant applause. When police arrived, students went limp, forcing the laborious dragging of hundreds, one-by-one, down several flights of stairs. By mid-day December 3, nearly 800 students had been hauled to the nearby prison farm in the largest mass arrest in California history.[12]

Following more bumbling obfuscation by the administration, the academic senate stepped into the chaos to support the students and bring victory to the FSM. Beyond affirming the right of free speech inside the university gates, the students' triumph at Berkeley presaged a growing liberalization of American higher education. More immediately, it foreshadowed for the New Left a far greater struggle ahead against the most powerful machine on earth.[13]

"We Must Name That System": The Antiwar Movement

On the evening of March 24, 1965, two weeks after the first American combat troops landed in Danang, people began to file into Angell Hall Auditorium on the campus of the University of Michigan for the first "Teach-In" on the Vietnam War. More than 3,000 students and Ann Arbor citizens attended the all-night event. Three principal speakers and 13 seminars covering various dimensions of Vietnamese history and culture, as well as the Johnson administration's policy of escalation in Southeast Asia, inspired vigorous debate. "On that night, people who really cared talked of things that really mattered," said Professor Marc Pilisuk. "Facts were demanded and assumptions were exposed." Students who never spoke up in class challenged their professors. Pilisuk and other faculty organizers noted that the spirit of probing inquiry carried into their classrooms in the days that followed.[14]

The teach-in was a tactical "stroke of genius," as SDS leader Carl Ogelsby put it.[15] Campus teach-ins proliferated across the nation; by the end of spring semester, more than 100 had been held. The largest was the 36-hour marathon at Berkeley attended by 35,000 people. Enlivened by performances from San Francisco-area musicians and comics, the Berkeley event was also notable for who did not appear—State Department representatives who could have defended the administration's policy. For many attendees, two empty seats and a "Reserved for the State Department" placard spoke volumes of an indefensible policy in Southeast Asia. Even as the war escalated, the teach-ins succeeded beyond organizers' expectations, producing the first serious crack in the Cold War consensus that led the nation into Vietnam.[16] Participants brought an awakened understanding of American policy into barrooms, living rooms, and the streets, stirring debate over Vietnam and U.S. foreign policy more broadly. Questions erupted over Lyndon Johnson's decision that spring to send 23,000 marines to the Dominican Republic, allegedly to prevent a Cuban-style communist dictatorship. The imperial adventure reprised the "gunboat diplomacy" that had long characterized U.S. policy in Latin America. It was clear to critics then, and confirmed decades later, that Johnson knew there was no communist threat. [17] After Tonkin Gulf, duplicity about U.S. actions overseas got easier for the president.

Amid the teach-ins that spring, SDS sponsored the first antiwar demonstration in Washington. Although dwarfed by events in the late sixties, the 20,000 in attendance made it then the largest peace demonstration in American history. The day was highlighted by the address of SDS president, Paul Potter, whose disturbing questions hung over the balance of the war:

> What kind of system is it that allows decent men, good men, to make the decisions that have led to the thousands and thousands of deaths ... in Vietnam? What kind of system is it that justifies the United States or any country seizing the destinies of the Vietnamese people and using them callously for our own ends? ... We must name that system. And we change it and control it, or else it will destroy us.[18]

As the war progressed, American casualties mounted, in tandem with the Johnson administration's call for higher draft quotas. In 1966 the draft became an increasing focus of the antiwar movement. Wealthy, well-connected Americans found a way to avoid serving, including future presidents and vice-presidents who would one day advance bellicose policies from the White House.[19] Higher education brought a draft deferment, but for non-college working-class young men, the choices were limited: refuse and face imprisonment and a hefty fine, head for Canada, or report for duty. Applications for Conscientious Objector status, the Peace Corps and VISTA soared, as did interest in religious vocations. Thousands faked or *caused* an array of afflictions, including inserting hypodermic needle marks for a drug addiction ruse, dropping ink on a cigarette, said to produce spots on the lung simulating tuberculosis. Shooting yourself in the foot was not off limits.[20]

As troop deployment and the body count on both sides mounted, U.S. policy appeared locked in perpetual escalation. Frustration and anger inside the antiwar movement grew accordingly. In mid-October 1967, Stop the Draft Week demonstrated both its growing numbers and intensifying temperament in events across the country. On Monday, October 16, more than 250 young men solemnly walked down the aisle of Boston's Arlington Street Church to refuse their draft cards, 60 of whom burned them over a candle. In Oakland, California police arrested 123 nonviolent protesters for blocking the draft induction center. Soon after dawn the next day, 10,000 protesters barricaded the entrance, many sporting helmets and shields. Suddenly a small army of Oakland's finest, armed with riot gear, came at them with no interest in arresting anyone. As the *San Francisco Chronicle* reported, "police surged down the street, their hard wooden sticks mechanically flailing up and down, like peasants mowing down wheat."[21] The brutality of the police, along with the visceral reaction of some protesters who trashed parts of downtown Oakland, offered a shocking preview of what was to come.[22]

On Thursday at the University of Wisconsin, SDS's target was Dow Chemical, chief manufacturer of napalm. Dow employment recruiters were met with hundreds of protesters swarming their tables, shouting "down with Dow!" A police riot squad stormed in, Billy clubs flying. "Girls began to scream, and both men and women students staggered sobbing from the building, many with blood dripping from head wounds." With tear gas in the air, the assault spilled outside the Commerce Building, where a gauntlet of police pummeled the students. Some in the crowd of more than 2,000 began chanting "off the pig" and, with mimicked fascist salute, "Sieg Heil! Sieg Heil!" That triggered more rage from police, some of whom were World War II veterans.[23] Seventy-six students were treated for injuries. The havoc divided the city of Madison for many years to come. While the majority of the campus community condemned the assault, the Wisconsin state assembly voted 94–5 for a resolution calling for the expulsion of protest leaders. "Long haired greasy pigs," sneered an assemblyman. Another called for SDS leaders to be shot for inciting insurrection.[24]

Stop the Draft Week culminated Saturday in the nation's capital. Organized by the National Mobilization Committee to End the War in Vietnam, 100,000 people attended an afternoon rally at the Lincoln Memorial, 35,000 of whom stayed for the ensuing March on the Pentagon, one of the era's indelible moments. Streaming across the Arlington Memorial Bridge that afternoon was a kaleidoscopic mélange of quietly determined pacifists, radical student protesters, black power militants, white mainstream liberals, and counterculture hippies. The latter's presence lent a carnival-like, theater-of-the-absurd atmosphere to the proceedings. Fearful of being maced, the hipsters brought a concoction called lysergic acid crypto ethylene (LACE), which "[made] you want to take off your clothes, kiss people and make love."[25] Arcing the Pentagon that afternoon was a symbolic culmination to the Summer of Love and the impossibly naïve belief that only *love* could end the war. The transcendent balm of marijuana filled the air, San Francisco's legendary Diggers distributed free food, and protesters chanted "we love you!" and "come join us!" to heavily armed soldiers defending the Pentagon. Beat guru Allen Ginsberg was there, along with a band of Shoshone medicine men. Abbie Hoffman and Jerry Rubin, flamboyant media stars of the hippie-protester hybrid strain of the movement known as "Yippies," planned an airdrop of daisies and then the big finish: an encircling exorcism of the Pentagon's demons, followed by a levitation of the world's largest office building. Hoffman and Rubin calculated that 1,200 linked protesters would do the trick (Figure 7.1).[26]

With shouts of "Hey, Hey LBJ, How many Kids Did You Kill Today?" ringing across the land all week, an unamused Lyndon Johnson insisted no effort be made to interfere with the planned protest, but also fortified Washington with military police, federal marshals, and tear gas-loaded flamethrowers. The 82nd

Figure 7.1 Anti-Vietnam War demonstrators during the March on the Pentagon in Washington DC demanding an end to the conflict on October 21, 1967.

Airborne were put on standby. The General Services Administration negotiated with Hoffman and Rubin the permitted height of the Pentagon's levitation (three feet, down from the planned 300!). It was hard years later to find anyone who would swear it had not happened ("*spiritually* levitated," Rubin insisted).[27] Photographically indelible were scenes of smiling hippies placing flowers into the barrels of MPs' rifles. Attempts at civil disobedience near the building's entrance were met with 600 arrests, among them Dr. Benjamin Spock and author Norman Mailer. Sporting a dark blue three-piece pin-striped suit for the occasion, the Jewish American Mailer found himself at one point tensely engaging members of the American Nazi Party, whose counter-protesting presence that day did nothing to lend moral legitimacy to the Vietnam War, or defuse the combustible tension that hung in the air.[28]

It began to ignite by mid-afternoon. Antiwar militants led a vanguard toward the Pentagon's plaza, tearing down the fence cordon. Twenty or so found their way into the building where they met a wall of soldiers who tore into them, janitors mopping up blood trails the next morning. With a crowd of Pentagon bureaucrats and Army snipers on the rooftop, the scene was spinning dangerously out of control. "It was terrifying. Christ yes, I was scared," admitted one of the onlookers—Secretary of Defense Robert McNamara, who was by then tormented by the war. Like many American fathers—including Paul Nitze, whose son was in the crowd—McNamara's relationship with his son suffered because of Vietnam. Just before midnight, a thick **V** of soldiers of the 82nd waded into the remaining crowd of several thousand and let loose. "The brutality was horrible," said one eyewitness later. "Nonresisting girls were kicked and clubbed." Young women's faces were bashed with rifle butts. "The look on the face" of one soldier beating a girl, said another onlooker, "could only have been that of someone having an orgasm."[29] There were nearly 700 arrests. No body count of the injured was offered by authorities.

After Stop the Draft Week, the once ebullient power of nonviolence and "participatory democracy" seemed quaintly inadequate to mounting body bags and what seemed a reactionary police state. The movement turned increasingly toward making the cost of further escalation the ungovernability of America at home; "glue in the keyholes," said Berkeley activist Suzy Nelson.[30] The point-of-no-return feeling was magnified by the revolutionary rhetoric of the Black Panthers. Taking hold inside the movement that fall was a seductive and dangerous bravado that induced fantasies of revolution bearing little relation to the power equation on the ground. Mutinous machismo in the streets, literal pissing in the face of the American military—that happened, too, at the Pentagon—would not win the hearts and minds of the American mainstream. Yet the paradox of these years was that even as the majority of the World War II generation looked at street demonstrations in revulsion, the movement's position that the war should end was increasingly that of the nation. As images of body bags and napalm attacks flooded living rooms, as returning soldiers confronted Americans with the savagery of the war, the percentage of citizens telling pollsters they favored a withdrawal nearly doubled between July and the March on the

Pentagon (Figure 7.2). The Johnson administration faced a widening "credibility gap." By late 1967 nearly half of Americans believed it had been a mistake to send troops to Vietnam in the first place.[31] LBJ's own national security team was wavering. "Ho Chi Minh is a tough old S.O.B.," McNamara admitted. "He won't quit no matter how much bombing we do."[32]

Almost three years into the war, the U.S. military establishment faced an antiwar movement of expanding weight. Business leaders, actors, lawyers, mothers, high school students, aging veterans, and decorated retired generals like David Shoup were among those voicing opposition to the war.[33] On April 15, 1967, a small group of young veterans, standing behind a makeshift, "Vietnam Veterans Against the War!" banner, marched with 100,000 more in New York City toward the United Nations calling for the war's end. In the crowd was Jan Barry Crumb, who had written a letter to McNamara that contained his service medals. Veterans across the country found each other and elected Crumb president of Vietnam Veterans Against the War (VVAW). In November 1967, a VVAW letter in the *New York Times* declared,

> that true support for our buddies still in Viet-Nam is to demand that they be brought home (through whatever negotiation is necessary) before anyone else dies in a war the American people did not vote for and do not want.[34]

Over the next five years, the organization became enough of a force to be swept up in J. Edgar Hoover's notorious Counterintelligence (COINTELPRO) Program. From the late 1960s on, COINTELPRO's surveillance and sabotage activities aimed at destroying the Black Panthers and what Hoover believed were dangerous elements of the antiwar movement, including American

Figure 7.2 The Vietnam War entered the living rooms of Americans through nightly televised news coverage.

Courtesy of the Library of Congress

veterans. Denounced by some veterans, the VVAW nevertheless disarmed some of the invective of zealous patriots who claimed that any criticism of the war undermined the war effort. The organization lent credibility to the cause of ending the war, and the national security establishment and its allies knew it.[35]

A still greater threat was the GI movement inside the military. In November 1965, Lieutenant Henry Howe marched in an El Paso, Texas peace march, and was quietly court martialed. In February 1966, *Ramparts* published a damning article entitled, "The Whole Thing Was a Lie!" Written by retired Special Forces Master Sergeant Donald Duncan, the essay condemned the U.S. alliance with the regime in Saigon and the growing opposition it faced among the South Vietnamese. Duncan then testified about the systematic use of torture against suspected Viet Cong at the "International War Crimes Tribunal" convened in 1967 by 94-year-old British Nobel Prize-winning philosopher and activist Bertrand Russell in Stockholm. Following testimony of napalm attacks and the widespread killing of civilians, the tribunal found the U.S. guilty of violating the Nuremberg principles articulated by chief prosecutor, Robert H. Jackson. As Jackson declared and the Russell Tribunal reaffirmed, crimes against humanity were to be prosecuted uniformly:

> If certain acts and violations of treaties are crimes, they are crimes whether the United States does them or whether Germany does them. We are not prepared to lay down a rule of criminal conduct against others which we would not be willing to have invoked against us.[36]

With no official standing, the Russell Tribunal was ignored or trashed in the press as a "farce" of "anti-American propaganda." Still, it put another crack in the national consensus on the war, and set the stage for a series of gut-wrenching public testimonials of war crimes by Vietnam veterans.[37]

Nuremberg had already emerged in the GI movement with the case of the "Fort Hood Three." On June 30, 1966, at the Community Church in downtown Manhattan, David Samas, James Johnson, and Dennis Mora held a press conference announcing their decision to refuse service in a war they considered, "immoral, illegal, and unjust."[38] At his court martial, David Samas declared he would not replicate the defense of Nazi officers that they were "just following orders."[39] Despite the U.S. military's threat of severe reprisals against any additional such actions, GI resistance multiplied. "I follow the Fort Hood Three. Who will follow me?" asked Ronald Lockman. At a "pray-in" for peace on a South Carolina military base in April 1967, resisters made clear this was a decision of conscience for which they were willing to accept consequences. By the time the Fort Hood Three were released three years later, GI resisters' coffeehouses had mushroomed around the country, and hundreds of underground newspapers were disseminating the voice of the antiwar soldier throughout the ranks.[40]

The actions of the Fort Hood Three also raised the entangled issues of class and race in Vietnam. All working-class young men, Samas, Johnson, and Mora offered a portrait of American diversity—Lithuanian-Italian American, African American, and Puerto Rican—which figured prominently in their decision. "We know that Negroes and Puerto Ricans are being drafted and end up in the worst of the fighting all out of proportion to their numbers in the population," they declared, "and we have firsthand knowledge that these are the ones who have been deprived of decent education and jobs at home." In 1966, nearly one-quarter of the casualties in Vietnam were African American, more than double the population at home.[41]

The connections between the war and racial injustice had been made by SNCC, the Black Panthers, and most famously, Muhammad Ali, heavyweight boxing champion of the world. A devout member of the Nation of Islam, Ali refused his draft notice in 1966, declaring:

> My conscience won't let me go shoot my brother, or some darker people, or some poor hungry people in the mud for big powerful America. And shoot them for what? They never called me nigger, they never lynched me, they didn't put no dogs on me, they didn't rob me of my nationality, rape and kill my mother and father … Shoot them for what? How can I shoot them poor people? Just take me to jail.[42]

On April 28, 1967, outside the Houston induction center where he refused to respond to his renounced "slave name" Cassius Clay, Ali announced that he could not, "be true to my beliefs in my religion by accepting such a call. I am dependent upon Allah as the final judge of those actions brought about by my own conscience."[43] Ali was convicted of draft evasion, fined $10,000, and sentenced to five years in prison. Stripped of his boxing crown at the height of his career, Ali spent the next four years appealing his conviction and speaking out on the war. In June 1971, the U.S. Supreme Court unanimously ruled in Ali's favor, determining that the draft board had illegitimately denied his application for Conscientious Objector status. One of the most polarizing figures of the decade, Ali was detested by many older white Americans. Journalist David Susskind spoke for many of them, sneering that Ali was a "a disgrace to his country, his race, and what he laughingly describes as his profession … He is a simplistic fool and a pawn."[44] Millions of young Americans, however, revered Ali for his courage and sacrifice.[45]

Decisions of conscience resonated in American religious communities, where there was deepening opposition to the war. Yale University chaplain William Sloane Coffin founded "Clergy and Laity Concerned About Vietnam," a broad coalition of religiously minded opponents of the war. Mainline Protestantism remained divided, and yet the longer the war dragged on, the greater the number of Episcopalians, Methodists and Presbyterians joining Coffin in denouncing the war. "A growing consensus among mature, morally sensitive people," urged *The Christian Century*, a Protestant magazine in January 1968, "is that the spiritual integrity of the United States cannot be secured by our present policy in Vietnam."[46] Most evangelicals, on the other hand, generally removed from politics for nearly a half-century by the 1960s, remained steadfast in support of the Cold War policies of presidents of both parties. Indeed, the antiwar movement became a fertile seedbed for the rise of the religious right in the 1970s. Conservative evangelicals welcomed into their churches growing legions of disaffected Mainline Protestants, alienated by public ministers like Coffin who took liberal positions on the war, poverty, the women's movement, and racial injustice.[47]

Religiously grounded opposition could be quite literally incendiary. Near nightfall on November 2, 1965, a devout Quaker named Norman Morrison sat down with his infant daughter near the river entrance of the Pentagon, not far from Robert McNamara's window. Setting his daughter aside, he doused himself with kerosene and lit a match. Morrison went up in flames "like the whoosh of a small rocket fire."[48] Mimicking the actions of the Vietnamese Buddhist monks, Morrison was followed a week later by Roger LaPorte, an activist in Dorothy Day's Catholic Worker Movement, who self-immolated at the United Nations.[49] Three years later the Catonsville Nine, a group of Catholic activists led by the brother priests Daniel and Philip Berrigan, poured homemade napalm over hundreds of draft files stolen from the Catonsville, Maryland Selective Service board, and set them afire. "Some property has no right to exist," Daniel Berrigan declared. The American Catholic Church banished Berrigan to South America for his radical brand of Catholic activism, further elevating his status with legions of liberal antiwar Catholics.[50]

The most prominent religious intellectual in the nation, Reverend Martin Luther King, had been relatively muted in his criticism of the war. That ended April 4, 1967 with an address to an overflowing throng at the Riverside Church in New York City. Casting aside concerns that a frontal assault on the war would sever his relationship with President Johnson, King delivered the most controversial oration of his public life. "A time comes when silence is betrayal," King began. "The world now demands that we admit that we have been wrong from the beginning of our adventure in Vietnam." King acknowledged that in urging residents of the urban ghetto to remain nonviolent, that he had no answer to their questions about the nation's horrific actions in Vietnam. "And I knew that I could never again raise my voice ... without having first spoken clearly to the greatest purveyor of violence in the world today: my own government."[51]

King's immersion in the problems of the urban north had helped forge his thinking on the war, no episode more critical than what happened the previous year in Chicago. The SCLC's Chicago Freedom Project targeted the discriminatory practices of city lenders and real estate companies that maintained an impenetrably segregated residential housing system. King moved with his family into a slum apartment on the city's west side and launched a series of boycotts and demonstrations focused on white employers in African American neighborhoods who managed to not have a single black employee. On August 5, 1966, King led a march of 700 demonstrators through the white ethnic stronghold of Marquette Park. The seething racism was evident in the signage: "King would look good with a knife in his back." Firecrackers, bottles, and bricks rained down on the marchers. King was struck with a rock, falling to one knee. For all the violence King had seen in the South, Chicago was different. "I have never seen anything so hostile and so hateful as I've seen here today," King said.[52]

What he witnessed in Chicago and elsewhere fueled King's evolution about the entwined nature of economic security, social justice, and racial fear, and the necessity of a Marshall Plan-scaled, multi-racial commitment on poverty. That could never happen as long as the war in Vietnam raged on. The war was draining funds and national energy away from a War on Poverty that had become increasingly marginalized in the Johnson administration. By the time he came to Riverside that evening, King was convinced that the United States needed to move toward a democratic socialist system, one not consumed by expensive overseas military adventures. There was, too, the striking image of white and black soldiers in Vietnam—side by side, said King, "as they kill and die together for a nation that has been unable to seat them together in the same schools," nor live in the same Chicago neighborhood. An unsparing history of the war followed: its colonialist roots, the denial of elections and repressive Saigon regime, and now the savage "madness" of the American war. Quoting a Buddhist leader, King's scathing attack went straight to the heart of why the war was being lost: "The Americans are forcing even their friends into becoming their enemies."

It was altogether a searing indictment of not just the war in Vietnam, but what the civil rights leader warned America was becoming: an imperial power permanently fortified for war, "approaching spiritual death" due to exorbitant military spending, a nation on the wrong side of a global struggle pitting wealth and might against impoverished people around the globe, and ultimately democracy itself. King's trenchant, transcendent analysis extended far beyond the rice paddies of Vietnam, attacking the very foundations of modern America:

> I am convinced that if we are to get on the right side of the world revolution, we as a nation must undergo a radical revolution of values. We must rapidly begin … the shift from a thing-oriented society to a person-oriented society. When machines and computers, profit motives and property rights, are considered more important than people, the giant triplets of racism, extreme materialism, and militarism are incapable of being conquered.[53]

The Washington Post declared that King had "diminished his usefulness to his cause, his country, and his people." *Time* called it "demagogic slander that sounded like a script for Radio Hanoi."[54] A liberated King left Riverside on the final journey of a life that would end exactly one year later.

The Radical Possibilities of the Counterculture

Perhaps the least understood dimension of the sixties' tumult, the counterculture was long ago reduced by politicians, the media, and Hollywood to a cartoon image of hippies obliviously awash in free love, psychedelic drugs, and good rock and roll. The caricature's many roots include the moment in 1966 when California gubernatorial candidate Ronald Reagan took aim at the university-sanctioned Vietnam Day Committee's dance featuring three rock bands and movies playing simultaneously at opposite ends of a gymnasium—consisting, Reagan declared,

> of color sequences that gave the appearance of different colored liquid spreading across the screen, followed by shots of men and women … [and] their nude torsos, and persons twisted and gyrated in provocative and sensual fashion. The young people were seen standing … with glazed eyes consistent with the condition of being under the influence of narcotics. Sexual misconduct was blatant.[55]

The lurid details were "so contrary to our standards of human behavior that [Reagan] couldn't possibly recite them to you." Reagan was pleased to try, however, featuring them in his larger assault on the "mess at Berkeley" that got him elected governor. One year later, CBS newsman Harry Reasoner brought cameras into Jerry Garcia's kitchen for a special report on San Francisco's Haight-Ashbury district amid the celebrated 1967 "Summer of Love." Pressing him to elucidate the aspirations of the counterculture, Reasoner elicited this from the Grateful Dead lead guitarist: "We're not thinking about revolution or war or any of that … We would all like to be able to live an uncluttered life. A simple life, a good life, you know, and like think about moving the whole human race ahead a step."[56]

Notwithstanding that glimpse of the counterculture worldview, Reasoner's "The Hippie Temptation" spent most of its hour warning of the alleged terrors of LSD. A pillar of the media establishment, Reasoner conveyed journalistic bemusement with the hippies, but made clear his judgment in the end: "They depend on hallucination for their philosophy. This is not a new idea, and it has never worked."[57] By the time the report aired, hippiedom's magical moment had already passed. *Time* had done a cover feature and thousands of wandering young souls had come to the Haight with flowers in their hair, some better prepared than others for the adventure. The production of hippie exploitation films began. Tie-dye and dayglo fashions found their way to department stores. TV's *Dragnet* offered viewers "Blueboy," an episode in which a hopelessly lost hippie mixes LSD with barbiturates in an effort to go "farther out," overdosing in the process. The media misrepresentation and over-exposure of hip inspired the legendary Diggers—theatrically minded community anarchists of the Haight who disseminated free food, medical care and promoted works of guerilla street art—to stage at the end of 1967 a mock "Death of Hippie" funeral in the neighborhood's Buena Vista Park.

Underneath the facile image of the counterculture lies not a movement, but a galaxy of ideas, impulses, and inclinations that comprised one of the wildest adventures in American cultural history. Distinct from the serious-minded activists of the antiwar and civil rights movements—judgmentally termed "politicos" by some—counterculture hippies had grown from the same fertile soil of deep questioning of postwar America. They shared with activists the same generational values, including a serious interrogation of the nature of work in modern society, an avowed rejection of the materialist ethos, an intuitive suspicion of authority, and a respect for black culture. Activists and hippies were moved by the same rock music, much of it colored by both a counterculture aesthetic of introspective searching, as well as visions of a more humane, just future that demanded active engagement with the world.[58] Each possessed an affection for the soothing, revelatory properties of marijuana, and a desire to live with greater awareness of and respect for the natural world. The question of the hour was *how*, as Garcia put it, the "whole human race was to be moved ahead a step." For hippies, it seemed pointless to continue trying to change a political and economic system embedded in a spiritually vacant, depraved culture. Energy was more usefully spent transforming one's consciousness, reaching for a new understanding of self and one's place in the world, and *living the revolution … being* the change, "living it the way you thought it ought to be."[59] It became a truism that at some point radiating outward from the counterculture's center of love and creative energy a critical mass of consciousness would manifest in the larger society.

For its inhabitants, the hippie mecca of Haight was a "joyful bohemian village" one never wanted to leave. "It was just heaven on earth," recalled Paul Kantner of the Jefferson Airplane, San Francisco's preeminent psychedelic band.[60] Much of what took root in hippie epicenters like the Haight and Greenwich Village spread to communities across the western world. Many people experimented with ancient, holistic medical treatments like yoga and meditation. Young women practiced natural childbirth and breastfed babies, and virtually everyone embraced their sexuality with less inhibition. Gardens were planted in abandoned lots. In Amsterdam a band of cultural anarchists known as the "Provos" launched the first bicycle-sharing program. Countless others, some inspired by the Beatles' exploration of Transcendental Meditation, explored Eastern and other alternative spiritual paths that provided what seemed a truer journey of enlightenment than the punitive Judeo-Christian experience of their youth. Jesus Christ himself was reimagined as a figure of liberation who preached love, peace, and few material possessions.

Many in the counterculture sought out life in experimental communities that mushroomed across both rural and urban America. Wherever people ventured, living communally or not, young hippies found their way to Stewart Brand's *Whole Earth Catalog*. Designed as an interactive regular publication to which readers would contribute, the *Whole Earth Catalog* offered probing essays on life's big questions, while answering "practical questions about how things work."[61] It delivered an endlessly expanding trove of illustrated instruction on subjects ranging from raising chickens and goat husbandry to designing one's own renewable energy system to planning new communities. Aspiring to "help people live outside the system of multinational conglomerates and automobile-choked cities," the *Whole Earth Catalog* focused on ecological systems and imagining new integrated means of building community. Companies producing niche seeds, machines, and other products for a wide range of occupations found new customers across the country. An encyclopedia for more conscious living, the catalog underscored the counterculture's central role in cultivating environmentally responsible practices that would later be accepted into the mainstream. Featuring the first-ever "Earth rise" photograph taken by Apollo 8 astronauts—Brand having lobbied NASA since 1966 to release an image of a fragile blue planet from deep space—the cover of the *Whole Earth Catalog* symbolized the rising environmental consciousness of the late sixties, as well as the sense of celestial possibility that persisted since the Kennedy era. Subtitled "access to tools," the *Whole Earth Catalog*, as many, including Apple founder Steve Jobs have observed, provided the essential framework of the World Wide Web. "It was sort of like Google in paperback form, 35 years before Google came along: it was idealistic, and overflowing with neat tools and great notions."[62]

To middle America, distinctions between the two halves of the youth revolt were irrelevant, dissolved in the chaos on their TV screens. For young people, the differences were real, especially early on. As Berry Melton put it, "[The politicos] were going to go march on Washington. We didn't even want to know that Washington was there."[63] As the war grinded on, many who were quick to cast judgment on the counterculture for their utopian unrealistic dreaming realized that on some level perhaps the hippies were the true realists. It was they who recognized the obvious: that the immensity of the western imperial project wreaking hell in Vietnam would not be stopped by street demonstrations. In the cauldron of the late 1960s, the tactical tension between hippies and activists as they stood at the barricades of a well-armed establishment proved dangerous at times, as at the Pentagon. But the synergy could also induce wondrous possibility. For many who were there, the "Human Be-In—Gathering of the Tribes" in San Francisco's Golden Gate Park in January 1967, was such a moment. Organized ostensibly to bring SDS antiwar activists across the bay at Berkeley together with the hippies of the Haight, the Be-In promised an ecstatic "union of love and activism" that could end the war. The underground newspaper *Berkeley Barb* did nothing to tamp down expectations:

> In unity we shall shower the country with waves of ecstasy and purification. Fear will be washed away; ignorance will be exposed to sunlight; profits and empire will lie drying on deserted beaches; violence will be submerged and transmuted in rhythm and dancing."[64]

As if they had all been awaiting the sublime occasion, 20,000 souls appeared. Many who saw the event on TV recall one image: Timothy Leary, the deposed Harvard psychology professor and LSD evangelist, angelically bathed in a flowing white gown, urging the crowd to "Tune In, Turn On, and Drop Out." That was the least of the day's marvels. The Diggers nourished thousands with turkey sandwiches sliced from the flock of renown psychedelic chemist, Augustus Owsley Stanley III, who also conjured up a bounteous helping of his finest LSD for the occasion. The throng reveled in the music of the Jefferson Airplane and the Grateful Dead, the poetry of Gary Snyder, and Buddhist incantations from

Allen Ginsberg. "The air seemed heady and mystical. Dogs and children pranced around in blissful abandon."[65] Painted, flower-festooned bodies danced, and cymbals, flutes, and redolent incense and marijuana filled the air. No one seemed surprised in the least when a man floated down from the clouds on a parachute dispersing LSD tabs like Johnny Appleseed.

A precipitator of the climactic Summer of Love, the Be-In might also be seen as the psychedelic summing up of all the creative currents charging the air of San Francisco's hip community since the arrival of LSD (lysergic acid diethylamide). Synthesized in 1938 by Swiss chemist Albert Hoffman, by the mid-1950s LSD, along with other psychoactive drugs, as suggested earlier, was being tested for its psychotherapeutic benefits in treating a range of addictions and mental disorders at Saskatchewan's Weyburn Hospital and Harvard's Center for Personality Research. It was clear from the instant of Hoffman's first legendary trip on April 19, 1943—when, as he reported, "everything glistened and sparkled in a fresh light ... [and] the world was as if newly created"—that LSD-25 contained mystical properties.[66] Whether prescribed in clinical settings or taken outside the lab, LSD and the entire family of psychedelic drugs had the capacity to induce not only extraordinary pictorial visions, but also a suspension of ego that invited a sense of wonder and revelatory understanding of self and the world that transcended earthly experience. In 1953, author and philosopher-mystic Aldous Huxley offered himself for testing to Humphrey Osmond, the leading psychotherapist at Weyburn. Anxious to expand a shrinking worldview, Huxley found euphoric delight in the seeming infinite expansion of consciousness wrought by mescaline. He had glimpsed, he said, "what Adam had seen on the morning of creation—the miracle, moment by moment, of naked existence."[67]

Perhaps the most intriguing, and provocative episode in LSD's pre-counterculture history concerns painter and bohemian socialite Mary Pinchot Meyer. The ex-wife of CIA official Cord Meyer, Mary Pinchot Meyer enjoyed a passionate love affair with President John F. Kennedy, who reportedly was beguiled by her intellect, beauty, and inspired social vision.[68] According to CIA operative James Angleton who was bugging Meyer's Georgetown townhouse, Meyer also introduced John F. Kennedy to marijuana and LSD, after which they made passionate love. In the spring of 1962, Mary Meyer paid a visit to psychedelics proselytizer Timothy Leary at Harvard, where she sought guidance in carrying out an audacious plan to have key players in Washington's national security establishment drop LSD in hopes of avoiding nuclear Armageddon. Meyer was convinced that once turned on, such men would come to their senses and seek world peace.[69] Less than a year after Kennedy was killed, Mary Meyer was found dead in a wooded area outside Washington. Her murder was never solved, but evidence pointed toward rogue elements of the CIA, and the entire episode added another layer of intrigue to JFK's assassination.[70]

Beyond that bizarre saga, the CIA's role in the journey of LSD into the counterculture is one of the more delicious ironies in the story. Believing that LSD had potential as a mind-control interrogation drug, the CIA in 1960 conducted a series of human experiments with it at the Menlo Park Veterans Hospital near

Stanford, where one of the orderlies—aspiring author and Olympian wrestler Ken Kesey—happily volunteered. LSD doses soon traveled out the door to Kesey's friends in Palo Alto's Perry Lane bohemian neighborhood.[71] By 1964 Kesey had written the hallucinogenic-inspired *One Flew Over the Cuckoo's Nest* and was packing a cross-country supply of LSD into an old school bus he and a band of adventuresome companions known as the "Merry Pranksters" painted psychedelic dayglo. With the exhortation "FURTHUR" painted on the bus's destination plate, Kesey and friends pointed toward New York City with "Cowboy Neal" Cassady at the wheel of the bus. Immortalized by Tom Wolfe in *The Electric Kool-Aid Acid Test*, the journey of the Merry Pranksters tested the outer edges of their consciousness and aesthetic vision, and blew the mind of small-town America.

Upon their return, Kesey and the Pranksters began organizing a series of "Acid Tests," a traveling psychedelic jamboree held initially at Kesey's La Honda ranch, and then staged in various venues of the Bay Area. Featuring the music of a band known at the start as "The Warlocks" but the Grateful Dead by the time they ended in December 1966, the Acid Tests were less musical performance than full-immersion spontaneous, LSD-enhanced "happenings" of art and consciousness. Psychedelically kindred spirits danced while Kesey and the Pranksters saturated the atmosphere with strobe lights and occasional stream-of-consciousness, absurdly intelligible commentary blared over the sound system. As Jerry Garcia recalled, "It was magic, far out, beautiful magic ... What life should be, really."[72]

By the 1967 Summer of Love, LSD was illegal and Kesey was on the lam in Mexico. Dismissed from Harvard for playing fast and loose with his experiments, Timothy Leary's antics popularized hallucinogenic drugs for a youth culture that was often ill-prepared for the spiritual and intellectual odyssey they delivered. Outside sympathetic settings where the social and actual chemistry was untainted, bad trips happened. Precise assessments remain elusive, yet imagining the sixties and all that it bequeathed to American culture *without* LSD is inconceivable. LSD was, said Grateful Dead drummer Bill Kreutzman, "one hell of a door to walk through. You don't outgrow it. You learn what it has to teach you and grow from it."[73] From the Beatles' mid-1960s psychedelically enriched transformation to the brilliance of Brian Wilson and the Beach Boys' *Pet Sounds* album, the mind-opening influence of LSD on the era's music, on the wondrous experimentation with sound and layering of harmonies and instrumentation, is a tale unto itself. The very definition of a musical instrument was shattered. Wilson, for example, employed plastic orange juice cups in "God Only Knows," the "greatest song ever written," according to Paul McCartney.[74] Stewart Brand's vision of the *Whole Earth Catalog* came courtesy of an LSD journey. Leary's former partner Richard Alpert became yoga master Ram Dass and in 1971 published *Be Here Now*, a seminal spiritual text of the era that served as a guide for countless westerners' forays into yoga and eastern religions. As Steve Jobs recalled, the birth of Apple in the hippie epicenter owes much to the deprogramming, transfigurative properties of LSD.[75]

More than all of that, the greatest legacy of psychedelics was and remains their capacity to induce contact with the sacred. In whatever manifestation, psychedelic travelers report back astonishing glimpses of understanding—not just of themselves, but whatever divinity lies on the other side. Since 2006, renewed clinical testing with psychedelics of terminally ill patients struggling with their mortality has reaffirmed the psychological and spiritual value of such revelatory experiences.[76] For most, psychedelic drugs open the door to those transcendent values that were always the heart of the counterculture—and which are, inevitably, hopelessly impossible to articulate: a way of being in the world that aspires to greater understanding, empathy and *love* of humanity and the natural world. Love and an abiding interconnectedness in a broken world, after all, lay at the root of so much of the undeniably positive cultural legacies of the hippies that carried well into the next century, from environmentally responsible lifestyles to reimaging how we care for ourselves. More than essential, in the end *love*, said writer Michael Pollan after one of his excursions, *was everything.*[77]

Notes

1 Students for a Democratic Society, "Port Huron Statement," June 15, 1962, https://history.hanover.edu/courses/excerpts/111huron.html, retrieved October 14, 2018; Michael Kazin, "The Port Huron Statement at Fifty," *Dissent*, Spring 2012, www.dissentmagazine.org/article/the-port-huron-statement-at-fifty, retrieved October 14, 2018.
2 A place established by the Congress of Industrial Organizations.
3 Jim Bloch, "Port Huron Statement Could Have Been Finalized Elsewhere," The Voice, September 12, 2012, www.voicenews.com/news/port-huron-statement-could-have-been-finalized-elsewhere/article_26df063a-7396-5c2c-82eb-bda358775137.html, retrieved October 12, 2018.
4 Students for a Democratic Society, "Port Huron Statement."
5 Judith Karpova, in David Hoffman, *Making Sense of the Sixties*, (Washington, DC: WETA, Public Broadcasting System, 1991), Episode 2 of 6, "We Can Change the World"; David Anderson, *The Movement and the Sixties: Protest in America from Greensboro to Wounded Knee* (New York: Oxford University Press, 1995), 25; Sarah Zimmerman, Jamie Ehrlich, and Emily Feigenbaum, "'A Special Problem': The University of Chicago's Troubled History with Sexual Assault, Harassment, and Campus Safety," *The Chicago Maroon*, May 1, 2017, www.chicagomaroon.com/article/2017/5/1/special-problem-university-chicagos-troubled-histo; Frank T. McAndrew, "Controlling the Conduct of College Women in the 1960s," *Psychology Today*, February 15, 2017, www.psychologytoday.com/us/blog/out-the-ooze/201702/controlling-the-conduct-college-women-in-the-1960s, retrieved October 17, 2018.
6 David Lance Goines, 1993, *The Free Speech Movement: Coming of Age in the 1960's* (Berkeley, CA: Ten Speed Press, 1993), 49.
7 Mark Kitchell, *Berkeley in the Sixties* (San Francisco, CA: Kitchell Films, 1990, documentary film, 117 minutes).
8 Kitchell; and Chip Gibbons, "Resisting HUAC: A Grassroots Success Story," *Defending Rights and Dissent*, November 19, 2015, https://rightsanddissent.org/news/resisting-huac-a-grassroots-success-story/, retrieved October 17, 2018.
9 Kitchell; and David Burner, "The Berkeley Free Speech Movement, 1963–64," in *Making Peace with the Sixties* (Princeton, NJ: Princeton University Press, 1996), www.writing.upenn.edu/~afilreis/50s/berkeley.html, retrieved October 17, 2018.

10 Kitchell.

11 Mario Savio, "Sit-in Address on the Steps of Sproul Hall," December 2, 1964; at www.americanrhetoric.com/speeches/mariosaviosproulhallsitin.htm, retrieved October 17, 2018.

12 Burner.

13 Kitchell; and Anderson, 101–105.

14 Tom Wells, *The War Within America's Battle Over Vietnam* (Berkeley, CA: University of California Press, 1994), 23–24; and Louis Menashe, ed., "Berkeley Teach-In:Vietnam," Voices and Documents, recorded at the Berkeley Campus of the University of California, KPFA (Washington, DC: Smithsonian Folkways, 1966), 1–2, https://media.smithsonianfolkways.org/liner_notes/folkways/FW05765.pdf, retrieved October 18, 2018.

15 SDS leader Carl Oglesby's characterization, quoted in Wells, 24.

16 Menashe, 2–3.

17 Alan McPherson, "Misled by Himself: What the Johnson Tapes Reveal About the Dominican Intervention of 1965," *Latin American Research Review* 38, no. 2 (June 2003), 127–146.

18 Paul Potter, "The Incredible War," April 17, 1965, https://voicesofdemocracy.umd.edu/potter-the-incredible-war-speech-text/, retrieved April 5, 2021.

19 Dick Cheney and Bill Clinton, George W. Bush, and Donald Trump employed a combination of college draft deferments, the National Guard, and faked bone spurs, respectively, to avoid service.

20 With help from his brother Duane and a lot of whiskey, southern rock musician Gregg Allman was among them. See Richard Scott, "Draft Dodging in the U.S. Now Socially Acceptable," *The Guardian*, April 12, 1966, www.theguardian.com/century/1960-1969/Story/0,,106464,00.html, retrieved October 18, 2018.

21 Wells, 191–193; and Reese Erlich, "Lessons from Stop the Draft Week," Antiwar.blog, September 28, 2017, www.antiwar.com/blog/2017/09/28/lessons-from-stop-the-draft-week-50-years-ago, retrieved October 18, 2018.

22 Anderson, 179.

23 Anderson, 177; and Bob Lawrence, "A Turning Point: Six Stories from the Dow Chemical Protest on Campus," https://1967.wisc.edu/profiles/bob-lawrence, retrieved October 18, 2018.

24 Wells, 93–194; and Gayle World, "50 Years Ago, 'Dow Day' Left Its Mark on Madison," *Wisconsin State Journal*, October 8, 2017, https://madison.com/wsj/news/local/education/university/years-ago-dow-day-left-its-mark-on-madison/article_47f7dc75-e30a-5a16-8cf1-044eebc66f18.html, retrieved October 18, 2018; and Anderson, 177.

25 "Protest: The Banners of Dissent," *Time*, October 27, 1967, http://content.time.com/time/subscriber/article/0,33009,841090-9,00.html, retrieved October 19, 2018.

26 Stephanie Buck, "The Plan to Levitate the Pentagon was the Perfect Absurdly Inspiring Protest for the Time." *Timeline*, February 26, 2017, https://timeline.com/pentagon-exorcism-ae0aad1b55c5, retrieved October 19, 2018.

27 Pat Thomas, "'Out Demons, Out!': The October 1967 March on the Pentagon," *Nightflight*, October 21, 2015, http://nightflight.com/out-demons-out-the-october-1967-march-on-the-pentagon, retrieved October 19, 2018.

28 Buck.

29 Wells, 200–203; and Anderson, 178–179.

30 Kitchell.

31 "Changes in Attitudes about Vietnam, 1967," Cornell University, Roper Center for Public Opinion Research, https://ropercenter.cornell.edu/public-support-vietnam-1967, retrieved October 20, 2018.

32 Quoted in Anderson, 162.

33 Anderson, 166.

34 Gerald Nicosia, *Home to War: A History of the Vietnam Veterans Movement* (New York: Random House, 2001), 15–23; and Jan Barry Crumb, "When Veterans Protested the Vietnam War," *Vietnam Full Disclosure*, April 19, 2017, www.vietnamfulldisclosure. org/veterans-protested-vietnam-war, retrieved October 21, 2018.

35 Laura Blumenfeld and Dan Balz, "FBI Tracked Kerry in Vietnam Vets Group," *Washington Post*, March 23, 2004, A7.

36 Robert H. Jackson, International Conference on Military Trials, London, July 23, 1945, https://avalon.law.yale.edu/imt/jack44.asp, retrieved October 21, 2018.

37 Wells, 141–143; and "Donald Duncan," obituary in *Medic in the Green Time*, http:// medicinthegreentime.com/donald-duncan, retrieved October 21, 2018.

38 "Statement of the Fort Hood Three," June 30, 1966. At Zinn Education Project, www.zinnedproject.org/news/tdih/fort-hood-three, accessed October 20, 2018.

39 Derek Seidman, "We Will Not Be Part of This Unjust, Immoral, and Illegal War': Remembering the Fort Hood Three," Zinn Education Project, *Huffington Post*, n.d., at www.huffingtonpost.com/the-zinn-education-project/we-will-not-be-part-of-th_b_10753178.html, retrieved October 21, 2018.

40 James Lewes, *Protest and Survive: Underground GI Newspapers during the Vietnam War* (Westport, CT: Praeger, 2003); Laura Smith, "When the Fort Hood Three Refused to go to Vietnam, they Sparked a Revolution," *Timeline*, November 30, 2017, https:// timeline.com/when-the-fort-hood-three-refused-to-go-to-vietnam-they-sparked-a-military-revolution-f981e39301a1; and Marcus Karl Adams, "The War Within: The Soldiers' Resistance Movement during the Vietnam Era," thesis, Department of History and Philosophy (Ypsilanti, MI: Eastern Michigan University, 2008), 6–12, https://commons.emich.edu/cgi/viewcontent.cgi?referer=https://timeline.com/when-the-fort-hood-three-refused-to-go-to-vietnam-they-sparked-a-military-revolution-f981e3930 1a1&httpsredir=1&article=1208&context=theses, retrieved October 21, 2018.

41 "Statement of the Fort Hood Three,"; and Christian G. Appy, *American Reckoning: The Vietnam War and our National Identity* (New York: Penguin, 2015), 139.

42 Bill Siegel, dir., *The Trials of Muhammad Ali*, documentary film (Kartmequin Films, 2013).

43 DeNeen L. Brown, "'Shoot Them for What?' How Muhammad Ali Won His Greatest Fight," *Washington Post*, June 16, 2017, www.washingtonpost.com/news/retropolis/wp/2018/06/15/shoot-them-for-what-how-muhammad-ali-won-his-greatest-fight/?utm_term=.b19ba7096181, retrieved October 21, 2018.

44 Krishnadev Calamur, "Muhammad Ali and Vietnam," *The Atlantic*, June 4, 2016, www.theatlantic.com/news/archive/2016/06/muhammad-ali-vietnam/485717, retrieved October 21, 2018.

45 Dave Zirin, "'I Just Wanted to be Free': The Radical Reverberations of Muhammad Ali," *The Nation*, June 4, 2016, www.thenation.com/article/i-just-wanted-to-be-free-the-radical-reverberations-of-muhammad-ali/, retrieved October 21, 2018.

46 Edward B. Fiske, "Religion: The Clergy on Vietnam," *New York Times*, January 7, 1968, www.nytimes.com/1968/01/07/archives/religion-the-clergy-on-vietnam. html?xid=PS_smithsonian, retrieved October 21, 2018.

47 David Mislin, "How Vietnam War Protests Accelerated the Rise of the Religious Right," *Smithsonian*, May 3, 2018, www.smithsonianmag.com/history/how-vietnam-war-protests-spurred-rise-christian-right-180968942, retrieved October 21, 2018.

48 Wells, 58.

49 Isaac May, "Forged in the Fire: Norman Morrison and the Link Between Liberal Quakerism and Radical Action," *The Graduate Journal of Harvard Divinity School*, Spring 2014, https://projects.iq.harvard.edu/hdsjournal/book/forged-fire-norman-morrison-and-link-between-liberal-quakerism-and-radical-action,　　　　retrieved October 21, 2018.

50 Anderson, 203, 381; and "'The Vietnam Years': How the Conflict Ripped the Nation's Religious Fabric," *Religion News Service*, September 8, 2017, https://religionnews.com/2017/09/08/the-vietnam-years-how-the-conflict-ripped-the-nations-religious-fabric, retrieved October 21, 2018.

51 Martin Luther King, Jr., "Beyond Vietnam—A Time to Break Silence," April 4, 1967, Riverside Church, New York City, www.americanrhetoric.com/speeches/mlkatimetobreaksilence.htm, retrieved October 22, 2018.

52 Frank James, "Martin Luther King, Jr. in Chicago," *Chicago Tribune* (January 3, 2008); at www.chicagotribune.com/news/nationworld/politics/chi-chicagodays-martinlutherking-story-story.html, retrieved October 22, 2018.

53 King, "Beyond Vietnam," 1967.

54 "A Tragedy," *Washington Post*, April 6, 1967; *Time* quoted in Mary Susannah Robbins, *Against the Vietnam War: Writings by Activists* (Lanham, MD: Rowman and Littlefield, 2007), 109.

55 Ronald Reagan, San Francisco Cow Palace Speech, May 12, 1966, quoted in Michael W. Flamm and David Steigerwald, *Debating the 1960s: Liberal, Conservative and Radical Perspectives* (New York: Rowman and Littlefield, 2008), 147.

56 Harry Reasoner, Narrator. Columbia Broadcast System News, Special Report, *The Hippie Temptation*, August 22, 1967.

57 Reasoner, *The Hippie Temptation*.

58 See Michael J. Kramer, *The Republic of Rock: Music and Citizenship in the Sixties Counterculture* (New York: Oxford University Press, 2013).

59 Jentri Anders, in Kitchell.

60 Paul Kantner, in Bob Sarles, Christina Keating, and Matt Friedman, prod., *Fly Jefferson Airplane* (United Kingdom: Eagle Rock Entertainment, 2004).

61 Robert Horvitz, "Exploring Whole Earth: Whole Earth Culture," *Whole Earth Catalog: Access to Tools and Ideas*, www.wholeearth.com/history-whole-earth-culture.php, retrieved October 25, 2018.

62 Steve Jobs, 2005 Stanford Commencement Address, quoted by Carole Cadwalladr, "Stewart Brand's Whole Earth Catalog, The Book That Changed the World," *The Guardian*, May 4, 2013, www.theguardian.com/books/2013/may/05/stewart-brand-whole-earth-catalog, retrieved April 6, 2021; see Fred Turner, *From Counterculture to Cyber Culture: Stewart Brand, the Whole Earth Network, and the Rise of Digital Utopianism* (Chicago, IL: University of Chicago Press, 2006).

63 Melton, in Kitchell.

64 *Berkeley Barb*, quoted in Anderson, 172.

65 Helen Swick Perry, "The Human Be-In," in Alexander Bloom and Wini Breines, eds., *Takin' It to the Streets: A Sixties Reader* (New York: Oxford University Press, 2003), 271.

66 Albert Hofmann, *LSD: My Problem Child* (Santa Cruz, CA: Multidisciplinary Association for Psychedelic Studies, 2009), 51.

67 Aldous Huxley, *The Doors of Perception, and Heaven and Hell* (New York: Harper and Row, 1963), 17.

68 Herbert Parmet, *JFK: The Presidency of John F. Kennedy* (Norwalk, CT: Easton Press, 1986), 305.

69 Timothy Leary, *Flashbacks: An Autobiography* (Boston, MA: Houghton Mifflin, 1983), 128.

70 David Talbot, *Brothers: The Hidden History of the Kennedy Years* (New York: Free Press), 207, 195–202.

71 Michael Pollan, *How to Change Your Mind: What the New Science of Psychedelics Teaches Us About Consciousness, Dying, Addiction, Depression, and Transcendence* (New York: Penguin, 2018), 206.

72 Jerry Garcia, quoted in David Gans and Peter Simon, *Playing in the Band: An Oral and Visual Portrait of the Grateful Dead* (New York: St. Martin's Press, 1985), 42.

73 William Kreutzman, quoted in Gans and Simon, 46.

74 "Album Liner Notes," http://albumlinernotes.com/Party_Stack-O-Tracks.html; Paul McCartney quoted at www.songfacts.com/facts/the-beach-boys/god-only-knows, retrieved June 10, 2021.
75 Pollan, 175, 205; W. J. Rorabaugh, "The Hippies Won the Culture War," *History New Network*, September 27, 2015, https://historynewsnetwork.org/article/160407, retrieved October 27, 2018.
76 Pollan, 331–358.
77 Ibidi, 251.

Further Reading

Anderson, David. *The Movement and the Sixties: Protest in America from Greensboro to Wounded Knee*. New York: Oxford University Press, 1995.

Bloom, Alexander, and Wini Breines, eds. *Takin' It to the Streets: A Sixties Reader*. New York: Oxford University Press, 2nd ed., 2002.

Burner, David. *Making Peace with the Sixties*. Princeton, NJ: Princeton University Press, 1996.

Cottrell, Robert C. *Sex, Drugs, and Rock and Roll: The Rise of the 1960s Counterculture*. Lanham, MD: Rowman and Littlefield, 2015.

Davis, James K. *Assault on the Left: The FBI and the Sixties Antiwar Movement*. Westport, CT: Praeger, 1997.

Flamm, Michael W., and David Steigerwald. *Debating the 1960s: Liberal, Conservative and Radical Perspectives*. New York: Rowman and Littlefield, 2008.

Goines, David Lance. *The Free Speech Movement: Coming of Age in the 1960's*. Berkeley, CA: Ten Speed Press, 1993.

Hall, Simon. *Peace and Freedom: The Civil Rights and Antiwar Movements of the 1960s*. Philadelphia, PA: University of Pennsylvania Press, 2005.

Hoerl, Kristen. *The Bad Sixties: Hollywood Memories of the Counterculture, Antiwar, and Black Power Movements*. Jackson, MI: University Press of Mississippi, 2018.

Huxley, Aldous. *The Doors of Perception, and Heaven and Hell*. New York: Harper and Row, 1963.

Kramer, Michael J. *The Republic of Rock: Music and Citizenship in the Sixties Counterculture*. New York: Oxford University Press, 2013.

Leary, Timothy. *Flashbacks: An Autobiography*. Boston, MA: Houghton Mifflin, 1983.

Lemke-Santagelo, Gretchen. *Daughters of Aquarius: Women of the Sixties Counterculture*. Lawrence, KS: University Press of Kansas, 2009.

Lewes, James. *Protest and Survive: Underground GI Newspapers during the Vietnam War*. Westport, CT: Praeger, 2003.

Nicosia, Gerald. *Home to War: A History of the Vietnam Veterans Movement*. New York: Random House, 2001.

Pollan, Michael. *How to Change Your Mind: What the New Science of Psychedelics Teaches Us About Consciousness, Dying, Addiction, Depression, and Transcendence*. New York: Penguin, 2018.

Robbins, Mary Susannah. *Against the Vietnam War: Writings by Activists*. Lanham, MD: Rowman and Littlefield, 2007.

Totter, Andrew J., ed. *Light at the End of the Tunnel: A Vietnam War Anthology*. Lanham, MD: Rowman and Littlefield, 2010.

Turner, Fred. *From Counterculture to Cyber Culture: Stewart Brand, the Whole Earth Network, and the Rise of Digital Utopianism*. Chicago, IL: University of Chicago Press, 2006.

Wells, Tom. *The War Within America's Battle Over Vietnam*. Berkeley, CA: University of California Press, 1994.

8   1968

The Rupture

Even a half-century later, a select list of the extraordinary events of 1968 retained a capacity to shock the historical imagination: the Tet Offensive that brought the deadliest fighting of the Vietnam War and its political turning point at home; the assassination of Dr. Martin Luther King, Jr., triggering violent uprisings across the nation and deadly state reprisals; unprecedented upheaval at Columbia and dozens more American universities, echoed in democratic rebellions all around the world; the assassination of Senator and presidential candidate Robert F. Kennedy that induced unspeakable grief; the courageous but polarizing human rights protest of Tommie Smith and John Carlos at the Mexico City Summer Olympic Games; a "police riot" against unarmed protesters in the streets of Chicago at the Democratic National Convention—itself a chaotic circus that signaled the demise of postwar liberalism as a viable political force; the protest of the Miss America pageant that marked the rising vitality and intersectional power of the women's liberation movement; a presidential election in which one candidate conspired with a foreign government to ensure his victory; and most ominously, the emergence of a brand of conservative politics fueled by racial fear and resentment. A year of turmoil and anguish unequaled in the twentieth century, 1968 left behind a breach in American society that proved difficult to comprehend, much less repair.

Vietnam, January 30

Late in November 1967, General William Westmoreland spoke to the National Press Club and announced, "We have reached an important point where the end begins to come into view." Citing a litany of challenges plaguing the communists, he spoke of a "transition to a fourth and final phase," of "making progress," of an "enemy [whose] hopes are bankrupt."[1] Two months later, in the wee hours of January 30, came the Tet Offensive, a highly coordinated assault of the North Vietnamese Army and the National Liberation Front that began on the occasion of the Tet lunar holiday. In the ensuing weeks, Americans watched an enemy allegedly "on the ropes" lay siege to military bases, villages, and major cities throughout South Vietnam, including the ancient capital of Hue. After fierce ground combat and massive air strikes, American and ARVN forces "liberated"

DOI: 10.4324/9781003160595-8

the rubble of Hue. American casualties in some units exceeded 50 percent, levels not seen since D-Day.[2] The NLF sent 35 battalions into Saigon, far short of the force needed to take the city, but more than enough to present Americans at home with the shocking specter of embattled GIs defending their own embassy. The fight produced Eddie Adams's Pulitzer-winning photograph of the Saigon police chief appearing to execute a VC suspect in cold blood, raising new questions about the kind of government America was defending.

Elsewhere, marines defending the base at Khe Sanh were pounded for 77 days and nights by NVA artillery, taking heavy casualties and triggering nightmarish imaginings in the oval office of a climactic defeat akin to the French at Dien Bien Phu. As Michael Herr wrote, the military command rendered Khe Sanh, a "false love object" that could not be lost. Following events obsessively from the White House, Johnson determined—as if defending the Alamo—that there would be no "Dinbinfoo" on *his* watch.[3] At tremendous cost, the Marines hung on, only to see commanders abandon the base, repositioning American forces elsewhere. Whether in-country or watching it unfold on the nightly news, the logic of American strategy became more difficult to comprehend with each passing day. Following a devastating assault to retake the village of Ben Tre that killed at least 500 civilians, an American major reportedly told the AP's Peter Arnett why the village had to be leveled: "We had to destroy the village in order to save it."[4] The veracity of the retort was later challenged, but in the moment, it rang chillingly true. Pursuing the question of what victory would look like, NBC's Frank McGee concluded that the nation "must decide whether it is futile to destroy Vietnam in the effort to save it."[5]

By late February American commanders had beaten back the Tet Offensive and all but declared victory. North Vietnamese hopes for an uprising in the South failed to materialize. Rumors filtered out of Washington that Westmoreland was requesting an additional 206,000 soldiers to finish off what he claimed was a weakened communist enemy, news that was met with shock and disbelief by most Americans.[6] J. Edgar Hoover warned the president of the security repercussions at home if he chose to escalate the war further. The yawning credibility gap between the pronouncements of officials and what citizens were seeing with their own eyes, became a chasm after the venerable CBS news anchor Walter Cronkite declared in a late-February broadcast that the United States was now "mired in stalemate," confirming the growing belief that the war could not be won.[7] The weeks ahead brought a collapse of public confidence in the war effort; by mid-March, one of four Americans supported Johnson's handling of Vietnam. In the New Hampshire primary, Minnesota's Democratic Senator Eugene McCarthy came within 230 votes of defeating the president in a surging antiwar candidacy. Like the Tet "victory," the president's narrow win was perceived as defeat. It only got worse when Robert F. Kennedy jumped into the race, and then LBJ's "Wise Men" of advisors began urging a partial bombing halt as a first step in changing course. Johnson, stunned and isolated, turned to National Security Advisor Walt Rostow, who offered up his previous recommendation of a ground invasion of North Vietnam and Laos, which in the spring of 1968 was nothing short of madness.[8]

On Sunday, March 31 at 9 p.m., Lyndon Johnson addressed the nation. He announced a partial bombing halt to try and lure Hanoi toward peace talks, prolonged the fable of Americans only ever wanting peace in Vietnam, bemoaned the deepening division in the country, and then dropped the bombshell: he would "not seek, nor would [he] accept the nomination" of the Democratic Party for president.[9] Despite ongoing U.S. bombing, the North Vietnamese responded favorably to the invitation and talks commenced that summer. Fueled by Tet, opposition to the war had forced the beginning of a painfully protracted five-year peace process to end the war. The offensive also helped drive from office a man who had once been one of the most popular and effective presidents in American history.

Memphis, Tennessee, February 1–April 4

Late in the afternoon of February 1, Echol Cole and Robert Walker, employees in the Memphis Sanitation Department's predominantly African American workforce, took shelter from a cold rain in the back of their decrepit garbage truck. Within minutes, faulty wiring triggered the operation of truck's compressor and pulled the men into the truck, crushing them to death. This horrific accident instantly became a metaphor for the city's treatment of black men. Paid so poorly that most had second and third jobs and nearly half qualified for welfare to support their families, black sanitation workers were given no benefits, no unemployment, health care or pension. With no access to showers enjoyed by their white counterparts, black men went home stinking, their clothes lined with maggots—"walking buzzards," some called them.[10] The deaths of Cole and Walker triggered a strike ten days later, an action Mayor Henry Loeb declared illegal. Hundreds of sanitation workers marched anyhow, demanding collective bargaining rights under the American Federation of State and County Municipal Employees. Following a massive protest at city hall, city council voted to recognize the union but Mayor Loeb vetoed the measure, prompting a demonstration on February 23 in which police turned Mace and tear gas on strikers and supporters.[11]

Memphis ministers led by James Lawson made a concerted effort to reassert the nonviolent spirit of the campaign. Despite those intentions, a tinderbox atmosphere pointed to the potential for violence, a fact brutally underscored by the "Orangeburg (South Carolina) Massacre" of February 8 in which police shot and killed three black South Carolina students and wounded 30 more after a series of peaceful protests against the continued segregation of a local bowling alley.[12] The night after the Macing, Rev. Lawson addressed a crowd at Clayborn Temple, declaring that "at the heart of racism is the idea that a man is not a man, that a person is not a person. You are human beings. You are men. You deserve dignity." As strikers marched out the doors, many carried signs distilling Lawson's message: "I AM A MAN." In the following days, strikers marched silently with

Figure 8.1 At the age of 71, sanitation worker Ben Jones was still working in 2008, so that he could pay off the mortgage on his house. Jones holds a replica of the sign 'I AM A MAN' that many strikers carried during the Memphis sanitation workers' strike of 1968 in Memphis, Tennessee.

Carl Juste/Miami Herald/Tribune News Service via Getty Images, www.gettyimages.co.uk/detail/news-photo/at-the-age-of-71-sanitation-worker-ben-jones-is-still-news-photo/112892641?adppopup=true

the placards slung over their bodies—a profound, defiant invocation of their humanity (Figure 8.1).[13]

Lawson reached out to unions and religious leaders around the country—including Dr. King, who saw in Memphis the embodiment of his recently announced Poor People's Campaign. The campaign envisioned a series of economic boycotts and sit-ins, culminating in an encampment in Washington of thousands of poor blacks, whites, Mexican American farmworkers and Native Americans that summer—all directed toward demanding of congress a bold anti-poverty program. King arrived in Memphis on March 18. Speaking to a throng of 12,000, he called for an interracial general strike on the city. He returned ten days later to a scene of alarming pandemonium. As King began leading a march of thousands toward Beale Street, a look of stupefying dread fell over him. Carried forward by Lawson, his aides and the onrushing crowd behind him, King heard the sound of store windows cracking. Interspersed with the marchers were members of "The Invaders," a local group of militants who had no interest in maintaining a nonviolent march. With shouts of "Burn it down baby!" in his ears, King found himself at the head of what appeared to be a mob. For the first time in his public life, King was forced to abandon a march descending into chaos. Police officers were among the injured, one 16-year-old was killed, and downtown Memphis was "littered with bricks and broken glass and dappled with blood," as a local reporter observed.[14] By nightfall, 4,000 Tennessee National Guardsmen were guarding a city under martial law. Shaken, King nevertheless vowed to return.

The civil rights leader faced mounting division inside the movement and withering assault from the press, members of congress, and the Johnson administration over the Poor People's Campaign. Events in Memphis hardly reassured that chaos would not engulf the nation's capital. Nor did it help that Stokely Carmichael, now heading a "Black United Front" in Washington DC, engaged in reckless talk of leading King's planned "tent city" masses in a confrontation with city and federal officials. Worse still, since the Israeli "Six Day War" of June 1967, Carmichael and H. Rap Brown joined other black radicals in spewing anti-Semitic rhetoric as they allied with the cause of Arabs and Palestinians, poisoning King's efforts to bolster Jewish support for the campaign. In late March, he journeyed to the Catskill Mountains of New York, where rabbis and other Jewish leaders greatly moved him by singing "We Shall Overcome" in Yiddish. For his part, King denounced the anti-Semitism and called for a UN-led effort to ensure the security and peace of Israel and its Palestinian and Arab neighbors.[15]

Into this cauldron dropped the "Kerner Report," the published findings of the National Advisory Commission on Civil Disorders that Johnson had ordered after four summers of urban rebellion. Following extensive testimony garnered from months of hearings, the Kerner Report concluded that more than any other force in American society, racism lay at the root of urban poverty and violence. Despite the progress of the Civil Rights era, the report declared that, "our nation is moving toward two societies, one black, one white—separate and unequal." The Kerner Report called for sweeping measures to confront the deep-seated racism that permeated the economic and political institutions of American cities, beginning with police departments. In calling for programs that went beyond the War on Poverty, Kerner implicitly affirmed the need for a Poor People's Campaign—and though it rejected their militancy, even the anti-racist, community empowerment agenda of the Black Panthers.[16] It stunned the man who ordered it, Johnson receiving the recommendations as a personal affront and an indictment of his administration's failures.[17]

On April 3, King returned to Memphis. Deeply distressed, under intensifying harassment by the FBI, he could hear the footsteps. It had been four years since the FBI had tried to convince him to commit suicide, and after King's scathing opposition to the war, J. Edgar Hoover was not alone in wanting his elimination from American public life.[18] That night, speaking to a crowd of strikers and supporters who braved a pounding rain to hear him, Dr. King offered this grim assessment:

> The nation is sick. Trouble is in the land; confusion all around ... But I know, somehow, that only when it is dark enough can you see the stars. And I see God working in this period of the twentieth century in a way that men, in some strange way, are responding.
>
> Something is happening in our world. The masses of people are rising up ...

Let us rise up tonight with a greater readiness. Let us stand with a greater determination. And let us move on in these powerful days, these days of challenge to make America what it ought to be. We have an opportunity to make America a better nation.[19]

Then came the haunting crescendo:

Like anybody, I would like to live a long life—longevity has its place. But I'm not concerned about that now … I've seen the Promised Land. I may not get there with you. But I want you to know tonight that we, as a people, will get to the Promised Land. And so I'm happy, tonight. I'm not worried about anything. I'm not fearing any man! Mine eyes have seen the glory of the coming of the Lord![20]

The assassination of Martin Luther King, Jr. the next evening as he stood on the balcony of the Lorraine Motel was followed by weeks of rioting in more than 100 cities. Sixteen thousand people were arrested, several thousand injured, the ruins of whole city blocks smoldered, and 43 black citizens lay dead. Another lone gunman, James Earl Ray, was found guilty of King's murder. Questions were raised immediately about the possible complicity of the FBI, and in 1976 the House Select Committee on Assassinations found evidence pointing to possible co-conspirators. In a 1999 civil lawsuit brought by King's family against a Memphis café owner named Lloyd Jowers, using the "preponderance of evidence" standard of a civil trial, a jury concluded that members of the Memphis Police Department, the FBI, and the U.S. 111th Military Intelligence Group had conspired to murder Dr. Martin Luther King, Jr.[21] Although the Justice Department in 2000 reasserted that Ray acted alone, for many black Americans, the Jowers trial confirmed their first instincts: white America pulled the trigger.

Following her husband's funeral, on April 8, Coretta Scott King led a peaceful march through Memphis and the sanitation workers won union recognition from the city. The Poor People's Campaign drew 3,000 souls to the nation's capital for a six-week encampment demanding an anti-poverty program. But in a fearful climate of white backlash, neither Congress nor a besieged Johnson administration heard their pleas.

Columbia University, April 23–30

At Columbia University in late April, the antiwar movement and Black Power struggle became entwined in a series of dramatic actions that threatened the leadership of one of the nation's premier research institutions. Since 1965, Columbia's Society for Afro-American Students (SAS) had been protesting the planned construction of the university's new gymnasium in Morningside Park, a space enjoyed by neighboring residents of predominantly black Harlem. Beyond the gym's design that envisioned a rear "Gym Crow" lower entrance for black residents, the project continued the university's longstanding encroachment on the community. Simultaneously, Columbia's SDS chapter had been waging a campaign against the university's multiple links to the U.S. military, led by the Institute for Defense Analyses (IDA). In late 1967, the high-handed administration of President Grayson Kirk imposed a ban on all indoor protest, further inflaming activists.

The anger began to boil over April 23, 1968, as 500 black and white student radicals marched toward the gym construction site. Rebuffed by police and a large group of conservative students, they found their way to Hamilton Hall, renamed it "Malcolm X Hall," took a dean hostage, and spontaneously assumed command. After prolonged arguments over strategy, the more disciplined black students ultimately demanded their white radical-anarchist allies move on so they could determine their own fate. The next morning, SDS radicals commandeered Low Library, answering the phone in the president's office, "We're sorry, but President Kirk will not be in today … Columbia is under new management."[22] Within 48 hours, waves of students seized three more buildings.

The Strike Coordinating Committee's demands to the university's board of trustees included termination of the gym's construction, severing ties with the IDA, and ending the ban on indoor demonstrations. As with so much that had transpired over the past decade and a half—Montgomery, Greensboro, the Berkeley FSM, the MFDP—what was happening that week at Columbia went beyond the prosaic operations of the university, inflated by its larger context. Writing for *Ramparts*, Tom Hayden saw in the events a "new tactical stage in the resistance movement" that began the previous fall. The radicals viewed themselves as "internationalist and revolutionary" guerillas aiming to disrupt the operation of the "war-machine."[23] "We can hope for and possibly win certain reforms within the university," the strike leaders wrote, "but the ultimate reforms we need—elimination of war and exploitation—can only be gained after we overthrow the control of our country by the class of people on Columbia's Board of Trustees."[24] The forces of institutional and racial oppression were suddenly, indissolubly linked, the struggles for justice at home and to end imperialism abroad, one. As SAS leader Bill Sales declared at Malcolm X Hall,

> There's one oppressor—in Low Library, in Albany, New York. You strike a blow at the gym, you strike a blow for the Vietnamese people. You strike a blow at Low Library, you strike a blow for the freedom fighters in Angola, Mozambique.[25]

At Columbia that week, it was hard to know whether this was world-transforming affinity, an LSD-inspired revolutionary vision, or just delusional folly.

The Columbia uprising saturated America's news coverage for the next week and dominated the underground press for months. It was all quite a spectacle: the revolutionary rhetoric of the occupying students; pitched verbal battles between supporters, conservative students, and a divided faculty; Harlem residents, H. Rap Brown and Stokely Carmichael encamped at Malcolm X Hall; counter-demonstrations by rightwing groups; the arrival of left luminaries

Norman Mailer, Susan Sontag, Abbie Hoffman, and—in the spirit of anarchist Emma Goldman who disdained any revolution that did not dance—the Grateful Dead.[26] One could almost forget the inevitable crackdown was coming. Just after midnight on April 30, the NYPD stormed in, producing 148 injuries, 700 arrests, and a staggering 372 complaints of police brutality. Construction of the gym was stopped, Columbia ended its IDA relationship, President Kirk was soon gone, and a new University Senate with faculty and student participation helped lead to a more liberalized institution. America went on, as did its malignant adventure in Vietnam.

Judgments of the Columbia radicals come easy: reckless, arrogant, nihilistic. Republican presidential candidate Richard Nixon leveled broadsides at the radicals and tied them to the discredited policies of liberalism, while J. Edgar Hoover stepped up FBI persecution of all antiwar activity. Historical empathy demands that we imagine how seductive, how exhilarating the possibility—the *necessity* of revolution—must have seemed that spring of 1968. The earnest efforts of activists to stop the war with peaceful protest and active resistance had been ignored. From the barricades of Columbia, radicals viewed a liberal administration that was napalming villages as hopelessly morally bankrupt. The indiscriminate violence of NYPD "pigs" only amplified and thickened the New Left perception of *Amerika* as an out-of-control fascistic police state.[27] Like pro-Saigon South Vietnamese peasants whose village had just been bombed, students formerly allied with the conservative "Majority Coalition" suddenly became anti-establishment insurgents. "My attitude changed as soon as the cops charged," said freshman Corwin Moore. "Whatever enmity I had against the demonstrators, I now have against the administration."[28] Moore did not specify *which* administration—Low Library or the White House; in the incendiary climate, they had congealed as one.

The wider context convinced the would-be revolutionaries they were part of a world-changing epic. From January to June, nearly 40,000 students at more than one hundred American universities participated in at least one major demonstration. In March, 15,000 Mexican American students in Los Angeles staged the largest high school walkout in American history. The adrenaline of students surged as they looked around the world and saw young people leading dozens of democratic protest movements. From Paris to Pakistan, Rome to Seoul, variously authoritarian or unresponsive governments and university administrations across the ideological spectrum found themselves under siege on a range of issues: Vietnam, workers' wages, a range of university and local issues, and most fundamentally, democracy itself. Many ended in state violence. The "Prague Spring" led by Czechoslovakia's reform-minded Slovak president Alexander Dubček was crushed in August when Soviet tanks rolled through the streets. In October, just days before Mexico City was to host the summer Olympic Games, government forces slaughtered several hundred students in the Tlatelolco Massacre. Though it did not end that way in Paris, it might have. The height of the uprising—the "Night of the Barricades"—was so threatening French President Charles de Gaulle secretly prepared for the possible use of troops to retake the city. On the rebel side of the barricades, Dany Cohn-Bendit remembered it this way:

> People were building up the cobblestones because they wanted—many of them, for the first time—to throw themselves into a collective, spontaneous activity. Thousands felt the need to communicate with each other, to love one another. That night has forever made me optimistic about history. Having lived through it, I can't ever say, "It will never happen …"[29]

Los Angeles, June 5

When Senator Robert F. Kennedy announced his run for the presidency on March 16, establishment Democrats attacked him as the "ruthless opportunist" opponents always claimed him to be. Kennedy, critics charged, only jumped into the race after Eugene McCarthy had proven Lyndon Johnson's vulnerability, and his antiwar candidacy would further fracture the party over Vietnam.[30] He would also divide young radicals who had gone "clean for Gene" and energized the McCarthy campaign. A supporter of Johnson's policy initially, Kennedy had moved decisively against the war. In February 1967, Bobby met with the president to discuss his proposal for an American withdrawal. Dismissing the plan out of hand, Johnson instead intensified the bombing—a strategic decision that carried the added bonus of a vindictive reply to the man he called a "grandstanding little runt."[31] In a speech on the Senate floor days later, Kennedy proposed a cessation of bombing and bore in on the matter of the war's responsibility: "It is our chemicals that scorch the children and our bombs that level the villages. We are all participants."[32]

Two days after he entered the race, Kennedy flew to Kansas. He had not yet made his first campaign appearance, but the news had made it to Topeka. Legendary New York reporter Jimmy Breslin was there to capture the mayhem:

> [They] tore at Robert Kennedy. They tore the buttons from his shirt-cuffs … They tore at his suit-buttons. They reached for his hair and his face. He went down the fence, hands out, his body swaying backwards so that they could not claw him in the face, and the people on the other side of the fence tried to pull him to them.[33]

So it would be for the next 81 days (Figure 8.2). United Farmworkers leader Cesar Chavez was among those who noticed how Robert Kennedy's hands were marked with bloodied scratches from the crowds constantly clawing at him.[34] The challenge of appreciating the preternatural energy that surrounded the RFK campaign, what that season of renewed hope meant in America, has only grown with time. Across the ideological spectrum Americans flocked to a candidacy whose vitality evoked that of his brother. As John caught the idealism of the early sixties, the less polished Bobby evinced a youthful elan and

Figure 8.2 US Senator Robert F. Kennedy (1925–1968) campaigns for the Presidency, Los Angeles, California, 1968.

Lawrence Schiller/Polaris Communications/Getty Images, www.gettyimages.co.uk/detail/news-photo/american-politician-us-senator-robert-f-kennedy-campaigns-news-photo/167717445?adppopup=true

reckless valor befitting this moment. A fearless campaign took him from the same West Virginia coal country his brother traveled to forsaken Native American reservations to the poorest barrios of the Southwest. In the senate, Kennedy had been advocating for the plight of Mexican American farmworkers. That March, he joined Cesar Chavez in a Catholic Mass of Thanksgiving that ended Chavez's hunger fast.

Wherever he went, Kennedy listened and bound himself to the struggles of working people and the forgotten. "He could see things through the eyes of the poor," Chavez observed, "like he was ours."[35] Demonstrating a vulnerability uncommon among public figures, Kennedy had grown in his understanding of racism since entering public life. A pivotal moment had come in 1963 at a meeting with a group of 11 civil rights leaders organized by James Baldwin. Then-Attorney General Kennedy intended to convince his audience of all the progress his brother's administration had achieved on civil rights, while warning them of the challenges of a divided Democratic Party and growing black nationalism. What he got was a fierce rebuke and an education about the realities of the urban ghetto. The tense exchange went on for three hours and proved a defining moment.[36]

Five years later on the night of the King assassination, Kennedy was campaigning in Indianapolis. Told on his way into the city that King had been killed, Bobby overrode the mayor's counsel to avoid the predominantly black neighborhood where he was to speak, for fear a riot would erupt like those breaking out around the country. From the back of a flatbed truck in Broadway Park,

Senator Kennedy informed the crowd of King's murder and then stilled the combustible moment. With tender grace, he referenced his brother's death for the first time publicly, and then invoked the wisdom of his favorite poet, Aeschylus, words he had leaned on since November 1963: "In our sleep, pain which cannot forget falls drop by drop upon the heart until, in our own despair, against our will, comes wisdom through the awful grace of God." And then, as if he had no doubt it would be heard, came this appeal:

> What we need in the United States is not division; what we need in the United States is not hatred; what we need in the United States is not violence or lawlessness; but love and wisdom, and compassion toward one another, and a feeling of justice toward those who still suffer within our country, whether they be white or they be black ...
>
> And let's dedicate ourselves to what the Greeks wrote so many years ago: to tame the savageness of man and make gentle the life of this world. Let us dedicate ourselves to that, and say a prayer for our country and for our people.[37]

Indianapolis was the only major city in America that did not explode in violence. Less remembered but equally emblematic was a late-night meeting with Black Panthers in Oakland, California in the closing days of that state's crucial primary. He spoke a few words and then the Panthers let loose, Kennedy absorbing the anger of black men too long unheard by white politicians. The next day after a speech in West Oakland, as a simmering crowd encircled Robert Kennedy's car, the Panthers drew a cordon around his vehicle, allowing him to move forward.[38]

Amid one of the most troubled moments of our history, Kennedy ran to "heal the divisions" in the nation, reminding Americans that they yet shared "a common concern for each other," but also being unafraid to challenge them. Speaking to a group of local service club men in Vincennes, Indiana, Kennedy strayed from his prepared text and the issue most of the men gathered wanted to hear about—the need for more law and order in the country. Instead, as journalist Thomas Congdon, Jr. summarized, he told the club members—

> big, heavy men, most of them, and still occupied in shoveling in their lunch—the Senator from New York spoke of children starving, of "*American children, starving in America.*" It was reverse demagoguery—he was telling them precisely the opposite of what they wanted to hear.
>
> "Do you know," he asked, voice rising, "there are more rats than people in New York City?"
>
> Now this struck the club members as an apt metaphor for what they had always believed about New York City, and a number of them guffawed.
>
> Kennedy went grim, and with terrible deliberateness said, "*Don't ... laugh ...*" The room hushed. There were a few more hushed questions, and finally he escaped to confused applause."[39]

Here was an authentic politician who in dark times spoke hard truths and tried to summon Americans' best instincts.

Kennedy also possessed a capacity for philosophical, moral questioning that endeared him to many in the New Left. At the University of Kansas, Kennedy offered reflections on the meaning of what is calculated in the Gross National Product. GNP, he said, counts:

> air pollution and cigarette advertising ... It counts the destruction of the redwood and the loss of our natural wonder in chaotic sprawl. It counts napalm and counts nuclear warheads and armored cars for the police to fight the riots in our cities ... the television programs which glorify violence in order to sell toys to our children.

GNP did not measure, Kennedy lamented,

> the health of our children, the quality of their education or the joy of their play. It does not include the beauty of our poetry or the strength of our marriages, the intelligence of our public debate or the integrity of our public officials. It measures neither our wit nor our courage, neither our wisdom nor our learning, neither our compassion nor our devotion to our country, it measures everything in short, except that which makes life worthwhile.[40]

This, in sum, is why so many Americans who were alive in 1968 will never shake the haunting impact of the assassination of Robert F. Kennedy when it came that June night in the kitchen pantry of the Los Angeles Ambassador Hotel following his victory in the California primary. It came with the shock and horror one might expect—and yet given the ricocheting horrors of the era, the temptation, even then, was to say *of course* Bobby Kennedy would be cut down. Todd Gitlin aptly termed it the climax of the sixties' "murder of hope."[41] Perhaps equally anticipated if not definitively answerable, were the questions surrounding the official verdict that convicted assassin Sirhan Sirhan pulled the trigger. Compelling expert evidence emerged from independent (of the LAPD) investigators indicating that the number of shots fired in that pantry pointed clearly to two shooters.[42]

In those dark days of June 1968, other questions hung heavy in the air: What kind of country had America become? What *now*? As RFK's funeral train made its way from St. Patrick's Cathedral in New York City to Arlington, Americans by the thousands stood along the tracks and poured out their grief—as much for themselves and their country as for the slain senator. One Kennedy volunteer, Arthur Levine, recalled:

> It all fell apart. *Everything* had fallen apart ... I can't ever remember a time of feeling less hopeful about the country, or feeling sadder ... I waited five, six hours just to walk past his coffin. And talking to people in the crowd ...

the level of sadness, the horror, the lack of belief that this could possibly be happening.[43]

Chicago, August 28

The violent chaos that erupted in Chicago in late August was foretold when thousands of antiwar protesters announced plans to descend on the Democratic National Convention and Mayor Richard Daley fortified his city for insurrection. An old-school urban boss, Daley had ordered his officers to "shoot to kill" arsonists after the King assassination.[44] As the convention approached, the mayor denied protesters a permit for street demonstrations, sequestered them in Lincoln Park and forbid their sleeping overnight, ordered his 12,000-man police force to stockpile massive amounts of mace and tear gas, and instructed commanders to draw up battle plans involving the riot squad, the Illinois National Guard, and troop reinforcements from as far away as Fort Hood.

A seven-foot-tall fence topped with barbed wire ringed the Conrad Hilton, where Vice-President and Democratic nominee Hubert Humphrey and most of the several thousand delegates were staying. Manhole covers were sealed, partly to guard against Yippie Abbie Hoffman's threat to drop LSD into the city's drinking water supply. Inside the convention hall police stationed themselves on a catwalk with rifles. Walter Cronkite reported that, "The Democratic convention is about to begin in a police state. There just doesn't seem to be any other way to say it."[45] Russian tanks blowing into Prague that week deepened the mood of impending doom.

On day one the Yippies introduced their nominee for president: "Pigasus," a 125-pound pig. Nightly sweeps after the 11 pm curfew through Lincoln Park produced ferocious police assaults upon the unarmed encampment. As blood spilled from the parks and into the streets, volleys of bottles and rocks flew from the crowd. The strangely anachronistic singing of "We Shall Overcome" by one contingent of nonviolent protesters was drowned out by "Seig Heil! Seig Heil!" Inside the convention hall, delegates narrowly approved a hotly debated resolution supporting the Johnson-Humphrey administration's continued prosecution of the war, enraging McCarthy and Kennedy delegates—this, as Senator Abraham Ribicoff of Connecticut angrily denounced the "Gestapo tactics" of Mayor Daley's police and called for the convention to adjourn and reconvene in another city. Americans watching the mayhem at home could read the vile reply from the mayor's lips: "YOU MOTHERFUCKER JEW BASTARD! GET YOUR ASS OUT OF CHICAGO!" [46]

The climax arrived Wednesday, the penultimate night of the convention. At a permitted rally in Grant Park, opposite the Conrad Hilton, hundreds were beaten, maced, or tear-gassed, the smell of which saturated downtown Chicago. Hubert Humphrey caught a whiff in his hotel suite while showering. The sustained assault swept up not only demonstrators, but dozens of reporters, as well as innocent Chicagoans going about their business. The only real surprise that week was that no one was killed. Amid a peaceful sit-down by thousands of demonstrators, the crowd chanted, "the whole world is watching." Indeed they were, and 56 percent of the country thought the police acted with justifiable force.[47] Others expressed outrage over citizens savagely beaten in an American city while trying to stop a barbaric war that no longer seemed half a world away. Somehow, the Chicago convention managed to nominate Hubert Humphrey, but it was better remembered as the perfect metaphor for a nation coming undone.

Atlantic City, September 7

Organized by the New York Radical Women, the protest on the Atlantic City boardwalk outside the Miss America Pageant immediately became one of the defining events of the women's liberation movement. Roughly 400 women marched, many tossing bras, mascara, false eyelashes, girdles, stockings and other oppressive trappings of modern American womanhood into a "Freedom Trash Can." The women carried placards with messages like, "CATTLE PARADES ARE DEMEANING TO HUMAN BEINGS," and, "CAN MAKE-UP HIDE THE WOUNDS OF OUR OPPRESSION?" For the protesters and for those cheering them on from afar, Miss America stood as an emblem of the objectification of women's bodies for male pleasure, a "Degrading Mindless-Boob-Girlie Symbol." Some of the women bought tickets to the pageant, affording them an incursion into the hall where they unfurled a large "WOMEN'S LIBERATION" banner before they were banished.

Protesters saw in the pageant a packaged nexus of much else that was wrong with America. It was "racism with roses," women said, a stinging rebuke to the uniform whiteness of the contestants year after year. Because Miss America went on tour to "entertain" the troops in Vietnam, she was a "military death mascot," an instrument of American militarism—as well as of consumerism, given that she was deployed by pageant sponsors to sell their products. In addition, said feminists, the pageant was ageist and inherently conformist, excluding older women and those with opinions about world affairs they were willing to express. Finally, for women like Robin Morgan, the protest in Atlantic City provided the opportunity to break free of a patriarchal antiwar movement increasingly shot full of dangerous, chest-beating machismo.[48] There would be larger protests in the women's movement. But it was the 1968 Miss America demonstration that first dramatically distilled women's rising demand for their humanity and dignity, while staking an imaginative claim on the intersectionality of their condition.

Mexico City, October 16

Five weeks later, at the 1968 Summer Olympic Games in Mexico City, black Olympians Tommie Smith and John Carlos earned the gold and bronze medals in the 200-meter track and field event. They strode to the podium to receive their medals shoeless, black socks pulled high and each sporting one black glove. As the Star-Spangled Banner was performed, they bowed their heads in mourning to the ongoing deaths of black Americans at home, each raising one fist in unity with the Black Power struggle to address poverty and confront racism. Expressing solidarity with Carlos and Smith, silver medal winner Australian Peter Norman wore the badge of the Olympic Project for Human Rights. Organized by sociologist and activist Harry Edwards, the Human Rights Project was a global, multi-racial cry for justice. Among other demands, the initiative had called for black athletes to boycott the games and for participants from Rhodesia and South Africa, both governed by white minority regimes, to be barred from the Olympics.

Hailed by activists at home and around the world, Smith and Carlos were immediately suspended from the Olympic team and endured a ferocious wave of death threats and vitriol from the media, the *LA Times* likening their defiant protest to a "Nazi-like salute." Their lives would never be the same, the monetary rewards and professional opportunities afforded to winning Olympians surrendered in a single moment. Decades later, Carlos maintained no regrets. In one's life, he said in 2012, "all that matters is … whether you're prepared to do what it takes to make change. There has to be physical and material sacrifice. When all the dust settles … the greatest reward is to know that you did your job when you were here on the planet."[49] Their action may have left them forsaken on the medal stand, but Smith and Carlos were hardly alone. Led by Muhammad Ali, NFL running back Jim Brown and NBA star Bill Russell, other black athletes were speaking out against the war and injustice at home. UCLA basketball great Lew Alcindor—soon Kareem Abdul-Jabbar—shaken awake by reading Malcolm X and by the events four years earlier in his native Harlem, opted to boycott the 1968 games in Mexico City. A year earlier, Abdul-Jabbar had joined a summit of black sports stars in Cleveland to voice support for the maligned Ali. "Hearing Ali's articulate defense of his moral beliefs and his willingness to suffer for them," he later recalled, proved pivotal in his decision to "take a stand" and stay home, despite fierce opposition from his own coach.[50]

America, November 5

"They oughtn't to be doing this. This is treason," Lyndon Johnson fumed to Senator Everett Dirksen on November 2.[51] "They" was a ring of individuals secretly working on behalf of presidential candidate Richard Nixon to sabotage the peace talks between the United States and the government of North Vietnam that might end U.S. involvement in the war. In the last days of October, U.S. intelligence agencies alerted Johnson to the shocking discovery that Nixon himself had been behind a clandestine plot to persuade the South Vietnamese government of Nguyễn Văn Thiuệ to reject the proposed plan of American diplomats in Paris before the U.S. election on the assumption that such an announcement would carry Hubert Humphrey to victory. Humphrey had risen from the ashes of Chicago, the turning point being a nationally televised speech on September 30 in which he called for a ceasefire as a first step to ending the war.[52] McCarthy endorsed him, many antiwar activists closed ranks, and

Humphrey cheered on the encouraging reports from Paris. By late October, he had closed the gap with Nixon from 18 points to two. U.S. diplomats had convinced the Soviet Union to pressure Hanoi to accept the participation of the Saigon regime in the talks in exchange for a bombing halt, which the president announced October 31. He then awaited word from Paris of a framework for peace that could push Humphrey over the top.

Johnson was not counting on Nixon's scheme aimed at undermining the talks. Secretly informed of the progress in Paris by Henry Kissinger—a longtime foreign policy advisor to both Democrats and Republicans, and in 1968 part of the president's team in Paris—Nixon ordered aide Bob Haldeman to "monkey wrench" the negotiations.[53] They turned to Anna Chennault, a major Republican fundraiser and ardent anti-communist champion of nationalist China with close ties to the regime in Saigon. In what became known as "the Chennault Affair," the Republican doyenne made clear to Saigon officials that a dramatic announcement in Paris would likely deliver victory to Humphrey, who would withdraw U.S. forces. As any objective observer had long known, that meant certain defeat for South Vietnam. "Hold on, we're gonna win … just hang through the election," the FBI wiretap recorded Chennault telling the regime's U.S. ambassador, assuring him that Nixon was determined to fight on in Vietnam. Saturday, November 2 brought the headline: SAIGON OPPOSES PARIS TALK PLANS. Humphrey's momentum plateaued in the last 72 hours, and Nixon pulled off a razor-thin victory.[54]

An enraged Johnson considered exposing Nixon's perfidy, but feared the ramifications of having illegally wiretapped Chennault. He also lacked evidence of Nixon's complicity, which did not emerge until decades later.[55] The Chennault Affair was a clear violation of the Logan Act that prohibits any candidate from interfering in U.S. government negotiations with a foreign power. It was a crime arguably far worse than all the rampant lawlessness unearthed in Watergate, for the Paris Peace Accords ultimately signed in January 1973—with Kissinger, Nixon's Secretary of State, serving as lead U.S. negotiator—differed little substantively from the agreement he had helped sabotage four years earlier. More than 22,000 Americans and over a million Vietnamese and Cambodians died in the interim.

Any presidential candidate's willingness to conspire with a foreign power to win an election was unseemly and illegal, but in the case of Richard Nixon and his campaign mantra of "law and order," carried rich irony. Defeated in his 1962 bid for California governor, Nixon had launched his rebirth as a national candidate with a string of harangues against the "lawlessness" sweeping the nation, hitching himself to the rising rightwing of the Republican Party. Inspired by the fervor of Barry Goldwater's 1964 ill-fated run, intellectually grounded in the caustic brilliance of William F. Buckley and writings of Russell Kirk, buoyed by the nation's demographic shift westward, and fueled by the turbulence of the era, California conservatives Nixon and Ronald Reagan began the slow but steady capture of the Republican Party from its more liberal northeastern center. Goldwater's *Conscience of a Conservative* called for lower taxes, voluntary Social

Security, and smaller government of two essential responsibilities: maintaining law and order, and defeating "international communism." In his deplored but ultimately seminal 1964 acceptance speech, Goldwater inveighed against "the license of the mob and of the jungle," and declared that "extremism in the defense of liberty is no vice." A 30-minute paid spot called "Choice" crudely played to the white backlash simmering in the country. "In your heart, you know he's right," by adding, "Yes, extreme right," answered liberals.[56]

But that was the faraway land of 1964. In the vortex of 1968, Goldwater appeared to many Republicans a prophet in the wilderness. Echoing the Arizona senator, in 1966 Nixon ranted against the "mob rule"—induced, he claimed, by the "doctrine of civil disobedience." The destruction liberalism had wrought all started with actions "not only wrong but potentially dangerous."[57] Two years later, Nixon won the nomination with racially coded calls for law and order, telling "forgotten Americans" all they wanted to hear about themselves: they were the "non-shouters, the non-demonstrators, that are not racists or sick, that are not guilty of crime that plagues the land. This ... is the real voice of America in 1968."[58] Physiologically ill-suited for television and contemptuous of the press, Nixon engaged a young media genius named Roger Ailes who devised a campaign that effectively sealed him off from journalists and remade his image. Ailes concocted a series of reporter-free events with average Americans asking Nixon supposedly serious policy questions, and then had Nixon make a cameo for the season-opener of the irreverent pioneering television comedy, *Laugh-In*. His memorable utterance of the show's stock laugh-line, "Sock-it-to-me," helped soften Nixon's wooden form.[59]

Nixon's campaign played to white resentment and fears of social disorder, amplified by rightwing firebrands like his Nazi-sympathizing speechwriter Pat Buchanan. There was also his vice-presidential nominee, former Maryland governor, Spiro Agnew. A bomb-throwing demagogue Nixon brought on to solidify his lurch rightward, Agnew railed against antiwar opponents as "nattering nabobs of negativism."[60] Far shrewder was political strategist Kevin Phillips, whose brilliantly cynical "Southern Strategy" envisioned Nixon exceeding the 55 percent of Southern white votes earned by Goldwater by stoking the resentment of "Negrophobic" Democrats. In a strategy soon replicated nationwide, Republican candidates, said Phillips, should forget ever winning "more than 10 to 20 percent of the Negro vote." They would not need to if they won the votes of aggrieved whites. As Goldwater put it back in 1961, "we ought to go hunting where the ducks are."[61] Refurbishing McCarthy-era anti-intellectualism, "forgotten whites," Phillips contended, had grown resentful of "upper-crust talk about equal justice for blacks" while they convinced themselves there would never "be a Polish president of General Motors."[62]

A line of attack that cast the white working class as put-upon suited Nixon's innate prejudices, notwithstanding a moderately liberal record on civil rights. His opposition to "forced busing" to advance school integration and appeals for "law and order" stood as a rebuke to civil disobedience and reinforced the growing acrimony of white Americans. "I pledge to you, we shall have order in the

United States," Nixon intoned in a campaign ad.[63] His launch of the "war on drugs" cynically fused the law-and-order message with the southern strategy, as John Ehrlichman, Assistant to the President for Domestic Affairs and Watergate co-conspirator, later made clear:

> The Nixon campaign in 1968, and the Nixon White House after that, had two enemies: the antiwar left and black people. You understand what I'm saying? We knew we couldn't make it illegal to be either against the war or black, but by getting the public to associate the hippies with marijuana and blacks with heroin, and then criminalizing both heavily, we could disrupt those communities. We could arrest their leaders, raid their homes, break up their meetings, and vilify them night after night on the evening news. Did we know we were lying about the drugs? Of course we did.[64]

Also in the race was well-oiled George Wallace, whose raw, segregation-forever racism had been filling Alabama air for a decade. Running under the banner of the American Independent Party and an appeal to, "Stand Up For America," Wallace's class-coded racialized appeal rendered Nixon a rank amateur and forced him to cede most of the Deep South. Wallace denounced the Supreme Court, the "take-over of your schools," and the Voting Rights Act—"one of the most tragic, most discriminatory pieces of legislation ever enacted," he fumed.[65] Wallace's campaign won broad support among white working-class Americans. After Bobby Kennedy's assassination and the disaster in Chicago, legions of union men fled Humphrey for Wallace. In the historic steel town of Homestead, Pennsylvania, union officials gauged near-unanimous support for Wallace in parts of the mill. In mid-September, when Wallace hit 20 percent in national polls, one United Auto Workers official disabused a reporter of any notion that his rank and file were voting for Wallace because of his populist economic plan: "The men in the plants want to zap the negroes by voting for Wallace. It's as simple as that."[66]

Most voters told reporters and themselves that it was the governor's call to increase Social Security, Medicare, and the minimum wage, his straight talk about traditional virtues like hard work and self-control supporters believed were under assault in 1968. Standing for Wallace was to deliver a middle finger to protesters, as well as the media, the Washington establishment, and campus intellectuals. Wallace partisans roared as their man ranted against the "sissy britches [and] intellectual morons" of the press, and the "pointy-headed professors who can't even park a bicycle straight."[67] With primal indignation, Wallace partisans saw themselves as a persecuted class in an America under siege from black radicals, the college educated, hippies, and foreign aid (a favorite foil of Wallace). The Wallace phenomenon revealed deep cultural fissures in the American polity, a breach between those Americans to whom country singer Merle Haggard famously paid homage in 1969's big crossover hit "Okie from Muskogee," and a privileged "elite" encouraging chaos in American streets.[68] Although he would seek redemption with black Americans later in his political life, in 1968 there was no denying the racism. The manager of a Polish American club in Webster, Massachusetts, said to Tom Turnipseed, Wallace's campaign manager: "'When George Wallace is elected president, he's going to line up all these niggers and shoot them.'"[69]

One could not run for president in 1968 and stand for an open-ended prosecution of the war; even Nixon, while furtively upending the Paris peace talks, alluded to a "secret plan" to wind down the war. Wallace said little about the war, stating vaguely that if there was no substantial progress within his first 90 days on the job, he would bring American troops home. His vice-presidential candidate, retired General Curtis LeMay, was a different story. Having recently written that Operation Rolling Thunder might have to annihilate "every work of man in North Vietnam," bombing the country "back to the Stone Age" in order to win the war, now on the stump he confidently told reporters he did not "believe the world would end if we exploded a nuclear weapon" in Asia.[70] On election day, for more than ten million Americans desperate to end the war and roll back the clock at home, LeMay was not a deal-breaker.

There seemed to be no vanishing point on the political horizon of 1968. Further right than Nixon or Wallace were the Birchers, as well as growing numbers of well-armed white vigilantes. Self-described "Loyal Americans for Law and Order," the Newark, New Jersey North Ward Citizens Committee organized after the city's 1967 rebellion and patrolled their neighborhood with an armored vehicle and a large cache of weapons. Their leader was former marine and future state senator, Anthony Imperiale, who railed against the followers of "Martin Luther Coon" and warned, "if the black panther comes, the white hunter will be waiting."[71] The Birch Society now stood 100,000 strong. William F. Buckley, founder of the influential conservative journal *National Review*, and the man who nurtured the growth of Young Americans for Freedom—a group with far greater membership than SDS for most of the decade—saw danger ahead. The erudite Buckley knew that the quackery of Birchers could eventually, if left unchecked, poison the conservative movement. What he could not see was that the race-baiting, anti-Washington demagoguery of Wallace and his own man Nixon portended a fissure in American democracy that would prove difficult to mend.

Notes

1 General William Westmoreland, quoted in James M. Lindsay, "TWE Remembers: General Westmoreland Says the 'End Begins to Come Into View,'" Council on Foreign Relations, November 21, 2017, www.cfr.org/blog/twe-remembers-general-westmoreland-says-end-begins-come-view-vietnam, retrieved April 8, 2021.
2 Tom Bowman, "Military Victory but Political Defeat: The Tet Offensive Fifty Years Later," National Public Radio, Morning Edition (January 29, 2018), www.npr.org/2018/01/29/580811124/military-victory-but-political-defeat-the-tet-offensive-50-years-later, retrieved October 28, 2018.
3 Michael Herr, *Dispatches* (New York: Random House Vintage International, 1991), 105–107.

4 The Arnett quote is found in many places, including Michael Walzer, "Destroying to Save," *Dissent*, January 15, 2018, www.dissentmagazine.org/blog/destroying-to-save-mosul-raqqa-civilian-casualties, retrieved April 8, 2021.

5 McGee quoted by George C. Herring, "The Tet Offensive," in Andrew J. Rotter, ed., *Light at the End of the Tunnel: A Vietnam War Anthology* (Lanham, MD: Rowman and Littlefield, 2010), 95.

6 Julian Zelizer, "How the Tet Offensive Undermined American Faith in Government," *The Atlantic*, January 15, 2018, www.theatlantic.com/politics/archive/2018/01/how-the-tet-offensive-undermined-american-faith-in-government/550010, retrieved April 8, 2021.

7 Cronkite, February 27, 1968, quoted in Don Oberdorfer, *Tet! The Turning Point in the Vietnam War* (Baltimore, MD: Johns Hopkins Press, 2001, 1971), 251.

8 Tom Wells, *The War Within America's Battle Over Vietnam* (Berkeley, CA: University of California Press, 1994), 250–252.

9 President Lyndon Baines Johnson, "Address to the Nation Announcing Steps to Limit the War in Vietnam," March 31, 1968, www.lbjlibrary.net/collections/selected-speeches/1968-january-1969/03-31-1968.html, retrieved April 7, 2021.

10 Laurie B. Green, *Battling the Plantation Mentality: Memphis and the Black Freedom Struggle* (Chapel Hill, NC: University of North Carolina Press, 2009), 277.

11 Ibid., 256.

12 David Anderson, *The Movement and the Sixties: Protest in America from Greensboro to Wounded Knee* (New York: Oxford University Press, 1995), 191.

13 Irwyn L. Ince, Jr. *The Beautiful Community: Unity, Diversity, and the Church at Its Best* (Downers Grove, IL: Intervarsity Press, 2020), 51; and Steven A. Reich, *A Working People: A History of American American Workers Since Emancipation* (New York: Rowman and Littlefield, 2013), 141–143.

14 Barney Sellers, from the compilation, "Martin Luther King and the Memphis Sanitation Strike, 102 Photos," *The Commercial Appeal*, February 22, 2017; https://www.commercialappeal.com/picture-gallery/news/local/2017/01/11/martin-luther-king-and-the-memphis-sanitation-strike/96460288/; retrieved September 7, 2021.

15 Irwin Unger and Debi Unger, *America in the 1960s* (St. James, New York: Brandywine Press, 1988), 130–131.

16 *Report of the National Commission on Civil Disorders* (Washington, DC: 1968), 1–15.

17 Karen Grigsby Bates, "Report Updates Landmark 1968 Racism Study, Finds More Poverty and Segregation" (National Public Radio: Morning Edition, February 27, 2018), www.npr.org/2018/02/27/589351779/report-updates-landmark-1968-racism-study-finds-more-poverty-more-segregation, retrieved June 10, 2021.

18 Beverly Gage, "What An Uncensored Letter to M.L.K. Reveals," *New York Times Magazine*, November 11, 2014, www.nytimes.com/2014/11/16/magazine/what-an-uncensored-letter-to-mlk-reveals.html?_r=1&referrer=, retrieved April 9, 2021.

19 Martin Luther King, Jr., "I've Been to the Mountaintop," Mason Temple, Memphis, Tennessee, April 3, 1968, www.americanrhetoric.com/speeches/mlkivebeentothe-mountaintop.htm, retrieved October 30, 2018.

20 Ibid.

21 The definitive account is William F. Pepper, *An Act of State: The Execution of Martin Luther King* (New York: Verso, 2018).

22 Anderson, 196.

23 Tom Hayden, "Two, Three Many Columbias," *Ramparts* (1968), in Alexander Bloom and Wini Breines, eds., *Takin' It to the Streets: A Sixties Reader*, 2nd ed. (New York: Oxford University Press, 2002), 333–335.

24 The Columbia Strike Coordinating Committee, "Columbia Liberated," in Bloom and Breines, 336–337.

25 Anderson, 194–196.

26 More precisely, the Dead performed a free concert when it was all over, on May 3. "Grateful Dead, Columbia University, 1968.Yeah," Bahr Gallery, n.d., www.bahrgallery.com/links/grateful-dead-columbia-university-1968-yeah, retrieved April 7, 2021.

27 See any number of first-hand accounts in Paul Cronin's excellent, *A Time to Stir: Columbia '68* (New York: Columbia University Press, 2018).

28 Moore, quoted in Unger and Unger, *America in the 1960s*, 189.

29 Dany Cohn-Bendit, quoted in Ronald Fraser, *1968: A Student Generation in Revolt* (New York: Pantheon, 1988), excerpted in Bloom and Breines, 364.

30 Arthur M. Schlesinger, Jr., *Robert Kennedy and His Times*, vol. 2 (Boston, MA: Houghton Mifflin, 1978), 898.

31 David Talbot, *Brothers: The Hidden History of the Kennedy Years* (New York: Free Press, 2007), 346–347; and Jeff Shesol, *Mutual Contempt: Lyndon Johnson, Robert Kennedy, and the Feud that Defined a Decade* (New York: W. W. Norton, 1997), 3.

32 Robert F. Kennedy, "Remarks on the War in Vietnam," United States Senate, March 2, 1967; *Congressional Record*, S. 2995–3000.

33 Jimmy Breslin, "With Kennedy in Kansas," *New York Post*, March 18, 1968, quoted in Schlesinger, Jr., *Robert Kennedy and His Times*, 900.

34 Jean Stein and George Plimpton, eds. *American Journey: The Times of Robert Kennedy* (New York: Harcourt Brace, 1970), 282–283.

35 Schlesinger, 834.

36 Karen Grigsby Bates, "The Education of Bobby Kennedy—On Race," National Public Radio, Code Switch, June 5, 2018, www.npr.org/sections/codeswitch/2018/06/05/616942962/the-education-of-bobby-kennedy-on-race, retrieved April 7, 2021.

37 Senator Robert F. Kennedy, "Statement on the Assassination of Martin Luther King, Jr.," Indianapolis, Indiana, April 4, 1968, www.jfklibrary.org/learn/about-jfk/the-kennedy-family/robert-f-kennedy/robert-f-kennedy-speeches/statement-on-assassination-of-martin-luther-king-jr-indianapolis-indiana-april-4-1968, retrieved April 7, 2021.

38 John Siegenthaler, as recorded by Jean Stein, August 27, 1968, 38, Stein Papers, quoted in Schlesinger, 949; and John Glenn with Nick Taylor, *John Glenn: A Memoir* (New York: Bantam, 1999), 342.

39 Thomas B. Congdon, Jr., *The Saturday Evening Post*, June 29, 1968, in Pierre Salinger, Edwin Guthman, Frank Mankiewicz, and John Siegenthaler, eds., *"An Honorable Profession": A Tribute to Robert F. Kennedy* (Garden City, NY: Doubleday and Co., 1968), 90.

40 Robert F. Kennedy, "Remarks at the University of Kansas," March 18, 1968, www.jfklibrary.org/learn/about-jfk/the-kennedy-family/robert-f-kennedy/robert-f-kennedy-speeches/remarks-at-the-university-of-kansas-march-18-1968, retrieved November 1, 2018.

41 Todd Gitlin, *The Sixties: Years of Hope, Days of Rage* (New York: Bantam, 1987), 311.

42 William Turner and John Christian, *The Assassination of Robert F. Kennedy: The Conspiracy and Coverup* (New York: Carroll and Graf, 2006), xxiv–xxv.

43 Arthur Levine, in David Hoffman, prod., *Making Sense of the Sixties*, (Washington, DC: WETA, Public Broadcasting System, 1991), "In a Dark Time," episode 4 of 6.

44 David Taylor and Sam Morris, "The Whole World Is Watching: How the 1968 'Police Riot' Shocked America and Divided a Nation," *The Guardian*, August 19, 2018, www.theguardian.com/us-news/ng-interactive/2018/aug/19/the-whole-world-is-watching-chicago-police-riot-vietnam-war-regan, retrieved April 8, 2021.

45 Quoted by Taylor and Morris.

46 William Manchester, *The Glory and the Dream: A Narrative History of America, 1932–1972* (New York: Bantam Books, 1973), 1142–1144; Lawrence S. Wittner, *Cold War America: From Hiroshima to Watergate* (New York: Praeger, 1974), 294–296; and Nancy Kurshan, "The Whole World Was Watching: Chicago '68 Revisited," *Counterpunch*, August 17, 2018, www.counterpunch.org/2018/08/17/the-whole-world-was-watching-chicago-68-revisited, retrieved November 2, 2018.

47 Gallup, cited by Taylor and Morris.

48 Olivia B. Waxman, "'I Was Terrified': Inside a History-Making Protest with the Women Who Took on the Miss America Competition," *Time*, September 7, 2018, https://time.com/5387623/miss-america-protest, retrieved June 18, 2021.

49 Gary Younge, "The Man Who Raised a Black Power Salute at the 1968 Olympic Games," *The Guardian*, March 30, 2012, www.theguardian.com/world/2012/mar/30/black-power-salute-1968-olympics, retrieved June 19, 2021.

50 Johnny Smith, "The Reign of Lew Alcindor in the Age of Revolt," *The Undefeated*, March 30, 2018; https://theundefeated.com/features/lew-alcindor-kareem-abdul-jabbar-ucla-boycot-1968-olympics, retrieved June 23, 2021.

51 Lyndon Johnson and Everett Dirksen, November 2, 1968, "The Turning Point, 1968: The Chennault Affair," University of Virginia Miller Center, https://millercenter.org/the-presidency/educational-resources/turning-point-1968, retrieved November 3, 2018.

52 Vice-President Hubert H. Humphrey, Address to the Nation on Vietnam, Salt Lake City, UT, broadcast on NBC, September 30, 1968, www2.mnhs.org/library/find-aids/00442/pdfa/00442-02747.pdf, retrieved November 3, 2018.

53 "H. R. Haldeman's Notes from October 22, 1968," *New York Times*, December 22, 2016, www.nytimes.com/interactive/2016/12/31/opinion/sunday/haldeman-notes.html, retrieved November 3, 2018.

54 Charles Kaiser, *1968 in America: Music, Politics, Chaos, Counterculture, and the Shaping of a Generation* (New York: Weidenfeld & Nicholson, 1988), 251–253.

55 Jason Daley, "Notes Indicate Nixon Interfered with 1968 Peace Talks," January 2, 2017, www.smithsonianmag.com/smart-news/notes-indicate-nixon-interfered-1968-peace-talks-180961627, retrieved November 3, 2018.

56 Barry Goldwater, 1964 acceptance speech, Republican National Convention, San Francisco, July 17, 1964; Matthew Dallek, "The Conservative 60s," *The Atlantic* (December 1995), www.theatlantic.com/magazine/archive/1995/12/the-conservative-1960s/376506, retrieved November 2, 2018; and Josh Zeitz, "How Trump is Recycling Nixon's 'Law and Order' Playbook," *Politico Magazine*, July 28, 2016, www.politico.com/magazine/story/2016/07/donald-trump-law-and-order-richard-nixon-crime-race-214066, retrieved November 4, 2018.

57 Richard Nixon, "If Mob Rule Takes Hold in the U.S.," *U.S. News and World Report*, August 15, 1966, in Bloom and Breines, 294–296.

58 Richard Nixon, "Speech Accepting the Republican Nomination," August 8, 1968, www.c-span.org/video/?4022-2/richard-nixon-1968-acceptance-speech, retrieved November 4, 2018.

59 Rick Perlstein, *Nixonland: The Rise of a President and the Fracturing of America* (New York: Scribner and Sons, 2009), 234–235, 330–332.

60 Joseph P. Coffey, *Spiro T. Agnew and the Rise of the Republican Right* (Santa Barbara, CA: ABC-CLIO Press, 2015), see especially 118–119.

61 Quoted by Editorial Board, "Mr. McCain's Message on Race," *New York Times*, April 21, 2000, www.nytimes.com/2000/04/21/opinion/mr-mccain-s-message-on-race.html, retrieved April 8, 2021.

62 James Boyd, "Nixon's Southern Strategy: It's All in the Charts," *New York Times*, May 17, 1970; Kevin Mattson, *Rebels All! A Short History of the Conservative Mind in Postwar America* (New Brunswick, NJ: Rutgers University Press, 2008), 93–94; and Ian Haney López, *Dog Whistle Politics: How Coded Racial Appeals Have Reinvented Racism and Wrecked the Middle Class* (New York: Oxford University Press, 2014), 17–27.

63 "Law and Order," Nixon Campaign Ad, https://vimeo.com/224660754, retrieved April 8, 2021.

64 Quoted in Dan Baum, "Legalize It All: How to Win the War on Drugs," *Harpers* (April 2016), https://harpers.org/archive/2016/04/legalize-it-all, retrieved April 8, 2021.

65 Quoted in Bryan Lyman, "George Wallace: A Segregationist Stand for America," *USA Today Network*, August 16, 2018, www.usatoday.com/story/news/nation-now/1968-project/2018/08/16/stand-up-america-george-wallaces-chaotic-prophetic-campaign/961043002, retrieved November 5, 2018.

66 Quoted in Lewis Chester, Godfrey Hodgson, and Bruce Page, *An American Melodrama: The Presidential Campaign of 1968* (New York: Viking, 1969), 705.

67 Rich Lowry, "From Wallace to Trump: A Journey of Demagoguery," *My San Antonio* (March 26, 2016), www.mysanantonio.com/opinion/commentary/article/From-Wallace-to-Trump-a-journey-of-demagoguery-7090284.php, retrieved November 5, 2018; and Dan T. Carter, *The Politics of Rage: George Wallace, The Origins of the New Conservatism, and the Transformation of American Politics* (Baton Rouge, LA: LSU Press, 2000), 379, 425.

68 Merle Haggard, Roy Burris, and Roy Edward Burris, "Okie from Muskogee" (New York: Capitol Records, July 17, 1969).

69 Bryan Lyman, "A Segregationist Stand for America," *USA Today Network*, April 1, 2018, www.usatoday.com/story/news/nation-now/1968-project/2018/08/16/stand-up-america-george-wallaces-chaotic-prophetic-campaign/961043002, retrieved October 30, 2018.

70 Chester, Hodgson, and Page, 695.

71 Paul Goldberger, "Tony Imperiale Stands Vigilant for Law and Order," *New York Times* (September 29, 1968); and "Black Power/White Backlash," *Rise Up Newark*, http://riseupnewark.com/chapters/chapter-3/part-3/black-power-white-backlash, retrieved November 5, 2018.

Further Reading

Carter, Dan T. *The Politics of Rage: George Wallace, The Origins of the New Conservatism, and the Transformation of American Politics*. Baton Rouge, LA: LSU Press, 2000.

Coffey, Joseph P. *Spiro T. Agnew and the Rise of the Republican Right*. Santa Barbara, CA: ABC-CLIO Press, 2015.

Cronin, Paul. *A Time to Stir: Columbia '68*. New York: Columbia University Press, 2018.

Duberman, Martin. *Stonewall*. New York: Penguin/Plume, 1994.

Fraser, Ronald. *1968: A Student Generation in Revolt*. New York: Pantheon, 1988.

Gitlin, Todd. *The Sixties: Years of Hope, Days of Rage*. New York: Bantam, 1987.

Green, Laurie B. *Battling the Plantation Mentality: Memphis and the Black Freedom Struggle*. Chapel Hill, NC: University of North Carolina Press, 2009.

Haney, López Ian. *Dog Whistle Politics: How Coded Racial Appeals Have Reinvented Racism and Wrecked the Middle Class*. New York: Oxford University Press, 2014.

Kaiser, Charles. *1968 in America: Music, Politics, Chaos, Counterculture, and the Shaping of a Generation*. New York: Weidenfeld & Nicholson, 1988.

Kurlansky, Mark. *1968: The Year that Rocked the World*. New York: Random House, 2004.

Longley, Kyle. *LBJ's 1968: Power, Politics, and the Presidency in the Year of America's Upheaval*. New York: Cambridge University Press, 2018.

Mattson, Kevin. *Rebels All! A Short History of the Conservative Mind in Postwar America*. New Brunswick, NJ: Rutgers University Press, 2008.

Oberdorfer, Don. *Tet! The Turning Point in the Vietnam War*. Baltimore, MD: Johns Hopkins Press, 2001, 1971.

O'Donnell, Lawrence. *Playing with Fire: The 1968 Election and the Transformation of American Politics*. New York: Penguin, 2017.

Pepper, William F. *An Act of State: The Execution of Martin Luther King*. New York: Verso, 2018.

Perlstein, Rick. *Nixonland: The Rise of a President and the Fracturing of America*. New York: Scribner and Sons, 2009.

Reich, Steven A. *A Working People: A History of American Workers Since Emancipation*. New York: Rowman and Littlefield, 2013.

Salinger, Pierre et al., eds., *"An Honorable Profession": A Tribute to Robert F. Kennedy*. Garden City, NY: Doubleday and Co., 1968.

Schlesinger, Jr. Arthur M. *Robert Kennedy and His Times*, vol. 2. Boston, MA: Houghton Mifflin, 1978.

Shesol, Jeff. *Mutual Contempt: Lyndon Johnson, Robert Kennedy, and the Feud that Defined a Decade*. New York: W.W. Norton, 1997.

Stein, Jean, and George Plimpton, eds. *American Journey: The Times of Robert Kennedy*. New York: Harcourt Brace, 1970.

Turner, William, and John Christian. *The Assassination of Robert F. Kennedy: The Conspiracy and Coverup*. New York: Carroll and Graf, 2006.

Unger, Irwin, and Debi Unger. *America in the 1960s*. St. James, NY: Brandywine Press, 1988.

9 Richard Nixon and the Resilience of American Democracy

Despite the unifying moment of the Apollo 11 moon landing in July, 1969 otherwise brought no end to the turmoil. Campus demonstrations surged. Black and Chicano students at San Francisco State led a "Third World Liberation Front" in an unprecedented 134-day strike against institutional racism. The shutdown, which triggered bloody street clashes, a thousand arrests, and the firing of two dozen faculty members, led to the establishment of Black and Ethnic Studies programs, and increased hiring of faculty of color.[1] Entirely different battle lines were drawn that spring at nearby Berkeley, where students and community activists labored to transform a vacant university lot into beautified green space. "People's Park" assumed for its creators mythic significance: an unfettered free speech zone, a tangible expression of ecological consciousness and the value of land once "liberated" from capitalist control, and for some a romantic affinity with the land's original inhabitants, the Costanoan Indians. Berkeley poetry professor Denise Levertov called it "a little island of Peace and hope in a world made filthy and hopeless by war and injustice."[2]

Governor Reagan saw the matter differently. He seized control of the park with a fence, inciting counterproductive stridency among park defenders. In a desperately futile action on what came to be remembered as "Bloody Thursday," students tried to reclaim it, only to be pummeled with teargas, nightsticks, and buckshot from deputy sheriffs that ended with one student dead and 62 hospitalized. Burnishing his "law-and-order" credentials, Reagan declared martial law and deployed the National Guard.[3] A few days later, in a subsequent peaceful protest on Sproul Plaza, National Guard helicopters fired tear gas down on peaceful protesters. Ruth Rosen, who had resisted the "collective hallucination … of revolutionary struggle," recalled this as the moment she succumbed:

> I started hearing the sounds of a helicopter and it came closer and closer, and the sound got louder and louder. And suddenly the helicopter swooped down over the whole campus, and I thought, 'we're going to be shot at, we're the Viet Cong.'[4]

City residents caught friendly fire, with one man blinded and school children hospitalized.[5]

DOI: 10.4324/9781003160595-9

On August 9–10, the shocking murders of actress Sharon Tate and four others inside a luxurious Beverly Hills home by members of the "Manson Family" riveted Americans' attention, much of the media coverage insinuating dark fears about the dangers of hippiedom. Behind the killings lay the loathsome Charles Manson, a failed would-be musician who had gathered a constellation of mostly women followers and induced them to commit mass murder. Lurid details of their descent from a free-loving, LSD-dropping hippie commune into violent cult madness seemed to many Americans a twisted reverberation of the youth rebellion.[6] All the trappings of the youth revolt appeared in the media's coverage, capped by Manson's warped interpretation of references from the Beatles' *White Album* that the killers etched in blood at the scene. As Manson's defense attorney summarized, it was the "lifestyle of the 36-year-old hippie cult leader that was on trial."[7]

A few days later came Woodstock. The "Aquarian Exposition: 3 Days of Peace and Music" would likely have been a footnote to the era if its planners had gotten their expected crowd of 50,000. When ten times that figure appeared, the epic gathering of the "Woodstock Nation" came to symbolize for many the truest expression of the counterculture's benevolent spirit. Altamont, headlined by the Rolling Stones that December at a California speedway, became its demonic antithesis. An ill-tempered sense of doom was palpable, particularly when the Hell's Angels were engaged as "security" for the event. Seeing members of the Angels clubbing people with pool sticks, Marty Balin, lead singer of the Jefferson Airplane, attempted to intervene and was knocked unconscious. Later, Mick Jagger looked on in horror from the stage as an Angel stabbed a black man to death. Two other deaths and scores of fights and drug overdoses further marred the event. As the Airplane's drummer Spencer Dryden recalled, Altamont was not the beginning of the end of the sixties, "it *was* the end."[8]

Beyond the agonizing public breakup of the Beatles, there were other indications the terminus had been reached. At their conference in June, the Students for a Democratic Society splintered into warring camps, arguing over the best strategy to end the war, and for increasing numbers of radicals, to topple by any means necessary the institutions of American power. The most notorious faction, the Weather Underground Organization (WUO), called for an alliance of the working class, the black struggle, and "the oppressed peoples of the world."[9] Determined to engage in urban guerilla warfare, WUO leaders called for 20,000 to show up in Mayor Daley's Chicago in October for what they called "Days of Rage." Three hundred showed up. "This is an awful small group to start a revolution," one averred. Armed with crude weapons and outfitted in "shit-kicker boots," the radicals surged hellbent into downtown Chicago, smashing store windows, overturning cars, and clashing with police. One city official was beaten senselessly and paralyzed in the rampage. Chicagoans looked on in disgust, as did many nonviolent antiwar activists. Pacifist Dave Dellinger noticed that most of the property destroyed belonged to the working and lower classes—the very people the WUO aimed to win over.[10] There was a fine line between righteous bravado and madness. And yet it was growing more difficult to resist the collective lurch toward incendiary action. Decades later, Weather Underground radical Bill Ayers offered this defensive reflection of his actions:

> Every day that the war went on, 2,000 innocent people would be killed ... That meant that if we couldn't stop it by Friday it would be 10,000, and so on ... I think it was a very difficult time to know what to do ... [the Days of Rage] was a colossal failure ... [But] we were making decisions in the middle of things, and anyone who thinks they knew what should have been done in 1969 is probably kidding themselves.[11]

Months later, three WUO leaders blew themselves up in a Greenwich Village townhouse while cooking explosives. The Weather Underground's fevered extremism made them a central target of Hoover's COINTELPRO well into the 1970s.

When U.S. Senator George McGovern accepted the Democratic nomination for president in July 1972, he implored Americans to "come home."[12] What they were to return *to* was very much a matter of perspective. One month before McGovern spoke, a burglary at the Watergate Hotel in Washington cracked open the door to the "secrecy and deception in high places" the Democratic nominee warned about that night, a scandal of corruption that would destroy the president he could not defeat at the ballot box. By the summer of 1972, the country was engulfed in what historian Walter Karp characterized as a "vast, chaotic upheaval that was mainly democratic in spirit, purely democratic in its outcome, and deeply threatening to the nation's political establishment."[13] The dynamic outbreak of social change movements that spilled out of the sixties inherently endangered the political order, even as it demonstrated the resilience of American democracy at a moment of grave constitutional crisis triggered by both the Watergate affair and the Vietnam War.

The Madman ... and the Theory

The contorted ethical reasoning of the Weather Underground had nothing on Richard Nixon and Henry Kissinger that summer of '69. Even as the president began drawing down U.S. forces, he and National Security Advisor Henry Kissinger intensified the bombing to staggering proportions. Nixon spoke of "peace with honor" but determined privately not to be "the first president of the United States to lose a war."[14] In March he authorized B-52 bombing runs over Cambodia at a time when Prince Norodom Sihanouk's government and his nation's neutrality were fragile. Sihanouk faced both the growing communist insurgency of the Khmer Rouge, and growing U.S. impatience with NLF sanctuaries and NVA command centers in eastern Cambodia along the South Vietnamese border. Nixon would go after them himself. Code-named "Breakfast," the operation was to be first on a "Menu" of increasingly ferocious operations aimed at forcing Hanoi to the peace table on American terms. Knowing public disclosure of a wider war would be met with condemnation, the bombing of Cambodia was orchestrated in secret—a truly impressive feat when one considers the horrific scale: from January to August 1973 alone, American pilots hit 33,945 sites.[15] Official documents recorded NLF targets in South Vietnam, when in fact aircraft turned west toward Cambodia. On Kissinger's orders, documents were destroyed and the circle of men privy to the "dual reporting" system remained tight.[16] The bombing took the lives of more than 150,000 Cambodians.

Operation Menu did not stand in isolation, but rather was part of Nixon's larger strategy—what he called "the madman theory," as he explained to aide Bob Haldeman:

> I want the North Vietnamese to believe that I've reached the point that I might do anything to stop the war. We'll just slip the word to them that "for God's sake, you know Nixon is obsessed about Communism. We can't restrain him when he's angry—and he has his hand on the nuclear button"—and Ho Chi Minh will be in Paris himself in two days begging for peace.[17]

In July 1969, Kissinger conveyed to Hanoi's negotiators in Paris and to their Soviet patrons that unless they made substantial movement toward the U.S. position by November 1, Nixon would be compelled to take "measures of great consequence and force." Intended as a "savage decisive blow" and code named "Duck Hook," the plan called for widespread bombing of population and industrial centers, the mining of harbors, bombardment of the dike and levee system essential to North Vietnamese rice production, a ground invasion of the North, and the use of tactical nuclear weapons on supply routes.[18] Four days of this savagery, Kissinger insisted, and Hanoi would cry uncle. "I can't believe a little fourth-rate power like North Vietnam doesn't have a breaking point."[19] On October 10, Nixon ordered nuclear-armed aircraft sent to civilian airports, deployed and readied for launch submarine-based ballistic missiles, commenced strategic targeting of North Vietnamese, Soviet, and Chinese cities and military installations. Then the three-day climax, code-named Giant Lance: on October 27, 18 B-52s armed with nuclear weapons took off from their bases along the West coast, crossed over Alaska and in 18-hour shifts, and flew in ovals over the Arctic Circle toward Soviet airspace.[20]

The nuclear risk was real, but the belief that withdrawing ground forces gave Nixon the political space to launch a major escalation, was pure apparition. That was made clear in the Vietnam Moratorium, the largest demonstration against the war. On October 15, an estimated two million Americans participated in the first of what was to be monthly Vietnam Moratoriums, where business as usual would cease until U.S. troops were withdrawn. Americans leafletted, attended teach-ins, church services, and vigils. Flags flew at half-mast, church bells tolled, the names of dead American GIs were read aloud. Soldiers in Vietnam were among those wearing black armbands to signify solidarity with the Moratorium. Involving all sectors of American society, the Moratorium received positive press coverage. As advisor Patrick Moynihan reported to Nixon: "The Moratorium was a success ... in style and content it was everything the organizers could have hoped for. The young white middle class crowds were sweet tempered and considerate: at times even radiant ... The movement lost no friends," he added. [21]

As historians have documented, the Moratorium "cast a pall over Nixon's planning" and in large part forced the decision to shelve Duck Hook.[22] On November 3, the president delivered an Oval Office speech reaffirming his commitment to U.S. withdrawal while decrying the "vocal minority" of opposition in the streets. He praised the "Silent Majority" of loyal, flag-waving Americans who refused to buckle while their president continued his efforts to "win the peace." Then he admonished, "Let us understand: North Vietnam cannot defeat or humiliate the United States. Only Americans can do that."[23] Press coverage ran resoundingly in Nixon's direction following the Silent Majority speech. Speechwriter Pat Buchanan orchestrated a public relations effort, complete with "Silent Majority" bumper stickers. "We've got those liberal bastards on the run now," Nixon crowed.[24]

Seizing the moment, Buchanan engineered a scheme that winter to exploit the popularity of country music star Johnny Cash, who endorsed Nixon's Vietnam policy on his television program. Buchanan saw a golden opportunity. Country legend Cash, so he and Bob Haldeman thought, *was* the Silent Majority, and to pull him into the Nixon orbit would solidify the president's support in the heartland. "This is culturally *us*!" Buchanan later recalled. "Let's bring Johnny Cash to the White House!" That Nixon was not a fan was irrelevant. As the big date of April 17, 1970 approached, Nixon issued two requests to Cash: "Okie from Muskogee," Merle Haggard's red, white, and blue anti-hippie number, and "Welfare Cadillac," a satirical harangue on welfare recipients. Cash agreed to learn them. But neither Pat Buchanan nor the 250 Nixon partisans who packed the East Room that night really knew Johnny Cash, an authentic rebel patriot. Champion of the oppressed, Cash's music in the late 1960s increasingly reflected social causes, including Native Americans and prisoner rights. Cash visited Vietnam that winter and returned agonizing over the reality of the war. "I'm in a search mode right now. I'm troubled about what's happening here," he confided to a friend. "I was raised in a Baptist church in Arkansas, I know what's right." There would be no "Okie from Muskogee" that night. Instead, the highlight was a brave performance of a new Cash composition called, "What Is Truth?" The song offered a pointedly probing defense of the youth rebellion that made Nixon and his fellow Republicans squirm and suggested the delusive nature of the Silent Majority.[25]

Whatever middle ground on which a "peace with honor" plurality may have stood had been collapsing for months. Nine days after Nixon's speech, Seymour Hersh published his first report on the My Lai Massacre. Nixon's fury at the revelations dripped with his notorious anti-Semitism. "It's those dirty rotten Jews from New York who are behind it," he fumed.[26] That month, a half million Americans surrounded the Washington Monument in the Moratorium March, an event perhaps best remembered for Pete Seeger leading the crowd in a stirring, prolonged rendition of John Lennon's recently released, "Give Peace a

Chance." Seeger remembered it as a "huge ballet, flags, banners, signs, would move to the right ... and then to the left for the next measure. Parents had children on their shoulders, swaying in rhythm."[27]

The clandestine bombing of Cambodia, meanwhile, seeded unforeseen ramifications at home. In May, a *New York Times* story about the bombing, based on information leaked from National Security Council staffer Morton Halperin, prompted Kissinger and Nixon to order the FBI to conduct warrantless wiretaps on Halperin and 13 other individuals in an effort to stop any further leaks.[28] Halperin was talking that fall to Daniel Ellsberg, the military analyst who a few years earlier produced for Robert McNamara a complete history of U.S. actions in Vietnam—soon known as the Pentagon Papers. The experience of compiling the documents had moved Ellsberg to sharply question the war. Now the news from Halperin about Cambodia and the darker plans of Kissinger and Nixon jolted him. That fall at a War Resisters League meeting, Ellsberg met activist Randy Kehler, recently sentenced to prison for draft resistance. "[That] he was going to jail as a very deliberate choice—because he thought it was the right thing to do," Ellsberg said, "just really tore my life in two."

> There was no question in my mind that my government was involved in an unjust war that was going to continue and get larger. I left the auditorium and found a deserted men's room. I sat on the floor and cried for over an hour, just sobbing.[29]

Within days, Ellsberg, aided by a colleague Anthony Russo and his young daughter, worked by night to make copies of the highly classified Pentagon Papers, and then agonized for over a year about how to release them. When excerpts began appearing in June 1971 in the *New York Times* and *Washington Post*, Nixon and Kissinger erupted, fearing further exposure of the Cambodian operation, and knowing that their continued release would further sap public support. The administration filed suit, arguing that national security concerns trumped the First Amendment, an argument that met a stinging rebuke from District Court Judge Murray Gurfein:

> Security also lies in the value of our free institutions. A cantankerous press, an obstinate press, a ubiquitous press must be suffered by those in authority to preserve the even greater values of freedom of expression and the right of the people to know.[30]

Secrecy and deception, it turned out, ran deep and wide in the Oval Office. One of the first indications came with the trial of Ellsberg and Russo for violating the Espionage Act. Ellsberg was set free when it was revealed that he had been the target of persecution by the "Plumbers" unit of Nixon political operation. Determined to plug security leaks, the Plumbers included former CIA operatives G. Gordon Liddy and E. Howard Hunt and were headed by Nixon adviser John Ehrlichman. The trial disclosed brazenly criminal conduct, including wiretapping, burglarizing Ellsberg's psychiatrist's office, plans to assault him at an antiwar rally, and an offer to the trial judge of the FBI directorship that sure smelled like a bribe. Nixon himself was bullish on plans to burglarize or fire-bomb the Brookings Institution, Morton Halperin's new employer. "The bizarre events have incurably infected the prosecution," wrote Judge William Byrne in May 1973 in dismissing the charges against Ellsberg and Russo.[31] Judge Byrne didn't yet know the half of it, for in the chain of events from Cambodia–Duck Hook to Halperin and Ellsberg lay the genesis of criminality that ended at Watergate and Nixon's resignation a year later.

While the Watergate scandal marinated, the war went on without mercy. In Cambodia, Sihanouk was overthrown in March 1970 by Lon Nol. Sihanouk then joined forces with Pol Pot and the Khmer Rouge, which exploited the former leader's continued popularity among the peasantry to ultimately drive Lon Nol from power in 1975. Operation Menu was well underway when on April 30, 1970, Nixon announced in a televised address a U.S.-led ground "incursion" into Cambodia on a mission to "clean out" communist strongholds. "This is *not*," Nixon assured viewers, "an invasion of Cambodia"; he was expand-ing the war in order to end it. Further, Nixon declared that, "If, when the chips are down, the world's most powerful nation ... acts like a pitiful, helpless giant, the forces of totalitarianism and anarchy will threaten free nations and free insti-tutions throughout the world."[32] In that moment, the fusion of presidential ego and imperial hubris that had led the nation into Vietnam reached its crescendo. Compounding the barbarism of the bombing, the U.S. invasion continued to drive Cambodians into the arms of the Khmer Rouge-led insurgency. What Nixon and Kissinger unleashed further destabilized the government in Phnom Penh and helped open the gates of hell to the Cambodian "killing fields."[33] Between 1975 and 1979, more than two million Cambodians perished in one of the worst genocides of the twentieth century.[34]

What opponents saw plainly in Nixon's action was an illegal expansion of the war. The campuses exploded. Following an antiwar demonstration on the cam-pus of Kent State University on May 1 and the burning of the ROTC building, Ohio Governor James Rhodes deployed the National Guard. On Sunday, May 3 Rhodes labeled antiwar demonstrators, "the strongest, well-trained militant revolutionary group that has ever assembled in America." They were more dan-gerous, he declared, "than the brown shirts and the Communist element ... the worst type of people that we harbor in America." He pledged "to eradicate this problem"[35] Following a noon demonstration the next day, most of the several hundred students began to disperse. Some taunted soldiers with insults and rocks. After briefly huddling, at 12:24 p.m. a contingent of soldiers positioned at the crest of Blanket Hill knelt and fired 67 rounds in 13 seconds. Four students were killed and nine injured, the nearest victim falling 60 feet from the Guard's position. Martin Scheuer, the father of Sandra Scheuer, one of the slain, later compared the inflammatory rhetoric of Rhodes and reactionary violence to that of Nazi Germany from which he had fled.[36] Ten days later, police fired 150 rounds into a women's dormitory at the predominantly black Jackson State College, killing two students and wounding 12. On August 29 in Los Angeles, at the Chicano Moratorium March against the war, journalist Ruben Salazar was killed by a tear gas projectile fired by police into a local bar where Salazar had gone following the march. As at Kent and Jackson State, suspicions lingered for decades about complicity on the part of the state in the killing of Salazar, who had become a thorn in the side of the white LA power structure for his reporting on police abuses against Mexican Americans.[37]

Reaction to Kent drove the national divide deeper. There was on the one hand grief and horror. And yet a Gallup poll indicated that nearly 60 percent supported the Guard's actions, lining up with Nixon who suggested the students brought the violence on themselves. On May 8, a large group of construction workers in Manhattan at the site of the World Trade Center assaulted a group of students mourning the Kent shootings and condemning the Cambodia invasion. The "Hard Hat Riot" was followed by a march of 100,000 rank and file workers in support of the war. Union officials traveled to the White House a few days later to present the president with an honorary hard hat.[38]

"I Am Not a Crook"

At 2 a.m. on June 17, 1972, the nightwatchman at the Watergate Hotel complex in Washington, DC, noticed the latch taped down on the door leading to the Democratic National Committee (DNC) headquarters. A five-man Plumbers unit had gone into the DNC that night primarily to repair a surveillance bug planted weeks prior. Two of the men carried address books bearing the White House phone number of E. Howard Hunt. FBI investigators soon revealed that Hunt and G. Gordon Liddy, finance counsel for the Committee to Re-elect the President (CRP), had directed what Nixon's press secretary dismissed as a "third-rate burglary attempt." In September, as Liddy, Hunt, and the burglars were indicted by a federal grand jury, *Washington Post* reporters Bob Woodward and Carl Bernstein began publishing an explosive series of stories linking a massive campaign of CRP political spying—paid for by a fund controlled by its chairman, former Attorney General John Mitchell. An investigation would reveal that Mitchell, the nation's highest law enforcement officer of a "law and order" administration, had authorized the Watergate break-in.

The inquiry would come too late for George McGovern. Declaring "Peace is at Hand," Nixon rolled to a landslide. One month later, with peace talks stalled he and Kissinger unleashed the heaviest air assault of the entire war, the 12-day "Christmas Bombing." American B-52s filled the skies over Hanoi, killing nearly 1,700 North Vietnamese, the majority civilians. "Immense incandescent mushrooms" appeared over factories, transportation facilities, residential areas, and a hospital, producing ghastly images of victims and medical personnel. While Nixon and Kissinger defended the action as an affirmation of American credibility that would advance the cause of peace, most of the world saw it differently. The *La Monde* in France compared the bombing to the infamous annihilation of Guernica by the Nazi Luftwaffe, while at home the *St. Louis Dispatch* spoke for many in abhorring the "new madness."[39] The Paris Peace Accords were signed three weeks later. In June, congress voted to end all U.S. military action in Southeast Asia.

By the time of Nixon's inauguration, the trial of the Watergate burglars was under way. Questioning by Judge John J. Sirica produced nothing of consequence regarding White House links to the operation. But in mid-March, Sirica received a presentencing letter from James McCord, one of the five, informing him that the burglars had been paid for their silence with CRP hush money. Hunt went to White House Counsel John Dean, threatening to expose even deeper, "seamy things," and demanding further payment. When Dean conveyed that news to Nixon, he flatly replied, "you could get a million dollars. And you could get it in cash." Dean warned Nixon of a "cancer" on his presidency and looked for a deal from federal prosecutors.[40]

In the meantime, after a U.S. Senate Select Committee began investigating the scandal, Nixon announced the resignations of Dean, Haldeman, Ehrlichman, and Attorney General Richard Kleindienst. The house cleaning did nothing to stop the train now rolling down the track. In mid-May, new Attorney General Elliot Richardson appointed Archibald Cox as Special Prosecutor to investigate criminal misconduct in the Watergate scandal. The more public inquiry unfolded on Capitol Hill with the televised committee hearings. For weeks that summer, the greatest constitutional crisis in modern American history unfolded live on TV, witness after witness disclosing criminal conduct of the White House. Viewers learned of a campaign of politically driven espionage, sabotage and "dirty tricks" to "ratfuck," as Donald Segretti put it, Nixon opponents: wiretapping, money laundering, burglaries, IRS tax audits, shaking down donors in exchange for political favors, planting salacious stories in the press about Nixon political opponents, and bagmen[41] delivering Mitchell's illegally raised campaign cash to political saboteurs in paper sacks.[42]

Day after day the revelations spilled out—through the hearings, the press, a grand jury weighing prosecution of Nixon aides, and the Ellsberg Trial. The Nixon White House compiled an "enemies list" of several hundred politicians, journalists, labor and business leaders, sports figures, and celebrities—against whom the Nixon White House applied varying degrees of the "available federal machinery" to "screw" them, as John Dean testified.[43] Nixon's Immigration and Naturalization Service worked overtime to deport ex-Beatle and antiwar activist John Lennon and keep him from a concert tour he and Jerry Rubin were planning—at which they would register young people ahead of the 1972 elections.[44] As the hearings continued, Tennessee Republican Senator Howard Baker famously asked Dean, "What did the President know and when did he know it?"[45]

He knew a lot as it turned out, much of which was recorded on an extensive White House taping system, a bombshell disclosed mid-summer. Immediately came the demand from Cox and the committee for the tapes. In October, Judge Sirica ordered their release, triggering the scandal's turning point. On October 20, Nixon ordered his Attorney General Elliot Richardson to fire Cox. Refusing the order, Richardson resigned. Hours later, Deputy AG William Ruckelshaus refused Nixon and was fired. The president then turned to Solicitor General Robert Bork, who fired Cox and moved to abolish the office of Special Prosecutor. Nixon's "Saturday Night Massacre" shocked the nation. "A government of laws may be on the verge of becoming a government of one man," Richardson declared.[46] As congress demanded a new special prosecutor, Nixon went into hiding. Making an appearance a few weeks later in Florida, the president blustered, "I am not a crook." The White House released several tapes, one containing a suspicious 18½ -minute gap. After more Nixon stonewalling, impeachment proceedings formally commenced in May 1974 in the House Judiciary Committee.

Beyond approving three articles of impeachment, the committee hearings were further enshrined in memory by the opening speech of newly elected Texas Congresswoman Barbara Jordan, the first African American woman elected from the South. Jordan delivered a spellbinding allocution on Nixon's crimes, situated against the essential purposes the Founders invested in the mechanism of impeachment, reminding Americans that the "President is impeachable if he attempts to subvert the Constitution."[47] Jordan's powerful oration came July 25, 1974—the day after the Supreme Court ruled unanimously that Nixon surrender the tapes. August 5 brought the "smoking gun" recording of June 23, 1972 in which Nixon discussed with aides how to quash the FBI investigation.[48] Republican defenders began to abandon him (though not entirely[49]), and on August 8, Richard Nixon became the first U.S. president to resign his office. Ascending to the presidency was Vice President Gerald R. Ford— appointed the previous fall upon the departure of Spiro Agnew, who had also resigned in disgrace over unrelated corruption charges.

Born of Richard Nixon's profound insecurities and his fear and loathing of political adversaries, Watergate also was a manifestation of the enlarged power of the presidency that had been growing since Harry Truman. The exigencies of the Cold War had produced an unprecedented concentration of power in the executive branch. Nixon's war in Cambodia was an extension of what happened in the Tonkin Gulf, his use of intelligence agencies to spy on Americans had origins in Hoover's abuses. There was no precedent for recklessly putting the nation's nuclear weapons delivery system on high alert, which happened again in October 1973. Four days after the Saturday Night Massacre, with Nixon drinking heavily and rambling incoherently to Kissinger about his imminent demise, the Secretary of State assembled the National Security Council, except for the president and his vice president. On Kissinger's agenda: how to respond to the Kremlin threat to send a joint U.S.-Soviet force to intervene in the Yom Kippur War between Israel and Arab states. If the U.S. did not join, warned Soviet Ambassador Anatoly Dobrynin, the Russians would go it alone. Kissinger led the NSC in rebuffing Dobrynin in favor of another nuclear gambit—initiating preparations for a massive attack on the Soviet Union. Working in secret, unelected leaders in the White House took the nation to the precipice of nuclear war while the president drank himself to sleep.[50] This was concentrated power exponentially squared.

Nor had Nixon been checked in the exercise of *Realpolitik*, Kissinger's overall approach to foreign policy. Though rooted in containment, *Realpolitik* aimed to liberate American actions from the pretense of considerations of democracy and human rights, focusing squarely on the "realistic" advance of U.S. national interests. Its more enlightened moments came in 1972 when Kissinger and Nixon advanced détente with the Soviet Union centered on nuclear arms control, and then achieved a stunning diplomatic opening with the People's Republic of China. Despite the communist regime's tyranny—then still engaged in a murderous "Cultural Revolution" against its own people—Kissinger and Nixon hoped the move would induce the Chinese to pressure Hanoi toward the U.S. position at the Paris Peace talks. Although that goal proved illusory, the opening with China did lead to U.S. diplomatic recognition in 1979.

Realpolitik's cold-blooded pragmatism led the Nixon and Ford administrations to strengthen U.S. alliances with authoritarian strongmen around the world, from the Philippines' Ferdinand Marcos to Indonesia, where Kissinger and President Ford pushed arms sales and then looked the other way as the regime invaded East Timor, committing massive human rights crimes. From 1970 to 1973, Nixon and Kissinger secretly funneled millions through the CIA to destabilize and ultimately assist military forces in Chile to bring down that nation's democratically elected president, Salvador Allende, who had moved to nationalize much of the Chilean economy, including the U.S.-controlled copper industry. Bemoaning the events, Kissinger mused, "I don't see why we need to stand idly by and watch a country go communist due to the irresponsibility of its own people."[51] Using institutions like the World Bank and the U.S. Export–Import Bank, the U.S. strategy wrought havoc on the economy and destabilized Chilean society, setting the stage for the September 11, 1973 overthrow of Allende led by General Augusto Pinochet and a cabal of fascist strongmen. For the next 17 years, the Pinochet dictatorship resulted in the deaths of more than 3,500 Chilean dissidents.[52]

Reform and Renewal

From the Kennedy assassination through the traumas of Vietnam and Watergate, the civic faith that once bound Americans in shared purpose to their government was badly frayed by the time of the nation's bicentennial. After Nixon's resignation, just over one-third of Americans trusted their government, a precipitous fall of nearly 40 percent from the late 1950s. President Ford furthered the slide just weeks into his presidency when he issued an executive pardon of Richard Nixon. To many Americans, the clemency reeked of a quid pro quo arrangement with the disgraced former president. Although no evidence emerged that Ford's action was anything other than an effort to end what he called the "national nightmare" of Watergate, the perception lingered, and two years later factored into Ford's narrow loss to former Georgia governor Jimmy Carter, who ran for president promising Americans he "would never lie to ya." Not everyone was buying the pledge. Nearly one-half of eligible voters stayed home that election day, a drop of nearly ten points since 1960.[53]

Responding to the crisis of civic fealty, congress moved to enact a series of wide-ranging reforms aimed at restoring trust in government, strengthening democracy, and weakening the powers of what seemed an unchecked executive branch. Ostensibly curbing the president's authority to engage Americans in hostilities abroad, the War Powers Act aimed at restoring congress's war-making powers. After Watergate and investigative journalists exposed the unconstitutional abuses of the FBI, CIA, and National Security Agency, in 1975 the Church Committee[54] hearings revealed that U.S. intelligence agencies had planned and carried out assassinations of foreign leaders, spied on millions of Americans, manipulated the news media, and sabotaged the outcomes of foreign elections.[55] In the wake of the revelations, Congress created Select Committees on Intelligence in the House and Senate to oversee covert operations, providing at least a mechanism of democratic accountability. The Foreign Intelligence Surveillance Act established a (FISA) court to oversee any act of surveillance requested on an American citizen, thereby creating a safeguard against presidential abuse. "It is the right of the American people to know what their government has done—the bad as well as the good," declared Senator Church.[56] In 1974, Congress strengthened the Freedom of Information Act (FOIA) permitting Americans to request documents pertaining to the actions of their government. Likewise, the Presidential Records Act (1978) mandated that all communications and records pertaining to presidents belong to the American people. Finally, the Inspector General Act posted IG watchdogs inside of federal agencies to ensure ethical behavior of public officials and fiscal accountability.

This unprecedented "season of reform," strengthened the founders' ingenious framework in which co-equal branches of government would check likely abuses of power by the other.[57] The efficacy of the laws ultimately depended on the ideological bent of elected officials, the will of Americans, and the judicial test of constitutionality. A series of post-Watergate campaign finance reform measures aimed at limiting the influence of big money in politics reinforced the latter point. In a landmark decision in 2010 (*Citizens United vs. FEC*), the laws were eviscerated by a conservative U.S. Supreme Court that argued that limits on campaign contributions were an unconstitutional restraint of free speech.

Participatory Democracy Lives On

The social change movements that grew out of the sixties were shaped by varied historical and contemporary forces. To one degree or another, however, all intersected with the African American human rights struggle, the era's wellspring of activism. For Japanese Americans, rising black consciousness stirred a desire to confront memories of the internment camps.[58] Interned with his family at Topaz, Utah, in the mid-1960s Richard Aoki became a founding member of the Black Panther Party. For many Japanese and Chinese Americans, as for recent refugees from Southeast Asia, the Vietnam War invited historical connections to other episodes of U.S. imperialism against Asian peoples, while also cultivating a positive pan-Asian American identity.[59] Indeed, the effort to claim a long-denied cultural identity grounded the struggle for "Yellow Power." Rejected by the late sixties was the term "oriental," imposed by a dominant white culture. "Oriental was a rug that everyone steps on," Aoki insisted.[60] Led by eloquent voices such as poet-activist Janice Mirikitani, Asian American women confronted an internalized self-loathing and desire to be blond and blue-eyed. With pride and dignity, they began celebrating their own cultural histories and life stories. They demanded an end to representations of exotic geisha girls and cheap hookers—an image often reinforced by returning GIs that invited sexual assault against Asian American women.[61]

Mexican Americans expressed a renewed cultural pride born of a history of conquest and resistance dating to the pre-Columbian civilization of *Aztlán*, as well as the Mexican American War. For a new generation, *Chicano* evoked a pre-1846 borderless region of the American Southwest and northern Mexico. "Chicano describes a beautiful people," declared Armando Rendon in the Chicano Manifesto, "a unique confluence of histories, cultures, languages, and traditions."[62] However one defined it, the term demanded a reckoning with a history marked by imperial domination. In a land that once belonged to their ancestors, Mexican American youth in the Southwest grew up as alien second-class citizens. Chicano consciousness confronted this history, along with degrading stereotypes of Mexican Americans in popular culture. By the mid-twentieth century, a history of dispossession and racism manifested in poverty, infant mortality, and in many areas, segregation. "No dogs, Negroes or Mexicans," read signs in restaurants and movie theatres in Texas. In areas of large Mexican American populations, voting rights were often restricted or municipal election districts so badly gerrymandered that not a single Latino could be elected to city council. It was rare to see a Mexican American policeman, or a citizen serve on a jury. Institutions were permeated with xenophobic intolerance. Despite the Bilingual Education Act of 1968, many school districts in the borderlands of the southwest prohibited children from speaking Spanish. As Sal Castro, an East Los Angeles social studies teacher observed, "If a kid speaks in Spanish, he is criticized. If a kid has a Mexican accent, he is ridiculed. If a kid talks back, in any language, he is arrested." It was Castro who in March 1968 organized the massive "Blowouts" of students from East LA schools.[63] The strike soon spread to other western cities.

That same defiant spirit fired the Alianza Movement of Reies Lopez Tijerina in northern New Mexico, which demanded the federal government remedy the Anglo theft of land and water rights guaranteed to Mexican American families by the 1848 Treaty of Guadalupe Hidalgo. In the decades after the Mexican American War, Spanish land grant rights that had descended to Mexican American families were routinely violated by white landowners in Texas, California and New Mexico. Once a fervent evangelical Christian preacher, by the 1960s Reies Tijerina had made extensive pilgrimages to traditional indigenous elders in the borderland region that convinced him his mission lay in working with poor New Mexicans to wrest back rightful ownership of their forebears' lands. After unsuccessful appeals to the state government in Santa Fe, Tijerina and members of a statewide land grant coalition determined to take radical action. In June 1967, they made an armed assault on the Tierra Amarilla County Courthouse that ended with a state policeman wounded before Tijerina and his men fled into the mountains. New Mexico politicians and national media branded Tijerina a communist revolutionary. Captured and briefly imprisoned, Tijerina nevertheless remained a heroic figure for many Chicanos.[64]

More broadly supported was the struggle of the United Farmworkers Union Organizing Committee (UFWOC), led by Cesar Chávez and Dolores Huerta. Chávez's strategy to advance *La Causa*—that is, justice and dignity for farmworkers—was grounded in Ghandian principles of nonviolence. Worker strikes and grape boycotts put economic pressure on the growers, while prayer pilgrimages and Chávez's hunger fasts drew national attention. Such actions reinforced farm workers' faith-based commitment to nonviolence, while sharpening the distinctions between UFWOC and more militant strains of the movement. The UFWOC faced a formidable array of opponents: politically powerful big growers, FBI surveillance, and the Teamsters Union. On one occasion, Chavez and a Catholic priest were arrested by officials for "violating the air space" of a grower as they flew in the reverend's plane trying to reach isolated farmworkers.[65] After a decade of perseverance and more than 1,000 strikes and other actions, in 1975 California recognized the right of farmworkers to unionize. The first union contracts won protections against the deadly health effects of indiscriminate pesticide spraying in the fields; since the 1950s, thousands of workers had been poisoned and hundreds killed from exposure.[66]

The Latinx struggle encompassed a wide spectrum of strategies and organizations. Arising out of a history of police brutality and inspired by the Black Panthers, the Brown Berets were established in 1967 in Los Angeles by David Sanchez around a program of armed self-defense and a variety of cultural and medical programs. In Chicago, moved by the social welfare work of Panther leader Fred Hampton, José Cha Cha Jiménez organized the Young Lords to address a range of problems afflicting the Puerto Rican community. In New York City, the Young Lords' work included a "garbage offensive" that pressured the city to improve refuse management in Spanish Harlem. A peaceful occupation of a local church, influenced by the liberation theology of the era, urged its pastor to provide a free breakfast program. Pioneering intersectional activists, the Young Lords brought a feminist perspective to much of their work, confronted racism within the Puerto Rican community, and looked for common cause with the white working class and LGBTQ activists.[67]

Opposite on the continuum, tactically speaking, was the venerable League of United Latin American Citizens (LULAC), which worked largely through the courts on issues of school desegregation, job discrimination, and voting rights. Operating within the xenophobic framework of cultural assimilation on which both American "melting pot" mythology and early twentieth-century restrictive immigration law was based, LULAC argued for the legal rights of Hispano peoples based on a notion of their European whiteness. By the 1960s, that position seemed anachronistic to many. In New York City, the lightness of skin meant little as Puerto Ricans fought alongside black activists against what were fundamentally colonial racist attitudes affecting housing conditions and employment opportunities of both marginalized communities.[68]

No minority in America had a longer list of grievances against the U.S. government than Native Americans. Wars of conquest, broken treaties, and cultural dispossession had left Indian peoples with shockingly high rates of unemployment, poverty, infant mortality, alcoholism, and suicide. Life expectancy was 42, twenty-five years less that of white Americans. Seeking to dramatize these issues, on November 20, 1969, 79 members of "Indians of All Tribes" (IAT) sailed toward Alcatraz Island in San Francisco Bay to launch a peaceful occupation of what was then an abandoned prison. Leaders announced they were reclaiming Alcatraz in accord with an old treaty granting Indians access to "unused federal lands." Their objectives included the establishment of a Native American Studies cultural center and museum. Seeking to avoid a confrontation, the Nixon administration exercised patience, waiting the Indians out and allowing the occupation of Alcatraz to exhaust itself by June 1971.

Though it failed its immediate objectives, Alcatraz helped to fully ignite a "Red Power" American Indian Movement (AIM) that had been simmering for years. AIM "hit our reservation like a tornado," remembered Mary Crow Dog, "like a new wind blowing out of nowhere, a drumbeat from far off getting louder and louder."[69] From 1969 to 1973, the pace of Indian activism accelerated: Indians staged "fish-ins" to regain lost fishing rights; attorneys filed lawsuits seeking rectification of broken treaty obligations; activists peacefully blocked roads to seashores trashed by white tourists; the United Native Americans demanded the establishment of cultural centers and Indian education programs. In August 1970, AIM staged a peaceful takeover of Mount Rushmore National Monument in South Dakota's Black Hills, drawing attention to the government's violation of the 1868 Fort Laramie Treaty guaranteeing Lakota sovereignty of the sacred Black Hills. Following the discovery of Black Hills gold, the Grant administration had abrogated the treaty, igniting the last phase of the Indian wars that ended with the 1890 Wounded Knee Massacre of 150 Lakota men, women and children. In 1970, Dee Brown's best-selling *Bury My Heart at Wounded Knee* offered a searing account of the entire history of U.S. government deception and military savagery against Indian peoples. Arthur Penn's revisionist western, *Little Big Man*, turned on its head the mythology of General Custer's "Last Stand." Coming amid growing criticism of the war in Vietnam, these and other cultural works arraigning the righteousness of American frontier violence carried haunting resonance.

As the scope and tenor of Native American activism intensified, federal responsiveness to Indian demands evolved rapidly. In July 1970, President Nixon announced his support for Indian "self-determination," hastening the path toward a number of legislative remedies that had long been debated. A symbolic breakthrough came December 2, 1970 as the U.S. Senate voted 70–12 to restore the 48,000-acre Blue Lake Watershed of the Sangre de Christo Mountains to the Taos Pueblo Indians of New Mexico—the first time the United States government had ever restored title to Indians over lands in the public domain.[70] The bar was low, but Indians saw more progress under Nixon than any president since FDR. The administration increased the budgets of the Indian Health Service and the Bureau of Indian Affairs and hired more Native Americans in positions of leadership at the agency. Nixon supported reforms aimed at granting tribal governments greater sovereignty in managing their affairs, including the Indian Self-Determination and Religious Freedom Acts.[71] Some measures proved to be disappointments. Funds appropriated for the Indian Education Act, for example, were diluted by white school districts that suddenly counted many Indian children in their seats.[72]

What seemed a violent denouement to the American Indian Movement came in 1973 with a 70-day armed takeover by AIM of the Wounded Knee community on the Pine Ridge Reservation that left two Indians dead and one FBI agent paralyzed. The action brought into sharp relief tensions between militants and moderates in the struggle, as well as the criticisms of an entrenched tribal leadership seen by many as too cozy with white interests. An Indian Policy Review Commission established after the standoff achieved little. Overall, however, the activism of the period placed Native American issues on the nation's agenda, restored a measure of autonomy to Indian peoples, and brought some improvement to their lives.[73]

"Strictly a run of the mill fire," fire chief William Barry called it. True enough, the Cuyahoga River had burned before, a conflagration in 1952 causing ten times the destruction. But when it caught fire June 22, 1969, America was a different country. By then, citizens could recognize the befouled waterway from their own backyards, the Cuyahoga's condition being not so different from rivers and lakes across the nation. Beyond the fact that rivers are not supposed to burn, there was something uniquely appalling in the story. Cleveland's river, *Time* observed dryly, "oozes rather than flows." Someone who falls in it "does not drown but decays."[74] Coming near the close of a decade in which history seemed to speed up with every riveting image, news coverage of the fire helped galvanize the environmental movement—particularly coming as it did six months after what was then the nation's worst oil spill. In January, the blowout of a drilling rig off the coast of Santa Barbara, California produced hideous images of oil-soaked seabirds. Suddenly the Earthrise photograph—as poet Archibald MacLeish described it, "small and blue and beautiful in that eternal silence where it floats"—assumed amplified significance.[75]

Hoping he could harness the energy of the antiwar movement, Wisconsin Senator Gaylord Nelson announced a national day of "Teach-Ins" on the environment for April 22, 1970. Nelson tapped Harvard law student Denis Hayes as national organizer. As Hayes later remembered, the event that became Earth Day "organized itself."[76] Twenty million citizens participated, the largest outpouring of activism on a single issue in history. Americans across the political spectrum took part in events at 10,000 schools, 2,000 college campuses, and in 1,000 communities. Although some in the antiwar and black struggles criticized the event for diverting attention from arguably more urgent matters, overall the nation united around Earth Day. Americans demanded change, and generally speaking, they got it. Over the next several years, Congress would pass—with broad bipartisan support and bearing the signatures of Republican presidents—sweeping environmental reforms, including strengthened Clean Air and Water Acts, a Safe Drinking water Act, the National Environmental Policy Act, an Endangered Species Act, and the Occupational Safety and Health Act. Richard Nixon established the Environmental Protection Agency to oversee the substantial environmental progress Americans would make in the coming years.

In addition to the vigorous response from Washington, Earth Day bestowed one other thing: the tens of thousands of Americans who had been working since the postwar era on issues from suburban sprawl to forest, marine mammal and oceans protection to the rising problem of toxic waste coalesced into the force of "environmentalism." Organizations like the Natural Resources Defense Council joined established groups like the Sierra Club working to protect both wild places and public health. Others like Greenpeace applied the tactics of nonviolent civil disobedience and direct action to bold attempts to interdict whaling ships or disrupt nuclear testing. International organizations like Greenpeace reflected what was already clear in the 1970s—that even the most stringent measures enacted by individual governments had limits. The planetary nature of environmental problems was made clear in Stockholm, Sweden at the 1972 UN Conference on the Environment. Barely registering a mention in Stockholm was the "greenhouse effect" of a warming planet that over time demonstrated the immensity of the challenges. Even then, most environmentalists had few illusions of what they were up against—fighting what the elves in J. R. R. Tolkien's *Lord of the Rings* (a favorite of the counterculture) called "the long defeat." Building a movement, as Hayes put it that first Earth Day, "that values people more than profit ... will be a difficult fight."[77]

No movement had more far-reaching impact than the liberation struggle of American women. Some of the consequences are quantifiable—the hundreds of annual deaths that would no longer be suffered by women at the hands of illegal abortions after the 1973 *Roe v. Wade* decision, and the thousands more who would not endure life-altering health problems.[78] Or the dramatic increase in household income that came by cutting the gender pay gap in half.[79] Or the availability of family planning and women's reproductive health services that have allowed millions of women to delay child bearing, attain professional degrees, and earn higher salaries for themselves and their families. Americans can hardly remember a time when banks denied women credit simply because they were women. Thanks in part to the Equal Credit Opportunity Act of 1974, women injected fresh entrepreneurial blood into the economy, and by 2016 comprised nearly 40 percent of American business owners. Although Title IX of the Education Amendments Act of 1972 is mostly celebrated for equalizing access to sports programs by prohibiting gender discrimination at institutions receiving federal funds, its economic impact has been substantial.[80]

None of these gains came without women crashing the barricades of a deeply entrenched patriarchy, which were *everywhere*—even in supposed cornerstones of American liberalism, higher education, and the media. One illustrative episode involves venerable Yale University and its mulishness in complying with Title IX. Yale established a women's crew team that quickly proved more successful than the men's team, yet women endured a gross disparity in facilities, most strikingly in the lack of showers or bathrooms at the crew boathouse. Cold days found the sweat-soaked women of the crew team shivering their way back to campus. When several rowers fell ill while training for the 1976 Olympics, Chris Ernst, their captain and a future Olympian, led them into the office of the Yale women's athletic director. They proceeded to strip naked, revealing the words: "THESE ARE THE BODIES YALE IS EXPLOITING." The story shamed Yale into implementing the changes mandated by Title IX.[81]

Similarly, the women at *Newsweek* never thought of themselves as feminists until they made feminist history. In 1970 the newsweekly had a staff of 50 writers. Just one was a woman. Women who graduated with honors from journalism programs at top-flight institutions were relegated to the mailroom. More tenured female employees could be elevated to (fact-)"checkers"—or as the men called them, "dollies." Sex between bosses and young women hoping for promotion was not uncommon. Outrage mounted as new male reporters landed plum assignments for which women had done the investigative digging. In the spring of 1969, some of the women began meeting secretly, often in the restroom, to plot legal action. Black civil rights attorney Eleanor Holmes Norton bolstered their confidence, persuading them to file the first-ever class-action gender discrimination suit. Charging *Newsweek* with systematic violation of Title VII of the 1964 Civil Rights Act, Lynn Povich and 45 colleagues announced their complaint to the Equal Employment Opportunity Commission in a press conference March 16, 1970.[82]

Their timing was exquisite: at newsstands that morning was the latest *Newsweek* featuring a cover story, "WOMEN IN REVOLT!" about the rising feminist movement, an article that had been outsourced to a freelancer. The irony was not lost on the plaintiffs. Months later, *Newsweek* resolved the complaint August 26, 1970—the same day 50,000 women marched down New York City's Fifth Avenue in the Women's Strike for Equality (Figure 9.1). Organized by the National Organization for Women (NOW), the event celebrated 50 years since the 19th Amendment granting women suffrage. Thousands more women participated in events nationwide. Elementary school girls sat alongside aging grandmothers clad in the suffragette white of their youth. Some women staged "baby-ins" at their workplaces. Others attended rallies across the country at which among other things, they reprised the action at the Miss America Protest, depositing "objects of oppression" into "freedom trash cans." (No husbands were found amid the debris.) The Women's Strike demanded reproductive health care, expansion of child care for working women, and equal opportunity in employment and education. It was the largest demonstration for women's rights in U.S. history.[83]

Newsweek was not alone in riding the wave of media interest in women's issues, though the majority of the coverage ranged from condescending to contemptuous. Howard K. Smith at ABC opened his show the evening of the

Figure 9.1 March for women's liberation, 1971.

Universal Images Group/Getty, www.gettyimages.co.uk/detail/news-photo/protest-in-new-york-march-for-womens-liberation-united-news-photo/535783071?adppopup=true

Women's Strike with a wry smirk and the words of the soon-to-be-disgraced Vice President Agnew: "Quote. Three things have been difficult to tame. The ocean, fools, and women. We may soon be able to tame the ocean, but fools and women will take a little longer." CBS commentator Eric Sevareid upbraided the women for falling to a kind of mass hysteria. "Many movements grow by simple contagion," he lectured, "thousands discovering they are in pain, though they hadn't noticed it until they are told."[84]

Sevareid was more correct than he knew. Many of the women pouring into the streets that day did so after a personal awakening. Beginning in the mid-1960s, women everywhere attended "consciousness raising" sessions—endless, open, frank discussions about an endless range of private concerns. Held in living rooms and basements, in barrooms and, as the *Newsweek* women discovered, Ladies Rooms, consciousness-raising delivered epiphanies of insight about the relationship between a woman's privately held pain and the social and political underpinnings of women's experience in America. Consciousness raising allowed women to move to an enlarged understanding of their lived reality *as women*. "The relief at finding I was not alone was incredible," Barbara Susan remembered. "In consciousness raising I saw women who recognized that there was no such thing as a personal way of solving their problems so long as male supremacy in all its formal and informal forms still existed."[85] Women had long internalized feelings of low self-worth, a fact laid bare by Alice S. Rossi in her landmark 1970 expose on workplace discrimination. Rossi documented how women had learned to simply accept that less qualified men were rewarded ahead of them. One woman's surrender was typical: "Ask a man's opinion about your ideas, show gratitude for his help, make your points as questions, listen with respect and interest to his ideas, and in this way you may be accepted."[86] Consciousness raising in black-and-white, the essay also documented what Rep. Martha Griffiths (D-MI) had called the "specious, negative, and arrogant attitude" of the EEOC, which devoted far fewer resources to cases based on sex discrimination versus those invested in race-based complaints.[87]

Many women came to understand that it was patriarchy that lay at the root of their repressed ambitions. Pay inequity, professional doors slammed shut, the lack of child care, weight limitations for airline "stewardesses," workplace harassment, the failure of husbands to lift a finger at home, the myth of the vaginal orgasm—all were mere symptoms of male supremacy, "the oldest, most basic form of domination," as the liberationist Redstockings declared.[88] Women had even seen it inside the antiwar and civil rights movements, in the sexist attitudes of their revolutionary comrades. Patriarchy was most appallingly expressed in the painful realities of rape, incest, and domestic violence. Americans of the 1970s were not far removed from a world in which women were legally considered property, where rape was criminal because it defiled another man's property. What happened in the back seat of a '57 Chevy or the home was a "private" matter and no business of the state. In 1970, 15 states required a witness for a rape case to be prosecuted. Women who dared bring charges usually found themselves treated by police—and often their parents, family, and friends—as somehow complicit, facing questions that a half-century later remained depressingly familiar: "What were you wearing that night?" "How is it you can remember your rapist but no other details of that evening?" It is little wonder that an estimated 70–90 percent of rapes went unreported.[89]

The anti-rape movement emerged from consciousness-raising and public "speak-outs," where women voiced their private trauma. The first was held in 1971, simultaneous to the appearance of Susan Griffin's powerful essay, "Rape: The All-American Crime."[90] Griffin exploded the myths that had long shrouded "rape culture." Sexual crime was not, argued Griffin, the aberrant behavior of a few dangerous "psychos"—as inferred by Alfred Hitchcock in his acclaimed film of the same title.[91] Rather, it represented the logical ultimate expression of a misogynist strain in the culture that sanctioned "male dominance and female submission." As women knew all too well, "good boys" raped, too.[92]

Progress would be maddeningly slow. In the 1970s, "rape shield laws" began limiting a rape defendant's ability to impeach the victim's credibility with her sexual history. A series of much publicized trials of women who killed their assailants stirred public debate about sexual violence. By 1993, every state recognized that the sanctity of a home where a man had raped his wife did not afford him protection from prosecution.[93] By then, "domestic violence" and "date rape" had entered the vernacular. Established in the mid-1970s, "Take Back the Night Marches" continued to demand women's right to walk without fear. In March 1982, however, with a backlash against the women's movement gaining strength, women at the University of California at Davis were reminded of what they were up against. As historian Ruth Rosen recounted:

> When [the marchers] passed 'fraternity row,' they encountered a shocking display of hostility. While one young man backed a car straight into the crowd, another urinated on the marchers; several 'mooned' the women; some men threatened to rape them later.[94]

The patriarchy would not go easily.

Nor would homophobia. Fear and loathing of gay, lesbian, queer, bisexual, and transgender Americans was deep-seated and statutorily entrenched. LGBTQ+ Americans had long endured fines and imprisonment, police beatings and harassment on a daily basis, their constitutional and civil rights systematically denied simply for living and loving authentically. Public displays of affection between two members of the same sex was illegal almost anywhere. In New York City, it was against the law to wear less than three "gender-appropriate" garments in public. The Cold War era had given us the "Lavender Scare" and the American Psychiatric Association's designation of homosexuality as a mental disorder to be "treated" with a variety of remedies, from drugs and electric shock to "aversion therapy" in which doctors injected gay men with apomorphine to make them sick while looking at male nude photographs. Some urged pre-frontal lobotomies or brain-implanted electrodes to stimulate heterosexual "pleasure therapy."[95]

Queer Americans found refuge in "gay bars," though they rarely lasted more than a few months due to harassment from police and fines imposed upon the owners. Established in 1967, the Stonewall Inn in the Christopher Street neighborhood of Greenwich Village had been a target of raids by the "Public Morals" section of the New York City Police Department. The NYPD's morality cops had repeatedly busted the Stonewall and hauled off "sexual deviants," meeting little resistance. That ended with a raid that began at 1:20 a.m. on June 28, 1969. As police attempted the arrest of patrons and bartenders, the crowd fought back. Outside, a growing and "festive" crowd joined in, interdicting police efforts to load people into paddy wagons. A full-blown riot erupted, with several hundred angry members of the gay community heaving bottles, pennies, and other debris toward the cops, who took refuge inside the Stonewall. Police continued beating homosexuals and transgender individuals mercilessly. At one point, some in the crowd set fire to the bar. The flames were doused, but the crowd had swelled to thousands, spilling into Christopher Park. Short-lived calm by morning ended with renewed rioting that persisted for several days.[96]

Allen Ginsberg dropped by (of course!) to express his wonderment at the proceedings. "You know the guys there were so beautiful—they've lost that wounded look that fags all had ten years ago … We're one of the largest minorities in the country—10 percent, you know. It's about time we did something to assert ourselves."[97] Straight Americans were not ready to hear it, but Ginsberg's observation portended things to come. On June 28, 1970 "Christopher Street Liberation Day" brought tens of thousands of gay, lesbian, queer and transgender residents into the street for what became the first "Gay Pride Parade." By decade's end, more than 100,000 would march on Washington in the first national demonstration for civil rights for gay and lesbian Americans. Recognized in 2016 by President Barack Obama as a National Monument, Stonewall was "the Boston Tea Party" of the LGBTQ+ liberation movement."[98]

In the mid-1970s, openly gay and lesbian Americans began running for elected office. Most notable was Harvey Milk, an antiwar, human rights activist who moved to San Francisco in 1972, opening a camera store in the city's Castro District. After repeated harassment of gay and lesbian businesspeople, Milk established the Castro Village Association and Castro Street Fair to both advance the community's civil rights and nurture its revitalization. The association made the Castro District a vibrant magnet for queer citizens and a model for urban communities of sexual liberation around the country. Milk's courage and sense of humor, coupled with an inclusive vision and ability to forge partnerships throughout the city, made him a compelling public figure and helped him get elected to the San Francisco Board of Supervisors in 1977. Despite repeated death threats, Milk remained fearless, encouraging others to come out of the closet for their freedom. "We are coming out to fight the lies, the myths, the distortions," he declared. "We are coming out to tell the truths about gays, for I am tired of the conspiracy of silence, so I'm going to talk about it. And I want you to talk about it. You must come out."[99]

On November 27, 1978, Dan White, a former city supervisor and self-appointed defender of family values, assassinated Harvey Milk and Mayor George Moscone. Seeing it coming, Milk had hopes for his martyrdom: "If a bullet should enter my brain," he had said, "let that bullet destroy every closet door." Within hours, gay, lesbian, and transgender Americans around the country declared their sexual orientation openly. Others marched in Washington and elsewhere, shouting, "Harvey Milk lives!"[100] And he did, his life and martyrdom earning him heroic status as a great American human rights champion. Much fear and hatred remained, the struggle far from over, but the closet door had been broken wide open.

It is worth noting, finally, that the wave of civic activism in the 1970s encompassed other struggles: prison reform that came in the wake of several explosive riots; "Gray Power!" of senior citizens demanding oversight of nursing home care and changes in Social Security; a tenants' rights movement; and led by Ralph Nader, a fight to protect consumers from the willful deceit and malfeasance of corporations in marketing products that were injuring and in some cases, killing Americans. Where the exuberant irruption of civic engagement was taking the country, no one could say. Perhaps only one thing was certain: despite the constitutional crisis of Watergate that capped the traumas of the sixties, the inherent strength of American democracy had demonstrated its enduring capacity for regeneration.

Notes

1 Terry Anderson, *The Movement and the Sixties: Protest in America from Greensboro to Wounded Knee* (New York: Oxford University Press), 296–300.

2 Levertov, "Human Values and People's Park," in *The Daily Californian*, n.d., in Alexander Bloom and Wini Breines, eds., *Takin It to the Streets: A Sixties Reader*, 2nd ed. (New York: Oxford University Press, 2003), 474.

3 Jon David Cash, "People's Park: Birth and Survival," *California History*, 88, no. 1, 2010, 24–25.

4 Mark Kitchell, *Berkeley in the Sixties* (San Francisco, CA: Kitchell Films, 1990, documentary film, 117 minutes).

5 Bill Van Niekerken, "People's Park 50 Years Later, Unearthing Never-Before-Seen Photos," *San Francisco Chronicle*, May 15, 2019, www.sfchronicle.com/chronicle_vault/article/People-s-Park-Bloody-Thursday-50-years-later-13845759.php, retrieved June 19, 2021.

6 Judith Elain Bullis, "A Social-Psychological case Study: The Manson Incident (Portland State University, 1985, dissertation), see especially, 116–119, https://pdxscholar.library.pdx.edu/cgi/viewcontent.cgi?article=4571&context=open_access_etds, retrieved April 10, 2021.

7 Ibid., 116.

8 Spencer Dryden, quoted in Jeff Tamarkin, *Got a Revolution! The Turbulent Flight of Jefferson Airplane* (New York: Atria Press, 2003), 213.

9 Weather Underground, "Bring the War Home," n.d., in Alexander Bloom and Wini Breines, eds., *Takin' It to the Streets: A Sixties Reader*, 2nd ed. (New York: Oxford University Press, 2002), 382.

10 Tom Wells, *The War Within: America's Battle Over Vietnam* (Berkeley, CA: University of California Press, 1994), 366–369.

11 Bill Ayers, in "Days of Rage 1969," *Chicago Tonight* (Chicago, IL: WTTW, n.d.), www.youtube.com/watch?v=Y8AnF2RkMV8, retrieved November 14, 2018.

12 Acceptance Speech of Senator George McGovern, July 14, 1972, Democratic National Convention, Miami Beach, Florida, www.4president.org/speeches/mcgovern1972acceptance.htm, retrieved November 15, 2018.

13 Walter Karp, *Liberty Under Siege* (New York: Franklin Square Press, 1988), 3.

14 Stephen E. Ambrose, *Nixon: The Triumph of a Politician, 1962–1972* (New York: Simon and Schuster, 1990), 301.

15 Taylor Owen and Ben Kiernan, "Roots of U.S. Troubles in Afghanistan: Civilian Bombing Casualties and the Cambodian Precedent." *Asia Pacific Journal* 8, issue 26, no. 4 (June 28, 2010), https://apjjf.org/-Taylor-Owen/3380/article.html, retrieved November 15, 2018.

16 Seymour M. Hersh, *The Price of Power: Kissinger in the Nixon White House* (New York: Summit Books, 1983), 54–65; and Maurice Isserman and Michael Kazin, *America Divided: The Civil War of the 1960s* (New York: Oxford University Press, 2000), 265.

17 H. R. Haldeman with Joseph Dimona, *The Price of Power* (New York: Dell Books, 1978), 83; and Scott D. Sagan and Jeremi Suri, "The Madman Nuclear Alert," *International Security* 27, no. 4 (Spring 2003), 156.

18 Wells, 357; and Hersh, 125–133.

19 Hersh, 127; and Isserman and Kazin, 265.

20 William Burr and Jeffrey P. Kimball, *Nixon's Nuclear Specter: The Secret Alert of 1969, Madman Diplomacy, and the Vietnam War* (Lawrence, KS: University Press of Kansas, 2015).

21 Wells, 370–376.

22 Burr and Kimball, 310–313; see also summary of Kissinger–Nixon conversation, September 27, 1969 (George Washington University, National Security Archive),

https://nsarchive2.gwu.edu/nukevault/ebb517-Nixon-Kissinger-and-the-Madman-Strategy-during-Vietnam-War, retrieved April 11, 2021.

23 Richard Nixon, "Vietnamization ('Silent Majority') Speech," November 3, 1969, www.let.rug.nl/usa/presidents/richard-milhous-nixon/vietnamization-speech-1969.php, retrieved November 15, 2018.

24 Stanley Karnow, *Vietnam: A History* (New York: Viking, 1983), 600.

25 Sara Dosa and Barbara Kopple, directors. *Re-Mastered: Tricky Dick and Johnny Cash* (documentary, Netflix, November 2018).

26 Wells, 389.

27 Allan M. Winkler, *"To Everything There is a Season: Pete Seeger and the Power of Song* (New York: Oxford University Press, 2011), 35–36; and Wells, 392.

28 Hersh, 88–92.

29 Ellsberg, quoted in Wells, 362.

30 *New York Times Company v. United States* 403 U.S. 713 (decided June 30, 1971), https://caselaw.findlaw.com/us-supreme-court/403/713.html, retrieved November 16, 2018. Appointed by President Nixon, Gurfein had once clerked for Justice Robert H. Jackson, Chief U.S. Prosecutor at Nuremberg.

31 "Judge William Byrne, Ended Trial in Pentagon Papers," *Washington Post* (January 15, 2006), www.washingtonpost.com/wp-dyn/content/article/2006/01/14/AR2006011401165.html, retrieved November 17, 2018.

32 Richard M. Nixon, "Speech to the Nation on the Situation in Southeast Asia," April 30, 1970, https://millercenter.org/the-presidency/presidential-speeches/april-30-1970-address-nation-situation-southeast-asia, retrieved November 18, 2018.

33 See Ben Kiernan, *How Pol Pot Came to Power: Colonialism, Nationalism, and Communism, 1930–1975* (New Haven, CT: Yale University Press, 2004).

34 Herbert D. Bowman, "Not Worth the Wait: Hun Sen, the UN, and the Khmer Rouge Tribunal," *Pacific Basin Law Journal* 1, no. 24 (2006): 52–54, https://cloudfront.escholarship.org/dist/prd/content/qt4rh6566v/qt4rh6566v.pdf, retrieved November 18, 2018.

35 James A. Rhodes, "Speech on Campus Disorders," May 3, 1970, www.library.kent.edu/ksu-may-4-rhodes-speech-may-3-1970, retrieved November 18, 2018.

36 Susie Erenrich, ed., "Kent and Jackson State: 1970–1990," *Vietnam Generation* 2, no. 2, article 1 (1995), 47, https://digitalcommons.lasalle.edu/cgi/viewcontent.cgi?referer=www.google.com/&httpsredir=1&article=1058&context=vietnamgeneration, retrieved November 18, 2018.

37 Phillip Rodriguez, director. *Ruben Salazar: Man in the Middle* (Los Angeles, CA: City Projects, LLC, documentary film, 54 minutes, 2014).

38 Isserman and Kazin, 270.

39 Wells, 568–561.

40 Stanley Kutler, *The Wars of Watergate: The Last Crisis of Richard Nixon* (New York: Knopf, 1990), 276; and Wells, 569.

41 One of whom was a young Roger Stone, whose dirty tricks continued for decades until he was convicted of federal crimes during the Donald Trump era.

42 Carl Bernstein and Bob Woodward, *All the President's Men* (New York: Simon and Schuster, 1974), 132, 138.

43 John Dean Testimony, "Watergate: The Cover-Up," University of Virginia, Miller Center, excerpted at https://millercenter.org/the-presidency/educational-resources/watergate-cover, retrieved November 18, 2018.

44 Jon Wiener, "McCain, Nixon and John Lennon." *Huffington Post*, May 25, 2011, www.huffingtonpost.com/jon-wiener/mccain-nixon-and-john-len_b_126641.html, retrieved November 19, 2018.

45 Senator Howard baker, May 17, 1973, www.pbs.org/newshour/politics/remembering-howard-baker-whose-famous-question-embodied-watergate-hearings, retrieved April 17, 2021.

46 Richardson quoted in Kutler, 411.

47 Congresswoman Barbara Jordan, "Statement on the Articles of Impeachment," House Judiciary Committee, July 25, 1974, www.americanrhetoric.com/speeches/barbara-jordanjudiciarystatement.htm, accessed November 19, 2018.

48 Central Intelligence Agency, "News Views, and Issues," (Washington, DC, August 1974), various news accounts, at www.cia.gov/library/readingroom/docs/CIA-RDP77-00432R000100330002-9.pdf, retrieved November 19, 2018.

49 Ten of 17 Republicans on the House Judiciary Committee voted against the articles of impeachment, and even after Nixon's resignation, one-quarter of Americans still supported him.

50 James Carroll, *House of War: The Pentagon and the Disastrous Rise of American Power* (New York: Mariner, 2007), 354–355.

51 Quoted in Pamela Constable and Arturo Valenzuela, *A Nation of Enemies: Chile Under Pinochet* (New York: W.W. Norton, 1993), 23.

52 Mike Mason, *Development and Disorder: A History of the Third World Since 1945* (Hanover, NH: University Press of New England, 1997), 74–77.

53 Richard J. Barnet, *The Rocket's Red Glare: War, Politics and the American Presidency* (New York: Simon and Schuster, 1990), 352–353.

54 Chaired by Senator Frank Church (D-Idaho).

55 Church Committee Reports, Mary Ferrell Foundation, www.maryferrell.org/php/showlist.php?docset=1014, retrieved November 24, 2018.

56 "Intelligence Activities—Unauthorized Storage of Toxic Agents," Select Committee to Study Governmental Operations with Respect to Intelligence Activities (Washington, DC, September 16, 1975), www.maryferrell.org/showDoc.html?docId=1163#relPageId=5&tab=page, retrieved November 25, 2018.

57 Barnet, 352.

58 Amy Uyematsu, "The Emergence of Yellow Power," 1969, https://faculty.atu.edu/cbrucker/Amst2003/Texts/YellowPower.pdf, retrieved April 17, 2021.

59 Daryl J. Maeda. *Chains of Babylon: The Rise of Asian America* (Minneapolis, MN: University of Minnesota Press, 2009), 126.

60 In Diane Fujino, *Samurai Among Panthers: Richard Aoki on Race, Resistance and a Paradoxical Life* (Minneapolis, MN: University of Minnesota Press, 2012), quoted in "Yellow Power: The Origins of Asian America," May 8, 2017, https://densho.org/asian-american-movement, retrieved November 25, 2018.

61 Jacqueline E. Lawson, "'She's a Pretty Woman … for a Gook': The Misogyny of the Vietnam War," *The Journal of American Culture* 12, no. 3 (Fall 1989), 58–59.

62 Armando B. Rendon, *Chicano Manifesto* (New York: Macmillan, 1971), quoted in Bloom and Breines, 136.

63 Quoted in Anderson, 302, 305.

64 Rudy V. Busto, "Sacred Order, Sacred Space: Reies Lopez Tijerina and the Valle de Paz Community," in Gaston Espinosa and Mario T. Garcia, eds., *Mexican American Religions: Spirituality, Activism, Culture* (Durham, NC: Duke University Press, 2008), 90–99.

65 Anderson, 304.

66 Cesar Chavez, testimony before the Subcommittee on Migratory Labor of the Committee of Labor and Public Welfare. United States Senate, 91st Congress, 1st and 2d Sessions on Pesticides and Pesticides and Farmworkers, September 29, 1969 (Washington, DC: Government Printing Office, 1970), Part 6-B, 3396–3400; and Susan Ferris and Ricardo Sandoval, *The Fight in the Fields: Cesar Chavez and the Farmworkers Movement* (San Diego, CA: Harvest/HBJ Books, 1998), see especially Chapter 2–3.

67 Ed Morales, "The Roots of Organizing," *The Nation*, March 24, 2020, www.thenation.com/article/culture/young-lords-radical-history-johanna-fernandez-review, retrieved April 17, 2021; Morales offers a thorough critical review of Johanna Fernandez, *The Young Lords: A Radical History* (Chapel Hill, NC: University of North Carolina Press, 2020).

68 Sonia Lee, *Building a Latino Civil Rights Movement: Puerto Ricans, African Americans, and the Pursuit of Racial Justice* (Chapel Hill, NC: University of North Carolina Press, 2014).

69 Mary Crow Dog and Richard Erdoes *Lakota Woman* (New York: Grove Weidenfeld, 1990), 74.

70 Diana Rico, "The Final Battle: How the Taos Pueblo Indians Won Back Their Blue Lake Shrine," New Mexico History, http://newmexicohistory.org/events/1970-taos-blue-lake-returned-to-pueblo, retrieved November 28, 2018.

71 Melvin Small, *The Presidency of Richard Nixon,* American Presidency Series (Lawrence, KS: University Press of Kansas, 1999), 180–182.

72 Vine Deloria, Jr. ed., *American Indian Policy in the Twentieth Century* (Norman: University of Oklahoma Press, 1985), 252–253.

73 Ibid., 253–254.

74 Ted Steinberg, *Down to Earth: Nature's Role in American History* (New York: Oxford University Press, 2002), 293.

75 Archibald MacLeish, "Riders on Earth Together, Brothers in Eternal Cold," *New York Times*, December 25, 1968, A1.

76 Denis Hayes, "Earth Day at 40: Legacies and Lessons," Sister Maura Smith Earth Day Keynote Address, Mercyhurst University, April 21, 2010.

77 Denis Hayes, "The Beginning," in n.a., *Earth Day—The Beginning: A Guide for Survival* (New York: Environment Action, 1970), iii.

78 Rachel Benson Gold, "Lessons from Before Roe: Will Past Be Prologue?" *Guttmacher Policy Review*, March 1, 2003, www.guttmacher.org/gpr/2003/03/lessons-roe-will-past-be-prologue#, retrieved April 14, 2021.

79 Heather Boushey et al, "Families Can't Afford the Gender Wage Gap," Center for American Progress, April 20, 2010, www.americanprogress.org/issues/economy/news/2010/04/20/7707/families-cant-afford-the-gender-wage-gap, retrieved April 14, 2021.

80 Erica H. Becker-Medina, "Women-Owned Businesses on the Rise," March 23, 2016, U.S. Census Bureau, www.census.gov/newsroom/blogs/random-samplings/2016/03/women-owned-businesses-on-the-rise.html; Sarah Jane Glynn, "The New Breadwinners," Center for American Progress, https://cdn.americanprogress.org/wp-content/uploads/issues/2012/04/pdf/breadwinners.pdf; and Maha Atal, "Happy Anniversary Title IXFrom Girls' Sports to Women's Wages," June 22, 2012, *Forbes*, www.forbes.com/sites/mahaatal/2012/06/22/happy-40th-anniversary-title-ix-from-girls-sports-to-womens-wages/#1b9357692797, retrieved November 29, 2018.

81 Michael Stewart Foley, *Front Porch Politics: The Forgotten Heyday of American Activism in the 1970s and 1980s* (New York: Hill and Wang, 2013), 66–67.

82 Jessica Bennett and Jess Ellison, "Behind the 'Good Girls Revolt': The *Newsweek* Lawsuit that Paved the Way for Women Writers," *The Daily Beast*, September 11, 2012, www.thedailybeast.com/behind-the-good-girls-revolt-the-newsweek-law-suit-that-paved-the-way-for-women-writers; Susan Donaldson James, "*Newsweek* Still Wages Gender War, 40 Years Later," ABC News, March 23, 2010, https://abc-news.go.com/US/women-lag-40-years-newsweek-sex-discrimination-suit/story?id=10171005, retrieved November 30, 2018; see Lynn Povich, *The Good Girls Revolt: How the Women of Newsweek Sued Their Bosses and Changed the Workplace* (New York: Public Affairs, 2010).

83 Ruth Rosen, *The World Split Open: How the Modern Women's Movement Changed America* (New York: Penguin, 2006), 92–93; David M. Dismore, "When Women Went on Strike: Remembering Equality Day," *Ms. Magazine* Blog, August 26, 2010, http://msmagazine.com/blog/2010/08/26/when-women-went-on-strike-remembering-equality-day-1970; and Sally Edelstein, "Women's Equality Day," *Envisioning the American Dream*, August 26, 2013, https://envisioningtheamericandream.com/2013/08/26/womens-equality-day, retrieved November 30, 2018.

84 Smith and Sevareid quoted in Susan Douglas, *Where the Girls Are: Growing Up Female with the Mass Media* (New York: Three Rivers Press, 1993), 163.

85 Barbara Susan, "About My Consciousness Raising," in Bloom and Breines, 416.

86 Alice S. Rossi, "Job Discrimination and What Women Can Do About It," *The Atlantic*, March 1970, www.theatlantic.com/magazine/archive/1970/03/job-discrimination-and-what-women-can-do-about-it/304922, retrieved December 1, 2018.

87 Martha Griffiths, Statement on the floor of House of Representatives, June 20, 1966, *Congressional Record*, 13054, quoted in Rosen, 73.

88 Redstockings Manifesto, "Redstockings Women's Liberation Archives for Action," 1969, in Bloom and Breines, 413.

89 Foley, 68; and Rosen, 182–186.

90 Susan Griffin, "Rape: The All-American Crime," *Ramparts* 10, n. 3 (September 1971), 26–35.

91 See, among others, Jane Caputi, *The Age of Sex Crime* (New York: Bowling Green Press, 1988).

92 Griffin, 28-29. The essay was also published as "The Politics of Rape," *Oz* (London, 1971, Issue 41), 26-31.

93 Kyla Bishop, "A Reflection on the History of Sexual Assault Laws in the United States," *Arkansas Journal of Social Change and Public Service*, April 15, 2018, https://ualr.edu/socialchange/2018/04/15/reflection-history-sexual-assault-laws-united-states, retrieved December 1, 2018.

94 Rosen, 185.

95 Foley, 82; and Robert Colville, "The 'Gay Cure' Experiments That Were Written Out of Scientific History," *Mosaic*, July 4, 2016, https://mosaicscience.com/story/gay-cure-experiments, retrieved December 2, 2018.

96 Martin Duberman, *Stonewall* (New York: Penguin/Plume, 1994), 199–202.

97 Ginsberg, in Lucian K. Truscott IV, "Gay Power Comes to Sheridan Square," *Village Voice*, July 3, 1969, 1, www.columbia.edu/cu/lweb/eresources/exhibitions/sw25/voice_19690703_truscott.html, retrieved December 2, 2018.

98 Dennis Altman, *Homosexual Oppression and Liberation* (New York: Avon, 1973), 117.

99 Harvey Milk, "That's What America Is," Speech delivered at San Francisco Gay Freedom Day Parade, June 25, 1978, www.onearchives.org/wp-content/uploads/2015/05/1978_harvey_milk_gay_freedom_day_speech.pdf, retrieved April 15, 2021.

100 Milk Foundation, "Official Harvey Milk Biography," http://milkfoundation.org/about/harvey-milk-biography, retrieved December 2, 2018.

Further Reading

Ambrose, Stephen E. *Nixon: The Triumph of a Politician, 1962–1972*. New York: Simon and Schuster, 1990.

Barnet, Richard J. *The Rocket's Red Glare: War, Politics and the American Presidency*. New York: Simon and Schuster, 1990.

Bernstein, Carl, and Bob Woodward. *All the President's Men*. New York: Simon and Schuster, 1974.

Blansett, Kent. *A Journey to Freedom: Richard Oakes, Alcatraz, and the Red Power Movement*. New Haven, CT: Yale University Press, 2018.

Brownstein, Ronald. *Rock Me on the Water: 1974—The Year Los Angeles Transformed Movies, Music, Television, and Politics*. New York: Harper's, 2021.

Burr, William, and Jeffrey P. Kimball. *Nixon's Nuclear Specter: The Secret Alert of 1969, Madman Diplomacy, and the Vietnam War*. Lawrence, KS: University Press of Kansas, 2015.

Church Committee. *COINTELPRO: An Oral History of the FBI's Most Notorious Program*. Washington, DC: Government Printing Office, 1976.

Constable, Pamela, and Arturo Valenzuela. *A Nation of Enemies: Chile Under Pinochet*. New York: W.W. Norton, 1993.

Crow, Dog Mary, and Richard Erdoes. *Lakota Woman*. New York: Grove Weidenfeld, 1990.

Deloria, Vine Jr., ed. *American Indian Policy in the Twentieth Century*. Norman, OK: University of Oklahoma Press, 1985.

Dobbs, Michael. *King Richard—Nixon and Watergate: An American Tragedy*. New York: Alfred A. Knopf, 2021.

Downs, Jim. *Stand By Me: The Forgotten History of Gay Liberation*. New York: Basic Books, 2016.

Espinosa, Gaston, and Mario T. Garcia, eds., *Mexican American Religions: Spirituality, Activism, Culture*. Durham, NC: Duke University Press, 2008.

Fernandez, Johanna. *The Young Lords: A Radical History*. Chapel Hill, NC: University of North Carolina Press, 2020.

Ferris, Susan, and Ricardo Sandoval, *The Fight in the Fields: Cesar Chavez and the Farmworkers Movement*. San Diego, CA: Harvest/HBJ Books, 1998.

Foley, Michael Stewart. *Front Porch Politics: The Forgotten Heyday of American Activism in the 1970s and 1980s*. New York: Hill and Wang, 2013.

Fujino, Diane. *Samurai Among Panthers: Richard Aoki on Race, Resistance and a Paradoxical Life*. Minneapolis, MN: University of Minnesota Press, 2012.

Hersh, Seymour M. *The Price of Power: Kissinger in the Nixon White House*. New York: Summit Books, 1983.

Isserman, Maurice, and Michael Kazin. *America Divided: The Civil War of the 1960s*. New York: Oxford University Press, 2000.

Johnson, Loch K. *A Season of Inquiry Revisited: The Church Committee Confronts America's Spy Agencies*. Lawrence, KS: University Press of Kansas, 2015.

Karnow, Stanley. *Vietnam: A History*. New York: Viking, 1983.

Karp, Walter. *Liberty Under Siege*. New York: Franklin Square Press, 1988.

Kiernan, Ben. *How Pol Pot Came to Power: Colonialism, Nationalism, and Communism, 1930–1975*. New Haven, CT: Yale University Press, 2004.

Kutler, Stanley. *The Wars of Watergate: The Last Crisis of Richard Nixon*. New York: Knopf, 1990.

Maeda, Daryl J. *Chains of Babylon: The Rise of Asian America*. Minneapolis, MN: University of Minnesota Press, 2009.

McLean, Nancy. *The American Women's Movement, 1945–2000: A Brief History with Documents*. Boston, MA: Bedford-St. Martin's Press, 2009.

Povich, Lynn. *The Good Girls Revolt: How the Women of Newsweek Sued Their Bosses and Changed the Workplace*. New York: Public Affairs, 2010.

Rendon, Armando B. *Chicano Manifesto*. New York: Macmillan, 1971.

Rosen, Ruth. *The World Split Open: How the Modern Women's Movement Changed America*. New York: Penguin, 2006.

Sale, Kirkpatrick. *The Green Revolution: The American Environmental Movement, 1962–1992*. New York: Hill and Wang, 1993.

Small, Melvin. *The Presidency of Richard Nixon. American Presidency Series.* Lawrence, KS: University Press of Kansas, 1999.

Spears, Ellen Griffith. *Rethinking the American Environmental Movement, post-1945.* New York: Routledge, 2020.

Steinberg, Ted. *Down to Earth: Nature's Role in American History.* New York: Oxford University Press, 2002.

10 Confronting Limits, Turning Right

> The symptoms of this crisis of the American spirit are all around us. For the first time ... a majority of our people believe that the next five years will be worse than the past five years ...
>
> As you know, there is a growing disrespect for government and for churches and for schools, the news media, and other institutions. This is not a message of happiness or reassurance, but it is the truth and it is a warning.
>
> —President Jimmy Carter, July 15, 1979[1]

By the time Jimmy Carter spoke these sobering words, Americans had been living through what he termed a deepening "crisis of confidence" for a decade or more, depending on where one marked the onset. As if racial conflict, Vietnam, Watergate, three assassinations, and accelerating social change were not enough, from 1973–1975 thirty years of relatively uninterrupted growth and broadening prosperity came to an end with the most severe recession since World War II. The economic turmoil was made worse by spiraling inflation fueled by an "energy crisis," which in turn was triggered by the retribution of Arab states who had Americans over a barrel—more than figuratively. The perfect economic-foreign policy storm of events was hard to fully comprehend, and equally vexing for three successive presidents to solve. As Carter's address suggested, throughout much of the 1970s Americans felt themselves for the first time since World War II at the mercy of events beyond their control.

As we will see, Carter's speech served as the climax to an "age of limits"[2]: to presidential authority, the exercise of U.S. military power, and at least for now, the cheap energy that had fueled the postwar boom and the assumption of an ever-expanding middle class. A series of environmental crises further suggested that even the wonders of science and technology that helped make possible the miracles of the modern "American way of life" were fraught with potentially troubling consequences. The energy crisis that loomed over the seventies, together with the nation's worst nuclear accident, toxic waste disasters unfolding in Love Canal and countless other American communities, and the first major scientific reports about a changing global climate, all threatened to impose the ultimate limits—of a natural world under siege.

DOI: 10.4324/9781003160595-10

Diminished expectations did not sit well with most Americans. Nor did the idea that the country had been turned over to, as TV evangelist Jerry Falwell declared them, a "godless minority of treacherous individuals" who had brought their "godless liberal philosophies" from the streets of sixties activism into the halls of government.[3] The "New Right" coalition for which Falwell was a leading religious spokesperson was an ungainly but mighty amalgamation of evangelical and Catholic conservatives, big business interests, defense hawks, and organizations like Young Americans for Freedom. Constituting a potent cultural and political recoil to the sixties, they aimed at reversing much of the social, cultural, and political change that had transpired over the previous twenty years on issues ranging from abortion and school prayer to taxes, gun rights, environmental protection, and defense policy. By 1979 the rebranded conservatism of the New Right was well positioned to exploit the disquieting "truth" of Jimmy Carter and lead the country away from a raucous two-decade era of change and toward a very different future.

Limits to Growth

For most Americans, the Middle East had long been an incomprehensible, conflict-riddled region easily ignored. That indifference was disturbed on October 6, 1973, when Egyptian and Syrian military forces launched an assault on Israeli defenses in the Sinai Peninsula and the Golan Heights. Coming on the occasion of Yom Kippur, the attack had Israeli forces reeling. In the war's first days, Syrian forces reclaimed part of the territory they had lost to Israel six years earlier in the Six-Day War, while Egyptian soldiers crossed the Suez Canal before Israel Defense Forces (IDF) could counterattack. That they did, eventually extending Israeli territory north, winning a swath of Egyptian land west of the Suez, and occupying nearly all of its immense territorial gains from the Six-Day War, including East Jerusalem and the West Bank.[4] The Israeli counter offensive owed much to more than 22,000 tons of military weaponry provided by the United States that fall. Helping the IDF turn the tide, "Operation Nickel Grass" bookended the political cover the U.S. provided to Israel during the pivotal Six-Day War. In acquiescing to the preemptive 1967 attack on Soviet-backed Arab states—justified in Israel's view by Egypt closing the Straits of Tiran and threats from its nationalist leader Abdel Nasser—the Johnson administration hoped to confront what it perceived as Russian aggression and resist the rising force of pan-Arab unity in the region. Taking at face value Israeli promises that their attack intended no territorial aggrandizement proved devastating—not only for the destiny of displaced Palestinians, but to U.S. strategic goals of "peace and security" in the region.[5]

The Six-Day War yielded both territory and insecurity for Israel, now perceived by critics as an aggressor, while inciting greater support for the Palestine National Liberation Organization. For many Arabs and Palestinians, the 1967 conflict placed America decisively in Israel's corner, a position reinforced by what followed six years later. After the Yom Kippur War, Henry Kissinger led

U.S. diplomatic efforts that paved the way for the Camp David Accords of 1978, an historic peace agreement signed by Israel's Menachem Begin and Anwar Sadat of Egypt. President Jimmy Carter's persevering insistence that the two leaders keep at it when all appeared lost ultimately resulted in a pact that returned all of the occupied Sinai Peninsula to Egypt, and a broader regional "framework for peace." The agreement said nothing about the growth of Israeli "settlements" in Gaza and the West Bank, nor the fate of Jerusalem and Palestinians—critical issues that could only be solved with a combination of U.S. insistence and Israeli moderation.[6] From Carter forward, one U.S. administration after another would apply varying degrees of insufficient pressure on Israel to end its occupation of Palestine, while continuing to send to America's ally more foreign and military aid than any nation on earth.[7]

Americans at home minded less the details of the diplomatic table than the price of gasoline, which was sent soaring October 17, 1973 when the Organization of Arab Petroleum Exporting Countries (OAPEC) enacted an oil embargo against the United States and a number of its allies in retaliation for the U.S.-Israeli re-supply effort. By the time the embargo ended six months later, gas prices had nearly doubled. As supply ran dry, service stations in parts of the country closed, while others had lines wrapped around the block (Figure 10.1). Some states took to rationing for the first time since World War II. By shutting off the spigot, OAPEC had two goals: asserting greater control over prices charged by western oil corporations operating in their countries; and changing the policy of the U.S. and its allies toward the Israeli-Palestinian

Figure 10.1 Long lines at gas pumps during the oil crisis of the 1970s.

conflict—partly achieved when some European nations began asserting an independent course on the Middle East conflict. The impact of the embargo was made worse by Nixon's earlier decision to take the United States off the gold standard, sending the dollar plummeting and reducing revenues of Arab states where petroleum was priced in dollars. The pain was further magnified because the United States, for much of the century a net exporter of petroleum, was quietly reaching its peak domestic production in the early 1970s. By 1973, the ability to blunt the impact of a foreign embargo by tapping reserve production capacity at home was gone.[8]

Without thinking much about it, Americans since World War II had carried out with spectacular success the project of creating an auto-centric civilization heavily reliant on cheap energy, increasingly drawn from foreign sources: from 16.5 percent in 1960 to twice that by 1973, 50 percent by 1977. Consumption per capita was now two and one-half times higher than that of other advanced economies.[9] The least energy-efficient people in the industrialized world, Americans were consuming oil at a rate one million times faster than it was laid down by the dinosaurs, and much of it came from the Middle East. Surging energy prices sent overall inflation galloping upward. In such an inflationary cycle it was shocking to see economic growth slow to a recessionary crawl from 1973 to 1975. Before he was driven from office, Nixon launched "Project Independence," an initiative to free America over the long run from foreign oil dependency. But Americans drove in the short term, and measures like year-round daylight savings time and a 55 mph speed limit produced more frustration than oil savings.

Combined with ongoing environmental distress, the energy crisis bolstered arguments contained in a slew of best-selling books that warned of severe long-term consequences of unsustainable development. Most influential was *Limits to Growth*, published in 1972 by a team of researchers commissioned by the Club of Rome. The book utilized pioneering computer modeling and projected rates of population growth to caution against current rates of resource consumption and patterns of environmental pollution. "If the present growth trends in world population, industrialization, pollution, food production, and resource depletion continue unchanged, the limits to growth on this planet will be reached sometime within the next one hundred years," authors warned. Maligned by mainstream economists and conservative critics, the book's essential argument and many of its specific forecasts have proved frighteningly accurate.[10]

More immediately, President Ford worked with a post-Watergate liberal congress to enact the Energy Policy and Conservation Act that imposed the first Corporate Average Fuel Efficiency (CAFÉ) standards on the auto industry. In 1974, the gas-guzzling fleet of Detroit's "Big Three" carried an average fuel efficiency of less than 13 miles per gallon, a figure that would double by 1985. In the meantime, however, the U.S. auto industry, already troubled by poor decision making, labor disputes, and sometimes-deadly safety recalls, was caught flat-footed by smarter foreign competition. The industry's eventual recovery would be built on unorganized cheaper labor abroad, a diversification of assets into other sectors like defense, and the shedding of more than 250,000 jobs by 1982.[11] The Big Three did roll out fuel-efficient models, but most buyers found them inferior to European and Japanese compacts.[12] Moreover, many Americans would not reconcile themselves to an age of limits. The defiance was reflected in films like *Smokey and the Bandit* and radio hits like J. W. McCall's "Convoy" featuring speeding truckers defying witless lawmen. A national citizens band "CB"-radio craze and the continued popularity of American "muscle cars" raised a middle finger to police and the new gas-saving speed limit.[13]

Deeper underlying forces contributed to the nation's economic distress. The alarming news of the nation's first trade deficit in nearly a century highlighted the issue of deindustrialization. Quietly underway since World War II in the New England textile industry and West Virginia coal mines, the loss of manufacturing jobs was now being felt in auto, steel, glass, and beyond. Nixon's enactment of import tariffs seemed a futile gesture given the historic currents of change. Emerging by the late seventies were both the genesis of the Silicon Valley high-tech boom, and the grim outlines of a "rust belt" of shuttered mills and hollowed out communities from the Midwest to the Northeast. Emblematic of a growing urban crisis was Cleveland, Ohio. Much of its white population, industry, and business having moved to the suburbs, in December 1978 the city became the first in the nation to default on its loans since the Great Depression.

"A Government as Good as Its People"

It is hard to imagine anyone wanting to be president in such times. Yet there he was, James Earl Carter, the former Georgia governor and peanut farmer, earnestly urging "a government as good as its people."[14] It is fair to say the government Americans received in this troubled era may have suited them about right. That Carter's presidency was marred by his share of failures was not for any failing of intelligence, effort, or character. Much about Carter—his love of the outdoors, of rock and roll, the plainspoken and informal manner—caught the seventies mood. Although Americans grew weary of it, the president's Southern Baptist-grounded righteousness resonated with the spiritual awakening of the decade and led him to an incessant emphasis on virtues of honesty, honor, and morality not exactly enshrined in the Nixon era. The 1976 contest between Ford and Carter in which very few private dollars were raised—both campaigns counting on public money from the new income tax check-off—heralded a presidency marked by integrity.[15]

Carter promised, on every issue, *comprehensive*, expert-driven solutions to the nation's problems that were insulated from special interests.[16] The approach carried inherent challenges, including the fact that Carter often worked in isolation from Congress before announcing bold policies. The pattern was established just weeks into his presidency with a sudden announcement that he was recommending that 320 dams and other water projects slated to be built be reviewed for possible cancellation. Nineteen of them would be terminated immediately. Carter's dam "hit list" sent shudders through Washington. For senators and congressmen, especially those from the West, this was utter heresy. Some learned of the cancellation of dams in their districts through the media, magnifying their anger.[17] As we have noted, for nearly a half-century the Bureau of Reclamation and U.S. Army Corps of Engineers, their champions in congress, and western water lobbyists had engineered a dam-building juggernaut that made development of the arid west possible. Dams helped to win World War II and light the Vegas Strip. The lubricant of American politics for decades, water projects had been traded by presidents and legislators for votes on everything from food relief to the Civil Rights Act. Dams were the domain of the agencies and their congressional appropriators. The president's job was to show up for dedications, spooning out pablum to the assembled about progress and the advance of the American frontier.[18]

Carter had no interest in the role. A fisherman with a deep appreciation for wild rivers, he came to Washington having already successfully confronted the Corps of Engineers as Georgia governor.[19] He saw in the dam projects an early opportunity to demonstrate the seriousness of his pledge to eliminate wasteful spending. Many of the dams were pork-barrel boondoggles, their cost-benefit analyses propped up with creative accounting, or justified by add-ons like water-diversion channels into desert wilderness to encourage development. Some would irrigate areas where there was already surplus federal water flowing. Others destroyed fisheries or unspoiled stretches of river more valuable to the recreation and tourism industries than the promised benefit to agriculture.[20] Those facts mattered little that spring as Carter faced a storm of criticism for his unseemly incursion into an iron-triangular fortress. In the end, the president capitulated, all but one of the projects surviving. In targeting the dams, Carter had implicitly affirmed the subversive idea of limits to growth. That may have captured the mood of a decade in which environmentalism was widely embraced and nature-loving John Denver was one of America's most popular musical artists, but it did not sit well on Capitol Hill.

Carter's first address on energy came two weeks after his inauguration, amid one of the worst winters on record that was intensifying a natural gas shortage and forcing the closure of schools and factories.[21] Appearing in a cardigan beside a blazing fireplace, Carter urged Americans to lower their thermostats as the White House had done and announced an avalanche of initiatives. The tone was grim, the theme all that had been "lost" in America, including a "faith in joint efforts and mutual sacrifices." Wistful for "a time when we really felt united," the president invoked the unity of the World War II era and expressed hope that Americans were again "ready to help each other for the common good."[22] He was back weeks later, warning of "catastrophe" unless the nation acted on the threat of "rapidly shrinking resources." Carter tried to confront the cynical view that energy shortages were contrived by corporations to drive up price with government complicity. Borrowing a phrase of William James, the president declared the commitment on energy to be the "moral equivalent of war," and announced a National Energy Plan (NEP). Expansive and visionary, it contained a whopping 113 proposals—from expanded nuclear energy and coal mining to a tax on gas guzzlers and incentives for home insulation and solar energy. The plan would create jobs but require sacrifice, which he assured, would be "fair" (underscored six times!) and equally shared.[23] It was vintage Carter: equal parts scolding schoolmarm, moralizing preacher, and expert technocrat. Any inspiration was inadvertent.

Nevertheless, after months of hearings and debate, congress passed the sweeping National Energy Act (NEA), containing much of the president's plan. It offered incentives to increase production of natural gas, nuclear, and coal, and seed capital for "synthetic" fuels—a ghastly boondoggle if ever there was one. Overall, however, the theme was conservation, including efficiency tax credits and standards for appliances and automobiles, improved performance of federal buildings, and development of renewable sources such as wind, solar, and geothermal. It was the most far-reaching energy law in U.S. history, and proved instrumental in producing significant improvement in the nation's energy efficiency over the coming decades.[24] Carter's installation of 32 solar panels on the White House roof signified the administration's commitment to a goal of 20 percent of the nation's energy supplied by renewables at the end of the century. Speaking at the dedication, the president did not exactly inspire man-on-the-moon confidence: "A generation from now," said Carter, "this solar heater can either be a curiosity, a museum piece, an example of a road not taken. Or it can be just a small part of one of the greatest and most exciting adventures ever undertaken by the American people." The muted optimism proved prognostic: in 2000, just 7 percent of the energy consumed by Americans came from renewable sources.[25]

The energy issue receded briefly, but returned in November 1978 when oil workers in Iran went on strike, inflaming the long-simmering revolution aimed at driving Shah Reza Pahlavi from power. That event brought another reduction in Middle East oil and spike in gas prices, inflation, and interest rates. Long lines at service stations reappeared. Those events were followed in March 1979 with the worst nuclear power plant accident in American history. At Unit 2 of the Three Mile Island facility in Middletown, Pennsylvania, a valve critical to the plant's cooling system malfunctioned and caused part of the fuel core to melt, releasing over 800,000 gallons of radioactive steam into the environment. The more threatening stage of the accident occurred when fuel rods overheated, creating a hydrogen bubble in the reactor that came within 90 minutes of catastrophically exploding. As technicians worked desperately, residents of central Pennsylvania were first reassured the crisis was contained, and then sent conflicting messages from officials about whether to evacuate. Carter arrived days later to inspect the plant and offer reassurance.[26] But confidence in a technology once promised as safe and inexpensive—"too cheap to meter," the head of the Atomic Energy Commission once pledged—was severely shaken. TMI signaled the death knell for new nuclear plants and suggested that even the miracle of atomic-powered science had limits.

The "Crisis of Confidence"

By late spring 1979, the Carter White House was in crisis. Knowing it would lead to still higher prices, nevertheless the president urged deregulation of domestic oil prices in hopes of slowing consumption, thereby easing supply. Inflation soared, and Carter's poll numbers plunged into the 20s—worse than Nixon's during Watergate.[27] Still it was less the president's evaporating popularity than his failure to galvanize the nation on the issue that led him to cancel a planned speech on July 5 and head to Camp David for a spiritual-intellectual retreat to prepare an address that would be anything but ordinary. Often remembered as "the malaise speech" (though Carter never used the word), the "Crisis of Confidence" address of July 15, 1979 represented the climax to his sermonizing presidency, and for good or ill came to define it.

The speech arrived at the end of a decade of recrimination by public intellectuals of America's profligate culture of consumerism, a current of thought that intersected with concerns over resource exhaustion and environmental degradation.[28] Christopher Lasch's groundbreaking *The Culture of Narcissism: American Life in an Age of Diminishing Expectations* offered a provocative indictment of patterns of American life that were, he said, creating a nation of self-absorbed consumers, in the process eroding family and community relationships, along with virtues of empirical truth, faith, and the rewards of meaningful work.[29] The greatest failing of such a society, argued Lasch, was not its pathetic narcissism, but that it was "criminally indifferent to the welfare of the next generation and the generation after that." Seen in this light, consumerism was destroying not only the planet, but all that once made life worth living. Perhaps a little energy shortage was a necessary corrective to a nation deprived of deprivation. The *New York Times'* James Reston declared, "What America really needs is more shortages. We need to cut down, slow up, stay at home, run around the block, eat vegetable soup, call up old friends and read a book once in a while."[30] A similar tone was struck by sociologist Robert Bellah, whose work mourned the retreat from the public realm to socially isolating self-indulgence that came in the wake of the sixties. While author Tom Wolfe celebrated the restlessly searching consciousness of what he labeled the "Me Decade,"[31] Bellah saw a corrosive cynicism where self-was-all and the very idea of the public interest was in question, an overall atmosphere of portentous implications:

> [The] present mood betrays a desperation and even despair just below the surface that could result in the decisions ... being made in a mood of vindictiveness and repression rather than generosity of spirit, with the consequences that could lead to the end of free government in America.[32]

Following extensive conversations with Lasch, Bellah, and dozens more Americans of greater or lesser note, the president took to the air to deliver a stunning jeremiad. He began with a characteristic note of self-reproof of his own failings, along with a recitation of some of the advice he had received.

Carter then offered a litany of recent traumas—assassinations, a war gone bad, turmoil in the streets, political corruption, a dollar losing value—an earnest if inelegant way of getting to the historical root of the "deeper," "underlying" issue: a "crisis of confidence ... that strikes at the very heart and soul and spirit of our national will." The crisis was seen in the "growing doubt about the meaning of our own lives and in the loss of a unity of purpose for our nation." And then this critical appraisal of American materialism:

> In a nation that was proud of hard work, strong families, close-knit communities, and our faith in God, too many of us now tend to worship self-indulgence and consumption. Human identity is no longer defined by what one does, but by what one owns. But we've discovered that owning things and consuming things does not satisfy our longing for meaning. We've learned that piling up material goods cannot fill the emptiness of lives which have no confidence or purpose.

Again invoking World War II, Carter declared that solving the energy crisis could at once solve pressing economic concerns, chart a more secure energy-independent future, and set in motion a unifying "rebirth of the American spirit." Americans were "looking for honest answers, not easy answers; clear leadership, not false claims and evasiveness and politics as usual."[33] Coupled to the sobering realities, Carter offered up another bushel full of policies and aspirations. What most astonishes—and has generally been overlooked in the politicized narrative that calcified around the speech—is the overwhelmingly positive response the address received. Carter's poll numbers shot up. White House mail and phone calls expressed support for the president and volunteered specific ways Americans determined to battle the energy crisis.[34] In the days that followed, however, the president fired his entire cabinet, a move that instilled anything but confidence. His polls sank and Carter never recovered. Squandered in this moment was the chance to fully reckon with the consequences at home and abroad of an energy-ravenous society.

That lost opportunity is all the more striking in light of the environmental landmarks of Carter's final year. On December 2, 1980, President Carter, joined by biologist Mardy Murie and musician and activist John Denver, President Carter signed the Alaska National Interest Lands Conservation Act, the most significant preservation measure in the nation's history. Although it left most of the state open to development, the law set aside more than 56 million acres as protected wilderness and doubled the size of the Arctic National Wildlife Refuge. Nine days later, Carter signed the Comprehensive Environmental Response, Compensation, and Liability Act, better known as Superfund. Forcing the cleanup of hundreds of toxic waste sites around the country threatening public health, the law was triggered by the nightmarish events that unfolded in the community of Love Canal in upstate New York, where 20,000 tons of toxic chemical waste had been dumped adjacent to what in the 1950s had become a suburban community. In the late seventies, residents pressed stonewalling officials to relocate them after studies showed high rates of severe birth defects and cancers, respiratory, and neurological health problems. The largely white community of Love Canal captured the nation's attention, but the plague of environmental pollution disproportionately affected communities of color around the nation, a fact made clear in predominantly African American Warren County, North Carolina. Unfolding simultaneous to Love Canal, largely black and poor citizens employed sixties-style civil disobedience to demand action from public officials following the illegal dumping of tons of toxic waste. Though it gained little attention from either national media or major environmental organizations, Warren County helped launch the environmental justice movement.[35]

The "Pitiful, Helpless Giant"

Compounding Carter's plight was a series of troubling foreign policy crises—each shaped in some measure by the profound impact of Vietnam. In the post-mortem, Americans generally divided into two camps. "Neoconservative" defense hawks clung to the comforting fiction that the war could have been won had soldiers not been betrayed by the antiwar movement and hamstrung by Washington politicians. Here is the war according to Ronald Reagan in August 1980:

> A small country newly free from colonial rule sought our help in establishing self-rule and the means of self-defense against a totalitarian neighbor bent on conquest. We dishonor the memory of 50,000 young Americans who died in that cause when we give way to feelings of guilt as if we were doing something shameful, and we have been shabby in our treatment of those who returned. They fought as well and as bravely as any Americans have ever fought in any war.[36]

"For too long," Reagan declared, "we have lived with the Vietnam Syndrome"— the dark diagnostic emerging on the right that America lacked not the righteousness, but the will to defeat global communism—all because of the degenerate actions of the left. The Vietnam Syndrome became a metonymic catchall for a general American retreat from the world, and an eviscerated frontier warrior masculinity.[37] *Treating* it became a consuming objective for neoconservatives.

On the other side were those who had opposed the war, many of whom believed U.S. intervention in Southeast Asia had been a mistake from the beginning. Jimmy Carter was not among them. When asked whether the United States had a moral responsibility to rebuild a ravaged Vietnam, Carter's reply captured the ahistorical ignorance of many Americans: "The destruction was mutual ... We went there to defend the freedom of the South Vietnamese. And I don't feel that we ought to apologize or to castigate ourselves or to assume the status of culpability."[38]

At the same time, the president reflected the mood of contrition that hung in the air. On day one of his presidency, Carter unconditionally pardoned nearly a half-million men who had evaded the draft, reigniting divisions of the war. For many veterans and patriots, the amnesty was an endorsement of unpatriotic cowardice. Moreover, the president's larger focus on human rights as the cornerstone of American foreign policy underscored what one scholar has characterized as a "discourse of atonement" on Vietnam.[39] There would be no reparations for Vietnam, but neither would there be any more Vietnams. A consistent application of universal human rights, the president asserted, best served the security interests of the United States. Cold War foes with atrocious human rights records such as Cuba continued to be criticized, but so too were U.S.-allied authoritarian regimes in Chile and South Africa. The human rights emphasis made military action a last resort. In January 1979, amid the volatile instability of Iran's revolution after U.S.-backed dictator Shah Reza Pahlavi was forced from power, Carter was pressed about whether America might have done something to "save" the Iranian dictator:

> Certainly we have no desire nor ability to intrude massive forces into Iran or any other country to determine the outcome of domestic political issues. This is something that we have no intention of ever doing in another country. We tried this once in Vietnam. It didn't work well, as you know.[40]

In Central America Carter attempted to both protect American interests and transform the image of the United States from that of imperial overlord to defender of democracy. Those goals were embodied in the 1977 Panama Canal Treaties transferring control of the canal to Panama, while guaranteeing an American presence and the right to defend the canal's neutrality. Since its construction, the canal had become for many in the region a concrete symbol of the U.S. pattern of undermining Latin American nations' sovereignty. Treaty negotiations had commenced in 1964 following a protest over the right to fly the Panamanian flag alongside the stars and stripes. American soldiers fired into the crowd, killing 20 and injuring 500 in what became known as Martyrs Day. Over a decade in the making, the agreement granting Panamanian sovereignty over the Canal Zone fit squarely into Carter's vision, but the heavily publicized debate over its ratification[41] featured vitriolic invective from conservatives condemning the treaty as a sign of American weakness, a nation in retreat from its global frontier. Senator S.I. Hayakawa declared, "We should hang on to it. We stole it fair and square." Fellow Californian and presidential candidate Ronald Reagan proclaimed, fallaciously, the ten-mile-wide canal zone "sovereign United States territory just the same as … the states that were carved out of the Louisiana Purchase." "We bought it, we paid for it, it's ours, and we're going to keep it," he thundered.[42] We didn't. The Senate ratified the treaty, barely.

The Carter policy of "constant decency" was severely tested in Nicaragua and El Salvador—both ripe for a moralistic review.[43] In Nicaragua, the appalling human rights record of the ruling Somoza family went back to the 1930s. "He may be a son of a bitch, but he's our son of a bitch," FDR reportedly said in 1939 of Anastasio Somoza Garcia, the original family despot.[44] More recent was the repugnant behavior of the Somoza government in the aftermath of a 1972 earthquake that rocked the impoverished nation. International aid flowed to Nicaragua, only to be embezzled by military officials and cronies of the ruling Anastasio Somoza Debayle.[45] Somoza's regime was begging for a cutoff of U.S. aid, and in November 1978 Carter gave it to them. But then he tried vainly to redirect the Sandinista revolution away from its Marxist orientation[46] and toward a U.S.-friendly transition. With Sandinista forces storming the National Palace in Managua and assuming control of the country, Carter proposed a hopelessly inapt plebiscite on Somoza's rule. More ungainly efforts followed, including a White House meeting in which Carter urged Sandinista leadership to respect democracy—this, after decades of U.S.-backed repression. Months of congressional debate of U.S. policy in Central America ultimately, stunningly ended with the approval of a $75 million aid package for the *Marxist* government of Nicaragua, conditioned on its human rights performance.[47]

Carter's faltering efforts to stage-manage Nicaragua's revolution were inspired partly by events in El Salvador. The fraudulent election of Carlos Romero as president in February 1977 brought national protests, sparking a wave of government repression: a massacre of peaceful protesters in San Salvador, suspension of civil liberties, widespread torture, and disappearance and execution of antigovernment activists. Many of these activities were carried out by paramilitary "death squads" linked to the government, some trained at the U.S. School of the Americas. In 1977 Carter suspended military aid to the government, which responded by indicating it would refuse any support from Washington "for the sake of national dignity," weakening U.S. leverage.[48] The administration did manage to block lending for dam and other development projects so long as human rights crimes continued.[49]

Which they did. Yet Carter by late 1977 had expended much of his political capital on the dam debacle and the Panama Canal debate, and thus had little interest in elevating the fight over El Salvador. It did not bode well when Carter appointed as ambassador Frank Devine, a career foreign service officer indifferent at best to the president's human rights emphasis.[50] In early 1980 Devine was replaced by Robert White whose views were more aligned with Carter's, but by then the administration's foreign policy was reverting to traditional containment. Led by anti-Soviet National Security Advisor Zbigniew Brzezinski, Cold War hardliners feared a victory by the Sandinista-backed Farabundo Martí Front for National Liberation (FMLN) over the Salvadoran government would mean a Marxist triple threat in the region headed by Castro's Cuba. Cold War geopolitics ignored the bloody facts on the ground, where the vast majority of Salvadorans lived in poverty, exploited by a tiny elite backed by an authoritarian government. Anyone suspected of associating with or offering support to the FMLN simply disappeared—tortured and murdered with increasing frequency.

After a brief period of civilian rule and promises of improved human rights, a military junta seized power and once more, "mutilated bodies were appearing on roadsides."[51] As U.S. weapons continued flowing south and the state terror escalated, Catholic priests, including Archbishop Oscar Romero, spoke out against the government. They too, were counted among the victims. Celebrating mass on March 22, 1980, Romero beseeched the government and its patrons in Washington: "In the name of God, in the name of this suffering people whose cry rises to heaven more loudly each day, I implore you, I beg you, I order you: stop the repression."[52] Two days later he was assassinated from the pulpit. December brought the rape and murder of three Maryknoll sisters and a lay missionary by Salvadoran soldiers, an atrocity that finally triggered a suspension of military aid.[53] By then, Carter's human rights policy was in tatters and he had been soundly defeated by Reagan—thanks in part to events far outside the hemisphere.

In Iran, the president faced a dilemma of higher geopolitical stakes. Iran's Shah Reza Pahlavi held what Amnesty International declared in 1975 to be the worst human rights record in the world.[54] As the Shah's grip on power grew more tenuous in 1977, the regime's CIA-trained SAVAK made torture and assassination of political dissidents routine. The Carter administration sent signals to Tehran that continued U.S. arms sales were contingent on liberalization of the political climate. The Shah took several steps, "mostly for show," but enough to allow a broad liberal social reform movement in the country to gain strength—and to trigger the return of his worst instincts. Still, there was Carter during New Year's talks in Tehran straining to look the other way, and raising his glass in a toast to the "great leadership" of Iran that had made it the region's "island of stability."[55]

Such pretense could not last. Support for the liberal democratic reform movement faded while the theocratic rhetoric and promises of exiled leader Ayatollah Ruhollah Khomeini won over masses of impoverished young Muslims averse to any ideas born in the west from whence the shah's rule had come. American intelligence officials never saw it coming. While there had been contacts between U.S. operatives and liberal reformers in hopes of transitioning to a constitutional monarchy after the Shah—reports of his cancer being too persistent to deny— the CIA had long ignored the latent political potency of Islamic resistance in the region. The possibility that America's most well-armored neocolonial state in the Middle East, its greatest market for pricey U.S. weapons systems, the frontier "outpost at the heart of the world's oil supply," as Robert Dreyfuss has aptly put it, could fall was simply unthinkable. The reform movement was too easily dismissed as communist in orientation. Even after revolutionary forces seized control of the country in January 1979, national security officials were certain it originated from Moscow.[56] At last Carter distanced himself from the Shah and declared events "in the hands of the Iranian people."[57]

As the Islamic Republic came to power, Zbigniew Brzezinski first entertained fantasies that a strongman might lead a counterrevolution. By the summer of 1979, he was imagining the Ayatollah an anti-communist U.S. ally, envisioning the new Iranian theocracy as key to an anti-Soviet "arc of crisis" defending America's own advancing frontier of interests in the region. Forged by U.S. military bases and a chain of Muslim-dominant countries extending from Iran and Egypt to Kenya and bases in the Indian Ocean, here was a "security framework to reassert U.S. power and influence in the region." The scheme's opening gambit was a Brzezinski meeting in Algiers that fall with Iranian ministers who were open to a new American relationship.[58] It would be the last official meeting of the two countries for another three decades; as it happened, the "arc of crisis" was about to implode in troubles more immediate.

Following Carter's decision to admit the Shah to the U.S. for cancer treatment, on November 4, 1979 Iranian revolutionary students, with sub-rosa orchestration by the government, seized the American embassy in Tehran, triggering the 444-day "Hostage Crisis." The holding of 52 Americans consolidated Khomeini's power and strengthened the move toward a hardline theocracy.[59] At home, nightly images of burning U.S. flags and shackled, blindfolded Americans being led through the streets of Tehran enraged the country. Richard Nixon's warning a decade earlier that an America retreating from Vietnam would render it "a pitiful, helpless giant" seemed all too real. Indeed, Vietnam haunted the entire spectacle as captors lined the hostages' cells with images of ravaged Vietnamese children and whispered "Vietnam, Vietnam" in their ears.[60] In Iran, the "Conquest of the American Spy Den" served as comeuppance for the 1953 coup and preemptive defense against any attempt to reverse the revolution.

An embattled White House resisted Tehran's demands for extradition of the Shah and the return of Iranian assets frozen in U.S. banks. As hostage-takers threatened trials against alleged American spies, Carter's patience looked more like feckless incompetence. Some critics complained the crisis was due to the president abandoning "our friend."[61] Five months into the crisis, in April 1980 Carter authorized an ill-fated rescue mission that ended with eight dead Americans and the resignation of his Secretary of State. That disastrous low point of the Carter presidency was followed by the Shah's death in July and the invasion of Iran by Saddam Hussein's Iraq. These events expedited negotiations that ultimately ended with the hostages freed, in exchange for a U.S. pledge to return Iranian assets and respect the nation's sovereignty.

One month into the hostage crisis, the perception of weakness deepened when the Soviet Union invaded Afghanistan. Conservatives alleged that it was a vacillating, naïve foreign policy that had invited Soviet aggression. It mattered little to most Americans that, in contrast to U.S. behavior in the Cold War, this was the first time the Kremlin had sent Soviet troops into combat operations beyond Eastern Europe. The invasion appeared a transgressive expansion of a new communist frontier. One-half of Americans polled that winter of 1980 believed the Soviets invaded Afghanistan because "they now [had] military superiority over the United States and [could] get away with it."[62]

Few Americans appreciated their own country's decades of meddling in Afghanistan, through a combination of foreign aid, Peace Corps work, and far less benign intervention from Iran. But the Shah's fall terminated the U.S. military presence in Iran, heightening the strategic importance of Afghanistan. In addition, a socialist-leaning government headed by Mohammed Noor Taraki welcomed an alliance with the Soviet Union. In the spring of 1978—18 months before the Soviet invasion—the U.S. began supporting the convergence of conservative Islamic factions into a fighting force to contest Soviet interference. The CIA viewed the rightist "holy warriors" of the mujahideen as a more reliably anti-Soviet partner than indigenous Afghan elements. Osama bin Laden was among the zealots welcoming U.S. support in trying to oust Taraki. They got their wish in October 1979 when Taraki was assassinated by figures linked to his more extremist prime minister, Hafizullah Amin. Disliked by both Soviet officials and Islamists, Amin had met previous uprisings with bloody reprisals that killed thousands of innocent Afghans. Belying the U.S. media's depiction of events, the Kremlin intervened only reluctantly, the volatility of Amin's rule providing the final trigger. In late December the Red Army rolled across the border, took control of Kabul, assassinated Amin, and installed a new president.[63]

Declaring Soviet actions "the most serious threat to world peace since the Second World War," Carter intensified support for the mujahideen.[64] A series of largely unpopular actions followed: reinstatement of Selective Service registration, an embargo on wheat sales to Russia, and a U.S. boycott of the 1980 Summer Olympic Games being held in Moscow. The latter seemed especially wrong-headed, given the "Miracle on Ice" victory over the Russian ice hockey team by a squad of upstart Americans the previous winter. Carter withdrew the Strategic Arms Limitation Treaty II (SALT II) from Senate consideration, increased defense spending, and pressed for NATO's deployment of cruise missiles in Western Europe. More ominous was Presidential Directive 59, which updated the nuclear war plan and increased the number of Soviet targets—from 1,700 to 7,000. It was a stunning reversal for a president who came to office with stated intentions of ending the nuclear arms race.[65]

Finally, there was the "Carter Doctrine," in which the president asserted the right to use military force to defend the "vital interests" of the United States in the Persian Gulf region.[66] As historian Andrew Bacevich has summarized, Carter laid bare the reality that in the crises of Iran and Afghanistan, "a great contest for control of the region had been joined," one both layered onto the Cold War and standing apart as something more portentous. Carter would not ignite a major war in the Middle East, but did set in motion a major expansion of the U.S. military footprint in Central Asia and the Middle East. A Rapid Deployment Force soon swelled into the U.S. Central Command (CENTCOM), an entirely new edifice encompassing a necklace of U.S. military bases and installations extending from the Persian Gulf into Central Asia and East Africa—essentially an overlay of Brzezinski's "arc of crisis," enabling long-term pursuit of a neoconservative vision to dominate the rich oil and natural gas fields of the Gulf and Central Asia.[67] For the moment, the faltering attempt by Jimmy Carter to translate the chastening experience of Vietnam into a morally grounded American realism of overseas limits was sabotaged by blowback in Iran and his own maladroit response in Afghanistan.

Reagan and the Rise of the New Right

If two foreign policy crises, systemic economic disruption, and a renewed spike in oil prices were not enough to doom Jimmy Carter's reelection, he faced even stronger headwinds. Americans were heaving rightward, socially and politically.

As Bruce Schulman has argued, a conservative pendulum swing was presaged with the accelerating demographic migration to the "Sunbelt" and made visible in a range of culturally "reddening" phenomena. "The South's Gonna Do it Ag'n," howled the Charlie Daniels Band, one of many southern rock bands and country music artists flooding the air waves by the late 1970s. Americans embraced a newly romanticized redneck rebel culture, one befitting the embittered post-Vietnam era in which institutions and authority generally were treated with disdain. It was evident in Americans' fascination with the liberal-loathing, daredevil motorcyclist Evel Knievel, and through widespread public displays of the Confederate flag. As was true on U.S. military bases throughout Vietnam, the stars and bars waved well outside the South as a potent symbol of "rebel" resistance and antipathy—to racial progress, belatedly to antiwar radicals, and to a liberal federal government guilty of betraying soldiers in Vietnam and a declining white working class at home. The conservative turn was heard in the rise of televangelist southern preachers like Falwell. Even the displacement of the more eastern, urban, and cerebral "nation's past time" of baseball with the other religion of the South, football, portended a more pugnacious America.[68]

Politically, the culture shift was evidenced in a set of conservative prescriptions to right all that seemed to have gone wrong in America. Yet something more was afoot in the agitated late seventies, a reactionary politics auguring deeper divisions ahead. One epicenter of looming upheaval was the National Women's Conference (NWC) in November 1977 in Houston, Texas. Inspired by the UN declaration of International Women's Year in 1975 and supported by President Ford, the NWC promised a bipartisan celebration of women's progress over the previous decade, and a charting of future strategy. The big story emerging from the NWC was not the National Plan of Action it produced, but the vituperative attack conference delegates absorbed from conservative activist Phyllis Schlafly and 15,000 supporters. Decrying the gathering as "Federal Financing of a Foolish Festival of Frustrated Feminists," the antifeminist founder of the Eagle Forum led her multitudes in inflated harangues against the horrors of abortion rights, lesbianism—civil rights protections regarding sexual orientation winning delegates' support after an historic debate—and the Equal Rights Amendment. Then being debated and ratified by state legislatures[69]—the E.R.A., declared Schlafly, threatened individual rights, Judeo-Christian morality, and the nation's very survival. She railed at "women's libbers," the "aggressive females" who "hate men, marriage and children."[70] Telepreacher Pat Robertson ranted that the feminists told women to "leave their husbands, kill their children, destroy capitalism, and become lesbians," while Pat Buchanan dismissed the NWC as a "warmed-over hash of the radical liberalism that generally stunk up the '60s."[71]

In hindsight, the hyperventilating reads like an early tremor of the seismic shift that was coming in American political discourse. But in 1977, as historian Marjorie Spruill has recounted, the assault on feminism that cracked wide open in Houston stunned many Republican women. For decades, the GOP had included E.R.A. ratification in its platform; feminism was a bipartisan affair. Until it was not. Suddenly, prominent Republican feminists like former First

Lady Betty Ford and Jill Ruckelshaus became the target of opprobrium from across a spectrum of conservativism that was tilting rightward. The counter-demonstration in Houston included not only the Church of Latter Day Saints, but the John Birch Society and the Ku Klux Klan. Imperial Wizard Robert Shelton declared the Klan's mission in Houston "to protect our women from all the militant lesbians who will be there."[72] An original Bircher, Schlafly was incensed that feminists tried to discredit her by exposing the long-running association of the Klan with anti-feminist forces.[73] Yet the close affinity of the civil rights and women's liberation movements that was on full display in Houston and which had "inflamed many white women and men in the South," was cooking up a virulent intersectionality of forces on the right.[74] The ascendancy of a "gender-based" attack on feminism, gay and lesbian rights—conflated easily with liberalism—paralleled the rise of the New Right and crosscut the GOP's racist Southern Strategy. As New Right leader Paul Weyrich recalled, what most outraged evangelicals and galvanized Christian conservatives in these years was the decision by Carter's IRS Commissioner Jerome Kurtz in 1978 to strip non-profit tax-exempt status from private religious academies for refusing to adopt policies of non-discrimination.[75]

Mainstream Republicans and pro-family forces denounced such tactics and eschewed public association with the Klan, even as some welcomed their help surreptitiously. One official for newly elected congressman Newt Gingrich explained the political strategy this way: "We went after every rural southern prejudice we could think of," including the idea of women working outside the home. Tanya Melich, a Utah Republican and co-founder of the National Women's Political Caucus, stood horrified along with many of her colleagues as the Republican Party launched what she called "The Republican War on Women." Melich was especially appalled by the hard right turn of the GOP in the South, forming a "new partnership of racism and sexism in pursuit of Republican victory."[76] The party increasingly exploited the energy generated by figures like white supremacist and Schlafly devotee Richard Barrett who lamented the failure of white men to halt the progress of civil rights, and of "founding-American stock" white women to reproduce in sufficient numbers, warning of national "race suicide."[77]

The Klan surged in membership and activity in the post-Vietnam era, continuing a pattern following every military conflict since the Civil War.[78] As was true after World War I, the spike in the late seventies coincided with waves of immigrants reaching America's shores: Cuban "Boat People," Vietnamese and Laotian refugees, and Mexicans. In addition, the rise of far-right extremism was fueled by a damaged warrior ethos and a generation of psychologically wounded veterans.[79] Buffeted by economic challenges and a rapidly changing social environment, some veterans retreated to violent, often racist impulses. Along the southwest border, Huey Helicopter gunner-turned-white supremacist leader Louis Beam established paramilitary training camps and a Special Forces-like unit within the Klan, waged a terror campaign against Vietnamese fisherman along the Texas Gulf Coast, and formed the Klan Border Watch targeting undocumented migrants for harassment and assault. For none of these actions did he face consequences. Early on in Beam's domestic terror career, he collapsed neatly the war abroad and that which had just been joined at home:

> The mere fact I had returned from Vietnam didn't mean the war was over. It was going on right here in the States. I knew right then and there I had to get engaged again and fight the enemy … Over here, if you kill the enemy, you go to jail. Over there in Vietnam, if you killed the enemy, they gave you a medal. I couldn't see the difference.[80]

Eventually, the Klan robes wore thin and Beam went rogue, becoming a computer-savvy leader of the leaderless Aryan Nations, helping to pioneer white supremacy into the digital age. As Kathleen Belew has summarized, in these years Klansmen like Beam would "shed their white robes to don camouflage fatigues, neo-Nazis would brandish military rifles, and white separatists would manufacture their own Claymore-style land mines in their determination to bring the war home."[81] Border Patrol agents frequently discovered Viet Cong-style pitfall traps in the swampy Tijuana estuary, a locale known to white vigilantes as "Little 'Nam."[82]

New Right extremism drove the Republican Party to abandon the E.R.A. in its 1980 platform. They were just getting warmed up. Led by self-proclaimed pro-family conservatives like North Carolina Senator Jesse Helms, the congress defeated the proposed "Act to Prevent Domestic Violence," with Helms arguing that funding battered women's shelters would encourage more women to leave the home, undermining the American family. Helms then helped lead the Senate to reject the Convention on the Elimination of All Forms of Discrimination Against Women (CEDAW), endorsed by nearly every nation on earth.[83]

The new Republican Party arose from the smoldering ruins of the postwar liberal consensus that perished in Vietnam and from a nation forced, momentarily, to confront the possibility of limits. It came as a mutation of paleo-corporate Republicanism coupled to hawkish neoconservatism abroad and cynicism about government's role in advancing social progress at home. Most of all, it emerged in the embrace of social "wedge" issues that won over broad swaths of Evangelicals, blue collar Catholics, and rural Americans who came to see a Democratic Party surrendering its forty-year commitment to egalitarian economic policy and now beholden to a constellation of what Republicans contemptuously labeled "special interest" groups: feminists, civil rights advocates, and environmentalists. On the defensive, national Democratic leaders more and more slouched center-right on economic issues. Carter's indifference to labor and his opening the door on deregulation of major sectors of the economy did not bode well for the party's ability to hold working class voters. Democrats allowed the GOP to begin framing the national policy agenda. Many of the issues were driven by opposition to decisions of the Warren Supreme Court for over a decade, the rest from newly formed conservative think tanks: school prayer, gay rights, abortion, gun control, school busing, affirmative action.

Prayer, guns, business, and more money for the military they were for; most everything else they stood fervently against—nothing more so than taxes and what they funded—"big guv'm'nt," as Reagan put it contemptuously.[84] During the 1980 campaign, the California Republican went to Neshoba County, Mississippi to give a speech hailing "state's rights" and disparaging, as he called it, the "distorted balance of our government today by giving powers that were never intended in the constitution to that federal establishment." Speaking to an almost exclusively white audience a short distance from the site of the 1964 murder of Andrew Goodman, Mickey Schwerner and James Chaney, this was more foghorn than dog whistle. Indeed, a local GOP official had suggested the site to the campaign to help woo "George Wallace-inclined voters." The Klan offered Reagan a rare endorsement just days before the address. The campaign rejected it, but only after Carter's people raised the issue.[85]

Beyond race-baiting, the speech reflected the candidate's larger anti-Washington message, embodied in the former governor's declaration of support for the Sagebrush Rebellion. An amalgamation of monied western interests—big mining, timber, cattle, and other industries—alongside ranchers and farmers besieged by expensive credit and low prices, the Sagebrush Rebellion rose up in opposition to the expanded authority of environmental regulatory agencies. "Count me in as a rebel," Reagan declared.[86] Particularly loathsome was the Federal Land Management Policy Act (FLMPA) of 1976. While the FLMPA encouraged continued multiple use of vast western lands overseen by the federal Bureau of Land Management (BLM), it called for a deliberative public review process of management planning with an eye toward designation of less than 5 percent of BLM lands as federally protected Wilderness Areas. The law imposed a temporary stay on development of potential wilderness areas during the review period. Western governors and corporate interests were incensed. In 1979, western legislatures passed Sagebrush Rebellion Acts, claiming state sovereignty. The statutes were largely symbolic, but the Sagebrush Rebellion signified westerners' deep, historic distrust of Washington, which had intensified in the seventies. The proposed MX Missile program—a complex scheme to deploy nuclear missiles on underground rail cars—threatened to appropriate thousands of acres of rangeland. Additional vast sums of money, western water, and land were being squandered on the synthetic fuels program. There was also the "hit list" and a Carter proposal to rescind the environmentally destructive and fiscally irresponsible General Mining Law of 1872.[87]

Sagebrush Rebels meant business, in the halls of power and on the range. Sagebrushers "engaged in acts of defiance against the BLM, opening dirt tracks onto grazing allotments that had been closed, bulldozing new roads, overstocking their allotments, violating permit agreements, and refusing to pay grazing fees."[88] Federal land managers received death threats. The belligerence set the tone for episodic standoffs between armed westerners and federal land management officials that continued in the decades ahead. By 1980, corporate interests led by Richard Mellon Scaife and Joseph Coors were forming corporate "nonprofits" like the Mountain States Legal Foundation, dedicated to "individual liberty, the right to own and use property, limited government, and free enter-prise."[89] Funded mostly by big oil and gas corporations, they began funneling corporate lawyers to fill the offices of the Interior Department and Environmental Protection Agency of Republican administrations.

As with feminism and civil rights, a Republican Party that once led on issues of environmental conservation now disavowed those principles, coupling them-selves wholly to a revival of *laissez faire*. The Faustian bargain helped to deliver Reagan to the White House, and there was no going back. Production, not conservation, would rule energy policy. Advance the global American frontier, not retreat. As his oil and gas man on the presidential transition team put it after Reagan's victory, the energy policy of the incoming president would be, "more, more, more." The Great Communicator himself offered this spoonful of hokum to a 1983 graduating class: "There are no such things as limits to growth, because there are no limits on the human capacity for intelligence, imagination, and wonder," conflating geophysical fantasy with the American myths of "weight-lessness, limitlessness, deathlessness" as Greg Grandin has summarized.[90] Nature would have the last say on matters of limits, but there was no denying that the previous decade witnessed the political ground shifting under Americans' feet.

Notes

1 President Jimmy Carter, "Energy and the National Goals – a Crisis of Confidence," July 15, 1979, www.americanrhetoric.com/speeches/jimmycartercrisisofconfidence. htm, retrieved April 19, 2021.
2 The term "Age of Limits" owes to John Barrow, "Circumventing the Establishment," paper presented at the Conference on the Carter Presidency, Jimmy Carter Library (February 1997).
3 Jerry Falwell, "Introduction," in Richard A. Viguerie, *The New Right: We're Ready to Lead* (Washington, DC: The Viguerie Company, 1980), front (unnumbered) pages.
4 Charles D. Smith, *Palestine and the Arab–Israeli Conflict: A History with Documents*, 7th ed. (New York: Bedford St. Martin's Press, 2010), 316–317.
5 Ibid., 283–289.
6 Burton I. Kaufman and Scott Kaufman, *The Presidency of James Earl Carter*, 2nd ed. (Lawrence: University Press of Kansas, 2006), 150–153.
7 Jeremy M. Sharp, "U.S. Foreign Aid to Israel." (Washington, DC: Congressional Research Service, April 10, 2018), https://fas.org/sgp/crs/mideast/RL33222.pdf, retrieved October 4, 2018.
8 James Howard Kunstler, *The Long Emergency: Surviving the Converging Catastrophes of the Twenty-First Century* (New York: Atlantic Monthly Press, 2005), 42–45. Advanced hydro-fracturing technology eventually allowed the U.S. to begin reversing its oil production decline, although the levels reached prior to "peak oil" would never be seen again.
9 Daniel Horowitz, *Jimmy Carter and the Energy Crisis of the 1970s: The "Crisis of Confidence" Speech of July 15, 1979: A Brief History with Documents* (New York: Bedford St. Martin's, 2005), 6–7; and Robert A. Strong, "Domestic Affairs," the Presidency of Jimmy Carter, UVA Miller Center for the Presidency, https://millercenter.org/presi-dent/carter/domestic-affairs, retrieved April 25, 2021.
10 Graham Turner and Cathy Alexander, "*Limits to Growth* was Right: New Research Shows We're Nearing Collapse," *The Guardian*, September 1, 2014, www.theguardian. com/commentisfree/2014/sep/02/limits-to-growth-was-right-new-research-shows-were-nearing-collapse, retrieved April 25, 2021.

11   Christopher J. Singleton, "Auto Industry Jobs in the 1980s: A Decade of Transition," *Monthly Labor Review* (December 1992): 20.

12   Alena Sawyers, "1979 Oil Shock Meant Recession for U.S., Depression for Autos," *Automotive News*, October 13, 2013, www.autonews.com/article/20131013/GLOBAL/310139997/1979-oil-shock-meant-recession-for-u-s-depression-for-autos, retrieved November 17, 2018.

13   Bruce J. Schulman, *The Seventies: The Great Shift in American Culture, Society, and Politics* (Cambridge, MA: Da Capo Press, 2001), 126.

14   Jimmy Carter, *A Government as Good as Its People* (New York: Simon and Schuster, 1977).

15   Michael Kazin, "The President Without a Party: The Trials of Jimmy Carter." *The Nation*, July 5, 2018, www.thenation.com/article/president-without-party.

16   Schulman, 121–126.

17   Jonathan Alter, *His Very Best: Jimmy Carter, A Life* (New York: Simon and Schuster, 2020), 304–305.

18   Marc Reisner, *Cadillac Desert: The American West and Its Disappearing Water* (New York: Viking Press, 1986), see especially Chapter 5–8.

19   Alter, 183–185.

20   "Water Projects Compromise Reached," *Congressional Quarterly Almanac* (1977), https://library.cqpress.com/cqalmanac/document.php?id=cqal77-1203898, retrieved April 25, 2021.

21   Steven Rattner, "Pennsylvania Closes All Schools in Gas Shortage as Layoffs Grow," *New York Times*, January 27, 1977, A1, www.nytimes.com/1977/01/27/archives/pennsylvania-closes-all-schools-in-gas-shortage-as-layoffs-grow.html, retrieved April 26, 2021.

22   President Jimmy Carter, "Report to the American People on Energy," February 2, 1977, https://millercenter.org/the-presidency/presidential-speeches/february-2-1977-report-american-people-energy, retrieved November 5, 2018.

23   President Jimmy Carter, Address to the Nation on Energy, April 18, 1977, https://millercenter.org/the-presidency/presidential-speeches/april-18-1977-address-nation-energy; and Schulman, 127.

24   Steven Nadel, Neal Elliott, Therese Langer, "Energy Efficiency in the United States: 35 Years and Counting," (Washington, DC: American Council for an Energy-Efficient Economy, June 2015), www.aceee.org/sites/default/files/publications/researchreports/e1502.pdf, retrieved April 22, 2021.

25   David Biello, "Where Did the Carter White House Solar Panels Go?" *Scientific American* (August 6, 2010), www.scientificamerican.com/article/carter-white-house-solar-panel-array/#googDisableSync.

26   Chris J. Magoc, *Environmental Issues in American History: A Reference Guide with Documents* (Westport, CT: Greenwood Press, 2006), 293–295.

27   Horowitz, 16.

28   Kevin Mattson, *What the Heck Are You Up to, Mr. President? Jimmy Carter, America's "Malaise," and the Speech That Should Have Changed the Country* (London: Bloomsbury, 2009).

29   Christopher Lasch, *The Culture of Narcissism: American Life in an Age of Diminishing Expectations* (New York: W. W. Norton & Company, 1977).

30   James Reston, "Who Needs More Gas?" *New York Times*, November 11, 1973, Sec. E, p. 13, quoted in Horowitz, 8.

31   Tom Wolfe, "The 'Me Decade' and the Third Great Awakening," *New York Magazine*, August 23, 1976, http://nymag.com/news/features/45938, retrieved November 15, 2018.

32   Robert Bellah, "Human Conditions for a Good Society," in "Ideas in Transition: Ideas in America," 100th anniversary edition, *St. Louis Post-Dispatch*, March 25, 1979, 8–11, excerpted in Horowitz, 75.

33 President Jimmy Carter, "Address on the Crisis of Confidence," July 15, 1979, www.c-span.org/video/?153917-1/president-carter-address-crisis-confidence, retrieved Novembber 15, 2018.

34 Mattson, 159–161.

35 See Lois Gibbs, *Love Canal: My Story* (SUNY Press, 1982); and Robert Bullard, *Dumping in Dixie: Race, Class, and Environmental Quality*, rev. ed. (Boulder, CO: Westview Press, 2000), 30–32.

36 Ronald Reagan, "Restoring the Margin of Safety," Veterans of Foreign wars Convention, Chicago, IL, August 18, 1980.

37 Greg Grandin, *The End of the Myth: From the Frontier to the Border Wall in the Mind of America* (New York: Metropolitan Books, 2019), 201–219.

38 Quoted in Edwin Martini, *Invisible Enemies: The American War on Vietnam, 1975–2000* (Amherst, MA: University of Massachusetts Press, 2007), 45.

39 Robert J. McMahon, "Rationalizing Defeat: The Vietnam War in American Presidential Discourse, 1975–1995," *Rhetoric and Public Affairs* 2, no. 4 (Winter 1999), 529.

40 Vietnam and the Presidency," March 11, 2006. Introduction by Caroline Kennedy and Interview by Brian Williams with President Jimmy Carter, www.archives.gov/files/presidential-libraries/events/vietnam/pdf/transcript-04.pdf, retrieved June 8, 2019.

41 The first ever radio broadcast from the Senate chamber.

42 "To Unsteal the Panama Canal." *New York Times* (February 14, 1977), www.nytimes.com/1977/02/14/archives/to-unsteal-the-panama-canal.html; Howard Jones, *Crucible of Power: A History of American Foreign Relations From 1945* (Lanham, MD: Rowman and Littlefield, 2009), 223; and James M. Lindsay, "The Fight Over the Panama Canal Treaties," *The Water's Edge* (Council on Foreign Relations, March 16, 2011), www.cfr.org/blog/twe-remembers-fight-over-panama-canal-treaties.

43 Jimmy Carter, "Address on Foreign Affairs," University of Notre Dame, May 22, 1977, in Carter, *Keeping the Faith: Memoirs of a President* (New York: Bantam Books, 1982), 141.

44 Peter Winn, *Americas: The Changing Face of Latin America and the Caribbean*, 3rd ed. (Berkeley, CA: University of California Press, 2006), 544.

45 Among the outraged was legendary Pittsburgh Pirate centerfielder and native Puerto Rican Roberto Clemente. On New Year's Eve 1972, Clemente loaded an airplane with relief supplies headed for Managua, believing his revered stature throughout Latin America would allow him to face down the dictator and deliver the aid. The plane crashed into the sea shortly after takeoff. See Gilbert M. Joseph, "Close Encounters: Toward a New Cultural History of U.S.–Latin American Relations," in Gilbert M. Joseph, Catherine C. Legrand, and Ricardo D. Salvatore, eds., *Close Encounters of Empire: Writing the Cultural History of U.S.–Latin American Relations* (Durham, NC: Duke University Press, 1998), 31.

46 Named for Augusto Cesar Sandino, murdered in 1934 by Somoza following a revolt against the government and U.S. military occupation.

47 Office of the Historian, "Central America, 1977–1980," (Washington, DC: Department of State), https://history.state.gov/milestones/1977-1980/central-america-carter, retrieved April 25, 2021.

48 Robert Armstrong and Janet Shenk, *El Salvador* (Cambridge, MA: South End Press, 1999), 91.

49 Arthur Keith Miller, "Jimmy Carter's Policy Toward the El Salvador Civil War: The Demise of Human Rights as a Priority," Master's thesis, Harvard Extension School, 2017, 37, http://nrs.harvard.edu/urn-3:HUL.InstRepos:33825944, retrieved June 13, 2019.

50 Ibid., 39–44.

51 Belisario Betancur et al, *From Madness to Hope: the 12-year war in El Salvador:Report of the Commission on the Truth for El Salvador* (Washington, DC: United States Institute of Peace, 1993), 21.

52 Oscar Romero, "Archbishop's Homily, March 23," Confidential Cable, United States Embassy, El Salvador March 23, 1980, at http://nsarchive.gwu.edu/NSAEBB/NSAEBB339/doc06.pdf.

53 Miller, 57–64.

54 Mark J. Gasiorowski, *U.S. Foreign Policy and the Shah: Building a Client State in Iran* (Ithaca, NY: Cornell University Press, 1991), 157.

55 John Gilbert, "Jimmy Carter's Human Rights Policy and Iran: A Reexamination, 1976–1979a." *Madison Historical Review* 5, article 1 (2014), 11–12, https://commons.lib.jmu.edu/cgi/viewcontent.cgi?referer=&httpsredir=1&article=1029&context=mhr, retrieved June 13, 2019.

56 Robert Dreyfuss, *Devil's Game: How the United States Helped Unleash Fundamentalist Islam* (New York: Henry Holt, 2005), 215–217.

57 Quoted in Marvin Zonis, *Majestic Failure: Tthe Fall of the Shah.* (Chicago, IL: University of Chicago Press, 1991), 257.

58 Dreyfuss, 241, quoting Zbigniew Brzezinski, *Power and Principle* (New York: Farrar and Strauss, 1983), 446–447.

59 Dreyfuss, 241–242.

60 Christian Appy, *American Reckoning: The Vietnam War and Our National Identity* (New York: Penguin, 2015), 235.

61 Michael Schaller, *Reckoning with Reagan: America and Its President in the 1980s* (New York: Oxford University Press, 1992), 21.

62 Richard J. Barnet, *The Rocket's Red Glare: War, Politics, and the American Presidency* (New York: Simon and Schuster, 1990), 364.

63 Angelo Rasanayagam, *Afghanistan: A Modern History* (London: I.B. Tauris, 2005), 83–94.

64 The statement came in Carter's January 20, 1980 appearance on *Meet the Press*, quoted in Kristina Spohr, *The Global Chancellor: Helmut Schmidt and the Reshaping of the International Order* (New York: Oxford University Press, 2016), 110.

65 James Carroll, *House of War: The Pentagon and the Disastrous Rise of American Power* (New York: Houghton Mifflin, 2006), 363–373.

66 Jimmy Carter, "State of the Union Address," January 21, 1980, www.jimmycarterlibrary.gov/assets/documents/speeches/su80jec.phtml, retrieved June 14, 2019.

67 Andrew Bacevich, *The New American Militarism: How Americans Are Seduced by War* (New York: Oxford University Press, 2005), 179–185.

68 Schulman, 102–117; and Grandin, 209–210.

69 The E.R.A. ultimately fell three states shy of the necessary three-quarters required of a constitutional amendment.

70 Schlafly, quoted in Marjorie Spruill, *Divided We Stand: The Battle Over Women's Rights and Family Values that Polarized America* (New York: Bloomsbury, 2017), p. 111; and Phyllis Schlafly, "What's Wrong With Equal Rights for Women?—1972," January 1, 1972, https://awpc.cattcenter.iastate.edu/2016/02/02/whats-wrong-with-equal-rights-for-women-1972, retrieved June 18, 2019.

71 Robertson quoted in Michael Schaller, *Right Turn: American Life in the Reagan-Bush Era, 1980–1992* (New York: Oxford University Press, 2007), 41; Judy Klemesrud, "Women's Movement at Age 11: Larger, More Diffuse, Still Battling," *New York Times* (November 15, 1977), www.nytimes.com/1977/11/15/archives/womens-movement-at-age-11-larger-more-diffuse-still-battling.html, retrieved June 19, 2019; and Patrick Buchanan, "Where Jimmy Should File the Houston Agenda," *Washington Weekly*, December 8, 1977, quoted in Spruill, 231.

72 Ibid.; and Kathleen Belew, *Bring the War Home: The White Power Movement and Paramilitary America* (Cambridge, MA: Harvard University Press, 2018), 37.

73 Spruill, 242–244.

74 Ibid, 305.

75 Schaller, 33.

76 Tanya Melich, *The Republican War Against Women* (New York: Bantam, 1996), 108.

77 Spruill, 305–308.

78 Belew, 36–38.

79 James William Gibson, "Warrior Dreams," in Sonia Maasik and Jack Solomon, *Signs of Life in the USA: Readings on Popular Culture for Writers* (New York: Bedford St. Martins, 1999), 496–504.

80 Ron Laytner, "I Infiltrated the Ku Klux Klan … and Lived!," *Argosy* 387, no. 6 (August 1978), quoted in Belew, 35.

81 Belew, 32.

82 Grandin, 224.

83 Spruill, 296–297.

84 Ronald Reagan, *Speaking My Mind: Selected Speeches* (New York: Simon and Schuster, 2004), 398.

85 Ronald Reagan, "Speech at the Neshoba County Fair," August 3, 1980, www.youtube.com/watch?v=bnVdAC1ZkO8; and Joseph Crespino, "Did David Brooks Tell the Full Story about Ronald Reagan's Visit to Neshoba County?," *History News Network*, n.d., https://historynewsnetwork.org/article/44535, retrieved June 20, 2019.

86 Robert H. Nelson, "Why the Sagebrush Rebellion Burned Out," *AEI* [American Enterprise Institute] *Journal on Government and Society* (May/June 1984), 32, https://pdfs.semanticscholar.org/3f42/d4f91df6a9d3035f9cc31e5a50af189afe6a.pdf, retrieved June 20, 2019.

87 Jedediah S. Rogers, "Land Grabbers, Toadstool Worshippers, and the Sagebrush Rebellion in Utah, 1979–1981." (Brigham Young University M.A. Thesis, July 15, 2007), 25–33, Brigham Young University Scholars Archive, http://citeseerx.ist.psu.edu/viewdoc/download?doi=10.1.1.879.4276&rep=rep1&type=pdf, retrieved June 20, 2019.

88 Christopher Ketcham, "The Great Republican Land Heist," *Harpers* (February 2015), https://harpers.org/archive/2015/02/the-great-republican-land-heist,   retrieved April 26, 2021.

89 Mountain States Legal Foundation, https://mslegal.org, retrieved June 20, 2019.

90 Ronald Reagan, "Commencement Address, University of South Carolina, September 20, 1983," in Heather Lehr Wagner, *Ronald Reagan* (Philadelphia, PA: Chelsea Publishers, 2004), 26; and Grandin, 215–218.

Further Reading

Alter, Jonathan. *His Very Best: Jimmy Carter, A Life*. New York: Simon and Schuster, 2020.

Armstrong, Robert, and Janet Shenk, *El Salvador*. Cambridge, MA: South End Press, 1999.

Bacevich, Andrew. *The New American Militarism: How Americans Are Seduced by War*. New York: Oxford University Press, 2005.

Belew, Kathleen. *Bring the War Home: The White Power Movement and Paramilitary America Cambridge*, MA: Harvard University Press, 2018.

Betancur, Belisario et al. *From Madness to Hope: the 12-year War in El Salvador: Report of the Commission on the Truth for El Salvador*. Washington, DC: United States Institute of Peace, 1993.

Bullard, Robert. *Dumping in Dixie: Race, Class, and Environmental Quality*. Boulder, CO: Westview Press, rev. ed., 2000.

Carter, Jimmy. *Keeping the Faith: Memoirs of a President.* New York: Bantam Books, 1982.

Dant, Sara. *Losing Eden: An Environmental History of the American West.* Malden, MA: Wiley and Sons, 2017.

Dreyfuss, Robert. *Devil's Game: How the United States Helped Unleash Fundamentalist Islam.* New York: Henry Holt, 2005.

Gasiorowski, Mark J. *U.S. Foreign Policy and the Shah: Building a Client State in Iran.* Ithaca, NY: Cornell University Press, 1991.

Grandin, Greg. *The End of the Myth: From the Frontier to the Border Wall in the Mind of America.* New York: Metropolitan Books, 2019.

Horowitz, Daniel. *Jimmy Carter and the Energy Crisis of the 1970s: The "Crisis of Confidence" Speech of July 15, 1979: A Brief History with Documents.* New York: Bedford St. Martin's, 2005.

Joseph, Gilbert M., Catherine C. Legrand, and Ricardo D. Salvatore, eds., *Close Encounters of Empire: Writing the Cultural History of U.S.–Latin American Relations.* Durham, NC: Duke University Press, 1998.

Kaufman, Burton I., and Scott Kaufman. *The Presidency of James Earl Carter.* Lawrence, KS: University Press of Kansas, second edition, 2006.

Lasch, Christopher. *The Culture of Narcissism: American Life in an Age of Diminishing Expectations.* New York: W. W. Norton & Company, 1977.

Magoc, Chris J. *Environmental Issues in American History: A Reference Guide with Documents* Westport, CT: Greenwood Press, 2006.

Martini, Edwin. *Invisible Enemies: The American War on Vietnam, 1975–2000.* Amherst, MA: University of Massachusetts Press, 2007.

Mattson, Kevin. *What the Heck Are You Up to, Mr. President?: Jimmy Carter, America's "Malaise," and the Speech That Should Have Changed the Country.* London: Bloomsbury, 2009.

Melich, Tanya. *The Republican War Against Women.* New York: Bantam, 1996.

Rasanayagam, Angelo. *Afghanistan: A Modern History.* London: I. B. Tauris, 2005.

Reisner, Marc. *Cadillac Desert: The American West and Its Disappearing Water.* New York: Viking Press, 1986.

Schaller, Michael. *Right Turn: American Life in the Reagan-Bush Era, 1980–1992.* New York: Oxford University Press, 2007.

Schulman, Bruce J. *The Seventies: The Great Shift in American Culture, Society, and Politics.* Cambridge, MA: Da Capo Press, 2001.

Smith, Charles D. *Palestine and the Arab-Israeli Conflict: A History with Documents,* 7th ed. New York: Bedford St. Martin's Press, 2010.

Spruill, Marjorie. *Divided We Stand: The Battle Over Women's Rights and Family Values that Polarized America.* New York: Bloomsbury, 2017.

Viguerie, Richard A. *The New Right: We're Ready to Lead.* Washington, DC: The Viguerie Company, 1980.

Winn, Peter. *Americas: The Changing Face of Latin America and the Caribbean,* 3rd ed. Berkeley, CA: University of California Press, 2006.

Zonis, Marvin. *Majestic Failure: The Fall of the Shah.* Chicago, IL: University of Chicago Press, 1991.

11 The Reagan Revolution

> There he was, the old Charmer, the Actor, with his practised rhetoric, his histrionisms, his emotional appeal—and all the patients were convulsed with laughter. Well, not all: some looked bewildered, some looked outraged, one or two looked apprehensive, but most looked amused. The President was, as always, moving— but he was moving them, apparently, mainly to laughter. What could they be thinking? Were they failing to understand him? Or did they, perhaps, understand him all too well?
>
> —Oliver Sacks, "The President's Speech," 1986[1]

In *The Man Who Mistook His Wife for a Hat*, neurologist Oliver Sacks's description of aphasiacs' response to a speech from the fortieth president illuminates more about the Reagan era than most Americans then would have admitted. Aphasia patients cannot comprehend language, but nor can they be lied to. Keenly intuitive, they perceive a speaker's authenticity through non-linguistic forms. "Thus," wrote Sacks, "it was [Reagan's] grimaces," the theatrical "false gestures and ... tones and cadences of the voice, which rang false for these wordless but immensely sensitive patients."[2] Bemused aphasiacs laughed Reagan off, but as had been true since the days of P. T. Barnum, there were plenty of Americans predisposed to entertaining illusion. Many voters chose the former actor not for his policy positions, but because they were inclined to be teleported to happier times. With his perpetually sunny disposition, the "Great Communicator" spoke in mystical terms, evoking an America of small towns filled with respectful white citizens, where rags-to-riches mobility prevailed, and, save for the military, there was little need for government. After two decades of turmoil, millions of Americans ached for such a country.

It was Reagan's good Irish luck that his presidency coincided with the rise of an image-driven culture of celebrity that increasingly distorted, even vanquished reality. A telling moment came in 1984. After CBS's Lesley Stahl ran a story highlighting the contradiction between Reagan's appearance at the Special Olympics with his having slashed funds for mental health care and disability programs, top White House aide Richard Darman called to thank her for the "great piece." "Did you hear what I said? I killed you," Stahl said. "You people in Televisionland haven't figured it out yet, have you?" Darman snapped. "Nobody

DOI: 10.4324/9781003160595-11

heard what you said. When the pictures are powerful and emotional they override if not completely drown out the sound. Lesley, I mean it. Nobody heard you." Stahl later reviewed the tape without the audio. What she saw was a "magnificent montage of Reagan" replete with "flags, balloons, children, and adoring supporters—virtually an unpaid commercial."[3]

Patients in the aphasiac ward may have seen through such performances, but elsewhere a dissonance prevailed, between the emotional uplift projected by Reagan's charm and the reality of workers losing ground and opposed to much of what he was doing. Buoyed by, as Reagan staffer Michael Deaver acknowledged, the "most generous treatment from the press" of any postwar president, a conflicted public reelected Reagan and gave him a 70 percent approval rating when he left office in 1989, higher than any president since FDR.[4] For liberals that was bitterly ironic, for it was the combined legacy of Roosevelt and LBJ that Reagan set out to dismantle, along with the New Deal political coalition. Already frayed by the fallout of the sixties, the Democrats' federation of farmers, blue collar workers, and African Americans fully disintegrated in the 1980s under the weight of racial resentment, the appeal of the religious right, and the continuing decline of unions. The final blow was the weakened faith in government, which Reagan brilliantly exploited. "Government is not the solution to our problem," he proclaimed in his 1981 inaugural, "government is the problem."[5] Behind the populist rhetoric, Reagan aimed to wrest government from discredited liberals and deliver it over to a conservative coterie of investment bankers, defense interests, and western corporate "rebels" anxious to expand America's energy frontier. On that first night of the Reagan era, a group of businessmen reveled in the moment at a celebration in Midland, Texas. The lavish buffet featured a large cutout of the U.S. Capitol dome captioned: "OURS."[6]

Reaganomics

Reprised by every Republican president since Reagan, the formula is familiar: slash taxes, cut domestic programs, raise military spending, and deregulate. Reaganomics promised a tax cut-fueled utopia, with benefits "trickling down" to working people: soaring business investment would spur hiring and robust economic growth, while reduced taxes would allow Americans to keep more of their own money and replenish dwindling savings. More fabulous was the pledge that gushing tax revenues from a fully unleashed free market would eliminate a national debt approaching one trillion dollars in 1981. Virtually none of it happened. Soaring deficits forced Reagan to accept a series of tax *increases*, but they could not stanch the bleeding of revenue. Together with massive increases in military spending, the tax cuts nearly tripled the national debt.[7]

Rising deficits buttressed the urge to reduce federal spending. More bluntly known as "starving the beast," the strategy aimed at draining the federal treasury of revenue via tax cuts and wantonly driving up the deficit, thereby producing the political pressure necessary to eliminate popular domestic programs.[8] Its most extreme proponents sought to "drag government into the bathroom and drown it in the bathtub."[9] With acquiescence from congress, in 1981 Reagan delivered cuts to dozens of agencies, from the EPA to the Department of Veterans Affairs to the Solar Energy Research Institute—slashed by 80 percent.[10] He went after anti-poverty programs with fervor, often invoking the tale of Chicago "welfare queen" Linda Taylor to falsely insinuate both massive welfare fraud among America's poor, and that most recipients were lazy black women.[11] Reagan was never forced to explain the contradiction of vilifying programs benefitting the poor while providing billions in tax breaks and subsidies for corporations. Nor have those in congress who adopted the strategy acknowledged the cunning artifice of blowing up the deficit to eviscerate vital federal programs—at least not while they are serving. "I came to the House as a real deficit hawk but I am no longer a deficit hawk," ex-senator-turned-CNN-pundit Rick Santorum admitted years later. "I'll tell you why … Deficits make it easier to say no" to government spending.[12]

Other defects in the strategy were mathematical. Cuts in domestic discretionary spending, a relatively small share of the federal pie, went only so far in balancing the budget. Moreover, many programs created since the 1930s were now viewed by Americans and local officials as essential. Often forgotten from the Reagan era is that federal cutbacks forced state and local governments across the country to raise a slew of property, income, and other taxes and fees to offset losses from Washington, many of the increases disproportionately impacting those of lesser means. In addition, an increase in the payroll tax to preserve Social Security was more sorely felt by working Americans than the wealthy. The cumulative effect of it all was to leave middle- and lower- income Americans with a net federal tax *increase*, and to shift the total tax burden downward.[13]

Among the discordant phenomena of the Reagan years was his relationship with working class Americans. The former head of the Hollywood Screen Actors Guild, Reagan captured the votes of nearly half of blue-collar workers, and then became the most anti-labor president since Calvin Coolidge. In August 1981 Reagan terminated 11,000 members of the Professional Air Traffic Controllers Association (PATCO) after they went out on strike. Supported by most Americans desperate for a strong hand from their president, Reagan's action set the tone.[14] Employers enjoyed a National Labor Relations Board now tilted in their favor. The number of workers fired for attempting to organize their workplaces quadrupled by mid-decade. The combination of anti-union practices, technological innovation, and the flight of capital and jobs abroad caused union membership to plummet from 25 to 17 percent of the private sector workforce by 1990. Unions also faced an explosion of "concession bargaining," accepting wage and benefit cuts when management threatened a plant shutdown or to ship jobs overseas.[15]

Accelerated deindustrialization combined with surging oil imports to drive the nation's trade deficit from what had once seemed an alarming $36 billion to $170 billion in 1987. By then, however, the economic sea change was sinking deep into America's psyche: the nation that had long been the manufacturing powerhouse of the world was becoming a land whose economic health was now increasingly measured by "consumer confidence" and the fortunes of Wall Street. Workers' insecurity receded in the national dialog, muffled by an exploding world of privatized entertainment where one could hear requiems to blue collar America. On Japanese-made Walkmans, Americans listened to Billy Joel's mawk-ish elegy to the closing of Bethlehem Steel in "Allentown." Bruce Springsteen's "Born in the USA" offered the anguished cry of an unemployed Vietnam vet-eran, a tale of embittered working-class social isolation.[16] In historic Homestead, Pennsylvania, the *Mill Hunk Herald* dripped with righteous anger over corporate greed and the elegiac pain of communities who had seen too many mills and mines shuttered. An "industrial holocaust," said one ex-steelworker, was "destroy-ing families, destroying people's lives; it's destroying our future, and it's destroying America."[17]

The "Reagan Boom"

A recession in 1981–1982 brought the worst economic conditions since the Great Depression, with unemployment at nearly 11 percent, higher in the "Rust Belt."[18] Arriving in 1983, the "Reagan Boom" was masterfully celebrated in the president's "Morning in America" reelection ad the following year—a misty-eyed, red-white-and-blue spot that said nothing about Reagan, instead offering a saccharine portrait of small-town America that was "Prouder, Stronger, Better." Behind the Norman Rockwellian imagery lay troubling realities. The Reagan "boom" was severely imbalanced, looking nothing like that of the postwar era and recalibrating the very definition of a strong economy. Of 16 million jobs created in the Reagan era, just over half paid poverty-level wages. Employment in steel fell by 58 percent from 1982 to 1986.[19] Americans in former auto manu-facturing centers like Flint, Michigan repeated the mordant joke, "I know Reagan's created a lot of jobs; I've got three of them." Median family income remained flat and the inflation-adjusted value of the minimum wage (in the mid-1960s enough to support a family), declined 44 percent. For the first time since the 1920s, a greater share of the nation's income growth went to the top one percent than the bottom 90 percentile—a striking 40 versus 25 percent. Poverty surpassed 13 percent for the first time in a decade.[20]

African American unemployment remained more than twice the national aver-age. In addition, racially disproportionate drug laws and mandatory sentencing guidelines combined to triple the African American prison population between 1980 and 2000. As young black men were imprisoned for nonviolent crack cocaine and marijuana offenses, powder cocaine use by affluent whites soared with relative impunity, glorified in films like *The Big Chill*. An historically racist criminal justice system penetrated ever more deeply. Fully half of all prison inmates on death row by 1990 were African American.[21] Beginning in 1989, television viewers watched a manipulated version of that system in *Cops*. One of America's first "Reality TV" shows, the vicariously dangerous, immersive misrepresentation of policing reinforced racial stereotypes and white America's worst urban night-mares. *Cops* depicted the police as protagonists of violent, drug-infested cities, all that stood between white suburban enclaves and invariably black and brown criminals of the urban jungle. As police enacted their most heroic selves, suspects were criminalized by the action that seemed all too real. Like sensationalized local news coverage of urban crime, such media contortions furthered the distance between privileged white Americans and communities of color.

The eighties boom was uneven geographically as well. Sunbelt cities enjoyed surging federal investments in defense and aerospace. Bicoastal urban affluence took hold, thanks to a burgeoning technology sector and growth in advertising, health care, and the service industries. Meanwhile, Reagan's sanctified middle America hollowed out. Farmers who expanded operations over the previous decade when grain and land values were high suddenly faced the cruel combination of collapsing commodity prices and high interest rates. By mid-decade, one in six farmers faced foreclosure. Every week, nearly 500 farms were lost, many to large agribusiness operations. The region faced an epidemic of suicide. Even at the height of the recovery, unemployment in the heartland remained twice the national average.[22] Long severed from contact with the soil themselves, most Americans were only dimly aware of the farm crisis. In 1985, musicians Willie Nelson and John Mellencamp drew their attention with the first televised Farm Aid concert to assist struggling family farmers. Genuinely well intentioned, Farm Aid, like the Live Aid concerts and USA for Africa collaboration of artists to raise money for famine-afflicted Ethiopia, inadvertently augmented the Reagan philosophy that social problems could be solved not through government policy but private charity. In the same spirit, in May 1986 more than six million Americans participated in the spectacle of "Hands Across America," literally joining hands to fight growing homelessness. For those living on the streets of big cities and rural communities, it looked more like evening in America.

"How Much Is Enough?"

With growing bipartisan support since the late 1970s, deregulation—loosening the presumed chokehold of federal rules governing the private sector—promised to uncork a veritable geyser of wonders: feverish entrepreneurialism and competition, lower prices, increased profits, higher wages for workers. In 1980, vaguely populist promises to "get government off our backs" masked the risks of what Reagan had in mind: a wholesale assault on the myriad responsibilities of government agencies.[23] In 1988, the weakening of government's essential mission to safeguard the public interest was laid bare when the Savings & Loan Scandal broke wide open. Suddenly, taxpayers were on the hook for tens of billions of dollars due to the corruption of S&L managers. An exchange on the *Phil Donahue Show* from that era offered a window on two decades of deepening cynicism toward Washington, increasingly seen as an alien force. An indignant audience member shouted, with not a shred of irony, "Why should my money pay for a bailout? … Why can't the government pay for these debts instead of taxpayers?" Donahue's audience erupted.[24] The Framers of "the government" were well acquainted with the capacity of conniving opportunists to use the instruments of the state to further engorge themselves. James Madison argued that the constitution's separation of powers would guard against abuses of power by co-equal branches, and that in turn government was needed to regulate economic activities affecting the general welfare. In both public and private spheres, unfettered power was to be checked. "If men were angels," Madison said, "no government would be necessary."[25]

Charles Keating would not have been mistaken for an angel. Charged in 1976 by the Securities and Exchange Commission (SEC) with fraud, by 1984 Keating's company had purchased the Lincoln Savings and Loan, looking to take advantage of the Reagan administration's deregulation of the S & L industry. Like all Savings and Loans institutions, Lincoln was for decades a secure bank managed with limiting controls—among other things, on how much of the bank's deposits its managers could invest at one time, and in what kinds of enterprises. In 1982 congress passed the Garn–St. Germain Act, which eviscerated the Federal Home Loan Bank Board (FHLBB), the S&Ls' regulating agency. Senator William Proxmire called it "sheer bribery."[26] Keating poured Americans' savings into high-risk ventures ranging from malls and real estate to casinos and bull sperm banks. Some investments were leveraged with "junk bonds"—grossly inflated sham securities that lubricated much of Wall Street's corruption throughout the decade. "Always remember the weak, meek and ignorant are good targets," Lincoln internal documents directed.[27] By such deceit Keating raked in a cool $41 million over five years.

Ed Gray, appointed by Reagan to head the FHLBB, saw the iceberg coming. When he tried to re-tighten the rules, Gray was denounced inside the administration as a "re-regulator." To help keep government wolves from the door, Keating invested in politicians—the infamous "Keating Five," four Democrats and Republican John McCain. Keating showered the senators with sweetheart deals, luxuries, and Lear Jet excursions to lavish resorts. Gray warned of the looming insolvency of Lincoln but was bullied by the Keating Five until his term expired. Leaving nothing to chance, Keating generously paid a pin-striped economist named Alan Greenspan to certify the Lincoln's reputable practices and Keating's genius. When enough investments went belly up, the crime could be hidden no longer. Americans were left holding a $132 billion bag of debt (with interest, somewhere north of $400 billion).[28]

The S&L crisis signaled a rupture in banking—for forty years, a boring pillar of American economic stability. Following the financial collapse that triggered the Great Depression, the Glass–Steagall Act of 1933 built a firewall between high-risk investment securities and commercial banks where Americans kept their savings, while the SEC guarded against financial chicanery on Wall Street. In the 1950s the salary of an investment banker was just two or three times that of a unionized steelworker. When investment banks issued new stock, it was the partners' own money they put at risk, along with their integrity. The S&L disaster should have served as an ethics refresher for the Washington establishment. Instead, the bipartisan culture of corruption that made the scandal possible proved metastatic. Keating went to jail, but Greenspan's role in enabling the scandal was not only overlooked, but rewarded by Reagan with an appointment to head the Federal Reserve Board. For the next two decades, he loosened more rules that invited more licentious behavior. Meanwhile, deregulating insurgents opened up a multi-agency front. Don Regan, a former investment securities banker at Merrill Lynch with a loathing for Glass-Steagall, was appointed Treasury Secretary. Greenspan at the Fed, Regan at Treasury, and a Wall Street executive heading the SEC marked the beginning of a decades-long assault on regulatory oversight led by the titans of American finance.[29]

Deregulation goosed the largest wave of mergers since the 1920s, many of them hostile takeovers leveraged with junk bonds and made possible by insider trading. Leading the pack was corporate raider Ivan Boesky, whose brazen criminality was too much even for Reagan's SEC. Finally cornered in 1987, Boesky fingered junk bond financier Michael Milken, signaling the Wall Street party had gotten out of hand and the cops had arrived. Until then, the SEC, the Justice Department's Anti-Trust Division, and the Federal Trade Commission were dedicated to doing as little as possible. Between 1981 and 1987, 10,723 mergers went before the Anti-Trust Division; 26 were challenged.[30] Corporate raiders preyed on vulnerable companies, targeted them for leveraged buyouts, then often closed plants deemed unprofitable, leaving communities devastated. Frank Lorenzo used junk bonds to purchase struggling Continental Airlines, declare the company bankrupt, and break the unions. In the 1987 film *Wall Street* that dramatized the story of 1980s predatory capitalism, Gordon Gekko mentors young Bud Fox to be a "killer" of The Street—until Gekko uses him to secretly engineer the Lorenzo-like destruction of Fox's father's airline. He then confronts Gekko: "So tell me, Gordon: when does it all end, huh? How many yachts can you water-ski behind? How much is enough?"[31] For the real Gordon Gekkos of a new age of robber-baronism, the answers ran to infinity.

The real human drama gives lie to one of the era's great myths: that tax cuts and deregulation fueled new business investment, spurring good job creation. In not a single year of the decade did the percentage of national income going towards the purchase of new plants and equipment reach the three-four percent average that had been the rule since the 1950s.[32] The counterfeit nature of much of the eighties boom was temporarily exposed by the Wall Street crash of October 19, 1987. Five years of over-inflated, highly leveraged stock valuation and high-risk trading were compounded by market fears over dangerously high federal deficits, luring traders away from stocks and toward treasury bonds. The Dow tumbled 800 points, losing 13 percent of value—then, the single largest percentage drop in its history.

Deregulation worked its magic in virtually every federal agency, including a de-policing of the Defense Department, where Reagan's military buildup delivered a feast for the military industrial complex. By 1988, each of the nation's top ten military contractors was either convicted or pleaded guilty to multiple offenses, including defrauding the U.S. government, rigging weapons contracts, and bribing public officials. An independent watchdog discovered a shocking pattern of fraudulent procurement, highlighted by tales of $640 toilet seats and

$7,600 coffee makers. By 1985, 131 separate investigations of defense contractors from Rockwell International to Reagan's former employer General Electric found an epidemic of criminality.[33]

Killer Trees and Toaster Pictures

"You know, a tree is a tree—how many more do you need to look at?" snapped Governor Reagan in 1966 in opposing a proposed Redwoods National Park.[34] On the campaign trail 14 years later, the sagebrush rebel derided Jimmy Carter's clean air rules, warning that trees cause more deadly air pollution than cars and of the job-killing costs of environmental protection—the latter assertion as fallacious as the first. At the time, Japanese automakers boasted state-of-the-art pollution control and were eating Detroit for lunch. As Germany and Japan continued investing in a diversifying energy portfolio, Reagan retreated on renewable energy, signified in 1986 by his removal of the White House solar panels.[35] Again, the incongruity: Americans overwhelmingly supported environmental protection—and backed a president who brought deregulatory fervor to the Interior Department and the Environmental Protection Agency.

Reagan's Interior Secretary James Watt was a born-again Christian and an architect of the Sagebrush Rebellion. Watt pursued a policy of unbridled drilling, logging, mining, and cattle production on public lands. He also proved a bit of a rightwing crackpot, basing his fire sale of natural resources on a belief that The End was coming soon; hence, no need to protect them for future generations. Watt denied the all-American Beach Boys an opportunity to perform for the National Mall's Independence Day celebration because they attracted "the wrong element." Then he mocked the diversity of a recently formed advisory panel, which, he joked, had "every kind of mix ... three Democrats, two Republicans ... a black ... a woman, two Jews, and a cripple."[36] His final disgrace came via a federal grand jury involving influence-peddling at the Department of Housing and Urban Development.

The liquidation of public lands largely continued under Watt's more judicious successor, though not without resistance. The membership of environmental organizations doubled and doubled again in the eighties as they challenged administration policies. On public lands of the mineral-rich Colorado Plateau, federal agencies produced a severely compromised wilderness inventory that better resembled a "commercial and industrial zoning" plan. The same was true across the Great Plains and Rocky Mountain West. The Sierra Club and regional groups led by the Southern Utah Wilderness Alliance and "Resource Councils" comprised of conservative ranchers and liberal wilderness enthusiasts fought back, advocating more environmentally sustainable development throughout the West.[37] At the EPA, Watt disciple Anne Gorsuch Burford served as the agency's first woman administrator. It did not go well. Beyond taking a budgetary axe to her own agency, Gorsuch's tenure was marked by corporate favoritism and mismanagement of the Superfund program. Within the first year, Gorsuch was summoned before congressional committees investigating her and a top aide,

Rita Lavelle for conflicts of interest in sweetheart deals for polluters. Cited for contempt, Gorsuch and Lavelle refused to turn over documents and faced perjury charges. Both eventually resigned in disgrace.[38]

Things improved at EPA with the appointment of William Ruckelshaus as Administrator. One of the heroes of Watergate, Ruckelshaus returned briefly to a post he once held to restore the EPA's mission and public standing. The old-school conservative was there long enough to deliver several speeches on the looming threat of global warming, warning that the continued burning of fossil fuels would trigger a "succession of unexpected and shattering crises" that "threaten all we hold dear."[39] In Reagan's second term, Ruckelshaus was replaced by the business-friendly Lee Thomas, and by decade's end, Republicans had largely abandoned their party's conservation legacy, supplanted by idolatry of economic growth. From the Reagan era forward, most GOP politicians mocked environmentalists as "tree-hugging" job destroyers and laughably dismissed empirical evidence of a warming planet. Reagan's killer trees appeared in hindsight a cruelly ironic overture to all that followed.

The president's ability to sustain his high public standing is all the more jarring in light of the plague of corruption that characterized the Reagan White House. Across more than a dozen agencies, 138 administration officials were either convicted or subject to indictment or criminal investigation for official misconduct or criminal acts. Beyond the criminality, deregulation bore serious implications for the health of the democracy. Most critical was the communications industry where Reagan's Federal Communications Commission advanced on several fronts. The FCC raised the ceiling on how many television stations could be owned by one company. Portending greater media consolidation to come, the action signaled the beginning of the end of more than a half-century of a communications environment that protected divergent viewpoints and guarded against the concentration of ownership. "The widest possible dissemination of information from diverse and antagonistic sources is essential to the welfare of the public," wrote Supreme Court Justice Hugo Black in 1945 in a case involving a modest attempted acquisition by the Associated Press.[40] Reagan's FCC eliminated guidelines for stations to carry non-entertainment programming, and raised limits on how much advertising could be broadcast per hour. Television, said FCC Chairman Mark Fowler, was "just another appliance—it's a toaster with pictures." "It was time," he said, "to move away from thinking about broadcasters as trustees" of public discourse, and "to treat them ... as a business."[41]

Media deregulation continued with repeal of the 1949 Fairness Doctrine, which required that publicly licensed radio stations broadcasting programs of a singular viewpoint on an issue of public importance allow airtime for opposing views. In 1969 the U.S. Supreme Court declared the Doctrine "the single most important requirement of operation in the public interest" for a media outlet, an essential instrument of an informed citizenry that guarded against "monopolization" of ideas.[42] Alongside growing control of radio stations by conservative media giants, loss of the Fairness Doctrine allowed the AM talk radio format to

proliferate, its highly profitable but ideologically extreme content further eroding balanced and informed civil discourse.

Individualism in the Reagan Era

> Selfishness blights the germ of all virtue; individualism, at first, only saps the
> virtues of public life; but in the long run it attacks and destroys all others
> and is at length absorbed in downright selfishness …
>
> —Alexis de Tocqueville, *Democracy in America* (1835)

In many ways, the culture of the 1980s represented a rebuke of the 1960s ethos of
collective idealism and toward the values Alexis de Tocqueville saw coming nearly
two centuries ago: exaggerated American faith in self-reliance, selfish ambition,
and an atomized, narcissistic "individualism." Tom Wolfe distilled the essence of
the decade's materialist excesses in *Bonfire of the Vanities*, a classic novel of class-
conscious desire, racism, and greed. Wolfe framed eighties culture through the
hubris of Park Avenue high roller Sherman McCoy cruising in a $48,000 roadster,
juxtaposed with South Bronx youths whose necks were draped in Mercedes-
Benz hood ornaments—idols of irony and desire, of white affluence worlds away.[43]

Beyond Manhattan, as Reaganomics launched the upward redistribution of
wealth, Americans working longer hours at lower paying jobs turned inward,
toward an increasingly privatized culture. Echoing the withdrawal of federal
responsibility to solve social problems, citizens generally retreated from the public realm, drifting away from settings like union halls, fraternal clubs, and bowling leagues—trends later documented by Robert Putnam.[44] Middle-class
Americans connected less with one another and more with their Mastercard[45]
to support a lifestyle bedecked with entertaining diversions enjoyed in isolation:
video cassette recorders, Apple and IBM computers, Sony Walkman cassette
players, and computer video games. Residents of suburban enclaves walked amid
well-manicured landscapes or at shopping malls or went to Disney World—
places now considered public space.[46] The rising dominion of private interests in
American life was evident in corporate naming of taxpayer-funded sports stadi-
ums, in creeping "underwriting" of public broadcasting, in corporation logos on
human bodies: "Just Do It," Nike demanded.

Television, meanwhile, glamorized a shimmering opulence well beyond reach
of most viewers. Emblematic of the era was Robin Leach's brashly unapologetic
Lifestyles of the Rich and Famous that celebrated the new American plutocracy.
Leach offered audiences a seductive glimpse of the homes of super-rich enter-
tainers, athletes and business titans, animating viewers' "champagne wishes and
caviar dreams." The phrase captured well the spectacle of 1980s conspicuous
consumption. Advertisers sanctified consumer desire as essential to success,
rebranding the American "cult of individualism" for career-driven baby boomers.[47] L'Oréal cosmetics assured the price-hesitant, "Because You're Worth it."
"You Know You Want It," the alluring headphone-wearing brunette shill for
Walkman whispered, while Haynes underwear mimicked the U.S. Army's

"Be All You Can Be" with "Be all that. Be you." As Susan Douglas has argued, for American women, "the ability to spend time and money on one's appearance was a sign of personal success" and a vainglorious reinterpretation of women's emancipation. The sisterhood of women's liberation gave way to extravagant individualism, made possible by padded-shouldered business suits, weight loss "systems," and a relentless work ethic.[48]

Susan Faludi famously documented the anti-feminist "backlash" of the decade that took many forms, including Reagan budget cuts, an attack on reproductive rights, and media declarations that feminism had been "women's own worst enemy."[49] It was reflected in Hollywood depictions of career-oriented single women who were either lonely, pathetic melancholiacs, or aggressive femme fatales who got theirs in the end. Adrian Lyne's *Fatal Attraction* (1987) gave viewers both. Lyne's take on the women's movement revealed the malignant misogyny that ran through a number of his films:

> You hear feminists talk, and the last ten, twenty years you hear women talk about fucking men rather than being fucked, to be crass about it. It's kind of unattractive, however liberated and emancipated it is. It kind of fights the whole wife, childbearing role. Sure you got your career and your success, but you are not fulfilled as a woman.[50]

Fatal Attraction depicted a happily married lawyer, Dan Gallagher (Michael Douglas), whose weekend affair with a beguiling professional woman-cum-sociopathic temptress nearly destroys his suburban bliss. "Alex" (Glenn Close) lives a grim existence in an urban warehouse-like apartment and becomes obsessed with Dan, who is suddenly a victim fighting to save his marriage. The film struck a misogynist vein: as Dan and the wicked Alex wrestle for a kitchen knife, male viewers in many theatres yelled aloud, "Kill her, Michael! Kill the bitch!"[51]

In this climate, it is pathetic for its very noteworthiness that New York Congresswoman Geraldine Ferraro was selected in 1984 by Democrat Walter Mondale as his vice-presidential running mate—the first woman on a major party ticket. The campaign revealed both the sexism of the culture and the persevering vitality of the women's movement. On the day Ferraro was to debate her Republican opponent, George H. W. Bush, the vice president's press secretary noted that Ferraro came across as "too bitchy." The debate's moderator asked Ferraro whether she thought "the Soviets might be tempted to try to take advantage of you simply because you are a woman." Throughout the debate Bush lectured Ferraro on foreign policy with highhanded condescension. Ferraro finally snapped back. "Let me first of all say that I almost resent, Vice President Bush, your patronizing attitude that you have to teach me about foreign policy."[52] At one level, Ferraro's confident gravitas served as political analog to the armor-corseted sexuality and transgressive independence of eighties pop star Madonna, each embodying the challenges women faced in navigating a supposedly "post-feminist" society.

Much of the cultural energy of the decade seemed consciously directed toward repudiating the sixties. The image of young urban professional "Yuppies"—the beautifully sculpted and highly successful women and men who renounced their idealism for the good life—although mocked in some corners, was generally celebrated. And to be *celebrated*—if only for one's "well-knownness," as Daniel Boorstin once put it—went to the morally hollow center of much of 1980s culture.[53] Forget Madonna's music; her real genius lay in the art of self-promotion. "Who do I think I am, trying to pull this off?" she admitted of her sudden superstardom.[54] The self-aware construction of Madonna iconography was provocative, privacy-bearing, and ubiquitous in a society that was now so fixated on fame that stories about the Material Girl could masquerade as evening news. From the race- and gender-bending Michael Jackson to the Hollywood performance presidency to the pretense of big hair and lip-syncing synth-pop, Americans worshipped celebrity and embraced flashy deception, so long as it entertained.

The era's greatest counterfeit artist, Donald J. Trump, launched a thirty-year run of bamboozle that would take him to 1600 Pennsylvania Avenue. The Donald's ersatz creation story—the self-made billionaire genius, the shrewd deal-making real estate tycoon—was birthed amid the corrosive confluence of deregulated corporate greed and pretense of celebrity news as if it mattered. Was it his charm or shrewd business acumen that led to Trump's fabulous success? Is Marla more ravishing than Ivana? America was now a country that cared about such questions. And they were answered on *Entertainment Tonight* and in the pages of *People*, and *Time*. CNN's Larry King gave Donald the microphone frequently. On May 17, 1989 it was to reiterate Trump's full-page ad in the *New York Times* demanding the state execute the "Central Park Five," five black and brown men accused of raping a white woman in Central Park. "I hate these people, let's all hate these people, maybe hate is what we need if we're going to get something done," he declared.[55] In 2003, the world learned the five men had been wrongly convicted based on confessions coerced by the police. An unrepentant Trump refused to recant.

What lay ahead was impossible to know, but even then, when the faux gold on Trump Tower was still being plated, streetwise New Yorkers saw through the deception. Many knew that Donald had inherited his wealth, that his father Fred, arrested at a Klan rally in 1927, was so notorious a racist landlord that Woody Guthrie wrote a song about him.[56] The Nixon administration caught up with Fred and Donald in 1973, citing them for egregious violations of the 1968 Fair Housing Act. Young Don dismissed the allegations as "absolutely ridiculous."[57] Early Trumpologists knew that he lied unashamedly about anything, including the number of stories in Trump Tower.[58] From 1985 to 1995, he lost more money than any American alive.[59] His celebrity was a product not of business smarts but good fortune and a media-savvy gift for hoodwink at exactly the right time in American life. In his semi-autobiographical *The Art of the Deal*, Trump revealed to author Tony Schwartz the mad genius behind the myth:

The final key to the way I promote is bravado. I play to people's fantasies. People may not always think big themselves but they can still get very excited by those who do. That's why a little hyperbole never hurts. People want to believe that something is the biggest and the greatest and the most spectacular. I call it truthful hyperbole.[60]

The gilded trappings of Trumpland—the books, the private jets, helicopters and yacht, his gaudy, ill-fated casinos, the trophy wives—were all "props for the show." So, too, the bankruptcies, failed marriages, spurned business partners, and resulting negative press. Yet as Neal Gabler put it, "Trump's blockbuster was so good a show that not even failure could close it."[61] Indeed, in this new America the con was just getting started.

Cold War: The Sequel

Beyond those monuments to heroism is the Potomac River, and on the far shore the sloping hills of Arlington National Cemetery, with its row upon row of simple white markers bearing crosses or Stars of David. They add up to only a tiny fraction of the price that has been paid for our freedom … Their lives ended in places called Belleau Wood, The Argonne, Omaha Beach, Salerno … *and in a hundred rice paddies and jungles of a place called Vietnam* [emphasis added].

—Ronald Reagan, Inaugural Address, January 20, 1981[62]

With this grandiloquent crescendo to his inaugural, President Reagan was off on a mission to reassert American military righteousness. The rhetorical sleight of hand served first to conflate the indisputably sacred ground of past American heroism with the contested terrain of Vietnam. In fusing an honorable history to an indefensible war, Reagan was building the rhetorical scaffolding for a reprise of Cold War militarism that could defeat the "enemies of freedom." His hawkish foreign policy would be abetted by a mostly compliant congress, an indulgent press, a flailing Soviet empire, and an American populace that longed for the kind of myth-laden exceptionalism that was Reagan's forte. "The era of self-doubt is over," he proclaimed that spring. There is, the president declared, "a hunger on the part of the people to once again be proud of America, all that it is and all that it can be."[63] The question that loomed from 1981 to 1984 was how far Reagan might go to defend it.

Branded "Peace Through Strength," Reagan's policy toward the Soviet Union focused on the buildup of the U.S. nuclear arsenal. Despite swollen claims from the Reagan faithful when the Cold War ended that the bellicosity brought the ultimate victory of the West, the historical record indicates that U.S. militarism in the early Reagan years—as had been the case in the Kennedy era—only fortified hardliners in the Kremlin, delaying the Soviets' desire for improved relations with the West.[64] Anatoly Dobrynin, the Soviet ambassador who helped end the Cuban Missile Crisis, recalled that "the impact of Reagan's hard-line policy …

was exactly the opposite of the one intended by Washington. It strengthened those in the Politburo, the Central Committee, and the security apparatus who had been pressing for a mirror-image of Reagan's own policy."[65]

Spearheading the strategy was Secretary of Defense Caspar Weinberger, who approved virtually the entire wish list of the Joint Chiefs and weapons lobbyists, including new stealth fighter planes, 100 B-1 bombers, 100 MX missiles, antiballistic weapons, and an expansion of the Trident submarine program. Weinberger overhauled the doomsday U.S. nuclear war plan, which now called for a staggering 50,000 targets inside the Soviet Union.[66] In the spring of 1982, the leak of the classified, "Defense Guidance 1984–1988"—calling for the "nuclear decapitation" of Kremlin leadership, waging conventional and nuclear conflict simultaneously around the world, and declarations of U.S. victory with casualties in the millions—was met with public alarm.[67] That followed an interview by journalist Robert Scheer with Pentagon official T. K. Jones on the matter of Reagan's civil defense plan. Americans should not fear the prospect of nuclear war, said Jones. "Dig a hole, cover it with a couple of doors, and then throw three feet of dirt on top. It's the dirt that does it. If there are enough shovels to go around, everyone is going to make it."[68] Jones was not a lost character from Stanley Kubrick's *Dr. Strangelove*, but an advisor to the President of the United States.

The calendar turned to 1983, the gravest year of nuclear peril since 1962. Speaking to a group of evangelicals that spring, President Reagan called the Soviet Union the "evil empire."[69] As if to prove him right, that September the Soviet military shot down a Korean airliner that strayed into Soviet airspace. Reagan denounced it as a "crime against humanity."[70] Two months later, the U.S. and its NATO allies carried out Able Archer, an elaborate nuclear war exercise involving heads of state. With Soviet leaders already convinced the United States was preparing a first strike, the response to Able Archer was unprecedented: nuclear weapons were emplaced into delivery systems, aircraft in Poland and East Germany moved into "strip alert" prepared for takeoff, while Chief of the Soviet General Staff took to his underground command bunker.[71] Months later came the president's Strangelovian mic-check to a live Saturday radio address: "My fellow Americans, I'm pleased to tell you today that I've signed legislation that will outlaw Russia forever. We begin bombing in five minutes."[72] Few outside the room got the joke.

The decade ended not with Armageddon but a series of breathtaking events: a sudden thaw in U.S.–Soviet relations, the curbing of the nuclear arms race, freedom breaking out across the Soviet bloc, and a stunning fracturing of the Soviet Union itself by 1991. Often overlooked in the United States, Mikhail Gorbachev's election as General Secretary of the Communist Party in 1985 remains one of the pivotal moments of modern world history. It signaled a wave of internal reform and an end to the use of coercive force to maintain communist rule outside the Soviet Union. Gorbachev ended the Afghanistan war and urged further reductions in military expenditures to strengthen a feeble Russian economy. The liberalizing trend in Moscow came alongside equally important events in the Soviet orbit. A shipyard strike in Gdańsk, Poland, bravely supported by native son Pope John Paul II, evolved into a national *Solidarnosc* (Solidarity) movement for democracy. By 1985 *Solidarnosc* was pressing for free elections in Poland and emboldening the push for peaceful democratic change throughout the Soviet bloc.

Finally, but by no means least of the consequential forces at work, was the Nuclear Freeze, the largest peace movement in world history. Conceived in 1980 by Randall Forsberg, a young MIT researcher, the Freeze proposed an immediate halt to the testing, production and deployment of nuclear weapons as a first step toward abolition. By 1983, Freeze referenda had passed 370 city councils, dozens of counties, and won support in 23 state legislatures and the House of Representatives. On June 12, 1982, one million people turned out in New York City's Central Park demanding a Nuclear Freeze, with similar throngs throughout Europe (Figure 11.1). The march represented the climactic peak of a movement that proved far more influential than the media acknowledged, more important than activists themselves realized. Reagan dismissed the Freeze as a communist ruse, but could not ignore the three-quarters of Americans who voiced support, nor the major religious organizations and labor unions who endorsed it. Some of the evangelicals present for the "evil empire" speech were Freeze supporters. The fear that fueled the movement was brought home the night of November 20, 1983 in the ABC broadcast of *The Day After*, an all-too-real dramatization of a nuclear attack on Lawrence, Kansas. Watched by more than 100 million Americans, *The Day After* was felt viscerally in living rooms, discussed at length in classrooms, and replayed in nuclear nightmares. It did nothing to dampen support for the Freeze.

Reagan had to respond. All he offered in 1983, at least publicly, was the techno-fantasy of the Strategic Defense Initiative (SDI), the "Star Wars" missile defense system, which threatened to destabilize the security regime of Mutually Assured Destruction that long guarded against a nuclear first strike. The president's presentation of SDI came with a pledge that "nuclear war can never be won and must never be fought." Even that bare-essential declaration, coupled with the *defense* posture of SDI, represented movement from an administration that two years earlier spoke casually about nuclear "warning shots."[73] Moreover, Reagan was indeed moving. *The Day After*, along with a close-up look at the nuclear war plan, had left him shaken. Like Kennedy, he was horrified by defense intellectuals' cavalierly "[tossing] around macabre jargon about 'throw weights' and 'kill ratios' as if they were talking about baseball scores."[74] In February 1983, he asked Secretary of State George Schultz to arrange a secret meeting with Dobrynin—the first indication of Reagan's intentions for a rapprochement with the Soviets.

In Gorbachev he found a willing partner. From 1985 to 1988, four summit meetings over a broad range of U.S.–Soviet issues brought the first breakthrough in the arms race since Kennedy and Khrushchev. Despite Reagan's insistence on SDI, and neoconservative advisers repeatedly warning that Gorbachev was not to be trusted, in 1987 the two leaders signed the landmark Intermediate Nuclear

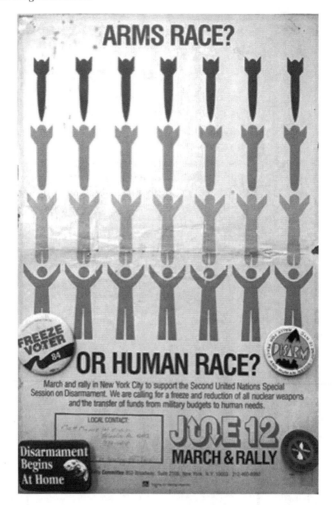

Figure 11.1 Poster and buttons from the March and Rally for the Nuclear Freeze, June 12, 1982, held in concert with the United Nations Special Session on Disarmament. An estimated one million people gathered on the Great Lawn of New York City's Central Park for the largest peace rally in history.

Courtesy of the author

Forces Treaty, the first nuclear arms control agreement to remove weapons already deployed, signaling more significant breakthroughs ahead.[75]

The "Moral Equivalent of Our Founding Fathers"

Within days of Reagan's inauguration, incoming Secretary of State Alexander Haig began feeding the media reports of a Soviet-Cuban communist plot to take over Central America, one that would eventually, warned Haig and UN Ambassador Jeanne Kirkpatrick, threaten America's southwest border. Kirkpatrick suggested the Maryknoll women raped and assassinated by Salvadoran death squads "were not just nuns," insinuating the "political activists" were up to no good in having sided with the "leftist" revolt of the poor.[76] So began an eight-year propaganda campaign to build public support for the Reagan administration's aggressive anti-communist intervention in Latin America. The linchpins were wars in El Salvador and Nicaragua, but the policy extended into South America, where the CIA intensified the "War on Drugs," deploying extra-judicial paramilitary torture and assassination against drug lords. Severe collateral damage resulted, with democratic movements in Columbia and Peru crushed and some of the cartels' business pushed north into war-ravaged Central America. None of it slowed the demand for drugs in the United States.[77]

In El Salvador, the Reagan administration overcame opposition from Democratic Speaker of the House Tip O'Neil to win congressional authorization of $6 billion in weapons, training, and other assistance for the governing military junta. The hideous civil war would drag on for 12 years, taking the lives of 75,000 Salvadorans and producing one million refugees. A UN Truth Commission later reported that nearly 85 percent of the torture, kidnappings and killings were committed either by the U.S.-backed regime or its death squads.[78] The most infamous atrocity took place December 10–11, 1981, when the Atlacatl Battalion, a Salvadoran Army unit trained by the U.S. School of the Americas, executed more than 900 unarmed men, women and children in the village of El Mozote. Elliott Abrams, Reagan's Assistant Secretary of State for Human Rights and Humanitarian Affairs, could not bring himself to acknowledge the massacre had even happened, nor condemn the U.S.-trained death squad leader who ordered Romero's murder. Reagan's policy had been "a fabulous achievement," Abrams said. Despite the killing and torture of thousands of Guatemalans, he praised the "considerable progress" on human rights made by that nation's despot, José Efraín Ríos Montt.[79,80] Reagan himself justified his policy with language that seemed to belong to another era: "Central America is simply too close, and the strategic stakes are too high, for us to ignore the danger of governments seizing power there with ideological and military ties to the Soviet Union."[81]

Reagan was right in one sense. Central America was indeed close enough for nearly one million victims of the wars he was fueling to walk more than a thousand miles to seek asylum in the United States. But granting political refugee status to Salvadorans and Guatemalans would have required admitting U.S. culpability in exacerbating the crisis. Thus, Reagan's Immigration and Naturalization Service (INS) invariably denied asylum applications, a policy that violated the 1951 Refugee Convention. Sixty percent of applicants from Iran and 40 percent of Afghans were granted refugee status in these years, while less than *three* percent of Salvadoran and Guatemalan asylum seekers were admitted. INS agents arrested thousands along the border, herding many into detention centers where they were pressured to return to their home countries or deported.[82]

U.S. policy in Nicaragua produced equally tragic consequences. In December 1981, in violation of U.S. law preventing hostile actions against non-threatening sovereign nations, Reagan secretly directed the CIA to mount armed "counter-revolutionary" (Contra) resistance against the Sandinista government. The directive came with an allocation of $19 million, allegedly to interdict the flow of weapons from Nicaragua to Salvadoran rebel forces—a wildly exaggerated charge. In April 1984, David MacMichael, a former lead CIA intelligence analyst in the region, asserted the agency had "systematically misrepresented" the weapons issue as a pretense for arming the Contras.[83] Nevertheless, the administration whipped up fears that Cuban-style universal health care in one of the poorest nations on earth somehow marked the beginning of communist domination of all Latin America, and eventually would threaten the security of Texas. The Contra army was formed from the "Fifteenth of September Legion," a rogue unit of the deposed Somoza National Guard that had decamped to U.S. client states Honduras, El Salvador, and Guatemala. From there they launched attacks on Nicaraguan health care clinics, assassinated local Sandinista officials, and engaged in torture and rape—enough to get them identified in 1982 by the Defense Department as a terrorist group.[84]

As the war escalated, the human rights group Americas Watch condemned Contra forces for having

> systematically violated the applicable laws of war. They have attacked civilians indiscriminately; they have tortured and mutilated prisoners; they have murdered those placed *hors de combat* [out of action due to injury] by their wounds; they have taken hostages; and they have committed outrages against personal dignity.[85]

Ignoring these and other corroborating reports, the White House went on the attack, orchestrating an elaborate, fallacious campaign to both discredit Contra opponents and smear the Sandinistas. One shadowy associate of Col. Oliver North, the National Security Council staffer running the operation, dressed up as a Catholic priest and lied to a congressional subcommittee about alleged Sandinista crimes. The FBI joined in, launching a campaign of political sabotage and harassment that was downright Nixonian, surveilling opponents of the administration's Central American policy and burglarizing offices of the Committee in Solidarity with the People of El Salvador (CISPES).[86]

The political calculus shifted in 1984 when reports emerged of a CIA campaign to bomb Nicaraguan harbors. Congressional leaders moved to terminate support for the Contras. Senate Republicans, some incensed at the deception, others that this was all endangering America's standing in the world, began withdrawing support. With Speaker O'Neil condemning the Contras as "marauders, murderers, and rapists," congress passed the Boland Amendment, prohibiting any further funding of their operations.[87] Having none of it, Reagan declared the Contras "the moral equal of our Founding Fathers," and ordered National Security Advisor Robert McFarlane to keep them alive "body and soul."[88]

In that moment Reagan seeded the worst scandal of his presidency, the Iran–Contra affair. This high romantic devilry began when a band of self-declared "cowboys" led by Oliver North orchestrated an illegal fundraising effort for the Contras that included skimming profits from CIA drug-running operations and soliciting contributions from rightwing millionaires. More infamously, North, McFarlane and his deputy devised a scheme to sell anti-tank and anti-aircraft weapons to Iran. In violation of U.S. and international laws, the Iran–Contra plot aimed at two completely unrelated goals. First, profits from the arms sales served as a cash stream for the Contras. A second objective was to win release of American hostages then being held in Lebanon by Iran-supported Hezbollah. Organized in response to the 1982 Israeli invasion of Lebanon, Hezbollah declared itself that country's quasi-governing defense force acting in support of the Palestine Liberation Organization (then headquartered in Beirut), and against the continued interference of Israel, the United States, and allied western powers in Lebanese affairs. In 1983 the United States and France led an international "peacekeeping force" that was tantamount to pouring gasoline on a raging fire. Engulfed in civil war for seven years, Lebanon had no peace to keep. Israeli, French and U.S. forces engaged in brutal fighting with various warring factions that brought mounting civilian casualties. That October, the suicide bombing of a marine base in Beirut killed 241 Americans, the largest single loss of military personnel since the Tet Offensive.

Reagan withdrew U.S. troops, but the saga was not over. In a desperate act of retribution, Hezbollah seized a small group of U.S. and French nationals and held them hostage. Thus by 1985 President Reagan faced the same quandary as Jimmy Carter, except here the only conceivable means of freeing American captives—short of the unthinkable, direct negotiation with a terrorist organization—was to deal secretly with Hezbollah's sponsor, Iran. The scheme netted little success: Iran received its arms, Hezbollah freed several hostages, then seized more. Meanwhile, propped up by the criminal activities of "the cowboys," the Contra war ultimately took the lives of more than 15,000 Nicaraguans, the vast majority civilians. The Iran–Contra Affair was diabolical genius, for which the masterminds and Reagan paid almost no price, despite a congressional inquiry and a special prosecutor investigation.

Apart from the Iran–Contra intrigue, the wars in Central America galvanized very different forms of law-breaking. In the summer of 1980, thirty Salvadoran migrants journeyed north across the Sonoran Desert. Just 17 survived, arriving in Tucson and Phoenix where INS officials moved to deport them without consideration of the 1980 Refugee Act, a law mandating protection for any refugee with "well-founded fear of persecution." In response, local church leaders began sheltering the first of what eventually became hundreds of thousands of Salvadoran, Guatemalan, and Honduran refugees fleeing the violence and chaos of the region. By 1983, a growing interdenominational network was providing sanctuary and assistance to asylum seekers. Despite INS efforts to sabotage their work and prosecute activists, the Sanctuary Movement spread nationwide to more than 600 communities.[89]

The persistence of grassroots activism was evident as well in the international movement to end the racist apartheid regime in South Africa. In the United

States, much of the energy emanated from college students who pressured boards of trustees and corporations to boycott South Africa. A victory came in 1986 with the passage of the Comprehensive Anti-Apartheid Act, which imposed tough economic sanctions on the government and called for an end to apartheid and the release of political prisoners including African National Congress leader Nelson Mandela. President Reagan and neoconservatives like Congressman Dick Cheney opposed the measure, calling Mandela and the ANC "terrorists."[90] But the tide had turned. "We are against tyranny, and Tyranny is in South Africa!," cried Senator Richard Lugar in breaking with the president, leading enough fellow Republicans to join Democrats in overriding Reagan's veto of the law.[91] It was an historic rebuke of both Reagan and the regime, and an important step toward a democratic South Africa.

"The Gay Plague"

Auto Immune Deficiency Syndrome (AIDS) was first felt in the gay community in the late 1970s, and by 1981 rising clusters of AIDS-related sickness and morbidity found their way into reports of the Centers for Disease Control. AIDS exacted a deadly toll, primarily on male homosexuals through sexual contact, but the AIDS HIV virus also found its way to heterosexuals and drug users exposed intravenously through blood transfusions or sharing of needles. As the body count mounted, the lone White House response was an offhand cruel joke from the president's press secretary about the "gay plague" that elicited laughter from journalists. Even when Hollywood legend Rock Hudson was dying of AIDS in 1985, Reagan said nothing, seemingly content to let the religious right speak for him. Jerry Falwell saw AIDS as "God's punishment for the society that tolerates homosexuals," while North Carolina Senator Jesse Helms declared "their deliberate, disgusting, revolting conduct ... responsible for the disease."[92]

Facing societal antipathy and surrounded by death, the gay community was prone to morbid powerlessness, yet managed to organize private networks of loving support. In 1980, screenwriter Larry Kramer, who lost dozens of friends to the disease, founded the Gay Men's Health Crisis which focused on comforting the dying. Fear and ostracism prevailed in most clinical settings. One notable exception was the bravely benevolent Ward 5B of San Francisco General Hospital, where nurses organized to treat AIDS patients, providing "dignity ... [and] radical compassion" to the suffering.[93] Especially frustrating was the niggardly federal funding directed to possible courses of treatment, as well as the dead-march pace of clinical trials for AIDS drugs. Personal grief and government insouciance combined to produce righteous anger. In 1987 Larry Kramer harnessed the rage to form the AIDS Coalition to Unleash Power (ACT UP), a direct-action organization that mounted a campaign of protest and civil disobedience directed at the federal Food and Drug Administration (FDA), pharmaceutical companies, the National Institutes of Health (NIH), and homophobic politicians. They were "united in anger," recalled filmmaker David France. "They would storm people's offices with fake blood and cover people's computers with

[it]. They locked themselves to politicians' desks. At one point, they barged into a meeting of a pharmaceutical company and turned over the shrimp cocktail tables." On October 11, 1988, ACT UP shut down the offices of the FDA in the largest act of civil disobedience since the Vietnam War. Their most creative action may have been cloaking Jesse Helms's home with a giant condom.[94]

Their efforts proved effective—in part because of the response of one public health official. Dr. Anthony S. Fauci, director of the National Institute for Allergy and Infectious Diseases (NIAID), felt the sting of ACT UP's vitriol in an open letter penned by Kramer in 1988 in the *San Francisco Examiner*. "Your refusal to hear the screams of AIDS activists early in the crisis resulted in the deaths of thousands of Queers," Kramer wrote. Rather than recoil, Fauci reached out to Kramer, opening up dialog with the community and soliciting advice on how to more effectively meet the crisis. Dramatic changes followed, including expanding the number of HIV-infected patients in clinical drug trials and direct participation by the afflicted in policy planning. Their relationship ultimately brought life-saving changes to the treatment not only of AIDS, but how all infectious diseases are managed on the national level. As Fauci adjudged when Kramer died in 2020, "in American medicine, there are two eras. Before Larry and after Larry," Fauci reflected.[95]

The efforts of ACT UP occurred alongside the very public AIDS battle of Ryan White, a young hemophiliac who had contracted the disease intravenously and endured vicious discrimination from students, parents, and school officials. Befriended by musician Elton John and other celebrities, the generous humanity of Ryan White and his parents evinced compassion toward all those afflicted by AIDS. Also cultivating greater empathy was the AIDS "Names Project" quilt, a project conceived by activist Cleve Jones. Each patch of the massive AIDS quilt, which grew to more than 48,000 names, memorialized a lost loved one. Dramatizing the individual humanity of victims, the quilt toured the country with its final display on the National Mall—the largest community art project in the world.[96] The clash of sixties-style vibrant activism with the growing strength of conservatism proved an overture to the looming "culture wars."

More menacing were the paramilitary activities of white supremacist self-declared patriots along the southwest border. Since the end of the Vietnam War, thousands of embittered nativist warriors—many of them neo Nazis or members of the Klan—channeled their militant anti-communist white nationalism into both mercenary support for Reagan's covert wars in Central America, and organized harassment and outright terror of communities of color in the Southwest.[97] On Independence Day 1986, twenty heavily armed "border angels" of the "Civilian Materiel Assistance (CMA)," a paramilitary group claiming thousands of members across the country, held sixteen asylum-seeking men, women and children at gunpoint before Border Patrol Agents arrived. The story sparked outrage, but the CMA and groups like it had only begun.[98]

Later that year, Ronald Reagan signed the Immigration Reform and Control Act that offered a path toward citizenship for 2.7 million undocumented residents—a gesture soon unimaginable in the Republican Party. Three years later, the outgoing president honored at least part of the law's intent with this high-minded nod to America's immigrant heritage: "And she's still a beacon, still a magnet for all who must have freedom, for all the Pilgrims from all the lost places who are hurtling through the darkness, toward home. We've done our part."[99] Indeed he had, but in ways more complex than he would have acknowledged—seeding with his foreign policy the rising tide of Central American migration, and the nativist backlash to it. Moreover, a decade that began with Reagan announcing his candidacy near the site of the murders of three civil rights workers, ended with former Klan Grand Wizard David Duke switching his political affiliation to Republican and winning a seat in the Louisiana state legislature. Reagan and newly elected President George H. W. Bush endorsed Duke's Democratic opponent, but there was no turning back. White grievance and extremism in the party of Lincoln had been set loose.

Notes

1 Oliver Sacks, "The President's Speech," in *The Man Who Mistook His Wife for a Hat* (New York: Harper and Row, 1985), 80.
2 Sacks, 80–84; adapted from Michael Schaller, *Reckoning with Reagan: America and Its President in the 1980s* (New York: Oxford University Press, 1992), 53.
3 David R. Tarr and Bob Benenson, *Elections A to Z*, 4th edition (Thousand Oaks, CA: Sage Publications, CQ Press, 2012), 317–318.
4 Seymour Martin Lipset, "The Elections, the Economy, and Public Opinion: 1984," *PS* 18, no. 1 (Winter, 1985), 28–38; and Frank Newport, Jeffrey M. Jones, and Lydia Saad, "Ronald Reagan from the People's Perspective: A Gallup Poll Review," *Gallup*, June 7, 2004, https://news.gallup.com/poll/11887/ronald-reagan-from-peoples-perspective-gallup-poll-review.aspx, retrieved June 1, 2020. The quote belongs to Assistant Chief of Staff Michael Deaver, in Schaller, *Reckoning with Reagan*, 66.
5 Ronald Reagan, "Inaugural Address," January 20, 1981, www.reaganfoundation.org/media/128614/inaguration.pdf, retrieved June 27, 2019.
6 Haynes Johnson, *Sleepwalking Through History: America in the Reagan Years* (New York: Anchor Doubleday, 1991), 131.
7 Among the many good studies of Reaganomics, see Jack Rasmus, *The Scourge of Neoliberalism From Reagan to Trump* (Atlanta, GA: Clarity Press, 2020), 57–75; Kim Phillips-Fein, *Invisible Hands: The Businessmen's Crusade Against the New Deal* (New York: W. W. Norton and Company, 2009); and Kevin Phillips, *The Politics of Rich and Poor: Wealth and the American Electorate in the Reagan Aftermath* (New York: Random House, 1990).
8 Bruce Bartlett, "'Starve the Beast': Origins and Development of a Budgetary Metaphor," *Independent Review* 12, no. 1 (Summer 2007), 5–26; and William Greider, "The Education of David Stockman," *Atlantic Monthly* (December 1981).
9 Clara Jeffery and Monika Bauerlein, "The Job Killers," *Mother Jones* (November/December 2011), www.motherjones.com/politics/2011/10/republicans-job-creation-kill, retrieved June 20, 2020.
10 Roy Rosenzweig et al., *Who Built America: Working People and the Nation's History, vol. II Since 1877*, 3rd ed. (New York: Bedford St. Martin's, 2008), 708; and Denis Hayes, "Earth Day at 40," Mercyhurst University, Erie, PA, April 22, 2010.
11 Ayana Byrd, "Code Switch Dives into Story Behind 'Welfare Queen,'" *Colorlines*, June 10, 2019, www.colorlines.com/articles/listen-code-switch-dives-story-behind-welfare-queen, retrieved June 28, 2019.

12 Ed Kilgore, "Starving the Beast," *Blueprint Magazine* (June 30, 2003), quoted by Douglas J. Amy, "Government is Good," http://governmentisgood.com/articles. php?aid=14, retrieved June 28, 2019.

13 Among the best of many studies documenting these patterns is Donald L. Bartlett and James B. Steele, *America: What Went Wrong* (Kansas City, KS: Andrews and McMeel, Universal Press Syndicate, 1992); see especially 40–63.

14 See Joseph A. McMartin, *Collision Course: Ronald Reagan, the Air Traffic Controllers, and the Strike that Changed America* (New York: Oxford University Press, 2011).

15 Rosenzweig et al 719–720. The author experienced this as an organizer for the Pennsylvania Nurses Association in 1989, seeing nurses threatened by hospital officials when they persisted in union activity, with impunity from the NLRB.

16 Christian G. Appy, *American Reckoning: The Vietnam War and Our National Identity* (New York: Penguin, 2015), 251–256.

17 Anne Marie Draham, "People and Power: The Struggle Continues," *Mill Hunk Herald* (Fall 1984), 59.

18 Richard C. Auxier, "Reagan's Recession," Pew Research Center, December 14, 2010, www.pewresearch.org/2010/12/14/reagans-recession/, retrieved June 22, 2020.

19 Johnson, 425.

20 Chad Stone et al., "Guide to Statistics on Historical Trends in Income Inequality," December 11, 2018, Center for Budget and Policy Priorities, www.cbpp.org/research/poverty-and-inequality/a-guide-to-statistics-on-historical-trends-in-income-inequality, retrieved June 28, 2019.

21 Algernon Austin, "For African Americans, 50 Years of High Unemployment," Economic Policy Institute, February 22, 2012, www.epi.org/publication/african-americans-50-years-high-unemployment/, retrieved July 5, 2019; and Rosenzweig et al., 716–717.

22 Johnson, 426–427.

23 Ronald Reagan, "Election Eve Address: A Vision for America," November 3, 1980, www.reaganlibrary.gov/11-3-80, retrieved June 6, 2020.

24 Quoted by Kathleen Day, "The Depression-Era Laws that Led to the 1980s Savings and Loan Crisis," *Zocalo* (Arizona State University, May 21, 2019), www.zocalopublicsquare.org/2019/05/21/the-depression-era-laws-that-led-to-the-1980s-savings-and-loan-crisis/ideas/essay/, retrieved July 1, 2019.

25 James Madison, *The Federalist 51*, published in the *Independent Journal* (February 6, 1788), www.constitution.org/fed/federa51.htm, retrieved July 1, 2019.

26 Charles Ferguson, *Predator Nation: Corporate Criminals, Political Corruption, and the Hijacking of America* (New York: Crown Publishing, 2012), 32.

27 "Charles H. Keating, Jr," *New York* Times, February 23, 2012, https://web.archive.org/web/20120223052045/http://topics.nytimes.com/topics/reference/timestopics/people/k/charles_h_keating_jr/index.html, retrieved July 1, 2019.

28 Ferguson, 27–32; and Tom Fitzpatrick, "McCain: The Most Reprehensible of the Keating Five," *Phoenix New Times*, November 29, 1989, www.phoenixnewtimes.com/news/phoenix-officer-suspended-over-cavity-search-11318316, retrieved July 1, 2019.

29 William Kleinknecht, *The Man Who Sold the World: Ronald Reagan and the Betrayal of Main Street America* (New York: Perseus, 2009), 103–127.

30 Ibid., 141.

31 Oliver Stone, director, *Wall Street* (Twentieth Century Fox, December 12, 1987).

32 Kleinknecht, 141–144.

33 Johnson, 177–178.

34 Robin W. Winks, *Laurance S. Rockefeller: Catalyst for Conservation* (Washington, DC: Island Press, 1997), 87–88.

35 Edward Roby, "The [Carter] Administration Responded Thursday to Reagan's Campaign Jabs," October 9, 1980, UPI Archives, www.upi.com/Archives/

1980/10/09/The-administration-responded-Thursday-to-Ronald-Reagans-campaign-jabs/6513339912000; on Japan and Germany, see Aleh Cherp et al., "Comparing Electricity Transitions: A Historical Analysis of Nuclear, Wind and Solar in Germany and Japan," *Energy Policy* 101 (February 2017), 612–628, www.sciencedirect.com/science/article/pii/S030142151630595X, retrieved July 3, 2019.

36 Quoted in Michael Schaller, *Right Turn: American Life in the Reagan–Bush Era, 1980–1992* (New York: Oxford University Press, 2007), 128–129.

37 Raymond Wheeler, "Strike and Counterstroke," in Ed Marston, ed., *Reopening the Western Frontier: Selections from High Country News* (Washington, DC: Island Press, 1989), 142–146. This observation is based also on the author's experience as an organizer for Wyoming's Powder River Basin Resource Council in 1985.

38 "Burford Resigns from EPA Post Under Fire," *Congressional Quarterly* (CQ Almanac, 1983), https://library.cqpress.com/cqalmanac/document.php?id=cqal83-1199176, retrieved July 3, 2019.

39 Nathaniel Rich, *Losing Earth: A Recent Earth* (New York: Farrar, Straus and Giroux, 2019), 114.

40 Quoted in John Light, "How Media Consolidation Threatens Democracy: 857 Channels (and Nothing on)," Moyers on Democracy, May 12, 2017, https://billmoyers.com/story/media-consolidation-should-anyone-care/, retrieved May 27, 2020.

41 Ibid., 141.

42 *Red Lion Broadcasting Co. v. FCC, 1969*, quoted in Steve Rendall, "The Fairness Doctrine: How We Lost It, and Why We Need it Back," Fairness in Accuracy and Reporting (FAIR), January 1, 2005, https://fair.org/extra/the-fairness-doctrine/, retrieved July 2, 2019.

43 Tom Wolfe, *Bonfire of the Vanities* (New York: Farrar, Strauss and Giroux, 1987), 77; and Bill Moyers, "Tom Wolfe: New York City and *Bonfire of the Vanities*," October 27, 1988, https://billmoyers.com/content/tom-wolfe/, retrieved July 4, 2019.

44 Robert Putnam, *Bowling Alone: The Collapse and Revival of American Community* (New York: Simon and Schuster, 2000).

45 Consumer debt, in fact, exploded during the decade, from $302 to $671 billion.

46 Sonia Maasik and Jack Solomon, *Signs of Life: Readings on Popular Culture for Writers*, 3rd ed. (New York: Bedford St. Martin's, 2000), 737–739; Susan Willis, "Disney World: Public Use/Private Space," in Maasik and Solomon, 744–756; and James Howard Kunstler, *The Geography of Nowhere: The Rise and Decline of America's Man-Made Landscape* (New York: Touchstone, Simon and Schuster, 1993), 220–221, 226.

47 This discussion leans on the analysis of Susan Douglas, *Where the Girls Are: Growing Up Female with the Mass Media* (New York: Random House, Three Rivers Press, 1994), 291–292.

48 Ibid., 246.

49 Susan Faludi, *Backlash: The Undeclared War Against American Women* (New York: Crown Publishing, 1991), see especially Chapters 1 and 9.

50 Adrian Lyne, quoted in Faludi, 121.

51 Ibid., 112.

52 Vice-Presidential Debate, Philadelphia, PA: League of Women Voters, October 11, 1984, https://awpc.cattcenter.iastate.edu/2017/03/09/1984-vice-presidential-debate-oct-11-1984, retrieved July 9, 2019.

53 Daniel J. Boorstin, *The Image: A Guide to Pseudo-Events in America* (New York: Macmillan, 1987; first published 1961), 57.

54 Quoted in Neal Gabler, *Life, The Movie: How Entertainment Conquered Reality* (New York: Alfred A. Knopf, 1998), 166–167.

55 Trump on Central Park Five, *CNN*, May 17, 1989, www.cnn.com/videos/politics/2019/06/06/trump-on-the-central-park-five-orig-js.cnn, retrieved June 23, 2020.

56 Mariel Loveland, "Trump's Dad was so Racist Woody Guthrie Wrote a Song About It," *Medium*, March 27, 2018, https://medium.com/@editors_91459/trumps-dad-was-so-racist-woody-guthrie-wrote-a-song-about-it-deea588fa11a, retrieved August 12, 2019.

57 David W. Dunlap, "1973: Meet Donald Trump (Looking Back)," referencing an archived story of October 16, 1973, www.nytimes.com/times-insider/2015/07/30/1973-meet-donald-trump/?smid=tw-share&_r=0&module=inline, retrieved August 12, 2019.

58 See Michael D'Antonio, *The Truth About Trump* (New York: St. Martin's Press, 2016); and Tim O'Brien, *The Art of Being the Donald* (New York: Warner Books, 2005).

59 Russ Buettner and Susanne Craig, "Decade in the Red: Trump Tax Figures Show $1 Billion in Business Losses," *New York Times*, May 8, 2019, www.nytimes.com/interactive/2019/05/07/us/politics/donald-trump-taxes.html?smtyp=cur&smid=tw-nytimes, retrieved May 27, 2020.

60 Donald J. Trump, *The Art of the Deal* (New York: Ballantine, 2015 reprint from 1986), 58; and *Frontline*, Interview with Tony Schwartz (Public Broadcasting System, n.d.), www.pbs.org/wgbh/frontline/interview/tony-schwartz, retrieved July 11, 2019.

61 Gabler, 157.

62 Ronald Reagan, Inaugural Address, January 20, 1981, www.reaganlibrary.gov/research/speeches/inaugural-address-january-20-1981, retrieved July 11, 2019.

63 "Transcript of the President's Commencement Address at U.S. Military Academy," reprinted in *New York Times*, May 28, 1981, www.nytimes.com/1981/05/28/us/transcript-of-the-president-s-commencement-address-at-us-military-academy.html, retrieved July 12, 2019.

64 James Carroll, *House of War: The Pentagon and the Disastrous Rise of American Power* (New York: Houghton Mifflin, 2006), 371–384.

65 Lawrence S. Wittner, "Did Reagan's Military Build-Up Really Lead to Victory in the Cold War," History News Network, n.d., https://historynewsnetwork.org/article/2732, retrieved July 12, 2019.

66 Carroll, 383; Ronald E. Powaski, *Return to Armageddon: The United States and the Nuclear Arms Race, 1981–1999* (New York: Oxford University Press, 2000), 86.

67 Raymond L. Garthoff, *The Great Transition: American-Soviet Relations and the End of the Cold War* (Washington, DC: Brookings Institution Press, 1994), 36–38.

68 Quoted in Dee Garrison, *Bracing for Armageddon: Why Civil Defense Never Worked* (New York: Oxford University Press, 2006), 168; from Robert Scheer, *With Enough Shovels: Reagan, Bush, and Nuclear War* (New York: Random House, 1982), 78.

69 Ronald Reagan, Speech to the National Association of Evangelicals, March 8, 1983, https://voicesofdemocracy.umd.edu/reagan-evil-empire-speech-text, retrieved July 12, 2019.

70 "Transcript of President Reagan's Address," *New York Times*, September 6, 1983, www.nytimes.com/1983/09/06/world/transcript-of-president-reagan-s-address-on-downing-of-korean-airliner.html, retrieved May 29, 2020.

71 Robert E. Hamilton, "ABLE ARCHER at 35: Lessons of the 1983 War Scare," December 3, 2018, Foreign Policy Institute, www.fpri.org/article/2018/12/able-archer-at-35-lessons-of-the-1983-war-scare/, retrieved May 29, 2020.

72 "Reagan 'Jokes' About Bombing Soviet Union, August 11, 1984," *Politico*, August 11, 2017, www.politico.com/story/2017/08/11/this-day-in-politics-aug-11-1984-241413, retrieved May 29, 2020.

73 Andrew Lanham, "Lessons From the Nuclear Freeze," *Boston Review* (March 14, 2017), http://bostonreview.net/politics/andrew-lanham-lessons-nuclear-freeze; Lawrence S. Wittner, "The Nuclear Freeze and Its Impact," Arms Control Association, n.d., www.armscontrol.org/act/2010_12/LookingBack#3, retrieved December 30, 2019; and Carroll, 385–390.

74 Jacob Weisberg, "Ronald Reagan's Disarmament Dream," *The Atlantic*, January 1, 2016, www.theatlantic.com/politics/archive/2016/01/ronald-reagans-disarmament-dream/422244, retrieved July 13, 2019.

75 Carroll, 413–414.

76 Richard J. Barnet, *The Rocket's Red Glare: War, Politics, and the American Presidency* (New York: Simon and Schuster, 1990), 376–385.

77 Juan Blanco Prada, "Reagan's Legacy in Latin America Marked by Failure, Obsession," *The Progressive*, June 16, 2004, https://progressive.org/op-eds/reagan-s-legacy-latin-america-marked-obsession-failure, retrieved July 13, 2019.

78 Raymond Bonner, "Time for a US Apology to El Salvador," *The Nation*, April 15, 2016, www.thenation.com/article/time-for-a-us-apology-to-el-salvador, retrieved July 13, 2019.

79 Neither this depravity nor multiple convictions in the Iran–Contra scandal kept Abrams from being rewarded with positions in subsequent Republican administrations.

80 Branko Marcetic, "The Tragic Life of the War Criminal Elliott Abrams," *Jacobin*, February 16, 2019, www.jacobinmag.com/2019/02/the-tragic-life-of-the-war-criminal-elliott-abrams, retrieved July 13, 2019.

81 Ronald Reagan, March 1983, quoted by Elaine Chen, producer, T. J. Raphael, ed., "How Justice for Slain Americans Took a Back Seat to Cold War Politics," Public Radio International, "The Takeaway," November 11, 2014, www.pri.org/stories/2014-11-11/how-justice-slain-americans-took-backseat-cold-war-politics, retrieved July 13, 2019.

82 Carroll, 402; and Susan Gzesh, "Central Americans and Asylum Policy in the Reagan Era," Migration Policy Institute, April 1, 2006, www.migrationpolicy.org/article/central-americans-and-asylum-policy-reagan-era, retrieved July 13, 2019.

83 "Ex-CIA Analyst Disputes U.S. Aides on Nicaragua," *Washington Post*, June 13, 1984.

84 Gary Marx, "Contra Chiefs' Dueling Peace Plans Put Rebel Chiefs in Limbo," *Orlando Sentinel*, September 6, 1987, www.sun-sentinel.com/news/fl-xpm-1987-09-06-8703120376-story.html, retrieved July 17, 2020.

85 Reed Brody, *Contra Terror in Nicaragua, Report of a Fact-finding Mission: September 1984-January 1985* (Boston: South End Press Collective, 1985), 10.

86 Barnet, 385.

87 John A. Farrell, *Tip O'Neil and the Democratic Century* (New York: Little Brown, 2002), 620.

88 Gerald M. Boyd, "Reagan Terms Rebels Moral Equal of Founding Fathers," *New York Times*, March 2, 1985, www.nytimes.com/1985/03/02/world/reagan-terms-nicaraguan-rebels-moral-equal-of-founding-fathers.html, retrieved July 13, 2019; and Lou Cannon, *President Reagan: The Role of a Lifetime* (New York: Public Affairs, 1991, 2000), 381.

89 Carroll, 402; and Judith McDaniel, "The Sanctuary Movement, Then and Now," *Religion and Politics*, January 21, 2017, https://religionandpolitics.org/2017/02/21/the-sanctuary-movement-then-and-now/, retrieved July 14, 2019.

90 Nick Wing, "Dick Cheney Didn't Regret His Vote Against Freeing Nelson Mandela, Maintained He Was a Terrorist," *HuffPost*, December 5, 2013, www.huffpost.com/entry/dick-cheney-nelson-mandela-terrorist_n_4394071, retrieved June 9, 2020.

91 Rick Ungar, "When Conservatives Branded Nelson Mandela a Terrorist," *Forbes*, December 6, 2013, www.forbes.com/sites/rickungar/2013/12/06/when-conservatives-branded-nelson-mandela-a-terrorist/#73479b53474d, retrieved July 14, 2019.

92 Patrick J. Buchanan, "Homosexuals and Retribution," *New York Post*, May 24, 1983, quoted in Kenneth J. Doka, *AIDS, Fear and Society: Challenging the Dreaded Disease* (New York: Taylor and Francis, 1997), 64; Christopher Reed, "Reverend Jerry Falwell," *The Guardian*, May 17, 2007, www.theguardian.com/media/2007/may/17/

broadcasting.guardianobituaries, retrieved July 14, 2019; and Senator Jesse Helms, "Remarks on Amendment No. 956, October 14, 1987, in *Congressional Record* 133, part 20: 27752–27754.

93 Matthew Jacobs, "*5B* Goes Inside the First Hospital Ward That Treated AIDS Patients with Dignity," *HuffPost*, June 15, 2019, www.huffpost.com/entry/5b-aids-documentary-dan-krauss_n_5d024856e4b0985c4198e844, retrieved July 14, 2019.

94 Nurith Aizenman, "How to Demand a Medical Breakthrough: Lessons from the AIDS Fight," February 9, 2019, National Public Radio "Shots", www.npr.org/sections/health-shots/2019/02/09/689924838/how-to-demand-a-medical-breakthrough-lessons-from-the-aids-fight; and Peter Staley, "In Memory of Jesse Helms and the Condom on His House," July 8, 2008, www.poz.com/blog/in-memory-of-je, retrieved July 14, 2019.

95 Matt Schudel, "Larry Kramer, Writer Who Sounded Alarm on AIDS, Dies at 84," *Washington Post*, May 27, 2020, www.washingtonpost.com/local/obituaries/larry-kramer-writer-who-sounded-alarm-on-aids-dies-at-84/2020/05/27/2afd55ce-a031-11ea-81bb-c2f70f01034b_story.html; and Donald G. McNeil, Jr., "'We Loved Each Other': Fauci Recalls Larry Kramer, Friend and Nemesis," *New York Times*, May 27, 2020, www.nytimes.com/2020/05/27/health/larry-kramer-anthony-fauci.html, retrieved May 31, 2020.

96 "The AIDS Memorial Quilt", www.aidsquilt.org/about/the-aids-memorial-quilt, retrieved July 14, 2019.

97 Greg Grandin, *The End of the Myth: From the Frontier to the Border Wal in the Mind of America* (New York: Metropolitan Books, 2019), 266–230.

98 Kathleen Belew, *Bring the War Home: The White Power Movement and Paramilitary America* (Cambridge, MA: Harvard University Press, 2018), 24, 78–80, 92–100.

99 Transcript of Ronald Reagan's Farewell Address to the American People, *New York Times*, January 12, 1989, www.nytimes.com/1989/01/12/news/transcript-of-reagan-s-farewell-address-to-american-people.html, retrieved July 14, 2019.

Further Reading

Bartlett, Donald L., and James, B. Steele. *America: What Went Wrong*. Kansas City, KS: Andrews and McMeel, Universal Press Syndicate, 1992.

Brody, Reed. *Contra Terror in Nicaragua, Report of a Fact-finding Mission: September 1984–January 1985*. Boston, MA: South End Press Collective, 1985.

Cannon, Lou. *President Reagan: The Role of a Lifetime*. New York: Public Affairs, 1991, 2000.

Faludi, Susan. *Backlash: The Undeclared War Against American Women*. New York: Crown Publishing, 1991.

Fitzgerald, Frances. *Way Out There In the Blue: Reagan, Star Wars, and the End of the Cold War*. New York: Simon and Schuster, 2000.

Fitzgerald, Frances. *The Evangelicals: The Struggle to Shape America*. New York: Simon and Schuster, 2017.

Gabler, Neal. *Life, The Movie: How Entertainment Conquered Reality*. New York: Alfred A. Knopf, 1998.

Garrison, Dee. *Bracing for Armageddon: Why Civil Defense Never Worked*. New York: Oxford University Press, 2006.

Garthoff, Raymond L. *The Great Transition: American-Soviet Relations and the End of the Cold War*. Washington, DC: Brookings Institution Press, 1994.

Johnson, Haynes. *Sleepwalking Through History: America in the Reagan Years*. New York: Anchor Doubleday, 1991.

Kleinknecht, William. *The Man Who Sold the World: Ronald Reagan and the Betrayal of Main Street America*. New York: Perseus, 2009.

Lucks, Daniel S. *Reconsidering Reagan: Racism, Republicans, and the Road to Trump*. Boston, MA: Beacon Press, 2021.

Mattson, Kevin. *We're Not Here to Entertain: Punk Rock, Ronald Reagan, and the Real Culture War of the 1980s*. New York: Oxford University Press, 2020.

McMartin, Joseph A. *Collision Course: Ronald Reagan, the Air Traffic Controllers, and the Strike that Changed America*. New York: Oxford University Press, 2011.

Phillips, Kevin. *The Politics of Rich and Poor: Wealth and the American Electorate in the Reagan Aftermath*. New York: Random House, 1990.

Phillips-Fein, Kim. *Invisible Hands: The Businessmen's Crusade Against the New Deal* New York: W. W. Norton and Company, 2009.

Putnam, Robert. *Bowling Alone: The Collapse and Revival of American Community*. New York: Simon and Schuster, 2000.

Rasmus, Jack. *The Scourge of Neoliberalism from Reagan to Trump*. Atlanta, GA: Clarity Press, 2020.

Rich, Nathaniel. *Losing Earth: A Recent Earth*. New York: Farrar, Straus, and Giroux, 2019.

Roth, Bbenita. *The Life and Death of ACT UP/LA: Anti-AIDS Activism in Los Angeles from the 1980s to the 2000s*. New York: Cambridge University Press, 2017.

Schaller, Michael. *Reckoning with Reagan: America and Its President in the 1980s*. New York: Oxford University Press, 1992.

Scheer, Robert. *With Enough Shovels: Reagan, Bush, and Nuclear War*. New York: Random House, 1982.

Schulman, Sarah. *Let the Record Show: A Political History of ACT UP New York, 1987–1993*. New York: Farrar, Straus, and Giroux, 2021.

12 The End of Nothing

History Lurches On

> Wherever the people are well-informed, they can be trusted with their own government.
>
> —Thomas Jefferson[1]

In the summer of 1989, Francis Fukuyama, deputy director of policy planning in George H. W. Bush's State Department, published an essay in *The National Interest* entitled, "The End of History?" Fukuyama argued that the unfolding implosion of the communist Soviet Union and its Eastern European bloc was delivering the conclusive turning point in modern world history:

> What we are witnessing is not just the end of the cold war, or a passing of a particular period of postwar history, but the end of history as such: that is, the end point of mankind's ideological evolution and the universalisation of western liberal democracy as the final form of human government.[2]

Fukuyama's triumphalist declaration of democracy's victory over communism, developed further in a 1992 book, *The End of History and the Last Man*, made him a public intellectual of some influence. Yet as critics pointed out, Fukuyama's overweening case for liberal capitalism's victory avoided entirely that summer's bloody crushing of democratic hopes in China's Tiananmen Square, as well as the yawning economic chasm between rich and poor. "The class issue," he concluded, "has actually been successfully resolved in the west ... the egalitarianism of modern America represents the essential achievement of the classless society envisioned by Marx."[3] Such near-sighted hubris belied the widening wealth gap in the United States, and between the affluent western industrialized world and much of the rest of the globe.

Still, Fukuyama's reading of the historic moment reverberated when the Berlin Wall came down that November, the sanguine outlook mirroring the national mood of the world's lone superpower. Indeed, the ideological conceit that characterized *The End of History* also defined the muscular neoconservativism Fukuyama had helped to cultivate as a member of the Reagan administration—a doctrine that would now shape American foreign policy.[4] It did so even as the winning atmosphere of 1989–1991 proved fleeting, the reassurance of

DOI: 10.4324/9781003160595-12

unifying national purpose, illusory. For even as Americans at home indulged in the new technologies that poured forth from the era's "dot.com boom"—the digital embodiment of liberal democratic capitalism's victory—other developments were sowing seeds of deepening division, insidiously undermining both civic faith and the informed citizenry that Thomas Jefferson knew was essential to democracy. The deregulated media environment bequeathed by Ronald Reagan would foment greater volumes of both information and ignorance, a fact made tragically clear on what became the existential crisis of the next century, one to shrink the Cold War's significance.

With ironic symmetry, in the same year Fukuyama declared with premature finality the demise of history, Bill McKibben published *The End of Nature*—the first general examination of the civilization-threatening menace of global warming. *The End of Nature* arrived just after the deadly hot summer of 1988 and the dramatic testimony on Capitol Hill of NASA climate expert James Hansen, a moment that produced substantive, bipartisan proposals to confront the threat. Throughout the 1990s, however, scientific fact would be overwhelmed by rising seas of disinformation and deception paid for by multinational fossil fuel companies. Parroted by the corporate media, global warming "skepticism" took hold, misleading the public and sabotaging the last genuine opportunity to tackle climate change for a generation.[5] Alas, McKibben's empirically based prophecy proved far more accurate than Fukuyama's. Moreover, before a new century dawned, prolonged drought and other impacts of climate change exacerbated a global refugee crisis, a preview of more social chaos and disruption ahead. The end of the natural world as we knew it[6] would further destabilize the liberal democratic order Fukuyama had declared all too soon.

"Kinder and Gentler"

In his speech accepting the Republican nomination for president in 1988, George Herbert Walker Bush called for a "kinder and gentler nation." Than what? asked Reagan disciples. The Republican Party of the New Right had long been suspicious of Bush, a well-bred New England-born-Texas oilman who began his political life as a moderate Republican in a party then full of them. Central to the bargain that earned Bush the vice presidency was abandoning the E.R.A. and reproductive rights for women. Still, the former Texas congressman and CIA director was no rightwing ideologue. When he died in 2018, his presidency would be viewed by many observers as one of the last moments in modern American history of civility and genuine bipartisan cooperation. It *was* that, and yet the record of political comity is more complicated, beginning with the 1988 campaign. Bush's opponent, Mike Dukakis, a decent man and effective governor of Massachusetts, proved a wooden technocrat on the stump who made the uncharismatic Bush look downright charming. Still, after 8 years of Republican policies, voters seemed ready for a change. That was evident early in the year when civil rights leader Reverend Jesse Jackson galvanized a broad, multiracial coalition of progressive activists around a strong run for the

Democratic nomination. Urging liberals to "Keep Hope Alive!" Jackson helped make Dukakis a clearer alternative to more trickle-down economics, and by mid-summer the Democratic nominee enjoyed a 17-point polling advantage.

The turning point came in September with the "Willie Horton" TV ads produced by the Bush team revealing the repellent story of William Horton. An African American inmate serving time in the mid-1970s for murder, Horton was released from a Massachusetts prison on the same kind of highly effective weekend furlough afforded to prisoners in many states. Failing to return to prison, Horton stabbed a man and raped his wife in their Maryland home. Raised in the deep South, Bush's campaign manager Lee Atwater knew what he had. "By the time we're finished, [voters will] wonder whether Willie Horton is Dukakis's running mate."[7] Produced by a Bush political action committee, the first ad featured grainy black-and-white shots of "Willie," as the words "kidnapping," "raping," and "weekend pass" flashed on screen and the narrator reminded voters of Bush's support for the death penalty, intoning darkly, "Weekend Prison Passes: Dukakis on Crime." The Bush campaign denied involvement, but then produced their own Horton spots cynically tapping racial fears.[8] Bush assumed a lead in the polls he never relinquished.

The Willie Horton episode kicked open a door of racial fearmongering in modern politics, for which Atwater later apologized on his deathbed. The saturated television coverage reinforced a familiar racial stereotype—as Horton summarized, "big, ugly, dumb, violent, black"—that was further ingrained on local news channels around the nation courtesy of a soaring black prison population. Beginning in the late 1980s African American males, facing gross social inequities and a racist criminal justice system, were incarcerated at rates between five and ten times that of whites. Americans in 1988 had no idea who William Horton was, nor would most have cared what circumstances led him down the road to prison, nor that he was a highly intelligent man who admitted he would have been terrified by the ads himself.[9]

Once in office, Bush's record on race continued years of inconsistency. Running for the senate in 1964, he opposed the Civil Rights Act, then four years later as congressman voted for the Fair Housing Act. President Bush would sign the Civil Right Act of 1991 after having vetoed a more comprehensive measure. That same year, Bush eloquently denounced former Klan Wizard David Duke's Republican candidacy for governor of Louisiana—itself a reflection of how some extremists were seeing in the Republican Party.[10] The Duke rebuke came months after he nominated Clarence Thomas to take the U.S. Supreme Court seat of Thurgood Marshall, the first black justice in the court's history—revered for his socially expansive interpretation of the constitution. Marshall's ideological opposite, Thomas had used his position as chair of Reagan's Equal Employment Opportunity Commission (EEOC) to oppose affirmative action and generally curb progress on confronting racial discrimination. Nevertheless, the Senate Judiciary Committee, chaired by Democrat Joe Biden, was poised to send the nomination on to the Senate for likely confirmation. Then came allegations of sexual harassment against Thomas from law professor

Anita Hill, a former EEOC subordinate. When Hill agreed to testify publicly, Biden postponed the vote, while working behind the scenes to accommodate his Republican colleagues "who were out to disembowel Hill," in the words of one committee staffer. In dramatic televised testimony, Hill charged that Thomas had boasted of "his sexual prowess" and "pornographic materials depicting individuals with large penises or large breasts, involved in various sex acts."[11] Two EEOC staffers corroborated Hill's testimony, but Biden left their accounts for the written record. Speaking first and last, Thomas angrily damned the spectacle as a "high-tech lynching."

Having lost a fight four years earlier over controversial Reagan nominee Robert Bork, Republicans "came with a purpose ... to destroy Anita Hill," recalled Biden staffer Cynthia Hogan. Arlen Specter suggested that Hill had perjured herself. Alabama's Howell Heflin drawled, "Ahr you a scorned wohh-man? Do you have a militant att-i-tude relative to the area of civil riights?" Smugly preening Oren Hatch of Utah alleged that Hill had drawn some of her accusations from *The Exorcist*, to which Hill was never given a chance to respond. "What happened is we got really politically outplayed," said Hogan.[12] Confirmed in the closest vote for a high court nominee in a century, Thomas would anchor the court's rightward lurch. The odious performance of the all-white male Judiciary Committee came at a time when there were two women in the entire senate. The spectacle incensed women around the country and sparked the first real discussion on sexual harassment in the workplace. It also motivated millions of voters the following year to help elect four new women to the senate— pathetically enough, sufficient for the media to label 1992 "The Year of the Woman."

One of the signature achievements of the Bush administration, the Americans with Disabilities Act (ADA) resulted from decades of lobbying and protest by the nation's disability community. The disability rights movement gained attention after the Vietnam War, as tens of thousands of physically disabled veterans faced severe readjustment challenges. One pivotal episode came in 1977 when Secretary of Health, Education and Welfare (HEW) Joseph Califano balked at adopting Section 504 regulations to ADA's antecedent, the 1973 Rehabilitation Act, that would require schools, universities and hospitals to grant accessibility rights to 28 million disabled Americans. In response to the stonewalling, the American Coalition of Citizens with Disabilities (ACCD), waged a sustained direct-action campaign. Activists sat in and occupied HEW offices around the country, including the 26-day "504 Sit-in" in San Francisco, the longest occupation of a federal building in history. The action won broad support, from labor unions and the Salvation Army to the Black Panther Party. Amid the occupation, activists flew to Washington to testify in support of Section 504 regulations. Within days, Califano relented and they were adopted.[13]

The struggle was hardly over. Early in the Reagan presidency, the Task Force for Regulatory Relief, led by Vice President Bush, took dead aim at the economic burdens of Section 504 claimed by the business community. When disability advocates rose up again, the Reagan administration was forced to yield.

In March 1990, with the ADA facing opposition in the Senate, dozens of activists crawled up the steps of the U.S. Capitol to dramatize the need for the law. President Bush indicated support and that summer signed the ADA, which "literally and figuratively opened countless doors" for one in four Americans, earning them civil rights protections in employment and other areas of public life.[14]

Los Angeles was a powder keg in the spring of 1992. The city had lost thousands of manufacturing jobs over the previous decade and a half. Unemployment among African and Latino Americans hovered between forty and fifty percent, with poverty rates near 30 percent. Compounding the economic challenges, race relations had improved only marginally since the 1965 Watts explosion, and in many respects had worsened with the arrival of Daryl Gates as police chief. In 1988, Operation Hammer, ostensibly a "sweep" of gang activity by the LAPD, resulted in the arrest of thousands, gang members and innocents both, as well as widespread property damage meant to terrorize whole communities.[15] In 1991–1992 when the merciless police beating of Rodney King was caught on videotape, replayed endlessly on television, and the nearly all-white jury in affluent Simi Valley acquitted the accused police officers, knowing observers of Los Angeles were less than shocked at what followed in the spring of 1992. Six days of rioting and looting left dozens dead, hundreds injured, 700 buildings burned to the ground, and one billion dollars in damage—some of it stretching thirty miles from its Southcentral LA epicenter. More than 16,000 were arrested in the worst civil unrest in U.S. history that was long in the making. As one participant put it: "My homies be beat like dogs by the police every day. This riot is all about the homeboys murdered by the police, about the little sister killed by the Koreans, about twenty-seven years of oppression. Rodney King just the trigger."[16]

President Bush toured the devastated city, met with residents, and pledged "an absolute responsibility to solve inner-city problems." Then in a nationally televised address, he appeared to dismiss those problems as an underlying cause of the riots. What happened in LA, declared Bush, was "the brutality of a mob, pure and simple."[17] Vice President Dan Quayle advised the city's (first African American) Mayor Tom Bradley to privatize LA's airport to raise funds to rebuild his city, while Bush offered to make LA a model city for "Weed and Seed"—a Justice Department anti-gang program dressed as economic and community development.[18]

Simultaneous to the events in LA, the country was crawling out from a recession triggered in large part by the weight of massive debt that left financial markets unstable and cash-starved. To the everlasting outrage of many in his party, in the summer of 1990 Bush cooperated with congressional Democrats and Republicans to negotiate a budget calling for tax increases. Whiting out his "read my lips" pledge of no new taxes from the 1988 Republican convention, Bush's action set the country on a path toward financial solvency, ultimately helping to free up venture capital for the digital tech boom. With that notable exception, Bush mostly remained a Reaganite—advancing deregulation and vetoing what would have been the first increase in the minimum wage in 12 years. In 1989, he abetted fossil fuel interests in allowing his chief of staff John

Sununu to sabotage U.S. support for what would have been a serious international agreement to address greenhouse gas emissions.[19] But the tax increase was
a Republican mortal sin that for the rising right flank of ideological purists
proved unforgivable. It exposed him as a faux adherent to the party's new dogma
being driven further right in the House of Representatives by insurgents like
Dick Armey and Newt Gingrich.

The tax increase prompted many who had voted for Bush to either stay home
in the 1992 presidential election, or pull the lever for Independent H. Ross
Perot. The eccentric Texas billionaire, who had built much of his Electronic Data
Systems fortune on government contracts, hollered against Washington, bad U.S.
trade deals, high taxes, and bloated deficits. Perot also trafficked in conspiracy
theories, including the falsity that Americans were still being held captive in
Vietnam. It was an altogether flaky anti-Washington celebrity candidacy of pet-
ulance that earned the votes of 19 percent of the electorate, presaging a successful run by another businessman 24 years later.

Republicans blamed Perot for Bill Clinton's victory that year, but nothing
could have saved George H. W. Bush—not successful military operations in
Panama and Iraq, nor his presiding over the victorious end of the Cold War.
Bush is rightly credited with signing with Mikhail Gorbachev in 1991 the first
START (Strategic Arms Reduction) Treaty, the most ambitious arms control
agreement in history that eliminated nearly 80 percent of all strategic nuclear
weapons then in existence. Yet his posture toward the Soviet leader and the dramatic events across Eastern Europe in the first year of his presidency—neither
gloating of Cold War victory, nor warming to Gorbachev's proposals for a stronger relationship—left the Soviet leader increasingly isolated, surrounded by anti-
west hardliners in the Kremlin. The White House was similarly populated with
ideologues like Defense Secretary Dick Cheney and policy deputy Paul
Wolfowitz who distrusted Gorbachev's every move. Even as Secretary of State
James Baker promised Gorbachev in early 1990 that in exchange for German
reunification NATO would not expand "one inch eastward," administration
officials were quietly moving toward extending membership in the alliance to
newly liberated Eastern European nations.[20] The result was a lost opportunity to
bolster whatever chance Gorbachev and moderates in the new government had
for building a more democratic Russia.

In the meantime, the Bush administration jettisoned two long-time allies—
Panama's General Manuel Noriega and Saddam Hussein in Iraq—with decisive
military actions that pronounced the U.S. as the lone superpower of, as the president declared, a "new world order."[21] Noriega and his drug-trafficking operations linked to Columbian cartels had proved useful to U.S. intelligence gathering
in Cuba and the ongoing conflict in Nicaragua. But by 1986, Noriega was
asserting a more independent foreign policy, including trying to broker a peace
to end the Contra War. Virtually overnight, Noriega went from reliable Cold
War ally to drug-dealing villain.[22] On December 20, 1989 Bush launched an
invasion of Panama that was cheered by Americans but produced a decidedly
different reaction in Moscow. While the U.S. invaded a sovereign nation and

overthrew its leader, there was Gorbachev renouncing the Brezhnev Doctrine's use of coercive military force in the Baltic States, allowing their independence and the continued dissolution of the Soviet Union—much to the embitterment of many Russian patriots and authoritarian revanchists like KGB officer Vladimir Putin. Increasingly under siege at home by 1990, Gorbachev put the contradiction pointedly to congressional leaders: "Why did you let your administration intervene in Panama if you love freedom so much?"[23]

Other incongruities prevailed in Iraq. Back in 1983, Reagan's Middle East envoy Donald Rumsfeld had flown to Baghdad and presented Saddam Hussein with a handwritten letter from the president. Reagan appealed for warmer relations with the dictator and offered U.S. assistance in interdicting the flow of arms to Iran against whom he was waging a brutal war. American generosity went much further. For the next seven years, the Reagan and Bush administrations orchestrated a subterranean network of U.S.-backed loans that allowed arms sales to Iraq—including chemical and biological weapons he would use against the Kurds at the end of the Iran-Iraq War. Intended to help ensure Iran was neutralized by war's end, U.S. support included components for Saddam's nuclear weapons program, as well as critical intelligence sharing and U.S. naval assistance as Iraq battled Iran in the Persian Gulf. The alliance continued right through the spring of 1990 as Saddam began threatening Kuwait with invasion.[24] Iraq had a long-simmering border dispute with Kuwait, which until 1961 had been an oil-rich Iraqi province providing the country with expansive port access. In the summer of 1990, Saddam's ministers understood from American officials that Iraq's goal of reattaching Kuwait was of no concern to the United States.[25] Until the invasion on August 2, 1990, when suddenly it was.

Saddam's invasion of Kuwait appeared to most Americans the "naked aggression" Bush declared it to be. The President and British Prime Minister Margaret Thatcher made reckless comparisons of Hussein to Adolf Hitler. A Madison Avenue public relations firm was engaged to market the war—efforts which included allegations of Iraqi soldiers taking babies from incubators in a Kuwaiti City hospital. Opponents saw it as a Persian Gulf oil grab. Among other antiwar exhortations, protest signs that fall read, "We Won't Die for the Price of Gas, Uncle Sam Go Kiss My Ass."[26] With the Cold War over, critics who had been calling for cuts in military spending and a "peace dividend" of renewed investment at home, saw in the war a well-timed effort to inject fresh life into the military industrial complex.[27] Operation Desert Shield, a UN-backed coalition effort, demanded the withdrawal of Iraqi forces from Kuwait and the defense of Saudi Arabia's territorial integrity.

In January 1991, the ultimatum was backed with military force in a six-week, made-for-CNN war, Operation Desert Storm. This would be no Vietnam. Restricted by the Pentagon from showing any of the 150 body bags returning to Dover Air Base, television cameras focused on high-tech weaponry leveling nighttime precision strikes on Iraqi forces with—so viewers were told—minimal civilian casualties. With the mission achieved, Bush declared, "by God, we've kicked the Vietnam Syndrome once and for all."[28] Respecting the UN resolutions, he withdrew soldiers from Baghdad and allowed Saddam to survive, despite objections of neoconservatives in the administration like Dick Cheney and Paul Wolfowitz. They, too, would live to fight another day. Together, Panama and Iraq served as a joint "Pentagon rescue operation" in the words of James Carroll, that helped revive a culture of militarism.[29]

"The Era of Big Government Is Over": The Neoliberalism of Bill Clinton

Bill Clinton's economic record contained something for everybody. He launched his presidency with an historic comprehensive tax increase that raised income and social security rates on high income earners and corporations, as well as a more regressive hike in the gasoline tax. Coming on the heels of the Bush tax hike, the package, together with Republican-driven spending cuts, put the nation on the road to fiscal solvency. By 1996 the federal treasury was running surpluses that were expected to continue well into the new century.[30] With a record 23 million new jobs, Clinton presided over falling rates of unemployment and poverty, ultimately reaching their lowest point since the early 1970s. Falling energy prices kept inflation in check. Outside of the black community, home ownership reached historic highs. The inclusion of the earned income tax credit helped lift incomes for the poor for the first time in nearly three decades, albeit modestly. Clinton economic policies were by no means a disaster for wealthy Americans. The gap between rich and poor widened further, dramatically.[31] Perhaps most revealing was the ratio between average CEO pay of Fortune 500 companies and the average pay for their non-supervisory workers—a disparity that in 1965 was 20 to 1; by 1980 it was 32 to 1; and after the Reagan years it had nearly doubled to 60 to 1. As Bill Clinton left the White House, the figure had ballooned to a staggering 383 to 1.[32]

Clinton made no apologies for such figures. He had run as a "New Democrat," pledging a final break with populist economic policies of the old Democratic Party coalition. In supporting the North American Free Trade Agreement with Mexico and Canada, he took on labor. "Ending welfare as we know it" alienated progressive organizations across the country, as well as members of his own cabinet. Though he vetoed the Republicans' first two attempts at welfare reform for their "draconian, punitive" nature, he ultimately collaborated with Republicans in returning much of the authority for revamped food stamp and cash support programs for the working poor who now faced a host of new requirements and limitations.[33] The most consequential manifestation of Bill Clinton's neoliberal economic philosophy was the decision to fill top Treasury posts with Wall Street executives Robert Rubin and Lawrence Summers. Along with Alan Greenspan, reappointed as Federal Reserve Chairman, Rubin and Summers advanced with gusto the strategy of financial deregulation begun under Reagan. Predictably, the late nineties brought a reprise of the 1987 crash: Internet-driven tech stocks, many grossly inflated in value, went bust.

The congenial deregulatory climate of the nineties accelerated the pace of change in the financial markets. As Charles Ferguson has summarized, "with astonishing speed, the financial sector's major components—commercial banking, investment banking, trading, rating, securities insurance, derivatives—consolidated sharply into oligopolies of gigantic firms" like Lehman Brothers and Bear-Stearns.[34] With backing from the White House, Wall Street assembled the "securitization food chain" that facilitated the bundling and selling of mortgages to pension and hedge funds. It was a ticking time bomb that would detonate long after Clinton left office. Satanic financial instruments like "credit default swaps" and "over-the-counter" derivatives ("OTCs") came along, ostensibly creating greater efficiencies, but the end result was an impenetrable, interlocked, and dangerously unstable system that was, as the world would learn in the crash of 2008, "vulnerable to both fraud and systemic crises."[35]

The warm embrace of Wall Street deregulation by Clinton and "centrist" Democrats in congress was crowned by two final moves. First, the suspiciously titled Commodity Futures Modernization Act effectively *banned* the regulation of OTCs, even as it vaguely promised they would be bound by "safety and soundness standards." If Brooksley Born had had her way, OTCs would have faced rigorous oversight. Chair of the Commodity Futures Trading Commission, by 1998 Born had concluded that the highly leveraged dark OTC market was dangerous and proposed its regulation when the phone rang one morning in her office. It was Larry Summers, who "had thirteen bankers in his office who were furious, and demanding that Born desist." "All the blood rushed from her face," said deputy Michael Greenberger who walked in to hear Born describe Summers's "shouting," bullying phone call. Rubin later attacked her proposal publicly. As Born later recalled, "I was astonished a position would be taken that you shouldn't even ask questions about a market that was many, many trillions of dollars in notional value—and that none of us knew anything about."[36] The deregulatory climax arrived in 1999 with the Gramm–Leach–Bliley Act that gutted the 1933 Glass–Steagall Act, destroying the firewall that for more than 60 years protected commercial banks from the investment securities market—a world by then shot full of derivatives and the opaquely named, "collateralized debt obligations." The gate for Gramm–Leach–Bliley had swung open the year before with the unholy amalgamation of entities that became Citigroup, a monstrous financial services firm to which Bob Rubin was personally linked.[37] The cumulative impact made possible much of the wild west securities market that helped bring down the world economy in 2008.

The final year of the millennium was fateful in other ways, not least for the protests of late November at the meeting of the World Trade Organization (WTO) in Seattle. As with NAFTA, Bill Clinton had championed U.S. membership in the WTO. While Clinton saw lower trade barriers through the WTO as a mechanism for global economic growth that could raise living standards, opponents viewed it as an opaque, undemocratic vehicle for advancing corporate globalization, a threat to environmental protection, workers' wages, and the vitality of local economies. WTO ministers in Seattle were greeted by 75,000 protesters, among them environmentalists, union members, anarchists, Zapatistas from southern Mexico, and a French sheepherder who had torn the roof from a Parisian McDonalds with his tractor. *The Nation* called it a "phatasmagorical mix … husky, red-jacketed steelworkers marching alongside costumed sea turtle impersonators, environmentalists with miners, human rights activists with small family farmers."[38] Oracles of the mainstream media saw something very different: a "Noah's Ark of flat-earth advocates, protectionist trade unions, and Yuppies," sneered the *New York Times's* Thomas Friedman. "Militant dunces parading their ignorance," *The Economist* observed. For his part, Clinton offered a vague pledge to link free trade with labor rights and to "put a human face on the global economy."[39] However one viewed the merits of the protests, what happened in the streets was shocking, as demonstrators were met with a police barrage of tear gas, concussion grenades, and rubber-coated bullets. Scores were injured and 600 arrested in the "Battle of Seattle" that conjured up memories of the late sixties. Critics of neoliberal globalization would look back on it as an overture to looming intersectional struggles for a more just world.[40]

Clinton's declaration in his 1996 State of the Union speech that the "era of big government [was] over" came with the caveat of exorbitantly high levels of military spending. Depending on how one did the calculations, annual defense-related spending by the Pentagon and other federal agencies was more than at least the next dozen nations on earth, and in 1998 ten times that of Russia. "We won the Cold War, but we're still spending at Cold War levels," said Lawrence Korb, an assistant secretary of defense under Reagan said in 1998. "How the hell did that happen?"[41] Beyond the inherent voraciousness of the military industrial complex, how it happened is that neoconservatives assumed command of the national discourse on America's role in a post-Cold War world. Distilled to its essence, the argument was that not only had history not ended, the new history was more dangerous than ever! The geopolitical volatility of the early nineties was undeniable. Within weeks of Clinton's inauguration, New York City's World Trade Center was bombed by figures associated with Osama bin Laden's newly organized terror unit, al-Qaeda. Three dozen wars erupted by mid-decade. And NATO expansion demanded ever greater volumes of weaponry for U.S.-allied states across Eastern Europe and beyond.

Despite his pronouncements of a more humane globalization, Clinton pursued a vigorous agenda of intervention. Whatever the merits of each military engagement, politically speaking, a muscular exercise of U.S. military power helped to inoculate the former "draft dodger" from accusations that he was weak on defense—the fallacious Republican charge that Democrats had been fending off since Vietnam—and also to divert attention from the relentless investigations into his private conduct. No matter the crisis, and even when events on the ground frustrated U.S. intentions—Mogadishu, Haiti, Iraq, bin Laden training camps in the Sudan, the fracturing former Yugoslavia—the dangers of the U.S. *not* acting always outweighed the risks. When the U.S. failed *utterly* to act in the Rwanda genocide, that, too, supported arguments for robust superpowerism, if only in hindsight. In 1998, as debate ensued over Saddam Hussein's alleged weapons of mass destruction and the possibility of another invasion of Iraq, U.S. Secretary of State Madeline Albright made like it was 1947:

> But if we have to use force, it is because we are America; we are the indispensable nation. We stand tall and we see further than other countries into the future, and we see the danger here to all of us. I know that the American men and women in uniform are always prepared to sacrifice for freedom, democracy and the American way of life.[42]

The national egotism was echoed by generals and neocon pundits who after the first Gulf War occupied semi-permanent seats on cable news outlets.[43]

On the premise of stopping ethnic cleansing by Serbian forces against Kosovar residents, Clinton approved a U.S.-led NATO operation in 1999 that lasted 78 days: 2,300 missiles and 14,000 bombs dropped on nearly 1,000 targets across Serbia, killing more than 2,000 civilians and displacing a million people. Notwithstanding the widespread human rights crimes that transpired in Srebrenica and other parts of the region, critics saw the administration's argument that the Balkan Wars threatened a contagion of European instability if left unchecked as cover for a larger agenda. Beyond giving added purpose to the expansion of NATO, the U.S.-western role in the breakup of the former communist Yugoslavia seemed to some progressives a cynical exploitation of the crisis to impose neoliberal capitalist policies—what journalist and activist Naomi Klein later called the "Shock Doctrine" of "disaster capitalism."[44] Within a decade, Balkan states were forced to accept the loss of state-provided services and the privatization of large swaths of their economies by transnational corporations.[45] The war and its aftermath brought opportunity to American energy companies. Before the first bombs dropped on Kosovo, Brown and Root (a Texas-based Halliburton subsidiary) began construction of Camp Bondsteel, employing Kosovars at two dollars a day. The largest U.S. military base constructed from scratch anywhere in the world since Vietnam, Bondsteel was the jewel in a necklace of U.S. military installations safeguarding oil and gas pipelines that stretched to the Caspian Sea.[46]

Never disappearing from the national security agenda was Iraq. Not long after American forces withdrew in 1991, neocon experts on cable news brought a steady drumbeat of warnings of Saddam Hussein's clandestine program of "Weapons of Mass Destruction," a term which suddenly, ominously landed in the national discourse. Fears that the Iraqi dictator was harboring chemical and biological—and many alleged, nuclear—"WMD" filled the news cycles. Close observers of the U.S.–Iraqi relationship quipped, "we knew he had WMD because we had the receipts." Allegations came thick and fast that Saddam was refusing to comply with UN disarmament resolutions. For much of the decade, American and British pilots flew more than 250,000 bombing sorties over Iraq, policing "no-fly zones" in northern and southern Iraq. The two nations won UN support for the most punishing sanctions regime in history, costing hundreds of thousands of Iraqi lives, the majority children. In May 1996,

CBS's Lesley Stahl asked Secretary Albright whether the punitive measures against Saddam for his alleged deceit was worth a half-million Iraqi children. "I think this is a very hard choice, but the price, we think the price is worth it."[47]

And yet, "in Haiti, in Somalia, and elsewhere, Clinton and his advisers had the stomach only to be halfway imperialists," complained leading neoconservative Robert Kagan. "When the heat was on, they tended to look for the exits."[48] That charge applied particularly to the 1998 Iraq Liberation Act, which made it official U.S. policy to seek the removal of Saddam Hussein from power, signaling an unprecedented willingness on the part of the United States government to launch preemptive military action against a nation that had neither attacked nor threatened America. Clinton signed the law but rebuffed the pressure to authorize an invasion, much of it coming from the neoconservative Project for the New American Century. PNAC leaders, including Kagan, Don Rumsfeld, Dick Cheney, and Paul Wolfowitz, would have the chance soon enough to arrange the operation themselves.[49]

Culture Wars

Toward the end of the nineties, American Studies scholar Nicolaus Mills wrote of what he perceived as unhealthy patterns of "meanness" that had emerged in our national life: "More prisons. More police. Less welfare. Decaying public schools … [while a] fortress America with gated suburbs and guarded apartment houses and private schools and private security forces" grew indifferent, said Mills, to the society outside the gates. These trends were leading inexorably toward a "country without shared hopes and obligations." When older Americans went to see the 1996 film *Independence Day* and the theatre's audience broke out in applause during the scene of the White House's destruction, they knew it was a different country from that of their youth.[50] The actual Washington was engaged in its own kind of corrosive self-destruction, evidenced by back-to-back government shutdowns in 1995–1996.

Patterns of behavior in any given cultural moment are easy to exaggerate if one goes looking for them, yet Mills was on to something. There was the impetuous incivility of rush hour drivers and parents at little league games surrendering to fits of rage. In the august halls of Congress, Dick Armey, Republican Majority Leader of the House of Representatives, smeared the openly homosexual Democrat Barney Frank as "Barney Fag." There were more calculated, sinister indicators: CEOs downsizing workers or refusing them benefits in order to inflate shareholder earnings; white supremacists engaged in the worst spate of southern black church bombings in decades; self-appointed border protectors chasing down migrants they could never see as fellow Americans. Although much of the spite emanated from the right, other elements reflected a loss of basic human decency bemoaned by liberals and conservatives. On *The Jerry Springer* Show—the most prurient, privacy-shattering, "boundary-punching" of all the daytime trash "talk" shows—one could be entertained by the humiliating airing of "sexy secrets," or women physically ambushing one another on stage as the host incited "participation" from an over-heated studio audience.[51] Meanwhile, 250,000 pay-per-viewers tuned in to a blood-sport spectacle called "Ultimate Fighting Championships," a vicious form of martial arts that one critic called "human cockfighting."[52] The longer the odiousness went on, the more inconspicuous it became.

Precise discernment of the sea change remains elusive. Mills worked his way toward "a culture in which cruelty wins out over compassion and 'civic empathy.'"[53] To be sure, this was not some thorny strain of American individualism. Bred in part by growing economic insecurities, a fearful egoism laced with caustic resentment about "others" who were somehow given undue advantage emerged in American society. The bitterness was growing especially toxic among white men, many displaced by the forces of deindustrialization or white-collar downsizing in the early nineties. Expressions of the "angry white male" were everywhere—a strain of the zeitgeist captured in the 1992 film *Falling Down* starring Michael Douglas. The movie tracked Douglas's character, William Foster—an angry, divorced, very well-armed Everyman—on a day-long trek across Los Angeles to his daughter's birthday party. Laid off from a missile production plant, Foster is an embittered victim of the end of the Cold War, his anger righteous and dangerous. He sports an early 1960s style crew cut that evokes, as Douglas put it, "the feeling that he came from another time, or he wished or he hoped for another time when things made sense."[54] Wreaking violence against a Korean American grocery store owner, a Mexican American gang, and fast food workers, Foster is lost in an urban multicultural wilderness that neither he, nor many of his white male viewers, understands.[55]

Another sign of the leavening malice was the militia movement, a loose but lethal confederation of virulently anti-government extremists, hard-core anti-abortionists, end-time Christians, gun rights zealots, white supremacists, and neo-Nazis. Most militia enthusiasts had read or were influenced by *The Turner Diaries*, a 1978 novel outlining the apocalyptic steps toward a revolutionary, regenerative race war. In the early nineties, the movement drew strength from various corners, including Bush's "New World Order" declaration —taken by the far-right not for its rhetorical vision of U.S.-led neoliberal hegemony, but as a shadowy threat of "globalism" emanating from the UN, backed by the forces of "global [read: Jewish] finance" and technology. The 1993 Brady Handgun Violence Prevention Act—a modest gun control law—enraged Second Amendment crusaders. Militia recruits were especially incensed at the use of force by federal agents in the November 1992 standoff at Ruby Ridge, Idaho, in which the wife and son of white supremacist Randy Weaver were killed. Months later, a 51-day government siege of David Koresh's Branch Davidian paramilitary compound of cult extremists in Waco, Texas ended in an assault that left 76 martyred dead. Soon the militia movement claimed 50,000 members in 47 states. The Southern Poverty Law Center tracking the rise of hate groups reported that support for the overlapping "Patriot" movement was 100 times larger.[56]

The nightmarish consequences of such extremism were brought home horrifically at 9:02 am on April 19, 1995 when a massive truck bomb exploded at the Alfred P. Murrah Federal Building in Oklahoma City, killing 168 people and wounded 500. The largest act of domestic terror in U.S. history, the blast was orchestrated by Timothy McVeigh, a Gulf War veteran whose social circles included the Michigan Militia and the Klan. Militia leaders around the country, then and long afterward, denied any white power associations—as had McVeigh himself, despite ample evidence to the contrary—insisting they were simply Second Amendment-defending patriots standing against an oppressive federal government.[57] As domestic terror metastasized in the years ahead, Americans would grow accustomed to such disavowals from white supremacist extremists.

Tracing direct causation for the cancerous rage was at best problematic. That was especially so when disinformation and conspiracy-mongering on the far-right fringe began echoing everywhere in the Clinton era, from right wing blogs and chat rooms to Capitol Hill to evening news coverage. No one had a louder, more mendacious megaphone than the king of talk radio, Rush Limbaugh. With vituperative bombast Limbaugh assailed the White House relentlessly. He stoked conservatives' antipathy over Hillary Clinton's failed "government takeover" of health care, tormented the Clintons for what was little more than poor investments in the failed Whitewater real estate venture, and speculated recklessly about the possible "murder" of deputy White House Counsel Vince Foster, which had been thoroughly investigated by police and ruled a suicide. Once the Limbaugh hurricane was over the warm waters of white male grievance, it would not be contained. His roar took aim at environmental "extremists" like the Sierra Club, "feminazis," and "the sixties gang" generally for imposing radical "elitism" and the evils of "political correctness" on the nation's campuses. Among his faithful millions of listeners, Limbaugh could count truck drivers, members of congress, and two Supreme Court Justices. More than any other figure, Limbaugh is responsible for the take-no-prisoners attitude that took hold on the right in the nineties. "Leave some liberals alive," he told the 1994 winning class of House Republicans (who named him an honorary member of the caucus), specimens—he said, "so we can show our children what they were."[58] The higher his star rose, the less certain one could be that he was joking.

By their own ethically challenged behavior, Bill and Hillary Clinton gave Limbaugh and the "vast right-wing conspiracy"[59] long arrayed against them plenty to work with. Over the course of four years, independent counsel Ken Starr's Whitewater investigation metastasized into a sprawling inquisition of the president's sexual misdeeds with a White House intern, *lying* about his sexual misdeeds, and a host of other trumped-up allegations that had little bearing on either what actually happened or his performance as president.[60] The entire affair—Clinton's impeachment and acquittal, Hillary's attack on her husband's accusers, and the "Starr Report" with its gratuitous, lurid references to the president's sexual hijinks—further degraded public discourse and did little to elevate debate about the serious issue of sexual harassment.

Just in time for the Clinton scandals came Fox News. Fox was the creation of two men: Rupert Murdoch, whose News Corp was already driving the media in Great Britain in the direction of tabloid journalism; and Roger Ailes, the man who had remade the thoroughly unlikable Nixon in 1968, produced Reagan's mawkish "Morning in America" ad, and collaborated with Lee Atwater on the Willie Horton spots. "Reagan campaign manager Ed Rollins called Ailes "our Michelangelo." In the1970s, Ailes worked on billionaire Joe Coors's Television News Incorporated, a short-lived operation where Ailes devised the basic elements of a "fair and balanced" television propaganda machine presenting itself as a populist alternative to the supposed control of the media by elite liberals. The early nineties saw Ailes deepening the cultural waste pool, helping to launch *The Maury Povich Show*, a cornerstone of the era's "trash TV" landscape, and consulting for the tabloid program, *A Current Affair*. His serious work came on behalf of Big Tobacco, for whom he masterminded a covert ad campaign aimed at destroying the Clinton administration's failed attempt at health care. Like a fascist villain from a 1930s Capra film, Ailes orchestrated a sham campaign of opposition from a paid "grassroots," many of them R. J. Reynolds-trained employees. "Ordinary Americans" fearful of losing their coverage were bused to the White House to express outrage, while others called in to the late-night TV program of Ailes's friend and ally Rush Limbaugh.[61]

This was the fear-driven, scorched earth politics Ailes brought to Fox when he and Murdoch teamed up in 1996, and what made the network by far the most profitable arm of the Fox empire. Murdoch invested heavily and got Fox into 25 million homes before airing his first broadcast. He promised Ailes free reign—free to impose on his reporters and broadcasters a rigid adherence to rightwing ideology. The canard of "fair and balanced" journalism was belied from the start in Murdoch's stated intent to create a conservative cable news channel to counter left-center CNN. From the start, it was the network "that confirmed all your worst instincts—Fox News' fundamental business model is driving fear," said Blair Levin, then chief-of-staff at the Federal Communications Commission. "The genius was seeing that there's an attraction to fear-based, anger-based politics that has to do with class and race." Talking with Ailes, said one of his associates, was "like you're talking to someone who's been under a rock for a couple of decades." Ailes packed heat in his desk drawer, established a workplace of intimidation where sexual harassment was rampant, and buried his newsroom in a subterranean windowless bunker. A modern incarnation of what Richard Hofstadter long ago identified as "the paranoid style" in American politics, Ailes was perpetually armed for combat and took no prisoners.[62] "What's fun for Roger is the destruction," remembered Dan Cooper, one of Ailes's founding team.[63] The destruction aimed at all Fox deemed threatening: brown people sneaking across the border, black men in the cities, outspoken women, environmental extremists bent on forcing Americans into caves with CFL lightbulbs …

Ailes destroyed the competition. Whether Fox viewers knew what was happening in the world was another story. Fifteen years after its debut, studies consistently showed viewers of the Ailes-Murdoch fear machine were "significantly (12 to 31 points) more likely" to hold factually incorrect views on everything from the state of the economy to the citizenship status of the president of the

United States. Another study indicated that Americans who watched no news at all were better informed than Fox viewers.[64] The analyses came from universities, which in Foxworld rendered them inherently suspect.

Fox and Limbaugh contributed mightily to the highly effective campaign of ignorance and disinformation on climate science. Major oil corporations employed the same researchers and public relations firm used by Big Tobacco to confuse the public about the dangers of smoking to speciously cast doubt on a warming planet—the facts of which they knew from their own scientific studies as early as the 1950s. False statements uttered by CEOs of major oil companies were echoed on Fox, and often in the reputedly "liberal" media.[65] The growing international scientific consensus on global warming was depicted as either alarmist or emanating from well-funded researchers or "special interest" groups who had an "agenda" to terrify the public. Republicans and more than a few Democrats torpedoed the faint efforts of the Clinton–Gore administration to address the issue.[66]

Republican consultant Frank Luntz, a sort of linguistic Svengali, played an important role in selling to the public GOP positions that were unpopular on their face. It was Luntz who in 1994 successfully marketed Newt Gingrich's "Contract for America," helping Republicans seize control of the House of Representatives. The once-uncontestable estate tax on inherited wealth, supported by wealthy Americans from J.P. Morgan to Bill Gates and imposed on the wealthiest one-tenth of one percent of citizens, is the most progressive levee in the U.S. Tax code. Repackaged by Luntz, it became the unjust, loathsome "death tax." Capital gains cuts and other generous tax abatement measures for the very top transfigured into "tax relief," "restoring the American dream" that would fuel "job creation and wage enhancement." Oil and gas drilling in environmentally sensitive areas like the Arctic National Wildlife Refuge—itself now referred to everywhere in the media by the clinically abbreviated "ANW[A]R"—was now "energy exploration."[67] In 2002, Luntz urged the Bush White House to swap out the threatening-sounding "global warming" for the softer, focus group-tested "climate change."[68]

Finally, there was the conservative assault on "political correctness," a term that became an all-encompassing metonym for the evils associated with "leftist" social change activism, particularly on the nation's college campuses. Those who urged more sensitive language to reference minority groups or those with physical or mental disabilities were derided as "PC thought police" restricting free speech. Simultaneously, conservative custodians of American exceptionalism ranging from Gingrich and Limbaugh to Secretary of Education William Bennett and National Endowment for the Humanities head, Lynn Cheney, opened up a central front of the Republican culture wars: attacking the post-sixties generation of "revisionist" history that was migrating from scholarly works into the public realm. Targeted for special punishment were the *National Standards for United States History*, a comprehensive compendium of guidelines and voluntary lesson plans crafted by more than 6,000 teachers, parents, business leaders, and scholars from across the nation. But because the standards incorporated Harriet Tubman into the teaching of the Civil War, the struggle of the labor movement into the Gilded Age, the awakening women's movement as part of postwar America—in sum, because the standards attempted to make more complete the teaching of U.S. history with the stories of under-represented groups, systemic racism, and episodes of conflict—they were maligned for "pursuing a revisionist agenda." By proffering, as Cheney alleged, a "great hatred for traditional history," they were undermining love of country.[69] The whole "PC" enterprise of American academia, Rush growled, put forward a dark view of the nation's history:

> Our country is inherently evil. The whole idea of America is corrupt. The history of this nation is strewn with examples of oppression and genocide. The story of the United States is cultural imperialism—how a bunch of white men imposed their will and values on peaceful indigenous people, black slaves from Africa, and women.[70]

This gross misrepresentation is worth quoting only because it gained so much currency as the decade wore on. One of the first signs came in 1991 when the Smithsonian's National Museum of American Art opened its exhibition, "The West as America." The show presented the epic story of westward expansion that confronted Hollywood's myth-laden West. The exhibit offered a complex narrative told from many points of view and fraught with conflict, winners and losers, and long-term consequences. It was slammed by the *Wall Street Journal* as an "entirely hostile ideological assault on our nation's founding and history," by columnist Charles Krauthammer as "tendentious, dishonest, and finally, puerile." Republican Senators damned the Smithsonian itself for its America-hating "leftist slant."[71]

They were just getting started. When the proposed script for the Smithsonian's National Museum of Air and Space Museum (NASM) exhibit commemorating the fiftieth anniversary of the dropping of the atomic bomb and the end of World War II was made public, the institution met a battalion of hyperventilating self-appointed guardians of historical truth. The Smithsonian's script envisioned a comprehensive, contextually rich exhibit that told the complex story of Harry Truman's fateful decision. Although the exhibition was to include episodes of Japanese brutality as well, the final part of the exhibition would have raised questions about the military necessity of the bomb decision and graphically depicted victims in Hiroshima and Nagasaki. "Biased," "anti-American," came the cries—and these were liberal voices at the *Washington Post* and *Boston Globe*.[72] The Air Force Association, a powerful representative of the aerospace industry deeply invested in how American air power was depicted, spared nothing in leading the attack. In the end, Martin O. Harwitt, the NASM's director, was fired, and the exhibit shrunken down to the fuselage of the *Enola Gay* that delivered the first bomb and minimal text—what Air Force historian Richard Hallion called little more than a "beer can with a label."[73] As Harwit reflected, the entire affair was "a symbolic issue in a 'culture war'" spilling out of all the social, economic, and cultural changes that had been under way since the 1960s. "To a number of Americans," Harwit said:

> The very people responsible for the script were the people who were changing America. The bomb, representing the end of World War II and suggesting the height of American power was to be celebrated. It was, in this judgment, a crucial symbol of America's "good war," one fought justly for noble purposes at a time when America was united. Those who in any way questioned the bomb's use were, in this emotional framework, the enemies of America.[74]

At bottom, the *Enola Gay* episode was emblematic of a steadily encroaching, emotionally driven war on reason, expertise, and empirical truth in America. The implications of where that assault was taking the country were chilling.

Notes

1 Thomas Jefferson to Richard Price, January 8, 1789, www.loc.gov/exhibits/jefferson/60.html, retrieved May 1, 2021.
2 Francis Fukuyama, "The End of History?" *National Interest* 16 (1989), 3.
3 Ibid., 7.
4 Although Fukuyama had signed on to a 1998 letter urging Bill Clinton to force a regime change in Iraq, in 2003 he parted ways with neoconservatism over the invasion.
5 Nathaniel Rich, *Losing Earth: A Recent History* (New York: Farrar, Straus, and Giroux, 2019), Epilogue.
6 Paraphrasing "The End of the World as We Know It," a popular REM song from 1987.
7 Roger Simon, "How a Murderer and Rapist Became the Bush Campaign's Most Valuable Player," *Baltimore Sun*, November 11, 1990, www.baltimoresun.com/news/bs-xpm-1990-11-11-1990315149-story.html, retrieved July 16, 2019.
8 Tali Mendelberg, *The Race Card: Campaign Strategy, Implicit Messages, and the Norm of Equality* (Princeton, NJ: Princeton University Press, 2017), 138–142, 150–152.
9 Jeffrey M. Elliott, "The 'Willie' Horton Nobody Knows," *The Nation* 257, no. 6 (August 23, 1993), 201–202; and Nicole Puglise, "Black Americans Incarcerated Five Times More Than White People—Report," *The Guardian*, June 18, 2016, www.theguardian.com/us-news/2016/jun/18/mass-incarceration-black-americans-higher-rates-disparities-report, retrieved July 16, 2019.
10 Stephen Holmes, "When the Subject is Civil Rights, there are Two George Bushes," *New York Times*, June 9, 1991, www.nytimes.com/1991/06/09/weekinreview/the-nation-when-the-subject-is-civil-rights-there-are-two-george-bushes.html, retrieved July 16, 2019.
11 Julia Jacobs, "Anita Hill's Testimony and other Key Moments from the Clarence Thomas Hearings, *New York Times*, September 20, 2018, www.nytimes.com/2018/09/20/us/politics/anita-hill-testimony-clarence-thomas.html, retrieved July 16, 2019.
12 Jane Mayer, "What Joe Biden Hasn't Owned Up to About Anita Hill," *The New Yorker*, April 27, 2019, www.newyorker.com/news/news-desk/what-joe-biden-hasnt-owned-up-to-about-anita-hill, retrieved July 16, 2019; and Jane Mayer and Jill Abramson, *Strange Justice: The Selling of Clarence Thomas* (New York: Houghton Mifflin Harcourt, 1994).

13 Joseph D. Whitaker, "Handicapped Plan Protest at HEW Offices in 10 Cities," *Washington Post*, March 30, 1977, www.washingtonpost.com/archive/politics/1977/03/30/handicapped-plan-protest-at-hew-offices-in-10-cities/381a72f0-1b3b-4479-9236-0f3cc7be7151/?noredirect=on&utm_term=.dcf11e532776; and Kara Mannor, "The ADA is not Bush Sr's Legacy. It Belongs to Disability Activists," *Truthout*, December 11, 2018, retrieved July 17, 2019.

14 Robyn Powell, "Why I Struggle Memorializing George H.W. Bush as a Liberal Woman with a Disability," *HuffPost*, December 5, 2018, www.huffpost.com/entry/opinion-george-bush-ada-disabilities_n_5c081e43e4b069028dc6060b, retrieved July 17, 2019.

15 John L. Mitchell, "The Raid That Still haunts L.A.," *LA Times*, March 14, 2001, www.latimes.com/archives/la-xpm-2001-mar-14-mn-37553-story.html, retrieved May 2, 2021.

16 Max Felker-Kantor, "The 1992 Los Angeles Rebellion: No Justice, No Peace," *Origins*, May 2017 (Ohio State University, 2017), http://origins.osu.edu/milestones/may-2017-1992-los-angeles-rebellion-no-justice-no-peace, retrieved July 16, 2019.

17 Ibid.

18 Mike Davis, "Who Killed Los Angeles? A Political Autopsy" *New Left Review* (January/February 1993), https://newleftreview.org/issues/I197/articles/mike-davis-who-killed-los-angeles-a-political-autopsy, retrieved July 16, 2019.

19 Rich, 149–174.

20 Joshua R. Itkowitz Shifrinson, "Russia's Got a Point: The U.S. Broke a NATO Promise," *New York Times*, May 30, 2016, www.latimes.com/opinion/op-ed/la-oe-shifrinson-russia-us-nato-deal--20160530-snap-story.html, retrieved July 16, 2019.

21 President George H.W. Bush, "September 11, 1990: Address Before a Joint Session of Congress," https://millercenter.org/the-presidency/presidential-speeches/september-11-1990-address-joint-session-congress, retrieved July 18, 2019.

22 William Blum, *Killing Hope: U.S. Military and C.I.A. Interventions Since World War II* (Monroe, ME: Common Courage Press, 2004), 296, 298.

23 Michael Beschloss and Strobe Talbot, *At the Highest Levels: The Inside Story of the End of the Cold War* (New York: Open Road Integrated Media, 1994), 272.

24 Alan Friedman, *Spider's Web: The Secret History of How the White House Illegally Armed Iraq* (New York: Bantam, 1993), 28–29, 166–168; and Hodding Carter, transcript, "The Long Road to War," PBS, *Frontline*, March 17, 2003, www.pbs.org/wgbh/pages/frontline/shows/longroad/, retrieved July 18, 2019.

25 Friedman, 160–168.

26 Nathaniel J. Hiatt, "In the Shadow of Vietnam, Students Brought the Gulf War to Cam pus," *The Harvard Crimson*, May 24, 2016, quoting the *Crimson's* December 6, 1990 edition, www.thecrimson.com/article/2016/5/24/1991-reunion-gulf-war-on-campus/, retrieved July 18, 2019.

27 Carroll, 435–437.

28 Maureen Dowd, "After the War: White House Memo; War Introduces a Tougher Bush to Nation," *New York Times*, March 2, 1991, www.nytimes.com/1991/03/02/world/after-the-war-white-house-memo-war-introduces-a-tougher-bush-to-nation.html, retrieved July 19, 2019.

29 Carroll, 437.

30 Andrew Soergel, "Which Presidents Have Been Best for the U.S. Economy," *U.S. News and World Report*, October 28, 2015, citing reports from the U.S. Bureau of Labor Statistics, www.usnews.com/news/blogs/data-mine/2015/10/28/which-presidents-have-been-best-for-the-economy; and Kimberly Amadeo, "President Bill Clinton's Economic Policies," *The Balance*, May 30, 2019, www.thebalance.com/president-bill-clinton-s-economic-policies-3305559, retrieved July 18, 2019.

31 Edmund L. Andrews, "Economic Inequality Grew in the 90s Boom, Fed Report," *New York Times*, January 23, 2003, www.nytimes.com/2003/01/23/business/

economic-inequality-grew-in-90-s-boom-fed-reports.html, retrieved July 18, 2019; and Emmanuel Saez and Gabriel Zucman, "Wealth Inequality in the United States Since 1913: Evidence From Capitalized Income Tax Data," *Quarterly Journal of Economics* 131, no. 2 (2016), 519–578.

32   Alyssa Davis and Lawrence Mishel, "CEO Pay Continues to Rise and Typical Workers are Paid Less," Report of the *Economic Policy Institute*, June 12, 2014, www.epi.org/publication/ceo-pay-continues-to-rise, retrieved July 18, 2019.

33   Chris Bury, "Interview with Robert Reich," PBS, *Frontline*, September 2000, www.pbs.org/wgbh/pages/frontline/shows/clinton/interviews/reich.html, retrieved July 18, 2019.

34   Charles H. Ferguson, *Predator Nation: Corporate Criminals, Political Corruption, and the Hijacking of America* (New York: Crown Business, 2012), 36–40.

35   Ibid., 40.

36   Charles H. Ferguson, producer, *Inside Job* (Documentary, October 8, 2010); Michael Hirsh and National Journal, "The Case Against Larry Summers," *The Atlantic*, September 13, 2013, www.theatlantic.com/business/archive/2013/09/the-comprehensive-case-against-larry-summers/279651, retrieved July 18, 2019; and Ferguson, *Predator Nation*, 44–45.

37   Timothy Noah, "Robert Rubin's Free Ride," *Slate*, January 9, 2009, https://slate.com/news-and-politics/2009/01/robert-rubin-s-free-ride.html, retrieved May 3, 2021.

38   Robert L. Borosage, "The Battle in Seattle," *The Nation*, November 30, 1999, www.thenation.com/article/november-30-1999-world-trade-organization-meeting-in-seattle-disrupted-by-anti-globalization-protests, retrieved July 18, 2019.

39   Quoted in Clyde Summers, "The Battle in Seattle: Free Trade, Labor Rights, and Societal Values," *Journal of International Economics* 22, no. 1 (2001), 61–62, 64.

40   Kevin Danaher and Roger Burbach, eds. *Globalize This! The Battle Against the World Trade Organization and Corporate Rule* (Monroe, ME: Common Courage Press, 2000), 7–12.

41   Quoted in Carroll, 473.

42   U.S. Secretary of State Madeline K. Albright, "Interview on NBC-TV *The Today Show* with Matt Lauer," February 19, 1998, U.S. Department of State, https://1997-2001.state.gov/statements/1998/980219a.html, retrieved July 19, 2019.

43   Andrew Bacevich, *The New American Militarism: How Americans Are Seduced by War* (New York: Oxford University Press, 2005), 89.

44   Naomi Klein, *The Shock Doctrine: The Rise of Disaster Capitalism* (New York: Henry Holt, 2008).

45   Karen Talbot, "The Real Reasons for War in Yugoslavia: Backing up Globalization with Military Might," *Social Justice* 27, no. 4 (2000), 94–116; and David Gibbs, "The Srebrenica Precedent," *Jacobin*, n.d., www.jacobinmag.com/2015/07/bosnian-war-nato-bombing-dayton-accords, retrieved July 19, 2019.

46   Francesca E. Morrison, "Paramilitaries, Propaganda, and Pipelines: The NATO Attack on Kosovo and Serbia, 1999," (Western Oregon University: June 7, 2007), 27–35, www.wou.edu/history/files/2015/08/Francesca-Morrison.pdf, retrieved July 19, 2019; and Kristina Luca, *Footsteps in Kosovo* (Victoria, BC: Trafford Publishing, 2004), 25.

47   "Democracy Now! Confronts Madeleine Albright on the Iraq Sanctions: Was It Worth the Price?" *Democracy Now!*, July 30, 2004, www.democracynow.org/2004/7/30/democracy_now_confronts_madeline_albright_on, retrieved July 19, 2019. As Albright made clear in other interviews, she regretted the cavalier dismissal of children's lives, but not the policy.

48   Robert Kagan, "The Clinton Legacy Abroad," *Weekly Standard*, January 15, 2001, quoted in Bacevich, 85.

49 Pierre Bourgois, "The PNAC (1997–2006) and the Post-Cold War Neoconservative Moment," E-International Relations, February 1, 2020, www.e-ir.info/2020/02/01/new-american-century-1997-2006-and-the-post-cold-war-neoconservative-moment/, retrieved June 20, 2021.

50 Nicolaus Mills, *The Triumph of Meanness: America's War Against Its Better Self* (New York: Houghton Mifflin, 1997), 7–12.

51 See James B. Twitchell, *For Shame: The Loss of Common Decency in American Culture* (New York: Macmillan, 1998); and Julie Engel Manga, *Talking Trash: The Cultural Politics of Daytime TV Talk Shows* (New York: New York University Press, 2003), 52–55.

52 Mills, *The Triumph of Meanness*, 43, 122–126.

53 Ibid., 10.

54 John C. Tibbits, *Falling Down: Conversations About the Film* (University of Kansas), https://kuscholarworks.ku.edu/handle/1808/7093, retrieved July 25, 2019.

55 Eric Avila, *Popular Culture in the Age of White Flight: Fear and Fantasy in Suburban Los Angeles* (Berkeley, CA: University of California Press, 2004), 238.

56 Kathleen Belew, *Bring the War Home: The White Power Movement and Paramilitary America* (Cambridge, MA: Harvard University Press, 2019), 192–193, 202–203.

57 Lou Michel, Dan Herbeck, "How Oklahoma City Bomber Timothy McVeigh Changed the Fringe Right," *The Buffalo News*, August 3, 2020, https://buffalonews.com/news/local/crime-and-courts/how-oklahoma-city-bomber-timothy-mcveigh-changed-the-fringe-right/article_35958e7b-7e95-50d7-bb60-58473cebf002.html, retrieved June 20, 2021.

58 Quoted in Jared Yates Sexton, *The People Are Going to Rise Like Waters Upon Your Shore: A Story of American Rage* (Berkeley, CA: Counterpoint, 2017), 53.

59 Famously used by Hillary Clinton in an inartful defense of her husband, the term encompassed everything from rightwing news sources like *The American Spectator* to arch-conservatives like Richard Mellon Scaife who had been trying to destroy the Clintons since their days in Arkansas.

60 Joe Conason and Gene Lyons, *The Hunting of the President: The Ten-Year Campaign to Destroy Bill and Hillary Clinton* (New York: Thomas Dunne Books-St. Martin's Press, 2000).

61 Tim Dickinson, "How Roger Ailes Built the FOX News Fear Factory," *Rolling Stone*, May 25, 2011, www.rollingstone.com/politics/politics-news/how-roger-ailes-built-the-fox-news-fear-factory-244652, retrieved July 22, 2019.

62 Richard Hofstadter, "The Paranoid Style in American Politics," *Harper's Magazine*, November 1964, https://harpers.org/archive/1964/11/the-paranoid-style-in-american-politics, retrieved June 20, 2021.

63 Dickinson, "How Roger Ailes Built …"; Richard Hofstadter, "The Paranoid Style in American Politics," *Harpers Magazine* (November 1964), https://harpers.org/archive/1964/11/the-paranoid-style-in-american-politics; and Jane Mayer, "The Making of the Fox News White House," *The New Yorker*, March 4, 2019, www.newyorker.com/magazine/2019/03/11/the-making-of-the-fox-news-white-house, retrieved July 23, 2019.

64 Jack Mirkinson, "FOX News Viewers are the Most Misinformed: [University of Maryland] Study," *HuffPost*, May 25, 2011, www.huffpost.com/entry/fox-news-viewers-are-the_n_798146; and "Fox News Viewers Know Less than People Who Don't Watch Any News: [Farleigh Dickinson University] Study," *HuffPost*, November 21, 2011, www.huffpost.com/entry/fox-news-viewers-less-informed-people-fairleigh-dickinson_n_1106305, retrieved July 22, 2019.

65 Benjamin Hulac, "Tobacco and Oil Industries Used Same Researchers to Sway Public," *Scientific American* (reprinted from *Climate Wire*, July 20, 2016), www.scientificamerican.com/article/tobacco-and-oil-industries-used-same-researchers-to-sway-public1, retrieved July 24, 2019.

66 Jean-Daniel Collomb, "The Ideology of Climate Change Denial in the United States," *European Journal of American Studies* (Spring 2014); https://journals.openedition.org/ejas/10305, retrieved July 24, 2019.

67 "Hurricane Irma and the Political Whirlwind," *Columbia Political Review*, December 3, 2017, www.cpreview.org/blog/2017/12/hurricane-irma-and-the-political-whirlwind, retrieved July 24, 2019.

68 Frank Luntz Memorandum to Bush White House, 2002, http://aireform.com/resources/archive-2002-memorandum-to-bush-white-house-by-gop-consultant-frank-luntz-17p/, retrieved June 20, 2021.

69 Michael Wallace, "Culture War, History Front," in Edward T. Linenthal and Tom Engelhardt, eds., *History Wars: The Enola Gay and Other Battles for the American Past* (New York: Metropolitan Books, 1996), 181–183.

70 Quoted in Wallace, 175.

71 Matthew C. Hoffman (of the corporate-funded Competitive Enterprise Institute), *Wall Street Journal*, quoted in Wallace, 180–181; Boorstin and Krauthammer quoted in Andrew Gulliford, "The West as America: Reinterpreting Images of the Frontier 1820–1920," *The Journal of American History* 79, no. 1 (June 1992), 199–208.

72 Michael Wallace, *Mickey Mouse History and Other Essays on American Memory* (Philadelphia, PA: Temple University Press, 1992), 278–279.

73 Paul Boyer, "Whose History Is It Anyway?" in Linenthal and Engelhardt, 116.

74 Barton Bernstein, "The Struggle Over History: Defining the Hiroshima Narrative," in Philip Nobile, ed., *Judgment at the Smithsonian* (New York: Marlowe and Co., 1995), 238.

Further Reading

Bacevich, Andrew. *The New American Militarism: How Americans Are Seduced by War*. New York: Oxford University Press, 2005.

Bacevich, Andrew. *America's War for the Greater Middle East: A Military History*. New York: Random House, 2017.

Beschloss, Michael, and Strobe Talbot. *At the Highest Levels: The Inside Story of the End of the Cold War*. New York: Open Road Integrated Media, 1994.

Coll, Steve. *Ghost Wars: The Secret History of the CIA, Afghanistan, and bin Laden, from the Soviet Invasion to September 10, 2001*. New York: Penguin, 2004.

Conason, Joe, and Gene Lyons. *The Hunting of the President: The Ten-Year Campaign to Destroy Bill and Hillary Clinton*. New York: Thomas Dunne Books–St. Martin's Press, 2000.

Danaher, Kevin, and Roger Burbach, eds. *Globalize This! The Battle Against the World Trade Organization and Corporate Rule*. Monroe, ME: Common Courage Press, 2000.

Draper, Robert. *To Start a War: How the Bush Administration Took America into Iraq*. New York: Penguin, 2020.

Ferguson, Charles H. *Predator Nation: Corporate Criminals, Political Corruption, and the Hijacking of America*. New York: Crown Business, 2012.

Filkins, Dexter. *The Forever War*. New York: Vintage Books, 2009.

Frederick, Jim. *Black Hearts: One Platoon's Descent into Madness in Iraq's Triangle of Death*. New York: Crown Publishing, 2010.

Friedman, Alan. *Spider's Web: The Secret History of How the White House Illegally Armed Iraq*. New York: Bantam, 1993.

Fukuyama, Francis. *The End of History and the Last Man*. New York: Free Press, 1992, 2006.

Judis, John B. *The Populist Explosion: How the Great Recession Transformed American and European Politics*. New York: Columbia Global Reports, 2016.

Klein, Naomi. *The Shock Doctrine: The Rise of Disaster Capitalism*. New York: Henry Holt, 2008.

Kornacki, Steve. *The Red and the Blue: The 1990s and the Birth of Political Tribalism*. New York: HarperCollins, 2018.

Linenthal, Edward T., and Tom Engelhardt, eds., *History Wars: The Enola Gay and Other Battles for the American Past*. New York: Metropolitan Books, 1996.

Manga, Julie Engel. *Talking Trash: The Cultural Politics of Daytime TV Talk Shows*. New York: New York University Press, 2003.

Mayer, Jane, and Jill Abramson. *Strange Justice: The Selling of Clarence Thomas*. New York: Houghton Mifflin Harcourt, 1994.

Mendelberg, Tali. *The Race Card: Campaign Strategy, Implicit Messages, and the Norm of Equality*. Princeton, NJ: Princeton University Press, 2017.

Mills, Nicolaus. *The Triumph of Meanness: America's War Against Its Better Self*. New York: Houghton Mifflin, 1997.

Rich, Nathaniel. *Losing Earth: A Recent History*. New York: Farrar, Strauss and Giroux, 2019.

Ricks, Thomas E. *Fiasco: The American Military Adventure in Iraq, 2003–05*. New York: Penguin, 2007.

Tooze, Adam. *Crashed: How a Decade of Financial Crises Changed the World*. New York: Penguin, 2019.

Twitchell, James B. *For Shame: The Loss of Common Decency in American Culture*. New York: Macmillan, 1998.

13 America Under Attack

> If we are to have another contest in the near future of our national existence I predict that the dividing line will not be Mason & Dixon ... but between patriotism & intelligence on the one side & superstition, ambition & ignorance on the other.
>
> —Ulysses S. Grant, 1875[1]

Gaining perspective on the recent past presents inherent challenges, and yet at least one thing was clear almost immediately about the distressing first decades of the twenty-first century: they were defined not by dramatic social change or reform, but by the continued disintegrating faith in once-shared American values and institutions. An era that began with a bitterly contested presidential election ended with a violent attack on the U.S. Capitol stemming from false claims of a stolen presidential election, reflecting a society more sharply divided than at any time since the Civil War. Other trends reflected the disquieting sense of a nation unraveling. None were more consequential than the ongoing collapse of social consensus, a centrifugal splintering of basic public understanding of empirical truth, of verifiable facts about issues confronting the nation. Americans accessed a veritable ocean of information and entertainment sources, but read far fewer newspapers, which had long been the bedrock of the informed patriotism to which President Grant alluded. The impacts of supplanting traditional local journalism with a profit-driven social media and cable news environment built less for comprehending a complex world than for national political battle were profound.

Meanwhile, growing dysfunctionalism in Washington failed to confront deepening economic insecurities, which only intensified with the 2008–2009 "Great Recession." That economic calamity helped to elect the nation's first African American president, climaxing a decade that had begun with the terrorist attack of September 11, 2001, the worst assault on American soil since Pearl Harbor. Resulting wars in Iraq and Afghanistan fought by a sliver of the populace provided, for a time, a veneer of national unity. But the federal government's Wall Street-friendly response to the economic meltdown stoked further anger and resentment in an increasingly crenellated political environment in which Americans came to view members of the opposing party as enemies. In the eye

DOI: 10.4324/9781003160595-13

of the storm was a racially charged recoil to both Barack Obama's presidency and demographic changes in the racial makeup of the nation. The cumulative weight of it all stoked the rise of a dangerously illiberal populism laced with white grievance.

Throughout the era Americans were barraged by a ceaseless stream of horrific events: 9/11, mass shootings, police killings of unarmed black citizens, rising hate crime and domestic terror, an unyielding wave of catastrophic wildfires and storms fueled by a warming planet. In 2020, there was no escaping the onslaught as the United States joined the world in quarantine lockdown caused by the COVID-19 global pandemic, which served as the cataclysmic finish to an era when America careened from one crisis to the next. Exacerbated by a bungled federal response, the pandemic produced calamitous economic impacts and a death toll exceeding half a million Americans.

By then, from many corners of the globe America looked like a ghostly skeleton of the flawed but broadly unified democracy of the postwar era. Having landed in what Susan Jacoby called *The Age of American Unreason*, the nation bore an unsettling resemblance to the dystopian society envisioned in Mike Judge's 2006 darkly comedic science fiction film, *Idiocracy*, a society marked by anti-intellectual civic ignorance and ethically vacuous commercialism. One telling moment came in 2010 when NBC *Today* host Matt Lauer questioned Vice-President Joe Biden about the wisdom of putting Elena Kagan on the U.S. Supreme Court, because, said Matt, that would make five justices on the court from either Harvard or Yale Law School, which, he opined, "sounded a little elitist." It may be that Lauer thought TV's Judge Judy should have been named instead; presumably he was not among the 10 percent of *college graduates* who believed she already was.[2]

Indeed, civic illiteracy and the concomitant relinquishing of verifiable facts upon which reasoned debate takes place in a democratic society was the most frightening development of the era. When White House spokespersons could speak of "alternative facts," others explain that migrant babies in cages at the border weren't babies in cages at the border at all, when one of the nation's major political parties was in thrall to conspiracy theories utterly severed from reality, the nation had landed in dangerous new territory. By 2020, the United States faced an epistemic crisis where, as one scholar of Vladimir Putin's autocratic Russia put it, "nothing is true and everything is possible." Thus did five-alarm warnings about the brittle, enervated condition of American democracy and a rising politics of authoritarianism arrive with terrifying force.[3]

The Guy You'd Rather Have a Beer With

The 2000 presidential campaign is remembered mostly for the disputed 537-vote margin by which George W. Bush ultimately won the state of Florida and the election, an outcome sealed when a 5–4 divided Supreme Court stopped the recount on December 12. The contest is notable for other reasons that shed unflattering light on the health of American democracy. Although the nation enjoyed relative prosperity, the bursting of the "dot.com bubble" and crash of the NASDAQ that year might have triggered serious debate about the dangerous nexus of market deregulation, insider political corruption, and the rising power of digital technology. It did not, and within a year Americans faced economic recession and learned of corporate malfeasance at Enron and Arthur Anderson. Together with rising home foreclosures and delinquencies on subprime mortgage loans driven by predatory lending, these were veritable billboards announcing the coming disaster of 2008.[4]

Instead of pressing the candidates on such questions, the mainstream media let Americans know that George W. Bush was fond of bowling with oranges on his campaign airplane, that polls indicated voters preferred having a beer with the Texas Governor over Vice President Al Gore.[5] Prominent media voices held the former Tennessee senator in thinly veiled contempt, depicting him as a self-important, boring policy wonk. In addition to Gore's earnest efforts on climate change (for which he was also derided), central to the portrait of a man who *knew things* was the claim that he had "invented the Internet." Gore had said no such thing, only that he had taken the lead as a senator in the 1980s to turn Web communications, then a tool confined to the U.S. military establishment and universities, into an "information superhighway" of enormous public benefit. Yet when Republican Congressman Dick Armey mocked the vice president's alleged claim, pundits and many news outlets took it at face value and piled on, reinforcing the campaign narrative of Folksy Bush v. Elitist Gore.[6]

The Florida recount battle foretold more trouble. Midway through, several hundred protesters descended on the Miami-Dade County recount, charging Gore a "sore loser" and alleging a sinister effort to miscount votes. Some assaulted Gore partisans and local elections officials. Although they appeared to many as ordinary Floridians seeking to preserve the integrity of their election, the protesters were bought and paid for by Bush corporate supporters and GOP operatives, including Watergate bagman Roger Stone. The chaos forced a suspension of that county's effort and reinforced the perception that Bush had won fair and square, a conclusion affirmed in the partisan Supreme Court verdict.[7] Whether he had or not, the *Bush v. Gore* decision led Al Gore to a moment of supreme grace, conceding that "the honored institutions of our democracy" had resolved the contest and offering his full support to the president-elect.[8]

9/11 and the Invasion of Iraq

"For God's sake, you're financing your own assassins!"[9] These words of warning, uttered by an Afghan official to a CIA operative amid the mujahideen's war with the Soviets, came to catastrophic fruition on the morning of September 11, 2001. A decade after the Afghan war ended, remnants of the Osama bin Laden-financed jihadi force had been reconstituted as the international terror network, al-Qaeda ("the Base"). Bin Laden had relocated back to Afghanistan where the Islamic fundamentalist Taliban was assuming control of the country. In the late 1990s, the U.S. maintained friendly relations with the Taliban, despite its bin

Laden alliance and the imposition of draconian rule far worse than the Islamic theocracy of Iran. Although the Taliban ran one of the world's most authoritarian governments, U.S. strategic aims in Central Asia fused with those of California-based Unocal, whose grand project to build a pipeline from Turkmenistan's natural gas reserves through Afghanistan overrode concerns over human rights.[10]

Bin Laden, meanwhile, seethed over American military bases in Saudi Arabia and larger U.S. policy toward Israel and the Palestinians and the Muslim world, and began planning a dramatic strike. The transactional relationship with the Taliban ended horrifically that crystal blue September morning as 19 jihadists, 15 of them Saudis, hijacked four aircraft, crashing two into the World Trade Center in Manhattan and a third into the Pentagon. A fourth was intercepted by its passengers and taken down over a field near Shanksville, Pennsylvania. Nearly 3,000 perished. In the years ahead, thousands more Americans died one-by-one—firefighters and other "first responders" who labored on the "The Pile" at Ground Zero, sickened by exposure to its deadly toxicity.[11]

Within days, George W. Bush stood on The Pile with a bullhorn alongside New York's finest. "I can hear you!" he shouted. "The rest of the world hears you! And the people … who knocked these buildings down will hear all of us soon."[12] "USA! USA!" came the crowd's roar, echoing the grief-stricken anger of Americans sporting yellow ribbon magnets and American flags on their SUVs, more unified than at any time since World War II. What Bush had not heard were warnings leading up to 9/11: "Bin Laden Determined to Strike in U.S.," read the briefing that August.[13] The government's post-mortem analysis focused on how intelligence officials did not "connect the dots"—not how U.S. policy had blown back in horror. By the time the 9/11 Commission released its report, America would be nearly three years into "Operation Enduring Freedom" in Afghanistan, a mission aimed at overthrowing the Taliban and capturing bin Laden. Evidence later emerged that the Afghan government had offered to hand over the al-Qaeda leader *before* the attacks. The CIA chief in Pakistan confirmed as much on the tenth anniversary of 9/11—by which time Enduring Freedom was embarking on its second decade.[14]

In 2015 the conflict became "Operation Freedom's Sentinel." The rebranding meant little to Afghans who had lost more than one million citizens fighting the Soviets, and by 2020, 150,000 more to a conflict in its nineteenth year—the longest in U.S. history. Endless combat in the land where empires since Genghis Kahn had gone to die reached a point when one could excuse Americans' indifference to a war whose purposes had become unclear. In 2019—eight years since bin Laden was taken out in a CIA-led operation in Pakistan—Washington reengaged the Taliban in "conditions-based" talks to withdraw the last of its troops, with U.S. envoy and one-time Unocal consultant Zalmay Khalilzad assuring Americans that it was a "peace agreement, not a withdrawal agreement."[15]

Khalilzad returns us to the fateful months after 9/11, for he was a signatory to the Project for the New American Century (PNAC) and its 1998 insistence on a U.S. invasion of Iraq. That mission was revived immediately in the days after the Towers fell. Defense Secretary Donald Rumsfeld and deputy Paul Wolfowitz, PNAC alumni, argued for attacking Iraq, not Afghanistan.[16] Bush opted for the Afghanistan-first strategy, even as he authorized planning for military action against Saddam Hussein. Simultaneous to the Afghanistan operation, administration officials mounted a public relations campaign aimed at persuading Americans that Saddam Hussein and his alleged WMD program posed an imminent threat to the United States, and that al-Qaeda enjoyed a shadowy relationship with Saddam's regime. The widely held assumption was that either of those offenses justified a preemptive invasion of Iraq. President Bush declared a global "War on Terror," an endless conflict to be waged "against evildoers," and then in January 2002 designated Iraq part of an "Axis of Evil" with Iran and North Korea. Nations would be "either with us or against us."[17] Neoconservatives echoed the threat endlessly on cable. Playing into bin Laden's hands, the coming war fueled the perception among many Muslims that the U.S.-British alliance constituted a plan to extend their century-long "humiliation and ... degradation" of the Islamic world, as bin Laden declared after 9/11.[18] The growing criticism of America undercut the post-9/11 global reservoir of sympathy, as well as Bush's own eloquence in condemning a spasm of Islamophobia that had erupted across the country.[19]

Many months after 9/11, invasion proponents saturating cable news sustained a sense of ongoing urgency, as did alarmist chyrons and the new ceaseless "news crawl."[20] Vice President Dick Cheney and other Bush officials typically referenced the 9/11 attacks in the same breath with dark warnings of Iraq's alleged cunning concealment of WMD, occasionally going big with ominous portents of "a mushroom cloud."[21] They implied repeatedly without evidence that Saddam Hussein and al-Qaeda were in league. It worked: by fall 2002, seven of ten Americans believed Saddam linked to the 9/11 attacks.[22] After weapons inspectors reported no WMD in February 2003, the White House sent Secretary of State Colin Powell to give a highly misleading presentation to the UN Security Council. Crowning one of the most shameful performances of an American statesman on a world stage: as Powell spoke, the UN tapestry reproduction of Pablo Picasso's antiwar masterpiece *Guernica* was ordered covered in a shroud.[23]

The March 2003 invasion was opposed by governments and millions of people around the world as a violation of the UN Charter prohibiting preemptive war. On February 15, 2003 some 30 million took to the streets. The UN refused to endorse the invasion. Germany and France opposed it outright, French Foreign Minister Dominique de Villepin proclaiming, "the United Nations must remain an instrument of peace, and not a tool for war."[24] Americans replied to French opposition by losing their minds, renaming French fries "Freedom Fries" and pouring French wine into waterways. When country music stars the Dixie Chicks performed in England and declared that they were "ashamed that the president of the United States is from Texas," Londoners roared their approval. Right-wing media denounced them as the "Dixie Sluts," the arch-conservative Clear Channel Communications banning them from their 1,200 radio stations.[25] Amid this jingoistic atmosphere, Americans accepted an intensified national security state of increased surveillance, resistance generally confined to civil libertarians on the right and the antiwar left. The new Department of Homeland Security was echoed in the widespread adoption of *homeland* into the discourse of national defense, a linguistic embrace of America's global imperium.

The American blunder into Iraq was launched with "shock and awe" bombing, obliterating Baghdad's defenses and forcing Saddam from power. He was soon tried and executed by the U.S.-led interim government. Ecstatic over the apparent victory, on May 1 the civilian commander-in-chief crashed a constitutionally guarded tradition by donning military garb in a speech aboard an aircraft carrier bedecked with a "MISSION ACCOMPLISHED" banner. Announcing that "major combat operations in Iraq have ended," the vainglorious performance was premature.[26] Even as Bush spoke, U.S. forces were facing the start of a violent insurgency that would ensnare them in a conflict lasting another eight years, one that fomented the rise of the Islamic State (ISIS). More than 4,400 Americans and well over 100,000 Iraqis died.

Shia militias tied to the U.S.-sponsored regime in Baghdad were charged with a wave of atrocities. Worse still, graphic evidence emerged of sadistic treatment of Iraqi prisoners by U.S. military guards at Saddam's notorious Abu Ghraib prison. Although dismissed as the aberrant behavior of a few "bad apples," the incidents were consonant with what the Bush administration called "enhanced interrogation techniques" long defined in international law as torture. In 2014, the U.S. Senate Select Committee on Intelligence released a summary of a classified report describing a range of human rights abuses to which detainees were subjected, including waterboarding, rectal rehydration, and containment in coffin-like boxes.[27] Beyond the price to America's soul, the Iraq misadventure cost taxpayers well over $2 trillion.[28] The war presented precisely the dreadful specter of "incalculable human and political costs" feared by Bush the elder when in 1991 he chose not to invade Baghdad. "Had we gone the invasion route," Bush wrote in 1998, "the United States could conceivably still be an occupying power in a bitterly hostile land."[29]

More evidence of Americans' vulnerability to media misrepresentation was provided by the "Swiftboating" of 2004 Democratic presidential candidate John Kerry. In contrast to a president and vice-president who evaded military service in Vietnam, Kerry had volunteered for duty. Serving with distinction on a Navy swift boat, Kerry returned home an impassioned opponent of the war. But in 2003 the longtime senator from Massachusetts, like most Democrats, had voted to authorize military force in Iraq. Running for president a year later, Kerry called the conflict misguided—an equivocation that damaged his credibility. Still, his military record bolstered Kerry's standing on national security—until a group of Vietnam veterans conspired with Republican operatives to produce the "Swift Boat" TV ads smearing Kerry as a lying, unAmerican coward. By the time Kerry responded, Fox led the media in beating the story senselessly. He never recovered.[30] Flayed in an ignoble campaign of gross distortion, Kerry was defeated by a president who had misled the country into a catastrophic war.

Here was the larger paradox: the nation fighting two costly wars, sending drones to attack people in several nations on two continents, spending (including the cost of past wars) more money on defense than every nation on earth combined, selling more weapons than any nation, and stationing military personnel on more than 600 bases and installations in nearly 150 countries, was the same people with almost no actual experience with, nor memory of real war. Hollywood films and video games of the era generally either glamorized war or desensitized viewers to the impact of new forms of combat being waged by the U.S. military. Even as athletic events and the culture at large became saturated with the veneration of soldiers and veterans, Americans lived in a surreal remove from the costs and consequences of both their immense global empire or the vast national security state that had emerged in the "homeland."

"Too Big to Fail"

At home, a Reaganomics rehash produced familiar consequences. Because modern Republican orthodoxy holds that there is never a bad time for tax cuts for the wealthy, the Bush administration delivered two rounds of massive tax "relief" tilted mostly toward the rich. As ever, Republicans sold the packages on the promise they would pay for themselves with revenue-generating growth. Arguments from liberals that the hard-earned budget surpluses of the 1990s be invested in pressing needs like education and infrastructure were dismissed, as were warnings that the tax cuts would turn surplus into deficits. Compounded by the costly conflicts in Iraq and Afghanistan, that is precisely what they did.[31] Deregulation fever ran high, the Bush administration weakening consumer, financial, workplace, and environmental protections across the board—sometimes to directly benefit corporate benefactors. In September 2000 the Clinton Justice Department brought a 97-count indictment against Koch Industries, the oil-gushing fortune of Sagebrush rebels Charles and David Koch, big donors of conservative causes and Republican politicians. A federal grand jury charged that Koch had deliberately released 90 metric tons of carcinogenic benzene from one its refineries and then lied about it to regulators. The verdict would have cost the Kochs $352 million in fines. Bush's Justice Department reduced the count from 97 to 9, resulting in a $20 million slap on the polluters' wrist.[32] In advance of the same fossil fuel-friendly agenda, Bush withdrew from the Kyoto Protocol to begin reducing carbon emissions, and Dick Cheney's secretive task force devised a national energy policy that leaned almost exclusively on fossil fuels and nuclear energy.[33]

"You can't overestimate what happens when you encourage regulators to believe that the goal of regulation is not to regulate." That nugget of wisdom summarizing the perils of financial deregulation dropped in September 2008 from Nobel Prize-winning economist Joseph Stiglitz as the nation sank into its worst economic crisis since the Great Depression.[34] As we have seen, in 1981 politicians effectively handed the keys of the nation's economic health and well-being over to bankers and financiers whose interests were fundamentally at odds with most Americans. One financial crisis built on the next, each one more severe than the last. In the spring of 2007—to paraphrase a rare moment of clarity from Fed Chair Alan Greenspan—the "irrationally exuberant" subprime mortgage bubble began to burst. Massively over leveraged chickens—"financial services" operations like Lehman Brothers and the financial insurance charlatans at AIG who had been propping up and profiting from the entire corrupted enterprise of the housing industry—came home to roost, either going bankrupt or otherwise seeking sheltered takeover or outright rescue from the Federal Reserve and Treasury. Having been globally interconnected by a web of highly complex financial instruments, the previously compartmentalized ship of the world economy was capsizing. By summer 2008, stock values began plummeting, unemployment inched up, and small businesses struggled for liquidity. Exploding foreclosures signaled a major crisis in the housing industry.

The Bush administration and Congress had no choice but to intervene. But as many critics argued, the approach taken to save a banking system deemed "too big to fail" was not the only fork in the road. Devised by many of the same people who had steered the ship into the iceberg, the rescue package was led by the $700 billion Troubled Assets Relief Program (TARP), the generous bank "bailout." Then came rescue of the auto industry. Relief for Detroit was both necessary and more than repaid. But that fact was lost in the stormy political aftermath, as help for automakers was conflated with the much-hated TARP, and the $831 billion American Economic Recovery and Reinvestment Act (the "Obama Stimulus"). Exacerbated by the fact that the U.S. Justice Department never brought a single culprit to justice for the greatest economic crisis in nearly 80 years, to millions of Americans the entire federal response smacked of corruption. The impunity was so thorough that it seemed a moral victory when one heard Greenspan admit to congress that he was wrong to assume that the "self-interest" of the "banks and others" would protect the stability of the system.[35]

When Barack Hussein Obama was elected forty-fourth president of the United States over Senator John McCain of Arizona that November, the mix of emotions across the country was overwhelming: a tearful wash of astonishment, pride, and hope—commingled with apprehension over the enormous pressure on him. Economic conditions had deteriorated further throughout the winter with tumbling stock values, skyrocketing foreclosures, and hemorrhaging jobs. A *Time* cover depicted the president-elect as FDR on his way to the inaugural. Not quite. Even if he had possessed the class-conscious disposition of Franklin Roosevelt, Obama confronted a very different political environment from that of 1933. For one thing, Obama's America was marked by an enervated union movement under siege for decades. And despite the undeniable charisma and community organizing background that helped elect him president, Barack Obama did not possess a natural affinity for the struggles of working people.

As one observer noted, just as the moderate conservative Eisenhower did not challenge the political consensus of the nation forged in the New Deal era, Obama did not attempt to reverse the "conservative, anti-government zeitgeist" that originated with Reagan.[36] Moreover, Obama faced a deeply divided nation and unprecedented obstruction from Republicans. On the eve of the 2010 mid-term elections in which Republicans seized control of the House of Representatives, Senate Minority Leader Mitch McConnell made explicit his intent: "The single most important thing we want to achieve is for President Obama to be a one-term president."[37] From health care to deficit reduction to immigration, Obama either proffered a position recently espoused by Republicans or gestured toward compromise, only to be rebuffed. It began when not one GOP House member supported the watered-down stimulus, despite an economy teetering on the edge of depression. Gathering at a luxury resort a few days later, Republicans watched video replay of the vote and gave themselves a standing ovation.[38] It continued this way for eight years, right through the Supreme Court nomination of Merrick Garland to replace conservative Antonin Scalia who died early in 2016. Despite Garland being a widely respected centrist, now Majority Leader McConnell refused to even consider the nomination, allowing the court a vacant seat for nearly a year until the election of the next president.[39]

Given the GOP blockade, Obama's genuine achievements are notable. On day one, he signed the Lily Ledbetter Act strengthening the ability of women to gain pay equity. He supported Elizabeth Warren's proposal to create the Consumer Financial Protection Bureau to protect consumers from predatory lending practices. Stymied by Republicans on climate change, Obama advanced a Clean Power Plan that imposed carbon emissions reduction standards on states, while granting them broad flexibility in attaining them. Fuel efficiency standards were strengthened for the first time since the Carter era. In 2015, his personal engagement with China helped rescue the Paris Climate Agreement. Despite an initially halting response to the months-long 2010 BP *Deepwater Horizon* disaster that gushed 200 million gallons of oil into the Gulf of Mexico, the RESTORE Act committed significant resources to the Gulf's restoration.[40]

Having seen George W. Bush fail to advance immigration reform due to GOP obstruction, Barack Obama pushed the issue to the backburner. Scorned by immigrant advocates as "deporter in chief," Obama unleashed the post-9/11 Immigration and Customs Enforcement (ICE) agency to round up and deport a record 1.2 million immigrants.[41] In 2012, however, Obama took executive action in advancing the policy of Deferred Action for Childhoods Arrivals (DACA). Nearly three quarters of a million young immigrant "Dreamers" brought to the United States illegally as children were suddenly protected and eligible for renewable work permits and a Social Security number.[42] DACA inflamed the right, which excoriated Obama for granting "amnesty" to "illegals" who would take jobs from Americans and burden public services. As DACA defenders predicted then, the evidence soon pointed in the opposite direction.[43]

President Obama demonstrated the ability to be moved on important issues. Most notable was his embrace of the struggle for LGBTQ rights, a sharp break from Bush who supported a constitutional amendment to ban gay marriage. After indicating early on that he was "evolving" on the issue, Obama made his support explicit in 2012—following his Vice President Joe Biden, but three years ahead of the landmark Supreme Court decision that prohibited state bans on same-sex marriage. He then issued executive actions on transgender rights, repealed the "don't ask-don't tell" policy prohibiting gays from serving openly in the military, signed hate crimes legislation, and appointed an historic number of LGBTQ Americans to federal positions. Obama reflected, but also shaped rapidly changing attitudes in the country on sexual orientation. "He revolution-ized the way America sees us," said Cari Searcy, co-plaintiff with her wife in the lawsuit overturning Alabama's marriage ban. "The policies and protections that our community gained under his administration changed our daily lives."[44]

Less dramatic were changes in federal drug policy. Obama was the first presi-dent since Jimmy Carter to spend less money on drug interdiction than on treatment and prevention. His Justice Department allowed states to advance marijuana decriminalization in violation of federal law. Sentences for non-vio-lent drug offenses were reduced, helping Obama to leave office with a lower federal prison population than he came in with.[45] That criminal justice record was mirrored inside the White House: not a single Obama official was indicted, seriously suspected of malfeasance, or forced to resign under a cloud of suspicion or conflict of interest. It was one of the most ethical administrations in history.

"Become a Part of the Mob!"

Notwithstanding these achievements and the very fact that America had elected its first black president, an equally true measure of where the country was headed was the anti-Obama reaction among Republicans and the far-right—forces that continued to meld. It began the summer of 2009 as Barack Obama, House Speaker Nancy Pelosi and Democrats in congress pursued passage of the Affordable Care Act (ACA). Derided as "Obamacare," the signature achievement of the Obama presidency differed little from various Republican plans for health care expansion floated since the Nixon administration. The ACA required unin-sured Americans to either purchase insurance on private exchanges or pay a tax to support the broadening of affordable access.[46] Still, the GOP went after the plan with a vengeance. Fox News personality Sean Hannity's Website invited followers to "Become Part of the Mob!", directing them to "Attend an Obama Care Townhall near you!" Defeated vice-presidential candidate Sarah Palin warned of "death panels" of grim-reaping government bureaucrats who would decide whether grandma would live or die. At congressional town halls that summer, constituents roared that the ACA would bring "tyranny!" Rush Limbaugh found a suspicious resemblance between the ACA's logo and Nazi insignia, inspiring some hysterically imaginative protest signs featuring Obamacare overlaid with swastikas. Others could have used spellcheck: "NO PUBIC OPTION!" "GET A BRAIN MORAN!"[47] Renowned for his cool, Obama was confounded by the rage. Visibly exasperated at one press conference that summer, the president described a letter he received from a rather confused citizen: "She said, 'I don't want government-run health care. I don't want social-ized medicine. And don't touch my Medicare.'"[48]

No celebrity crank was more successful at fusing legitimate anger over the bank bailout with unhinged Obamacare fury than Fox's Glenn Beck. Deploying chalkboard diagrams filled with circles and arrows and stickmen figures, professor Beck fingered all the mad socialist-communist plotters, somehow linking John D. Rockefeller and Woodrow Wilson to George Soros, the Hungarian American billionaire, to various Obama villains. Beck ingeniously inverted the depravity of Wall Street corruption brought on by decades of government deregulation, into a faux Everyman's economic populism that decried the abuses of … *too much* government!—ultimately circling in on the socialist plot of Obama and his connections to a nonprofit community organization called ACORN.[49] Leavened with occasional maudlin crying, the sweater-wearing patriot's maniacal performances warned that Obamacare would bring "the end of America as we know it."[50]

The Beck show was jet fuel for the Tea Party, a corporate-funded "movement" opposed to the bailouts which were now fused to the "government takeover" of health care. Tea Partiers were suddenly everywhere. Many wore colonial garb, others wielded placards warning of blood-soaked trees of liberty. Some brought guns, brandished thanks to "open-carry" laws being passed by numerous Republican-controlled state legislatures. The Tea Party agenda blended seamlessly with that of rightwing nonprofits "Freedom Works" and "Americans for Prosperity." FreedomWorks drew on the Koch brothers' coffers, the American Petroleum Institute, the tobacco giants, and undisclosed "dark" money. It launched a wave of anti-union campaigns in 2011–2013 even as the Tea Party hoi polloi they funded pretended to stand for the little guy.[51] Laced into the mix were spasms of old-school racism directed against Obama. A Tea Party protest near the White House featured one patriot declaring the president a Marxist, Islamist "traitor" who "funded al-Qaeda and … illegal sales of weapons to cross our borders from America into Mexico." From the crowd came a cry to, "Hang the traitor! We got rope. There's plenty of trees in the front yard … Wouldn't be the first one hung from one of them trees."[52]

More sustained gusts of racism came from birtherism—the thoroughly debunked but incessantly professed "theory" that the alleged socialist president was not American. By 2012 birtherism's chieftain was Donald Trump, who never missed an opportunity to mix racism with personal ambition. Nor was he prone to accepting facts that stood in the way of a good conspiracy. When the president took the unprecedented step of producing the long form of his birth certificate from the Honolulu hospital where he was born, Trump claimed he had sent his own private investigators to Hawaii. "They cannot believe what they're finding," he panted.[53] It was of course rubbish, but a growing plurality of Fox-watching Republicans believed it. Soon *The Apprentice* star was deploying this racist fallacy to mount a presidential campaign.

While the Tea Party consumed much of the media oxygen, real movements for change were unfolding. September 2011 brought Occupy Wall Street (OWS), birthed in Zucotti Park adjacent to Wall Street. Spreading to cities around the globe, OWS claimed to speak on behalf of the "99%" left behind in the recovery while raising broader economic justice issues, including unsustainable student loan debt and the continued decline of worker wages. "You Know Things Are Bad When Librarians Start Marching," read one protester's sign. Generally dismissed by the media, OWS succeeding in reframing the debate over an economy tilted toward the "1%," even as conditions remained unchanged. The titans of America's "Second Gilded Age"—Walmart, Amazon, and the Silicon Valley tech industry—worked to suppress worker wages, often through union busting tactics. In addition, the last six years of the Obama era saw a Republican-controlled congress imposing domestic spending cuts, which, combined with cutbacks in education and social services at the state level, served as a further drag on middle-class prosperity.[54] Economic recovery, slow at first, was eventually robust but tilted toward the wealthy as it had for three decades.

In West Virginia, a struggle to preserve historic Blair Mountain from the ravages of "mountaintop removal" (MTR) mining was supported by a coalition of union members, climate justice activists, and preservationists. Blair Mountain was the scene of the 1921 epic battle between coal mine operators and 10,000 miners and families fighting for union recognition that might earn them decent pay and better working conditions. Backed by U.S. Army troops, the powerful mine owners succeeded in crushing the largest uprising of Americans since the Civil War, killing hundreds of miners. Even in defeat, it proved a landmark event in the eventual success of the United Mine Workers of America. Ninety years later, the mountain, listed on the National Register of Historic Places, was targeted by mine owners for MTR, which had already blown the tops off hundreds of mountains in Appalachia and contaminated thousands of miles of waterways and had long been opposed by residents working for a more sustainable Appalachian future. In 2011, hundreds of activists, joined by Robert F. Kennedy, Jr. and musicians Ashley Judd and Kathy Mattea, marched 50 miles to the crest of Blair Mountain in an effort to protect the site and focus attention on the larger issues it symbolized.[55]

"We have never ceded this land," declared Joye Braun of the Indigenous Environmental Network, one of the Native American leaders who in 2016 joined the struggle of the Standing Rock Sioux to prevent construction of the Dakota Access Pipeline (DAPL). Standing Rock leaders declared the pipeline, being advanced by a Texas-based multinational to carry oil from western North Dakota to southern Illinois, violated the terms of the 1868 Fort Laramie Treaty guaranteeing the tribe "undisturbed use and occupation" of reservation lands and the Missouri River watershed threatened by the project. The nonviolent DAPL struggle, initiated by a group of Standing Rock teens through social media, galvanized a diverse coalition. By fall 2016, indigenous peoples from around the world were joined by environmentalists, labor and civil rights leaders, and military veterans at a massive encampment on the Missouri River aimed at protecting water and cultural resources. Tribal member Anna Lee reminded the head of the Army Corps of Engineers of the stakes: "Water to Native American people is the first medicine. Mni Wiconi: water is life." That winter, video footage of armed forces of the state of North Dakota and the company using attack dogs and water cannons against peaceful "Water Protectors" elevated the profile of the struggle, heightening pressure on the Obama administration. The Corps stayed construction on the pipeline, a decision soon reversed by Donald Trump.[56]

That a movement called Black Lives Matter (BLM) was even necessary in the twenty-first century was a damning statement of American race relations. It began in a Sanford, Florida gated community the night of February 26, 2012 when 17-year-old Trayvon Martin, walking to his father's girlfriend's house armed with an iced tea and a bag of Skittles, was shot and killed by neighborhood watch volunteer George Zimmerman. Arrested six weeks later, Zimmerman, with a history of racial profiling, was later acquitted of second-degree murder and manslaughter.[57] On the night of the verdict, Alicia Garza was sitting in a bar in Oakland, California with other anxious black patrons. "Everything went quiet, everything and everyone," Garza later said.

> And then people started to leave en masse. The one thing I remember from that evening, other than crying myself to sleep that night, was the way in which as a black person, I felt incredibly vulnerable, incredibly exposed and incredibly enraged. Seeing these black people leaving the bar, and it was like we couldn't look at each other. We were carrying this burden around with us every day: of racism and white supremacy. It was a verdict that said: black people are not safe in America.

That night Garza Facebook-messaged a "love note to black people," ending with, "I love you. I love us. Our lives matter." Days later, she and two activist friends were building a social media campaign around the Twitter #blacklivesmatter, inviting black Americans to share stories—of racial profiling, police violence, egregious disparities in the criminal justice system, and the unacknowledged value of African American lives.[58] As Sybrina Fulton, Martin's mother put it, "It's not taking away from anybody else's life, it's just putting emphasis on black lives because black lives seem so … disposable."[59] In the years that followed, the toll of unarmed black bodies killed at the hands of police kept piling up: Freddie Gray, Michael Brown, Tamir Rice, Eric Garner, Sandra Bland … a body count that powered the fundamental BLM demand to respect the humanity of black Americans (Figure 13.1).

There has never been a "good time" for a racial justice movement in America, but with growing antipathy toward the nation's first black president interlaced with Facebook- and Fox-amplified anger over the skewed recovery and Obamacare, BLM arrived with especially inauspicious timing. As local organizations, hip-hop artists, Hollywood celebrities, and eventually NFL quarterback Colin Kaepernick began championing the cause, many white Americans responded with indignation. "Blue Lives Matter!" read counter-protest signs, as if black men were engaged in an epidemic of killing police. When Barack Obama uttered a rare racially conscious statement—that "if he had a son he would look like Trayvon"—the right cried that he was "[pouring] gas on the fire."[60] White folk may have had Jay-Z on their iPods and twice helped elect a

Figure 13.1 Black Lives Matter art on the Miller & Chevalier building on Black Lives Matter Plaza in Washington, DC.

Courtesy of the Library of Congress

black president, but whether they were living in what many in 2008 had proclaimed a "post-racial" America was another matter.

"Make America Great Again"

Dylann Roof had heard enough of Black Lives Matter. On the evening of June 17, 2015, the 21-year-old walked into a prayer service at historic "Mother" Emanuel African Methodist Episcopal Church in Charleston, South Carolina and shot nine people to death. The remorseless Roof's self-proclaimed "bravery," augmented with photos of himself brandishing flags of the Confederacy and white supremacist regimes from colonial Africa, made him a memed idol in the far-right swamps of the Internet.[61] Escaping public attention in the immediate aftermath was this stunning example of white privilege: when Roof told police he was hungry, they stopped at a Burger King to order the man they called "very quiet" and "not problematic," a quarter-pounder.[62] The episode revealed a larger pattern: far right violent extremists like Roof—radicalized by many of the same online strategies at work in the recruitment of Islamic terrorists—were not only treated more humanely by police, but depicted in the media as "troubled," "disturbed" "lone wolves," a pattern that began with Tim McVeigh.[63] The wolf pack was growing. After 9/11, white supremacist, far-right extremism became the leading domestic terror threat, responsible for 71 percent of American terrorism deaths between 2008 and 2017.[64] But when the Department of Homeland Security sounded that warning in 2009, it was smeared by Republicans as an attempt to silence white conservatives.[65]

The horror in Charleston briefly overwhelmed the political news from Manhattan 48 hours earlier. After descending Trump Tower escalator, Donald Trump delivered an anti-immigration screed that announced his presidential candidacy and ensured this was no mere vanity campaign: "When Mexico sends its people, they're not sending their best … They're sending people that have lots of problems … They're bringing drugs, they're bringing crime, they're rapists, and some, I assume, are good people."[66]

Soon came the xenophobic promise to "Build that Wall!" on the southwest border, one that Mexico would somehow pay for. Chanted ceaselessly at his rallies, Trump's Wall fused the candidate's skill in tapping the base instincts of supporters with his legendary charlatanism. It was, perhaps, tragically fitting that Americans elected themselves a conspiracy-mongering racist reality TV star as president, for this cynically transgressive, socially dystrophic television genre was defined by core elements of Trump's biography: revenge-driven story lines, overwrought victimhood, the pervasive use of racist stereotypes and racialized plots, and the lie of the performance itself. A thousand miles apart on the GPS, Dylann Roof's blood-soaked infamy and Trump's gold-plated announcement served as opening acts to an era of extreme white identity politics.

The facts were known to the 63 million who voted for Donald Trump. Few were unaware he had criticized U.S. Senator and war hero, John McCain—"I like people who weren't captured, OK?"—that he had mocked a disabled reporter, that he was credibly accused by more than a dozen women of sexual misconduct and assault. "When you're a star, they let you do it. You can do anything … grab 'em by the pussy," he bragged on the infamous *Hollywood Access* tape released weeks before the election.[67] The bankruptcies were part of the man's genius, supporters believed, as was the fraud case brought by victims of "Trump University," which he used to slander the Indiana-born appeals court judge as "Mexican"—by definition, anti-Trump.[68] Voters certainly knew that after the San Bernardino December 2015 mass murder by an Islamic extremist, he declared, in performative third person to a cheering throng aboard the historic *USS Yorktown*: "Donald J. Trump is calling for a total and complete shutdown of Muslims entering the United States until our country's representatives can figure out what the hell is going on!" One man present "[liked] that he's not going to bullshit you," and was unafraid to mock "all this politically correct bullshit," while a woman was in thrall with the authoritarian tone: "It seems right because he's so … strong."[69] Antipathy toward "PC culture" prevailed at one "Make America Great Again" rally after another. In response to the candidate's rantings about Democratic opponent, former Secretary of State Hillary Clinton and her mishandled but thoroughly investigated emails, one heard interminable shouts of "Lock Her Up!" punctuated with the odd "Hang that Bitch!" Confederate flags were common, as were racist defamations of the president. Nazi swastikas appeared, along with an occasional, "Sieg Heil Trump!"[70]

Donald Trump did not conjure the fear and ignorance, nor the malevolent racism and misogyny. Present at America's creation, they had been merely tranquilized by the sixties. Nor did Trump concoct the mythology of whites as innocent victims of black, brown, and red treachery. As we have seen, white victimhood began to surge sporadically in the post-Vietnam era, around the time Trump began hammering away—at the Japanese, Iranians, brown immigrants, black urban criminals, Wall Street, and "stupid" Washington politicians. By 2016, all were villains to Fox-watching patriots. Many Republicans looked on in astonishment as the former New York Democrat swatted away his primary opponents. They should not have been. Although it had been just eight years since John McCain nobly corrected a supporter questioning Barack Obama's faith and patriotism, Trump in fact was the logical Republican end-game of a pattern going back decades. As Republican campaign consultant Stuart Stevens concluded, "Trump [wasn't] an aberration of the Republican Party. He *is* the Republican Party in purified form."[71]

It was easy to forget that the nation of John Lewis and Ella Baker was also the land of George Wallace and P. T. Barnum. And like the "penny press" of Barnum's day, the mainstream media cashed in with soaring ratings, giving the failed businessman a reported $5 billion worth of free media.[72] Demonstrating his true talent of self-promotion, Trump received unprecedented, incessant coverage of every MAGA rally, fact-free utterance, insult, and conspiracy re-Tweet. Bernie Sanders's run for the Democratic nomination packed arenas in often greater numbers than Trump's, but received a fraction of the coverage. At CNN and MSNBC, talking heads gushed over the Vermont Democratic Socialist's crowds, then sneered at policy positions like reducing military spending or raising wages of working people.[73] In the end, Trump's electoral college victory came despite receiving nearly three million fewer votes than Clinton. He won courtesy of slim margins in industrial states particularly vulnerable to a combination of white working-class economic insecurities, anti-Obama recoil, and a disinformation campaign that exploited Americans' deepening divisions. The fault lines were long-brewing: urban v. rural, communities of color v. white, college-educated professionals v. working class, CNN-MSNBC v. Fox. By 2016 the cleavages ran so deep that relatives were "unfriending" one another—on Facebook, and in life.

Few Americans knew it, but the schisms were being amplified by Russian operatives on fake Facebook pages and false accounts on Twitter. Analysts and scholars would grapple with the profound role of Facebook in the weakening of western democracy for decades to come. Even as it was happening, however, close observers of the social media platform like British investigative journalist Carole Cadwalladr already had a good bead on the destruction:

> Algorithmically amplified "free speech" with no consequences. Lies spread at speed. Hate freely expressed, freely shared. Ethnic hatred, white supremacy, resurgent Nazism all spreading invisibly, by stealth beyond the naked eye.[74]

Cadwalladr likened it to toxic sewage running beneath the streets of American democracy. The Russians simply punctured the lines. Their cyberattack on the 2016 U.S. presidential election was, as Americans later learned from Special Counsel Robert Mueller, "sweeping and systematic," reaching more than 125 million Americans. The Russian Internet Research Agency (IRA), a Kremlin-directed troll farm, interfered less with the goal of helping to elect Donald Trump—they were sure he would lose—but to sow doubt in the validity of the outcome. IRA Facebook pages falsely alleged that Hillary Clinton was conspiring to steal the election through a range of illegal activities. The Russians even readied a #DemocracyRIP for election night, prepared to "cripple" her presidency and enshrine Trump as an "outsider victimized by a corrupt political establishment and faulty democratic election process."[75] The Russians also hacked the computers of the Democratic National Committee and engineered the timely release of DNC emails. The finishing stroke came July 27, 2016, when Donald Trump implored a foreign adversary to meddle in an American election: "Russia, if you're listening, I hope you're able to find the 30,000 emails [of Secretary Clinton] that are missing." That evening, Russian operatives began hacking the computer server of the Democratic candidate.[76] By October, the FBI's counterintelligence investigation had uncovered much of this evidence—along with the fact that numerous Trump campaign officials welcomed Russian attempts to manipulate the election. President Obama sought to issue a bipartisan statement with Majority Leader Mitch McConnell expressing outrage at Russian behavior and warning of consequences, but McConnell refused.[77]

When FBI director James Comey refused to drop the Russian investigation, Trump fired him, triggering Mueller's inquiry. The nearly two-year-long special counsel investigation led to the indictment of dozens of Russians, Trump's campaign chairman, his deputy, former National Security Advisor, and personal attorney—the latter over another scandal stemming from the secret pre-election payoff of two women with whom he had had affairs. Despite clear evidence of Russian guilt, in July 2018 Americans beheld the astonishing specter of their president in Helsinki, Finland publicly siding with the malevolent despot Vladimir Putin over the authoritative conclusions of U.S. intelligence that Russians had attacked American democracy. As the Mueller report made clear, Trump had also on multiple occasions tried to obstruct justice and terminate the inquiry. Left unanswered were questions of motivation, what was driving him to reshape U.S. policy toward Russia and its commitment to NATO. One thing was clear: unlike every president before him, Trump's loyalties remained a legitimate question throughout his presidency. The Trump base was unmoved. The president and his team at Fox defamed it all as a "witch hunt," the work of anti-Trump "deep state" government bureaucrats. "If Jesus Christ gets down off the cross and told me Trump is with Russia," said one of the faithful, "I would tell him, 'Hold on a second. I need to check with the President if it's true.'"[78]

"Very Fine People"

Whether one voted for him or not, the ceaseless drama and chaos of the Trump presidency proved exhausting. There were the charges of brazen corruption of Trump, his family, and administration officials. A record-breaking number of cabinet members came and went. There were the lies—30,573 by one count—about matters large, petty, and in between.[79] It was an unceasing geyser of prevarication, a form of what Trump strategist and white supremacist Steve Bannon called "flooding the zone with shit."[80] The greater the volume, the more overwhelmed a scrutinizing press, the more doubt sowed in the mind of a divided public about "which side" to believe. America found itself in an abusive relationship with a president lying in the evening about things he had lied about that morning and then pretending that he had said none of it. In a moment of twisted Orwellian candor, he declared to a crowd of veterans in July 2018: "What you're seeing and what you're reading is not what's happening."[81]

As Bannon knew, the more straight-faced duplicity from the White House lawn—critics abused the term "gaslighting" from the classic film about a murderous master of psychological manipulation—the less media coverage of actual policies. Did it matter to supporters that Trump had not delivered on a promise to rebuild America's crumbling infrastructure? That he and congressional Republicans tried mightily to kill the Affordable Care Act without offering their promised alternative? Did they not care that the president cozied up to dictators, including one whose henchmen used a bone saw to dismember an American journalist? That he seemed to think abolitionist Frederick Douglass was alive, that George Washington's Continental Army "took over the airports" from the British?[82] Beyond criminal justice reform, Trump's agenda was largely that of corporate plutocrats and far-right ideologues: aggressive deregulation, draconian immigration policies, tax cuts for the wealthy, withdrawal from international agreements led by the Paris Climate Accord and a multilateral deal to keep Iran from building a nuclear weapon. He had pledged in his inaugural to confront socioeconomic "American carnage"—a grim portrait that was in fact objectively quantifiable. A U.S. Senate committee tabulated the "deaths of despair" attributable to suicide, drugs, and alcohol. That index of misery mortality had doubled from 22.7 per 100,000 in 2000 to nearly 46 in 2017.[83] Yet save a program to address a raging opioid crisis, Trump did little for the rural poor. He opposed a federal minimum wage increase—at $7.25 per hour, less than one-third its value in 1968.[84]

The president preferred playing to his strengths: rage- and conspiracy-Tweeting, in the process opening up new fronts in America's "cold civil war."[85] He singled out for special vitriol journalists and politicians of color and Republicans who turned on him or challenged his abuses of power. Amid a succession of historic wildfire seasons, Trump urged California officials to "rake" and "clean" their forest floor—like the "forest nation" of Finland. Finnish officials had said nothing of the kind.[86] Amusing for Twitter trolls, such imbecility was dangerous on a burning planet. By July 2019, the hottest month ever recorded, climate change was changing the very language of weather forecasting: "rain bombs," the winter "polar vortex," and "heat domes" that lingered into October all became part of a new reality of life on Earth—as did the psychological trauma of "climate grief."[87] Yet farmers facing the one-two punch of Trump's trade war with China and natural disasters that once were half-century events stood with their president who insisted it was all a Chinese "hoax" and that wind turbines cause cancer.[88] He could not resist attacking 16-year-old climate change activist Greta Thunberg, who helped power a global youth movement of climate justice.[89]

Trump insinuated himself into the growing movement to remove Confederate memorials from the public square. On August 11–12, 2017, hundreds of neo-Nazis and neo-Confederates marched on Charlottesville, Virginia in a "Unite the Right" protest to the planned removal of a Robert E. Lee statue. Some sported Trump gear. Many were armed with shields, helmets, clubs, and assorted firearms. Marching at night with torches in hand, shouting "Jews will not replace us!" "Blood and soil!", the chilling footage evoked Nuremberg 1934. They were met by thousands of overwhelmingly peaceful demonstrators. Anti-fascist militants and a contingent of the "Redneck Revolt"—a network of "pro-worker, anti-racist" rural folk[90]—came to protect them—anticipating correctly that local police would be overwhelmed.[91] One activist, Heather Heyer, was killed when a white supremacist drove his car into the crowd.[92]

Issuing an unequivocal statement condemning "Unite the Right" proved beyond Trump's capacities. After widespread criticism of his initial response, he dug deeper, averring that he was "not putting anybody on a moral plane. You had people that were very fine people on both sides."[93] World War II veterans saw it differently. "Many buddies lost their lives fighting to destroy that evil," said 91-year-old Army Staff Sgt. Alan Moskin, who helped liberate one of the death camps. "Too many. To see what recently occurred in our own country, I have little doubt they would be turning over in their graves."[94] As with Trump's election, the far right took Charlottesville as another affirming marker on the road to mainstreaming a movement that showed no signs of abating: in April 2019, arsonists destroyed much of the historic Highlander Folk School, leaving behind the mark of the fascist Romanian Iron Guard. Neo-Nazi Atomwaffen disciples were charged in multiple murders across the country.[95] At Pittsburgh's Tree of Life Synagogue, a white supremacist incited by Trump's warning of a border "invasion," and angry over the Jewish community's support for refugees, gunned down 11 worshippers. On August 3, 2019, an anti-immigrant gunman killed 23 at a Walmart in El Paso.[96] While the president was not responsible for the slaughter, he had unquestionably added his politics of aggrieved vengeance to an already volatile mix of racism and America's massive weapons arsenal, in the process giving further license to extremism.

Republicans on Capitol Hill responded with a varying mix of muted criticism ("I wish the president wouldn't Tweet so much"), ignorance ("I haven't read the Tweet"), and dissembling evasion. In the end, most embraced Trump out of fear of offending his supporters. Conscientious defectors were punished with mean Tweets and forced out by a Trumpified electorate. In return for his craven surrender, Majority Leader Mitch McConnell received a wave of conservative appointments to the federal judiciary. Neal Gorsuch purloined Merrick Garland's Supreme Court seat, and in 2018 Brett Kavanaugh was nominated to fill the seat of Anthony Kennedy. When serious charges of sexual misconduct came forward against Kavanaugh, his nomination hearing became a combative sequel to the Hill-Thomas episode, Christine Blasey-Ford testifying movingly of having been assaulted by Kavanaugh in her youth. Kavanaugh and his defenders spat back tirades of indignation and Republicans got their man on the court.

The hearing came amid the #MeToo Movement, which cast a spotlight on the sexual transgressions of powerful men in Hollywood, business, and beyond, infusing Blasey-Ford's account with greater potency. Just eighteen months earlier in the Women's March, millions expressed outrage at Trump's election, many committing themselves to active engagement in politics. In March 2018 young Americans took to the streets in the March for Our Lives, a massive demonstration against gun violence. The event was initiated by students of Marjory Stoneman Douglas High School in Parkland, Florida following a mass shooting there that cut short 17 lives, just the latest in the epidemic that had been raging for two decades. Altogether, the Trump backlash of vigorous engagement ensured the election of a record number of women in November 2018, and that the U.S. House of Representatives would be controlled by the Democrats who hoped to place a constitutional check on an obstreperous presidency.

2020

"I would like you to do us a favor, though." The president was speaking to Ukrainian President Volodymr Zelensky. The favor? To collaborate with Rudy Giuliani and other Trump operatives to smear Joe Biden, his likely opponent in the 2020 election. "Though" signaled the *quid pro quo*: if Zelensky refused, the $400 million in congressionally authorized military aid—desperately needed by Ukraine as it fought Russian aggression—would continue to be withheld. Three years of what many experts called impeachable offenses paled beside this: exploiting military assistance to a U.S. ally trying to wrest itself from its former overlords in Moscow—the same Russians who attacked American democracy—to help ensure your reelection. As many constitutional scholars argued, the mob-style extortion of the Ukrainian president went to the heart of the "betrayal of trust" of the office which the founders believed would demand impeachment.[97] The phone call took place July 25, 2019, the very day after Robert Mueller testified on Capitol Hill. Much anticipated by Trump critics, Mueller's appearance disappointed, and together with an "exoneration" his Attorney General William Barr claimed he had received in the report, reinforced Trump's belief that—as he lectured a group of high school students two days before—"I have an Article II [of the U.S. Constitution] where I have the right to do whatever I want to do as president."[98] It did not, of course, but Trump behaved like it did.

With Republicans slavishly beholden to Trump, the outcome of the impeachment trial was a forgone conclusion. The drama came in the presentation brought by the House of Representatives. Most damning was testimony from leading State Department and National Security Council experts in U.S. Russian policy who happened to be women and American immigrants, favored targets of Trump debasement. Marie Yovanovitch, U.S. Ambassador to Ukraine, grew concerned that the president's leveraging of foreign aid for personal gain was undermining Ukraine's ability to defend itself against an American adversary, as well as U.S. national security. For that, Yovanovitch was trashed in a disinformation campaign waged by Giuliani to everyone in Ukraine who could not avoid him and on Fox. Trump warned Zelensky that Yovanovitch was "going to go through some things." She was abruptly recalled as ambassador, ending a sterling 33-year record as a foreign service officer. For her testimony in the impeachment proceeding, she was Tweet-attacked *as she was testifying.*[99]

With decades of service to the United States, Ukraine-born NSC official Alexander Vindman testified to the "power disparity" evident in the president's phone call. Vindman recalled that his father, born under Soviet domination, feared the consequences of his son coming forth to testify in a gravely consequential proceeding against a sitting American president. Lieutenant Colonel Vindman reassured his father that he would be safe, because "this is America … and here, right matters."[100] But not to everyone. For some Republicans and Fox pundits, Vindman's immigrant background called his loyalty into question. Former top NSC Russian expert, British immigrant Fiona Hill reaffirmed America as a "beacon" of liberty, called such questions "deeply unfair," and castigated Trump sycophants for perpetuating the grotesque "fictional narrative" coming from Russian intelligence that it was Ukraine that attacked the 2016 election.[101] Even as he knew acquittal was coming, lead impeachment manager Representative Adam Schiff delivered a predictive closing entreaty to U.S. Senate jurors:

> You can't trust this president to do the right thing … What are the odds if left in office that he will continue trying to cheat? I will tell you: 100 percent. A man without character or ethical compass will never find his way.[102]

In early 2020, the Russia investigation and the Ukraine affair appeared as ghastly bookends to a four-year assault on American constitutional norms and institutions: the free press, smeared Stalin-style as "the enemy of the people"; open disdain toward the oversight responsibilities of congress; the attack of public servants who dared blow the whistle on administration wrongdoing; the fracturing of U.S. alliances abroad. Although federal law enforcement, intelligence agencies, and the judiciary remained relative bulwarks of integrity in the Trump era, they, too, were maligned, transformed, and in the case of the Justice Department, led by Trump loyalists. The attack on America from within produced a most unlikely political bedfellowship. Republicans, longstanding stalwart defenders of institutional order, followed Trump into a conspiratorial world where the United States government was a diabolical "deep state" scheming to destroy him. Democratic progressives, meanwhile, with a longstanding suspicion of law enforcement stemming from Vietnam era abuses, found themselves cheering Republican heads of the FBI and National Intelligence who were standing up to an authoritarian president. When left-leaning MSNBC could bring Bill Kristol, a neoconservative architect of the Iraq invasion, together with rapper Fat Joe, Americans knew they were living in a world turned upside down.[103] Policy disputes over the size of government or U.S. hypocrisy abroad shrank in significance as America's better angels from across the spectrum were summoned to a higher unifying cause: to save their democracy.

Emerging out of Wuhan, China, in late December 2019, the novel coronavirus (COVID-19) pandemic, officially declared March 11, 2020 by the World Health Organization, would have been an immense challenge for any president. With hundreds dying daily in hot spots like northern Italy and cases reported in dozens of countries, the WHO's declaration compelled many governments to issue stay-at-home orders in hopes of saving as many lives as possible. President Trump, while wisely halting travel from China and authorizing "Operation Warp Speed" to develop vaccines in what proved record time, at the same time repeatedly downplayed the threat. "It's going to disappear one day. It's like a miracle. It will disappear," he declared February 27—the first of countless such utterances in the weeks and months ahead. Privately, he was confiding to journalist Bob Woodward the truth of its lethality.[104] Even as the Center for Disease Control (CDC) and his COVID-19 task force advised Americans to wear masks, the president refused and mocked Democratic opponent Joe Biden for doing so.

Weeks into the crisis, Trump took command of the daily task force briefings where, among other things: he boasted of all the steps he had taken that had gotten the virus under control (it was not), suggested that doctors and nurses were pilfering N95 masks, said that if you removed the "Democrat-run" states and stopped testing for the disease, the COVID numbers were good—this, while the United States with four percent of the world's population had 20 percent of COVID deaths—mused that rays of ultra-violet "light inside the body" might kill the disease, and then the president of the United States said this:

> I see the disinfectant that knocks it out in a minute, one minute. And is there a way we can do something like that by injection inside or almost a cleaning? As you see, it gets in the lungs, it does a tremendous number on the lungs, so it would be interesting to check that.[105]

The catastrophic pandemic that would kill more than 500,000 Americans in little over a year and bring severe economic pain had many culprits, beginning with the initial opaque response from Chinese officials, and continued with shifting, sometimes conflicting information from the CDC. Even the revered Dr. Anthony Fauci, head of the National Institute of Allergy and Infectious Diseases, was not above error. Scientists, however, dealing with a virus unprecedented in nature, acknowledged missteps and self-corrected. This, Donald Trump could never do. Eventually, COVID lanced the bubble of the Trump Show presidency, as multiple White House officials, including the president, contracted the disease. Even then Trump continued to spurn public health measures and elevate pseudoscience, echoing the despots of the old Soviet Union.[106]

Quarantined lockdown brought out the best and worst of Americans. Frontline health care workers enduring shortages of personal protective equipment, watching patients die alone, and risking their own lives were hailed as heroes. Evoking the spirit of World War II, Americans sewed and donated masks to hospitals. Others contributed funds to beloved restaurants and nonprofits devastated by the shutdown. The pandemic shined sympathetic light on underpaid "essential workers" in grocery stores and elsewhere, who unlike most professionals, did not have the luxury of working from home. The loaves-and-fishes operation of humanitarian chef Jose Andres fed hundreds of thousands and helped keep restaurants afloat.[107] Phone calls to grandparents, phantom deliveries of groceries to the elderly, and other random acts of kindness abounded. A few weeks in, however, anger over lockdown restrictions spilled into the streets. In Denver, one woman confronted health care workers in scrubs with, "This is the land of the free! Go to China if you want communism."[108] Well-armed protesters inside the Michigan state capitol in Lansing, many sporting Trump regalia, demanded the state open up. The president piled on: "LIBERATE MICHIGAN," he Tweeted. Some of the same men were later charged with an attempt to kidnap Governor Gretchen Whitmer and start a civil war.[109] Overall, the disease heightened the tension between the idea of the common good and callous individualism, while exacerbating other pre-existing American afflictions. Conspiracy theories raged faster than the contagion, the working poor waited hours in food lines, and the wealthy became fabulously more so.[110]

"Man Dies after Medical Incident during Police Interaction"

That was how the Minneapolis Police Department reported the death of George Floyd to the public on the evening of May 25. The "police interaction" turned out to be the knee of officer Derek Chauvin on the neck of the 46-year-old African American father of five, his full body weight squeezing the life out of Floyd for nine minutes and 29 seconds. For much of the time, Chauvin's hand was tucked in his pocket as he stared icily into the cell phone camera of 17-year-old Darnella Frazer, who uploaded the video to Facebook.[111] Nearly three months into the pandemic, locked down Americans were suddenly transfixed by a twenty-first century lynching. Eight years on from Trayvon Martin, the murder of Mr. Floyd followed the deaths of Breonna Taylor during a blundering police raid in Louisville, Kentucky, and Ahmaud Arbery, chased and shot by three white Georgia men while jogging. The added layer of context was a pandemic impacting black and brown Americans disproportionately.

Overnight, Floyd's murder transformed Black Lives Matter into a global protest movement against police violence and racial injustice. Throughout the summer, extraordinary multi-racial demonstrations across the United States and around the world made for compelling viewing for locked down Americans. Binge-watching TV viewers suddenly sought race-related programming. Corporations and sports teams delivered a range of anti-racism gestures—some more genuine than others to be sure, but altogether signaling an unprecedented American reckoning with systemic racism. Notwithstanding sporadic incidents of violence, the uprising in the streets was overwhelmingly peaceful, one study indicating 93 percent of protests in more than 2,000 locations involved no violence. Many incidents of violence in fact were meted out by reactionary police, national guard, and vigilante white patriots.[112] Those facts did not stop the president, Fox, and others in the rightwing media from smearing the entire movement. Seeing clear opportunity to exploit racial fear, on June 1 the president and his attorney general deployed the military to expel protesters from Lafayette Square near the White House in order to stage a photo-op in front of St. John's Church. Concussion grenades and tear gas having cleared his path, the president stood Mussolini-like holding a Bible (upside down) to proclaim, "I am your president of law and order."[113]

He had no interest in restraining lawless cops, whose violence continued. In late August, shortly after Jacob Blake was shot seven times in front of his children in Kenosha, Wisconsin and left paralyzed for life, Doc Rivers, coach of the NBA Los Angeles Clippers, fought back tears to deliver these words in a postgame press conference:

> All you hear is Donald Trump and all of them talking about fear. We're the ones getting killed. We're the ones getting shot … denied to live in certain communities. We've been hung. We've been shot. All you do is keep hearing about fear.
>
> It's amazing why we keep loving this country, and this country does not love us back.[114]

At 11:25 am on November 7, 2020, the Associated Press declared the Democratic ticket of Joe Biden and Kamala Harris the winner of Pennsylvania, bringing an end to a long week of meticulous vote counting in the most consequential presidential election since 1864. Together with victories in Wisconsin and Michigan, the victory in Biden's native state secured the 270 electoral votes necessary to make him the forty-sixth president of the United States. Wins in Arizona and Georgia followed, fortifying Biden's triumph and delivering the first woman, African American, and South Asian American to the vice presidency. They promised to turn the corner on the virus, deliver needed economic relief, address systemic problems like racial injustice and climate change, and somehow, try and unite the country. A record 158 million Americans voted, nearly two-thirds of the electorate, the highest turnout since 1908. Because of the pandemic, a significant percentage of the vote came by mail, a system Republicans had advocated and utilized for many years. Chris Krebs, the Trump-appointed official responsible for ensuring the security of U.S. elections, called it the most secure in U.S. history, refuting claims of voter irregularities and widespread fraud.[115]

The claims came from the president, who soon fired Krebs. The baseless allegations had been coming since 2016 when Trump warned of a "rigged election" and even in victory claimed that "millions" of illegal votes had been cast. Alarm bells sounded throughout the fall of 2020 as Trump complained endlessly about voter fraud, and indicated he might not accept the peaceful transfer of power in the event of a loss. At 2:30 am on election night, he declared victory and called for an end to the vote counting. He was particularly aggrieved by votes pouring in from urban, predominantly black and brown Philadelphia, Atlanta, Detroit, and Milwaukee. In the days and weeks that followed, local officials across the country—Republican and Democrat—continued dutifully tabulating ballots, recounting, and then auditing the count in battleground states. Trump campaign officials and attorneys led by Rudy Giuliani waged battle in court, where judges—some Trump-appointed—handed them 60 defeats. Yet Trump's "Big Lie" continued to be amplified—by Trump and Trumpified Republicans across America. Some elected Republicans remained faithful to the constitution and to the integrity of an election they had overseen. In the face of death threats, Georgia officials withstood a likely illegal request from Trump demanding they "find 11,780 votes," one more than he needed to overturn the result.[116]

As the reality TV president refused to accept the truth of his defeat, he tried to get states whose legislatures were controlled by Republicans to reject the will of their voters and send a new Trump slate of electors. Republicans continued to either indulge his dangerous fantasy or promulgate the lie outright. Finally, as if scripting a series-ending big finish, Trump called on supporters to come to Washington on January 6, when congress would certify Biden's victory. "Be there. Will be wild," he Tweeted. It was. Following a morning rally at which Trump incited followers to march to the capitol and "fight like hell," they proceeded. Trump battle flags in hand, hordes of supporters—far-right extremists, military veterans, policemen, and elected GOP officials from around the country among them—mounted a violent insurrection on the United States Capitol. They called for the deaths of House Speaker Nancy Pelosi and other Democrats and built gallows to hang Vice President Mike Pence, who refused Trump's bidding and elected to fulfill his constitutional duty and preside over the vote certification. It was the first time the capitol had been breached since the War of 1812, the first time the treasonous flag of the Confederacy had ever been paraded inside the hallowed rotunda. Supporters of the "law and order" president wielded American and "thin blue line" pro-police flags as weapons against police officers defending the lives of elected officials—a number of whom had themselves played a role in inciting the mob. Five Americans were killed, including a capitol police officer; four subsequently committed suicide (Figure 13.2).[117]

Figure 13.2 Trump supporters clash with police and security forces as people try to storm the US Capitol on January 6, 2021 in Washington, DC.

Brent Stirton/Staff/Getty, www.gettyimages.co.uk/detail/news-photo/trump-supporters-clash-with-police-and-security-forces-as-news-photo/1230733998

Two weeks later, Joe Biden was sworn in as president amid a heavily militarized U.S. Capitol complex. As he and Vice President Harris moved forward on an ambitious progressive agenda, Donald John Trump became the only president in history to be impeached twice. All but seven Republicans in the Senate voted to acquit. A slim Democratic majority in congress passed President Biden's massive COVID rescue plan that included the largest commitment to address child poverty in half a century. The fate of the rest of his agenda, though widely popular even among Republicans, remained very much in doubt. Biden and Democrats faced rock-solid opposition from Republicans who remained captive of the man now golfing at his Mar-a-Lago resort in Florida. Though stripped of his Twitter and Facebook accounts and facing possible indictment for financial crimes, Trump retained a firm grip on a Republican base that believed he was the rightful president.[118] So deep in thrall were their voters that very few Republican congressmen or senators could summon the courage to vote for a 9/11-style commission examining the 1/6 attack on the capitol in which their own lives were threatened. One member of congress, photographed helping to barricade the doors of the House chamber that afternoon, declared that the attempted violent overthrow of the U.S. government looked for all the world like a "normal tourist visit."[119] As Matthew Dowd, chief strategist for the 2004 Bush–Cheney campaign, observed, his former political party had no "interest in [advancing] the common good," and had severed contact with the truth, with "a common set of facts" around which public policy is debated.[120]

What *did* interest proto-fascist Republicans, beyond waging unrelenting culture wars, was keeping people from voting. Attempts by GOP-controlled state legislatures to undermine the 1965 landmark Voting Rights Act had already been intensifying since the 2013 decision of the U.S. Supreme Court in *Shelby County v. Holder*. A 5–4 conservative majority of the high court determined that the law's most important provision requiring states with a history of discriminatory restrictive voting measures obtain "preclearance" from the U.S. Justice Department prior to implementing any changes that might impact access to the ballot. In her stinging, prescient dissent, Justice Ruth Bader Ginsburg wrote that, "throwing out preclearance when it has worked and is continuing to work to stop discriminatory changes is like throwing away your umbrella in a rainstorm because you are not getting wet."[121] The downpour of restrictions that followed—closed polling places, reduced hours, photo identification requirements, purged voter rolls—turned to a hurricane after the 2020 election. At this writing, Republican state officials had proposed nearly 400 antidemocratic measures across the country, speciously aimed at "election security." This, after an election in which Trump's own servile Attorney General William Barr said experienced no widespread fraud. Any objective observer could see their purpose: to restrict and suppress Democratic turnout, particularly in black and brown communities. Some measures sought authority to replace or supersede local and state election officials who, like Republicans in Georgia, Arizona and Michigan in 2020, remained faithful to the constitution and not their party.[122]

Eighty years removed from taking up the fight to preserve a democratic world from the threat of global fascism, Americans now faced an illiberal, antidemocratic malevolence from within. For millions of citizens, the third decade of the century dawned with profound trepidation, even grief, over the existential crisis of democracy now confronting their country. Still, there was irrepressible hope, always, in America. As the new president was fond of saying, it was never a good idea "to bet against the American people."[123]

Notes

1 National Park Service, "Ulysses S. Grant's Controversial Visit to Ireland," www.nps. gov/articles/000/ulysses-s-grant-s-controversial-visit-to-ireland.htm, retrieved May 12, 2021.

2 "Poll: Americans' Knowledge of History, Government in 'Crisis,'" *VOA News*, January 19, 2016, www.voanews.com/usa/poll-americans-knowledge-government-history-crisis; and Joel Stein, "We Have Become an Idiocracy," *Time*, May 12, 2016, https:// time.com/4327424/idiocracy, retrieved August 4, 2019.

3 Counselor to the President, Kellyanne Conway, NBC News, January 22, 2017; Rob Tornoe, "Trump to Veterans: 'Don't Believe What you're Reading or Seeing," *Philadelphia Inquirer*, July 24, 2018, www.inquirer.com/philly/news/politics/presidential/donald-trump-vfw-speech-kansas-city-what-youre-seeing-reading-not-whats-happening-20180724.html, retrieved May 18, 2021; Peter Pomerantsev, *Nothing is True and Everything is Possible: The Surreal Heart of the New Russia* (New York: Public Affairs, 2015); and Timothy Snyder, *On Tyranny: Lessons From the Twentieth Century* (New York: Crow, 2017).

4 Michael Scheer and Timothy A. Canova, "The Legacy of the Clinton Bubble," *Dissent* (Summer 2008), www.dissentmagazine.org/article/the-legacy-of-the-clinton-bubble, retrieved August 5, 2019.

5 Roper Starch poll, October 18, 2000, www.iol.co.za/mercury/world/voters-would-rather-have-a-beer-with-bush-49676, retrieved August 5, 2019.

6 Evgenia Peretz, "Going After Gore," *Vanity Fair*, September 4, 2007, www.vanityfair.com/news/2007/10/gore200710, retrieved August 5, 2019.

7 Paul A. Gigot, "Miami Heat: A Burgher Rebellion in Dade County," *Wall Street Journal*, November 24, 2000, https://web.archive.org/web/20060216081537/http://opinionjournal.com/columnists/pgigot/?id=65000673; and Rachel Maddow, "Reviewing the History of Fake Conservative Protests," MSNBC, August 4, 2009, www.youtube.com/watch?v=O5L4dXl4fns, retrieved August 5, 2019.

8 Al Gore, reprinted in *New York Times*, December 13, 2000; www.nytimes.com/2000/12/13/politics/text-of-goreacutes-concession-speech.html, retrieved May 28, 2021.

9 Quoted in Steve Coll, *Ghost Wars: The Secret History of the CIA, Afghanistan, and bin Laden, from the Soviet Invasion to September 10, 2001* (New York: Penguin, 2004), 182.

10 Stephen Kinzer, *Overthrow: America's Century of Regime Change from Hawaii to Iraq* (New York: Henry Holt, 2006), 271–275.

11 Erin Durkin, "September 11: Nearly 10,000 People Affected by 'Cesspool of Cancer,'" *The Guardian*, September 11, 2018, www.theguardian.com/us-news/2018/sep/10/911-attack-ground-zero-manhattan-cancer, retrieved August 6, 2019.

12 Kenneth T. Walsh, "George W. Bush's 'Bullhorn Moment," *U.S. News and World Report*, August 25, 2013, www.usnews.com/news/blogs/ken-walshs-washington/2013/04/25/george-w-bushs-bullhorn-moment, retrieved August 6, 2019.

13 Kinzer, 275–276.

14 Mujib Mashal, "Taliban 'Offered bin Laden for Trial Before 9/11,'" *Al Jazeera*, September 11, 2011, www.aljazeera.com/news/asia/2011/09/20119115334167663.html, retrieved August 7, 2019.

15 "Excellent Progress Reported in U.S.–Taliban Peace Talks," CBS News, August 6, 2019, www.cbsnews.com/news/afghanistan-excellent-progress-reported-us-taliban-peace-talks-today-2019-08-06, retrieved August 6, 2019.

16 "The Iraq War—Part I: The U.S. Prepares for Conflict, 2001" (George Washington University, National Security Archive), posted September 22, 2010, https://nsarchive2.gwu.edu/NSAEBB/NSAEBB326/print.htm#17, retrieved May 28, 2021.

17 All statements of public record from late 2001 to 2003; see for example, Joe Klein, "Why the 'War President' Is Under Fire," *Time*, February 15, 2004, http://content.time.com/time/nation/article/0,8599,591270,00.html, retrieved August 7, 2019.

18 George W. Bush, State of the Union, January 29, 2002, www.npr.org/news/specials/sou/2002/020129.bushtext.html, retrieved August 7, 2019; and Peter L. Bergen, *The Longest War: The Enduring Conflict Between America and Al-Qaeda* (New York: Free Press, 2011), 27.

19 George W. Bush, "Islam Is Peace," September 17, 2001, https://georgewbush-whitehouse.archives.gov/news/releases/2001/09/20010917-11.html, retrieved August 6, 2019.

20 Kat Stoeffel, "Ticker-Taped: The 9/11 News Crawl," *Observer*, September 6, 2011, https://observer.com/2011/09/ticker-taped-the-911-news-crawl, retrieved August 7, 2019.

21 Wolf Blitzer, "Searching for the Smoking Gun," CNN, from a September 8, 2002 interview with Dr. Condoleezza Rice, www.cnn.com/2003/US/01/10/wbr.smoking.gun, retrieved August 7, 2019.

22 "U.S. Public Thinks Saddam Had Role in 9/11," *The Guardian*, September 7, 2003, www.theguardian.com/world/2003/sep/07/usa.theobserver, retrieved August 7, 2019, citing a recent *Washington Post* poll.

23 Maureen Dowd, "Powell Without Picasso," *New York Times*, February 5, 2003, www.
    nytimes.com/2003/02/05/opinion/powell-without-picasso.html, retrieved August
    7, 2019.

24 Phyllis Bennis, "February 15, 2003: The Day the World Said No to War," Institute for
    Policy Studies, February 15, 2013, https://ips-dc.org/february_15_2003_the_day_
    the_world_said:no_to_war, retrieved August 7, 2019; and Phyllis Bennis, *Challenging
    Empire: How People, Governments and the UN Defy U.S. Power* (Northampton, MA:
    Olive Branch Press, 2005).

25 Nigel Williamson, "Free the Dixie Three," *The Guardian*, August 22, 2003, www.the-
    guardian.com/music/2003/aug/22/1; and Lindsay Ellis, "Movies, Patriotism and
    Cultural Amnesia: Tracing Pop Culture's Relationship to 9/11," *Vox*, September 11,
    2017, www.vox.com/2016/9/9/12814898/pop-culture-response-to-9-11, retrieved
    August 7, 2019.

26 George W. Bush, speech aboard the USS *Abraham Lincoln*, May 1, 2003, www.cbsnews.
    com/news/text-of-bush-speech-01-05-2003, retrieved August 7, 2019.

27 Senate Select Committee on Intelligence, "Committee Study of the Central
    Intelligence Agency's Detention and Interrogation Program, Together with a
    Foreword by Chairman Dianne Feinstein and Additional and Minority Views"
    (Washington DC: Government Printing Office, December 9, 2014), www.intelli-
    gence.senate.gov/sites/default/files/publications/CRPT-113srpt288.pdf, retrieved
    August 7, 2019.

28 Daniel Trotta, "Iraq War Cost U.S. $2 Trillion: Study," *Reuters*, March 14, 2013, www.
    reuters.com/article/us-iraq-war-anniversary-idUSBRE92D0PG20130314, retrieved
    August 7, 2019.

29 George H. W. Bush and Brent Scowcroft, *A World Transformed* (New York: Vintage,
    1999), 491.

30 Derek Buckaloo, "Swift Boat Veterans for Truth," Election of 2004 (Southern
    Methodist University, Center for Presidential History, n.d.), http://cphcmp.smu.
    edu/2004election/swift-boat-veterans-for-truth, retrieved August 7, 2019.

31 Emily Horton, "The Legacy of the 2001, 2003 'Bush' Tax Cuts," Center for Budget
    and Policy Priorities, January 3, 2013, updated October 23, 2017, www.cbpp.org/
    research/federal-tax/the-legacy-of-the-2001-and-2003-bush-tax-cuts, retrieved
    August 7, 2019.

32 Robert F. Kennedy, Jr., *Crimes Against Nature: How George W. Bush and His Corporate
    Pals are Plundering the Country and Hijacking Our Democracy* (New York: Harper
    Collins, 2004), 34–35.

33 James Carney and John F. Dickerson, "The Rocky Rollout of Cheney's Energy Plan,"
    Time, May 19, 2001, http://content.time.com/time/nation/article/0,8599,127219,00.
    html, retrieved August 7, 2019.

34 Mark Landler and Sheryl Gay Stolberg, ": Bush Can Share the Blame for Financial
    Crisis," *New York Times*, September 20, 2008, www.nytimes.com/2008/09/20/busi-
    ness/worldbusiness/20iht-prexy.4.16321064.html, retrieved August 7, 2019.

35 Thomas Frank, *Pity the Billionaire: The Hard-Times Swindle and the Unlikely Comeback
    of the Right* (New York: Holt/Metropolitan, 2012), 32–33, 36.

36 Elaine Kamarck, "The Fragile Legacy of Barack Obama," *Brookings*, April 6, 2018,
    www.brookings.edu/blog/fixgov/2018/04/06/the-fragile-legacy-of-barack-obama,
    retrieved August 8, 2019.

37 Quoted in Joshua Green, "Strict Obstructionist," *The Atlantic*, January/February
    2011, www.theatlantic.com/magazine/archive/2011/01/strict-obstructionist/
    308344, retrieved August 8, 2019.

38 Michael Grunwald, "The Victory of 'No,'" *Politico*, December 4, 2016, www.politico.
    com/magazine/story/2016/12/republican-party-obstructionism-victory-
    trump-214498, retrieved August 9, 2019.

39 With brazen hypocrisy, McConnell and the Republicans reversed themselves when liberal icon Ruth Bader Ginsburg died just weeks before the 2020 election and they rammed through Donald Trump's third Supreme Court nominee, Scalia protege, Amy Coney Barrett.

40 Keith Gaby, "Ready to Defend Obama's Environmental Record? Top 10 Accomplishments to Focus on," Environmental Defense Fund, January 12, 2017, www.edf.org/blog/2017/01/12/ready-defend-obamas-environmental-legacy-top-10-accomplishments-focus, retrieved August 8, 2019.

41 Stef W. Kight and Alayna Treene, "Trump Isn't Matching Obama Deportation Numbers," *Axios*, June 21, 2019, www.axios.com/immigration-ice-deportation-trump-obama-a72a0a44-540d-46bc-a671-cd65cf72f4b1.html, retrieved August 8, 2019.

42 Amelia Thomson-DeVeaux, "Will the 2020 Democrats Reject Obama's Immigration Legacy?" *Five-Thirty Eight*, July 31, 2019, https://fivethirtyeight.com/features/will-the-2020-democrats-reject-obamas-immigration-legacy, retrieved August 7, 2019.

43 Danielle Kurtzleben, "Fact Check: Are DACA Recipients Stealing Jobs Away from Other Americans," NPR, September 6, 2017, www.npr.org/2017/09/06/548882071/fact-check-are-daca-recipients-stealing-jobs-away-from-other-americans; and Lily Mihalik, "How Did DACA Affect Dreamers? Financial Independence, Bank Accounts, and Credit Cards," *Politico*, September 6, 2017, www.politico.com/interactives/2017/how-did-daca-impact-dreamers, retrieved August 8, 2019.

44 German Lopez, "'We Were Heard for the First Time': President Obama Leaves an Incredible Legacy on LGBTQ Rights," *Vox*, January 17, 2017, www.vox.com/policy-and-politics/2017/1/17/14214522/obama-lgbtq-legacy; "To LGBT Americans, Obama Will Always Be a Champion," *VOA News*, January 4, 2017, www.voanews.com/usa/lgbt-activists-obama-will-always-be-champion, retrieved August 8, 2019.

45 German Lopez, "How Obama Quietly Reshaped America's War on Drugs," *Vox*, January 19, 2017, www.vox.com/identities/2016/12/19/13903532/obama-war-on-drugs-legacy, retrieved August 8, 2019.

46 Robert Reich, "The Iron of Republican Disapproval of Obamacare," *Christian Science Monitor*, October 28, 2013, www.csmonitor.com/Business/Robert-Reich/2013/1028/The-irony-of-Republican-disapproval-of-Obamacare, retrieved August 9, 2019.

47 Ian Urbina, "Beyond Beltway, Health Debate Turns Hostile," *New York Times*, August 7, 2009, www.nytimes.com/2009/08/08/us/politics/08townhall.html; and Matthew Schafer and Regina Lawrence, "Sarah Palin's 2009 'Death Panel' Claims: How the Media Handled Them and Why That Matters," Nieman Lab, May 26, 2011, www.niemanlab.org/2011/05/sarah-palins-2009-death-panel-claims-how-the-media-handled-them-and-why-that-matters, retrieved August 9, 2019.

48 Bob Cesca, "Keep Your Goddam Government Hands Off My Medicare!" *HuffPost*, September 5, 2009, www.huffpost.com/entry/get-your-goddamn-governme_b_252326.

49 The Association for Community Organizations for Reform Now, which had done good work for 40 years on issues like housing and voter registration, did not survive this attack.

50 Frank, 64–65; Jared Yates Sexton, *The People Are Going to Rise* (Berkeley, CA: Counterpoint Press, 2007), 210–211; and Sean Wilentz, "Confounding Fathers," *The New Yorker*, October 11, 2010, www.newyorker.com/magazine/2010/10/18/confounding-fathers, retrieved August 10, 2019.

51 Frank, 75–80; and Jane Mayer, *Dark Money: The Hidden History of the Rise of the Radical Right* (New York: Anchor Books, 2017), 221–225.

52 "During Another Protest in Washington, the Tea Party Called for the Lynching of President Obama," *The Source*, December 15, 2014, http://thesource.com/2014/12/15/during-another-protest-in-washington-the-tea-party-called-for-the-

lynching-of-president-obama; Glenn Kessler, "A Look at Trump's Birther Statements," *Washington Post*, April 28, 2011, www.washingtonpost.com/blogs/fact-checker/post/a-look-at-trumps-birther-statements/2011/04/27/AFeOYb1E_blog.html, retrieved August 9, 2019.

53 Ben Smith and Byron Tau, "Birtherism: Where It All Began," *Politico*, April 22, 2011, www.politico.com/story/2011/04/birtherism-where-it-all-began-053563, retrieved August 9, 2019.

54 Robert Reich, "How Corporations Crush the Working Class," *Salon*, April 28, 2021, www.salon.com/2021/04/18/robert-reich-how-corporations-crush-the-working-class_partner; Nicole Karlin, "Silicon Valley is Primed for a Worker Uprising," *Salon*, January 6, 2020, www.salon.com/2020/01/05/silicon-valley-is-primed-for-a-labor-uprising; and Jordan Weissmann, "The 2010s Were An Economic Tragedy," *Slate*, December 27, 2019, https://slate.com/business/2019/12/the-four-mistakes-that-turned-the-2010s-into-an-economic-tragedy.html, retrieved May 20, 2021.

55 Melinda Tuhus, "The Blair Mountain Project," *In These Times*, May 16, 2011, http://inthesetimes.com/article/7306/the_blair_mountain_project; and Paige Lavender and Corbin Hiar, "Blair Mountain: Protesters March to Save Historic Battlefield," *HuffPost*, August 10, 2011, www.huffpost.com/entry/blair-mountain-march-protesters_n_875150, retrieved August 10, 2019.

56 Anna Lee, "Treaties Still Matter: Dakota Access Pipeline," Smithsonian Institution National Museum of the American Indian Native Knowledge, https://americanindian.si.edu/nk360/plains-treaties/dapl.cshtml; Nadia Prupis, "83 Arrested at Dakota Pipeline Protest, Frontline Camp Erected on Unceded Territory," EcoWatch (from Common Dreams), October 24, 2016, www.ecowatch.com/arrests-dakota-access-pipeline-2061419170.html, retrieved August 10, 2019; and Tara Houska, "Defending the Sacred: The Dakota Access Pipeline and the Fight for a Livable Future," Mercyhurst University, Monday, April 24, 2017.

57 Lizette Alvarez, "Zimmerman Case Has race as a Backdrop, But You Won't Hear It In Court," *New York Times*, July 7, 2013, www.nytimes.com/2013/07/08/us/zimmerman-case-has-race-as-a-backdrop-but-you-wont-hear-it-in-court.html, retrieved August 11, 2019.

58 Elizabeth Day, "#BlackLivesMatter: The Birth of a New Civil Rights Movement," *The Guardian*, July 19, 2015, www.theguardian.com/world/2015/jul/19/blacklives-matter-birth-civil-rights-movement, retrieved August 11, 2019.

59 Aliyah Shahid, "Conservatives Blast President Obama's Remarks on Trayvon Martin: He's Race Baiting!" *New York Daily News*, March 24, 2012, www.nydailynews.com/news/politics/conservatives-blast-president-obama-remarks-trayvon-martin-race-baiting-article-1.1050298, retrieved May 21, 2021.

60 Jamelle Bouie, "Racial Discontent is Rising, but That's Not Obama's Fault," *Slate*, July 15, 2016, https://slate.com/news-and-politics/2016/07/racial-discontent-is-rising-but-thats-not-obamas-fault.html, retrieved August 11, 2019.

61 Zack Beauchamp, "An Online Subculture Celebrating the Charleston Church Shooter Appears to be Inspiring Copycat Plots," *Vox*, February 7, 2019, www.vox.com/policy-and-politics/2019/2/7/18215634/dylann-roof-charleston-church-shooter-bowl-gang; Rachel Kaadzi Ghansah, "A Most American Terrorist: The Making of Dylann Roof," *GQ*, August 21, 2017, www.gq.com/story/dylann-roof-making-of-an-american-terrorist, retrieved August 11, 2019.

62 Simon McCormack, "Cops Bought Dylann Roof Burger King Hours After Charleston Shooting," *HuffPost*, December 6, 2017, www.huffpost.com/entry/dylann-roof-burger-king_n_7645216, retrieved August 12, 2019.

63 Caroline Mala Corbin, "Terrorists are Always Muslim but Never White: At the Intersection of Critical race Theory and Propaganda," *Fordham Law Review* 86, no. 2, article 5 (2017), 461–462, 466–467, https://ir.lawnet.fordham.edu/cgi/viewcontent.cgi?article=5437&context=flr, retrieved May 24, 2021.

64 Janet Reitman, "U.S. Law Enforcement Failewd to See the Threat of White Nationalism. Now They Don't Know How to Stop It," *New York Times*, November 3, 2018, www.nytimes.com/2018/11/03/magazine/FBI-charlottesville-white-nationalism-far-right.html, retrieved August 12, 2019.

65 Josh Israel, "Research Predicted This Wave of Right-wing Domestic Terrorism. Republicans Tanked the Report," *Think Progress*, November 26, 2018, https://think-progress.org/right-wing-domestic-terrorism-rise-obamas-dhs-warned-a57940206352; and Mehdi Hasan with Joy Reid, "AM Joy," MSNBC, March 17, 2019, https://archive.org/details/MSNBCW_20190317_140000_AM_Joy, retrieved August 12, 2019.

66 Time staff, "Here's Donald Trump's Presidential Announcement Speech," *Time*, June 16, 2005, https://time.com/3923128/donald-trump-announcement-speech, retrieved August 12, 2019.

67 Donald Trump, Family Leadership Summit, C-Span, July 18, 2015, www.youtube.com/watch?v=541Cg2Jnb8s; and Danielle Kurtzleben, "Here's the List of Women Who Accused Donald Trump of Sexual Misconduct," NPR, www.npr.org/2016/10/13/497799354/a-list-of-donald-trumps-accusers-of-inappropriate-sexual-conduct, retrieved August 12, 2019.

68 Z. Byron Wolf, "Trump's Attacks on Judge Curiel are Still Jarring to Read," CNN Politics, February 27, 2018, www.cnn.com/2018/02/27/politics/judge-curiel-trump-border-wall/index.html, retrieved August 12, 2019.

69 Donald Trump, December 7, 2015, in Sexton, 93–95.

70 Sexton, 109–110, 135–136, 165–166.

71 Stuart Stevens, *It Was All a Lie: How the Republican Party Became Donald Trump* (New York: Knopf, 2020), 4.

72 Emily Stewart, "Donald Trump Rode $5 Billion in Free Media to the White House," *The Street*, November 20, 2016.

73 Amy Goodman and Denis Moynihan, "How the Media Iced out Bernie Sanders and Helped Donald Trump Win," *Common Dreams*, December 3, 2016, www.common-dreams.org/views/2016/12/03/how-media-iced-out-bernie-sanders-helped-donald-trump-win, retrieved August 12, 2019.

74 Carole Cadwalladr, "If You're Not Terrified About Facebook, You Haven't Been Paying Attention," *The Guardian*, July 26, 2020, www.theguardian.com/commentisfree/2020/jul/26/with-facebook-we-are-already-through-the-looking-glass, retrieved June 21, 2021.

75 Ryan Broderick, "Here's Everything the Mueller Report Says About How Russian Trolls Used Social Media," *BuzzFeed News*, April 18, 2019, www.buzzfeednews.com/article/ryanhatesthis/mueller-report-internet-research-agency-detailed-2016; and William Saletan, "Trump Is Finishing Russia's Smear Campaign Against America," *Slate*, December 11, 2020, https://slate.com/news-and-politics/2020/12/trump-finishing-russia-plan-discredit-american-elections.html, retrieved May 23, 2021, quoting various U.S. Intelligence Agencies' Reports, 2017–2019.

76 Sabrina Siddiqui, "What the Mueller Report Tells Us About Trump, Russia and Obstruction," *The Guardian*, April 18, 2019, www.theguardian.com/us-news/ng-interactive/2019/apr/18/mueller-report-trump-russia-key-takeaways; CNN Library, "2016 Presidential Campaign Hacking Fast Facts," May 2, 2019, www.cnn.com/2016/12/26/us/2016-presidential-campaign-hacking-fast-facts/index.html, retrieved August 12, 2019.

77 Edward-Isaac Dovere, "Biden: McConnell Stopped Obama from Calling Out Russians," *Politico*, January 23, 2018, www.politico.com/story/2018/01/23/mitch-mcconnell-russia-obama-joe-biden-359531; Biden's version has been corroborated by multiple other sources.

78 Amanda Marcotte, *Troll Nation: How the Right Became Trump-Worshipping Monsters Set on Ratf*cking Liberals, America, and Truth Itself* (New York: Skyhorse Publishing, 2018), 65.

79 Fact Checker, "Trump's False or Misleading Statements Totaled 30,543 Over 4 Years," *The Washington Post*, January 24, 2021, www.washingtonpost.com/politics/2021/01/24/trumps-false-or-misleading-claims-total-30573-over-four-years, retrieved May 24, 2021.

80 Sean Illing, "'Flooding the Zone with Shit': How Misinformation Overwhelmed Our Democracy," *Vox*, February 6, 2020, www.vox.com/policy-and-politics/2020/1/16/20991816/impeachment-trial-trump-bannon-misinformation, retrieved May 24, 2021.

81 Donald J. Trump, "Address to the Veterans of Foreign Wars Convention," Kansas City, MO, July 24, 2018, www.bbc.com/news/av/world-us-canada-44959340/donald-trump-what-you-re-seeing-and-what-you-re-reading-is-not-what-s-happening, retrieved August 11, 2019.

82 Cleve R. Wootson, Jr., Trump Implied Frederick Douglass was Alive. The abolitionist's family offered him a 'history lesson,'" *Charlotte Observer*, February 2, 2017, www.charlotteobserver.com/news/politics-government/article130328199.html; and Kate Lyons, "Flight of Fancy: Trump Claims 1775 Army 'took over airports'," *The Guardian*, July 5, 2019, www.theguardian.com/us-news/2019/jul/05/flight-of-fancy-trump-claims-1775-revolutionary-army-took-over-airports, retrieved June 21, 2021.

83 Cited by Ross Douthat, "The Age of American Despair," *New York Times*, September 8, 2019, SR, 7.

84 Nicholas Kristof, "Can Biden save People Like My Pal Mike?," *New York Times*, February 14, 2021, SR, 7.

85 The phrase belongs is owed to Republican strategist Steve Schmidt, heard on "Deadline," MSNBC, October 20, 2020, www.youtube.com/watch?v=qW2ghgv9Or0, retrieved May 24, 2021.

86 Anu Partanen, "Op-Ed: Finland to President Trump: 'We Don't Rake the Forest Floor, but We do Other Things you Should Emulate,'" *LA Times*, November 18, 2019, www.latimes.com/opinion/op-ed/la-oe-partanen-finns-dont-rake-the-forest-floor-20181119-story.html, retrieved May 24, 2021.

87 Kate Yoder, "From 'Heat Domes' to 'Rain Bombs,' Climate Change is Changing How We Talk About Weather," *Grist*, August 3, 2016, https://grist.org/climate-energy/from-heat-domes-to-rain-bombs-climate-change-is-changing-how-we-talk-about-weather; and Jennifer Atkinson, "Climate Grief: Our Greatest Ally?" *Resilience*, August 27, 2020, www.resilience.org/stories/2020-08-27/climate-grief-our-greatest-ally, retrieved May 24, 2021.

88 John McCormick and Jesse Naranjo, "Iowa Farmers Stick With Trump Despite Trade War," *Wall Street Journal*, August 14, 2019, www.wsj.com/articles/iowa-farmers-stick-with-trump-despite-trade-war-11565775003; and Justin Worland, "Donald Trump Called Climate Change a Hoax. Now He's Awkwardly Boasting About Fighting It," *Time*, July 9, 2019, https://time.com/5622374/donald-trump-climate-change-hoax-event, retrieved August 16, 2019.

89 Ella Nilsen, "The New Face of Climate Activism is Young, Angry—and Effective," *Vox*, September 17, 2019, www.vox.com/the-highlight/2019/9/10/20847401/sunrise-movement-climate-change-activist-millennials-global-warming, retrieved May 24, 2021.

90 They took their name from the multi-racial, working-class origins of "redneck," which most historians date to the 1921 Battle of Blair Mountain when striking miners wore red bandanas.

91 Farah Stockman, "Who Were the Counterprotesters in Charlottesville?" *New York Times*, August 14, 2017, www.nytimes.com/2017/08/14/us/who-were-the-counterprotesters-in-charlottesville.html, retrieved May 24, 2021.

92 Dara Lind, "Unite the Right, the Violent White Supremacist Rally in Charlottesville, Explained," *Vox*, August 14, 2017, www.vox.com/2017/8/12/16138246/charlottesville-nazi-rally-right-uva.

93 Ben Jacobs, "Trump Reverts to Blaming Both Sides Including 'Violent Alt-Left'," *The Guardian*, August 16, 2017, www.theguardian.com/us-news/2017/aug/15/donald-trump-press-conference-far-right-defends-charlottesville, retrieved August 13, 2019.

94 Veronica Harris and Larry McShane, "WW II Veterans Disgusted by Neo Nazis at Charlottesville Protest," *New York Daily News*, August 26, 2017, www.nydailynews.com/new-york/wwii-veterans-disgusted-surge-neo-nazis-va-protest-article-1.3445232, retrieved August 13, 2019.

95 Sarah Jones, "At Fames Civil Rights Center, Fire Destroys a Building, But Not a Mission," *The Intelligencer*, April 6, 2019; and A. C. Thompson and Ali Winston, "Atomwaffen, Neo-Nazi Group Whose Members Have been Charged in Five Murders, Loses Some of Its Platforms," *Pro Publica*, March 6, 2018; www.propublica.org/article/atomwaffen-extremist-group-whose-members-have-been-charged-in-five-murders-loses-some-of-its-platforms, retrieved May 24, 2021.

96 Chas Danner, "Everything We Know About the El Paso Massacre," *The Intelligencer*, August 7, 2019, https://nymag.com/intelligencer/2019/08/everything-we-know-about-the-el-paso-walmart-shooting.html, retrieved May 26, 2021.

97 Michael Sozan, "The Founders Would Have Impeached Trump for His Ukraine-Related Misconduct," Center for American Progress, September 26, 2019, www.americanprogress.org/issues/democracy/news/2019/09/26/475114/founders-impeached-trump-ukraine-related-misconduct, retrieved May 25, 2021.

98 Christina Zhao, "'Article 2' Trends After Trump Falsely Claims It Grants Him Unlimited Powers as President: I Can 'Do Whatever I Want'," *Newsweek*, July 23, 2019, www.newsweek.com/article-2-trends-after-trump-falsely-claims-it-grants-him-unlimited-powers-president-i-can-do-1450798, retrieved May 25, 2021.

99 Alanna Vagianos, "Women and Immigrants, Demeaned by Trump, Take Center Stage at Impeachment," *HuffPost*, November 22, 2019, www.huffpost.com/entry/women-immigrants-trump-impeachment-hearings_n_5dd6b4dfe4b0e29d72807059, retrieved May 25, 2021.

100 Lieutenant Colonel Alexander Vindman, testimony before the U.S. House of Representatives Intelligence Committee, November 19, 2019, www.youtube.com/watch?v=AugBEf6gl90, retrieved May 26, 2021.

101 Roger Cohen, "Fiona Hill and the American Idea," *New York Times*, November 22, 2019, www.nytimes.com/2019/11/22/opinion/impeachment-inquiry-fiona-hill.html, retrieved May 26, 2021.

102 Dareh Gregorian, "Schiff's Powerful Closing Speech: 'Is There One Among You Who Will Say, Enough!'?" NBC News, February 3, 2020, www.nbcnews.com/politics/trump-impeachment-inquiry/closing-argument-democrats-say-not-removing-trump-would-render-him-n1128766, retrieved May 26, 2021.

103 Ari Melber, "A Year of Strange Bedfellows Against Trump," MSNBC: *The Beat*, December 28, 2018, www.youtube.com/watch?v=SnAGwA9zmI8, retrieved May 26, 2021.

104 "Trump Tells Woodward He Deliberately Downplayed Coronavirus Threat," National Public Radio, Morning Edition, September 10, 2020, www.npr.org/2020/09/10/911368698/trump-tells-woodward-he-deliberately-downplayed-coronavirus-threat, retrieved May 26, 2021.

105 Dartunorro Clark, "Trump Suggests 'Injection' of Disinfectant to Beat Coronavirus and 'Clean' the Lungs," NBC News, April 23, 2020, www.nbcnews.com/politics/donald-trump/trump-suggests-injection-disinfectant-beat-coronavirus-clean-lungs-n1191216, retrieved May 26, 2021.

106   Nicholas Kristof, "'A Colossal Failure of Leadership,'" *New York Times*, October 25, 2020, SR 4.

107   Jane Black, "Chef Jose Andres Embraces the Chaos," HuffPost, n.d., www.huffpost. com/entry/jose-andres-covid19-pandemic-world-central-kitchen_n_5fb689f4c5b 6f00bd84e1e8f, retrieved May 27, 2021.

108   Poppy Noor, "What Happened When Healthcare Workers Confronted Anti-lockdown Protesters—in One Photo," *The Guardian*, April 20, 2020, www.the-guardian.com/artanddesign/2020/apr/20/photograph-healthcare-workers-confronted-anti-lockdown-protesters-denver, retrieved May 27, 2021.

109   David Eggert, "Men Accused in Plot on Michigan Governor Attended Protests," Associated Press, October 10, 2020, https://apnews.com/article/virus-outbreak-donald-trump-michigan-gretchen-whitmer-gun-politics-8aff3b8db-0c03a80946e054d602f70fe, retrieved May 26, 2021.

110   Chuck Collins, "Updates: Billionaire Wealth, Job Losses, Pandemic Profiteers," Inequality.org, April 15, 2021, https://inequality.org/great-divide/updates-billion-aire-pandemic, retrieved May 27, 2021.

111   Ari Shapiro, "How Police Reports Became Bulletproof," National Public Radio: All Things Considered, May 26, 2021, www.npr.org/2021/05/26/1000598495/ how-police-reports-became-bulletproof, retrieved May 27, 2021.

112   Lois Beckett, "Nearly All Black Lives Matter Protests Are Peaceful, Despite Trump Narrative, Study Finds," *The Guardian*, September 5, 2020, www.theguardian.com/ world/2020/sep/05/nearly-all-black-lives-matter-protests-are-peaceful-despite-trump-narrative-report-finds; and "This Summer's Black Lives Matter Protesters Were Overwhelmingly Peaceful," *Washington Post*, October 16, 2020, www.wash-ingtonpost.com/politics/2020/10/16/this-summers-black-lives-matter-protest-ers-were-overwhelming-peaceful-our-research-finds, retrieved May 27, 2021.

113   Donald Trump, "I Am Your President of Law and Order," Associated Press, June 1, 2020, www.nytimes.com/video/us/politics/100000007168573/trump-floyd-pro-tests.html, retrieved May 27, 2021.

114   Kurt Helin, "Doc Rivers: 'We Keep Loving This Country, and This Country Does Not Love Us Back," NBC Sports, August 26, 2020, https://nba.nbcsports. com/2020/08/26/doc-rivers-we-keep-loving-this-country-and-this-country-does-not-love-us-back, retrieved May 27, 2021.

115   Amanda Macias, "Trump Fires DHS Cybersecurity Chief Chris Krebs," CNBC, November 17, 2020, www.cnbc.com/2020/11/17/trump-says-us-cybersecurity-chief-chris-krebs-has-been-terminated.html, retrieved May 27, 2021.

116   Michael D. Shear and Stephanie Saul, "Trump, in Taped Call, Pressured Georgia Official to 'Find' Votes to Overturn Election," *New York Times*, January 3, 2021, updated May 26, www.nytimes.com/2021/01/03/us/politics/trump-raffens-perger-call-georgia.html, retrieved May 27, 2021.

117   Robin Stein et al., "U.S. Capitol Riot," *New York Times*, March 22, 2021, www. nytimes.com/spotlight/us-capitol-riots-investigations, retrieved June 21, 2021.

118   Max Greenwood, "53 percent of Republicans Believe Trump is Rightful President," *The Hill*, May 25, 2021, https://thehill.com/homenews/campaign/555256-53-per-cent-of-republicans-say-trump-is-true-president-poll, retrieved June 21, 2021.

119   Thomas Colson, "A Republican Congressman Who Denied There was an Insurrection and likened Capitol Rioters to Tourists was Photographed Barricading the Doors Against Them," *Business Insider*, May 17, 2021, www.businessinsider. com/gop-rep-who-called-capitol-rioters-tourists-photographed-barricading-house-2021-5, retrieved May 28, 2021.

120   Matthew Dowd, "Biden Should Have Addressed Anti-democratic, Fantasy-land Trumpism in His Speech to Congress," *USA Today*, April 30, 2021, www.usatoday. com/story/opinion/2021/04/30/biden-should-have-held-trump-accountable-for-our-broken-democracy-column/7401028002, retrieved May 27, 2021.

121 Vann R. Newkirk II, "How *Shelby County v. Holder* Broke America," *The Atlantic*, July 10, 2018, www.theatlantic.com/politics/archive/2018/07/how-shelby-county-broke-america/564707, retrieved July 4, 2021.

122 Nick Corasiniti on Terry Gross's Fresh Air, "Voting Restrictions are Further Politicizing U.S. Electoral System, Journalist says," May 27, 2021, www.npr.org/2021/05/27/1000869614/voting-restrictions-are-further-politicizing-u-s-electoral-system-journalist-say, retrieved May 27, 2021.

123 Joe Biden, "Remarks as Prepared for Delivery by President Biden – Address to a Joint Session of Congress," April 28, 2021, www.whitehouse.gov/briefing-room/speeches-remarks/2021/04/28/remarks-as-prepared-for-delivery-by-president-biden-address-to-a-joint-session-of-congress, retrieved May 28, 2021.

Further Reading

Anderson, Carol. *The Second: Race and Guns in a Fatally Unequal America*. New York: Bloomsburg, 2021.

Anderson, Kurt. *Evil Geniuses: The Unmaking of America—A Recent History*. New York: Random House, 2020.

Ben-Ghiat, Ruth. *Strongmen: Mussolini to the Present*. New York: W. W. Norton, 2020.

Bender, Michael. *"Frankly We Did Win This Election": The Inside Story of How Trump Lost*. New York: Twelve, 2021.

Bergen, Peter L. *The Longest War: The Enduring Conflict Between America and Al-Qaeda*. New York: Free Press, 2011.

Campbell, Bradly, and Jason Manning. *The Rise of Victimhood Culture: Microaggressions, Safe Spaces, and the New Culture Wars*. New York: Palgrave Macmillan, 2018.

D'antonio, Michael. *The Truth About Trump*. New York: St. Martin's Press/Thomas Dunne Books, 2015.

Frank, Thomas. *Pity the Billionaire: The Hard-Times Swindle and the Unlikely Comeback of the Right*. New York: Holt/Metropolitan, 2012.

Hartman, Andrew. *A War for the Soul of America: A History of the Culture Wars, 2nd ed.* Chicago, IL: University of Chicago Press, 2019.

Hinton, Elizabeth. *America On Fire: The Untold History of Police Violence and Black Rebellion Since the 1960s*. New York: Liveright Publishing, 2021.

Horesh, Theo. *The Fascism This Time and the Global Future of Democracy*. Boulder, CO: Cosmopolis Press, 2020.

Lavin, Talia. *Culture Warlords: My Journey into the Dark Web of White Supremacy*. New York: Hachette Book Group, 2020.

Lozada, Carlos. *What Were We Thinking: A Brief Intellectual History of the Trump Era*. New York: Simon and Schuster, 2020.

Marcotte, Amanda. *Troll Nation: How the Right Became Trump-Worshipping Monsters Set on Ratf*cking Liberals, America, and Truth Itself*. New York: Skyhorse Publishing, 2018.

Mayer, Jane. *Dark Money: The Hidden History of the Rise of the Radical Right*. New York: Anchor Books, 2017.

McGhee, Heather. *The Sum of Us: What Racism Costs Everyone and How We Can Prosper Together*. New York: One World, 2021.

Rhodes, Ben. *After the Fall: Being American in the World We've Made*. New York: Random House, 2021.

Rhodes, Ben. *The World as it Is: Inside the Obama White House*. New York: Vintage, 2019.

Richardson, Heather Cox. *How the South Won the Civil War: Oligarchy, Democracy, and the Continuing Fight for the Soul of America*. New York: Oxford University Press, 2020.

Serwer, Adam. *The Cruelty Is the Point: The Past, Present, and Future of Trump's America*. New York: One World, 2021.

Sexton, Jared Yates. *The People Are Going to Rise Like Waters Upon Your Shore: A Story of American Rage*. Berkeley, CA: Counterpoint, 2017.

Snyder, Timothy. *On Tyranny: Twenty Lessons From the Twentieth Century*. New York: Crown, 2017.

Stelter, Brian. *Hoax: Donald Trump, Fox News, and the Dangerous Distortion of Truth*. New York: One Signal Publishers, 2020.

Stevens, Stuart. *It Was All a Lie: How the Republican Party Became Donald Trump*. New York: Knopf, 2020.

Index

Page numbers followed by 'n' refers to notes numbers.

Abdul-Jabbar, K. 187
Abrams, E. 267, 276n79
Acheson, D. 35; and Korea 37; role in and globalization of Truman Doctrine 27, 29
Affluent Society, The (Galbraith, J.K.) 100
Affordable Care Act ("Obamacare") 311, 319; *see also* Tea Party
Afghanistan: Soviet Union invasion of and war 239, 264; U.S.-CIA support of anti-Soviet mujahideen 239–240; U.S. war in, 2001–2021 (Operation Enduring Freedom) 302, 304–306
African American women and sexual terror, role of in Civil Rights Movement 84–85; *see also* Bates, D.; Montgomery (AL) Bus Boycott; Taylor, R.; Women's Political Council
Age of American Unreason, The 303
Agnew, S. 189
Ailes, R.: collaboration with "Big Tobacco" to stop health care reform 293; and Fox News 293–294; as Republican media guru 189, 293; *see also* Fox News
Alaska National Interest Lands Conservation Act 234
Albright, M. 289–290, 298n47
Alcatraz occupation (1969) 211
Ali, M. 160, 187
Allende, S. 207
Altamont 198
America First Committee 1
American Century, The 1–3, 44; *see also* American exceptionalism
American Dilemma, The 14
American exceptionalism 1, 58, 144, 294

American Indian Movement 211–212
American Nazi Party 135, 157
Americans with Disabilities Act (ADA) 282
Andres, Chef J. 324
Andy Griffith Show 111
anti-Dow campaign, University of WI 155
anti-fascism (World War II): and civil rights 6; *Don't Be a Sucker* 5; Leon Lewis 4–5; *see also* Wallace, H.
anti-intellectualism 54, 189–190
Aoki, R. 208–209
Armey, D. 284, 290, 304
Atwater, L. 281, 293
Auto Immune Deficiency Syndrome (AIDS) 270–271; *see also* Fauci, A.; Helms, Sen. J.; Kramer, L.
auto industry: Corporate Average Fuel Efficiency (CAFÉ) standards 229; and rescue of (2009) 309

Baker, E. 91, 317
Balkan Wars (1999) 289
Bannon, S. 319
Barnett, R. 108–109
Barr, W.: affirms secure 2020 election 328; misrepresents Mueller Report 322
Bates, D. 90
Beam, L. 242–243
Beatles, The: arrival in United States 128; break-up 198; and counterculture 164, 167; and Manson murders 198
Beat literary movement 79–80; *see also* Ginsberg, A., *Howl*; Kerouac, J., *On the Road*; psychedelic drugs
Bebop jazz 78–79

Beck, G. 312

Bellah, R. 233

Berkeley, University of CA, early 1960s 152; *see also* Free Speech Movement

Berlin crisis (1948–1949) 27, 34–35; *see also* LeMay, C.

Berlin Wall 114–116, 126; as symbol of Cold War's end 279

Berrigan, D. and P. 161

Biden, J. 303; and Hill-Thomas Hearings 281–282; and marriage equality, as vice-president 310; presidential inauguration of 327; and 2020 election 321, 323, 325–326

Bin Laden, O. 240; and al-Qaeda 1993 bombing of World Trade Center 288; and September 11, 2001 al-Qaeda attacks 304–306

Birmingham (AL) 7, 50, 84, 107–108

Birmingham campaign (1963) 110–112

"birtherism" 312

Bissell, R. 113–114

Black Hills 211

Black Lives Matter (BLM) movement 314–315; *see also* Roof, D.

Black Panther Party for Self-Defense 140; *see also* Lowndes County Freedom Organization

Blair Mountain (WV) 313

Blasey-Ford, C. 321

"Blueboy," *Dragnet* 163

Bonfire of the Vanities 260

Brady Handgun Violence Prevention Act 291

Brady, Judge T.P. 90

Brand, S. 164, 167; *see also* Earth Rise photograph; *Whole Earth Catalog*

Brown, H.R. 177, 179

Brown vs. Board of Education 88–89; and resistance to 89–90; *see also* Little Rock; Southern Manifesto

Bruce, L. 78

Brzezinski, Z. 237; and "arc of crisis" vision 238–239

Buchanan, P.

Burke, Admiral A. 114

Burroughs, W. 80

Bury My Heart at Wounded Knee (Brown, D.) 211

Bush, G.H.W. 261, 272, 279; campaign and disputed election of (2000) 303–304; declares "mission accomplished" prematurely over Iraq 307; and foreign policy 284–285; and presidency 280–284; reprises Reaganomics 308; and "War on Terror" 306; withdrawal from Kyoto Protocol 308; *see also* disability rights movement; Hill-Thomas hearings; Horton, W.; Iraq War (2003); Los Angeles Riots; Operation Desert Storm; September 11, 2001 terrorist attacks; START (Strategic Arms Reduction) Treaty

Cadwalladr, C. 318

Califano, J. 282

Cambodia 199–203; *see also* Kent State

Camp David Accords 228

Carmichael, S. 139, 177, 179

Carter, J. 208; Alaska National Interest Lands Conservation Act; and Carter Doctrine 240; emblematic of the seventies 230; first address on energy 231; human rights foreign policy 236–237; installs solar panels on White House 232; and National Energy Plan 232; pardons draft evaders 235–236; and Shah Reza Pahlavi 238; *see also* "Crisis of Confidence" speech; Dams, "hit list"; El Salvador; Nicaragua; Panama Canal Treaties

Cash, J. 81; and White House performance 201

Cassady, N. 79, 167

Castro, F. 113–114, 116

celebrity culture (1980s) 251, 262; *see also* Trump, D.

Central America refugees (1980s): and Sanctuary Movement 269; U.S. response to 267

Central Intelligence Agency (CIA): and Afghanistan, 304–305; and Central America (1980s) 267–269; and Chile, 207–208; and Cuba, 114–116; establishment of 29–30; and Iran and Guatemala (1953–1954), 65–67; and Iran (late 1970s), 238–239; and Kennedy assassination, 119; and LSD, Mary Pinchot Meyer, 166; and Patrice Lumumba, 113; and Vietnam (1950s), 142; and Watergate Plumbers, 202; *see also* Italy 1948 general elections

Chavez, C. 181–182, 210

Cheney, D. 169n19, 270, 284; and Iraq, 286, 290, 306

"Chennault Affair" 188

Chicago Democratic National
Convention (1968) 185–186
Chicago Freedom Project 161
Chile, 1973 coup d'etat 207
China: and COVID-19 323; and Korean
War 39–41; and McCarthyism 55;
Nixon opening 207; and nuclear
"brinksmanship" 65; and Paris Climate
Agreement 310; Tiananmen Square 279;
and Trump trade war 320; U.S. response
to collapse of Chiang Kai-shek's
government 35; and Vietnam 67, 127
Church Committee hearings 208
Churchill, W.: and Atlantic Charter 6; and
Greek Civil War 27–28; and Iran 65;
and "Iron Curtain" declaration 27; and
postwar view of America 20; and
Wallace, H. 6
Citizens United vs. FEC 208
civic illiteracy 303
civil disobedience as strategy for change
106, 153, 157, 213, 235, 270–271;
condemned by Nixon 189
Civilian Materiel Assistance 271
Civil Rights Act (1964) 105, 128–129
Civil Rights Acts (1957 and 1960) 91
Civil Rights Movement, early 1960s 92;
and Nashville campaign 106; and sit-ins
106–107; *see also* Battle of Oxford;
Birmingham Campaign; Congress of
Racial Equality; *Fire Next Time, The*;
Freedom Rides; Student Non-Violent
Coordinating Committee
Clarke, S. 91–92
Clark, T. 31, 49–50
Clean Power Plan 310
Clear Channel Communications 306
Clemente, R. 247n45
climate change and crisis 226, 280, 304,
310, 313, 325; and "climate grief" 320;
and disinformation campaign 294; and
Paris Climate Agreement 310, 319; *see
also* global warming; Thunberg, G.
Clinton, B.: as neoliberal "new Democrat"
286–288; scandals 292; signs 1998 Iraq
Liberation Act 290; use of military
power 288–290; *see also* Balkan Wars
(1999); deregulation of financial markets
(1990s); Whitewater investigation
Clinton, H.: charges "vast right-wing
conspiracy" 292, 299n59; effort to
reform health care 292; and 2016
presidential campaign 317–318

Coffin, W.S. 160–161
Columbia University Strike (1968)
178–181
Colvin, C. 86, 88
Comey, J. 318
Committee in Solidarity with the People
of El Salvador (CISPES) 268
conformity (1950s) 63–64
Congress of Racial Equality (CORE)
107–108, 131
Connor, E. "Bull" 107–108, 110–111, 152
Contract for America 294
Cooke, S. 128
Coors, J. 244, 293
Copland, A. 3
Cops, depiction of African Americans
254–255
counterculture 80, 140, 152, 162–168; and
March on the Pentagon 156; *see also*
Diggers; Haight-Ashbury; Human
Be-In; psychedelic drugs
Counterintelligence Program
(COINTELPRO, FBI) 158, 199
Cousins, N. 117
COVID-19 323–324
"credibility gap" 158, 174
"Crisis of Confidence" speech 226, 233–234
Cronkite, W. 111, 118, 174, 185
Cuba, early 1960s 113–114, 116; *see also*
Castro, F.
cultural conservatism of the 1970s 241
culture wars: and *National Standards for
United States History* 294–295; 1980s
roots 271; and political correctness 292;
Republican continuation of in Trump
era 328; Smithsonian National
Museum of Air and Space Museum,
Enola Gay exhibit 295–296; and "The
West as America" 294–295
Cuyahoga River fire (1969) 212

Dakota Access Pipeline (DAPL), struggle
against 313–314
dams: and Carter "hit list" 230–231; 1950s
boom era 60–61
Daniels, C. 241
Daniels, J. 139
Dass, R. 167
Day After, The (1983) 265
deindustrialization 230, 253, 291; and
"Rust Belt" 254; *see also* deregulation
Democratic National Convention (1948)
58–59

Democratic Party and demise of New Deal political coalition 252, 286

Denver, J. 231, 234

deregulation: and Carter era 233, 243; and Interior Department 258–259; Reagan era, promises of and corruption 255–257; Savings & Loan Scandal 256–257; *see also* deregulation of financial markets (1990s); disability rights movement; Federal Communications Commission; Greenspan, A.; *Wall Street* (1987 film)

deregulation of financial markets (1990s) 286–287

Detroit racial unrest (1943) 15

Diggers 156, 163, 165

Dirksen, E. 128–129, 187

disability rights movement 282–283

Dixie Chicks 306

Dominican Republic, U.S. intervention in 154

Domino, F. 82–83

"Doomsday Clock" 36

Double V 15

Dowd, M. 327

Dresner, Rabbi I. 129

drugs, war on 190; and Central and South America 267; drug laws, disproportionate impact on African Americans 254; *see also* psychedelic drugs

"Duck Hook" 200–201; *see also* Vietnam Moratorium

Dukakis, M. 280–281

Duke, D. 272, 281

Dulles, A. 65–66, 113–114

Dulles, J.F. 58, 65–66

Dylan, B. 83, 128, 135, 139

Earth Day (1970) 212–213

Earth rise photo 165

Edmonds, Mstr. Sgt. R. 17–18

Eisenhower, D.: and domestic policy 57; and "falling domino" principle in Vietnam 67; and integration at Little Rock 90–91; and Korea 42; and "lavender scare" 57; and New Look foreign policy 64–65; response to attack on Marshall, G. 55–56; response to Hiroshima 23n76

Ellsberg, D.: compiles *Pentagon Papers* 202–203; target of Nixon "Plumbers" Unit 203–205

El Salvador 236; and death squads 237, 267; El Mozote massacre 267; Farabundo Martí Front for National Liberation (FMLN) 237; and terrorism against religious leaders 237–238; *see also* Committee in Solidarity with the People of El Salvador (CISPES); O'Neil, T.; U.S. School of the Americas

End of Ideology, The (Bell, D.) 58

energy Crisis 226–230; and "age of limits" 245n2; Energy Policy and Conservation Act 229; inflationary cycle triggered by 229, 232; and National Energy Act 232; 1979 resurgence triggered by Iran crisis 232; *see also Limits to Growth*

Environmental Protection Agency, establishment of 213; and deregulation (1980s) 245; scandal at 258–259; *see also* Ruckelshaus, W.

Equal Rights Amendment 3, 104, 241; and abandonment by Republican Party 242–243

evangelical conservatives 160–161, 227, 242–243, 264–265

Evers, M. 112

Facebook 314, 324, 327; and role in deepening American schism 317–318; *see also* Cadwalladr, C.

Fair Employment Practices Committee (FEPC) 15, 49, 58

Falling Down (1992) 291

Falwell, Rev. J. 227, 241, 270

Fanfare for the Common Man 3

far-right domestic terrorism (2017–2020) 316, 320–321; *see also* Highlander Folk School

fascism (or proto-fascism) in America 3–5, 328

Fatal Attraction (1987) 261

Fat Joe 323

Fauci, A. 271, 324

Federal budget deficits 252–253, 257

Federal Bureau of Investigation (FBI) 50; and anti-communism 50–51; and antiwar activity 180; and Central American antiwar activity 261; and Chennault Affair 188; and exposure of McCarthy 56; and harassment of Chavez and Huerta 210; and harassment of King 177–178; and JFK assassination 119; and Nixon-Kissinger warrantless wiretaps 202; and response

to civil rights activists 107, 130–131; and surveillance of *Salt of the Earth* 52; and Watergate 204, 206, 208; and Wounded Knee standoff 212; *see also* Hollywood and the Cold War
Federal Communications Commission, and deregulation (1980s) 259–260
Federal Land Management Policy Act (FLMPA) 244
Feminine Mystique, The (Friedan, B.) 11, 103–104
Ferraro, G. 261
Fire Next Time, The (Baldwin, J.) 105–106
Floyd, G. 324–325
folk music 82–84; *see also* Highlander Folk School; Seeger, P.; "We Shall Overcome"
Ford, G.R. 206–207; and pardon of Nixon 207
Forrestal, J. 31, 33
Fort Hood Three 159–160
Fox News 292–294; and attack on Affordable Care Act 311–312; and Trump era 314, 317, 319, 322, 325; *see also* Ailes, R.
Frank, B. 290
Freedom Rides 107–108; *see also* Connor, E. "Bull"
Freedom Train 49–50, 68
Free Speech Movement (FSM) 152–154
Friedan, B. 11, 103–104
Fukuyama, F. 279–280

Garcia, J. 163, 167
Garland, M. 310, 321
"gaslighting" in Trump era 319
Gay (LGBTQ+) liberation movement: cultural homophobia and legal persecution 57, 217; and Milk, H. 218; Stonewall, 1969 217–218
GI Bill of Rights 60
GI Movement against the Vietnam War 159–160
Gingrich, N. 242, 284, 294
Ginsberg, A.: *Howl* 79; and Human Be-In 166; and March on the Pentagon 156; and psychedelics 80; and Stonewall 217
Ginsburg, R.B. 328, 331n39
Giuliani, R. 321–322, 326
Glass-Steagall Act 256, 287
globalization 287–288; *see also* United Nations Bretton Woods Conference; U.S. interests in Middle East

global warming 294; *see also* climate crisis; *End of Nature, The*; Hansen, J.; McKibben, B.; Sununu, J.
Goldwater, B. 110, 127, 134, 152, 188–189
Gorbachev, M. 264; allows dissolution of Soviet Union 284; criticizes U.S. over Panama 285; and negotiations on arms control 265–266, 284
Gore, A. 304
government shutdowns 290
Grant, C. and LSD 80
Grateful Dead 79, 163, 165, 167, 180
"Gray Power" 218
Great Recession (2008–2009) 302; auto industry rescue and economic recovery from 309, 312–313; banking system, collapse of and "bailout" (Troubled Assets Relief Program, TARP) 309; deregulation as a root cause 304, 308–309; *see also* Occupy Wall Street Movement
Great Society 126, 128, 140; and War on Poverty, impact 140–141
Greece 25; American Mission to Aid in Greece (AMAG) 28; and authoritarian government 28–29; Polk, G. 29; and roots of Civil War 27; *see also* Jackson, R.H.
Greenspan, A. 256–257, 286, 309
Guatemala: CIA Coup (1954) 66, 113; human rights crimes and refugees (1980s) 267–269
Guernica (Picasso) 306
Gulf of Tonkin, events and Resolution 127

Haight-Ashbury 163–165
Halberstam, D. 37, 106
Halperin, M. 202–203
Hands Across America 255
Hansen, J. 280
"Hard Hat Riot" 204
Harris, Sen., Vice-President K. 325
Hayden, T. 150, 179
Hayes, D. 212
Hearst, William Randolph 2
Helms, Sen. J. 243, 270
Herbert, Col. A. 145
Hersh, S., My Lai revelations 144, 201
Highlander Folk School 83; burning of (2019) 320
"Hippie Temptation, The" 163
Hill, F. 322

Hill-Thomas hearings 281–282; *see also* Biden, J.

Hiss, A. 54

Hitler, Adolf 2, 4, 11, 15, 28, 31, 34, 39, 57, 68, 110, 115, 129, 285

Hoffman, A. 156, 180, 185

Hollywood and the Cold War 51–52

Home front mobilization (World War II) 7–8; defense housing 8; and Victory Book Campaign 10

"Homeland," as indicator of American empire 307

Homestead (PA) 190, 254

Hoover, J.E. 31; abuses predating Nixon 206; and COINTELPRO 158; desire for King's elimination from public life 177; and Freedom Rides 107; and Freedom Train 50; intensifies persecution of antiwar activity 180; intervenes on behalf of ex-Nazis 51; and McCarthy era 52, 64; warns of further escalation in Vietnam 174

Horton, W. 281

House Un-American Activities Committee (HUAC) 31; fascistic, racist elements 54; and Hiss inquiry 54; Hollywood inquisition 51; persecution of John Garfield 52; *see also* Rankin, J.

Hudson, R. 270

Huerta, D. 210

Human Be-In 165–166

Humphrey, H.: at 1948 Democratic National Convention 59; 1960 campaign 102; and 1964 Civil Rights Act 128; and 1964 Democratic National Convention; and 1968 presidential campaign 185–188, 190

Hungary, 1956 uprising 68

hungry i, the 78–79

Hussein, S.: allegations of "weapons of mass destruction" 289, 306; and Kuwait invasion 285; Reagan entreaty for warmer Iraq relations 285; sanctions against 289–290; uses U.S.-brokered weapons 285; *see also* Operation Desert Storm

Idiocracy 303

Independence Day (1996) 290

Indian Self-Determination and Religious Freedom Acts 212

individualism: culture of (1980s–1990s) 260–261, 291; loss of (1950s) 78; reflected in COVID-19 response 324

in loco parentis 151

international democratic revolt (1968) 181

International War Crimes (Russell, B.) Tribunal 159

Interstate Highways and automobile dominance (1950s) 61–62

Iran: CIA coup (1953) 65; liberal reform movement dismissed by U.S. 238; Shah Reza Pahlavi, human rights record and toppled by Islamic revolution 238–239; *see also* Carter Doctrine; Iran-Contra Affair; Iran hostage crisis

Iran-Contra Affair 268–269; *see also* Lebanon, Israeli invasion of

Iran hostage crisis 239

Iraq War (2003) 305–307; *see also* Powell, C.; Project for the New American Century

Islamophobia 306

isolationism 26–27

Israel: 1948 recognition 20; *see also* Lebanon, invasion of; Six-Day War; Yom Kippur War

Italy, 1948 elections 31

Jackson, Rev. J. 280–281

Jackson, R.H., and Nuremberg Principles 29, 159

Jackson State shooting 203

January 6, 2021 insurrection and proposed bipartisan commission 326–327

Japanese Americans World War II internment and 442nd Regimental Combat Team 12

Jerry Springer Show, The 290

Jobs, S. 165, 167

John Birch Society and Birchers 57–58, 109, 191, 242

Johnson, L.B.: address on voting rights 138–139; "Daisy Girl" Commercial 127; decision to prioritize civil rights 126; Johnson Treatment 138; rescinds withdrawal from Vietnam 126–127; response to Mississippi Freedom Democratic Party 132–134; and "Wise Men" 174–175; *see also* Civil Rights Act; Great Society, The; Gulf of Tonkin episode; Selma Campaign

Jones, C. 271

Jordan, B. 206

Kantner, P. 117, 119, 164

Kavanaugh, B.: Supreme Court nomination and hearings 321

Kehler, R. 202

Kennan, George: Long Telegram 28; on regrets of containment policy 33–35

Kennedy, J.F.: and alleged "missile gap" 100; Alliance for Progress 113; American University Speech on Peace 117–118; anti-imperialist views as senator 112–113; assassination 118–120; and Carson, R. 102–103; inaugural address 101–102; and meeting with Quakers 115; New Frontier 100; 1960 primary campaign, WV 102; Pay Equity Act of 1963 105; Peace Corps proposed 101; policy in Berlin and Laos 116; President's Commission on the Status of Women 105; relationship with CIA and generals 113–114; relationship with Khrushchev 114–115; and response to civil rights movement 107–111; and Vietnam, decision to withdraw 116–117; *see also* Cuba; Partial Test Ban Treaty

Kennedy, Sen. R.F.: assassination and impact of 184–185; Indianapolis address following King assassination 182–183; 1963 meeting with civil rights leaders 182; presidential campaign 181–185; proposal for Vietnam withdrawal 181

Kent State 203; *see also* "Hard Hat Riot"

Kerner Report (National Advisory Commission on Civil Disorders) 177

Kerouac, J., *On the Road* 79–80; *see also* Cassady, N.

Kerr, C. 151

Kerry, J. "swiftboating" ad campaign against 307

Khalilzad, Z. 305

King, Jr., Dr. M.L. 92; assassination of 178; and Birmingham 110–111; Chicago Freedom Project 161–162; criticized for support of 1957 Civil Rights Act 91; "Declaration of Independence from Vietnam" 161–162; fall 1960 arrest and release 101; and Memphis Sanitation Workers Strike 176–178; and MFDP compromise in Atlantic City 134; and Montgomery Bus Boycott 86; Poor People's Campaign 178; in Selma (1965) 135–139

Kissinger, H.: and Cambodian bombing 199–200; and Chennault Affair 188; and destruction of documents 202; and Paris Peace Accords 188; *Realpolitik* 206–207; and Yom Kippur War crisis 206; *see also* Chile; Duck Hook; Halperin, M.

Kitchen Debate (American National Exhibition in Moscow) 100

Klan Border Watch 242

Klein, N. 289

Koch, C. and D. 308, 312; *see also* Tea Party

Korean War: atomic bombs and 42; background, 37–39; bombing campaign 42; boon to military budget 37; China's intervention 41; Chosin Reservoir 41; conclusion and impacts of 43; invasion of South Korea and U.S. military response 39–40; Jeju massacre 39; and MacArthur, General D. 40–42

Kramer, L. 270–271

Krebs, C. 326

Kristol, B. 323

Ku Klux Klan 14, 89, 107, 111–112, 129, 131, 135, 153; and David Duke 272, 281; and Fred Trump 262; and post-Vietnam surge 271; and Republican Party 242–244

labor movement and unions 7, 17; anti-communist assault on 50, 53; assault on in Greece 27; attack on during Reagan administration 253, 273n15; Congress of Industrial Organizations 53–54; conservatism of during Cold War 58; and Freedom Works' anti-union activity 312; Operation Dixie 54; at Seattle WTO protest (1999) 288; union busting in Silicon Valley 313; union vote in the 1968 election 190; weakness of in Obama era 309; *see also* Memphis Sanitation Workers Strike; Nelson, J.; United Farm Workers

Lasch, C., *The Culture of Narcissism* 233

Latinx struggle: Castro, S. and 1968 "blowouts" 209; Jimenez, J. and Young Lords 210; League of United Latin American Citizens (LULAC) 210–211; Rendon, A. and Chicano consciousness 209; Sanchez, D. and Brown Berets 210; Tijerina, R.L. and Alianza Movement 209–210; United Farmworkers Union 210

Lattimore, O. 55

"lavender lads" 57

Lawson, J. 92, 106, 175–176

Leary, T. 165–167

Lebanon, invasion of and attack on U.S. Marine barracks 269

LeMay, C.: Berlin Airlift 34; Cuban Missile Crisis 115; and Korea, 42; and 1968 campaign 191; and predictions of nuclear war 123n87; and *Seven Days in May* 119

Lennon, J. 201, 205

Levitt, W. 8; and Levittown 62–63

Lewis, J. 92, 317; Freedom Rides 108; and Nashville campaign 106; and Selma "Bloody Sunday" 137

Life (magazine) 1–2, 15; and reports on psychedelic drugs 80

Lifestyles of the Rich and Famous 260

Lily Ledbetter Act 310

Limbaugh, R.: and Affordable Care Act fear-mongering 311; aims to destroy liberalism 292; and culture war over history 294; promulgates Clinton conspiracy theories 292

Limits to Growth 229

Little Big Man (Penn, A.) 211

Little Rock (AR) standoff over integration (1957) 90–91

Los Angeles Riots (1992) 283

Love Canal 226, 234–235

Lowndes County Freedom Organization (LCFO) 139

LSD (Lysergic Acid Diethylamide): and Human Be-in 165–166; and Kesey, K., Merry Pranksters and Acid Tests, 167; and Luce, H. and C.B. 80; and misrepresentation in the culture 163; and Meyer, M. P. 166; and music 167; Pollan, M. 168; transcendent properties 166–167; and treatment of psychological disorders 80; *see also* psychedelic drugs

Luce, H. 1–2, 6, 10, 18; and LSD 80; *see also* American Century

Lumumba, P. 113

Luntz, F. 294

Madison, J. 256

Madonna 261–262

Mailer, N. 157, 180

Malcolm X 135–136

Manhattan Project 18, 36

Manson, C. 198

March for Our Lives 321

March on the Pentagon 156–158

March on Washington Movement 14

marriage equality, 2015 Supreme Court decision 311

Marshall, G.: attacked by McCarthy 55; *see also* Marshall Plan

Marshall Plan, The (European Recovery Program) 32–33

Marshall, T. 89, 107, 281

McCain, Sen. J.: attacked by Trump 316; defeated by Obama (2008) 309; defends Obama as candidate for president 317; one of "Keating Five" 256

McCarthy, Senator E. 174–181

McCarthy, Senator J. 35, 54; Army-McCarthy Hearings 57; condemned by Truman 55; and Tydings Committee 55; Wheeling, WV speech 55; *see also* Murrow, E.; Welch, J.N.

McConnell, Sen. M.: leader of Obama obstruction efforts 310; packs judiciary 321; refuses joint statement condemning Russian interference in 2016 election 318

McGovern, Sen. George 199–204

McKibben, B., *The End of Nature* 280

McNamara, R. 119, 127, 142, 157–158, 161, 202

Memphis Sanitation Workers Strike 175–176; *see also* King, Jr. Dr. M.L.

Meredith, J. 108–109

#MeToo Movement 321

Mexican Americans: *bracero* program 13–14; Dayton, WA strike 14; repatriation 14; Zoot Suit Riots 14

Mexico City Summer Olympic Human Rights Protest 186–187

Middle East, U.S. interests and 19–20, 36, 229; and growing U.S. military footprint 65, 240; and Truman 25–27, 39

militarism, culture of (post-Cold War era) 286

military Draft: avoidance of 155; as focus of antiwar movement 155; *see also* anti-Dow campaign, University of WI; March on the Pentagon

military industrial complex (Eisenhower, D. Farewell Address) 99; bomber and missile gap, allegations of 98, 100; and Gaither Report (*Deterrence and Survival in the Nuclear Age*) 98; and Kennedy assassination 119; post-Cold War era 285, 288; Reagan era 257

militia movement: and disavowal of white supremacy 292; Oklahoma City bombing 292; *Turner Diaries, The* 291

Mills, N., culture of "meanness" 290

Miss America Protest (1968) 186

Mississippi Freedom Summer 130–132; and Mississippi Freedom Democratic Party (MFDP) at Atlantic City Democratic National Convention 132–134

Mondale, W. 261

Montgomery (AL) Bus Boycott 85–88; *see also* Colvin, C.; Nixon, E.D.; Parks, R.; Robinson, J.A.

Morgan, R. 186

Morrison, N. 161

Mountain States Legal Foundation 244

Mountaintop removal mining 313

Mrs. Miniver (1942) 6

Mueller, R.: report of 2016 Russian attack on American democracy 318; testifies to congress 321

Munich appeasement, fears of (Korea) 39

Murrow, E.: exposes McCarthy 56–57; *See It Now* and departure from television 76–78

My Lai Massacre 144; and Vietnam War Crimes Working Group 145

Nader, R. 141, 218

Nash, D.: Freedom Rides 107–108; Nashville campaign 106

National Association for the Advancement of Colored People (NAACP) 84, 86–92, 108, 129–130

National health insurance proposals (1950s) 59

National Labor Relations Act 7

National Security Act 29, 114, 116–117

National Security Council 27, 29–30, 36, 42, 115, 202, 206, 268, 322

National Women's Conference (NWC) 241

Nazis (ex-) and U.S. intelligence agencies 50–51

Nelson, J. and United Electrical Workers (506) 53

Neoconservativism 235, 306; *see also* Cheney, D.; Project for the New American Century; Rumsfeld, D.; Wolfowitz, P.

New Right, The 227; Republican Party, impact on 242–243; *see also* National Women's Conference; Schlafly, P.

Nicaragua: Carter administration response to 237; Reagan administration Contra

War 267–268; Somoza dynasty and Sandinista revolution 236–237; *see also* Iran-Contra Affair

Nitze, P. 33, 36, 157; *see also* NSC-68

Nixon, E.D. 84–86

Nixon, R.: as anti-communist congressman 35, 54; Christmas bombing 204; "madman theory" 200; 1960 campaign 100–101; 1968 campaign 180, 187–190; "Operation Menu" 199–203; resignation 206; and "Silent Majority" 201, 220n23; *see also* Ailes, R.; American Indian Movement; Cambodia; Cash, J., White House performance; Chennault Affair; Duck Hook; "Hard Hat Riot"; Hiss, A.; Kitchen Debate; *Realpolitik*; Watergate affair

Noriega, M. 284

North American Free Trade Agreement (NAFTA) 286–287

North Atlantic Treaty Organization (NATO) 35, 240, 264, 284, 319

NSC-68 36–37, 40

nuclear–atomic weapons testing 74–76; anti-nuclear movement (1950s); *see also* Partial Test Ban Treaty

Nuclear Freeze Movement 265–266

Obama, B.H.: American Economic Recovery and Reinvestment Act 309; and immigration 310; and LGBTQ+ rights 310–311; moderate character of presidency 309–310; on murder of Trayvon Martin 314; presidency as mirage of "post-racial" America 314–315; and unprecedented obstruction to 310; *see also* Affordable Care Act ("Obamacare"); "birtherism"

Occupy Wall Street Movement 312–313

"Okie from Muskogee" 190, 201

O'Neil, T. 117, 267

Operation Desert Storm 285–286

Operation Enduring Freedom (Afghanistan war) 305

Opioid crisis, as indicator of deeper American traumas 319

Orangeburg (SC) Massacre 175

Other America, The (Harrington, M.) 102

Oxford, Battle of 108–109

Paint-by-number kits 64

Panama Canal Treaties 236

Parkland (FL) Marjory Stoneman Douglas High School 321

Parks, R. as investigator of sexual assault 84–85; and Montgomery Bus Boycott 86–88

Partial Test Ban Treaty (PTBT) 118

"Peace through Strength" policy: Reagan military buildup and shift toward arms negotiations 263–265; Strategic Defense Initiative ("Star Wars") 265

Pelosi, Rep. N. 311, 326

Pence, Vice-President M. 326

Pentagon Papers 202

People of Plenty (Potter, D.) 59

People's Park 197

Perot, H.R. 284

Phillips, S. 81

Pinochet, A. 207

Port Huron Statement 150–151

Post-Watergate democratic reforms 207–208; *see also* Church Committee hearings; *Citizens United vs. FEC* (2010)

Powell, C. 306

Presley, E. 81–82

Professional Air Traffic Controllers Association (PATCO) strike 253

Project for the New American Century 290; as proponents of Iraq invasion 305–306

psychedelic drugs 80, 162, 165–166

Putin, V. 285, 303, 318

Rankin, J. 54–55, 76

Reagan, R.: condemns counterculture 163; and distrust of government 252; environmental policies 258–259; "evil empire" speech 264; Immigration Reform and Control Act 271–272; inaugural address 252, 263; jokes of bombing Russians 264; "Morning in America" reelection ad 293; 1980 campaign speech in Neshoba County, MS and Klan endorsement 244; and Panama Canal 236; and People's Park 197; press treatment of 252; Reaganomics 252–255; and Republican Party rightward shift 188; and Sagebrush Rebellion 244; and Screen Actors Guild 51; and Vietnam Syndrome 235; *see also* deregulation; Nicaragua, Contra War; "Peace through Strength" policy

Reality TV 254, 316, 326

"redneck revolt" 320

Regan, D. 257

Republican Party: becomes party of far-right and Donald Trump 311–313, 316–317, 321–323, 326–327; Buckley, W 188; Kirk, R. 188; shift rightward (1990s) 284; *see also* culture wars; Goldwater, B.; Limbaugh, R.; New Right; Nixon, R.

Rivers, Doc 327

Robinson, J. 101, 129

Robinson, J.A. 85–86, 88

Rock and roll 80–82

Roof, D. 315–316

Roosevelt, Franklin Delano: and African American civil rights 14–15; "arsenal of democracy" 7; Atlantic Charter 6–7; Executive Order 9066 12; fireside chats 9, 15; "Four Freedoms" 2–3, 49; New Deal 1–2, 5–6, 9, 17, 31, 51, 54, 56, 58–59, 100, 252, 309; 1944 State of the Union ("Second Bill of Rights") message 15–16; relations with business during WW II 7–8; and Saudi King Abdulaziz (Ibn Saud) 19–20; and Wall Street Putsch 2

Rosenberg, J. and E. 54

Rubin, J. 156–157, 205

Rubin, R. 286–287

Ruckelshaus, J. 242

Ruckelshaus, W. 205, 259

Rumsfeld, D. 285, 290, 306

Rural America: farm crisis and Farm Aid 255; poverty 102, 319; rural voters shifting toward Republican Party 243

Sacks, O., *The Man Who Mistook His Wife for a Hat* 251

Sagebrush Rebellion 244, 258

Sahl, M. 78–79

Salazar, R. 203–204

Sanders, Sen. B. 317

San Francisco State Strike 197

Santa Barbara oil spill 212

Savio, M. 153

Scaife, R.M. 244

Schiff, Rep. A. 322

Schlafly, P. 241–242

Schlesinger, A. Jr. 100

Seeger, P. 83–84; and Vietnam Moratorium March 201

Selma campaign: Bloody Sunday 137; Clark, Sheriff J. 135–137; Dallas County Voters League 135; Jackson, J.L.; Johnson, Judge F. M. 137;

Liuzzo, V. 139; Montgomery march 139; "Turnaround Tuesday" 137–138; *see also* King, Jr. Dr. M.L.; Wallace, G.

September 11, 2001 terrorist attacks 302, 305; U.S. support for bin Laden and strategic aims in Central Asia and Middle East as precursor to 304–305; *see also* Operation Enduring Freedom

Serling, R. 77–78

Seven Days in May 119

shock doctrine 289

Silent Spring (Carson, R.) 102–103

Six Day War 177, 227

Smith, Senator M.C. 56

Solidarnosc 265

South African apartheid 36, 152, 269–270

Southern Christian Leadership Conference (SCLC) 88, 91–92; Citizenship Education Program 92; *see also* Baker, E.; Clarke, S.

Southern Manifesto 89

Southern Poverty Law Center 291

Soviet Union, actions of: Czechoslovakia coup, 1948 30–32; Poland 27

Spector, P. 128

Spock, B. 64, 75, 157

Springsteen, B., "Born in the USA" 254

Sputnik 1, impact of 98–99; *see also* Military Industrial Complex

Stahl, L. 251–252, 290

Stalin, J. 11, 27; and atomic bomb 28; and Greece 28; and Tito, J. 28; *see also* Percentages Agreement

START (Strategic Arms Reduction) Treaty 284

"Starve the beast" as Republican strategy 252

St. Augustine (FL) campaign 129

Stevens, S. 317

Stiglitz, J. 308

Stone, R. 220n41, 304

Strategic Arms Limitation Treaty II (SALT II) 240

Student Non-Violent Coordinating Committee (SNCC) 107–108, 130, 132, 134, 137–139, 160

Students for a Democratic Society (SDS) 150–151, 191; antiwar demonstration (1965) 154; and Columbia uprising 179; and Human Be-In 165; *see also* anti-Dow campaign; Port Huron Statement; Weather Underground Organization

suburbs: environmental impacts 62–63; racial discrimination (1950s) 62

Summers, L. 286–287

Sununu, J. 283–284

Superfund law (Comprehensive Environmental Response, Compensation, and Liability Act) 234, 258

Taft-Hartley Act 53, 58

Taxes, burden shifted in 1980s 253

Taylor, R. 84–85

Teach-Ins 154, 200, 212

Tea Party: alignment with Freedom Works and dark money interests 312; corporate agenda of 312; Koch Brothers 312

television (1950s): game shows 77; *Honeymooners, The* 64; *I Love Lucy* 77; *See It Now* 56; *The Twilight Zone* 77–78; *see also* Serling, R.

Tet Offensive 173–174, 269; *see also* Cronkite, W.; Kennedy, R.F.; McCarthy, E.

Three Mile Island 32

Thunberg, G. 320

Thurmond, S.: as 1948 Dixiecrat candidate 59; and 1957 filibuster 91

Tiananmen Square 279

Till, E. 85–86, 131

Tito, J. 28, 35, 67

Tocqueville, A. 260

Tolkien, J.R.R. 213

To Secure These Rights 58–59

Truman Doctrine of Containment: aid to Greece and Turkey 25; criticism from politicians and national security experts 26; economic interests embedded in 27; *see also* Acheson, D.

Truman, H.: centrism and 1948 reelection 53, 58; decision to use atomic bomb at Hiroshima and Nagasaki 18–19; Doctrine of Containment Speech 25–26; Fair Deal 59; and hydrogen bomb decision 36; and Korean invasion 38–39; Loyalty Review program 31; 1944 Democratic ticket and ascension to presidency 6; and race 58–59; and relations with labor 53, 58; relieves MacArthur of command in Korea 41–42; and non-response to Ho Chi Minh 67; *see also* Truman Doctrine

Trump, D.: and Article II constitutional power 322; attacks on free press and constitutional norms 322; avoids draft 169n19; background of and celebrity

culture 262–263; and "birtherism" 312; and border wall promise 316; calls climate change a "Chinese hoax" 320; campaign announcement 316; and Central Park Five 262; corruption of administration 319; and COVID-19 323–324; as expression of modern Republican Party 317; false claims of fraudulent 2020 election ("the big lie") 326–328; *Hollywood Access* tape 316; impeachment of (2019) 321–322; and Lafayette Square 325; lies tabulated 319; "Make America Great Again" rallies 316–317; media role in 2016 campaign success 317; and Muslim ban 317; policies of 319; promulgates white grievance and victimhood 317, 320–321; and Putin at Helsinki 318; Republicans' response to 321; and Russian assistance in 2016 election 317–318; second impeachment of (2021) 327; summons supporters to Capitol 326; Trump University fraud 316; and "truthful hyperbole" 263; unites defenders of democracy 323; *see also* Facebook; "gaslighting" in Trump era Reality TV; January 6 insurrection; "Unite the Right," Charlottesville; Vindman, Lt. Col. A.; Yovanovitch, M.; Zelensky, V.
Twitter 314, 317, 320, 327

United Farm Workers 210
United Nations: Bretton Woods Conference 44; UN Conference on the Environment Stockholm (1972) 213; Universal Declaration of Human Rights 16
"Unite the Right," Charlottesville (2017) 320–321
U.S. Central Command (CENTCOM) 240
U.S. School of the Americas 237, 267

Venona Project 54
Vietnam: body count fixation 143–144; "crossover point" 143; Dien Bien Phu 67, 112; Geneva Accords (1954) 66–67; Giáp, Võ Nguyên 142–143; "hearts and minds" 144; Ho Chi Minh 67, 142–143, 158, 200; Ia Drang, Battle of 143; National Liberation Front 68, 142, 173; Ngô Đình Diệm 67–68, 116, 145; Ngô Đình Nhu 68; Vietnamese history

as unheeded warning 67; Vietnam War 37; Westmoreland, W. 142–143, 145, 173; *see also* credibility gap; My Lai Massacre; Tet Offensive; Vietnam Moratorium; Vietnam Syndrome
Vietnam Moratorium 200–201
"Vietnam Syndrome" 235, 285
Vietnam Veterans Against the War (VVAW) 158–159
Vigilantism (1968) 191
Vindman, Lt. Col. A. 322
Voting Rights Act 139, 191, 328

Walker, E. 109
Wallace, Governor G.: 1968 campaign 190–191; "schoolhouse door" stand 111; and Selma voting rights campaign 136–138
Wallace, H.: criticizes Truman Doctrine 26; expanded role as vice president 3; 1948 Progressive Party candidacy 58; outspoken anti-fascist and anti-imperialist 3–4, 6; postwar outlook 19; Price of a Free World Victory (Century of the Common Man) speech 1–3; promotes hybridized farm animals 59; removed from 1944 Democratic ticket 6, 16
Wall Street 4, 7, 58, 254; deregulation and corruption of (1980s) 256–257; 1987 crash of 257; Putsch (1933) 2; *Wall Street* (1987 film) 257
Warren County (NC) 235
Warren, E., Consumer Financial Protection Bureau 310
Watergate affair 188, 190; Committee to Re-elect the President (CRP) 204–205; Dean, J. 205; Ehrlichman, J. 190, 202, 205; hearings of the U.S. Senate Select Committee 205; impeachment proceedings 206; "Plumbers Unit" 202–204; Richardson, E. 205–206; "Saturday Night Massacre" 205–206; Sirica, Judge J. 205; Watergate Hotel burglary 199, 204; *see also* Post-Watergate democratic reforms; Stone, R.
Watt, J. 258
Watts (L.A.) (1965) 139
wealth concentration and redistribution 7, 61, 260, 279, 286, 294, 324
Weather Underground Organization and "Days of Rage" 198–199; as COINTELPRO target 199
Weavers, The 83

Welch, J. N. 57
"We Shall Overcome" 83–84
Westmoreland, Genl. W. 142–143, 145, 173–174
White, R. 271
white backlash (1960s) 132, 134, 178, 189
white male victimhood (1990s) 291–292; *see also Falling Down*; Limbaugh, R.
white supremacist extremism: southwest border (1970s) 242–243; *see also* Civilian Materiel Assistance; Far-right domestic terrorism
Whitewater investigation 292
Whitmer, Gov. G. 324
Whole Earth Catalog 164–165, 167
Willoughby, Major General C. 41
Wolfowitz, P. 284, 286, 290, 306
women in World War II: as defense workers 10–12; Lanham Daycare 12; Women Airforce Service Pilots (WASP) 10
women's Liberation Movement: consciousness raising 215–216; *Newsweek,* Title VII class action lawsuit 214; "radical" feminism 216; *Roe v. Wade*, impacts of 213; Rossi, A., workplace discrimination

expose 216; sexual violence and rape 216–217; Women's Strike for Equality 214; Yale University Title IX episode 213–214; *see also* Equal Rights Amendment
Women's March (2017) 322
Women's Political Council (WPC) 85
Woodstock 198
Woodward, B.: and Trump's response to COVID-19 323; and Watergate investigation 204
World Trade Organization (WTO), Seattle protests against (1999) 287–288

"Yellow Power" 208
Yom Kippur War 227–228; and nuclear threat 206; and Organization of Arab Petroleum Exporting Countries (OAPEC), embargo 228–229; *see also* Camp David Accords; Energy Crisis; Kissinger, H.; Six-Day War
Young Americans for Freedom 191, 227
Yovanovitch, M. 322
Yuppies 262, 288

Zelensky, V. 321–322

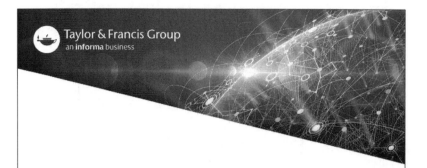